The Integrity of the Body of Christ

The Integrity of the Body of Christ

Boundary Keeping as Shared Responsibility

ARDEN F. MAHLBERG &
CRAIG L. NESSAN

CASCADE *Books* · Eugene, Oregon

THE INTEGRITY OF THE BODY OF CHRIST
Boundary Keeping as Shared Responsibility

Cascade Books
An Imprint of Wipf and Stock Publishers
199 W. 8th Ave., Suite 3
Eugene, OR 97401

www.wipfandstock.com

Paperback ISBN 13: 978-1-4982-3536-5
Hardcover ISBN 13: 978-1-4982-3538-9
Ebook ISBN 13: 978-1-4982-3537-2

Cataloging-in-Publication data:

Names: Mahlberg, Arden, F., and Craig L. Nessan.

Title: The integrity of the body of Christ : boundary keeping as shared responsibility / Arden F. Mahlberg and Craig L. Nessan.

Description: xii + 224 p.; 23 cm—Includes bibliographical references and index.

Identifiers: ISBN: 978-1-4982-3536-5 (paperback) | 978-1-4982-3538-9 (hardback) | 978-1-4982-3537-2 (ebook)

Subjects: LCSH: Pastoral theology. | Pastoral care. | Clergy. | Pastoral theology—Evangelical Lutheran Church in America. | Nessan, Craig L. | Cooper-White, Pamela | Cooper-White, Michael. | Title.

Classification: BV4011 M35 2016 (print) | BV4011 (ebook)

Manufactured in the USA

Contents

Foreword

IN OUR CURRENT CALLINGS, we serve at historic institutions of theological education. On July 1, 1863, the bloodiest battle ever fought on U.S. soil took place on and around the campus of Gettysburg Seminary. In the previous days, Robert E. Lee and the Confederate army had crossed the Mason-Dixon line, the border between Maryland and Pennsylvania. Lee believed that his advance into northern territory would overwhelm Union forces, cower the civilian population, and lead to a swift victory and permanent division of the nation. The Civil War was all about borders and boundaries; it was about who would govern which territory, whether a *United* States would prevail or the young country would be divided into two or more loose federations of autonomous and largely independent states. Above all, it was about whether or not boundaries would forever be established between races—an elite and superior (white) class ruling it over an enslaved, rights-denied underclass of African Americans and presumably other people of color as well. Would whites be allowed at will to cross personal boundaries, lay hands and legal claims of "property" upon persons of color?

A few decades later, near the end of the nineteenth century, a different kind of boundary battle took place at the still young Union Seminary in the City of New York. Though it was founded by Presbyterians in 1836, some six decades later Union's leaders had to make a determination of where doctrinal lines would be drawn and who would ultimately govern the school. Upset with teachings by one of the school's faculty members, who embraced the radical notion that not everything in the Bible might be literally true and verbally inspired by God, church officials deemed his teachings heretical and demanded his release from the school. Standing on the principles of academic freedom, scholarly self-determination, and a commitment to embrace and honor a wide spectrum of beliefs, Union's leaders decided to declare their independence from the Presbyterian

Church and become a freestanding, independent, and broadly ecumenical school for the preparation and formation of ministers and other leaders in church and society.

Throughout their illustrious histories, these two great institutions have had to engage in continuing discernment (and often hotly contested, prolonged debates) about boundaries. How rigidly would theological and confessional borders be drawn? Who would be allowed to teach? Could women as well as men, persons of color as well as whites, be allowed to become students and even faculty and senior administrators? Who would determine the style of worship at chapel services, and who might be allowed to preside at such services? What would be the nature of the relationship with other schools? Would it serve seminaries well to join with colleges and universities as the movement for accreditation gained steam? Could our schools accept the constraints and careful governmental monitoring that ensues in becoming eligible to administer U.S. federal student loans? What policies would guide governing boards as they steward endowment funds? Are some promising investments "off limits" by virtue of company products or labor practices?

Over the course of human history, persons, families, tribes, organizations, and nations have recognized the necessity of setting and stewarding borders or boundaries—those places where one individual, group, community, or public entity ends and another begins. Establishing and tending boundaries requires careful attention and constant vigilance. Many boundaries are good; they protect persons, other creatures, and property from being overrun, abused, and denied their rightful place in the universe. Some boundaries, like those within which and for which the Confederacy was established, cannot be allowed to stand and must be torn down, if they are allowed to be set up in the first place. Since its inception, humankind has had to engage in discernment regarding boundaries: Which are good and which are bad? Where should they be drawn, and with what degree of clarity? How rigidly should they be enforced? How do those in power enforce boundaries of their own making, and how are just boundaries reestablished when tyranny and abuse reign? Currently, our nation and others with the greatest resources are engaged in heated debates about how national borders should be monitored and patrolled, opened or closed. In sharp contrast to the spirit of the Statue of Liberty in New York's harbor, whose torch beckons and invites in the "huddled masses yearning to breathe free," some current politicians' campaign slogans shout, "Build a wall; keep them out!"

This is a book about stewarding borders, establishing, tending, and sometimes changing boundaries. Its authors—Prof. Craig Nessan and Dr. Arden Mahlberg—bring to bear their collective wisdom on a vast array of topics related to personal and professional boundaries. Each author in his own way has assumed a *calling* in which boundary tending lies at the very heart of the profession. A pastor, professor, and longtime seminary academic dean (Nessan) and a practicing clinical psychologist (Mahlberg) lead readers gently but insistently down a path into some of the most complex and vexing dimensions faced on a daily basis by their peers in many professions. Heeding their own counsel that boundary keeping is a communal endeavor, they reach beyond their own experience and insights to draw heavily upon the wisdom of others; readers will do well to follow the many tributaries that lead to other resources cited in the extensive footnotes.

The book is deeply *theological*; it makes the claim that God cares about how we relate to one another as individuals and communities. The Hebrew Bible portrays creation as a divine boundary-establishing activity. At creation, God "separated" things and beings. Where there was only an amorphous glob of borderless nothingness (*tohu va bohu* in Hebrew), God drew boundary lines between day and night, darkness and light, earth and sky, plants and animals, male and female. When boundaries were crossed, pain, enmity, and alienation occurred through the eating of fruit from a tree "across the border." But when some boundaries became oppressive and no longer served God's beloved, they had to be crossed. Jesus and his followers got in trouble when they transgressed some of the overly rigid religious laws that had become death-dealing rather than life-giving. St. Paul declared that in the overarching unity in Jesus Christ "there is neither Jew nor Greek, slave nor free, male nor female." (Gal 3:28) Explicitly Christian at its core, the book's insights and practical implications will nevertheless be relevant to readers of any faith tradition, and to those who ascribe to no spiritual creeds or religious beliefs.

As educators engaged in the formation of future "ministers" (we use the term broadly to embrace a wide range of vocations in which today's seminary graduates live out their callings), we are well aware that our institutions' and ecclesial bodies' requirements for "boundary training" courses or workshops are often met by sighs, groans, and eyerolls from our students. Such reactions frequently reveal resistance to engaging with difficult and challenging topics, some of which touch sensitive nerves within fledgling religious professionals. A significant percentage of students (especially women) have themselves been victims of boundary violations at the hands of family members, neighbors, strangers, teachers, clergy, or others least suspected of such crimes. Some who find their way to our schools have been on the offender side of a boundary violation and must come to terms with their culpability, which can provoke profound guilt and should result in serious self-examination regarding fitness for a calling in which temptations and opportunities to repeat such behavior will appear at every turn. Mahlberg and Nessan walk the fine line between a legalistic approach and an overly tolerant stance that has all too often marked the church's way of treating boundaries and boundary violations. Later chapters offer quite specific guidance on a vast array of issues that every person will encounter with some regularity, with particular focus on those unique to religious and therapeutic professionals involved in what prior generations of pastoral theologians commonly referred to as "the cure of souls."

The authors recognize that boundary tending is *contextual*. In our work with seminarians, clergy, and congregations over the decades, we have often witnessed colleagues get into trouble as they move from one ministry to another. Such troubles arise from a failure to recognize that boundaries are drawn differently in different places. Whereas unannounced drop-in pastoral calls may be appreciated and even expected in some contexts (we have tagged along with a "community promoter" on her round of spontaneous visits in Central American *campesino* villages), in other settings such a practice will be met with horrified looks and a chilly reception at the door. Just as preachers must exegete a text of Scripture (that is, must draw out of a passage its original meaning and what it might mean for us today), so pastoral counselors and other helping professionals must exegete their context to determine what words and actions are appropriate in that particular setting. Being a careful student of "where the boundaries lie" becomes particularly acute as one engages in cross-cultural ministry. As one example, direct eye contact in some cultures is the norm for conveying respect and authenticity; in other contexts such eyeball-to-eyeball exchange is regarded as presumptuous, offensive, or even flirtatious, particularly with a person of the opposite gender.

While every context undergoes change over time, the landscape for professionals has undergone seismic shifts in recent years with the advent of smartphones, with the dizzying array of social media, and with other developments made possible by the electronic revolution. Should one "friend" students, parishioners, or members of a youth group on Facebook? Do I widely disseminate my mobile phone number? How does one "keep sabbath" and "turn off and tune out" from time to time when serving among folks, who may launch search and rescue operations if a text message does not receive response within minutes? If Robert Frost's legendary poetic assertion is true, that "good fences make good neighbors," how does one even begin to conceive of building fences in the cyberspace neighborhood? No book can anticipate every boundary-tending matter that will be encountered in daily life and the exercise of a profession, but this one offers enough of a road map to help readers avoid many danger zones.

Boundary tending, as we have suggested, is deeply theological and highly contextual. While, as the authors delineate so compellingly, it is communal, it is also profoundly *personal*. Each of us brings our own history and unique set of life experiences to bear in our relationships and professional responsibilities. While there are no inherently gender-specific ways of responding to events and occurrences, socialization tends to shape women and men in different ways; this too varies by cultural context. Among the many gifts offered in the chapters that follow is a heavy dosage of attention to the whole matter of self-care. Often ignored if not outright derided by ecclesiastical officials frustrated at hearing anecdotal stories of the rare clergy who refuse to respond to a true emergency on a day off, this area should receive the kind of careful and compassionate attention the authors signal. While the "wounded healer" is an apt description of all who engage in spiritual and therapeutic callings, there are limits to just how much hurt and pain one can endure and manage in a redemptive fashion that may serve others.

Among the boundaries most difficult to reinforce among those of us in the helping professions are those that pertain to respecting our own human limitations and temptations, as well as the power conferred by our professional role. We hold a *fiduciary* trust—from the Latin word *fides*, which means both trust and faith! If airline crews and long-distance truck drivers must abide by strict limitations of time spent in the cockpit and cabin or behind the wheel, should enforced periods of rest and renewal not be even more rigidly monitored for those whose sharp retort or careless comments may cause someone in our care physical, psychological, and *spiritual* harm? No less than is the case for other professionals entrusted with high-level responsibilities, personal well-being and stewarding of the self is a life-and-death matter for those of us who engage in spiritual and mental caretaking. Some boundary crossings may appear mutual, but it is always the responsibility of the professional to maintain the appropriate line of familiarity—to cross sexual boundaries with a member of one's congregation, or to exploit a parishioner financially, is not only boundary crossing but violation.

Nessan and Mahlberg herein offer a solid foundation on which to build personal and communal codes of ethics. Good communicators that they are, the authors set forth a broad range of issues in an accessible manner devoid of "insider language." Even as the book will serve well in the classroom and professional gatherings of the clergy or counselors, so it can provoke lively conversations by parish councils as they set policies and fulfill their responsibilities to ensure that congregations are safe places for all. Doctors Mahlberg and Nessan invite us into honest and open conversations about matters that, despite receiving heightened focus in recent years, merit more frequent and in-depth examination. May such conversations flourish and help us all develop and sustain integrity and wholeness in our callings!

Pamela Cooper-White
Christiane Brooks Johnson Professor of Psychology & Religion
Union Theological Seminary, New York

Michael Cooper-White
President
Lutheran Theological Seminary at Gettysburg

Introduction

*"You shall love the Lord your God with all your heart, and with all your
soul, and with all your mind." This is the greatest and first commandment.
And a second is like it: "You shall love your neighbor as yourself." On these
two commandments hang all the law and the prophets (Matt 22:37–40).*

WE WROTE THIS BOOK after years of hearing people—clergy, seminarians, and their spouses—ask for a comprehensive resource on boundaries in congregational life. We wrote this book both for people who have
violated the boundaries of others and for people whose boundaries have
been violated. Readers have wanted to know how to create common language and how to establish common understanding about boundaries.
They want to develop a shared recognition of what boundaries are and of
how to think through boundary issues. Clergy and seminarians want to
know how to speak up to insensitive colleagues within the seminary or
church context.

While this is a book about boundaries and boundary keeping, it is,
more fundamentally, a book about love. Perhaps there is something paradoxical about that. While boundaries sound like constraints and boundary keeping sounds constricting, boundaries do far more than constrain.
Boundaries serve as doorways opening to wonderful experiences of love
that are not otherwise possible. Only within the safety, mutual accountability, and permission of love is free expression of our most creative
selves possible. When we monitor the health of our relationships with
persons, things, and functions (including with our own roles), we find
that some actions build relationships, some actions harm relationships
(or have potential to do so), and some (neutral) actions have little effect,
one way or the other, on our relationships.

We can group our actions into good, bad, or neutral in terms of their effects on our relationships. We might also color code our actions, just as traffic lights are color coded. A red light means, stop! A red action is one that if we do not stop it will do damage, or at least damage is possible. A green traffic light means, go! Do these things! They are good for relationships. Think of things that are good for a marriage, for example. Successful couples are willing to follow green-light practices and avoid red-light practices.

A yellow light means proceed with caution and be ready to stop. Professional drivers who see a yellow light want to know if it is fresh or stale. How long has the light been yellow? In relationships, yellow-light issues are those that require caution because you are being motivated by feelings, urges, and desires that may or may not be appropriate, may be helpful or may be harmful. Relationships succeed because people let green trump yellow most of the time—not necessarily all the time but much of the time. That is, we do not let our feelings dictate whether we will go to work in the morning, or whether we are willing to do what the job calls for. But relationships also succeed when folks are willing to slow down and prepare to stop at a stale yellow.

Boundary keeping is surprisingly difficult. You would think that good intentions would lead to constructive behavior. Most of us believe that because our motives are good, what we do is therefore justified. Or we think that when we do "the wrong thing" but nothing bad happens, it was not a bad decision. There is plenty of evidence that most of us want to do the right thing, but it has long been recognized that doing the right thing is not always that easy. Fortunately, today we have the benefit of some helpful research that we can apply to our own boundary keeping and that of our congregations and colleagues in ministry, whether ordained or laity.

Paul decried the fact that he did not understand why he acted contrary to what he wished he would do (Rom 7:15). Since World War II, social scientists have made laudable attempts at understanding how it is that people commit atrocities on the one hand, as well as how some people are able to do the right thing under adverse and threatening circumstances. In our approach to boundary keeping in this book, we hope to apply some of the things that have been learned so we can all do better, at least with boundary keeping in congregational life. Of course, we hope that the benefit will spread beyond our congregational lives, but we are confining our scope in this book to congregational relationships and functions.

Within congregational life, we set out to address with the broadest possible all relationships with persons, things, and roles. We do this because it is the health of the entire system that best shapes the health of the individual parts. For example, while the discussion of boundaries in the church rightfully gives prominent attention to sexual boundaries, especially the responsibility of clergy to safeguard from harm all those with whom they relate, the context that supports and enforces this involves focusing on the well-being of the other rather than how the other person can help you have pleasurable experiences. This means never objectifying others, not seeing them as a means to an end, and never misusing power at all, not just in the area of sexual gratification.

In our discussion we start with the fact that our judgment and decision making can only be as good as our awareness. We cannot respect a boundary that we do not recognize, nor will we effectively counteract an unhealthy personal motive that we do not recognize. Our awareness also shapes our sense of what is important and what is not important. We quickly make the point that once we start looking for them, we find boundaries everywhere, important boundaries, in all aspects of congregational life. We will examine the factors, such as time pressure, stress, and social and cultural dynamics, that routinely limit our awareness. We will look at ways to expand and clarify our awareness so we can act more lovingly, even in stressful circumstances.

We want it understood at the outset that boundary-keeping decisions in congregational life, which protect the well-being of others, can jeopardize one's own self-interest. To take a common example, we all want to be liked; in fact, it feels like we "need" to be liked. This is fine until that need overpowers boundary reasoning, which it easily can do.[1] Keeping and promoting good boundary practices may risk the loss of social support, the loss of friends, the loss of support from coworkers or colleagues, and even the loss of one's employment. In more minor circumstances, our setting boundaries may diminish our freedom and pleasure. Healthy interpersonal boundary keeping can bring loneliness instead of social resources that are precious to many people, especially clergy. Thus, to be a good boundary keeper one must be ready to sustain loss of resources and be comfortable with vulnerability. Virtually

---

1. Kerns, "Why Good Leaders Do Bad Things."

all boundary keeping involves loss, and virtually all boundary violations involve the acquisition of resources of one form or another, including the resource of power. Jesus was right: we must become willing to lose things for the sake of love, even love of self. In the Parable of the Sower (Matt 13:18–13) Jesus notes that "the cares of the world" choke the word of God to the point that it does not yield the fruits of love. These concerns can dim our awareness of the well-being of others. However, we will discover that when we are willing to take a loss on one level, other very important things become possible—for others and sometimes even for ourselves. We will invite you at various points in this process to reflect on your own motives, which can conflict with your own awareness of and prioritizing the needs of others.

How can we possibly counteract these strong forces? We bring to this discussion insights from the relatively new field of behavioral ethics, which is the scientific study of why we act ethically and why and how we act unethically. Most of this research has been done in the field of business. The task for the individual is the same regardless of the setting. We must live more consciously and intentionally, not letting the perverse forces of the psyche or the external organizational culture control us. We must recognize and understand what we are dealing with when we try to love consistently, one moment to the next, in all circumstances and with all people.

As we will discuss at various points throughout the book, living ethically requires that we learn when not to trust our own judgment and what to do instead. Our judgment, according to the research, is often shaped by forces beyond our conscious awareness, in the deep, primitive parts of the mind, where urges and desires activate our outward behaviors, sometimes before conscious decision making can even begin to occur. Ethical decision making is a much slower process than what it takes to generate feelings and urges. Often by the time the conscious mind gets involved, the train has left the station, and the conscious mind is left to construct a rationale for what we are already doing. The result is often self-deception rather than self-revelation.[2] The ego wants to preserve a positive image of the self. So researchers have come to characterize our ethics as being egocentric in nature.[3] Much of what we hear in boundary and ethics discussions is actually ego-based ethical reasoning, even when

2. Tenbrunsel and Messick, "Ethical Fading."

3. Epley and Caruso, "Egocentric Ethics."

it is couched as being based on compassion. For example, a pastor who is uncomfortable with conflict or distress in others will try to justify not insulting a person by requiring a background check. While it sounds caring to do so, it avoids the self-interest that it serves for the pastor.

When we do engage the conscious, rational process of ethical thinking with awareness of our own urges and desires, the result can be what Bazerman, Tenbrunsel, and Wade-Benzoi brilliantly characterize in the title of their article as "negotiating with yourself and losing: making decisions with competing internal preferences."[4] Bazerman and Tenbrunsel note: "Behavioral ethics research supports the argument that most people want to act ethically. Yet we still find ourselves engaging in unethical behavior because of biases that influence our decisions—biases of which we may not be fully aware. These biases affect not only our own behavior, but also our ability to see the unethical behavior of others."[5] So in many cases of decision making about ethical issues, there is very little internal negotiating going on. The self-interest of the ego takes off and musters the support of the rest of the self before our ethical, rational self even knows what is happening. As the phenomenon of ethical fading reveals, the ethical dimension of the self often is defined out of the situation entirely. Sometimes it is stress, especially time pressure, which limits our awareness and excludes ethical considerations. In order to get real negotiating to occur among the various parts of the self, we have to change our relationship to what occurs inside ourselves. In this book we will make this point both early and often.

We can become more consciously aware of what is going on inside ourselves, in order that these events have less control over us. One powerful approach we recommend is some form of meditation or prayer designed to increase awareness. This is different from what many people do for meditation when the motivation is relaxation. Relaxation can help with some things that seriously restrict awareness and thereby also ethical decision making, such as stress and time pressure. On the other hand, relaxation and stress release without increased awareness can simply assist a person in persisting with a life that is not well considered, in the same way that various forms of "numbing out" relaxation do. The purpose of increased awareness is greater self-control and freedom of choice, no longer being controlled by unhealthy habits, urges, or desires.

4. Bazerman et al., "Negotiating with Yourself and Losing."
5. Bazerman and Tenbrunsel, *Blind Spots*, 99.

With comprehensive awareness, we notice our urges and desires and how they contrast with our deeply held values. We have awareness of the present, past, and future. We have awareness of self, others, and God simultaneously.

Behavioral ethics researchers have some recommendations that have guided us in writing this book. Bazerman and Tenbrunsel, for example, conclude from their research that organizations will benefit from standards of practice that identify separately what is unethical from what is ethically desirable.[6] We will highlight how our biblical heritage is a resource for the church to do just that. We will pair "thou shalt not" with a positively stated alternative. In our final chapter we will summarize recommended practices. Bazerman and Tenbrunsel recommend a zero-tolerance policy for unethical behavior in order to reduce uncertainty. Furthermore, they also recommend continuing to move the standards to higher levels, which challenges us to grow ethically. Without that, as their research suggests, there is a tendency for standards of conduct to degrade—something we can identify also in the church. We note how Jesus raised the standards of the Ten Commandments. While there can be value in seeing the gospel as relief from the law, in fact Jesus raised the bar considerably in characterizing the alternative kingdom of God—particularly in the Sermon on the Mount.[7]

Bazerman and Tenbrunsel also note the following risk factors for unethical behavior within organizations: uncertainty in the system, isolation, and time pressure. Many of our churches and church leaders rate high on these risk factors. We recommend, as does the research, deliberately referring to the ethical standards in routine ways, in order to keep them in our conscious awareness. We also recommend particular practices that can help accomplish this same goal. Mary C. Gentile adds another useful approach from the business realm.[8] She teaches people to practice speaking up when they encounter ethically questionable practices, in order to increase the likelihood that theirs will become more

6. Ibid.

7. The authors choose to employ the term "kingdom" as the primary translation of the New Testament word *basilea*. Readers should note that in many places we employ the term "shalom" as a synonym for "kingdom." While "kingdom" may seem antiquated to some, it preserves the comprehensive claim and political character of what Jesus meant by God's kingdom activity in the world. In the New Testament, the kingdom is not a place but a mode of God's transforming presence and rule over all creation.

8. Gentile, *Giving Voice to Values.*

ethical communities. As Gentile notes, confidence that we can address unethical behavior in others and in our organizations will help us be more consciously aware of the ethical violations happening around us. This makes good sense psychologically. Her approach is elegant and brilliant. Gentile and others make the observation that the people who stand up to unethical behavior are people who were taught to expect that they would have to at some point in their lives. For Christians charged with living the alterative kingdom of God, how could it be otherwise?

James L. Bailey speaks of the alternative kingdom of God as a "contrast community."[9] The findings of behavioral ethics support the value of making explicit the contrasts between self-interest and best practices in our decision making. We recommend that readers begin to practice examining their ethical lives according to best practices while reading this book. When making decisions that affect others, ask yourself these questions: (1) What do I want, based on my feelings and desires? (2) Why do I want that? (3) What would it do for me? (4) How strongly do I desire that? (5) How important does it feel to me? (6) Why do I feel so strongly? (7) What best practices are called for and why they are they needed? and (8)Why are these best practices so important? By asking these questions before engaging in potentially unethical behavior, we let the rational, ethical part of the brain have a better chance of influencing our behavior. Throughout the book, and especially in our final chapter, we offer best practices as a resource to help guide us in good decision making.

It is hard to live in contrast with our environment, especially the contemporary social environment. We are strongly influenced by the social norms around us. For this reason behavioral ethicists recognize the need to create an informal culture of high ethical standards in our organizations (congregations, in the case of this book) in all aspects of their functioning. Formal codes of ethics and conduct, while essential, have less sway on us than the informal culture. You, our reader, are co-architect of the informal culture of your congregation and in the larger church—you, your coworkers, friends, colleagues and peers. We welcome your interest and participation in helping make our congregations more healthy and vibrant centers of love.

We express our heartfelt appreciation to those who reviewed our manuscript and offered constructive suggestions that have enhanced our work: Robert Albers, Wayne Menking, and Gary Schoener. We also

9. Bailey, *Contrast Community*.

are deeply grateful to Michael Cooper-White, President of the Lutheran Theological Seminary at Gettysburg, and Pamela Cooper-White, Christiane Brooks Johnson Professor of Psychology and Religion at Union Theological Seminary, for sharing their insights in the foreword and offering constructive advice for improving the book. We also offer thanks to the many people whose work we have built upon (as represented in references and bibliography) as well as to countless unnamed others from whom we have learned. The authors express our special gratitude to Halcyon Bjornstad for her assistance in proofreading and indexing. The editors and staff of Cascade Books have been excellent to work with in the editing and publication process, and we are grateful to each of them. The authors especially desire to express thanks to their wives: Arden to his wife, Linda Mahlberg, for her patience and support through the process of devoting many hours to this book; Craig to his wife, Cathy Nessan, for her steadfastness and support. We dedicate this book to those who have requested a resource like this, in the hope that it will contribute to forward movement for an ethical church. We especially dedicate this book to our children, whose generation calls us to accountability for bequeathing to them a church that more adequately demonstrates the integrity necessary to serve as a life-giving community for them, their peers, and future generations: Nathaniel and Nora Mahlberg; Benjamin, Nathaniel, Sarah, Andrew, Jessica, and Mary Nessan.

PART 1

Defining and Protecting Integrity through Boundaries

1

The Necessity of Boundaries for Creating and Sustaining Identity and Effective Mission

SCENARIO ONE: PASTOR A AND PASTOR B

EARLY IN HER MINISTRY at Grace Church, Pastor B. began to visit members who were unable to attend church. She was the new Associate Pastor and was eager to meet everyone. The pastor rang the doorbell at one of her first calls. A frail yet spirited elderly woman came to the door. "Are you Dottie?" Pastor B asked politely. She introduced herself and asked to come in. When they sat down, she said: "Everyone has told me, 'You will enjoy getting to know Dottie.'"

"Actually, Pastor, my name is Dorothy. I've always loved that name. It was my grandmother's name, but everyone calls me Dottie."

"Well," replied Pastor B, "Dorothy is a beautiful name. And, actually, I prefer to be called 'Pastor Blanchard,' if you don't mind."

Pastor B. realized that she was in the same boat as Dorothy. Her name was Susan Blanchard. When the call committee decided to extend her the call to be Grace Church's first Associate Pastor to work with Pastor Alvez, a member of the committee declared excitedly, "Now we have a 'Pastor A' and a 'Pastor B!'" Everyone laughed. But the names stuck! When Pastor Blanchard raised her disquiet in private with Pastor Alvez, he brushed it off. He thought it was cute. She, however, felt uneasy, like she was not in control of her own identity. Should she assert herself over this issue with her new colleague and congregation? "Pastor B," in contrast to "Pastor A," was by definition second-best. It was not that she needed to be first, but according to her understanding this was supposed to be a nonhierarchical copastorate.

Pastor Blanchard came to discover that many of the members of Grace and also many members of the local community had been given nicknames by others, like "Stub," "Baldy," "Skinny," and "Nutsy." When she began to inquire in private, many of them did not like their nicknames but nonetheless had resigned themselves to them.

"She'll always be Dottie to me," the church secretary said when Pastor Blanchard told her about Dorothy's preference. Names convey messages and communicate images. "Dorothy" does not evoke the same meanings and images as "Dottie." Pastor Blanchard did not like the implications of being labeled "Pastor B."

Who has the right to decide what one is called? This is a boundary issue of great significance. The question about who has the right to define one's core identity in life leads us into the central theme of this book: the myriad boundaries questions we encounter in Christian community. Naming others can be a form of domination. Conquering cultures routinely rename those they have come to dominate, instead of using the native people's own names for themselves. Cult leaders often rename their members as part of asserting their control. Bullies engage in name-calling to intimidate their victims. One of the first steps leading to dehumanization and violence is stealing the name of another person or group and substituting a degrading epithet (for example, "cockroach" or "vermin") for their valued name.

As Pastor Blanchard considered the issue of naming more fully, she became disturbed by the realization that she, Pastor Alvez, and their clergy colleagues had been educated, trained, and socialized to label parishioners. As Pastor Alvez was orienting Pastor Blanchard, he said: "We do have three alligators in the congregation and one clergy wannabe." He proceeded to identify the people he felt had a history of criticizing their pastors in ways that did not seem could ever be satisfied except by their removal; he also talked about those members who sometimes could be satisfied with specific things but who were preoccupied with figuring out how they could always get what they wanted. This type of labeling (alligators, clergy killers, and clergy wannabes) reduces ambiguity and complexity. It makes us feel like we have got the person figured out. But once we have categorized another, we see and relate to the label and lose site of the person in all of their rich complexity. Therefore, labeling is a violation of a person's identity boundary.

BOUNDARIES, BOUNDARIES EVERYWHERE!

Boundaries are fundamental structures that establish and preserve identity. Boundaries protect the essential nature of things, while also contributing to their definition.[1] *A guiding question for respecting boundaries is, who does this belong to?* The Ten Commandments begin with an identity boundary. We are commanded to know and acknowledge who God is, as well as to remain clear about who God is not. It is God alone who defines God's nature, not us. We are neither to construct our own image of God nor to behave as if anything other than God is God. We are not to use the name of God in ways that diminish God's being or identity. We are to use God's name to preserve God's being and identity for us and for others. God's identity belongs to God, not us.

Similarly, we are also commanded to respect the identity of others. Bearing false witness is one form of creating a false image of the other. This includes saying a person's name with a negative inflection. We are also enjoined to respect our own identity as a person created in God's image.[2] Jesus encouraged each one of us, "Let your light shine!" In the Parable of the Wise and Foolish Bridesmaids, when the women who let their lamps go out came to join the party, they were told, "Truly I tell you, I do not know you" (Matt 25:12). Attitudes and practices that protect and nurture our core identities are essential to living as Christ calls us to live.

One of our deepest longings is to express who we are: to be known, understood, and accepted just as we are. When other people project their own images upon us and have agendas for who they want us to be, we feel unsafe and withhold who we really are. By adolescence, most children who are still creating stories or artwork as a form of self-expression have stopped showing them to anyone else. It is so easy to form our own images of others and to justify them to fulfill our own agendas. For example, a pastor might peg a young person as a future pastor and become overinvested in that outcome. The young person would not want to disappoint such an influential person in his or her life. When others act like they are authorities about who we are, on some level we feel we are unsafe, even if

1. Cf. Olsen and Devor, *Saying No to Say Yes*, 4–7.
2. Harbaugh et al., *Covenants and Care*, 119–21.

their image of us is flattering: "I can tell that you are the kind of girl who will make a man very happy." On the other hand, when others criticize us, they attack our very being. One's identity is unsafe in either case. Who does one's identity belong to?

While we are quick to form impressions and to set agendas for others, a part of us longs to know others deeply for who they are. Allowing the self to be "self" and the other to be "other" establishes the delightful conditions for the meeting of an I and a Thou. How we treat a stranger respectfully becomes the model for how we treat each and every person, since here we approach the other without presuming already to know who they are. We ask their name and invite them to tell us about themselves. We err in such encounters, however, if we too quickly form an impression, thereby creating a false image, one based upon our own construction. Exploring who others are in deliberate conversation by listening to them gives us the benefit of an entirely different way of seeing things, something wholly "other" from our own hasty perceptions. While the impulse of the anxious mind is to reject what is foreign and different, the secure and open mind responds to differences with respect, fascination, and curiosity.

Respecting boundaries is so essential to the spiritual life that it is a key part of the prayer Jesus taught his followers: "and forgive us our trespasses, as we forgive those who have trespassed against us." This is territorial language, the language of boundaries and borders. While the translation can be "sins," "debts," or "trespasses," we note that the major thrust of the Ten Commandments has to do with disturbing or violating established boundaries, which the word "trespass" reflects.

Various types of boundaries are associated with different parts of our being, as we will explore in the chapters ahead. We have a physical boundary that protects our health, which, if violated, will result in death. We are commanded not to kill. Life does not belong to us—it belongs to God. It is not ours to take. We are not to take from others their possessions or their loved ones. We are even commanded not to steal with our imaginations—not to covet or desire what others have. Does it not feel like a kind of theft when we have something precious and sense that someone else wants to possess it instead of being happy for us? "Do not commit adultery!" Again hear the warning about a boundary violation. With marital infidelity, you are not just going where you do not belong (even if invited); you are stealing from your own marriage what rightly belongs to it—vital energy whose absence damages the marriage, even if the partner is not consciously aware.[3] We are also commanded to protect the boundary around sacred time—to keep the Sabbath holy, uncontaminated by thoughts about work, outside responsibilities, or the secular values of the dominant culture that distract us from the sacred values of the culture of God.[4]

The commandments have to do with respecting boundaries. So they tell us what not to do instead of telling us what to do. Thereby, they delineate boundaries in ways that would not be as clear, if the same content were merely put in positive terms. For example, "Do not covet what belongs to your neighbor," clarifies a boundary. Taking the same content and putting it positively could translate as: "Be grateful for what you have." This may communicate somewhat the same idea but misses the lesson about boundaries: To whom does this belong? Put even more positively, God could have commanded us to be happy for our neighbor for the good things they have to enjoy. Again this surely is a part of what it means to fully love our neighbor, but it misses the truth about boundaries.

Beyond the discipline of boundary keeping, translating the commandments positively as did Jesus *builds bridges across boundaries* that would not be possible without first respecting the boundaries for what they are. The commandment to "love the Lord your God with all your heart, and with all your soul, and with all your mind, and with all your strength" (Mark 12:30) builds a bridge to God; God is accessible and can be totally engaged. To "love your neighbor as yourself" (Mark 12:31) reveals the bridge not only between people, but between us and Christ. To recognize that how we treat the least important person (Matt 25:40) is the same as how we treat Christ requires both a boundary and a bridge. Boundaries beget bridges. Respecting the boundaries defined in the Ten Commandments, while adding love, strengthens each person's uniqueness, their capacity to love, serve, celebrate, and create, giving us the conditions ripe for spiritual community.

Spiritual community depends on bridges between and among us. Paul taught the followers of Jesus to understand themselves as a mystical body, the very body of Christ. Each one has a unique and important function that when linked to others is like the complex organism of the

3. Harbaugh et al., *Covenants and Care*, 123–24.
4. Brueggemann, *Sabbath as Resistance*, chap. 1.

human body.[5] To live as members of Christ's body requires both the ability to be a unique person, on the one hand, and the capacity to unite with
others without damaging them, on the other. The standards are high and
the challenge significant.

We all know what it feels like to be violated. If you have ever had a
purse stolen or your car broken into, you have felt violated. If you have
ever had people say hurtful things about you to others or misrepresent
you, as happens in gossip, you have felt a boundary violation. Gossip is
by nature problematic when it comes to boundaries. Barbara J. Blodgett
defines *gossip* as "informal, evaluative discourse about someone not present who is a member of the speaker's social group. These features—the
informality, the absence of the person being talked about, the evaluative
or judgmental nature of the discourse, and the relational context—are
ones I take to be necessary and sufficient features of gossip."[6] Perhaps
you have experienced even worse violations. It is now widely recognized
that abusive violations of a person's integrity can wound that person in
profound ways for a very long time.[7] As a consequence of abuse, parts
of the self can be cut off and the individual can turn against themselves
or others. Among the many consequences, the abuse can so negatively
impact a person's relationship with God that it impairs their capacity to
trust the gospel.[8]

A car that has a few things wrong with it can run safely at forty-five
miles an hour. When you try to drive it ninety miles per hour, however,
it will perform badly and may even be dangerous. The demands of the
godly life are at least that challenging. Every part of the vehicle needs
to be in top condition. Therefore we can cultivate awareness of and care
even for subtle boundaries, not just the obvious ones. As scientists learn
more about the impact of boundary violations on our lives, they coin
new terms: "microviolations," "micro-insults," and "micro-incursions."[9]
These are the kinds of behaviors that are not easily detected but do have
significant impact on our sense of safety, our willingness to disclose ourselves freely, and our ability to do our best work. These relatively small,
apparently minor, violations damage our spirit, especially when they are

5. Nessan, *Shalom Church*, 34–36.

6. Blodgett, *Lives Entrusted*, 88.

7. See Fortune, *Love Does No Harm*, 35, for reflections on the meaning of "harm."

8. Fortune, *Is Nothing Sacred?*, 110–11.

9. Cf. Sue, *Microaggressions and Marginality*.

persistent. What we would call toxic environments at work, home, or church result from accumulating subtle violations. Such events seem so small that people can disagree about whether one person is being overly sensitive or the other person is being overly insensitive. Is it something, or is it nothing?

Before mechanical sensors of air quality were invented, coal miners would bring a caged canary with them into the mine, because canaries are more sensitive to dangerous gasses than humans. As long as the canary was singing, the miners were fine. But as soon as the canary stopped singing, the miners knew to get out fast. Like the proverbial canary in the coal mine, some people are more sensitive than the rest of us when it comes to toxicity in the psychological and spiritual environment. These persons are more strongly affected by attitudes, language, and behaviors that are actual boundary violations, though these violations may not be so obvious to others. Others might regard these people as being thin-skinned or overly sensitive, especially with regard to behavior that seems to have become the norm. People who grew up in family systems where boundaries were not respected can become numb to violations of their own boundaries and to their violating the boundaries of others.[10] The sensors inside us need to be cleaned, repaired, and activated to their full capacity.

How many rabbis and priests in Jesus's time had some minor, nagging qualms about money changing in the temple? Undoubtedly there were some, but most would have been shocked by Jesus's bold assertion that the integrity of the temple was being violated by commercial activity that had become routinized. Habituation dulls our capacity to sense harmful elements. As rust weakens iron, so microviolations weaken the spirit and impair our capacity to do God's work, especially when they are allowed to continue unchecked. Attending to micro-issues proactively allows us to get better and better at Christ-like community. We will not "let our light shine," as Jesus urged us, if we fear someone around us will disrespect or invalidate us.[11]

Respecting others involves a sense of the sacred. The apostle Paul tells us that the human body is the temple of the Holy Spirit (1 Cor 6:19). My body is not wholly mine. We are advised to approach the body as sacred space. Thomas Merton also spoke about the sanctity of human

---

10. Halstead, *From Stuck to Unstuck*, chap. 3.
11. Bailey, *Contrast Community*, chap. 3.

subjectivity.[12] Our subjectivity is central to who we are. It is the experience of interior dwelling that we have been given, and which we create and occupy. It includes our attitudes, values, impressions, perceptions, beliefs, feelings, and thoughts. It also includes our sacred experiences, entrusted to us by the Holy One. We treat our own subjectivity as being sacred, when we do not contaminate our state of consciousness through negativity toward self or others.

Dorothy accurately detected that her identity boundary had been violated when people renamed her instead of granting her the simple courtesy of asking her how she wished to be called. She respected her boundary by telling Pastor Blanchard how she wished to be called but failed to protect her identity boundary with others, perhaps sensing that her preference would not be respected. The result: Dorothy was not as fully at home in Christian community as she might have been. Nor was Pastor Blanchard, who also chose not to make an issue of her moniker after she failed to get the support of Pastor Alvez. Because of his expressed attitude, Pastor Blanchard faced the risk of alienating him and others in the congregation simply by exercising the right to choose her own name. The result? She also became tentative in other areas of self-expression. She treated those people differently, whom Pastor Alvez labeled as alligators and clergy wannabes, interpreting their behavior otherwise than the behavior of those not so labeled. Even microviolations have real consequences for the body of Christ.

PROTECTING AND PRESERVING THE IDENTITY AND MISSION OF THE CHURCH

Boundary issues are pervasive in the life of the church. Often when we hear the word, "boundary," we think chiefly, if not exclusively, about sexual boundaries in ministry. God knows that maintaining clear and proactive sexual boundaries is an imperative of the first order for healthy ministry.[13] The extent and magnitude of sexual boundary violations throughout the Christian churches has permanently harmed countless victims and their families—women, men, and children—each one precious to God. The failure of the churches to hold leaders accountable for sexual abuse and to remove offenders from public service has further

12. Merton, *Seeds of Contemplation*, chap. 2.

13. Cf. Hopkins and Laaser, eds., *Restoring the Soul of a Church*.

complicated the church's integrity. Moreover, these abuses have brought scandal and suspicion to everything the church does. This book certainly advocates for vigilance and accountability in maintaining and respecting sexual boundaries at every level of the church's life—beginning with the ethical responsibilities of the clergy.[14]

At the same time that we insist on clarity about sexual boundaries, in this book we extend the argument for wise boundaries to encompass a broad array of church practices by *including all church members* (laity, lay staff, and clergy) and *every dimension of human life* (thought, word, and deed). For church professionals not to exploit church members for their own ends is only the beginning. In virtually every human encounter and human activity in the life of the church, we either express the identity of the church by living according to the values of God's kingdom or not. Are we being the church, or are we being something else? There are necessary boundaries that are rightly observed, if we are to relate to one another with the respect due to those made in the image of God and redeemed by Jesus Christ. What is more, it is crucial that we recognize and tend these interpersonal boundaries for the sake of preserving and safeguarding the integrity of the church's core mission of bringing the Gospel of Jesus Christ to the world in word and deed.

Boundaries can be detected at every human interface. As we have already seen, there are boundaries that involve "naming" and "labeling" persons. Furthermore, there are many boundaries involving the use of language in appropriate and edifying ways. There are boundaries involving inflection of voice and innuendo of speech. There are boundaries entailed in written communication, both private and public: handwritten notes, newsletter announcements, professional correspondence, e-mails, messages social networks, blogs, text messages, and a host of other electronic means. There are boundaries involving propriety and respect in the assembly for Christian worship and at other church gatherings for congregational, council, and committee meetings. There are boundaries involved in childcare and youth ministry. How we do these things with integrity as church will be different than how others might do them in secular society.

Pastors must follow accepted professional practices in visitation, counseling, and all other private meetings with people. There are boundaries involving a wide range of public behaviors: for example, what one

14. Cf. Jung and Stephans, eds., *Professional Sexual Ethics.*

buys and where one purchases it, what movies one attends and which DVDs one rents, or whether one drinks alcohol in public. Pastoral ministry is public in a way that requires careful attention to boundary crossings that might compromise the effectiveness of the pastoral role and the church's ministry.[15] Maintaining clear boundaries can assist all members of the church to preserve clarity about roles, avoiding dual relationships and role confusion. We will go so far in this book as to suggest that we maintain proper boundaries by reflecting not only on our words and actions but even on how we 'think about' others in a salutary way. This is only a beginning list of how defining boundaries affects our life together with others in the church.

Because the range of issues involving boundaries is so broad, it is important to offer a working definition of the term 'boundaries'. *Boundaries protect the essential nature of persons and things, while at the same time contributing to their definition. Boundaries are therefore necessary for the faithful expression of identity. In the life of the church, boundaries are intentional limits placed on thoughts, words, and deeds to safeguard the protection of persons and to guard and protect the integrity of the church's identity and mission. Furthermore, boundaries set limits on behavior in order to protect things of value.* What is at stake in tending boundaries is preserving the integrity of each person as made in God's image, the value of holy things set aside for God's purposes, the identity of the church as the body of Christ, and the mission of the church in extending God's reign. Conversely, boundary violations put at risk the integrity of persons, the proper use of holy things, the core identity of the church, and the church's mission.

Boundaries protect persons and thus allow for the faithful expression of their true identities as members of the body of Christ! Each person has been created in the image of God and is precious to Jesus Christ. For this reason, it is essential that we relate to other persons in thought, word, and deed with the respect owed to those with such status. It is now widely recognized that traumatizing a person by violating their boundaries through abuse can wound that person in profound ways for a very long time. Furthermore, research has shown that abusing children negatively impacts their relationship with God as adults.[16] Again, as rust weakens iron, microviolations weaken the spirit, especially when the microviola-

15. Everist and Nessan, *Transforming Leadership*, 116–17.

16. Salter et al., "Development of Sexually Abusive Behavior in Sexually Victimized Males," 471–76.

tions are allowed to continue. Even micro-incursions demoralize people's vitality. It is wise to assume that when someone objects to something, even where we see no problem at all, at least a microviolation may have taken place. Listening to those who complain or express hurt feelings is one way to increase our own sensitivity, asking questions in order to see things from another's point of view. If someone objects, it is wise to assume they have a valid point, even if you do not readily understand it. If we are the offending person, this means checking our defensiveness to consider what the other is expressing.

Moving from micro- to extreme violations, such as when a person has been assaulted, the impact is likely to include dissociation to reduce the pain.[17] Dissociation is a disengagement from what is happening. The victim of an extreme violation becomes somewhat, if not totally, unconscious and may not even remember what happened. If conscious, the victim becomes numb. As they experience the violation, they may feel like they have become an outside observer of what is happening to them, as if they are watching someone else. They may literally experience being outside their body. While this is extreme, micro-incursions have the same effect on a smaller scale. If we undergo a microviolation, to some degree we become less present and engaged. We may freeze up at a church meeting and be unable to fully participate because of the alarm that is sounding inside us in response to critical language or harsh tones.

A member might hesitate to participate fully in a fellowship after witnessing a pastor exploiting relationships with members—for example, pursuing members for private business interests. Agents at church-based insurance companies may seek privileged access to members or membership lists. Or a pastor might seek a clergy discount from a church member who works at a car dealership. Here the relationship between pastor and parishioner is exploited in the interest of financial benefit. This boundary also is obscured when church members in business voluntarily offer clergy discounts or other favors to their pastor.

Boundaries protect holy things! While not as damaging as infractions involving persons, boundary violations can also involve the misuse of property. For example, the church council president decides, without asking permission, to use the fellowship hall for a private Christmas party for her family and friends. Or a member who lives in the neighborhood borrows the church's lawn mower, and so it is missing when a member

17. Cf. Karjala, *Understanding Trauma and Dissociation.*

of the property committee comes to use it to mow the church's lawn. Or the chair of the property committee enters the parsonage when no one is home, in order to borrow coffee creamer for a church meeting. Or the pastor borrows folding tables and chairs for a family graduation party and returns the tables dirty, and one of the chairs with a broken chair leg. In each of these cases, self-interest leads to disrespect for things set aside for the church's 'holy' use.

Boundaries preserve the church's identity! What is the church? The church is the people of God, the communion of saints, the fellowship of the baptized, and the body of Christ. Each of these images points to the intrinsic identity of the church in relationship to the triune God. The church discovers its true identity exclusively grounded in God's grace revealed in the person and work of Jesus Christ by the power of the Holy Spirit.[18] The church lives in obedience to the Great Commandment: to love God with all one's heart, soul, mind, and strength and to love the neighbor as oneself. One constant temptation in the life of the church is to substitute some other identity to replace core Christian identity. Thereby the church serves as a social outlet for the enjoyment of the members, or as an organization to provide services for those who pay their dues. Or the church gets construed as a business venture that only has value when it makes a profit. Or the church exists primarily to perpetuate the building and provide a cemetery. So many false identities threaten to overtake the church's identity as the people of God in Christ Jesus! Good boundaries clarify, protect, and preserve the true nature of church so that it can fulfill its mission of living the Great Commandment.

Boundaries preserve the church's mission! The mission of the Christian church is to proclaim the gospel of Jesus Christ, to serve a world full of neighbors as disciples of Jesus Christ, and to care for God's creation as faithful stewards. The church exists not for its own self-interest but to mediate God's life-giving presence to the world through the message of the gospel and ministry of service for the well-being of others. Primary venues for the church to embody this mission are evangelism, ecumenism, global service, and social ministry. Wherever church leaders or members distort Christ's mission to serve self-interest, a boundary has been crossed and the intended purpose of the church becomes compromised. One of the great challenges that undermines the integrity of the church and its mission is the misrepresentation of the gospel by those

---

18. Nessan, *Beyond Maintenance to Mission*, 6–10.

who represent it publicly. Hypocrisy by church members and misconduct by clergy obscure the intention of the gospel as Christ's message of unconditional forgiveness, mercy, and grace. "If any of you put a stumbling block before one of these little ones who believe in me, it would be better for you if a great millstone were fastened around your neck and you were drowned in the depth of the sea" (Matt 18:6).

THE PURPOSE OF THE CHURCH
AND ITS MINISTRY

Boundaries are essential to the life of the church and its ministry, in order to preserve the church's core identity and mission. There are a variety of ways to describe the basic purpose of the church. Consider the following affirmations: The church exists to follow the Great Commandment of loving God and loving the neighbor as oneself; the church serves as an instrument for the arrival of God's kingdom in this world; the church lives for the sake of proclaiming to others the good news about Jesus Christ as Lord and Savior of the world; the church seeks to follow the way of Jesus Christ through faithful discipleship; the church is the body of Christ in the world and makes Christ present to others. Each of these descriptions reveals aspects of the church's true identity and mission. In concise formulations, each of these statements expresses the spiritual purpose of the church: how the church serves God's intention to bring life, wholeness, fulfillment, and salvation to the world.

There are several paradigmatic ways the church incarnates this fundamental purpose, enacting its identity and mission—through worship, prayer, education, community life, stewardship, evangelizing, ecumenism, global connections, and social ministry.[19] The center of the church's life is in the communal gathering of God's people for worship.[20] At worship we reclaim our identity in Christ and become the people God intends us to be—through confession and absolution, praise, hearing the Word, voicing our convictions in the creed, praying, sharing the peace, presenting an offering, breaking bread, and receiving blessing. The pattern of the Christian life is rehearsed in the things of worship: trusting God's promises for our lives, learning to praise God, attending to God's Word, becoming those who care for the things for which we pray, shar-

19. Ibid., 8–10.
20. Ibid., chap. 4.

ing God's peace with one another and the world, generously stewarding
the gifts God has bestowed, and partaking of the Lord's Table where all
are welcome and there is enough for all. We are sent from worship to be
agents of God's shalom in our daily lives.

The church also exists to pray for the needs of all people and the
creation itself. We pray for God's mercy and healing in a broken world,
where suffering threatens to overwhelm us. The church teaches members
the way of discipleship as a primary educational task. At church we learn
what it means to follow Jesus in our daily lives. By living with one another
in community, the church learns what it means to live under the cross,
where the weak and lonely, the sick and marginal ones have privileged
place.[21] In this community we recall that it is the Crucified One who
binds us together in love. We learn to experience Jesus Christ himself
as we relate to one another in the church and as we go out into the local community to encounter Jesus Christ in the least of these. Moreover,
the church knows the true meaning of stewardship, where everything we
receive is a gift given to us from God's generosity. As stewards the very
posture of our lives is that of thanksgiving for all the kindness God has
showered upon us.

In its life of service, the church responds to God's goodness by sharing the good news of Jesus Christ in words and deeds. Evangelizing involves the church in speaking boldly, genuinely, and authentically about
what God has done for us in Jesus Christ. Christian people are to testify to
others about what God has done in their lives in order that others might
believe (Rom 10:10–13). The work of evangelizing encompasses both
personal conversations with others and testimonies given in public worship services. Glory is also given to God wherever Christians of different
traditions and denominations are reconciled to one another as brothers
and sisters. Beyond the scandal of denominational divisions, Jesus prays
that the church be one (John 17:20–21). Therefore ecumenical relations
belong centrally to the church's mission. Christians also build connections with one another across the globe in partnerships and cooperation
that mutually enhances our life together. The catholicity of the church is
manifest wherever Christians throughout the world pray for one another,
join in worship together, participate in Christ-centered community, and
live in mutual service to one another. Lastly, the church partakes in social
ministry—both acts of charity to relieve human suffering and the work

---

21. For a pastoral approach to the theology of the cross, see Menking, *When All
Else Fails*, 74–81.

of advocacy to transform the structures and policies that hold people in subjugation. Through these manifold expressions the church fulfills its God-given purpose.

Those who serve as ministers of the church—meaning both the clergy and laity—have as their Christian vocation the fulfillment of the church's purpose in the various ways described in the previous paragraphs. Biblically and theologically, these are the reasons why the church exists: to reveal the presence and the way of God to others in this world. For the laity, this means trusting the good news of Jesus Christ at the center of life, and following the way of Jesus Christ in discipleship by thought, word, and deed. The Christian vocation encompasses all arenas of life: one's family, the workplace, at church, and as member of local and global communities.[22] As a Christian, one's very identity is centered in Jesus Christ and one's whole existence is offered as spiritual worship of God (Rom 12:1–2).

Pastors have a particular calling among the baptized: to serve as ministers of God's Word and sacraments among God's people. This vocation involves faithful teaching and preaching of the Christian faith, stewardship of worship among the Christian community, and sharing the presence of Christ with others in pastoral care. Because of the nature of professional ministry and how these leaders represent God before the world, pastors and other ministers who work for the church are held to a high ethical standard. The failure to reflect the highest Christian values on the part of pastors and other ministers brings special scandal upon the church and its mission. Without expecting Christian perfectionism, there is an expectation that both Christian laity and especially Christian pastors and lay professionals represent with integrity the reality of God's own ministry in the world.

Boundaries are designed to safeguard the church's identity and mission. Worship takes place for the praise of God, not to sell products. Prayer is for entreaty to God, not gossip. Christian education is for learning the meaning of discipleship, not bragging about one's accomplishments. Christian community is for the mutual strengthening of the members in the faith, not cruising for a date. Stewardship is about gratitude to God, not for tax benefits, gaining influence with the pastor and congregation, or pride about one's generosity. Evangelizing is for sharing the good news, not manipulating people with guilt. Ecumenism is for

---

22. Fortin, *Centered Life*, 83–84.

building up the whole body of Christ, not demonstrating the superiority of one's own tradition. Global partnerships are for mutual accompaniment in the Christian faith, not creating dependency relationships. Social ministry is for sharing with those in need, not obtaining a sense of one's own righteousness or the promotion of political agendas.

The church's central purpose—to worship God and minister to the world in the name of Jesus Christ—is undercut by thoughts, words, and actions that compromise or contradict the stated purpose of the church as articulated in this chapter. When Christians, whether ministers or laity, engage in domestic abuse, cheat on taxes, operate according to unfair business practices, discriminate in hiring, tell lies, fail to maintain the safety of an automobile, or litter in public places—each of these behaviors violates a boundary by misrepresenting the will of God for human life in the spirit of Jesus. Another cause for consternation is valuing secondary identities over the primary one. This especially includes the privileging of certain ethnic and cultural heritages over baptismal identity, whereas it is baptism that properly provides the fundamental basis of Christian community. Eric H. F. Law comments:

> To be interculturally sensitive, we need to examine the internal instinctual part of our own culture. This means revealing unconscious values and thought patterns so that we will not simply react from our cultural instinct. The more we learn about our internal culture, the more we are aware of how our cultural values and thought patterns differ from others. Knowing this difference will help us make self-adjustments in order to live peacefully with people from other cultures.[23]

Engaging in intentional processes to increase diversity in congregational life must become an urgent priority.[24] Other secondary matters also are often sources of conflict in congregations, such as conflict over music and styles of worship. Often when people feel loss about their secondary identities, they do not know who they are anymore and fall out of touch with their primary identity, similar to how a person may feel lost after retirement. Such behaviors contradict Christian identity and obscure God's purposes for the world.

Likewise when Christian pastors or ministers neglect their families, fail to pay their bills, manipulate their relationships with others out of

---

23. Law, *Wolf Shall Dwell with the Lamb*, 9.
24. Cf. Law, *Sacred Acts, Holy Change.*

self-interest, misrepresent their competence, break confidences, exhibit professional jealousy, complain about parishioners to their colleagues, or display rage in public, such behaviors contradict their public vocation as representatives of God and bring scandal upon the church in its professed identity and mission.[25] These examples illustrate the variety of ways that Christian pastors and ministers can overstep boundaries to the detriment of the church's identity and mission. The Christian life—for laity, pastors, and other ministers—is abounding with ethical boundaries to preserve the church in fulfilling its central purpose of bearing witness to the reality of God in this world.

Becoming "canaries in the church" requires us to keep our eye on the church's core identity and mission so that we can better know how to fulfill it, detect what is harmful, and keep ourselves from violating it. At the close of this chapter we have mentioned examples of how personal interests that can conflict with the church's core identity and mission. Many of these will be explored in the remainder of this book. Having introduced in this chapter particular facets of the boundaries needful for preserving the identity and purpose of the church, we next discuss boundaries in relation to the matter of entrustment: the imperative that the church be a safe place for us to be in Christian community together.

25. Bush, *Gentle Shepherding*, chap. 2.

2

Entrustment

SCENARIO TWO: CONFIDENTIALITY BREECH

THE EVENING AFTER A youth event as she was relaxing, Marge shared with her husband, Larry, how upset she was with the new youth leader. She complained that he was disorganized and immature. She did not give any details but simply shared how upsetting the youth outing was for her. Maybe she was just in a bad mood, she wondered aloud. They then went on to discuss other things before going to bed.

The following morning, Larry stopped for coffee at the local restaurant and saw Elle, who invited him to join her at her table. Elle is a member of the Youth Ministry Committee. As they talked, Elle shared with Larry how excited she was with the new youth leader and the creative ideas and talents he brings. Larry shared with her Marge's negative impressions of him. Elle asked for details, but Larry only had Marge's generalizations and conclusions to share. Elle did not like Marge and did not trust her. After the coffee, Elle promptly called Clarissa, the council representative, and warned her that Marge and Larry were trying to get rid of the new youth director. Clarissa called Marge and confronted her with the charge.

All these people were affected by information about Marge's subjective state and did different things with it. When Marge shared her feelings with her husband, Larry, she assumed he would not tell anyone else and not make anything of it. For her, venting was the end of it. The matter was so unimportant to her that she did not even clarify that she did not want Larry to tell anyone else. She just assumed that Larry understood where she was coming from and that she could trust Larry to not violate the implicit conditions under which she was sharing with him.

When talking with Elle, Larry treated Marge's sharing as something of his own, essentially hijacking it, an appropriate description even though his intentions were favorable toward Marge. The term *hijacking* applies here because he took the material she shared, which belonged to her, and made it his own, grabbing ownership, and feeling free to make his own decisions about its use. While he was not completely sure that Marge would be fine with his passing along her feelings, he believed it was important that a member of the Youth Committee know that there was some disgruntlement about the new youth leader. Larry fell prey to the temptation of "substitution of judgment." He substituted his own judgment in place of Marge's.

Elle, who neither liked Marge nor trusted her, hijacked Larry's sharing and used it for her own ends, which were controlled by her feelings of dislike and distrust. She then reframed the material with a new spin: "Marge and Larry are trying to get rid of the new youth director." Her motive was to stop them by generating negative feelings toward them. Elle believed she was doing the right thing in trying to protect the youth director.

Clarissa, the council member, also took ownership of the material by making her own judgment about what to do with it. Elle did not want her to confront Marge, suspecting that the source of the information would be traced to her.

THE NATURE OF ENTRUSTMENT

Our God-given identity is something we are entrusted to claim and protect. We are entrusted with the care of our bodies, our minds, our perceptions (insights and concerns), our passions, our spirits, and with all of the resources at our disposal. We are also entrusted with the care of others—their bodies, their minds, their perceptions (insights and concerns), their passions, their spirits and their resources—alongside other responsibilities we have assumed. We are also entrusted with God's intentions and mission for our lives. We are called to live out faithfully the Great Commission. In this chapter we will look at the process of entrustment, what it means to be entrusted, and what it takes to be faithful to that trust.[1]

Entrustment is not a process that transfers ownership and rights to another. It is a process of placing something in another's care. The rights are retained by the owner of the material, whatever the content of that material. Confidential communications, for example, belong to the person who originates them.[2] What I tell you does not become yours to do with as you please. Entrustment carries conditions. Even without an explicit pledge of confidentiality, what is shared with us remains the property of the speaker, unless it has been spoken publicly. We experience this whenever our own trust is violated. Marge rightly experienced that her trust in her husband had been violated. He had no right to hijack her material and substitute judgment, allowing his own judgment about the use of the material to trump hers. Larry rightly felt his trust in Elle was violated by her hijacking of the information and using it for her own emotionally driven ends.

Church leaders too often feel entitled to the ownership of whatever subjective and objective material is shared with them. This allows them to exercise their own judgment, a process that has led to a breakdown of trust and a reduction of material being entrusted to the church. Blodgett observes: "Confidences should not be an occasion to exacerbate anyone's vulnerability or create a power struggle . . . When one person tells a secret to another, or to a group, a trust relationship is immediately implied. Often, however, the issues of risk, vulnerability, and power relevant to the relationship are not immediately obvious."[3] Fewer souls are entrusting themselves, their children, their material resources, and their time to the care of the church and its ministers. Perhaps this is for good reason.

People in positions of ongoing trust are subject to the subtle and insidious temptation of thinking that in order to care for others, they must transcend the weaknesses of those in their care. This involves the process of "splitting," whereby one separates problems from solutions, instead of looking for both in the same place.[4] If I am entrusted to help you, I come to believe that when you are confused, then I must be clear and know

1. Cf. Blodgett, *Lives Entrusted*, chap. 1.

2. Everist and Nessan, *Transforming Leadership*, 135–38.

3. Blodgett, *Lives Entrusted*, 53.

4. Cf. Guggenbuhl-Craig, *Power in the Helping Professions*, chap. 7.

what is best for you. If you are feeling weak, I must be strong. If you are sick, I must be well. The result of this splitting leads me to feel not only entitled to the information you share but also obligated to substitute my judgment for yours as I search out help for you. This behavior becomes so routine that leaders no longer notice they are hijacking someone else's confidences. They truly believe it belongs to them and that they are right in exercising their own power or discretion. Not only do they believe they are right in doing so, but they believe it is necessary and faithful to do so, because in the splitting process they have come to deny the other person's strengths. The whole situation becomes increasingly distorted as they deny their own weaknesses and vulnerabilities, while accentuating the weaknesses and vulnerabilities of others.[5]

Mother Teresa made the mistake of sharing in writing her emotional and spiritual weakness and vulnerability with her spiritual advisor.[6] Several times she made it clear that she did not want her writings published after her death: they were confidential. Nevertheless after her death, the Vatican directed someone to compile materials on her life and make the case for sainthood. Her spiritual advisor turned the letters over to the care of the investigator, who in turn decided to publish some of them. His judgment trumped hers. He believed others who were struggling in faith could learn from her struggles. Perhaps he was right. But whose material was this? She did not relinquish the right to have her judgment overturned, even after her death. Her sacred and sensitive material was hijacked, albeit with good intentions. Good intentions are often the basis for bad boundary decisions. No wonder people no longer trust church authorities, even though they are full of good intentions.

ENTRUSTMENT IN THEOLOGICAL PERSPECTIVE

The Christian life begins with faith or trust in God. Entrusting one's life to the care of God is at the heart of the Christian journey. The God of the Scriptures has been revealed as a God worthy of trust. God has proven trustworthy through a history of keeping promises to God's people. God promised to Abraham against mighty odds to make of his descendants a great nation and a blessing to all families of the earth (Gen 12:1–3). God made a covenant with the house of David to establish God's kingdom

5. Peterson, *At Personal Risk*, 122–27.
6. Cf. Kolodiejchuk, ed., *Mother Teresa*.

forever (2 Sam 7:12–16). In the fullness of time God fulfilled the promise of sending a Messiah to fulfill the promise of establishing God's peaceable kingdom (Isa 11:1–9). The promises made by God to the people of Israel came to fruition with the coming of Jesus Christ (Heb 1:1–4). Jesus's birth fulfilled the promises made in the Scriptures of old (Matt 2:22–23). The life and death of Jesus Christ revealed the fulfillment of God's promises in a profound yet unanticipated way (Luke 24:32). From the beginning to the end of time, God's Word is "trustworthy and true" (Rev 22:6). God has been revealed throughout all time as one in whom we can place our ultimate trust.

Jesus Christ expresses to us the unwavering promise: "I am with you always, to the end of the age" (Matt 28:20). The way of entrustment begins with entrusting our lives to the promises of God. Do we dare to rely on God for favor and protection and deliverance through all the chances and changes of life? The Christian faith affirms that God is truly trustworthy, abiding with us even "through the darkest valley" (Ps 23:4). The journey of faith is always therefore the way of the cross. God's people are not spared experiences of suffering, which require cross bearing. Yet we are invited to trust in God's kindness and mercy, even when all evidence of our lives points to the absence of God's presence. Truly, our own feelings may deceive us; there are many experiences that would lead us to conclude that God has abandoned us (cf. Matt 27:46). Yet our final hope is in God's faithfulness to us, come what may. Human entrustment is predicated on our entrusting all that we are to God's promises—our bodies, our minds, our perceptions (insights and concerns), our passions, our spirits, and our resources. The testimony of the generations witnesses to God's trustworthiness, even unto eternal life.

God is trustworthy as the One who has our best interests always at the fore.[7] God is no trickster who puts us in predicaments to see whether we will stumble. The Christian insistence on the centrality of faith is based on the conviction that God is fundamentally worthy of our trust. For the church, its ministers, and members, this means that faithful ministry and mission is also predicated on our reflecting, as adequately as we are able, God's own trustworthiness. Establishing a climate of trust in the church is a high priority for credible ministry.[8] For God's sake ministers and people of faith are called to build trust with one another by inten-

---

7. Cf. Cooper-White, *Shared Wisdom*, 189–93.

8. Everist and Nessan, *Transforming Leadership*, chap. 1.

tionally relating in ways that promote the welfare of the other, not by taking advantage of another's trust in order to assume power over the other or in order to attempt to control them. Attentiveness to boundaries is a prerequisite for establishing and fostering the trustworthy environment which is indispensable to life-giving ministry in the church.

The first priority at the beginning of a new ministry by a Christian leader is to build a covenant of trust with God's people in that place. There are many core practices that can assist both leader and people to establish and nurture a trustworthy climate, reflective of the God of ultimate trustworthiness. In the following pages we articulate six key practices.

The *first practice* for establishing mutual trust is prayer. The minister takes time to pray faithfully and fervently for the people among whom one is called to minister.[9] Likewise, the people enter into the relationship with a new minister by praying earnestly for her/his welfare. Bringing these mutual petitions to our trustworthy God locates the unfolding relationships in the nexus of God's compassionate care. People of faith should not underestimate the efficacy of prayer for creating the climate in which fruitful and long-lasting ministry can endure. Prayer nourishes the new relationships in a spirit of goodwill and expectation that will bear good fruit.

A *second practice* indispensable to the building of trust involves the posture of appreciative inquiry. New relationships take time to grow. This necessitates intentionality about exploring the history of the new partner by investigating written materials and engaging in strategic conversations in a spirit of appreciative inquiry. Church histories, annual reports, minutes from meetings, and old newsletters each can provide insight into what has shaped this people to become who they are. Appreciative inquiry suspends judgment in getting to know other people by choosing to focus on their strengths and gifts rather than on their weaknesses and problems.[10] Effective engagement in appreciative inquiry takes time. Just as a good friendship deserves a serious investment of spending time together, so building trust between minister and people takes more intentionality and active engagement in appreciative inquiry than we usually imagine.

9. Lathrop, *Pastor*, chap. 5.

10. Cf. Snow, *Power of Asset Mapping*. The process of asset mapping is based on the method of appreciative inquiry.

A *third practice* basic to the art of ministry and the fostering of trust is the skill of listening. Active listening grounds all pastoral care.[11] People are hungry for a caring person to take the time to listen carefully to the stories of their lives. Active listening poses leading questions to invite people to go deeper in exploring the meaning of what has been experienced, both in times of joy and especially in times of sorrow or struggle. Good listeners then sit back with attentive ears to hear and enter into the unfolding narrative. Listening is one of the most precious gifts we can give to another person, an incarnation of the gospel. Effective pastoral care almost always involves more active listening than wise speaking. Perhaps no other practice will be more effective in building a climate of trust than the ability to enter into the stories of others through genuine listening. Listeners are able to knit what they have heard into the ongoing relationships with people as their lives continue to unfold. What has been heard endures in the memory and becomes wisdom for drawing people more deeply into life-giving participation in the faith community.

James Glasse wisely described our *fourth practice* as "paying the rent."[12] On the one hand, paying the rent involves faithfulness in ministry with and for people day after day, week after week: visiting the shut-ins, making hospital calls, ministering to the grieving, teaching confirmation, showing up at congregational events, preparing well for worship, preaching solid sermons, and giving generously of one's time and resources to the life of the church. Demonstrating authentic love for the people through steadiness over time fosters a trustworthy heart and contributes to the climate of entrustment. A trustworthy pastor invites the trust of people. Paying the rent, however, also means being a faithful steward of one's own life.[13] Attending to one's own spiritual wellness, physical fitness, emotional balance, and sharp intellect finally are indispensable to sustaining healthy ministry. Ministers are called upon to lend much of themselves to the care of others. Ministers are finite creatures who can easily become exhausted in body, mind, heart, and spirit. In order to have one's energy sustained and joy renewed, one must engage in a routine that establishes a baseline of health. Taking care of one's own health in its various dimensions is fundamental to paying the rent each day, week, and month.

11. Hedahl, *Listening Ministry*, chap. 1.

12. Glasse, *Putting It Together in the Parish*, 56.

13. Everist and Nessan, *Transforming Leadership*, chap. 9.

A *fifth practice* invites both ministers and people into a process of imagining the future together. We become what we imagine. This is one of the core convictions of Christian faith. Jesus in his ministry invited both disciples and the crowds to imagine a world in which God is alive and active, affecting who we are and what we do. Jesus described this divine involvement as the in-breaking of God's kingdom.[14] His teaching and ministry challenged people to open their eyes to see and believe what God was doing: forgiving, healing, casting out demons, feeding the hungry, bringing good news to the poor. One of the life-giving activities that most opens up the horizon of the future to congregations is imagination. Resistance to change can best be overcome as people begin to imagine themselves otherwise. As Willie Jennings describes it, "theological identity enters imaginatively into various social forms and imagines the divine presence joining, working, living, and loving inside boundary-defying relationships."[15] Juxtaposing our lives in relationship to the past—through the biblical narrative, Christian history and the story of the local church—opens up new horizons of possibility. Leaders can appeal to the imagination by telling stories from the Bible, remembering significant events in the Christian past, or recalling significant undertakings in the history of the congregation. Sometimes this process of imagining the future together can be furthered by inviting an outside facilitator to serve as midwife for the process. Living by faith in God always entails imagining what God is seeking to make of us.

A *sixth practice*, always needful, is forgiveness. What do we do when trust breaks down? Both ministers and people suffer under the burden of sin. It is not a question of whether but only of when we will find ourselves estranged from one another. Not only major boundary violations in speech and action undermine the trust necessary for vital ministry. Micro-infractions also eat away at the entrustment between pastor and people. Violations of trust can be committed on all sides of the relationship between pastor and people. We do not always keep our promises. We do not always tell the truth. We do not always interpret the behavior of others in the kindest way. We do not always turn the other cheek when offended.

Although the ritual of confession and absolution is prominent in congregational worship, the actual practice of forgiveness is rarely so

---

14. Perrin, *Jesus and the Language of the Kingdom*, 32–56.

15. Jennings, *Christian Imagination*, 291.

easy. The practice of forgiveness requires the humility to admit one's own failings. The practice of forgiveness requires mutuality of goodwill to heal the breech. The practice of forgiveness requires believing in God more than in the malice of the one who has hurt us. The realization of forgiveness in the life of the church depends in many ways on the scale of the infraction and on the willingness of the estranged parties to engage in the process of reconciliation.[16] When major violations occur, or if the parties are unwilling to practice confession and forgiveness, the climate may become so damaged that mutual entrustment is no longer possible. Such instances, for example in cases of sexual abuse, need to ensure that victims suffer no additional harm in any efforts at truth and reconciliation.

THE CASE FOR BEST PRACTICES

One of the important outcomes of the practices mentioned above is humility. Humility makes us more trustworthy because we do not just look to ourselves and our own experience for guidance in making decisions that affect others entrusted to our care. Humility leads to the willingness to look beyond one's self for direction, beginning by placing God above self. The practice of gratitude helps us to look beyond ourselves toward those to whom we are indebted. The humble, grateful person is always aware of how much we are indebted to others, even as praise may come their way. We can see this, for example, in some athletes who first give thanks to God for their talents and also for the support of their parents and coaches before they receive praise for themselves. We see this in scholars who begin their public lectures by praising their teachers and mentors, acknowledging the legacy that was handed down to them and upon which they have built. Praise and reward that is not shared with those from whom one has received such gifts results in ego inflation and a sense of entitlement, as if *I* am the source of all this goodness rather than the beneficiary or conduit. On the other hand, suffering that is not handled in a healthy way can also lead to a sense of entitlement: "I have suffered so much for the church; I have given so much. It isn't fair for me to have to pass up this opportunity for pleasure, companionship, or happiness."

---

16. Bash, *Forgiveness*, chap. 9.

Another important outcome of such practices is the ability to surrender—to submit our will to God and our own self-interest to the protection of others. There remains great wisdom in the Serenity Prayer:

> God, give us grace to accept with serenity
> the things that cannot be changed,
> Courage to change the things
> which should be changed,
> and the Wisdom to distinguish
> the one from the other.[17]

Without the healthy ability to surrender, one tends to denigrate or devalue best practices in favor of individual, and thereby often distorted, judgment.

Humility, surrender, and compliance play crucial roles in making good decisions. While one is always called upon to employ one's informed professional judgment in the practice of ministry, we do well to beware our tendency to privilege one's own self-serving bias with its accompanying distortions.[18] Apart from best practices, overreliance on one's own individual judgment frequently leads to destructive outcomes. In the remainder of this chapter we provide rationale for the imperative of following "best practices" in ministry as a prelude to summarizing in detail many such best practices in the final chapter. Professions that are highly entrusted with the care of others establish best practices not only to guide decision making but to override the hazards of individual judgment. Professions do this, not because they regard their members as incompetent, but out of conviction about our universal tendencies toward self-deception, which lead to bad decisions. Professionals who value best practices tend to be those who willingly recognize that their own thinking is also susceptible to error, just like everyone else's. One's own brain is an essential resource, but it is fallible and subject to systematic error. It is foolish not to recognize this, trusting instead one's own judgment in all circumstances. A big part of what we are trusting, after all, is the brain's capacity to reason accurately.

Professional airline pilots have done a great deal to understand and compensate for brain error. They learn very early that the brain can mislead them about such basic yet crucial matters as where they are in

---

17. Brown, ed., *Essential Reinhold Niebuhr*, 251.
18. Cf. Ubeda. "Consistency of Fairness Rules," 88–100.

space relative to the earth.[19] For a pilot, following best practices means recognizing that especially when flying in clouds one will be fooled by one's senses or "gut feelings." The key to staying alive, and keeping one's passengers safe, is to rely on the flight instruments and believe their accuracy. Pilots are also keenly aware of their own fallibility, and recognize the inherent risks in trusting one's memory. Best practices include strict adherence to checklists and standardized procedures; by following them a pilot is less apt to overlook critical items necessary for the safety of a flight. Pilots also learn what happens to the brain when it is subjected to a great deal of stress. Thereby they learn rules to follow under various circumstances, instead of naively following what the brain is telling them to do in any given moment.

Pilots also routinely experience the limits of information processing. In flight simulation, for example, when pilots practice dealing with emergency situations, a curious thing takes place. The flying pilot, the nonflying pilot, and the trainer occupy the flight simulator. There may also be another pilot simply observing. In the midst of an emergency, the people in those various roles take in different amounts of information. How much information the brain takes in depends on the amount of responsibility held by each person. The less responsibility you have, the more information you can process, insofar as responsibility is a source of stress. The brain protects itself from overload by setting limits on the incoming information. Unfortunately, the person who takes in the most information is the observer, followed by the trainer, then the nonflying pilot, and finally the pilot—in descending order of responsibility.

Pilots learn that stress impairs their ability to make good decisions. Therefore they learn to trust best practices even more than trusting their own brains. They learn, specifically, when and how the brain can mislead them and what to do about it. The pilot is entrusted with the safety of those on board. This is more important than the pilot's feelings.

Compare this to how the minister is entrusted with the well-being of those in her charge. In Christian community, members are likewise entrusted with the well-being of one another and of the pastor. While in the church daily boundary perceptions and boundary decisions may be less intense than for pilots handling an emergency, what we have learned through the scientific study of critical decision making can be helpful to decisions made in the parish. Good decision makers understand that

19. "Sensory Illusions in Aviation."

decision making is more about process than outcomes, even when the process involves intuition. Being a good decision maker means you use a sound decision-making process.

Many people believe and act like the only test of a decision is the outcome, not the process. This false belief can lead eventually to bad outcomes, even though it may not do so initially. For example, a young man decides to invest $1,000 in the stock market but could not decide where to invest it. He pins up the financial pages, closes his eyes, throws a dart, and buys the stock that was struck randomly. Within three months, he has tripled his investment. "This is the best decision I ever made," he concludes. But was it a good decision? When people invest in a prolonged up market, they can falsely come to believe that they are good at investing, while in fact they merely invested under favorable circumstances. Bad decisions can have benign or sometimes even favorable outcomes. The conclusion that one has made a good decision simply provides faulty reinforcement for sloppy decision making and encourages neglect of best practices that work well in both favorable and unfavorable circumstances.

Who bears the responsibility for establishing best practices? The ethics of piloting comes to mind as a good example here, as does medicine. Professional pilots and prescribing health care professionals take responsibility not only for those in their direct care but also for the safety of other passengers and patients. When a piece of equipment or a medicine does not perform as the collected data suggest it should, they give their input to those in charge. Responsibility is shared across the profession. It is not just a hierarchical system. A person lacking a participatory sense of the self will tend to act as an outside critic rather than a contributor or potential contributor to the bettering of the profession. An outsider regards responsibility for best practices and codes of ethics as belonging to "them" not "us." Such a person is also likely to regard the profession's rules as an imposition from the outside rather than an aid in becoming more trustworthy and an agent for caring for others beyond their immediate charge.

Relying on the formal exchange of experiences, such as research, gives equal weight to all pieces of information. This is an important way to counteract the human brain's bias to weigh information based primarily on where it is located in time and space.[20] The brain shows a bias of *propinquity* (nearness in space and time) in the following ways:

20. For the following, cf. Roberto, *Art of Critical Decision Making.*

1. In judging how likely a bad event is to happen to us, we give more weight to events that we have personally experienced rather than those experienced by others: "It has never been a problem for me to drive without my seat belt. I even got in an accident once and wasn't hurt."

2. If a bad thing has not happened to us, we tend to make decisions as if it never will.

3. In judging how likely a bad event is to happen to us, we give more weight to events that others have experienced when they occurred in our physical proximity, while giving less weight to the same event if it happened far from where we are.

4. We give more weight to events that happened recently than to events that happened further back in time.

Another major source of bias cited in the literature on decision making, is called the *self-serving bias*. This is extremely common, and it behooves us to recognize it in ourselves. Through the self-serving bias we take excessive credit for favorable outcomes while shedding blame when things go wrong. We also give more importance to data that support our beliefs or desires than to data that contradict us. Moreover, we are biased to believe that we are better than others (*overconfidence bias*). This is a form of bias that needs to be countered by the very humility and surrender previously mentioned.

We believe that we can succeed where others have failed. It is almost universal that people who knowingly violate codes of ethics or best practices believe that while the rule is good, they somehow will be able to manage the situation in such a way so that no one gets hurt ("I'll get the money back before anyone notices it's gone"). Or if they are willing for others to be hurt (as many are), they somehow become convinced that they will manage not to get caught. The self-serving bias also leads us to rationalize our decisions, putting them in a favorable light. A common rationalization argues that our intentions were good, even though our actions may have been errant. A self-serving bias also leads some to claim the right to forgiveness when caught in an indiscretion and at the same time to fault others for any lack of leniency and forgiveness. Again, humility and surrender are the responsible stances, not entitlement.

Internal pressure from feelings and emotions are a common impetus for bad boundary decisions. The actual desire to help is very common in the helping professions. It may seem like this is due to the pressure of another's needs or interests. Often, however, the inability to say no to an inappropriate or unworkable request is more internal to the person in the helping role than to the person making the request. The requesting person may easily accept the boundary when it is compassionately and skillfully established.

Internal pressures from feelings, emotions, and unmet personal needs can also wreak havoc. Loneliness, sadness, resentment, guilt, depression, and anxiety can override rational decision making, especially when people are not well versed in ethical and moral reasoning. Employing the concept of Marcia Riggs, we are called as ambassadors of Christ to become "religious ethical mediators": "This ministry of reconciliation is a ministry of mediation for people of faith who understand that being created in the image of God, recreated in Christ, is to live as moral beings in relationship with others as an experience of cross-cultural encounter."[21] Even with such training, however, the lust for sex (as seen, for instance, in the scandal of sexual abuse in churches), the greed for money, and endemic racism are forces powerful enough to cause great damage.[22] The unmet social and interpersonal needs for power, affiliation, comfort, support, and being understood, alongside unmet intimacy needs and prejudiced cultural conditioning, can interact with the self-serving bias to justify inappropriate actions.

The tendency is to engage in wishful thinking and best-case scenarios instead of in worst-case reasoning that best practices take into account to protect people from harm. Unfortunately, people who make boundary decisions from best-case scenarios may discover reinforcement in doing so, because their actions may make them more popular with certain people, as long as they are lucky enough to not have a bad outcome. Bad outcomes in the church often remain hidden from view for a long time, either through victims' reluctance to come forward or through perpetrators' deliberate secrecy and cover-up. By contrast, people who make decisions on worst-case thinking will cause less damage but may also be less popular in the short run, unless others are educated about the reason for best practices. Conscientious boundary keepers objectively monitor

21. Riggs, "Living as Religious Ethical Mediators," 250.
22. Gaede, ed., *When a Congregation Is Betrayed*, 25–27.

their own vulnerability and stress (factors that tend to limit awareness) and promote long-term thinking over short-term considerations.[23]

The study of bad decisions also demonstrates that social norming plays a strong role. Parishioners often encourage boundary violations without full knowledge of or appreciation for the importance of boundaries. Clergy colleagues can exercise a powerful influence against the maintenance of best practices. The power of the group is such that we are uncomfortable when our actions are different from the actions of those we are with and of those with whom we identify. If others are doing it, it must be okay. If I seem to be the outlier, maybe it is because I am just being overly cautious or rigid. Yet groups need alternative voices, or they easily fall prey to *groupthink*, a subtle group process that leads members to feel there is really only one way to think about things.

When ministers experience other ministers labeling their parishioners, gossiping about them, maintaining involvement with former parishioners, or otherwise not following best practices, the tendency is to follow suit. Behavior established by senior members of a norming group is a major factor contributing to how behavior drifts away from established best practices. This is not to say that best practices cannot change over time. Professional associations do treat codes of ethics, for example, as living standards that change as more information is gathered and conditions change.[24] But such changes are implemented through a formal process.

As members of a norming group, many clergy actively devalue best-practice standards with colleagues (and interns) with comments such as these:

- "Rules are made to be broken."
- "There is an exception to every rule."
- "It is the spirit of the law, not the letter of the law that matters."
- "Rules are just guidelines."
- "Don't be legalistic."
- "Boundary rules don't apply in small towns; you can't avoid violating them."
- "Times have changed; nobody does that anymore."

23. Cf. Cooper-White, *Shared Wisdom*, 58–60.
24. Trull and Carter, *Ministerial Ethics*, chap. 8 and Appendixes A–E.

These comments are actual invitations to disregard best practices in favor of some alternative—usually feelings and desires or local precedents—when best practices are intended to trump all of those.

This does not mean that best practices as rigid rules must always prevail, but the burden of proof is always on the side of those violating the best practice rather than on those observing it. There must be a clear and compelling reason to do something other than following the rule. Ignorance or lack of understanding are among the most common excuses for violating best practices: "I don't see why it's such a big deal; I've done it before and nothing bad happened." Note well the self-serving nature of these comments. The professional standard is that if someone is considering violating a best practice, this should only be done after consulting a person well versed in the issues, someone in a position to be objective and poised to tell them what they do not want to hear. A friend or close colleague obviously does not meet these criteria. To justify violating a particular boundary, there must be an important principle that reasonably outweighs the standard boundary, such as safety. With confidentiality in youth groups, for example, the youth may be advised to tell an adult when another young person threatens suicide or harm to someone else. As we will see in later chapters, there are situations where being trustworthy results in the consideration of different boundaries that compete for primacy. What is untrustworthy is to allow personal desire to trump best practices.

Many of the factors that lead to poor decisions came into play in the famous 1996 Mount Everest disaster.[25] Two teams with highly trained and experienced guides did not follow the established "Two O'Clock Rule" of the mountain. The rule states that during your summit attempt, regardless of whether you have made the summit or not, you turn back by 2:00 p.m. at the latest. This is not a recommendation or a guideline. It is a rule articulating a best practice established from years of cumulative experience. All Everest climbers know it. Descending in the dark or in a storm is extremely hazardous and puts not only yourself but others at risk. But in this case neither of the leaders had experienced any bad weather on recent climbs, and no bad weather was forecast. The radio chatter among the climbers was confident and mutually encouraging. They had invested a lot of money and months of preparation, and this was their last day. They knew they could do it. Though they had been schooled in the bias

---

25. Cf. Roberto, *Art of Critical Decision Making*.

of the "sunk cost effect" ("I've invested too much in this effort to give up now"), most did not turn back at 2:00 p.m. Only four of the thirty four climbers turned back as the rule dictated. They were the outliers in the group. Eight people died, and many others barely escaped with their lives in the brutal storm and darkness that followed.

Another factor involved in this tragedy that applies to congregations was the fostering of dependence. People who feel that others are dependent on them easily fall prey to feeling they should get their way, while those who feel dependent on them will tend to defer to the powerful person. Large contributors to the church, in time or money, may want and be given a bigger vote than others.

The temptation to violate best practices is great, even though practices are based on cumulative and wise collective experience. Those who are entrusted with the care of others hold a special obligation to be trustworthy in protecting others from harm. The lesson is to know enough not just to trust one's own judgment, because one's brain is subject to bias. No one is exempt from these biases, not even those who are most skilled at what they do. A trustworthy leader is one who understands these biases and limitations in judgment and who relies instead on established best practices. If you follow them like a reliable map, you will get a predicable outcome, not in terms of social approval but in terms of safety and trustworthiness. To expect others to trust us when we are not fully trustworthy is another expression of self-serving bias.

It is important not just to know what the best practices or rules are but also to understand the principles and reasoning behind them, because the principles and reasoning act as a steady guide, especially in murky situations. As we explore the myriad boundary issues involved in congregational life and congregational leadership, we consider both the what and the why of best practices, returning to a concluding and comprehensive articulation of best practices in the final chapter. Having here examined identity boundaries and ownership issues regarding subjective states, we turn next to the significant theme of role integrity.

3

Role Integrity

IN THE MUSICAL COMEDY *Church Basement Ladies*, the ladies in charge of the funeral dinner found themselves in a quandary. The widowed pastor's young new wife brought vegetarian lasagna. However, they are Scandinavian. They wondered if she is Catholic. Lasagna is not who they are. Should they serve it or freeze it for another time, running the risk of offending her and the pastor? Which is more reflective of who they are: welcoming and appreciating differences or ethnic exclusivity?

We know that on Sunday mornings people want to spend time with other people who are most like themselves. If they cannot find such a group, they may not attend church. The apostle Paul's stance toward this dilemma was, in effect, "Go ahead and be who you are; keep your differences and don't require others to be like you."

While the initial reflex of the church basement ladies was to protect the cultural integrity of their congregation (others in the congregation might even see them as having that unstated responsibility!), they did recognize that the primary role for members of the body of Christ is to live according to the culture of God, which is radically welcoming. Whatever role one plays in one's congregation, we are called to be subservient to the primary role of living the Great Commandment: to love God and neighbor. When this commitment is kept alive and fully embraced, any conflict of interest can be informed by what is most essential.

CLARITY ABOUT PRIMARY
AND SECONDARY ROLES

The healthiest and strongest organizations are those in which the primary purpose is so infused in the members and the commitment is so strong, that there is mutual accountability, which is carried out respectfully. If the preacher slips and uses ridicule in a sermon, every member sees it is their responsibility to point it out directly to the pastor. When a Sunday school teacher gets frustrated with disciplinary problems and begins to use the fear of God as a weapon, any parent will feel empowered to kindly address the matter with him. When a member of the leadership team is frequently late for meetings and arriving ill prepared, any other team member will feel responsible lovingly to address it.

We all have different identities; from them come different roles and functions. In different contexts, they carry different weight. Being clear about those identities helps inform us about which are primary and which are secondary. The church basement ladies got it right. The pastor's new wife was welcomed, and her food contribution was appreciated. The work of the kingdom goes well when our thoughts, words, and actions are informed by proper prioritizing. What is challenging to the work of the church is that very often improper prioritization makes primary roles and interests secondary to other personal roles and interests. It takes intentional effort not to act from secondary personal roles and interests.

In *Church Basement Ladies*, when Mavis was charged to recruit people to prepare and serve the funeral meal, personal interest might have led her to ask her friends and avoid asking those she found personally disagreeable. Yet when she intentionally embraced her role as a member of the body of Christ, she realized that a key feature of the culture of God is inclusion: that all are welcome and treated equally; priority is given even to the least important person. There are no cliques in the body of Christ. Mavis asked those who had not recently served and helped create a welcoming space for them.

Unconsciously prioritizing friendships over inclusion is a common reason that people are excluded from church activities. The church comes to feel like a closed circle.[1] Before and after worship on Sunday mornings, personal interests draw us to socialize with those we know and like, leaving out strangers. On church outings, this dynamic can become even

1. Cf. "The Parable of a Life Saving Station" originally appeared as Wedel, "Evangelism—the Mission of the Church to Those Outside Her Life," 24.

more pronounced by creating an insider group that is experienced as exclusive. When there is a free afternoon or evening on a mission trip, for example, people readily want to spend time with those whom they personally like the most. Personal friendships get in the way of serving the common good of the whole group. People can be reminded not to do that.

Dual relationships negatively affect both laity and clergy in the church.[2] When parents participate as chaperons on a youth mission trip in which their own child is a member, both the parents and child can be reminded before the trip that during these days the role of chaperon has primacy over the parental role. In fact, insofar as possible, the parental role needs to be suspended so the child can have the same type of experience that the other youth have, free from "being parented," which is qualitatively different from being supervised by an objective adult. In order to avoid boundary issues, parents in these circumstances do well to exclude themselves from disciplining their own child, leaving it to other adults. This includes recusing themselves from decisions involving the discipline of their own child.

It is common to think of these situations in terms of a conflict of interest. But this is merely a subset of situations in which multiple identities and roles can produce what we could name as the clouding of interest. In any situation of multiple roles, clouding can occur. What is called for is clear prioritization, giving priority to the role one has assumed for the church, informed by the values of the culture of God.[3] This requires a great deal of self-awareness. What hat am I wearing now? Is this the hat I should be wearing in my responsibility to the church? What role am I assuming? What role is influencing the feelings and thoughts I am having right now? With awareness often comes the realization that it may not be clear what role we are assuming.

Am I functioning as a dad on the youth trip by thinking my son should not be punished, because I do not like how that reflects on me? Am I being objective in thinking the offense is so minor that it should be ignored? Given that I am not sure, as well as that others cannot be certain whether we are being objective or not, the right thing in this circumstance is gracefully to defer to others. At every level in the church we are helped by clear understanding about situations in which a person should

2. Fortune, *Love Does No Harm*, 82–84.

3. Gula, *Just Ministry*, chap. 5.

identify their dual role and recuse themselves. All parties also may adopt a stance of mutual accountability in order to assume responsibility for gracefully pointing out perceived conflict or clouding of interest, which the other person is not able to perceive or acknowledge.

The goal is the protection of the integrity of the primary role, which includes avoiding even the appearance of favoritism, impropriety, or inappropriateness. This is one reason codes of ethics for professionals include the prohibition of behavior "unbecoming" a member of that profession. All roles in the church involve the inherent value of integrity and trust. For example, parents who drink on the youth outing compromise the effectiveness of their primary role by undermining and essentially violating that primary role. The pastor who makes suggestive comments toward a youth will not be seen by that young person as pastor any longer. While pastors in training (for example, interns) are taught to "embrace your pastoral identity," many come to resent it over time and want to "take it off" or "put it on" as it suits their personal interests, rather than serving in the primary role of pastor.

The quintessential example is the pastor who relates to a parishioner out of personal intimacy needs or interests.[4] The pastor has the primary responsibility to protect the integrity and effectiveness of the pastoral role for all concerned, including someone to whom they may be attracted. This is, of course, an obligation for all those who assume any role in the church, that they enhance and protect the integrity and effectiveness of that primary role for all concerned. The role does not serve you; you serve the role. When a pastor relates affectionately toward a parishioner, the pastor can no longer relate to that person in an unclouded way, because s/he has mixed a highly charged personal interest (that even changes how the brain functions!) with an objective professional role.

For example, Pastor Terry begins to see Chloe as a good candidate for leading Vacation Bible School when he never did previously. Before long, Chloe no longer has a pastor. If she reciprocates the romantic interest, she is no longer capable of seeing Terry as her pastor; Terry has become Terry, the romantic interest. This dynamic is even more pronounced if the love relationship is acted upon and subsequently turns sour. Now Terry is the one who hurt her, which contradicts the role of pastor. Even if Chloe does not reciprocate Terry's romantic interest but only detects it, consciously or unconsciously she also has lost her pastor,

---

4. Everist and Nessan, *Transforming Leadership*, chap. 10.

because she can no longer trust that Pastor Terry can relate to her within the expectations of his professional role.

If roles become cloudy by being mixed together, so does judgment. The pastor and parishioner in love may try to bargain. What if the parishioner leaves the church? Then perhaps their relationship would not be unethical? For a long time this ploy has been tried by many professionals and has been rejected by ethics commissions, who steward both the integrity of the profession and the well-being of persons. The problem is that this ploy is self-serving; it is not serving the integrity of the professional role. Upon further examination, why should the parishioner leave and not the pastor? After all, it is the pastor who has abandoned his primary role in favor of personal interest. But that still would not make it ethical. The boundary violation has already occurred when the pastor allowed himself to feel, think, and act affectionately toward the parishioner. When the professional allows himself to continue the personal relationship under different conditions, he is further invalidated as a professional, because of the failure to demonstrate the self-control that is expected of a pastor. When push comes to shove, he has chosen personal interest over protecting the integrity of the pastoral role.

We are all subject to temptations of various sorts that risk violating the integrity of our primary roles. A board member can recognize an opportunity for a relative to get a job at the church and can create an inside track. A church secretary, who is a member of the church and upset that her daughter was informed by the parish education committee that she will not be confirmed because she did not complete the requirements, is tempted to come to work the next day and complain to the pastor instead of remaining in her role and doing her work. As parent she may wish to advocate for her child, but she needs to take this up with the parish education committee. It is very difficult, if not impossible, for church employees who are members of the congregation not to contaminate their work roles with their personal concerns as members.

DEVELOPING STRATEGIES FOR MAINTAINING ROLE CLARITY

Because temptations are so prevalent, we are wise to plan for how to address them and the concomitant clouding of judgment. It helps to recognize that keeping boundaries includes watching not only our words and actions but our very thoughts. Our outer actions flow from inner sources. Taking responsibility for our actions requires an increased awareness of our inner life. Since the Great Commandment is about love, let us consider the example of anger.[5] Often people who get treatment for an anger problem feel that their anger outbursts "just happen" to them. How can they be responsible for things they cannot control? They only feel capable of controlling themselves after they have done or said harmful things. What they do well to learn (and can learn!) is to increase their awareness of the inner states that breed anger. People can learn to become more aware of the beliefs and attitudes that tell them they are in danger, which lead to lashing out to defend themselves. People can learn to recognize when they are dwelling on perceived offenses and fueling the fire with past memories and damning generalizations. People can learn to slow time down so they can intervene within microseconds to stop themselves from initiating an angry action. This is possible to learn.

Self-control begins with the control of one's attention. At every moment in time we face the decision of where to direct our attention. When Pastor Terry first recognized that he was having personal feelings toward Chloe, he was at a decision point. Such a decision has consequences. There is a saying that goes: "Where we direct our attention, the rest of us is bound to follow." A dramatic example of this phenomenon involves the state law prescribing that when you see an emergency vehicle ahead on the side of the road, you are to vacate the lane next to them. The reason is that emergency vehicles stopped along the side of the road are more likely to be hit by drivers than nonemergency vehicles. Why? Because our eyes are attracted to them, and we unconsciously tend to steer in the direction where our eyes are looking.

Self-control begins with controlling where we place our attention. Self-control means saying no to the self and taking that no as the answer.[6] All boundary keeping involves a firm no. It is the essential skill of all boundary keeping. Pastor Terry, to be faithful to his pastoral role, must prevent himself from dwelling on his feelings toward Chloe so that he does not fuel his desire through mental and emotional energy. He must not allow his imagination to explore what it would be like to be with Chloe. Dwelling on urges and desires leads both consciously or

---

5. Whitehead and Whitehead, *Transforming Our Painful Emotions*, chaps. 4 and 5.
6. Cf. McGonigal, *Willpower Instinct*, chap. 3.

unconsciously to establishing the conditions to act them out. That is the natural flow of energy that must be stopped.

There is a spiritual discipline called custody of the eyes, which is being used by therapists who work with people with sex addictions. The concept of custody of the eyes is also being used in spiritual retreats to help people learn to keep focus.[7] On a retreat (usually a silent retreat) custody of the eyes as a discipline encompasses not looking into the eyes of the other retreat participants or at any printed words, so as to keep focus on one's retreat. Roman Catholic worship leaders historically were taught custody of the eyes by keeping their eyes on the altar and cross as much as possible, both for the benefit of maintaining one's own attention on worship and for guiding the worshipers to do the same. It is hard for worshipers to be disciplined when the worship leader is not.

Custody of the eyes and the control of attention has wide implications for every ministry role. People working with youth do not allow themselves to gaze at a young woman's breasts, for example, even if they think she would not notice. Sexualizing anyone in the congregational community is a role violation, because it objectifies the other person and uses them for one's own gratification. In all church functions, to take our attention away from the matters at hand, even briefly, disrupts the effectiveness of the event.

Why does this matter so much in ministry? While inattentive driving threatens the body, inattentive ministering impoverishes the soul. One of the key ways we demonstrate that someone is important to us is by giving them our undivided attention. A family meal without a TV or other electronic device is remarkably different from a meal that includes these. Without such distractions, attention can be fixed on those present (including one's own full presence) in order to know what to share. When the pastor or Stephen Minister[8] does not establish a mental boundary when visiting with someone and allows the mind to wander during the visit, even a very brief lapse can bring a complete collapse in understanding what the other person is talking about. You do not have as meaningful a visit with that person if you let your mind wander to other things. You damage the value of the encounter when you vacate your role and ask them a question whose purpose is to satisfy your personal curiosity.

7. Armstrong, *Through the Narrow Gate*, 79.

8. Stephen Ministries, founded in 1975, trains laypeople to minister in their congregations as one-to-one counselors and pastoral caregivers.

In times of need people notice when you switch out of your proper role with them by either talking about yourself or asking them questions out of personal rather than professional interest. Molly, for example, told Ellen (her Stephen Minister) about a painful experience at a recent family reunion in Colorado. Since Ellen was planning a reunion for her own family, she asked Molly where the reunion was held and about the accommodations. While Molly was gracious, she felt the loss of focused attention on her distress. People do notice. People know when you mentally vacate the room, even briefly. One can sense it. Consciousness creates a field that projects around us. When we are fully present, people perceive our presence; when we lapse, they feel our absence.

No role in ministry is too insignificant to warrant mindful presence. The custodian who pulls the bell rope and focuses on the sacred call to worship knows that faithful performance of this role means not just pulling the rope but praying for people to come to worship and celebrate the Sabbath. She recognizes the difference from those other times when she was focused merely on getting back to bed. It was not just a matter of pulling the rope. Because we have become so accustomed to split awareness, we do not always notice the difference until we are forced to do so. At first young people at camp or on a mission trip get out of sorts, when not allowed to use their electronic devices to distract themselves. After a few days, however, they experience the world around them more fully and settle more deeply into themselves and their relationships with others.

The committee chair who is fully mindful in leading a meeting will not only be able to manage the agenda but will also be aware of what is unspoken and unexpressed by those present at that meeting. The Sunday school teacher who is mindful is not just focused on the curriculum and discipline but can tune in to sense what is going on with each of the children in order to connect in a caring way, even briefly, with what they are experiencing.

Pastor Terry is no longer ministering to Chloe when he lets his attention wander out of his pastoral role with her. He needs to exercise custody of the eyes with Chloe as well as with others for whom he may experience sexual attraction. This is not just a matter for clergy; it also applies to parishioners to remain faithful in their roles. Women clergy in particular complain about people looking at them sexually while they are performing their role. Even worse is for someone to put it into words: "Pastor, you look so cute in your collar!" This is a boundary issue that begins with control of attention and custody of the eyes, based upon custody of thoughts and desires.

Those who serve in the helping professions recognize that personal feelings can interfere with adequately serving others, whether the feelings are attraction or repulsion.[9] When that happens, the responsibility of the professional is to get consultation to try to clear up the personal feelings in order to be faithful to the professional role. Pastors are under more pressure than other professionals to resolve and control their clouded and conflicted feelings since they cannot refer the parishioner to another church the way a counselor can refer a client to another counselor.

Pastors and parishioners are most at risk for violating the integrity of their roles when their personal needs are not adequately met.[10] If Terry allows relations with his wife to go sour, he is more at risk of becoming inappropriate with the Chloes in his congregation. If Chloe has done the same in her marriage, she is more at risk of being exploited by Pastor Terry. If Mavis is not spending enough time with her friends outside of church, she is more at risk of using church events to spend time only with them, instead of attending to her primary church role of promoting inclusive fellowship. If Wendy is not tending to her finances or her gambling problem, she is more at risk of "borrowing" money from the youth fundraiser. She may even put herself into the position of being asked to be the treasurer for that account.

The better we are at appropriately meeting our own needs, the less we are at risk of using our church roles to satisfy those needs and so violating role integrity in the process. In our personal lives, personal needs and interests take precedence. In our church roles, those specific roles take precedence over our personal interests. Many would like to believe that the church should take care of their personal needs, but that is a form of using the church, not serving Christ through the church. This is a matter of role integrity.

As Susan Nienaber observes, "The healthiest congregations have the lowest tolerance for inappropriate behavior. Unhealthy congregations tolerate the most outrageous behavior."[11] What do we do about bad behavior? Do we tolerate it or confront it? The optimal work of the church also encourages the ability to say no to others. When the pastor allows

9. Peterson, *At Personal Risk*, chap. 3.
10. Harbaugh et al., *Covenants and Care*, chap. 3.
11. Sevig and Watson, "Bullying the Pastor."

someone to take too much time, the pastor then have less time for other things. When the meeting leader allows people to come late, waiting for them before starting, or allows the discussion to become pointless, the chair is failing to protect the integrity of that role.

The point here is not to be rigid, since rigidity can be both inconsiderate and less adaptive than flexible discipline. Disciplines that are overly rigid tend to break down because they do not flex when circumstances are different than normal. But many people who argue for flexibility really want no discipline, standards, or accountability at all. They argue for unconditional acceptance, meaning tolerating everything. Discipline is more sustainable when it is clear and consistent, while also taking conditions into account. When road conditions hold people up, for example, you might well wait a bit to start a meeting, while under normal circumstances you would start precisely on time.

More significant and challenging issues of flexibility and adaptability of boundary keeping occur when we consider that some people are at risk of violating boundaries due to psychological or medical conditions that can damage social perception, judgment or impulse control. Head injuries can do all three. Cognitive limitations can interfere. Developmental disabilities such as Asperger's syndrome and other autism-spectrum disorders can interfere with a person's ability to interpret other's behavioral cues. They may also be quite rigid and unskillful in applying behavioral rules. Personality disorders also complicate interpersonal decision making. There are people without a conscience who are motivated solely by self-interest. ADHD makes it harder for a person to conform their behavior to boundaries and interpersonal agreements. With regard to such conditions, boundary setting while respecting the identity boundaries of these persons means not identifying them with their condition. The condition isn't who they are; it is a condition that they have. Setting boundaries with people having these conditions calls for both grace and skill. People with these conditions may also be challenged in setting boundaries with others.

Some personalities are built in such a way that saying no to others makes them very uncomfortable. In many communities, this can be fairly common. They would rather accommodate others than disappoint them. Or they can feel they have no viable alternative since they need to continue to live with the person they may wish to stand up to. Some people with weak boundaries take on the feelings of others and have difficulty not feeling bad themselves when the other person feels bad. These people have an innate tendency to minimize the importance of boundaries since boundary keeping makes them very uncomfortable. They can also twist the notion of "loving others" to mean always doing what others want. The result over time, however, may be resentment toward those who want things from them, or even burnout.[12]

Role clarity and mutual accountability are required for the high level of functioning, which the Great Commission demands. Churches often have an aversion to both. We hate job descriptions for various reasons: They are a lot of work to produce, and they tend to become outdated. We also do not particularly enjoy being held accountable or holding others accountable. However, churches, like secular organizations, function best when it is clear who is responsible for what. Job descriptions end up reducing stress, including the stress of pastors, insofar as pastors are being evaluated by people in any case. It is unavoidable. Is it really better not to have unrealistic or ill-defined expectations: "What are we paying the pastor to do anyway?"

Job descriptions protect people from being unfairly evaluated. In many cases, pastors are expected to do whatever someone else has not done, while many of the things left undone are not in anyone else's job description.[13] Or if they are, that person is not held accountable for them, because in the church we hate to hurt people's feelings. By contrast, the best functioning organizations normalize mutual accountability. Within a culture of mutual accountability, feelings need not be hurt, because holding another accountable for their behavior is not the same as attacking the person. The more routinely and lovingly it is done, the more accountability can evoke gratitude instead of hurt feelings from the one holding the job. Clear job descriptions also help us objectively evaluate our own work performance.

In the work of the kingdom, all roles are informed and infused by the Great Commission. Worshipers cannot fill their roles when they just passively show up for worship and are unprepared to participate. The role of worshiper, like all other roles, is either filled fully, partially, or minimally. Like worship leaders, worshipers have a vital role in helping to create the optimum conditions for worship. When ready to fully engage and contribute, to read and sing, when ready to hear the lessons and the sermon deeply, worshipers enhance the worship experience for all

12. Lehr, *Clergy Burnout*, chap. 2.

13. Cf. Bacher and Cooper-White, *Church Administration*, 148–49 and Appendix F.

involved. Outside of worship, members have a role to play in hospitality for new people and responsibility for fostering an inclusive fellowship for one other, including for those at the edges of the social system.

The role of the religious education teacher, when informed by the Great Commission, is not just to teach the curriculum with competence; this role also encompasses understanding each student's relationship with God in order to nurture it. The communion deacon is not just a distributor of the elements; the role also entails engaging the "communion of saints." The acolyte is not just about lighting candles at one point and snuffing them out at another: the acolyte helps to evoke reverence and awe.

When each person knows well their particular role, including how and where it fits with other roles, and when together we fully live into these roles with a sense of call, beautiful things begin to happen. It is like playing jazz, where rules, conventions, and shared expectations create the conditions for beautiful expression and improvisation. You can truly let your light shine in a collaborative way when you are willing to take your turn within the ensemble. Jazz requires courage and creativity, built on a foundation of self-discipline, careful listening, and communication with others.

Ours has been dubbed the information age. We have ready access to all kinds of information and opinions from virtually anywhere in the world. Access to information has been put to positive ends (such as influencing governments via Twitter to prevent violence and injustice) to criminal ends (such as stealing personal and confidential data) to other evil ends (such as cyberbullying, which leads to violence toward the self and others). When Arden decided to finally get a smartphone, his daughter, who had had a couple of years of experience with smartphones, informed him, "Dad, to have a smart phone you need to have the self-discipline to let questions go unanswered. Otherwise you will be on it all the time!"

Prior to the information age, there were boundary quandaries from the fishbowl effect. In many communities, it seemed, everyone knew everyone else's business for good or for ill. The good occurs when we watch out for and care for our neighbors, even beyond what they intentionally reveal to us. The ill occurs where we jump to faulty conclusions and in other ways do harm to our neighbors. It really never was everyone, however, who kept track of that was going on in the community. Some people meddled, pried, and stuck their noses where they do not belong. They were up to no good, just satisfying their curiosity and perhaps a need for power in gossip circles. By contrast, in traditional societies people designated as elders of the tribe are required to know what is going on with everyone in their charge, in order to care for the welfare of the individual and simultaneously the group. The welfare of individuals and the welfare of the community are intertwined. The elder needs to know people better even than they know themselves: for example, knowing who can marry whom based on family trees, without causing problems through inbreeding. So what is the difference between meddling and serving as an elder? An elder acts from a legitimate and agreed-upon role in the community and is doing so responsibly. An elder is not acting in secret.

It takes a village. It still does! Robert M. Franklin, with regard to restoring hope in African American communities, makes reference to "the central local institutions in villages as 'anchor institutions'—the institutions that have an enduring presence and operate to stabilize people amidst chaos and rapid transition."[14] He names the three primary anchor institutions as church, family, and school. Enduring institutions of the village are characterized by their effectiveness according to specific criteria: innovative capabilities, governance and leadership, information flow, culture and values, adaptive response, risk structure, and legitimacy.[15]

We might ask ourselves to what degree congregations are genuinely equipped to serve as enduring institutions for anchoring future generations to live out their calling as the body of Christ with integrity? Some use of social media by young people keeps track of and cares for members of their group who are in trouble. You do not let friends hurt themselves or others. You do not let brothers and sisters in the body of Christ venture into harm. The prevention of harm is one principle that trumps confidentiality and privacy. In our discussion of boundary keeping, we affirmed that in violating a boundary, there must be a principle that overrides keeping the boundary as one normally would. In this case the conflict is between confidentiality and assuming the role of one who cares for others in order to prevent harm. In this spirit, the parents who hear from others in the community that their daughter is using drugs would be appreciative. To say something could appear to be sticking one's nose in someone else's business, while not doing so would be to fail to fulfill the

14. Franklin, *Crisis in the Village*, 4.
15. Ibid., 12–13.

role of community or congregation member on behalf of others and on behalf of the whole.

Into the information age came HIPAA: the Health Insurance Portability and Accountability Act. HIPAA places controls on the transfer of medical information on the part of patients and on the part of those who have direct roles to care for them medically. No one else can have access to a patient's medical records without the patient's consent. Given their care role, medical professionals are allowed, unless prevented by state law, to exchange information about the patient among themselves, in order to assess and coordinate care on behalf of the patient. A person with power of attorney over medical decisions also has a legitimate role to access medical information about a patient. A person who is on the staff of the medical facility is only to access a patient's medical records if they are in a direct care role with that patient.

The computer system monitors who accesses what and for how long. A staff member who accesses the records of a friend or relative will be fired. Because of the temptation and potential consequences, the computer systems have an additional level of protection for records of alcohol and drug treatment and mental health treatment, and for the records of public figures. For the sake of the patient safety, emergency access can be had by an unauthorized staff member via a preset procedure referred to as "breaking the glass" (taken from the notion of having to break the glass to access a fire alarm or fire extinguisher).

Faith communities desire to be caring communities, but when someone joins a congregation, are such persons giving consent to others in the community to keep track of them beyond what they reveal? That certainly could be part of the covenant. If it were, however, accessing information about another person would have to be part of a caretaking role, not based on personal curiosity. Staying in role would require that the caretaker turn away from gossip, unless the caretaker needed to inform a person who was a victim of the gossip. Maintaining the caretaker role would mean refraining from looking up out of curiosity what the minister's family paid for their home, even though it is a matter of public record. By contrast, for a covenanted caretaker it would be in role—exercising due diligence—to look up the driving record of someone who would soon be driving a vehicle on a congregational outing.

Another measure for legitimately accessing information about a parishioner or staff member would be that you inform the person that you did so, just as the hospital monitors digitally the accessing of patient records. If you feel the need to keep your access secret, it would not be legitimate. This also applies to doing a Google search on someone or poking into social media about them. The fact that information is publicly available does not mean that it is morally correct to access it. If you need such information to fulfill your agreed-upon role toward the person and the congregation, and if you are willing to inform them of it, it may be sound boundary keeping.

Accessing electronic information can take on a compelling quality that interferes with good self-care boundaries. Keeping your finger on the pulse of late-breaking news can become a way of life. Many teens want to keep their cellphones on all night so they can keep connected with friends at all times. This is simply not healthy. If a friend is at risk in the middle of the night, parents should be informed. Some people monitor emergency radio communications as a hobby. They want to be in the know about such things, while it has no bearing on any agreed-upon role that they have in the community. While this is legal, it is not ethical to do whatever they want with that information. The temptation to misuse information is great. An important act of self-discipline and spiritual discipline in the information age is knowing when not to use information, when to turn away from a screen, and when to turn off your device or go offline in order to do other important things uninterruptedly.

FOSTERING MUTUAL ACCOUNTABILITY

Just as many other professional organizations have standards of accreditation, and just as professions have periodic reviews to maintain certification, so churches do well to develop clear structures of accountability,. Annual audits and personnel reviews, while appearing to be an additional burden, actually secure the integrity of the church's identity and mission. Building a climate of accountability creates the conditions for synergy in an organization. The members of a band have to be able to hear each other in order to play together and create something new. In an organization this begins with mutual accountability and communication, asking the question about who is doing what with their time, talents, and resources (financial and otherwise). Keeping track of such information allows congregational leaders conscientiously to budget the use of available resources and to identify the additional resources that are needed.

Many pastors, however, object to accountability as itself a kind of boundary violation, holding that competent and responsible professionals should not have to answer to others, especially to laypeople. To the contrary, most professionals are answerable to others, and it is good that they are held accountable, though professionals may not like being evaluated any more than anyone else. Physicians, for example, have their work reviewed by accrediting bodies. Would you want to visit a surgeon whose work was not reviewed by anyone, or who was not accountable to anyone? Although no one likes it and many balk, without accountability standards of practice tend to decrease. When we believe others should "just trust us," what are we asking them to trust? What is our realistic appraisal of human nature?

Mutual accountability means that everyone is called to account for their own areas of responsibility, not just the paid staff. Shared accountability is different from micromanaging or excessive monitoring, which most often is driven by anxiety or control issues rather than inspired by the Great Commission. It is imperative that each member understands both their own role and the roles of others. But who should define roles in the church: (a) the pastor or lead pastor, (b) the church's lay leadership, (c) the congregation itself, (d) the clergy as guild, (e) the denomination, (f) the person occupying each role, (g) the Bible, or (h) all of the above? In practice, congregational roles are social contracts fashioned by all stakeholders. This is why formally defined roles eventually tend to give way to informal definitions. They are shaped by external and internal pressures over time. Congregational members and staff judge each other based on what they think they should be doing, whether or not it is in the formal description. Roles are agreements among people.

Unrealistic expectations are a major source of failure in relationships. A pastor cannot live up to everyone's expectations.[16] The running joke is that pastors are expected to do a long list of things at any time of day or night, inclding interrupting their vacation to do these things; and on top of all, the pastor must "walk on water." However, when roles are defined by a select group without everyone having input, expectations likely will not correspond with what those in power have decided. Expectations become coherent when all stakeholders help shape role descriptions. Through the crucible of such input, expectations become more realistic. But it also needs to be acknowledged that in some cases

16. Everist and Nessan, *Transforming Leadership*, 59–60.

the unrealistic expectations come from the occupant of the role—for example, from the pastor him- or herself.

Fidelity to the congregational role is similar to fidelity to the role of a spouse. It is not just defined by one's self, but it is relationally defined. One test of fidelity to the role of spouse can be measured by this question: if one's partner were able to view one's interactions with others, would they feel betrayed or not? Is one having an emotional affair or just a friendship? We can delude ourselves if we only stay in touch with our own point of view. One of the measures of accountability is to raise questions about the common tendency toward self-justification and self-delusion.

As with the role of spouse or parent, congregational roles may include a list of tasks or functions. But they are more than that! Informed by the Great Commandment, all roles are about love: expressing love for God and neighbor. The pastor's first responsibility is to love the people with God's own love, and it is the congregant's first responsibility to love one another, including the pastor, with this same love. Role descriptions, if reduced to a list of tasks, do not capture the spirit of a role any more than you can create a task list for being someone's spouse. Complex relationships require more than just breaking them down into tasks and assigning the tasks to people. While task definition may be important, it is merely the skeleton around which sinew needs to grow so that a fuller synergy can emerge.

Roles constitute the functional units of the congregation. Respecting role boundaries makes for better fulfillment of the congregation's mission. To simply ask more often, whose role is this? Whose decision is this? can itself contribute to better functioning. For example, a group of Sunday school teachers take it upon themselves to clean up the storage room where educational materials are kept. They come across some obviously used materials that they had not seen before. They figure no one would be using them again and throw them out. The question, whose is this? would have revealed that these teachers did not get to decide the fate of those materials. If they had asked, they would have discovered that the materials were being kept for vacation Bible school. Would it have been their role to take it upon themselves to throw out materials owned by the church? Communication is a two-way street. The vacation Bible school staff had not communicated to anyone that they had intentions for the used materials.

When flowers were ordered for Easter, someone had to ask, whose role is it to water them and care for them? No one had been assigned that role. Two-way communication allows the body of Christ to become not just a collection of roles or organs but an organism that is greater than the sum of its parts.

Some insects and other crustaceans have compound eyes composed of up to thirty thousand separate lenses pointed in slightly different directions, an arrangement that is especially good at detecting movement. The brain of such creatures takes the information from each lens and puts together a composite, a mosaic, in order to construct a complete view of the world. Single-lens eyes such the human eye also gather bits of data. Inside the eyeball thousands of photosensitive cells send their information to the brain, each by its own nerve. Every part must communicate what it is sensing in order to have healthy vision.

The early Christians constructed their worldview and view of Christ by valuing personal witness: "What did you see?" "What did you hear Jesus say?" "What did you experience?" "What healing have you received?" Hearing each one's point of view creates a more complete picture. This is another aspect of the primary role we have as a Christian—to bear witness to what we have seen and heard so that others may be transformed by it. We also have the responsibility to create a culture of respect and safety so that each and every person's witness is valued. Where this climate is fostered, Christian community can move to a new level. In the next three chapters we turn our attention to the implications of healthy boundaries for the life of the Christian community.

PART 2

Integrity of Community

4

Integrity in Worship

SCENARIO FOUR: PRIVATE WORSHIP WAR

DRIVING TO CHURCH, MARTIN and Barbara expressed their dread of another Sunday at St. Paul's. Pastor Hulteen had driven them to the edge of dropping out. "I just can't stand how he leads the service," Martin complained. "And his sermons are unbearable," Barbara added. It was just not the way they liked it. They were used to having things done a certain way. After all, they were charter members of the church. The last pastor had conformed to their expectations in nearly every way. But Pastor Hulteen did not listen. He had told the congregation that when they entered the church, they should be quiet and pray. The tradition at St. Paul's had always been that this was a time for fellowship and getting caught up with your friends. He had also told them that worship was not a spectator sport, so they should not applaud for any reason, even for the children's choir. How impudent! How would the children and other performers receive recognition for sharing their gifts? They would not be surprised to see members stop participating.

During the entire worship service, Martin and Barbara silently seethed. What awful hymns! They could barely even listen to the pastor's voice, let alone pay attention to what he said. When it came time for the passing of the peace, they made sure to turn in the other direction when he came down the aisle. At communion, they were especially glad that they sat on the side of the lay communion assistant, so they did not have to receive the bread from him or look him in the eyes. As they went through the line after the service, Martin said, "Nice sermon, Pastor." Barbara just smiled and nodded her head. Then they made a bee line for their friends, most of whom were also charter members. "What are we going to do?" asked Barbara. "Maybe all of us should boycott until he changes his ways," added Martin. "It just doesn't feel like church anymore," replied one of their closest friends. They all agreed that something had to be done to demonstrate their frustration and discontent. "I am going to stop going up for communion," Martin declared. "And we are going to stop giving our offering to the general fund," Barbara chimed in. The group of friends agreed that they too were going to send a message to the pastor.

As soon as they got in their car, Barbara breathed in deeply and sighed, "That was a good Sunday morning." "Finally we are getting somewhere," Martin agreed. Both were glad to have such good friends at church, who would see to it that things got back to normal again. The sermon on this Sunday had been titled "Speaking the Truth in Love." The prayers had focussed on the theme of reconciliation. The congregation had celebrated Holy Communion in the name of Jesus for the forgiveness of sins. The closing hymn had been "Blessed Be the Tie that Binds." "How much should we reduce our offering?" asked Martin. "Let's give it all to the building fund," proposed Barbara, not missing a beat.

INTEGRITY OF WORSHIP: DELINEATING THE ULTIMATE BOUNDARY

After receiving the Ten Commandments for the second time, Moses came down from the mountain transformed. Everyone could tell. His countenance had changed. He was glowing (Exod 34:29–35). He had encountered God and had done so on God's terms. But this was not Moses's first transformation. Much earlier in his life, before Moses began to lead the Israelites, God called Moses to his special mission. At the burning bush, God told Moses he was standing on sacred ground and to take off his sandals out of respect. Moses took off his sandals. God reminded Moses that God was God and he was not. Moses respected that boundary. And so, he was transformed (Exod 3).

The most sacred of all boundaries is the distinction between God and creatures. God is God and we are not. The first commandment given by Moses was "I am the LORD your God, who brought you out of the land of Egypt, out of the house of slavery; you shall have no other gods before me" (Exod 20:2–3). As an observant Jew, Jesus gave his disciples the Great Commandment in this form: "You shall love the Lord your God with all your heart, and with all your soul, and with all your mind. This is the greatest and first commandment. And a second is like it: 'You shall love your neighbor as yourself'" (Matt 22:37–39).

Whenever and wherever human beings attempt to transcend the primordial boundary established by their creatureliness, they fall into sin and idolatry. The power of sin, taking over our lives in manifold ways, deceives us into believing that the self is god. Thereby I place myself at the center of all existence and assert that my own will accords with the divine intention for the world. There is no end to the mischief and evil of which human beings are capable as soon as they seek to defy this original boundary by claiming their own divinity.

Only God gives life. When human beings strive to express their transcendence over creation, inevitably they transgress the limit that God has established as the fundamental boundary between heaven and earth. Believing that I myself am the center of the universe, I seek to order the world self-centeredly and at the expense of others, a state of affairs that inexorably leads to death, not life. If I am god, then all others should bow to my will and obey my commands. In a world where many view themselves as distinct centers of divine power there emerge intractable conflicts among these gods, each one thinking the ego's own views deserve universal acclaim and acknowledgement.

Feminist theologians such as Rosemary Radford Ruether have criticized such an analysis of the human condition as reflecting male bias.[1] While the original sin of men may be selfishness, feminist theologians contend that the original sin of women is submissiveness. If men tend to assert themselves at the expense of others in hubris, women tend to denigrate themselves through the inability to accept and claim their full status as human beings. Only by affirming their created goodness as those created in God's own image can women overcome the socialization process that attributes to them second-class human status. The sin of pride in men finds its converse in the sense of humiliation in women. Therefore feminist scholar Carol Lakey Hess calls for intentional "conversational education" to counteract and transcend entrenched patriarchal patterns by recovering "(1) the thread of recovering women's experience of caring

---

1. Vaughn, *Sociality, Ethics, and Social Change*, 193.

and connection and (2) the thread of promoting women's capacity for voice and differentiation."[2]

In both pride and humiliation there is a fundamental transgression of the goodness of the creation. For many men, this entails claiming too much for the self; for many women, too little. If men are tempted to transcend the qualitative difference between God and humans by thinking themselves divine, women are tempted to deny the goodness of what God has created in them. In both cases the distinction between God and the creature is distorted in destructive ways. The first distortion leads to the exploitation of creation on the part of humans; the second leads to the loss of self-respect and abdication of one's worth as a valued member among those created in God's image. Both distortions disrupt the intended relationship between God and human beings in demonic ways.

Worship is the human activity that most reorients human beings to live according to God's original creative purpose.[3] The very act of worshiping God reestablishes human beings in the role afforded them from the creation of the world. Human beings are neither gods unto themselves nor humiliated creatures unworthy of being. At worship those who think too highly of themselves are instructed to let God be God and are set free from all presumption. At worship those who claim too little for themselves receive the affirmation of their created goodness and are restored as those made in God's own image. Worship of the One who is truly God grants to humans their status as creatures—nothing less and nothing more. We were created to serve as stewards of God's creation, responsible for tilling and keeping the garden (Gen 2:15) in which God graciously placed us for nourishment, enjoyment, and life.

Observing the boundary between God and created humanity establishes the fundamental limit for acknowledging and honoring all other boundaries. When we recognize the ultimate boundary between God and human creatureliness, we receive the perspective by which we may acknowledge the boundaries that must be respected in our relations with other creatures, including other human persons. The practices of worship assist us in honoring the infinite qualitative distinction between God and creatures, free us from distorting our created role, and teach us to observe

---

2. Lakey Hess, *Caretakers of Our Common House*, 182.

3. Lathrop, *Holy Things*, 2–4.

the primordial boundary without which we as humans will violate God's purposes.[4]

BECOMING TRANSFORMED BY THE PRACTICES OF WORSHIP

Worship involves many distinct elements designed to connect us with essential truths and states of being important for our relationship with God, including our capacity to do God's work. We might think of the elements of worship as being comparable to the Stations of the Cross, in that each has its own meaning and integrity. We are challenged to enter fully into each element of worship and then transition, sometimes very quickly, into the next worship element that builds upon the previous. The worship leader has the responsibility to work with others in designing the worship service and presiding in such a way that facilitates the full participation of those who gather in the pattern of worship toward soul-restoring and reorienting states of being.

Before worship, worship leaders must carefully transition from the matters of personal life into the right attitude for worship—into the right mind, the right heart, and the right energy. After the service they have occasion to connect with those who were engaged in worship as deeply as possible, even though brief encounters. These postworship relationships also require the right mind, heart, and energy. Worship leaders must seek to discern what is going on with each soul present at worship, be they known members or guests, in terms of their current pastoral needs. If there are multiple services, worship leaders must then set previous experiences aside, in order once again to be in the right state of soul to effectively lead worship each time. Psychologists call this *state shifting*. It involves the important skill of shifting from one state of consciousness to another at will. State shifting is an essential skill in pastoral ministry. Also essential is controlling one's attention during worship to keep focus on worship. The worship leader is challenged to both lead worship and to participate personally as an engaged worshiper as fully and meaningfully as possible.[5] The spouse and family of the pastor are also challenged to enter into worship mode and not be evaluating.

4. Cf. Kierkegaard, *Concluding Unscientific Postscript*, 313.

5. Schmit, *Sent and Gathered*, 114.

Worshipers must also engage in state shifting if they are to engage worship in the most meaningful way possible. Without state shifting, worshipers tend to keep the mental state and mood in which they entered worship, or something close to it. Pastor Hulteen as worship leader, although perhaps clumsily, was trying to help St. Paul's worshipers more fully engage the integrity of each element of worship. He was trying to help parishioners experience worship as something different from secular performance that calls for applause as a show of approval. When worshipers interrupt the silence after a musical piece with applause, for example, they effectively undermine the function of worship music (which is to lead worshipers into deeper communion with God and one another); applause turns the focus away from worship and toward the performers themselves.

Musicians themselves recognize that music needs to linger to reach its full effect, especially when challenging lyrics are involved. As the musician knows, rests and silences before, during, and after the music are major factors in enhancing music's effectiveness as means of state shifting. The silence after the music provides a moment of liminality, a thin space, when many worshipers can more easily enter into the Spirit's presence and guidance through the musical offering. Those who applaud deprive themselves and others of such experiences of liminality. Worshipers who applaud after a section of worship are also switching roles from worshipers to audience members—two entirely different stances.[6]

Pastor Hulteen also desired that the children in the children's choir experience their singing as a contribution to worship, something different from the performances they may do in school. Some parents even want to treat their child's participation in worship as a photo opportunity. When they do so, they are not in worship mode; instead they undermine their child's emerging understanding of worship, as well as distract others who are themselves hopefully in worship mode. There also may be instances where other lay leaders in worship may succumb to the inordinate temptation to draw attention to themselves and their own performance. Such *hijacking* of worship out of one's personal need for recognition also undermines the integrity of worship by shifting the focus away from the relationship between God and the assembly.

Worshipers can more fully engage worship from the very beginning by making a transition from fellowship to worship at least a few

6. Cf. ibid., 117–25.

minutes before the formal call to worship. The musical prelude is meant to ready the mind and heart for worship. It can only do so if one enters into worship by listening to the prelude or to the silence, not treating it as background music or as the occasion for conversation, as one would at a bar or nightclub. The worshiper also finds that one can go deeper into the music and lessons of the service when one reads and contemplates them before the start of worship.

Worship begins with the invocation of God's presence in the midst of the worshipping congregation. The assembly and each participant enter worship in the presence of the Living God.[7] This shifts us into recognition of our identity as those who were created by God, gathering now in the presence of the One who created us. This fundamental relation is underscored through the rite of confession of sin and absolution. We confess before God that we have sinned in thought, word, and deed, by what we have done and by what we have left undone. We are creatures begging mercy and pardon from the only One with the power to forgive us. The divine-human relation is nowhere more starkly portrayed as when we tell the truth about our existence by admitting we are sinners in need of God's forgiveness in Christ. Our identity is defined as those who are forgiven sinners and who therefore owe God gratitude by extending the same generous forgiveness to those who have offended us.

But these are mere words that we mouth when our minds and hearts are elsewhere. They become meaningful when we have spent time before and during worship in self-examination, comparing our thoughts, words, and actions of the previous week to what Jesus calls us to be and do. It is very challenging for us to acknowledge, for example, that we routinely engage in unjust practices at work, in our relationships, and as part of God's creation, when these practices are in fact more in line with conventional wisdom reinforced daily by the society around us. Worship juxtaposes such conventional reality and the countercultural coordinates of God's own kingdom.[8] In this regard Rebecca S. Chopp summons the church to become a "community of emancipatory transformation."[9] After we realize how implicated we are in violating the way of Jesus by our acquiescence to conventional social expectations, we can put meaningful

---

7. Lathrop, *Holy Things*, 113–15.

8. For the following, Nessan, *Beyond Maintenance to Mission*, 42–49.

9. Chopp, *Power to Speak*, 71–74.

content to our confession and experience deep gratitude in response to the worship leader's proclamation of God's forgiveness.

Many of us must also prepare our hearts to fully accept the precious gift of forgiveness. When we engage worship with our whole being, it becomes transformative for the choices we make about our thoughts, words, and deeds in the days ahead, including in our choices to hold others accountable and extend forgiveness toward them. When confession and forgiveness are offered in a mindless way, we publicly purport to confess our sins and accept God's grace when this is not really the case. So we lull ourselves into believing we are doing something when really we are not entering into and trusting God's promises.

In the passing of the peace, we are challenged to act as God's agents of love and grace to all who are assembled, regardless of how we might have felt about them before worship. To do so requires that we see each worshipper as equal in the presence of God, not selecting out some for special treatment because of who they are to us outside of worship— friend, family member, lover, or coworker. We may want to ignore or avoid others because of how we feel about them. Our inner state in relationship to God during the passing of the peace shows us how far we have come, or have yet to go, in living the kingdom.[10] During worship (and in the Christian fellowship that precedes and follows worship), not only are we called to outwardly and visibly treat each person as someone precious to God, but we are called to bear each person in our hearts with divine care as we extend God's peace to them. Undoubtedly, this practice requires a deliberate transition.

Dietrich Bonhoeffer in *Life Together* proposes that it takes the spiritual discipline of seeing the other through the eyes of Jesus Christ rather than through our human eyes: "Now other people, in the freedom with which they were created, become an occasion for me to rejoice, whereas before they were only a nuisance and trouble for me."[11] These disciplines of integrity in worship expand our capacity to live lives of love well beyond our human limitations.

At worship we sing praises to God. God is worthy of our praises as the Author and Sustainer of our lives. We learn at worship that we were created to praise God; we exercise this praise through our hymns until our entire lives become songs of praise. Many of us can grow by

---

10. Nessan, *Shalom Church*, 79.
11. Bonhoeffer, *Life Together*, 95.

increasing our capacity for praise and celebration, becoming less self-conscious and concerned for how we look to others, in order to let loose the joy that passes understanding. We attend to God's Word at worship through readings from Scripture and the preaching of the pastor. Thereby we acknowledge that it is the Word of God that lends orientation and direction to our lives as we navigate the challenges and dilemmas we face every day.

Protecting the integrity of the sermon is a challenge for all concerned, from the preacher's preparation and delivery to the hearing of the sermon by those assembled. In preparing the sermon, the preacher protects the integrity of the sermon by maintaining good boundaries. Preachers must set aside a host of private agendas that can contaminate the process, from the desire to impress people or win their loyalty to the impulse to lecture or scold those who oppose them. The question about whether the preacher should set aside political agendas is worthy of reflection. Does the addressing of political issues violate the integrity of the sermon, or is it a necessary aspect of prophetic preaching? While the preacher does well to avoid partisanship regarding political parties, addressing the urgent social issues of our time corresponds to the Scripture's own engagement with such questions.

Respecting the integrity of each sermon requires that the preacher spend prayerful time in study and reflection in order to discover what the Spirit is speaking to this people through these texts, even when they may have preached them many times before.[12] Even more challenging may be texts that preachers find personally disturbing or baffling. The point is to bring the reading of God's Word alive for worshipers to hear in a way that has integrity for the congregation as a whole and for each person assembled.

Those hearing the sermon must, in worship mode, set aside their conventional likes and dislikes.[13] They are called to set aside cultural and educational trappings to hear God in the thoughts and speech of the preacher, as mediated by the Holy Spirit. Not only the Bible readings but also the words of the preacher become for us the Word of God in the act of preaching. Self-control begins with control of attention. Keeping attention on the sermon, with openness to the Spirit, may help amplify what the preacher says, bringing awareness of thoughts, images, and

12. Lathrop, *Pastor*, chap. 2.

13. Samuel D. Giere has provided a useful resource for the hearers of sermons: *With Ears to Hear*: http://www.withearstohear.org/.

memories associated with our personal hearing of the Word. Some of the thoughts we bring to the sermon enhance our understanding, while other thoughts must be let go as mere distractions. Barbara and Martin have fallen prey to putting their attention on their own likes and dislikes about Pastor Hulteen and his style of preaching, giving it more importance than the biblical text and how God is speaking to them through this Word. Sermons, like worship music, are not performances, and we degrade them when we treat them as such.

We confess a creed at worship, using ancient forms that have guided the people of God over the generations. These creeds are affirmations of core beliefs, things for which we stand and for which the martyrs died. Each successive rehearsal of worship further elaborates the boundary between God and our lives, establishing our accountability to God in all things. Each element requires that we be fully present to it. Thus we enter into prayer to God at worship, presenting intercessions for God's care and concern. These, however, are not just petitions we hand over to God. If these are the things for which we dare pray, then they serve also as a mission statement for ourselves and the church in its outreach and ministry. In this way the prayers of the church are a commitment on the part of those who pray to give their lives to exactly those things for which they pray. This only happens when we enter into prayer with our whole, conscious being. The offering of the church also clearly defines the relationship between God and creature. God has provided everything we are and have. As creatures we owe to God only thanksgiving for every gift we have received. Therefore the basic posture of the creature is one of gratitude to God, demonstrated by generosity toward the world of neighbors God has given us to serve.

In the meal, the Lord's Supper, the church gathers at the table to remember and receive the presence of Jesus Christ in bread and wine. This is the banquet of the kingdom of God. At this meal we receive the gifts of Christ's forgiveness, deliverance from evil, and the reality of eternal salvation. Here all are welcome, calling upon those communing to subordinate our everyday tensions and differences with others to our unity in the presence of Christ. At this meal there is enough for all. There is no shortage of either food or grace in the economy of God.[14] The body and blood of Christ are given and shed for you! Each person receives from Christ sustenance for living and hope in the face of dying. We are

14. Nessan, *Shalom Church*, 93.

precious, although sinful, recipients of God's mercy in Christ. Nowhere do we find our lives defined more clearly and profoundly by what has been accomplished for us by Christ Jesus than in the sharing of the Lord's Supper.

PASSING FROM THE BOUNDARY ZONE OF WORSHIP INTO SERVING IN DAILY LIFE

Worship concludes with a benediction and the sending. We receive the blessing of the triune God—grace, love, and hope. The face of the Lord shines upon our way. Moreover, we are sent to live as creatures defined by all the practices of worship. We are sent to serve the Lord, share the good news, and be generous to the poor. Christ himself is with us. Thanks be to God!

Worship easily can be faked. But then it is not really worship. We can sit through the whole thing and say all the right words without engaging our hearts, minds, or souls. It is tempting to do so, since engaging worship with our full being can take us out of our comfort zone, translating us out of conventional reality into the presence of Holy God. We may like to keep our emotions in a narrow range of control, while worship calls us to surrender control to the Spirit. We are called to transcend our conventional sense of ourselves. While we may feel timid, we are called to sing boldly. Make a joyful noise! While we may be shy, we are called to engage in the passing of the peace. While we may be loud and domineering, we are asked to be silent and yield to God's presence.

Worship involves making ourselves vulnerable—vulnerable to God and before others. As essential as vulnerability might be to the life of faith, our humanness does not like it. We do not like having our lives engaged so fully or our feelings affected so deeply as they are when we fully engage in each element of worship. We may cry with tears of immense joy and gratitude or with tears of great pain and disappointment. We may sing out of tune. We are certain to become emotionally uncomfortable— guaranteed! We may embarrass ourselves. Therefore the worship space must be a safe place, safe from our own self-criticism and safe from the judgment of others. It is to be sanctuary. And we must help make it a sanctuary for others. We are invited to stretch our awareness vertically to engage the transcendent presence of God and horizontally to engage in community with others. Worship fully engaged is thereby the most psychospiritually challenging activity of the week.

The sanctuary is a sacred space for worship and for the protection of what is sacred to us. We take off our shoes and enter with respect. Boundaries are kept by what is allowed at worship and what is not. Nothing is to be located in a sanctuary that summons our allegiance to anything other than God. No symbols are allowed that serve private interests or are promotional in nature, even those of nonprofit or fraternal organizations. The sanctuary is protected from anything that might distract us from the worship of God alone.

Within the practice of worship, keeping the integrity of each part means recognizing the boundaries within the elements of worship and making successful transitions between them in order that we participate fully and mindfully with our whole being. At worship our lives are oriented by the primordial boundary that defines our existence: the relationship between Creator and creatures, Savior and sinners, Spirit and those in need of the life only God can give. The boundary between the life-giving God and our finite lives provides the fundamental orientation for how we are to live in relationship to other persons. The God who created us, forgave our sins in Christ, and gives us life by the power of the Holy Spirit is the One who holds us accountable for observing life-giving boundaries in relation to all the persons we encounter in our daily affairs.

Since God is the source of life for us, as experienced in every practice of worship, we are to be conduits of life for the people who are entrusted to us in all arenas of our lives: family, daily work, local community, and global connections. The boundary between God and humans, established at the creation of the world and exercised through the practices of worship, undergirds all the boundaries we must respect in our dealings with other people every day of our lives and with the creation itself. God holds us accountable to relate to others honorably and to be concerned about their welfare and life, just as we are creatures who owe everything to God. We are not gods. Worship, in all its diversity of elements, reinforces that God is God, the One who in Jesus Christ finally comes again to judge the living and the dead. Our core identity and mission are clarified by what we do at worship. We are to fear, love, and trust in God above all things. And we are to love our neighbor as our self. This overarching truth, as established at worship, grounds and safeguards every boundary with which we are entrusted in our lives as creatures in God's world!

5

Bearing Witness: Integrity in Interaction and Communication

SCENARIO FIVE: BEARING FALSE WITNESS?

Maria: "I'm thinking Steven would be a good person to work with our youth group. He is such a nice guy."

Megan: "But haven't your heard? He is a sexual abuse survivor, and sexual abuse survivors are more at risk of abusing others. We shouldn't take the chance.

Claire: "How do you know he is a sexual abuse survivor?"

Megan: "Evelyn, the church secretary, told me."

Beth: "Isn't it odd that Steven and Fey don't have any children? They've been married eight years."

Joanne: "I heard Fey doesn't want to have children."

Megan: "Maybe she doesn't trust him with children?"

Claire: "Is it really true that sexual abuse survivors are more at risk of abusing others?

Megan: "That's what I heard on *Oprah*."

Joanne: "Well, my husband, Jim, was molested by his older brother for a couple of years, and you can't tell me he isn't safe with kids. That's ridiculous!"

Megan: "Well let's ask Pastor about it!"

RELATIONAL PERSONHOOD

What does it mean to be a human being? A foundational understanding about who we are as human beings is indispensable for clearly naming, analyzing, and honoring the boundaries necessary for flourishing human communities, including faith communities. Theologically speaking, our understanding of human beings derives consequently from our concept of God as the One who created us. Although after the Enlightenment human beings have been increasingly conceptualized as individuals, especially as individuals who have capacity for intellectual reasoning, a Trinitarian understanding of God—and of human beings as those created by this triune God—gives a qualitatively different shape to our interpretation of human being.

In modernity the human being has been depicted primarily as an individual, as one who has unprecedented capacity for reasoning.[1] This definition of the human has contributed to expanded human understanding and the discovery of vast knowledge, based especially on the fruitfulness of scientific method for formulating and testing hypotheses. Such knowledge is reliable and sure insofar as scientific findings can be quantified with mathematical precision. Thereby modernity has tended toward reductionism in its view of the human, stressing the achievements of atomistic, reasoning individuals as the drivers of history. In our contemporary, postmodern world, one of the chief characteristics affecting human life is the transforming of individualism into "hyper-individualism."[2]

In multiple ways, contemporary society takes the autonomy of the individual as the presupposition for every form of technological innovation—in electronic communications, information systems, transportation, education, health care, and virtually every other arena of contemporary life. Our lifestyles have become extremely individualized. Consumerism caters to the desires of the individual and the affinity groups into which individual desires may lead us to congregate. How much we see ourselves as individuals is revealed by how we make decisions. Who do we consider when we make decisions? How much do we act from self-interest? How much focuses on, what's best for my family? How much is based on my personal affiliations, my tribe? How much

---

1. Cf. Borgmann, *Crossing the Postmodern Divide*, 37–47, on "ambiguous individualism."

2. Beck. *God of One's Own*, chaps. 7 and 8. For a description of what he names "monadic relativism," Jameson, *Postmodernism*, 412–13.

relates to, what's best for others affected by my decision? Or what's best for God's work in the world? Hyperindividualism locates the self in a position of inflated importance at the expense of other considerations in all the decisions that we make, large and small.

In contrast to the hyperindividualist tendencies of the postmodern world in which we are immersed and by which we are often overwhelmed, theological anthropology, following belief in the triune God, views human beings not as individuals but as *persons*. Just as the One God is constituted through the dynamic interrelationships among the three persons of the Trinity in life-giving mutuality (*perichoresis*), so human beings find their fulfillment not in the pursuit of individualizing agendas but through relationships of mutual consideration and mutual accountability.[3] Catherine Mowry LaCugna writes: "Everything comes from God, and everything returns to God, through Christ in the Spirit. This *exitus* and *reditus* is the choreography of the divine dance that takes place from all eternity and is manifest at every moment in creation."[4] One imaginative depiction of the relational character of the Trinitarian persons is the icon of the Trinity by Andrei Rublev (ca. 1360–ca 1430). The Holy Trinity is portrayed as three remarkably identical persons seated at table around a common vessel, in full communion with one another and inviting the viewer(s) to join their communion.

The Latin word *persona* refers to the "masks" we wear as human beings always in relation to other persons. As those created in the very image of God (Gen 1:26), we are made for life-giving relationships with God, other human beings, and all of God's creation. In the words of Dwight N. Hopkins, "the *imago dei* unfolds outward into the *missio dei*. We are called to exhibit healthy humanity by recognizing this divine image and sharing liberating evangelism with others."[5] We exist as persons, donning masks, always in relationship to others, which relationships provide fulfillment and meaning for our lives. Social-scientific research has demonstrated that it is not wealth, status, or even health that ultimately makes people happy. Rather, human happiness is grounded in the quality of the relationships we have with others. The quality of our relationships with other people is the crucial factor whether we experience joy in living. Is it not providential that the Christian church engages exactly in the "relationship business," with love as the guiding principle?

3. LaCugna, *God for Us*, chap. 8.

4. Ibid., 274.

5. Hopkins, *Being Human*, 185.

Jesus Christ reveals and re-presents true human being. Jesus existed in life-giving relationship with God through worship and prayer, the intimacy of which was indicated by his naming God as *Abba*, Daddy, in relation to his own Sonship. Moreover, Jesus instructed his followers to address God as *Abba* in prayer, reminding us of our shared lineage, that we are sisters and brothers. Jesus welcomed all people to live in communion with God, inviting us to share table fellowship with one another in his presence (Mark 14:22–25). Following in the way of Jesus, the early church "devoted themselves to the apostles' teaching and fellowship, to the breaking of bread and the prayers" (Acts 2:42). Jesus revealed his way to his followers both by the witness of his life in ministry and by teaching what it means for us to live in relation to others.

Family-systems theory provides a constructive framework for reinterpreting how the Christian understanding of justification by grace through faith contributes to self-differentiation, in contrast to the hyper-individualism of contemporary society. In systems theory "self-differentiation" and "nonanxious presence" derive from two human capacities: (1) the ability to constitute a centered self and (2) the ability to relate to others in life-giving ways.[6] The distortion of either of these capacities leads to disfunction: an inadequate sense of self undermines one's ability to relate to others, resulting in either inability to enter into and maintain life-giving relationships with others ("cut offs") or overidentifying oneself with particular others (enmeshment). In systems theory the way toward self-differentiation involves close examination of one's family of origin and family dynamics, especially as schematized through a genogram. Through insight into established patterns of emotional reactivity, one is able to attain a greater measure of self-differentiation and nonanxious presence.

The doctrine of justification by grace through faith in Jesus Christ provides a theological grounding for self-differentiation and nonanxious presence that both respects the insights of systems theory and transcends them.[7] While it is imperative that church leaders come to understand the emotional patterns that inform how they relate to others based on the patterns from their family of origin, there is an ultimate source for self-differentiation and nonanxious presence that comes to us as a gift of God in Jesus Christ. Trusting in God's grace serves both as a spiritual

6. For an accessible summary related to self-differentiation, see Richardson, *Becoming a Healthier Pastor*, chap. 5.

7. Nessan, "Surviving Congregational Leadership," 390–99.

foundation for self-acceptance and as a source of freedom to relate to other persons, which is created at worship (through Word and sacrament) and fed by spiritual practices. One's relationship with God, based on the gift of justification by grace through faith in Jesus Christ, grounds self-differentiation in God's acceptance of us for Christ's sake and provides a source of nonanxiety and peace deeper than the world gives (John 14:27). This is why the practices of Sabbath discussed in the next chapter are so crucial to the well-being of church leaders and members.

God's creation of human beings, we know today, took place through a long evolutionary process. Although the Genesis creation stories capture lasting truth about who we are as persons created in the very image of God and about the power of sin over human life as a consequence of "the fall," it is vital today that we attend to the insights of evolutionary science regarding human nature in order to fathom the dilemmas we face in following the teachings of Jesus—especially the radical imperatives of the Sermon on the Mount. Through our evolutionary inheritance we share many basic instincts, drives, and tendencies with our relatives in the animal kingdom. These include not only regulating the body (as with respiration or blinking) or satisfying bodily appetites (by gathering or hunting for food) but also engaging in behaviors instrumental to social relations. For example, human beings have an unprecedented capacity for face recognition, an ability that assisted humans to interpret social relations with acuity amid the complexities of human relationships, some of which might have threatened our very survival.[8]

Similarly, human beings inherited from our animal ancestors many primal instincts and drives in relation to behaviors such as aggression, social hierarchy, sex, and the avoidance of pain. When threatened by others, human beings are hardwired to respond aggressively, through emotional intensity, facial expressions, bodily posture, verbal warnings, and physical readiness to (defend from) attack.[9] As other species do, human beings also participate in symbolic displays and ritualized behavior to establish social hierarchy, especially among their sexual rivals of their own gender. One attains a sense of security in life by dominating and subduing one's rivals.

8. Cf. Bates and Cleese, *Human Face.*
9. Nessan, "Sex, Aggression, and Pain."

In terms of human sexuality, men and women have distinctive strategies for "success" according to our evolutionary inheritance.[10] Males of the species are genetically most successful through sexual behaviors that propagate sperm promiscuously, impregnating as many females as possible. Females of the species are most successful through the selection of genetically "strong" sexual partners and through mating strategies that will protect offspring from danger into adulthood (the age when they can themselves begin to propagate). Regarding the function of experiencing pain in evolutionary perspective, human beings share with other animals both the perception of pain and well-developed behaviors linked to pain avoidance.

Much human behavior is fruitfully explained in terms of how we relate to others based on such primal instincts and drives. Commonly, the reports we hear or read about in the news can be interpreted insightfully according to the instincts and drives we share with other animals. What complicates these impulses, however, is the evolution of the human mind. With the emergence of the neocortex and the human mind's unprecedented capacity for reflective self-consciousness, what once was natural for other animal species has become a moral and religious problem for the human being.[11] Because of human awareness about how, for example, our aggression or sexual behaviors can do harm to others (and have ramifications for our own well-being), human beings face moral and religious dilemmas based on our peculiarly human cognizance about how what we do affects others, either negatively or positively. This human mindfulness unveils the dislocation of the human animal. Whereas other creatures do what comes naturally without violating conscience or accruing blame for their aggressiveness or sexual behaviors, human beings are morally culpable for their actions. The human condition entails accountability for living responsibly with behaviors that are innate and natural in other species.

The evolution of the human mind also has opened the path to the development of human culture as one of the most powerful influences upon human behavior. Whereas other species, especially the higher primates, have rudimentary cultural practices, human beings have developed complex symbol systems to shape and direct human history. Kathryn Tanner comments: "to a particular group of people, *culture*

---

10. Cf. Ridley, *Red Queen*, chaps. 6 and 7.

11. Nessan, "Sex, Aggression, and Pain," 452–53.

tends to be conceived as their entire way of life, everything about the group that distinguishes it from others, including social habits and institutions, ritual, artifacts, categorical schemes, beliefs, and values."[12] Socialization into a particular culture or subculture significantly shapes what we consider normative human behavior. One of the functions of human culture is either to endorse or resist the primal instincts and drives that motivate human action. This means that cultural elements (such as stories, rituals, or values) can work upon the human person to either accentuate or resist the evolutionary impulses that are deeply embedded in our human psyche. For example, culture can either endorse expressions of human aggression against enemies in a time of war, or culture can promote nonviolent means of conflict resolution. Culture can titillate innate human sexual drives through advertising images in the marketing of products, or culture can set limits on the sexualizing of human persons as objects to motivate consumption.

Religions, with their warrants about what we are to regard as ultimate in life, are powerful shapers of cultural values. For this reason, as Musimbi Kanyoro argues, we need a vital "cultural hermeneutics" for interpreting particular cultural phenomena.[13] Religious beliefs and practices, as elements of human culture, can either endorse or curb innate human impulses regarding aggression, hierarchy, sex, or pain. Appeals to religious traditions can provide warrants for either just war or principled nonviolence, dictatorship or participatory democracy, polygamy or celibacy, corporal punishment or restorative justice. In relation to Christian beliefs and practices, the Bible too can function to shape human culture variously, depending on one's interpretive lens. Christian leaders appeal to the Bible to pray for the victory of "our" nation over its enemies, to authorize varied forms of ecclesial government, to combat or allow committed same-gender sexual partnerships, or to support or oppose the death penalty. In each of these instances, it is useful to consider how the innate instincts and drives that condition human behavior are either authorized or resisted by religious teachings.

Further, religion can either reinforce the cultural values within which it exists, or religion can contrast and conflict with them. When it does contrast, its adherents need clear direction from the religion in order to not be overly influenced by the dominant culture. The boundary

---

12. Tanner, *Theories of Culture*, 27.

13. Kanyoro, *Introducing Feminist Cultural Hermeneutics*, chap. 5.

practices we are exploring in this book are in most cases not in line with the practices of the dominant culture in which we find ourselves: this contrast gives us all the more reason to be clear about them, to teach about them, and to refer to them explicitly. Without such clarity, behavior will inevitably drift toward the norms of the dominant culture rather than toward what is spiritually derived.

The teachings of Jesus make strenuous demands on human beings to live not according to the norms of our animal ancestors but according to those potentialities that belong to the evolution of the human mind and culture in fostering life-giving relationships with God, other persons, and God's creation. We find especially in the Sermon on the Mount the most radical of Jesus's teachings about what it means for the church to be a "contrast community" to both our animal nature and the dominant culture.[14] With regard to striving for power in a social hierarchy, Jesus teaches that those who are great must become as a child (Matt 18:1–5). This is how love works; it makes us subservient to it and gives us the desire to elevate others. With regard to sex, Jesus teaches his disciples that they not only are to avoid adultery but also are not to look with lust at other persons (Matt 5:27–28), which would be to objectify them. Regarding avoidance of pain, Jesus instructs his disciples to take up the cross and follow him (Matt 16:24–26). The goals of love must become stronger than the urge to avoid pain and loss.

Regarding aggression and retaliation—the taking of an eye for an eye or a tooth for a tooth—Jesus teaches his followers to turn the other cheek, to love our enemies, and to pray for those who persecute us. (Matt 5:38–47). Being oppressed and mistreated does not excuse one from the command to love. Those who use and abuse others remain themselves in need of love and generosity. However, as we show love and generosity, we must always insist that those who have been harmed remain safe. To experience compassion in response to aggression can open the perpetrator to life-changing transformation. The oppressed and mistreated can serve on the front lines of the campaign of love and compassion, provided that they have been involved in a process of truth and reconciliation with the perpetrator about what has occurred. It is important that we reframe reconciliation from a matter of individual forgiveness to a process of communal reconciliation in the form of restoring right relationships and justice.[15]

14. Bailey, *Contrast Community*, chap. 1.
15. Cooper-White, *Cry of Tamar*, 253–62.

Human beings are best understood not as individuals but as persons! Individuals pursue self-interest while persons are made for life-giving relationships with others and with creation in the presence of the triune God. Following Jesus means following his way in the things that make for life, peace, and shalom. According to Randy S. Woodley: "Shalom is always tested on the margins of society and revealed by how the poor, oppressed, disempowered, and needy are treated."[16] This way of discipleship places us in tension with many values endorsed by our culture and even by many conventional religious beliefs and practices. It pits Christian community against the dominant culture that competes in shaping our thoughts, beliefs, and behaviors. The moral assumptions we make based on our innate instincts and drives, even as these may be endorsed by culture and religion, often mislead us about the higher righteousness to which we are called as Christians (Matt 5:17–20). Only comprehensive attention to boundaries in all areas of life—in thought, word, and deed—can grant us life—true life, eternal life.

THOUGHT, WORD, AND DEED

We are relational beings called to love with our whole beings in relation to God, others, and self. Hopkins underscores the relational character of human persons:

> Relationality names the living presence of others in the self and the self in others . . . Each self, in this regard, internalizes prior human experiences from a massive span and scale of time and place. Likewise, each day during the self's sleeping and non-sleeping, conscious and subconscious moments, the individual takes in, through reason, intuition, the five senses, and spiritual avenues, a flood of information from others.[17]

The Great Commandment to love everyone and to do so unconditionally engages us in caring for the relational integrity and effectiveness of ourselves and others. This begins with our basic posture toward others, which Jesus addresses with the command to love. He did not just say to act according to love outwardly. Universal and unconditional love is a posture of the whole being, an inner and outer state of welcoming openness to all others, an eager invitation to know and be known. Good

16. Woodley, *Shalom and the Community of Creation*, 15.

17. Hopkins, *Being Human*, 99.

boundary practices cultivate this holistic posture of love in ourselves and in others. By necessity, it includes what we do within our hearts and minds, not just what we do overtly.

How we think about others can either strengthen or weaken our capacity to love them. What we say to another person can either strengthen or weaken their capacity to love themselves. What we say about someone to another person can either strengthen or weaken that person's capacity to love the other. How we think about ourselves, and the nature of our self-talk, can either strengthen or weaken our capacity to love ourselves. The same is true of our capacity to love God.

The mission of "doing no harm" in relationship to others involves keeping various types of boundaries. To apprehend self and others accurately in our mind and heart, with no false images, requires the absence of bias from preconceived ideas. Sloth (that is, laziness) loves bias. It wants hasty conclusions and generalizations, because taking each person at each moment in an open manner requires effort. Laziness would rather speculate than abide in a state of not knowing. It would rather judge than be uncertain. The stressed mind has the same tendency, since it wants to expend as little energy as possible. It wants to categorize people and secure them in those categories, rather than to go through the trouble of getting to know people as they are. The Christian directive against making false images as "impression building" pits this tendency of the human brain against secular culture, which promotes and reinforces impression building. The spiritual discipline of tolerating and even embracing "not knowing" is well described in the fourteenth-century Christian text *The Cloud of Unknowing*.[18]

What we experience in life involves an interaction between what happens objectively and what we bring to it subjectively. Fundamentally, when I encounter a person, what category do I put them in—the ingroup or the outgroup? Are they one of us, or not? The human brain wants to know, while Jesus tells us to treat everyone as being within the ingroup. Jesus instructs us to consider all people our neighbors and, even more fundamentally, our sisters and brothers. Everyone is in the ingroup; no one is in the outgroup. Jesus says as much in the Lord's Prayer. The word *Abba* implies that we are all in the same family. When we hold on to this truth and are filled with love, there is no bias; there is only charity.

18. Walsh, ed., *Cloud of Unknowing*.

Because we cannot know the extent of our subjective distortions in perceiving the other, some people advise that we operate with the *principle of charity*. The principle of charity operates according to the values not only of truth and honesty but also of helpfulness and kindness. The principle of charity conflicts with the wiring of the human brain to keep us safe. The safest thing is to assume the worst about someone else, not to assume the best. Martin Luther, for example, encouraged us to interpret another person's actions "in the best possible light."[19] But is this not naive charity at the expense of the truth? When we put our own behavior in the best possible light, for example, the result can be unhealthy denial of our genuine intentions and actions. With others, it can lead to allowing someone to persist in taking advantage of us or of others, because we do not want to think ill of them. It can lead to our turning a deaf ear to a complaint against someone whom we want to trust rather than investigating the matter out of concern for someone else's well-being. It could lead to irresponsible trust rather than due diligence—for example, in congregational youth protection policies.

An alternative is the *principle of truth in love*. Unconditional love toward the self creates safety so that we can see ourselves realistically, as we really are. It does not provoke defensive denial in us. It does not provoke shame but rather compassion for our human and animal natures. Unconditional love and acceptance does not hide from unpleasant truths but rather increases our capacity to apprehend the truth, which strengthens and protects our relational nature. In contrast, denial puts a person at undue risk of misbehavior while shame evokes the urge to withdraw from others. In shame we may well turn on ourselves with abusive self-talk and hurtful overt behavior justified by our negative attitude. In both cases life-giving relationships are damaged rather than enhanced, thus failing the test of love.

A healthy use of the principle of charity allows for accurate and truthful representation so that each person can contribute maximally, including ourselves. Each person legitimately has a different point of view and a different set of abilities and skills. The more points of view that contribute, the more fully we can apprehend the full truth. This view is consistent with the research, which shows that decisions tend to be better when more people contribute to them rather than fewer people. Truth is

19. See Luther, *Small Catechism*, "Explanation of the Eighth Commandment," 1160–67.

beyond the comprehension of any single mind, so we need the benefit of as many points of view as possible.

The spreading of the good news and therefore our very understanding of Christ depended upon the willingness of those who had encountered the risen Christ to bear witness to what they had directly seen and heard for themselves. To know what was going on, the disciples needed to hear from the women who saw the empty tomb and the angel who spoke to them. They needed to hear from those who encountered Christ on the road to Emmaus. A person's willingness to bear witness is enhanced when they know they will be met by a caring, listening ear. Sadly, surveys show that a vast majority of Americans have had meaningful spiritual experiences that they have not shared with others. We lose out from that reluctance. Unfortunately, it is common that when one does share such experiences, the listener does not respond with charity but rather puts their own spin on the other person's experience. To have the enormous benefit of another's experience, an attitude of open, nonjudgmental listening is needed. This respects boundaries. As Paul Tillich famously observed, the first duty of love is to listen.[20]

Listening requires mental, emotional, and even theological discipline.[21] We must set aside the filter of our own beliefs and experience in order to understand the other. If we approach others with the presumption that they are wrong because their beliefs are different from our own, we are incapable of understanding them. Philosopher Donald Davidson suggests that understanding requires applying the principle of charity, by which we assume the truth of what the other is saying.[22] Without that assumption, we are unable to understand the person, as we remain constricted by our own point of view and thus misrepresent the ideas of the other. Similarly, psychiatrist David Burns has found that it works best to first agree with someone who is upset with us.[23] When we subsequently are able to explain their point of view and perhaps even amplify it, the person feels understood and relaxes, thereby being more able to hear a different point of view from their own. Burns, who has widely taught this technique, also finds (as Davidson too would predict) that this act

20. These quotable words are widely attributed to Tillich, but they look like a composite: "In order to know what is just in a person-to-person encounter, love listens. It is its first task to listen" (*Love, Power, and Justice*, 84).

21. Hedahl, *Listening Ministry*, chap. 9.

22. Davidson, *Essential Davidson*, 234–35.

23. Burns, *Feeling Good Handbook*, chap. 21.

of agreement helps us enter into the mindset of the upset person. While students may initially object that they cannot agree to what they do not think is true, Burns advises that this objection falls away with repeated use of the technique. People learn from their own experience that the commitment to finding truth in another's viewpoint leads to just that. There invariably is truth in what the other is saying, while initially it might not appear to be so. Application of the principles of charity and seeking the truth in love can result in more people feeling safe enough to share what they have seen and heard, so all can benefit from it. In short, good boundary keeping helps us perceive the truth.

While this approach is not easy, it is also not easy to apprehend the truth of our own experiences. What we experience is the product of the interaction between what has happened externally and what we bring to events subjectively. This interaction constitutes our perception and experience. In order not to misinterpret events or create false images of others, we must approach each situation and person free from bias, free from hasty conclusions about the present, and free from faulty conclusions about the past. The subjective state we bring to experience is our inner world, the psyche, which we compose from the raw materials of the thoughts, feelings, memories, impulses, desires, urges, and images that impress us. We select from the vast array of inner experiences available to us those to which we give importance and priority, those on which we choose to dwell, and those which we choose to let go. This often unconscious selection process creates our disposition and predispositions. Our thoughts, feelings, and predisposition either help or hinder our being able to see the truth. What we do in our inner world matters. Good internal boundary keeping helps.

Thoughts that increase stress simultaneously reduce awareness, including awareness of the feeling states of others, thereby reducing the capacity for empathy and related empathic responses. Such thoughts make the situation in which one finds oneself seem worse than it really is (thinking, for example, "This will never work!"). Negative thoughts can make our own capacity seem less than it really is (for example, "I'm an idiot; what am I doing?"). We may also misperceive what others are doing and ascribe to them negative motives that are not actually present.

Enhancing and protecting our relational capacity takes into account how we relate to others in the privacy of our own minds and imaginations. Every thought about another person is an opportunity to love or not to love. Being loving enhances relatedness, while unloving thoughts and feelings damage our capacity to love. Love is a subjective state of heart, mind, and soul that regards and treats all others as part of one's ingroup. All are to be regarded as neighbors, not as aliens. Every thought is an opportunity to objectify and exploit, or to resist doing so. Lust provides one example of using another for our own pleasure, even if only in our imaginations.

In the other direction, jealousy and resentment cast us into the outgroup by our failure to participate in the joy of a sister or brother. Shame likewise casts us out from shared community. For a follower of Christ, the litmus test of our inner state is similar to the test for our actions: do we show love and the capacity for inclusiveness in relation to community with others?

While it belongs to our human-animal nature to have objectifying thoughts and feelings toward others, we are given the capacity to control where we put our attention. With each thought we can decide to dwell on it or not. We can either keep our attention on it or turn away. Spiritual practices like *centering prayer* and *welcoming prayer* exercise and strengthen our capacity to control our own attention; thereby we protect and enhance the capacity for relatedness in our own minds and hearts. As we gain control of the environments we create and inhabit, certain kinds of thoughts are more likely to occur in our minds. An important part of self-control is monitoring the environments into which we imagine ourselves. It is like controlling an appetite by not going to an all-you-can-eat buffet.

Jesus gives us a concrete way to assess our love: how we treat the least important person. Jesus said that how we treat "the least of these" is how we treat him (Matt 25:40). We perhaps care least about those we perceive as harming us. Since love is meant to bring us together, those most in need of my love may be exactly those who inflict harm on others and exploit others for their own gain. Thus, without perpetuating their own harm, victims are called upon by Jesus to love those who harm them. This advances love, adds love where it is missing. When perpetrators experience love, they may be transformed. In contrast, when we hate or harm them in return, we do nothing to increase their capacity for love. Further, when we harm them, we harm those who care about them—everyone in their family. As one who regarded himself as the brother of all, Jesus is harmed when we harm others. Likewise, Jesus is given joy when we give joy to others. Some have even taken this in a metaphysical sense—that Christ dwells in each of us: The Christ in us honors the Christ in others.

In this way, we do not favor those for whom we have personal affinity over those for whom we do not. This is the discipline of *love equality*. To see the other person through the eyes of Christ is to see them through the eyes of love. This is the Christian standard. To love is to bear witness to Christ, especially when it is most difficult to do so. We recall the opportunity for witness that was afforded to an Amish community. The community immediately extended forgiveness to a man who killed their schoolchildren, even as they also extended compassion to his family. They immediately recognized that his was the act of a troubled soul.[24]

Another test of whether a thought enhances life-giving relationships or not involves asking whether it meets the following four criteria:

1. Is it honest? Many in our culture believe that if a thought is honest, then it is healthy to think it and perfectly fine to say it to someone else. But that is not enough when our concern is for also for the other person.

2. Is it true? How certain are we that it is true? If we are not certain, then holding the thought and sharing it with others is being careless with the welfare of the other person about whom we are speaking. The same applies to thoughts about ourselves. As we stated above, speculation or predisposed interpretations about behavior do not meet the standard of certainty of truth. In our opening scenario, Megan passed along a rumor that Steven had been sexually abused and did so by labeling him ("a sexual abuse survivor"). She also speculated to herself about his trustworthiness and passed along that speculation to others. None of this passes the test of truth in thought or word.

3. Is it kind? The principle of compassion toward self and others precludes unkind thoughts, feelings, and actions as unworthy of our time and energy. Unkind thoughts damage our subjective relationship with a person. To verbalize them to others is to potentially damage another's relationship with that person and so to harm that person.

4. Is it helpful? Some thoughts and words may meet the above criteria but are simply not helpful in a situation. In those cases, the loving thing is to let them go.

24. See Doblemeier, dir. *Power of Forgiveness.*

Prayer and meditation are practices that help condition our hearts and minds to be loving. In the Lord's Prayer Jesus taught us to regard all others as part of the ingroup to which we all belong.[25] When someone asked Jesus how they should pray, his instruction was to pray not as an individual but rather as a "we" praying on behalf of an "us." He addressed the prayer to the One who created us all, our common "parent" or *Abba*, as in the voice of a small child. In this prayer, we pray for love and compassion to reign on earth. We pray that all persons will have their basic needs met. Compassion comes from a shared sense of vulnerability, with which this prayer connects us. In that regard, it is interesting to note that when Jesus was asked, "Who is our neighbor?" in effect the answer was that our neighbor is anyone and everyone (Luke 10:36–37). We are all from the same neighborhood. In the parable of the Good Samaritan, the person in the story who stopped to help the man who was beaten and robbed was someone who was himself highly vulnerable to being attacked on that road. The man he helped was from a group of people who treated him as an enemy. When we lose our sense of shared vulnerability, we lose our capacity for empathy. And so this prayer reminds us of the utter dependency on God that we all share in common. In this prayer, we pray for healing in broken relationships through acts of forgiveness. We are in this together, and together we shall remain. There are no outsiders.

Another spiritual practice that enhances life-giving relationships is the blessing of others. When we consider who is suffering in the world and extend our blessing toward them in our prayer life, we enhance our relatedness with each other. Since we are also encouraged to "bless the LORD, O my soul" (Psalm 103), we get the amazing reminder that blessing can even come from us to the Lord. This is one expression of our love of the Lord. We are not relegated merely to request that the Lord bless us or someone else. We are the agents. Even more sobering in this regard is Jesus's statement that if we do not forgive someone, they are also not forgiven in heaven. We act on behalf of the whole by how we relate to others, so this is both a huge responsibility and a vast opportunity.

We have been through an era in North America when people have wanted to believe that our inner lives do not matter: for example, that it is fine for someone during sex to fantasize about being with someone other than their partner, if doing so gives them more pleasure. Some have wanted to believe that infidelity does not hurt anyone if the partner never finds out about it. Some have wanted to believe that taking what does not

25. Cf. Bailey, *Contrast Community*, chap. 10.

belong to us does not matter if the other party can afford to lose it and never finds out who took it. What makes something wrong is "getting caught." But attitudes and secret actions do matter. This is why Jesus's Sermon on the Mount and Luther's Explanation of the Ten Commandments include our thoughts and feelings in the same moral category as outward actions. There are boundaries to be respected in both arenas.

To summarize, here are seven types of individual boundaries to be respected in our covert (internal) actions:

a. *Identity boundaries.* We respect a person's identity boundaries when we internally and externally regard them according to their core identity as a distinct and unique person, a child of God, and as someone for whom Christ died. We do not simply view people as objects for our use or according to what they can do for us. We do not create false images of others either in our own minds or in the way we communicate about them to others. We think of them and refer to them with the name they wish us to use, not using labels or nicknames they do not offer. We do not generalize about them, which leads to misinterpreting their behavior. We do not speculate about them; instead we stick to what we know for sure.

b. *Physical boundaries.* We do not imagine exploiting the person by sexualizing them in our mind or fantasizing about them in ways that turn them into objects for our own ends.

c. *Will boundaries.* We do not mentally consider how we can dominate or control another person. When we make a request of another person, we inwardly and outwardly respect no as an answer without demanding explanations or judging their reasons.

d. *Emotional Boundaries.* We inwardly and outwardly allow others to have their own feelings and thoughts without invalidating them or deciding for them what they should think or feel.

e. *Mental Boundaries.* We appreciate the importance of other people's thoughts as an important expression of their identity. We do not criticize others inwardly or outwardly for what they think or believe, but rather seek to understand and learn from them.

f. *Resource boundaries.* We do not covet the resources others have or lay claim to them in any way, including their physical resources, money, time, and talents. We do not impose guilt or manipulate others to use their resources in the way we desire.

g. *Spiritual Boundaries*. We do not judge another's relationship with God or interpret another's spiritual experiences. We do not invoke God's action toward the other person without their consent. We do not decide for others what they should believe or practice spiritually. We do not use God to manipulate, correct, or condemn others even in our own minds.

Speaking is a form of action. All of the above apply also to how we speak to another and what we say about them to others. Jesus taught his followers to discipline what they say. For example, Jesus tells his disciples not to swear using oaths but rather to simply let "your word be 'Yes, Yes' or 'No, No'!" (Matt. 5:37). Moreover, Luther taught us not to "tell lies about our neighbors, betray or slander them, or destroy their reputations. Instead we are to come to their defense, speak well of them, and interpret everything they do in the best possible light."[26]

Returning to our opening scenario, we see many kinds of boundary violations. Megan "reports" to others that Steven is a sexual abuse survivor, which, if true, is not her information to share. But she does not really know it to be true; she is simply passing along what she has heard from the church secretary, which is unfair to Steven (and might well put the church secretary at risk of losing her job for violating this boundary). Megan then generalizes about sexual abuse survivors being more at risk for abusing others. Even if her generalization were valid, which it is not, it would be prejudicial and unfair to Steven. Beth and Joanne then talk about Steven and Fey not having children and engage in speculation about it, imposing false images of them.

BEARING WITNESS, TESTIMONY, GOSSIP

The dominant culture values power and influence. Every opportunity to speak is an opportunity to gain power and influence. We are advised by business consultants that if we wish to be successful, we should treat ourselves as we would a commercial object, because in fact we are a commercial object. We need to sell ourselves in order to have others desire us socially and vocationally. If we are not successful, we need to "rebrand" ourselves according to what would be more successful, look the part, and act the part. To get a job, you need to figure out what the employer wants and then shape your resume and yourself to fit it. Once in the job,

26. Luther, *Small Catechism*, "Explanation of the Eighth Commandment," 1161.

the project of shaping and selling one's self continues by our performing the actions the employer desires. In this course of action, while material success may be forthcoming, demoralization occurs internally. Moral injury may occur if one violates one's deepest values, which includes the spiritually derived value about doing good in the world rather than the culturally assumed value of making money.

In order to prevent ourselves from feeling bad, we learn from the dominant mental health community the art of *reframing*. Reframing, when applied without integrity or moral guidance, easily becomes the practice of thinking about what we are doing in a way that prevents us from feeling guilty, rather than finding words that reflect the truth of the situation. Thus there may be ways that reframing is "helpful" in keeping us going, but really not true. Similarly, a manipulative person will put a spin on another person's words, in order to create the appearance of support, when in fact it is a stealthy ploy to alter what the other person has said. Another example of this is telling others what they think about something in order to appear to have their approval of your own idea: "I know you'll agree with me that . . ." This is pure manipulation.

The standard in court is to tell the truth and nothing but the truth. As Sargent Friday famously said, "Just the facts, ma'am; just the facts." To tell the truth and only the truth takes the spin out of things, because spin is a form of manipulation and deception. It is an interpretation. Manipulation damages life-giving relationships by treating others as objects to get what one wants. It also damages life-giving relationships by risking loss of trust on the part of the other. Self-deceptive reframing even damages our relationship with ourselves, making ourselves less trustworthy in our own eyes.

To not interpret what we perceive in order to keep to the facts requires a deliberate sustained campaign. It is well worth the effort. It is hard enough to accurately report what you see and hear in an auto accident, let alone the extraordinary events reported in one's spiritual experience. In bearing witness and testifying to what we have seen and heard that has spiritual and religious import, we again have enormous responsibility and enormous opportunity. Take, for example, the story of the empty tomb reported in John 20. Mary visited the tomb where Jesus was buried and saw that the entrance was no longer covered by the stone that had enclosed it. She interpreted that it had been "rolled away" and that someone had "taken" the body of Jesus. This was all misleading interpretation. It would have been factual to state simply that she found the tomb empty and did not know what had happened. To remain factual requires a willingness to not know and to say that one does not know. Comfort with not knowing is essential to the ability to know the truth and report it accurately.

"God came to me in a dream last night and told me the pastor has to go. He is destroying the church." But when Ed's friend asked him to say exactly what happened in the dream, it became clear that Ed had distorted the actual dream material into the interpretation he wanted and was giving it authority from beyond. We can distort our dreams instantaneously. In recalling them, thinking about them, writing them down, and telling them to others, they filter through lenses constructed from our own perceptions of reality based on assumptions, fears, and desires. Sticking to the facts is hugely important.

When we listen to another's testimony, we are also challenged not to interpret. To assert "Oh, that is a God moment!" or "There are no co-incidences" is to tell other people what they should believe about their own experiences. In doing so, we make it our own and impose it on the other person, a boundary violation. The sad result is that people do not feel safe in sharing spiritual experiences with others. Neither do we want others to distort it, nor do we want others to think we are crazy, because we had an extraordinary experience. On the other hand, respecting our own boundaries can mean, at least temporarily, keeping extraordinary experiences to ourselves. Mary told no one about the message that she was pregnant with Jesus but kept it safe in her heart where she could come to understand it free from the contamination of other points of view. This was wise.

When we communicate with others, we are carefully attuned to how they are reacting and tend to adjust what we are saying in order to get approval. Without those visual and auditory cues, social media have trained users get their entries "liked" in order to get "friended." We are constantly being judged "thumbs up" or "thumbs down." This setup works against integrity. It easily results in a sense of self that is shaped by the dubious interpretations of others regarding our actions online. In no way does this enhance life-giving relationships, because the object presented to ourselves and others is a constructed self, not who we really are. It is a deliberate fabrication. It appears, however, to give us power about what we want in life, except, of course, the deep desire to be known and loved just as we are. When churches use social media, this should only be on the terms of the gospel, not involving "liking" and "friending." "Thumbs up" and "thumbs down" was a Roman practice, not a Christian one. The sanctity of the psyche must be respected for God's unconditional love to prevail.

Some clergy rationalize their speaking ill of others as healthy "venting." Many people still feel that venting, which involves complaining about others, is helpful psychologically in order that things "do not build up." Clergy groups support and may even encourage this. The mental health field has long since abandoned this approach, however, as it neither matches current understandings of how the psyche works nor accords with the research. Research instead verifies that venting negative feelings toward others simply reinforces those feelings, which is what behavior theory predicts. Venting is deceptive, because initially we may feel better after doing so. But as we know, many unhealthy behaviors initially bring pleasant feelings.

When we want to express our feelings, it is best to always follow the same rules that we would if we were expressing those feelings directly to the person (or persons) who evoked those feelings. Even when they are not in the room, using "I" statements to express own our feelings is far healthier in every respect than making "they" statements about others. The latter lead to cynicism. Venting with "they" statements can also be attractive because it leads to a sense of intimacy and support with the people to whom we are talking. But this is false intimacy whenever the subject is "they" instead of "I." Internally, the same principles and considerations apply. When in the privacy of our own thoughts we think in terms of "you" or "they," we create false intimacy even within ourselves. We feel like we are being honest with our own feelings, when we are actually avoiding self-reflection by endorsing our own projections upon others. Venting also issues from a selfish motive, an ego motive, rather than the motive of bringing out the best in ourselves and others. Whatever the activity, the final criterion is, does this make us more loving, more able to serve, or less so? You will know them by their fruits.

This chapter has examined theological foundations, anthropological evidence, and best practices of boundary keeping in order to guide us in preserving the church's integrity both through our internal processing and through our interactions with others. As we have indicated, the practice of Sabbath is crucial for the centering of our lives necessary for maintaining wise boundaries in thought, word, and deed. The next chapter focusses on the meaning of Sabbath shalom for the sake of preserving the integrity of the body of Christ as a shared responsibility.

6

Sabbath Shalom: A Day in the Kingdom

SCENARIO SIX: SUNDAY CHURCH MEETINGS

RENALDO WAS RELATIVELY NEW to Lord of Life but was well liked and quickly voted into leadership positions. He had a very busy business and family life, as did many other members of the leadership team. For this reason he initiated having meetings after the first service on Sunday mornings, so people would not have to make an extra trip to the church for another meeting. The initial response was very positive and they encouraged other congregational committees to follow suit.

THE NATURE OF SABBATH

Sabbath is in many ways the crown jewel of all boundary keeping. It belongs to the first of the Ten Commandments. In the first Genesis creation story, Sabbath is the goal of creation, coming after the creation of everything else, as the very crown of all creation. But the meaning of Sabbath's value has been elusive. Most obviously and conventionally, it is about the need of the body and soul for rest. Sabbath is, in part, the antidote to "the cares and riches and pleasures of life that choke the spirit" (cf. Luke 8:14) As Michael Kerper notes, "Without a generous amount of leisure, the spirit dies." Further, he says, "And when this happens, faith communities become lifeless museums used for 'holy days.'"[1]

---

1. Kerper, "Loss of Leisure Time, Loss of Faith."

Less apparent, especially to the busy mind preoccupied with the things of this earth, Sabbath (as itself a product of creation) is the threshold to a dimension of creation that is not readily accessible. Sabbath, fully engaged in by us, demonstrates that good boundaries not only prevent bad things from happening through the choking of the spirit but help create the conditions for wonderful things to happen that would not otherwise be possible, when the spirit is fully functioning. Walter Brueggemann believes that the first table of the Ten Commandments clarified for the Israelites that Pharaoh was not their god.[2] They no longer needed to serve Pharaoh; now they were to serve God. The commandment to keep the Sabbath naturally follows as a reminder to worship God above all things. After the Sabbath commandment comes the basics of what it means to care for God's people rather than to exploit them.

Every person, every place, and every time reveal aspects of the Divine. Without this awareness, we know less about God. Sabbath, when entered into deeply, helps us connect with the Divine in all persons, places, and times because it allows us to look past the blinders imposed by our usual preoccupation with "function": What do I need from you? What can I get from you? What can you do for me? What do you want from me? What do I need or what can I get from this place I am in? All these considerations are suspended in the practice of radical Sabbath, allowing us to see and appreciate everything that is. It is a time to relate to others, to our own true selves, and to the living God according to the values of the kingdom.

Sabbath turns off the usual sense of purposefulness we normally bring to our work and to the other tasks that we need to do to survive. We refrain from "using" what others do or say. When we suspend viewing others as objects for our own use, we are better able to see their genuine identity, the "who" of the person and not just their "what for." In Sabbath we also relate differently to ourselves. We put aside the ways we tend to objectify ourselves by "branding" ourselves. When we are in our conventional mode of relating to ourselves and others, our awareness is constricted to functional value. We are focused on task, which excludes awareness of other dimensions.

Stress further constricts our awareness, especially time pressure. Under time pressure, we are more likely to walk past someone in need than stop to help them.[3] This is our usual state of mind. In this mode, those

2. Brueggemann, *Covenanted Self*, 49–51.
3. Cf. Darley and Batson, "From Jerusalem to Jericho," 100–108.

who can contribute something to us get more of our positive attention, because of their advantage to us. People who are neutral to us do not count, and those who are in our way often get treated poorly. This approach is light-years away from loving our neighbor and treating the least of these as we would treat Jesus. Other natural objects are also thought of in terms of their potential usefulness to us, not as ends in themselves.[1] A tree is not at thing of beauty; it is potential lumber. The world of nature becomes occupied with things we can possess, because we are operating with a "production and acquisition" frame of mind. We entirely squelch true mindfulness as we strive merely to get by functionally in the world. Thereby the spirit becomes choked and thereby the work of the kingdom.

The intent of Sabbath is easily co-opted to simply serve the cares, riches, and pleasures of life. To remain effective, the body and the brain need rest. The anxieties of our cares and "urgent" priorities both serve to keep us from taking Sabbath breaks or, if we do, motivate us to compromise Sabbath. We keep working the treadmill instead of engaging in something that might threaten to be disruptive of our established way of life. Our behavior may appear like Sabbath as a kind of rest from work, but in actuality there is little or no sense of the Divine in our rest. Brueggemann describes this as going "through the motions of Sabbath."[4] Renaldo wanted to use Sabbath time to get church business done, during which he and the other leaders would principally relate to each other in terms of their congregational functions, not according to their true personhood. Sabbath is elegant in design.

Sabbath instruction tells only what not to do, not what to do. We are to keep the time holy, which is a matter of quality, not content per se. Without resting in God, rest can merely serve to support the status quo. We are commanded simply to rest from our work and to grant that rest to others as well. Why is this so hard?

If you have ever been to Cloquet, Minnesota, you have probably had the odd pleasure of seeing the only gas station in the world designed by the famous architect Frank Lloyd Wright. Mr. Wright, as they called him, was a utopian. He did not design buildings to accommodate how people live and work; he designed them purposely to shape how people live and work in accordance with certain ideals. In the homes he designed, for example, the bedrooms are very small, really just sleeping chambers, because he did not want people to isolate themselves from others. You are not allured to want to hang out in one of his bedrooms but rather are

4. Brueggemann, *Sabbath as Resistance*, 62.

attracted to the great room with its welcoming large hearth, where you will be in the company of the rest of the family.

Cloquet was to be the site for an entire utopian community that Mr. Wright envisioned. But the only building that was ever constructed was the gas station. He designed it with a second-floor lounge where weary travelers could rest. As with deep Sabbath, however, rest was not the only goal for the lounge: it was to provide a place of rest so that relaxed folks could notice and enjoy the beautiful view of the forests of northern Minnesota. What do you suppose the travelers' lounge is used for now? Storage! Travelers today do not want to stop and rest; they want to stop and go. They scarcely care about beauty; they want to get to their destination as quickly as possible. Similarly, God's rest stop at Sabbath is largely going unobserved.

To a large degree we are afraid to stop due to our attachment to "the cares and riches and pleasures of life." We fear that we will lose something, not accomplishing what we think needs to be completed. We become anxious that our families will lack for something. All boundary keeping involves loss, or the risk of loss, of the good for the sake of the best. Our occupations, which are meant to serve us, instead actually enslave us when we are afraid of losing them. Our possessions do the same when we are unwilling to risk losing them. We do not understand how we can slow down or stop for any significant period of time. It just does not seem practical or even possible, at least to the anxious mind. The anxious mind, like that of Pharaoh, always expects something more, demands more and more work from us. In fact, we increasingly feel we must always be multitasking in order to get everything done that is important to us.

But suppose we do stop, then what? Here is the elusive part. For those who are adept at setting the boundaries to enter deeply into Sabbath, there is beauty, awe, wonder, and joy to connect with aspects of God and God's creation that normally are obscured by our busyness and preoccupation with the practical, utilitarian concerns of the material world. Why do some people, however, who try to stop and to rest quickly become bored and restless for their usual preoccupations and sources of stimulation? Rest can seem tedious, even depressing. Rob Bell, in his book *Velvet Elvis*, describes his own early attempts at keeping Sabbath.[5] He initially became depressed. Rather than turning back, Bell persisted and broke through the fog of depression to experience the joys of Sabbath. Bell's experience is not unusual.

5. Bell, *Velvet Elvis*, 116.

In the early 1900s a psychiatrist recognized that some of his patients became depressed on Sundays. He called it Sunday Neurosis.[6] Others also struggle with Leisure Sickness, the phenomenon that some people feel less happy during vacations.[7] Typically, however, these are transitory phases of adjustment that open a path to the benefits of actual Sabbath keeping, when we learn to set aside our usual concerns and recover from the toll they take on us. Many of us experience that the first few days of vacation are spent catching up on sleep. There may be a period of less mental clarity or even sluggishness until we emerge on the other side, at last able to experience things we would not experience otherwise.

Camp counselors report that when campers, particularly youth, are deprived of their electronic devices, for the first couple days they get bored and restless. They grumble and complain. They must go through withdrawal from artificial stimulation. Then after a couple days, other dimensions of the natural world open up to them. They are able to appreciate the stillness of the woods, the scent in the air, the amazing flight of the birds, the aliveness of the clouds, and the depth and grandeur of the night sky—none of which were previously accessible to their awareness, given the state of their preoccupations.

The dimension of reality Jesus named the kingdom of God, which some now refer to as the shalom of God, requires a certain state of consciousness in order to perceive and enter. In the shalom of God, unconditional love is shared in life-giving relationships with all—with neighbors, with self, with the Lord God, and with all God's creation. The lens of unconditional love suddenly makes all reality clearly accessible. It provides the "eyes to see and ears to hear." It is an awareness of everything around us and in us, which is difficult to maintain all the time. Normally, the mind gives value and priority to certain things over others in terms of our attentiveness, thereby distorting our perception through the exercise of judgment. In contrast, nonselective compassion engages everything willingly.[8] In our everyday lives, priority is given to utilitarian matters. Realistically, except for the mystics, there is no way to be aware of the holiness of all reality and its glory apart from Sabbath. It rarely happens any other way.

When we look at what the most expansive states of awareness require, we find that our energy must be on the high side rather than the

6. Frankl, *Man's Search for Meaning*, 112.

7. Vingerhoets et al., "Leisure Sickness," 311–17.

8. Cf. Nussbaum, *Upheavals of Thought*, chap. 6.

low side—something that Sabbath helps to create. Awareness takes energy. It also takes energy to sustain a positive mood. Our energy must be calm rather than agitated in order for us to have fullest awareness. When water is clear and calm and the air is clear and calm, you can see deeply through both into the nighttime sky. Our consciousness must be clear rather than foggy, and our awareness must be broad rather than narrowed by utilitarian concerns. Both of these qualities of consciousness are more available in deep Sabbath and invite entry into loving awareness of the shalom of God. If we use Sabbath merely for recovery, in order to get ready to go back to work, we miss out on this most blessed gift, while possibly believing that we actually are keeping Sabbath. That is just scratching the surface of Sabbath. "Sabbath is not simply the pause that refreshes. It is the pause that transforms."[9]

Here is where we must add something to our typical understanding of Sabbath as merely resting from our work. Martin Luther wondered whether a man passed out on the floor on Sunday was keeping Sabbath. He was, after all, resting from his work. What was missing? He was not keeping the Sabbath holy. Holy intent involves neither becoming unconscious (in order to recover, numb out, "veg out," or forget), nor simply doing what feels good (for example, enjoying the benefits of our labor through consumption). Sabbath is not payday. A holy intent and focus can help carry us into awareness of God's shalom and assist us in avoiding lesser interests that do not have shalom qualities. This is possible, however, only if we are prepared.

Entering into the sacredness of time brings with it feelings of vulnerability, as it did for Rob Bell. Is that surprising? Do not all encounters with the holiness of the sacred involve vulnerability? Brené Brown's conclusion from studying vulnerability is that it is the doorway to many very special things, including intimacy.[10] We would add that vulnerability is the threshold to deep Sabbath. Of course, awareness of the sacred threatens the comfortable confines of the ego and the pursuit of ego interests. Becoming comfortable with our own vulnerability aids in the experience of Sabbath, just as it does with other forms of boundary keeping. If there is no zone of vulnerability, it is probably not deep Sabbath. In deep Sabbath, we invite others to enter as well by reducing their sense of risk through our own good boundary keeping. When we purposely refrain

9. Bruggemann, *Sabbath as Resistance*, 45.

10. Brown, *Daring Greatly*, 104.

from regarding what others say and do in terms of our own self-interest, they can feel safer to explore and share who they really are.

Left to our own devices, most of us respond to vulnerability and other forms of emotional discomfort by backing off rather than leaning into it. We turn on our smartphone, laptop, or TV to avoid the initial discomfort of silence and apparent aloneness. We say "apparent" because in the reality of God's shalom, there is no such thing as being alone. We are always surrounded by God's creation. When the ego is motivated to reduce its discomfort, we rationalize doing what brings us pleasure and enjoyment in the free time of Sabbath. Again, our relationship to our feelings is crucial for living a faithful life. When we let ego-based feelings control us, we deprive ourselves and others of what is possible, instead of riding the waves of the Spirit.

Sabbath is a state of being. Boundary keeping is fundamentally about love. When we love someone, we give them time and attention. In the case of Sabbath, it is about fully receiving God's love even with awareness of our unworthiness, realizing that God's unconditional love is beyond any sense of being worthy or unworthy. It can neither be earned, nor can it be lost. We are referring here to unconditional love as grounded in God and directed toward the Self, not love of ego and its trappings: loving God, loving our neighbors, and loving ourselves. Sabbath helps us increase our awareness in all dimensions—physical, emotional, mental, and spiritual—making us more able to love.

There is something paradoxical about Sabbath, which reflects the paradoxical nature of unconditional love itself. Sabbath is both a gift and a commandment, a delight and a duty. It is a gift of love, which we have a duty to receive. It is a gift for us and yet it belongs to God, because we belong to God. Our lives belong to God and our time belongs to God. When we refuse the gift of Sabbath, we steal from our relationship with God and thereby also intrinsically from our relationship with ourselves. When we encroach on another's Sabbath time, we steal from them as well as from God. Renaldo's practical considerations in doing the business of the congregation after worship, during what is Sabbath time, is a form of theft, no matter how well intentioned.

Like Sabbath, love is both a gift and a commandment: the greatest commandment. It is both grace and law. The ability to accept ambiguity and apparent contradiction comfortably is also required of those living God's shalom. Deep Sabbath and unconditional love change our likes and dislikes. Like and dislike considerations are subordinated to holiness.

All self-discipline involves the subordination of likes and dislikes to something of greater value. Self-discipline is, after all, the ability to get ourselves to do what we do not feel like doing and, conversely, to get ourselves to do things that we do not feel like doing. With what we might call "God-discipline" rather than self-discipline, we yield to holiness and the commands of love.

Complete awareness requires holding all things together, including contradictory things, instead of excluding some for the sake of others. Reality is not an either/or. The ability to hold together conflicting things is essential to living and working in a way fully informed by Christian values (rather than, for example, isolating business decisions from those values). It is also critical to our ability to recognize the truth. Researchers have discovered that our willingness to believe their findings is based on whether or not we like the implications of the data, a phenomenon called "solution aversion."[11] In order to acknowledge the truth, we must recognize and be able to suspend our personal likes and dislikes.

There are two versions of the Sabbath commandment in the Bible. In Exodus 20:3, Sabbath is referred to as a reality to be remembered, harkening back to the first Genesis creation story, according to which the seventh and final day of creation was a day of rest for God. Sabbath is the goal of creation. The ostensible reason for us to keep Sabbath is as a remembrance of God's original ordering of creation. In Deut 5:15, the reason given for keeping Sabbath is for the Israelites to remember their freedom, that the Lord delivered them from slavery. Now they were free to serve God, not Pharaoh. These reasons—God's ordering of creation, gratitude, and the celebration of freedom—inform deeper levels of Sabbath keeping.

The Sabbath commandment is brilliant in that it only tells us what not to do with it; it does not tell us what to do with it. We are to not work. People of faith over the centuries have put great effort ("great work") into defining both what work is and what it is not. For our purposes, we will understand work to be anything that carries a sense of obligation to the things of this earth, anything that is on a to-do list, anything we are not free not to do, or anything that advances such obligations. Thinking about work, for example, is work. The mind can engage in work even while the body is resting. While we cannot stop ourselves from having such thoughts, we do control how we relate to such thoughts once they

11. Cf. Campbell and Kay, "Solution Aversion."

occur. We can simply turn away from thoughts of work during Sabbath time. No, it is not easy, but with practice it can be done.

As people seeking to honor Sabbath, we have a tendency to "bargain" with it and interpret this as freedom to pursue our likes and dislikes. Doing this, however, only strengthens the part of the self that attends to likes and dislikes. Hence the value of considering holiness. A soaring eagle is free only by having rapport with the air current, sensing and responding to air's subtle movements. One of the lessons of Sabbath is that the greatest freedom comes with the consideration of holiness: "Since I enjoy mowing the lawn, it isn't a chore; it is a pleasure. Doesn't that count for Sabbath time?" By the criterion of freedom alone, the answer would have to be that it could only be considered a Sabbath activity if you are free never to mow the lawn, not just today but ever again. Given our attachment to the cares of the world and our anxiety about there being more things to do than there is time for us to do them, it is understandable that we want to bargain for counting things on the to-do list as Sabbath. Getting tasks done is one strategy for reducing stress. Renaldo and the others liked the time savings from killing two birds with one stone on Sunday mornings. The stressed mind, as we have mentioned, becomes short-term in its thinking. The secularization of Sabbath wants to turn it into a mere self-care practice to serve the purpose of sustaining the status quo with its narrow interests, instead of challenging the status quo with an awareness of the awe and wonder of things and people beyond their usefulness.

We can enter into sacred places as tourists or as pilgrims. If you have ever been to any of the great cathedrals, you may have noticed this difference. You also can see this difference in awesome natural spaces like a redwood forest. Some people enter these spaces in a preoccupied state of mind, still talking about the last thing they saw on their itinerary or about where they want to go to lunch. They may take a few pictures and barely notice where they are. Just like a stone skipping over the water, the faster we go, the more we just glance across the surface of things. Others may see the money to be made if only they could cut down the trees or sell things to the tourists. By contrast, others enter sacred spaces as a destination, not just an attraction along the way. These are the pilgrims. They are interested in forming a meaningful relationship with the space itself and what inhabits that space. They are able to engage the Divine presence. They have prepared their minds and hearts to be fully present, fully receptive, and fully prepared to engage what is there with their entire being.

Awe, wonder, and beauty are open to them, as is the subtle movement of the Spirit. In Sabbath we can enter the sacredness of time either as tourists or as pilgrims. What we experience depends on our approach. We prepare for entering into the depths of Sabbath by slowing down, resting, and opening up before entering into it—not just using Sabbath to recover from our tiring endeavors.

Sabbath contrasts with other uses of time in that it is not utilitarian. Utilitarian interests have an extrinsic objective. They aim to go from point A to point B. In Sabbath time, there is no point B. An example is the archetypal Sunday drive. How can you distinguish a Sunday driver? They drive like they have all the time in the world and as though they do not know where they are going. Both are true. Sunday drivers are actually interested, as Mr. Wright hoped, in the beautiful scenery around them. And it is true that they do not know where they are going. Arden's mother used to say, "Let's just get in the car and see where it takes us." On a Sabbath drive, at any given intersection you could choose any option, not just continuing in the direction you were headed. Sabbath is antihabit, anti-inertia, counter–status quo. In this state of openness, you explore. Even when you go nowhere and stay put, you become aware of more and more aspects and dimensions of the place where you happen to be.

All kinds of activities can have this Sabbath quality. In a Sabbath walk, for example, you also do not know where you are going. You are exploring, engaging, and interested in relating to whatever is encountered. It differs from purposeful walking, in that it has no point B. It differs from an exercise walk in that it has no objective. While an exercise walk may be refreshing and healthy, it is purposeful and therefore lacking this Sabbath quality of nonutility. Holy freedom is a characteristic of everything related to Sabbath. It does not need to have anything to show for it.

BOUNDARIES AND SABBATH

In Sabbath, good boundaries open up new possibilities. Another great example is Sabbath talk. In utilitarian communication, one aims to transfer information from one mind to another mind. The goal is to do so as efficiently and effectively as possible. This is useful and even feels great when one is understood correctly. In Sabbath conversation, however, when the sacredness of time is respected, there is no time pressure.

When two people both are freed from the usefulness of what is said, whether now or later, there is safety to disclose freely. Sabbath conversation can wander without feeling like anything important was lost. This is precisely the kind of conversation that can lead to intimacy through vulnerability. It is the kind of talking some people can do in a car, while driving a long distance with a trusted companion. It starts and stops. It goes hither and yon. Campfires invite Sabbath conversation. In one such talk, after sharing an idea, Arden remembers his son saying, "I didn't know you felt that way." Arden replied, "I didn't know either. I've never had that thought before just now." Much of our talking is merely reporting rather than mutual exploration and discovery. This joy of discovery is made possible by the conditions of deep Sabbath: freedom from the distractions of one's usual concerns, holy intent, freedom to explore, and freedom from possessing or using what we encounter.

In our exploration of the different types of boundaries, we began with identity. Sabbath appeals to claiming our ultimate identity: who we are separate from our functions in the world. By remembering and engaging with God, we remember who we really are on the most fundamental level: we recall an identity that can never be lost. All other identities can be lost. Furthermore, we connect with our inherent freedom. When we grant Sabbath to others, we rest from relating to them according to their functional identities. If someone asks Arden on Sunday morning, "Aren't you Dr. Mahlberg?" he is likely to say, "Not today." Sabbath is broken by relating to others in their functional roles and is kept when we relate to others as wholly other than that, in the spirit of Buber's I-Thou relation.[12]

More challenging for many clergy is to separate who they are as persons from their identities as pastors or ministers, since those are thought to involve the whole person. Far from it! This belief is an excuse for not delving more deeply into the self and justifies the belief that clergy are somehow different from other people. Many clergy deeply long to be known as persons in distinction from their role and the stereotypes and assumptions that may go along with the role. Clergy spouses do also.

To rest from our work and engage otherwise, all part of the Self must disengage from work. Take the example of clergy. One part of disengaging is mentally resting from our work. Comedian Bob Newhart once observed that comedians are never really on vacation. No matter where they are, they are looking for material. This is as much an occupational hazard for preachers and teachers as it is also for writers—to be constantly looking for insights and material. One is always "on duty." Without an explicit Sabbath discipline all prayer, meditation, and devotional time, as well as

12. Cf. Buber, *I and Thou.*

other personal and family recreational time, can be spent mining for material, insights, or life lessons to use in sermons, Bible studies, or counseling. When one tries to mine Sabbath experience for work purposes, it is a violation of the integrity of Sabbath. It requires discipline to differentiate and safeguard personal time with God from its professional use, no matter how brilliant the insights.

Part of the preparation for going into Sabbath time is the reminder not to put to use any insights or material that comes up. There is precedent for relating to God differently during Sabbath. In the Jewish tradition, some distinguish between Sabbath prayer and non-Sabbath prayer. Sabbath prayer does not include petitioning God or asking God for anything, which would treat God in a utilitarian manner as someone from whom you want something. Sabbath prayers are prayers of thanksgiving. Similarly, clergy may find it helpful to distinguish relating to God in their work mode from encountering God in Sabbath, which is to be protected from professional use. Likewise, Sabbath can be a time to refrain from speaking for God.

Beyond physically resting from work and mentally resting from work (and from other areas of responsibility), one also needs to learn how to rest from work emotionally, to put down what we carry in our hearts. Resting from ministry emotionally means, in part, giving over the sense of responsibility that is usually carried. We simply must take significant rest breaks from the caring that is part of the job, as well as breaks from the trauma and suffering with which we have to deal. Some cannot go home and watch more suffering on TV. A good practice is to look back and debrief the past work period to see if there are feelings that remain undigested and, if so, to deal with them intentionally. If we do not do so, the result will be compassion fatigue, an inability to care. Instead of caring, we become cynical, resentful, and bitter toward those we are called to serve. This is true for any caregiver, professional or otherwise. It would seem odd that Sabbath time would be a time to stop caring. Jesus, after all, did heal on the Sabbath. But here it makes good sense for helping professionals to discover rest from their work by giving their caring concerns over to God for the duration of their Sabbath time. This frees you to have energy and time to care about other things and other people in personal rather than professional ways. Emotionally resting from our work and from other burdens of caring opens us to experience emotional states not as available when we are in work mode, for example, delight. Isaiah says to "call my Sabbath a delight" (Isa 53:13). Emotionally resting from caring work, we are more capable of engaging a broader range of feeling states, like delight, love, joy, and playfulness.

Spiritually resting from our work involves putting aside our primary call. We are in receiving mode. In doing so, we are not only refreshed, but we have time and energy to discover and engage in the other things we are called to do, in other roles that have importance for God's presence in our lives. Parent, friend, lover, writer, inventor, gardener, artist, naturalist, photographer, woodworker—God created us to be so complex and multifaceted that no earthly role, however important, can contain all of us. Sabbath is a time for exploring all the rest of what God calls us to be, the rest of who we are. When we are not getting enough time away from our daily work mindset, we lose track of the fact that we have other calls. Many pastors complain that they feel called to get involved in something that their congregation has no interest in, like justice work. When the pastor decides to do it anyway, even on their own time, they become more fully alive. Also, having a date with one's significant other in a committed relationship is a time to set aside other issues and just enjoy each other's company. Sabbath is a time to set aside one's issues with God and just enjoy God's company.

One of the occupational hazards of professional ministry is the objectification of God. We know that worship can be harder for clergy when they are worship leaders, because they must keep tracking in a work mode. They cannot just lose themselves in the experience. Even when clergy are worshipers in the pew, it can be similar to the difference between a nonmusician at a concert and a professional musician. The nonmusician listens with the emotional or experiential part of the brain, letting the music move them in a receptive mode. By contrast, the professional musician listens with the analytical part of the brain. The professional musician may even be "playing" the music, or "conducting" it with micromovements of the muscles. They are in active "work" mode, not receptive "being" mode. So when clergy and other worship leaders are in the pew, the challenge for them is to switch off the work mode and switch on the experiential. One's professional relationship with God can become devoid of an experienced faith component, given the constant pressure of speaking for God, speaking about God, and representing God in some responsible way. The professional minister can begin to encounter Holy Scripture exclusively in an analytic and utilititarian manner, not as an experience to ponder for the feeding of one's own soul.

In the novel *A New Kind of Christian*, Brian McLaren has his character Neo observe that "Talking about God for pay always threatens to work against really loving God . . . The people who talk the most about God are the ones most in danger of taking [God] for granted, of letting God become just a comfortable word in their lexicon, a piece of furniture, rather than a reality, a friend, a constant surprise."[13] This is strong stuff. In Buber's I-Thou relationship, we stay with and savor the vastness and inexplicability of the Other, reaching well beyond what we have experienced or have yet understood about the Other. We respect the inexpressible nature of the Other that cannot be reduced to the categories of language. Sabbath rest from the work of ministry includes the soul's being with God in ineffable mystery, not trying to reduce this mystery to words or to use it in any way.

Dual relationships are always complicating. To lend money to a friend can risk the friendship. Working for or with family members can risk the integrity either of the family role or the business role. Many a farm boy has grown up feeling that they only had working relationships with their fathers, not personal relationships. What happens in the boss-employee relationship during the day can be hard to set aside after work is done in order to pick up a father-son relationship. Sometimes after work you would rather not spend any more time with each other. Spouses who work together are challenged to learn to set the boundaries necessary to keep the roles separated so that each can adequately flourish. Many clergy couples who work together, for example, go to bed and talk shop. Rarely do they have set staff meetings with each other, like they would if they were not married to each other. They do not see the need for it, since they can always talk shop. On their days off, they may wish to go their separate ways. Their personal relationship becomes weakened by poor boundaries.

Like the farm family, some clergy would rather not spend their free time with the same people they work with. Some clergy admit to not wanting to spend Sabbath time with God. In their meditation practice, some clergy prefer to have a nonspiritual focus rather than a spiritual one. Beyond that, many clergy contend with the desire to spend non-work time in secular—and possibly even unholy—pursuits, to get as far away from work mode as possible. Some refer to this as "carnalling out," pursuing carnal interests as a break from "the holy life." We can get tired of being good, especially when there is a sharp contrast between

13. McLaren, *New Kind of Christian*, 167.

how we would like to act and the constraints of the role we occupy. In this circumstance, switching from religious or spiritual work mode to Sabbath mode can feel unfulfilling, too much like more of the same, too much "not me." This is a barrier to Sabbath keeping, not only for spiritual workers but for others in the helping professions. We get tired of being good. We long to engage in "conduct unbecoming" our professions. This involves splitting off parts of ourselves for the sake of indulging our appetites, impulses, urges, and desires. Usually this involves numbing our consciousness rather than fostering clear and heightened awareness. This is a serious condition calling for the kind of disciplined attention professional consultation can provide.

The answer is not to degrade Sabbath. There can be much fulfillment within Sabbath when all parts of us are integrated within holy intent. In some Jewish traditions, for example, the strong recommendation is for married couples to make love on the Sabbath. When we consider that the Sabbath way of doing things is to savor them, unhurried and not goal-directed, Sabbath lovemaking can be the best of all, because of the greater awareness and integration of relating the body with our deepest values. Likewise Sabbath eating can be the best of all. Sabbath conversation becomes a delightful discovery process about the self and the other. On Sabbath we do fast from some things, things related to work, in order to feast on others. It can be a time of holy indulgence, with the whole of us involved, in contrast to the habitual multitasking and halfheartedness whereby a part of us is dissociated or split off so that many experiences are less than satisfying.

The examined life allows us to be more fully integrated within the clarifying awareness of the Spirit. Within the safety of God's unconditional love, we can see more fully how our actions relate to core values of the kingdom. Retreats tend to serve that purpose, allowing people to see what they cannot see when they have their nose too close to the page. Most people's experience is that they are better able to connect with the big picture when they "get out of the office," so to speak. We must find the conditions that will short-circuit habitual ways of thinking, feeling, and acting in order to attain greater awareness.

There are whales that periodically stop swimming, raise their heads up vertically out of the water as far as they can, and then slowly turn 360 degrees before lowering themselves back down into the water. They may then change their course or direction. Though they live in the water, they are apparently orienting themselves to landmarks above the water. One instruction for the Christian life is to be in the world but not of the world. This means, like the whales, that we take our bearings from a different element than the one we usually inhabit, the one we might think of as conventional reality, the lowest common denominator. Unfortunately, the church inevitably absorbs and even emulates aspects of the dominant culture. Part of the value of a Sabbath-modeled sabbatical, in contrast to an approach patterned after academia, is to get some distance from the usual mindset and worldview of one's work in order to return with new eyes to see and new ears to hear on the other side of habituation. Weekly Sabbath subverts the kind of habituation that results in no longer recognizing the incursion of the dominant culture into the church, most notably the secular business model or entertainment worship model. Regular Sabbath keeping accentuates the contrast community, also between the shalom of God and dominant church culture.

It might actually be harder for pastors to recognize the value of a radical reorientation than it is for laypeople. Church members often know how they compromise their Christian values in their work by either simply giving in to temptation or feeling powerless to do otherwise. All of us conspire to remain oblivious to the ways we work and live in violation of the kingdom. And so we keep our heads in the water and try to reduce the dissonance between the kingdom and how we live, masking our awareness of the contrast by overworking, numbing ourselves with TV or computer games, consuming, or dulling our awareness with alcohol or drugs. Taking intentional Sabbath breaks to reorient to God and to one's soul can be very unsettling to our comfortable lives.

The 2002 *Time* magazine "Person of the Year" was shared by three people who blew the whistle, exposing misconduct in the organizations for which they worked: the FBI, Enron, and WorldCom. Others knew of the problems these employees encountered but chose to go along with them. The *Lutheran* commented on the article that two of the three were Lutherans, who credited their faith with guiding them to do the right thing and giving them the courage to deal with the consequences. The motto of whistle-blowing is "Commit the Truth." Regarding the 2014 revelations of dangerous, dishonest appointment practices at the Veteran Affairs hospitals, Representative Jeff Miller remarked, "At great risk to themselves and their families, whistleblowers dare to speak truth to power."[14] Jesus said the truth shall set us free. By contrast, the slogan of

14. Mockenhaupt, "Confessions of a Whistleblower." Unlike Rep. Miller, we are not using the label "whistle-blower" as it brands the person, rather we use the term

secular society is, "Go along to get along," which often entails participating in dishonesty and greed for the sake of self-interest. The only way to gain the perspective that what we normally are doing is inconsistent with our core values is to fully step out of that context and set it aside for a period of time, entering into the holy and noticing the contrast when we come back. It helps to "go away" as far as possible from the usual world we inhabit. The routine of weekly Sabbath can help us avoid getting too far off course so that we do not have to confess that we made a lot of money but lost our soul. For others it may be, "I helped a lot of people, but I lost myself." "I had a good career, but I was a stranger to my children." And so on . . . This is an obvious challenge for most church members. Many of our people suffer from moral injury or soul injury, incurred from doing things in their work that violate their core values. Clergy are also significantly at risk for not stepping far enough away from church culture in order to recognize how off course we may have strayed.

As deep Sabbath strengthens our compassionate relationship with all that is, we become more courageous to follow the way that compassion inspires. Courage is another quality that is required for living shalom. Jesus said we must be willing to lose much, even our own lives, to advance the cause of love. The people who rescued Jews during the Nazi domination of Europe risked their own lives and the lives of their spouses and children. They did so for the sake of love. People risk losing their lifestyles by being truly generous. Many risk losing their jobs when they refuse to "go along to get along" at work. People lose friends and social support when they act contrary to the status quo. The courage that it takes to break through one's vulnerability and enter into deep Sabbath can carry over into the rest of one's life. In fact, it is our conviction that deep Sabbath fuels the desire and hones the ability to keep good boundaries in general.

Careers that are meant to serve us become our masters. Legitimate priorities, such as care for our families become distorted by anxiety and social comparisons. This is what Jesus warned us about. As Jesus was tempted by the devil to use his powers for personal and earthly gain, so are we tempted to use our talents and abilities for the things of this earth that we will ultimately lose anyway. With Sabbath reorientation, it can feel like we risk losing them already now.

Perhaps Sabbath is a commandment instead of a recommendation, because God knows that we will lose our bearings when engaged in the

"whistle-blowing" to characterize the action.

things of this earth. We need regular interruptions of the Spirit to break the world's spell over us: the spell of fear and insecurity; the spell that we have no choice but to adopt the values of Wall Street; the spell of greed that businesses must keep expanding, that more is better and bigger is better; the spell that there are winners and losers in life, as measured by material possessions and earthly power; the spell that if you are not the best, you are a loser; the spell that sacrificing your health and happiness for success (playing hurt) is admirable; the spell that sacrificing integrity for success is necessary; the spell that social approval is more important than God's approval.[15] Yes, this spell, as promoted in our work culture, the media, and our mass-marketed entertainment seduces us to put other things before God and God's universal love. To not lose our way, and to keep our spirits free, we desperately need Sabbath breaks from these sources of persuasion so that we can examine the assumptions and beliefs that actually shape our thoughts and actions. How else will we be reminded that we are here to do God's work, the work of love for everyone and everything? How else can we keep track of what that work might entail as our lives unfold?

Sabbath reminds us about the true nature of time and its purpose. Time is precious because it is sacred, not because it is limited in quantity, which is what our anxiety tells us. The word "time" has the same root, *tempus*, as the word "temple." Time is a meeting place for us to be with God, and for God to be with us. There is no need for time to make us anxious. Clocks were not invented by employers or unions; they were invented by Christian monks to keep track of the times for them to stop working and pray together. Clockmaking was motivated by faithfulness. Clocks and calendars need not enslave us or stress us; they can help liberate us by reminding us to set everything else aside and spend time with God at designated times and on designated days.

John Calvin said, "On Sabbath we cease our work so that God can do God's work in us."[16] A big part of that work is for God to reorient our bearings, and for us to pay attention. Since Christianity is the majority religion in our society, we can easily forget that our culture is not driven by spiritual values. We easily lose sight of how strongly we are influenced by the values and worldview of the dominant culture, in which we live, work, shop, and play. It is easy, even most natural, to spend our nonwork

15. Anderson, *Just a Little Bit More*, chap. 5.
16. Quoted in Thomas, *Even God Rested*, 162.

or "Sabbath time" as consumers. We merely switch from being producers (at work) to consumers (in our free time). If we spend our Sundays watching TV, reading the paper, or going to a movie, we continue to be submerged in the culture that sees people as consumable objects to be used, exploited, dominated, or ridiculed. And we may even begin to see ourselves as products to be sold to them.

What finally makes people happy? A significant body of research into the source of human happiness contradicts our most basic assumptions. Contrary to everything we have been socialized to believe and to pursue, the things we think make us happy may not really deliver.[17] From the time of watching our first advertisement, we are immersed in a force field that persuades us that the ability to buy things and purchase services will make us happy. While it is true that having a certain minimum income is necessary for survival, accumulating excess does not appear to increase happiness. In fact many people with very high incomes suffer inordinately from high rates of depression and suicide.

Does status then make us happy? Consider people in high-status positions—CEOs, managers, movie stars, senior pastors, university presidents, and those in high political offices. Are such people happier than others? Is the president, likely occupying the most powerful and prestigious position in the world, a happy person? With high status comes enormous responsibility and tremendous stress to perform and not fail: this is not a formula for happiness! Then perhaps it is one's health that makes you happy? You would think this would be the case. However, those of us enjoying good health seem to take it for granted until we face a health crisis of some magnitude. Only those who have suffered serious illness may be truly in a position to see good health as a prerequisite to human happiness.

What finally makes people happy are relationships: what we have called life-giving relationships. Life-giving relationships begin with our relationship to God, the Maker and Giver of all life, the source of shalom. Happiness also derives from life-giving relationships with others—the kind of gratuitous, serendipitous relationships fostered by Sabbath time with others. And it is especially urgent in our time of environmental crises to recognize that human happiness depends on our developing a new life-giving relationship to God's creation, a relationship based on the intrinsic value of the natural world, not based on our instrumental use of nature. Wonder, amazement, and awe typify such life-giving encounters

17. See Ched, prod., with Engel, dir., *Human Spark*.

with creation. These are the contours of shalom: life-giving relationships with God, other persons, and creation itself. This is what we were finally made for and these quality relationships, the essence of Sabbath, are what make us happy.

In Sabbath mode we can more easily relate to everyone, including God, according to an I-Thou relationship, instead of in an I-It manner, treating people merely as objects or as functions. A trucker who stopped regularly at the same diner had the waitress come over, recognize him, and say, "Oh, you're the corned beef." If she were to have one foot in the kingdom of God and the other in work, she might have said, "Joe, you're late today. Is everything going okay?" Likewise, the lives of children have become strongly oriented away from enjoying life-giving relationships to building resumes for future success. We see the parental task as building up children's market value instead of helping them to find God's calling. The inculcation of these values is so insidious that we do not recognize that we have lost our way. Or we believe we have no choice.

A nutritional therapist who is sensitive to Sabbath values was at a conference of professionals where the focus was the "war against fat." She was disturbed by the way people were talked about. Fat is the enemy; the patient was characterized as the adversary against whom the professional wages the war based on the fat in another person's body. In all of our work, it is too easy for people to become objects or functions and stop being to us children of God or citizens of the kingdom of God. The same thing can happen with objects. A Sabbath-sensitive young man had worked for a couple of independent bookstores, where the employees love books and know about them. For them and the store owners, the goal was to help customers get just the right book for their needs or interests. Then this same young man got a job for a multinational bookstore chain, where books are not even referred to as books but instead as "products." Books became exchangeable products, and the goal was to "move product." It is not surprising that young adults refer to such jobs as "soul-sucking."

A Sabbath perspective also may reveal to employers that they have become like Pharaoh, demanding more and more productivity while reducing the resources workers have to meet those goals. Corporate leaders may become morally unsettled by the practice of keeping for themselves the profits from increased productivity rather than sharing them with the employees through commensurate increases in compensation. Employers may find themselves realizing that they could in fact hire more people in order to benefit their fellow citizens of the kingdom who are without employment. Supervisors may cringe that they are forcing employees to train others, here or abroad, to do their jobs at lower pay and then terminating that trainer-employee. People may come to question their participation in practices that are deceptive, dishonest, or exploitative of other people. Some may realize they work for corporations that engage in predatory practices. How can our economy become informed by Sabbath values, transforming human labor into a more life-giving environment, providing sufficient, sustainable livelihood for all?[18]

TRANSITIONING OUT OF SABBATH

Good boundary keeping is essential to entering into meaningful, deep Sabbath. Specifically, it takes the ability and willingness to set aside our ego-based concerns and identities. Learning how effectively to make that transition determines the depth of the Sabbath relationship. As Barbara Brown Taylor has observed, in Sabbath we do not rest because our work is done, we rest "as if" our work is done.[19] The transition out of Sabbath is also important. As Oscar Romero noted, "The spiritual life does not remove us from the world, but leads us deeper into it."[20]

Just as worship culminates in a sending, deep Sabbath inspires a kind of "sending forth" with the intention and desire to continue what has been experienced and transformed by the Sabbath. Since Sabbath is not work, one does not need to have something to show for it in terms of a product. Partaking of the shalom of God connects us with uncon- ditional compassion, inspiring and motivating certain ways of living, as Jesus described in his parables. As we leave behind our tendency to ob- jectify others, we discover we care about people who once were seen only as the means to an end when we are in work mode. Sabbath, as worship does, helps us access states of being that serve as a reservoir to inform and reshape whatever comes next. Therefore, healthy transitioning out of Sabbath helps us integrate the resources of Sabbath into the rest of our lives.

We draw attention to three themes: retain, inform, and inspire. Living in the shalom of God, we retain what we have gained to inform our thoughts and to inspire loving actions. Preachers decry the fact that

18. Evangelical Lutheran Church in America, A Social Statement on "Sufficient, Sustainable Livelihood for All."

19. Taylor, Leaving Church, 228.

20. Nouwen, Making All Things New, 55.

great sermons on Sunday do not necessarily carry over into making a difference on Monday. One reason for this involves the limitations of the human mind. The phenomenon is called "state-specific learning," which is part of a larger pattern of the mind that connects things by association. What we learn in one external context may not transfer in our minds to another setting, because the same associations are not present in the new setting. What is learned in the classroom may need to be relearned in the field, because it may not automatically occur to the student on their own.

State-specific learning carries the risk of compartmentalization. When compartmentalized, "what we experience in Sabbath stays in Sabbath" and does not interact with the rest of our lives. The transfer value needs to be carried out intentionally and deliberately. Resources such as Mary Gentile's *Giving Voice to Values* increase the likelihood of addressing value clashes at work by a process of rehearsing behavior outside of that setting.[21] It primes the mind to recognize ethical problems at work that would otherwise go unnoticed. Whether or not we use this specific program, ending Sabbath prayerfully and mentally by exploring how to apply Sabbath values to the rest of the week helps to prime the pump. Becoming more comfortable with vulnerability can help us to be more willing to be indicted and transformed by the gospel. Deliberate spiritual practices throughout the week can keep this alive.

One such practice is care for "the least of these." Jesus said that how we treat the least important person is how we treat him (Matt 25:40). Under stress and busyness, we lose track of whom we regard as least important. Psychologist Robert Levine has studied our "pace of life" and found overall that in the cities with the fastest pace (like New York City) people are less helpful to others than in slower-paced cities.[22] In a frequently cited experiment with seminary students, some of whom had just prepared to give a talk on the Good Samaritan story, the only predictor of who would stop and help someone in need was how much time pressure they felt.[23] When we claim paying attention to those who are the least important as a spiritual practice, that intention and awareness can guide our choices and behavior. Usually our decisions are based on who is most important, not on who is least important. Yet as we increasingly realize from the practices of deep Sabbath, unimportant people are much affected by our actions.

21. Gentile, *Giving Voice to Values*.

22. Levine, *Geography of Time*, 162–63.

23. Cf. Darley and Batson, "From Jerusalem to Jericho," 100–108.

To keep track of how we are doing, we can use an adaptation of the Prayer of Examen. Since we are more able to be aware of things through the lens of unconditional love and compassion, we begin by focusing on the realization that God loves us unconditionally. We are accepted by God just as we are. Unconditional acceptance does not mean liking everything about oneself or approving of all of your behavior. It is unconditional. To whatever degree you can, trust in that promise and savor it. Enjoy how good it feels to be understood and accepted just the way you are. You are neither worthy nor unworthy of unconditional acceptance. You cannot earn it, nor can you lose it. Enjoy how good that feels. Now from this viewpoint, look over the last 24 hours. Notice which people you were most loving and open toward, including yourself, and how that felt. Now notice which people, including yourself, you were least loving toward. Who did you most disregard? Imagine what it would have been like to give more consideration to that person, and be more compassionate.

Many people are now using the concept of mini-Sabbath to set aside brief times throughout the day to serve as Sabbath breaks. These can be both planned ahead of time or practiced as circumstances allow, such as when one is stopped in traffic or forced to wait for some other reason. Rather than using such time "productively," one can receive this interruption as the gift of a mini-Sabbath, time for reconnecting us with the values of the kingdom and helping us see how to live Sabbath more fully each day. Breathe out the stresses and conventional ways of relating to persons and things in your everyday life! Breathe in deeply the shalom of God that makes all things new!

In part 2 of this book, we have examined in detail indispensable boundary themes related to the advancement of the foundational identity and mission of the Christian community: the integrity of worship, the integrity of interactions and communication, and integrity in the practices of Sabbath. In part 3 we turn our attention to topics that focus directly on the integrity of persons: the pastor as person, boundaries as a shared responsibility of church members, and a concluding chapter on best practices in preserving boundaries for the sake of preserving the core identity and mission of the church.

PART 3

Integrity of Persons

7

The Pastor as Person

SCENARIO SEVEN: PASTOR-OF-THE-YEAR AWARD

WHEN PASTOR JON CAME to Lord of Life five years ago, the congregation was struggling. While the challenges were great, he was confident because the situation called for just his set of talents, experiences, and passions. His last call had gone badly due to disgruntlement on the part of a small group of parishioners, which left him baffled and hurt. Lord of Life was welcome relief. He developed and identified new leaders and created new programs in the community. Due to his leadership, membership grew and giving increased.

The denominational leadership was so impressed and wanted to help inspire other pastors to greatness, so that they decided to inaugurate a Pastor-of-the-Year award to be given at their annual meeting. The denominational magazine decided to write a story on it as well and asked to interview Pastor Jon's wife and sixteen-year-old son. After a painful discussion, they agreed to the interview but also to be truthful with the reporter. "There's not much I can say about my dad," his son told the reporter. "I don't see him very much." His wife commented, "Frankly, I have been living the life of a single parent, except I don't get to date. I wish I could." After the interviews with his wife and son, the denominational magazine decided not to run the story and the district leadership was left in a quandary.

PROTECTING THE PASTOR'S IDENTITY
AND ROLES

Like every Christian, a pastor has received a core identity from God in Christ through the gift of baptism. At baptism God made the person, who later in life assumed the role of pastor, the recipient of all baptismal gifts in Christ: forgiveness of sins, deliverance from evil, and eternal life. At baptism by the power of the Holy Spirit, the person who later was ordained to ministry of Word and sacrament received unconditional belovedness as God's child for Christ's sake.[1] The gospel of Jesus Christ grounds all the baptized, including pastors, in their core identity as persons in relationship with God. One of the most difficult challenges facing those who serve in ordained ministry is keeping their lives primarily oriented to this baptismal identity rather than confusing this core affirmation with their "working" role as a pastor of the church. Much confusion and dis-ease in the lives of pastors is a consequence of allowing one's role as pastor to displace one's identity as a baptized child of God.[2]

When pastoral identity takes priority over all one's other roles in life, tending one's own baptismal identity in Jesus Christ through involvement in the practices of Sabbath, as articulated in the last chapter, often becomes neglected. While pastors know the importance of Sabbath and advocate to others commitment to Sabbath, often they find themselves failing to practice what they preach. The lure of pastoral ministry as a source of self-fulfillment and the emotional "need to be needed" lead to unhealthy patterns that undermine one's relationship with God, relationships to one's primary community of family, and even one's own health.

The call to pastoral ministry is a call to a particular role within the life of a faith community and the wider church. This role is specific, not all-inclusive of the person, and it is not to be confused with one's baptismal identity. Moreover, it is only one of several roles in which the pastor as person is called to serve in life. Other crucial roles include as a family member (in various capacities, depending on the particular relation—as son or daughter, as a spouse, as a parent, as an aunt or uncle, as a cousin, and so forth) as a friend, as a hobbyist, as a club member, as a neighbor, or as a citizen. Among these others roles is the one assumes by virtue of one's work: the role as pastor. While this role is important for the sake of the identity and mission of the church, the pastor not only

1. Nouwen, *Life of the Beloved*, chap. 3.
2. Cf. Harbaugh, *Pastor as Person*, chap. 1.

must acknowledge the responsibilities belonging to this call but also must place limits on this role. As comprehensive and far-reaching as the role of parish pastor is, it does not contain the whole person. As a pastor, one assumes the duties belonging to the pastoral office—the ministry of Word and sacrament, at the call of a particular congregation or agency of the church. Pastoral ministry is a leadership role within the life of the church among the people of God, who themselves are also called to Christian service by their own baptisms in the various roles they assume in their lives.

Each pastor brings unique personal characteristics to service as a church leader: parents, birthdate, place of birth, gender, ethnicity, appearance, height, weight, personality type, multiple intelligences, life experiences, education, and a host of other factors. These are the biological and biographical features that make each of us the unique persons that God has created us to be. These are also the factors that God employs whenever a distinctive person, with particular experiences and character, assumes the pastoral role.[3] It is vital for well-being in ministry that the pastor can affirm the unique features of personhood in assuming the pastoral role. There is no single way that every pastor is supposed to function. Different persons embody the pastoral role differently according to their God-given circumstances, abilities, and experiences. There is freedom in being able to claim and affirm one's own uniqueness without falling into debilitating comparisons with other pastors, who are simply different from each other in so many ways. Such differences are to be celebrated as belonging to the variety of gifts in the body of Christ.

At the same time there are professional and institutional expectations that belong to the pastoral office. To the pastor is delegated authority for serving as a public representative of God and the church; the pastor is someone held accountable to a letter of call and the standards of conduct belonging to a church body.[4] The pastoral authority that one exercises is finally above all accountable to God in Christ, whose Word one proclaims and whose sacraments of grace one shares with God's people. The call to the ministry of Word and sacrament orbits around some centering pastoral practices: *preaching the gospel*, especially at worship; *teaching and sharing God's Word*—not only in formal classes or Bible studies but whenever one speaks to others (for example, in church meetings, hall-

3. Everist and Nessan, *Transforming Leadership*, 56–57.
4. Ibid., 57–58.

way conversations, pastoral visitation; through church communications, e-mail, or social media); *presiding at worship and over the sacramental life of the congregation*; and in *the many forms of pastoral care*. While pastors are asked to get involved in many other aspects of church life and activities, these central things that most cohere with Word and sacrament ministry provide the plumb line for prioritizing the use of one's time as a pastor of the church. While the demands placed upon the pastor may seem endless and exhausting on the one hand and enticing on the other, setting clear boundaries about what is central and what is secondary is necessary for balanced life as a person, especially in order to fulfill the responsibilities belonging to one's many other vital roles and to lead a healthy, balanced life.[5]

Even as the pastor is called upon to fulfill these duties assigned by the church, well-being in life necessitates role clarity about what belongs to the pastoral office in relation to all the various other roles we assume in life. These encompass our connection to God, family members, friends, and other nonwork relationships. Baptismal identity means living out one's care for the neighbor not only by what one does in the work of pastoral ministry but by caring the members of your family, friends beyond the membership of the church, residents in your local community, and those to whom you are connected all over the world—all of whom are neighbors whom we are called to love according to the Great Commandment (Matt 22:37–40).[6] As we discussed in the last chapter, practicing Sabbath is crucial to a balanced life for all people, including pastors. Providing pastoral care and service to others is no substitute for engaging in spiritual practices that nourish the soul of the religious professional as person.

Perhaps the most neglected neighbors in the lives of pastors are the pastor's family members.[7] While we might understand theoretically that the primary community in which God has placed us is our own family, in practice it is easy for pastors to prioritize relationships to church members above one's family relationships. Family members are always at a disadvantage in competing for the pastor's time, insofar as time spent in relationship with church people can easily be rationalized as a "holier" or more urgent use of the pastor's time. As Thomas Merton commented: "Douglas Steere remarks very perceptively that there is a pervasive form

5. Trull and Carter, eds., *Ministerial Ethics*, chap. 3.

6. Brueggemann, *Sabbath as Resistance*, chap. 6.

7. Harbaugh et al. *Covenants and Care*, chap. 4.

of contemporary violence . . . activism and overwork. The rush and pressure of modern life are a form, perhaps the most common form, of it innate violence. To allow oneself to be carried away by a multitude of conflicting concerns, to surrender to too many demands, to commit oneself to too many projects, to want to help everyone in everything, is to succumb to violence. The frenzy of our activism neutralizes our work for peace. It destroys our own inner capacity for peace. It destroys the fruitfulness of our own work, because it kills the root of inner wisdom which makes work fruitful."[8] We must come to know the line between faithfully filling the pastoral role and foolishly exceeding it.

OUR MULTIPLE SELVES

Psychologists talk about an "Observer" part of the self that notices and observes without judgment or reactivity. It is this part of the self that allows us to consult with our deepest values before we act or respond to a situation. Roberto Assagioli refers to it as a "point of pure awareness."[9] It is without content, free and flexible. People learn to access the Observer self in meditation and types of prayer (for example, centering prayer). We also have other parts of ourselves that have substance and interests. I invite you to make a list. Take a piece of paper and list the numbers 1 through 20 in a column on the left side of the paper. Now on the top write "I am." Proceed to finish the sentence 20 different ways!

Typically from this exercise people will list affiliations that we identify with, such as, "I am a Christian." We name roles, like "I am a father," or "I am a good friend." We also name qualities, like "I am kind and considerate." We may also identify characteristics like "I am a musician" or "I am an avid reader." This and similar exercises can assist us to identify parts of ourselves that seek expression outside of our work roles. Free time for Sabbath also helps us notice these roles. When we value them, we want to create and protect time and energy for them.

It also behooves us to look for the history or motives behind some of the roles and qualities with which we strongly identify: "I am a helper," for example. Where does that come from? We must accept that we cannot and do not have completely healthy motives for doing many of the good things that we do; nor fortunately must we. But we do have to do our best

8. Merton, *Conjecture of a Guilty Bystander*, 81.
9. Cf. Assagioli, *Psychosynthesis*.

to be responsible for those motives. This requires that we be conscious of them. Only in this way can we keep track of the unhealthy motives so that we do not act based on them.

This is a challenge for everyone, not just pastors. A parishioner may wish to be council president in order to elevate his or her status in the community or to pad a resume. This person may also genuinely wish to serve God and to help the congregation be more faithful. This is not an either/or. But we do violate our church role when we put personal interest above the interests of the church or of God An example of placing personal interest above community interest would be organizing a trip to climb a mountain when you know no one else in your group will be fit enough to make it except for you. The pastor or group leader, however, gets a free trip out of the deal. A different trip would be more rewarding for everyone. Far better would be to discern what is needed in the congregation and find a trip to meet those goals.

There are several potentially unhealthy personal motives for going into the ministry that can lead to boundary issues:

Perpetuating certain things that were important for you as a child (such as filling helping role in an alcoholic family where parents did not provide adequate supervision). The child may have come to gain a sense of safety from being in control when it seemed no one else was in control. The "need to be needed" is another common reason for entering pastoral ministry. Some pastors found refuge in the church as children and felt acceptance there far more than anywhere else. The unhealthy motive is then to perpetuate that acceptance, which in the pastoral role becomes an unrealistic expectation.

Compensating for what was missing in childhood is also an unhealthy motive for ministry and a source of unrealistic expectations. Here are some possible forms of unhelpful compensating:

1. The need to be loved: the congregation is supposed to love you.

2. Difficulty making friends: with the congregation you have a ready social life.

3. Feeling unimportant: now you have people for whom you are important.

4. No one listens to me; now you have a captive audience.

5. A feeling powerlessness: now you have power.

6. A lack of status: now you have status, at least in some circles.

Recognizing our personal motives can help us keep them from having undue influence. When Henri Nouwen was writing *The Wounded Healer*, the Jungian analyst Güggenbühl-Craig was working on a similar book, *Power in the Helping Professions*.[10] He gives us an important warning for our well-being as helping professionals and for the well-being of those we help. We must not split archetypes. Healing and sickness are parts of one archetype. As many pastors know from clinical pastoral education, it is tempting for helpers to believe that if I am helping you and you are weak. I cannot be weak. I must be strong. If you are confused, I cannot be confused. I must be certain. If you are powerless, I must be powerful. Thus we deny the attributes in ourselves of those we help, believing that those qualities render us useless in being able to help. In the process of this splitting, we also deny the other person's strength, knowledge, and wisdom. And so we set up the dynamics for abusing our own power. Everyone in a position of congregational leadership would do well to discover their personal motives. One way to do so is to ask what you hope a particular role will do for you.

Dealing with contrast and conflict also requires the capacity to draw upon one's multiple selves. The individuals who compose congregations and those who work professionally with them can greatly benefit from expressions of individual differences in perceptions, priorities, values, beliefs, ideas and even preferences. When these are expressed unnecessarily as personal attacks, however, the person being attacked with criticism or contempt needs to protect his or her emotional boundaries. One constructive way to do this is not to identify oneself as the target but rather to sidestep the attack by adopting a neutral, third-party perspective on the matter. This promises a better outcome than either allowing oneself to be injured or counterattacking with defensiveness. While the parishioner may make the issue with the pastor personal by using critical "you" statements, the pastor may choose not to buy into that definition of the situation by taking it personally. Every criticism might instead be reframed as a request, which potentially reveals something important about the parishioner and potentially adds something of value to the community if the content can be identified and protected in the process.

The objective, third-party point of view is the stance a mediator must be able to adopt in order to arbitrate a disagreement. We can effectively mediate the disputes in which we are personally involved by

---

10. For the following, see Güggenbühl-Craig, *Power in the Helping Professions*.

intentionally positioning ourselves in that role, although it is inherently a dual role.[11] We must be able to understand and express not only our own point of view but also that of the person bringing the complaint. When and only when the other person has been heard and understood can that person also begin to understand the pastor's point of view. The steps are these: 1) sidestep the criticism so you do not identify yourself as the target; 2) adopt the posture of a mediator; 3) listen, inquire, and check to make sure that you understand the person correctly and that the person comes to believe that you do understand; and 4) only then express a contrasting point of view, if you have one. In order to know the best outcome to a conflict, the mediator must know from each party (1) what they want, (2) why they want it (the rationale), (3) how strongly they feel about it, and (4) why they feel as strongly as they do. The first two parts are usually concrete, factual, and framed rationally, while the last two are more emotionally based. If a person feels strongly about something, there is usually something in their past history that informs and shapes it. With enough safety, this can be discovered. For example, congregational conversations involving people's feelings about sexual orientation have had a peaceful and positive outcome, when people share their personal thoughts behind their own viewpoint in a safe and supportive context.

In any conflict situation, a person needs to decide which of the five basic options to adopt, as identified by Thomas and Killmann: avoiding, accommodating, competing, collaborating, and compromising.[12]

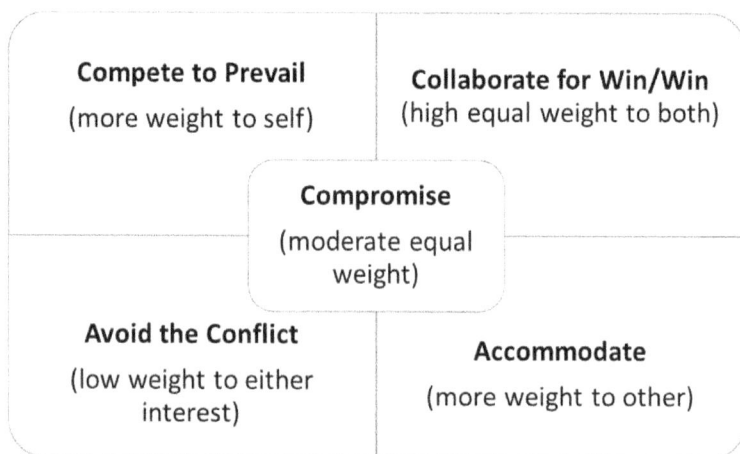

Compete to Prevail (more weight to self)	Collaborate for Win/Win (high equal weight to both)
Compromise (moderate equal weight)	
Avoid the Conflict (low weight to either interest)	Accommodate (more weight to other)

---

11. Cf. Everist, *Church Conflict*, chap. 5.

12. The table is adapted from Thomas and Killmann, Conflict Mode Instrument, http://www.kilmann.com/conflict.html/.

It is important to be comfortable and skillful at using all of the options according to which of them is most appropriate in a given situation. Our comfort level may depend on the context. For example, in the stereotypical abuse situation, a person may be overly accommodating at work and then become overly aggressive in getting one's own way at home. It can go the other direction as well. In the process of getting more comfortable with all the options, it is helpful to examine early life experiences from each person's family of origin as well as from other contexts, such as school. While some children learn to stay quiet and passive in family conflict out of fear of making things worse for themselves and others, other children learn that they can easily get their own way by insisting on what they want. However your family system responded to passivity or assertiveness on your part and whatever you may have learned about how to engage in conflict, it is important to recognize your own tendencies and patterns so you can increase your repertoire of responses to address various situations.[13]

When pastors talk about their comfort level with conflict, they usually think about unwelcome conflict initiated by someone else. They rarely think about the healthy need for they themselves to actually initiate contrast or conflict. Obviously, it is essential at times to do just that, not only to negotiate conflicted situations in ministry but also to think clearly and sustain meaningful time and energy for personal life. Many people attracted to the ministry are attuned to accommodating others rather than creating contrast or conflict. Because of this tendency, some pastors may either avoid raising conflict; and when they do create contrast or conflict, they do so with an edge or awkwardness that makes it less effective. Recall how Jesus supported saying no to others as the wise thing in the parable of the Wise and Foolish Virgins (Matt 25:1–13). For those with the habit of saying yes automatically in response to a request, it is recommended that the first response be one of buying time. For example, one can say something like, "Let me get back to you on that" so there is ample opportunity to make a good decision. If the request has merit but one already has a full schedule, the advised rule is only to say yes after you can identify what you would be able to give up to make time for it.

If you agree to talk to a church member in the grocery store, what are you giving up? For those with families, you are in essence making a decision for other family members to delay dinner and deprive them of

13. Halstead, *From Stuck to Unstuck*, chap. 6.

your presence. A practice to follow in tending boundaries is to ask, who does this belong to? In the case of time, one does well to ask, to whom or what does this time belong to? If your current time slot belongs to your family, you are imposing your decision on them by overstaying at the grocery store. It is useful to think this way about the different parts of oneself. Your pastor self is deciding to deprive your personal self of the allotted time by delaying dinner or some other involvement. Whoever the time belongs to deserves to have their needs and interests be your priority during that time. To think of your "personal self" as a separate self may seem strange, but it is useful. Since comfort comes with practice, look for opportunities to say no and set limits.

When a leader is willing and able comfortably to establish contrast and initiate conflict with another person, it assists others in the faith community to do the same.[14] Without this culture of honoring both the personal and the community, people will try to hide and withhold parts of themselves, to the detriment of themselves and the community. When they do initiate contrast or conflict, it may be carried out awkwardly or in an unhealthy way. It is actually fairly uncommon for people to be comfortable, graceful, and diplomatic in creating contrast. So we can learn to help each other out. One way to do so involves establishing and maintaining good identity and feeling boundaries. In constructively initiating contrast, one person informs the other person about something important to them and may make a request. These "I" statements are easy to hear. To fully inform the other person about what is relevant means telling them what you are wanting, why you are wanting it, how strongly you feel about it, and the reasons why you feel about it to that degree. Only with that information can the other party possibly know how much weight to give to what you are wanting in comparison to the weight given to what they themselves might want.

If equal weight is given to both parties, you know that it is important to work towards a compromise or a win/win outcome. If the information leaves you deciding that the other person's needs or wants are greater than your own, then you accommodate them. If you judge that what you need or want for some reason deserves the greatest weight, you initiate and hold your ground. It works best in the negotiation process if you proceed to share all of the relevant information about what you want, why you want it, how strongly you feel about it, and why you feel so strongly.

14. Cf. Menking, *When All Else Fails*, 68–70.

THE PASTOR AS PERSON   133

The first reason why is usually based on information or reason, while the last reason why is usually based more on personal experience. For example, the first reason why might be to avoid breaking a promise, and the final reason why might be to avoid harming the person to whom you made the promise.

In poorly executed conflict situations a person will employ "You" statements as accusations or complaints, making it about the other person—for example, the pastor. The pastor has the choice whether to accept being identified as the target or not. If you the pastor do choose to be identified as the target, you will become hurt or defensive. Those are about the only two options when one feels under attack. If, however, the pastor does not choose to be identified as the target, then the pastor can choose to take a more objective stance, essentially playing the role of mediator in the dispute. Even though the pastor may be personally involved in the conflict, choosing a mediating approach is the most desirable for all involved. Only from this vantage point, that of the Observer self, can one possibly know how much weight to give to the different aspects of the conflict. From this vantage point, one can advocate for one's own position with adequate emotional self-control, so as not to be careless about the feelings of others.

STEWARDING THE PASTOR'S LIFE

There are some advantages to a job where you punch in and punch out. You know when you are working and when you are not. It helps you not think about work when you are in bed, for example. It is also helpful to have a job with prescribed hours and a clear job description for everyone's benefit. That way you know when you are supposed to be working or not, and what your responsibility is or is not. How do you tell when someone is overfunctioning or underfunctioning without some demarcation in these areas? Certainly pastoral ministry can be like that. But should it be like that?

Pastor Jon's new call to Lord of Life was the perfect storm: falling prey to the temptation of overwork, John risked neglecting other important parts of his life. He felt he had something to prove. Lord of Life was his chance to prove it. There was an open slate for his creative talents. He had the vision to improve things beyond what anyone had seen before. He would get lost in these creative tasks and lose hours of time without

realizing it. He enjoyed walking around the church late at night and seeing the improvements he had made—not just in the aesthetics and order-
liness of the building but also in the programming that took place in each
space. It was a source of joy and pride. He no longer felt like the failure as
he had in his last call, where his efforts were resisted and not appreciated.

Our talents and passions desire an outlet. The parish ministry is
great for that because there is such a variety of things to do—from preaching to teaching to interpersonal endeavors to artistic projects to music to
organization, to much more. The list is endless. At Lord of Life, Pastor
Jon had a large "sweet spot" between what he wanted to do and what the
congregation wanted from him. While in many ways it is a desirable situation to have a large sweet spot, it also presents the temptation to overdo.
When the sweet spot is smaller, it is clearer to the pastor that important
parts of the self will need time and energy for expression outside the role.
When the majority of interests can be met within the ministerial role, it
takes more self-discipline to achieve healthy balance and awareness of
who you are and who you should be outside that role.

Pastor Jon was also finally beginning to enjoy a sense of job security
as his efforts got approval from the congregation and now even from the
wider church. Always in his life he had felt the pressure of anxiety from
unfinished tasks, which in many congregations are endless. While some
people use avoidance to temporarily reduce stress, others like Pastor Jon
use overworking, always working in order to check items off the to-do
list. The healthy alternative is setting time limits on work. But this will
result for some pastors in having to learn to tolerate the stress of unfinished tasks. The mental exercise of "one thing at a time" helps with this
tendency, as does having a ritual of closure at the end of a work period:
debriefing what was done, affirming it, and setting basic plans for the
next work period. This helps reduce the anxiety of unfinished tasks. The
consideration here is not about how much time it takes to complete all
the tasks; it is what amount of work is fair and healthy. It is not the pastor's
responsibility to compensate for the congregation being understaffed, as
Lord of Life was when Pastor Jon arrived.

Many pastors come from a family system where some form of addiction or other dysfunction is evident.[15] This background puts one at

15. The following two paragraphs are adapted from personal correspondence
between the authors and Robert H. Albers, who is contributing author of the clergy
education curriculum called *Spiritual Caregiving to Help Addicted Persons and
Families*, published by the Substance Abuse and Mental Health Services Association in

risk of falling into any of several unhealthy patterns: (1) making *heroic efforts* to make up for the dysfunction by accomplishing something to "redeem" the family and family name, or to make up for the dysfunction by engaging or overengaging in salvific ministry; (2) dealing with the dysfunction by *acting out* and getting into trouble, which can sometimes be helpful by bringing outside attention to the dysfunction in the family (The anxiety occasioned by the dysfunction can eventuate in such persons becoming addicted or getting in trouble with the law.); 3) *withdrawing* from the system, often engaging in fantasy thinking or becoming a loner: this behavior sometimes leads one to be deemed a social misfit or antisocial; and 4) *deflecting attention* from the stressful situation by being funny or cute, or in some other manner seeking a lot of attention and thereby drawing attention away from the addiction as the "elephant in the room."

While not precluding other patterns, many seminary students and pastors often have a high need for achievement. When such persons become pastors or lay professionals, they tend to see their task as "fixing" other people. This is not to judge them, for usually they are unaware of how the social matrix in which they have grown up has shaped them. Their investment in "fixing" prevents them from being able to establish appropriate boundaries, because they have adopted this role already in childhood as a way of coping with the dysfunction in the family. These people not only feel the need to fix things, but they claim responsibility for everything that occurs in the system, even if they are not responsible. Often they feel like failures if they cannot fix the dysfunction in their families or in their parishes. If parishioners assume that the pastor can "fix" them, then the members become hostile when the pastor is unable to accomplish that goal, and the dynamics of shame enter the picture. Almost invariably, these people, who some would say have a "messiah" complex, become disenchanted with ministry because a little voice inside them accuses them of being failures. They are also prime candidates for workaholism, which damages not only their health but their relationships as well. Theologically, such persons have little sense of grace and in essence have supplanted God in their lives by assuming that they can heal, when healing is entirely the province of God and not their responsibility. While a pastor can help to facilitate healing, they are not responsible for the healing.

2007. For a copy of the handbook, see http://www.nacoa.org/clergy.htm/.

Different types of backgrounds place us at risk of developing blind spots and habits that work against good boundary keeping beyond our self-awareness. One such background comes with growing up in a family with alcoholism—with the denial, secrecy, powerlessness, and lack of safety that is often involved. Research indicates that people with this background are not a homogeneous group; everyone with this background does not have the same tendencies.[16] This is important because otherwise we can be subject to stereotyping and profiling people based on this background, which would violate an individual's identity boundaries. Given that caution, it remains prudent for people who grew up with alcoholism in their families to evaluate themselves for the following tendencies, identified by Janet Geringer Woititz, which can interfere with healthy boundaries.[17]

1. Having to guess what normal is.

2. Having difficulty following a project through from beginning to end.

3. Tending to lie when it would be just as easy to tell the truth.

4. Judging oneself without mercy.

5. Experiencing difficulty with having fun.

6. Taking oneself too seriously.

7. Having difficulty with intimate relationships.

8. Overreacting to changes over which one has no control.

9. Constantly seeking approval and affirmation.

10. Feeling somehow different from other people.

11. Being either superresponsible or superirresponsible.

12. Showing extreme loyalty, even in the face of evidence that loyalty is undeserved.

13. Being impulsive and locking into a course of action without giving serious consideration to alternative behaviors or possible consequences. This impulsivity leads to confusion, self-loathing and loss of control over their environment. In addition, it can lead to an excessive amount of energy cleaning up the mess.

16. Hinrichs et al., "Personality Subtypes in Adolescent and Adult Children of Alcoholics."

17. Adapted from Woititz, *Adult Children of Alcoholics*, xxvi–xxvii.

Clearly such behaviors by pastors can lead to misunderstanding, conflict, and many boundary violations.

It is not emotionally easy to stop working when the pastor is feeling pressure of one sort or another. When there is the feeling of pressure, it is important to look for the source of that pressure in order to identify and solve the problem. This takes careful self-examination, which requires more objectivity than most of us have. This usually means it is essential to consult with an objective, outside person. Questions might be phrased as follows: Who is this for? In what way might this actually be self-serving? In many cases, the pressure is internal to the pastor (for example, a pattern learned in one's family of origin or an anxious posture toward the world). Overwork is then self-serving in the sense that it is a way to relieve pressure or anxiety. While congregations benefit in a codependent way, the result of pastoral overwork is inevitably unhealthy. Overfunctioning on the pastor's part begets underfunctioning on the parishioners' part. Ways to address this anxiety, other than overwork, can be found. Even when the pastor feels pressure to avoid criticism, and feels this as a realistic threat, it is still self-serving to try and reduce stress by overworking. The more comfortable a pastor gets with criticism, the less pressure one feels. If they keep trying to reduce the pressure by overworking, they will remain enslaved by the anxiety.

A similar internal motive is to avoid irrational guilt. Perfectionism is a source of internal pressure, though it may have originally been learned in order to protect the self from criticism by a parent. Perfection becomes a way to feel safe from criticism, and it may actually work, at least to some degree, with some people, though not all. The external circumstances can also provide pressure when, for example, a congregation is in decline and it seems like saving the situation can only be accomplished by overwork on the part of the pastor. While it is easy to say that it is not all the pastor's responsibility, the pastor's self-interest can get involved, since saving the congregation can mean saving one's own livelihood and career path. How stressful this seems depends on the perception of one's options.

An important principle for creating an environment conducive to healthy boundaries involves evaluating whether unmet personal needs are pressing to be met (inappropriately) within the pastoral role. Given the situation many ministers are in, it is much easier for them to meet their own social needs within the pastoral role with parishioners than outside the role with nonparishioners. As humans we tend to take the easy path, which leads to parishioner-based friendships that, as we mentioned earlier, end up depriving the parishioner of a pastor. The more church members are your friends, the less they will see you as their pastor. The pastor's responsibility is to protect the integrity and effectiveness of the pastoral role for others, not to pursue one's own self-interest. Being a friendly, sociable pastor is different from needing to become buddies with church members so that they forget you are the pastor. This is admittedly a challenging situation for pastors. It means meeting one's social needs outside the role in a way that does not compromise the effectiveness of the pastoral role. Often there is no easy solution.

In addition to the unhealthy long-term motives mentioned above (the desires to be loved, to be important, to have an audience, and to have power and status), unmet needs based on situational factors can also lead to boundary problems. A pastor's unmet needs for psychological, spiritual, and physical intimacy put him or her at risk of inappropriate thoughts, feelings, and actions toward parishioners, who might be able and even willing to meet those needs at the expense of the integrity of the pastoral role. Since our motives are often unconscious, it is best to rely on best practices to protect boundaries for the sake of preserving the church's identity and mission. Following best practices helps us detect when we are putting others or ourselves at risk. Many pastors who are not trained in counseling, for example, set a three-session limit on the number of counseling sessions they will have with a parishioner. If the situation calls for more than that, the pastor refers the parishioner to a mental health professional. When the pastor feels tempted to make an exception and go beyond three sessions for some reason, this is an indicator that it is time to consult with someone who can be objective about the situation.

Realistically, every area of personal need and interest, which could press to be met inappropriately or excessively within the pastoral role, needs a plan for addressing it in the pastor's personal life. This includes such things as planning regular dates with a spouse, setting aside time with one's children or ensuring time with the whole family. It includes intentional plans to stay in touch with friends and figuring out how to make new friends. Due to the lack of motivation that comes with fatigue, it is even necessary to plan time to discover, explore, and pursue hobbies and interests. Oddly, as we emphasized in the last chapter, we must make a plan for taking free time.

Pastors and other professionals might wish that they could be anonymous in their personal lives. Everywhere they go, however, people will recognize them. A pastor is not free to "be myself" in ways that might reflect poorly on the ministry. One might at least like to be able to go to the grocery store and not have others want to talk to them as their pastor. Protecting personal time from opportunities for spontaneous ministry means having comfort with diplomatic assertion. When a parishioner wants pastoral conversation in a grocery store or after a late meeting at church, it may well be an opportunity for good ministry, but it is even more a time to move along with one's personal life by continuing to shop or going home. Good boundary keeping on the part of pastors can help parishioners become more intentional about deciding to arrange for a pastoral appointment rather than following a spontaneous impulse to talk about a personal matter with their pastor as, for example, it might occur to them in the grocery store. The pastor can also learn to say, "This seems really important, so please call me in the morning at the office so we can set a time to talk." It does not have to be "now or never."

Some people who hoard are afraid if they throw something out, they may later find they need it. There is always the risk of loss in all good boundary keeping. We can learn to become comfortable with that possible loss rather than seeking to avoid it by overdoing.

Good boundary keeping between work and the rest of life, and between the self and one's roles, helps create and maintain time and energy for one's personal life. It helps to make clear transitions, intentionally making closure with work before leaving work, which also helps prepare the way for the next time one returns to work mode. An essential phase in this transition is to set everything else aside and connect for a few minutes, as best as possible, with the Observer self. Just before entering the home (or into whatever activity comes after work), you put your full self into what comes next, with the attitude and energy that belongs to this new time. When entering into relationship with a small child, for example, one wants to be able to fully concentrate on that person and match their enthusiasm about seeing you. The same is true for adults in our lives or even for pets. If one is returning to an empty home, then it is a matter of activating and engaging the other parts of the self by giving them priority. This requires that we quickly recover our energy (if it as depleted from work) or calm our energy (if it was agitated at work).

Paradoxically, the most effective ways to recover energy involve some expenditure of energy. As most of us experience, doing nothing and being passive (for example, by watching television) may be attractive to the stressed mind, such passive activities do not lead to recovery. Instead, mild to moderate exercise, even a walk around the block, will quickly reinvigorate. Talking with someone, listening to upbeat music, or doing some tasks around the house also can be helpful. While it may be great to listen to our feelings in shaping how we spend our free time, this does not work so well with the stressed mind, since it seeks short-term fixes that tend not to be satisfying in the long run. Because of that, most busy people find value in planning in advance how they will spend their time, including their personal time.

The integrity and health of one's personal life is also preserved by keeping personal matters out of work. Having one's personal life encroach at work results in getting behind at work, which then can increase pressure to violate personal time in order to catch up. Marital conflict that is not contained at home will distract the pastor from work. Texting or making phone calls can be a way to continue an argument or to try to resolve it. Often, however, letting the conflict wait for the next good time together actually helps resolve it. Some people have a lot of difficulty taking a break from conflict. If a person wants a good outcome to conflict, however, they must have the emotional self-control necessary to wait for that time. This may require changing one's own capacity for anxiety, so it has less control over us.

The transitioning process described above can help keep one's personal life from interfering with one's functioning at work. (To review, the transitioning process entails getting temporary closure with your home life, taking a brief mental rest break for refreshment, and then turning toward what you will be entering at work so you can fully engage with it.) While it is important that all parts of the self inform and enrich the other parts, not keeping them largely separate and distinct is like painting each stroke of a picture with the color that results from mixing together all the colors on the pallet. A painting is more beautiful when each color has its own distinctiveness. Having examined the integrity of the pastor as person in this chapter, especially focussing on the boundary between work and the rest of the pastor's life, we turn next to a discussion of boundaries as the shared responsibility of church members.

8

Boundaries as Shared Responsibility
by Church Members

SCENARIO EIGHT: FRAN'S OVERINVOLVEMENT IN THE CHURCH

AFTER TWO YEARS AT St. Mark's, Pastor Christina made a home visit to the church's most active member, Fran. Fran was in her fifties, with very high energy. After her divorce at age thirty-five, Fran poured herself into St. Mark's. She was extremely generous with her time and was involved in virtually every aspect of the ministry. In each area she did great things and naturally assumed leadership to the gratitude of others. She was now in her final year of her second term on the Leadership Team. The Constitution only allowed two consecutive terms. They had been doing vision setting, and when it came her turn to speak, Fran said she wanted the church to continue to be a place where she could participate every day of her life. The contrast was striking; everyone else on the team had voiced a vision for the future of the congregation based on their sense of the needs of the community and had said nothing about themselves personally.

Pastor Christina came to the disturbing realization that the congregation and Fran at some point had developed an unhealthy relationship. She also realized that Fran's contributions in the church were largely motivated by self-interest, even while they also did benefit others. Fran had shaped church programs to fit her own interests, based on what she needed or wanted rather than discerning what the church needed from her that she could contribute. Pastor Christina raised her pastoral concerns with Fran and helped her see how she could benefit from having more of a life for herself outside the church. They agreed that Fran would take a six-month sabbatical from church involvement other than attending worship.

PROTECTING THE IDENTITY AND ROLES OF CHURCH MEMBERS

The sacrament of baptism is the entrance rite for membership into the church, the body of Christ.[1] Baptism grounds our identity in God's divine promise in Christ, a reality that is deeper than all the other characteristics by which human beings are judged: race, class, gender, age, or sexual orientation. As bell hooks comments, while these identifying characteristics indelibly contribute to who we are, affect how we understand ourselves in relationship to others, and condition how others treat us, we are summoned by God to existence in "beloved community" beyond all hierarchy.[2] Baptism serves as the primal "ordination" for all Christians. This is just as true for those who later are ordained into pastoral ministry as for those who are laypersons in the church. Laity and clergy both benefit from orienting the entirety of their lives in relation to the promises God made to them in Christ at baptism, claiming this sacrament as their rock and foundation through the chances and changes of life. The church would be enriched if all baptized Christians trusted and claimed baptism as the source of their own core identity for life, an identity that grounds and informs all the other roles they assume in all their arenas of life. At baptism the baptized person receives every gift that is freely bestowed by the grace of God in Jesus Christ. These gifts include the promises of forgiveness, deliverance from temptation, and the hope of eternal life. As a recipient of such amazing belovedness, every Christian grounds life in gratitude for the richness of God's blessings. One central purpose of the practicing of Sabbath through worship is to keep reclaiming these promises as the core of one's identity for all of life.

At the same time that church members as baptized persons are recipients of God's abundant gifts of forgiveness, life, and salvation in

1. Cf. Marty, *Baptism*.
2. hooks, *Killing Rage*, 263–65.

Jesus Christ, the baptized are given a commission about what it means to live out their baptismal vocation in the world. One liturgical articulation of this commission poses this question to the baptized: "Do you intend to continue in the covenant God made with you in holy baptism: to live among God's faithful people, to hear the word of God and share in the Lord's Supper, to proclaim the good news of God in Christ through word and deed, to serve all people, following the example of Jesus, and to strive for justice and peace in all the earth?"[3] Those affirming their baptism answer: "I do, and I ask God to help and guide me." This promise serves as the foundation for all church membership and Christian service to the world. Those thoughts, words, and behaviors that would lead us to compromise or deviate from these promises are the very matters from which boundaries are intended to protect us.

This baptismal commission sets forth the central provisions for the Christian life that guide the discussion of boundaries in this entire book. The true purpose of the congregation is to serve the mission of God by bringing the good news of Jesus Christ to the world and by sharing the love of Christ with others by our words and actions. Whenever church members are tempted to shift the purpose of the church toward some narrower or self-serving agenda, the integrity of the church's identity and mission is compromised, undermined, and even contradicted. We explore in this chapter how God's baptismal gifts to us and our baptismal promises to God must be preserved by church members through attention to boundaries in thought, word, and deed, in order that the God-given identity and mission of the church remain primary, not only for the relationships among those who belong to the Christian community, but also for the integrity of the church's witness to the world.

The churches of the Reformation committed themselves to what Martin Luther called the universal priesthood. This expression affirms that it is not only those ordained as pastors ("priests") who are accountable to standards of Christian practice; rather all Christians have inherent responsibility to live their lives in accordance with the teachings and way of Jesus Christ. Every Christian as a follower of Jesus is called to represent with integrity the good news of God's mercy and love by assuming the mind of Christ, speaking charitably, and living a life of service to others.[4] While captivity to sin inevitably also affects church members, nothing undermines the credibility of the Christian message more than hypoc-

3. "Affirmation of Baptism," *Evangelical Lutheran Worship*, 237
4. Wingren, *Luther on Vocation*, 28-37.

risy. God has given the law as a curb on human sinning in order both to prevent us from harming others and to help preserve the common good.[5]

Too often we operate in the church with a double standard. While clergy are rightly held to a high standard for living their lives according to the way of Jesus Christ, many church members fail to acknowledge how they themselves, like all church members, are to be held accountable to a comparable standard of behavior. The failure on the part of church members to maintain the integrity of the church's identity and mission as their own responsibility erodes the effectiveness of the church's life and integrity. If the universal priesthood accords to all Christians equal status before God by virtue of baptism, so also all Christians stand equally accountable in the presence of God in Christ for the conduct of their lives.

Not only does the Christian life encompass what happens within congregations, but it extends into all arenas of life. Christian freedom means not only that we have been freed by Jesus Christ *from* sin, death, and the power of the devil but that we have been freed *for* service to all the neighbors God gives us in our lives.[6] Jesus teaches, as in the parable of the Good Samaritan that all people are neighbors God has given us to serve—with no exceptions. Each person is made in God's own image. Each person is one for whom Jesus Christ died on the cross. Each person is one for whom Jesus Christ is risen from the dead. Each person we encounter is a neighbor. For Christ's sake the baptized are called to look upon, speak about, and act toward each and every person as a neighbor. The priesthood of all believers thus takes on the character of universal neighborliness, the neighborliness of all believers.

This means that we discover neighbors wherever we go, in every arena of life. One primary arena God has given us for serving neighbors is our own family. Too often we overlook that the members of our own family are as much neighbors, whom God has given us to serve, as those people we encounter in other life arenas. This is a particular hazard for church members, not only pastors, who may value what they do for the church more than they value what they do for the people in their own families. Grandparents, parents, aunts, uncles, siblings, cousins, spouses/partners, children, grandchildren, and all other relations are among those neighbors, whom God has given us as neighbors. God has put us in primary relationship with these family members for the sake of protecting them from harm and for preserving the common good. Only when we

5. Cf. Wingren, *Creation and Law*, pt. 2, chap. 2.
6. Cf. Luther, *Freedom of a Christian.*

are good stewards of the neighbors who are members of our own family can we be genuinely free to attend to neighbors in other arenas of life, including in church involvements.

God also gives us neighbors to serve in the arena of daily work. For young people this may mean serving neighbors in the daily work of attending school or college. For those who are employed, neighbors are all those persons who are affected by our labor. Formally, we serve neighbors through the fruit of what we do for a living—providing goods or services, or both, according to the purpose of one's employment. Whether one is employed in business, sales, medical care, construction, education, technology, government, food service, or any other job, we serve neighbors by the very goods and services provided through our work. We will not here explore the challenges many people today face in finding daily work that is both a good use of their own aptitudes and meaningful for the sake of others—let alone fairly compensated. These are ethical questions deserving their own careful consideration. Here we simply assert that what one does for a living is intended to be of service to others as a contribution to the public good.

Through the arena of one's daily work one also enters into interpersonal relationships with other people, who are also, each one, neighbors God gives us to serve. We come to know them not only as customers or clients but as human beings, who have the same gifts, challenges, and concerns universal to all. Through these relationships church members also have an opportunity to care for neighbors in need. By observant, active listening we attend not only to what is said by others but can invite them to share their deeper thoughts and feelings. As appropriate, such relationships become occasions for expressing and offering genuine care to people in their hour of need. Happiness in life derives above all from life-giving relationships with other people. The contacts we develop with others, fellow workers and the people we encounter at work, can become the opportunity for extending life-giving concern about their welfare and concrete expressions of help.[7]

One's local community is also an arena for Christian neighborliness. The erosion of community participation in recent decades has been cited by sociologists as one sign of societal decline.[8] Christians live out their baptismal vocations not only by through the social ministry of their congregations but by how they invest themselves in community

7. Cf. Kaptein, *Workplace Morality*.
8. Cf. Putnam, *Bowling Alone*.

service to neighbors through other involvements and activities.[9] Civic organizations, service clubs, scouting, and other forms of public engagement do genuine good for the sake of neighbors in need. Helping young people, the sick, the aged, the grieving, the hungry, the homeless, the imprisoned, the addicted, or those facing other life crises is a concrete expression of neighbor love. Moreover, these are situations that deserve not only our charitable service but also our active engagement in the responsibilities of citizenship. Willie James Jennings calls us to join a movement for "truly cosmopolitan citizenship": "Such a world citizenship imagines cultural transactions that signal the emergence of people whose sense of agency and belonging breaks open not only geopolitical and nationalist confines but also the strictures of ethnic and racial identities."[10] Christian people serve God by becoming active as cosmopolitan citizens by voting, becoming educated about social issues, and advocating for legislation and policies that preserve the common good for all people. Church denominations provide social statements and advocacy resources to assist church members in becoming thoughtfully involved in serving neighbors through responsible citizenship.

This chapter focuses on the boundaries most directly related to being a church member: it discusses those behaviors and practices that can protect and promote the congregation's genuine identity and mission. However, by observing best practices in church membership that guard against those things that distract from and undermine the way of Jesus Christ, we believe that the baptized will be empowered to serve their neighbors more effectively in all the other arenas of daily life as well—in family, daily work, local communities, and civic engagement. Through references to research about human nature and case material, we will explore issues such as motivation, communication, and conflict in congregational life on the way to recommending best practices for stewardship of the self and honoring boundaries for the sake of generative and faithful congregational mission.

9. Cf. Franklin, *Crisis in the Village*, 132–69.
10. Jennings, *Christian Imagination*, 10–11.

CHURCH MEMBERSHIP THAT PRESERVES GOD'S PURPOSES FOR THE CHURCH

As we saw in the last chapter, good boundary keeping for pastors involves a delicate balancing act among many integral factors involved in who they are as human beings. The same applies for parishioners. As with clergy, it is also the case for parishioners that their roles in the church are not intended to compensate for inadequacies in their personal lives, but rather to help inspire and strengthen members to live their lives in the world with love of God, love of neighbor, and love of self, and to do all of these in community together. The congregation is not necessarily to be an outlet for a person's specific interests and talents, except insofar as they serve the larger purpose. Otherwise, for example, a musician without adequate outlets will want to perform, or an artist will want the church to exhibit his or her artwork. While music and art are important parts of ministry to be sure, they can be offered in self-serving ways rather than in ways that really serve the community. Talents and interests seek outlets. When there are not adequate outlets other than the church, those interests will press until they are met, perhaps in unhealthy or inappropriate ways within the church. How do we tell the difference between healthy participation in congregational life and unhealthy use of the congregation for personal ends?

It is important to try to understand our motives, including those that might be unhealthy. However, experimental psychologists are not very impressed with our own ability to accurately perceive our personal motives.[11] We tend to think of ourselves as being more virtuous than we really are. Nevertheless, we can still come to greater self-awareness for the sake of the whole. Some motives will be conscious, as with a person who wants to become an executive or wants promotions at work and needs public service to fill out their resume. Such persons will want to position themselves to be on the leadership team, to become an officer, and to leave a record of their service. Some motives are less conscious. A person who felt unaccepted as a child except at church runs the risk as an adult of expecting excessive time and attention from church staff, instead of developing other social outlets. The same is true for involvement in other social activities, whenever a person comes to feel the church "owes them" something. Any time we feel the church "owes us something" should give

11. Cf. Sternberg and Fiske, eds., *Ethical Challenges in the Behavioral and Brain Sciences*, 219–26.

us pause for self-examination rather than engaging in the criticism of the church and its members.

A second way to detect whether our motives are healthy involves our response when we do not "get what we want," considering not only our outward behavior but also our inward attitude, thoughts, and feelings. As we have seen, we can violate boundaries by our thoughts, words, and deeds. Refusing to take no for an answer, even internally and without outward expression, is a boundary violation involving the will. Typically, however, when one cannot accept not getting one's way, this dissatisfaction finds outward expression by withdrawing or by withholding something, if not in outright hostility. According to 1 Cor 13:5, love does not insist on its own way. In Fran's case, getting her way was more a matter of opportunity and persistence than obvious self-assertion (combined with a lot of misplaced yielding on the part of others). One telltale sign is that Fran always would refer to St. Mark's as "my church," not "our church." As is often the case with clergy sabbaticals, during Fran's six months off, the congregation saw others step up in healthy ways to the benefit of both the congregation and Fran. While others previously had felt that their efforts were not as good as Fran's, what may have been lost in quality was more than made up for in improved esprit de corps.

Finding healthy levels and forms of member involvement within a congregation requires mutual trust and discernment both by the individuals involved and by others affected in the church. Such discernment takes seriously the needs of the congregation in preserving its identity and mission, as well as in perceiving what a particular person has to offer and is called to offer. This includes consideration of when it is one's turn to step up and meet a need. For the sake of the integrity of the church's identity and mission, congregation members are called to mutual discernment about when to listen, when to speak, when to act, when to not act, when to persist, when to yield, when to compromise, and when to search for a win/win outcome.

Individuals of many species, from humans to insects, differ greatly in their levels of being assertive, exploratory, aggressive, and in taking initiative toward others and their environment; there are also comparable differences in passivity, yielding, submissiveness, and receptivity. In some circumstances, assertiveness has more survival value, and in other situations passivity has more survival value. In any given social situation, the dynamics of dominance and submission come into play. At one extreme, people insist on getting their own way. At the other extreme, people let others take advantage of them and others. Both are boundary violations of different kinds. An example from driving in traffic shows us the value of both assertiveness and yielding. Driving in traffic is the largest scale cooperative activity, in which most of us routinely engage. Tempo, spacing, and flow are each factors involved in participating well in driving. Connecting with the flow of traffic takes good concentration and generalized awareness to know what each situation calls for at any given moment. Sometimes the context calls for us to be assertive, while other times to yield. The best thing for the sake of other drivers is to remain predictable. If we yield when it is our turn to go, we are disruptive. When we force our way unpredictably, we are disruptive. Likewise in the flow of congregational life, there are times to step up and be assertive and times to yield.

While dominance and submission as character traits may be natural to human beings, they are not simply to be perpetuated in Christian community because they can interfere with and undermine the core identity and mission of serving the way of Jesus Christ. In Christian community, even passive people must be willing to contribute their viewpoints in clear and direct ways for the sake of communal discernment, serving as the eyes and ears of the Spirit. As we have mentioned previously, just as insect eyes can have thousands of separate lenses whose inputs combine to create what the insect sees, so the congregation needs the input and influence of each person. Each person also needs to be willing to step up at the appropriate time. This approach can take us out of our personal comfort zones and require us to act uncharacteristically for the good of the whole. A domineering person chooses to remain silent based on discernment and requests the input of others. A passive person chooses to speak with authority about their point of view to the betterment of the common ministry. This is what it means to fulfill one's role as parishioner without squelching another's role. Initiative without receptivity is like a bull in a china shop. Receptivity without initiative withholds needful gifts, remaining passive and inert. In some congregations people with dominance in the community are deferred to by others who always wait for their opinion; they are given virtual veto power. While the council may deliberate without them, the final decision becomes, "Let's see how Ed feels about this. We can't do it without his support."

Accurate discernment about how much initiative to take requires an adequate exchange of information so that a member can know when they have something to contribute. Too often, if someone is informed at all, it is only after a leadership team or committee has already come to a decision. This then places the person who has a contrasting viewpoint into a disruptive role rather than into the constructive one they could have played if they had been consulted earlier in the deliberation process.

It is always disruptive, regardless of the stage in the process, when members wish to have anonymous input. Some congregations have the practice of not allowing any anonymous input or even input coming through a third party because of the disadvantage such input places on those who receive such input. First of all, we know that accuracy is lost whenever information is delivered secondhand. In such a case, there is no opportunity to get direct clarification so that others might be able to determine how much weight to give to such input.

In some cases individuals act more like consumers toward their congregation than like participants in its ministry. The stress of time pressures is one widespread reason for this. Another involves the needs of members not otherwise being met; this might happen in an aging congregation. Based on a consumer mentality, serving the human needs of the members becomes an end in itself; from a participant or discipleship viewpoint, meeting the needs of the members has the final purpose of equipping them for ministry to others.[12] The contest between the consumer and the discipleship attitudes sometimes comes to expression in relation to funerals, weddings, or confirmations. Through these celebrations self-interest rather than discipleship is too often promoted. At a wedding, for example, the church's mission involves having the couple's marriage grounded in the horizon of God's ministry in Christ, so that the marriage is a resource that benefits others, not just the couple. This calls for a different kind of worship service than simply complying with what the couple may want or like. Very often, however, the couple does not share, or sufficiently share, the mission of the church so that the requirements or wedding policies of the congregation come into conflict with what the couple wants.

Confirmation is another occasion where conflicts may ensue between member as consumer and member as participant in the larger ministry and mission of the congregation. In all honesty, some parents think they have an obligation to get basic religious instruction for their children and then "let them decide." Parents want children to receive such instruction with as little disruption as possible. Other parents

---

12. Foss, *From Members to Disciples*.

frankly just want to get their children a "diploma" to satisfy grandparents or other family members. For this same reason they may have gotten their children baptized in the first place, although parents also may be hedging their bets that the children need to be baptized in order to get into heaven. The consumer mentality is made even more difficult when you add to it a sense of entitlement. Because the parents are members, the congregation "owes them" what they want, which almost always comes into conflict with the integrity of a confirmation program. By analogy, consumers are free to shop around and get the best deal. When there is a conflict between the confirmation requirements and what the child or family wants according to their own interests, the better those particular members are able to deal with their own stress, the more easily they will see things from the viewpoint of the pastor and the congregation's mission, not remaining locked into their perception of their own needs. In contrast to such disgruntled consumers of confirmation, there are also many families, students, and parents, who do approach confirmation as an opportunity for participation in the church's ministry and mission.[13] The boundary question, whose is this? helps us realize that the confirmation program does not belong to the family. It belongs to the congregation, and the congregation has a right to set participation requirements for the program.

In a parallel manner, it is useful to examine carefully the question, whose wedding is this? It may seem obvious that the wedding "belongs to" the couple and their families. However, when it is being done as a religious service, a holy rite, the church is responsible for the mission integrity of the service and necessarily has considerations that parishioners (as consumers) unfortunately may not have adequately considered. The trained clergy, who are well educated about such matters, often take the heat for seeking to protect the integrity of the wedding's religious purpose. It is most useful for congregations to adopt clear policies that designate the expectations of for Christian wedding and to abide by those standards. It is helpful for church members to receive and learn about the congregation's requirements so that they can more fully understand and respect them, refraining from pressuring the pastor to violate the requirements or best practices in relation to all religious services, including baptisms, confirmations, weddings, or funerals.

13. Everist, *Church as Learning Community*, chap. 5.

When parishioners seek to disregard such requirements, they are violating the boundaries of the congregation itself and its ministry, not just the pastor's boundaries. Policies define the boundaries needed to preserve the integrity of the church's identity and mission. The same applies to the question of who is to preside at a wedding. In the consumer mindset, the couples want to choose. Some may even want a previous pastor, who has moved on, since they knew and liked that pastor and may not know the current pastor as well. But if the previous pastor does the wedding, it is in violation of the congregation's boundary. A former pastor has responsibility not to interfere with the ministry effectiveness of the current occupant of the pastoral role.[14] For the previous pastor to even ask the current pastor about it is unfairly putting pressure on the current pastor. In another variation, members may want a relative who is also a pastor to perform the ceremony, again making the function personal rather than respecting the mission of the church. Marriage in the church is a religious rite, not a personal ceremony. Many people do not understand that. If the couple wants a civil ceremony, the service could be performed by a justice of the peace. As a religious rite, it is performed by the pastor of the congregation, the person designated by the congregation for that role.

Similar reasoning applies to funerals. Funerals held in a church do not just belong to the family and friends of the deceased to conduct as they wish, or with whomever they want to preside. Perhaps even more than with weddings, the parishioner as person may want the funeral to be performed by a previous pastor who best knew their loved one. The family may also want the current pastor to come back from vacation instead of having the supply pastor, whom they may not know. Yet a funeral in church is a worship service, and so the church rightly has requirements to protect the integrity of that process. "Whose is this?" A worship service falls within the care of the church. That in no way sets limits on what else a family may wish to do as part of their remembrances, in order to make connections with one another outside the worship service.

Especially surrounding funeral services, parishioners may treat the church as a vending machine, expecting the church to compensate the family for the church's inadequate emotional self-care, desiring church involvement to reduce their stress and distress. Many people very easily want their church to be a place of refuge, solace, comfort, and reassurance.

14. Everist and Nessan, *Transforming Leadership*, 141–42.

"Come to me, all you that are weary and carrying heavy burdens," Jesus said, "and I will give you rest" (Matt 11:28). Yes, but it was also the case that Jesus challenged people, not just telling them what they wanted to hear. That is, after all, why they killed him. The very first day of his ministry, they wanted to throw him off a cliff, they were so upset by what he said (Luke 4:29).

Parishioner as consumer of a service from the church puts the congregation and its leaders in a bind: "Give me comfort"; "Don't disturb me"; "Don't challenge me"; "Don't call me out"; "Don't preach sermons that make me or others think you are talking about me." Clergy and laity unconsciously collude to avoid what it disturbing. Parishioners do not want to be upset, and pastors do not want to upset parishioners. After all, the members are the ones paying the pastor's salary! Should the pastor not always do what the members want? The ability to respond to the difficult challenge of loving Lord, neighbor, and self requires a high tolerance for becoming disturbed about the world as it is. Otherwise religion can begin to function as the opiate Karl Marx thought it was. Given the stress of our lives, we easily may not have the capacity to be aware of all the terrible things that could be addressed right in front of our eyes, let alone in faraway communities. We want to shut off our awareness in order to not become overloaded. An alternative is to come together in order to increase our tolerance for disturbing things, including disturbing realizations about ourselves.

When the parishioner's self-care is inadequate, they will look to the church to reduce their stress; they will look to the church to reduce their uncertainty. They will be intolerant of pastors and other church members who challenge them, because that increases their stress rather than decreases it. They will be intolerant of anything new, because adjustment involves the stress of the unknown. They will be intolerant of people holding them accountable, because self-reflection is hard work. By contrast, when we get our self-care needs met outside the church, we can accept, and even welcome, when the church challenges us to grow in our capacity to minister for the sake of others. Then we can welcome mutual accountability and the process of knowing and being known just as we are and just as we are becoming.

When parishioners join hands to face ugly realities through mission and ministry, it is a beautiful thing. When self-interest is set aside, as it is by observing the Sabbath, then emerges the needed mutual, unconditional support and trust that allows freedom to reign so that new dimensions of God's purposes can to be discovered and explored within community. Synergy can happen in unexpected and delightful ways. There is a paradoxical aspect to this. With the command to love God, love neighbor, and love oneself, and with the setting aside of self-interest, there is an increase in the love of God and love of neighbor. But there is also an increase in the love of self, when this means love of the self as a child of God, love of the self beyond all roles, beyond all stressors, beyond all likes and dislikes.

The spiritual discipline of setting aside self-interest in Christian community helps bring awareness to aspects of the true self that we ourselves benefit from exploring and that others benefit from when we do so. For example, many people who attend high school reunions notice that after a few years, people are willing and interested in talking to people who were outside their social circle in high school. When they do so, they are amazed to learn how interesting and wonderful these people really are. In relating to them now, they are not relating with their old selves but rather with their just-now-being-discovered selves. When at church we just congregate with those we already know and like, we likewise set limits on the true self who dwells deep within.[15] When we relate in Christian community equally, without playing favorites, something special can happen for all involved. The love of the Lord, love of neighbor, and love of self all converge into one celebration of life.

PRACTICING BOUNDARIES IN LOVING OTHERS AND OURSELVES

One way that we extend love to others is by protecting them from harm. Best practices, as described in this book, are ways of creating safety for all involved. Given the complexity of human existence, with all the unknowns of our shadow sides, it is more loving to set boundaries with others than to set before them open temptations. It is actually more caring toward children not to leave them alone in a candy shop. It is more caring toward those handling our money not to leave them alone with other people's money. It is careless toward all involved not to have safeguards in place. The part of the self that takes offense at not being trusted is the ego, not the soul.[16] Why give to the ego so much power? It is respectful to

15. Merton. *New Seeds of Contemplation*, chap. 4.
16. Ibid., chap. 7.

acknowledge everyone's weaknesses. Every day in the news we encounter yet another story about a person having done a horrible thing, which those who know the person would not have predicted. Every day, in the confidence of therapists' and pastors' offices and in confessional booths, ordinary people reveal how shocked they are by their own behavior, not having realized that they were capable of doing such harm. Every night countless girls discover that nice boys are capable of selfish aggression against them. Every day people are shocked to discover what their spouses and partners have done behind their backs.

Given all this, it seems more loving and caring toward the self not simply to trust the self but rather to draw upon best practices to protect some parts of the self from other parts of the self. It is an act of care to monitor the different parts of ourself. Many of us must set limits on how we allow parts of ourself to talk to other parts in the privacy of our own minds. Love of self means not being careless with ourself. Care for our future self means putting limits on destructive tendencies of our current behavior. The research on self-discipline and willpower is reinforcing the long-held tradition within the world's religions that self-control requires control of our environment, because willpower is weaker than the power of temptation.[17] The great religions agree that we cannot know what we are capable of until faced with the temptation. The well-known proverb states that "pride comes before the fall." Such pride is based on self-deceit, the self-deceit of recovering alcoholics, who boldly declare that you could place a bottle of whisky in front of them and they would not drink from it. This is careless talk. We do not want to believe our own vulnerability any more than we want to believe that our neighbor is capable of incest. But being faithful means facing up to reality. It is caring toward ourselves to say no if offered a free buffet. It is caring toward ourselves and others to not go to a "gentleman's club" for an outing with friends.

Currently, respect for our shared vulnerability is growing due to the work of Brené Brown.[18] It is careless to deny how vulnerable we are as human beings. It is also careless to be afraid of our vulnerability. The best way to respect our vulnerability and the vulnerability of others is to recognize and respect boundaries with ourselves, with others, and with God. An extremely helpful tool for doing so is the adoption of codes of ethics and best practices, to which we turn in the next chapter. Before doing so,

17. McGonigal. *Willpower Instinct*, chap. 3.
18. Brown, *Daring Greatly*.

we want to touch on the role of best practices in care for ourselves, that is, love toward ourselves.

Best practices in care for or stewardship of the self are well recognized. Here we point to the basic principles. The first is the motive of love and care—not only for our present self but especially for our future self. While not brushing our teeth today may not hurt us immediately, it takes a risk with our future health. We do not need to calculate the odds about getting cavities or gum disease in our particular case. We accept it as careless not to brush our teeth and as caring to do so. We do not need to think it through every day. It is a healthy habit. Just as driving can be a spiritual practice, when we recognize that we hold other people's well-being in our hands when we drive, so it is with many other aspects of our own lives. In many varied activities we hold our own well-being in our own hands. Valuing healthy practices comes more easily when we are in touch with God's unconditional love for us. When we are mindful of God's love for us, we more easily remember to care for others when we are driving. So we also remember more easily to care for ourselves. Daily spiritual practices that connect us with God's unconditional love help to motivate and reveal loving ways of relating to ourselves. Practices of caring for ourselves then are not a hassle. Rather they have importance, because we are important to God and our future selves are important to God. We choose to practice them, whether we feel like it or not, because it is the loving thing to do. It is at the same time also loving toward others, because reducing our own stress, for example, allows us to be more aware of the needs of others, more patient, more kind, and more able not to insist on our own way. We thereby also care for our congregations by caring for ourselves. This does not mean, however, that we withhold from pastors and congregations all awareness of our needs, as when we are hospitalized and decide not to inform the pastor about it. Sharing such information is not about placing a demand, but rather allowing the pastor and congregation to fulfill their God-given mission in offering pastoral care.

Following best practices and living by healthy habits assist us in recognizing that without them we fall prey to letting current feelings take control over us. In chapter 5 we identified several distinguishable types of boundaries: identity, physical, will, emotional, mental, resource, and spiritual boundaries. Each of these boundaries summons us to respect and protect others. However, they also apply to caring for ourselves.

Best practices with regard to our own *identity boundaries* are those that keep us in touch with our core identity as a child of God. We do not misrepresent ourselves toward others through dishonesty, nor do we misrepresent ourselves to ourselves. This is challenging, because we want to maintain a positive view of ourselves. Therefore we may tend to deny our faults rather than, with the help of God's unconditional compassion, see ourselves as we really are. We refrain from calling ourselves names: "You idiot! What were you thinking?" To engage in such derogatory self-talk is careless with our identity. We also avoid creating false or incomplete images of ourselves to ourselves. Love of self begins with accurate self-image. As in the case of Sabbath freedom, however, all we know about ourselves is our past, not what we are capable of in the future. The fact that we have not yet done something does not mean we never will. So, as one example of careful practice, we might drop the expression "I can't . . ." and replace it with "I have never . . ." or "I have yet to . . ." In relation to congregational life, we care for our identity boundaries by not allowing others to misrepresent us, or refer to us by names other than those of our own choosing. We also care for our identity boundaries by not using our professional, social, or psychological identities in congregational life—not doctor, not mayor, not incest survivor but rather child of God.

Caring for one's *physical self* includes maintaining healthy physical boundaries in relation to others, not letting our self be exploited or even touched in unwelcome ways. For some people with arthritis, this can mean not letting others grab their hands in a handshake, since it is painful. Caring for one's basic physical needs is an expression of love toward self. This includes protecting sleep from encroachment by such things as worry. The old image of a child saying prayers while kneeling beside the bed is instructive. Here one's cares are handed over to God even before getting into bed. Best practices of care toward self can be carried with us wherever we go. While traveling, for example, some people wisely continue their exercise routine regardless of where they are, as well as other aspects of their daily regimen. They tend to feel better and also function better with others because of this activity.

Physical body boundaries also include our appearance. Asking of our body the question, whose is this? can help us acquire freedom of self-expression in our physical appearance. The adolescent girl who spends two hours preparing her face and hair before she goes to school is giving others control over her appearance. As relational beings, it is caring to consider how others will react to our appearance, but that is only one consideration. The other is our own identity and ownership of our bodies.

Healthy *will boundaries* allow the will to assert itself appropriately without violating another's will. Assessment of the health of the will involves checking in with different arenas of one's life. People who feel powerless or jacked around at work can compensate by being overly aggressive at home, and vice versa. With regard to the will and congregational life, it is important that we use the will to contribute and participate as helpfully as possible, neither holding back (to the detriment of the congregation's mission) nor overextending the will to encroach on others or on congregational boundaries. Care for one's own will involves how we exercise it in different circumstances and different parts of our lives. To protect oneself from being controlled by another person, it is helpful to practice saying no. Best practice for a person who has trouble with this is to respond to another's request first by buying time, saying something like "Let me get back to you on that." And when saying no, it is helpful to not give a specific reason, since the other person may argue about it. "It doesn't work for me to do that" should be sufficient. The attitude here is that you are simply informing the other person of your decision. They do not get to vote on your decision. If a person continues to push, address that rather than the specifics, saying, "I would like you to respect my decision."

To protect ourselves from being controlled by inner forces—such as appetites, urges, desires, and emotions, best practices include avoiding certain tempting circumstances, especially when we are alone. Often our behavior is constrained by the possibility of being detected by others, so when we are alone our will is more at risk of being overpowered by temptation. Holding ourselves accountable both to ourselves and others, as with an accountability partner, is another way to care for the exercise of our own will. As with other aspects of our self, the will can be strengthened, so merely protecting its potential weakness is not the total answer. Deliberately choosing to do something different, as long as it is a realistic goal, is one way to strengthen the will. Lenten fasting is a way to strengthen the will, as can the practice of some kind of weekly fast. Daily spiritual practices also strengthen the will. Sustaining a good practice does not take as much willpower as starting a new one, even if the intent is for the new practice only to be done briefly. With a healthy, skillful will we strengthen and protect all dimensions of ourselves. We do not let our mental selves be controlled by unhealthy inner forces, including the urge to dominate others, and we do not let ourselves be dominated by what others think of us or want from us. We also respect the integrity of the other's will and the integrity of congregational boundaries and role boundaries.

With *emotional boundaries*, we protect the integrity of our own and others' feelings and emotional space. We pay enough attention to our feelings to find accurate ways to portray and describe them to ourselves and others. We do not jump to conclusions or speculate about what they might be, based on past experience. Excitement and anxiety can feel similar, for example, but to mistake excitement for anxiety is to hamper ourselves. We can deny our feelings also in order to protect our self-image: "I wouldn't want to think of myself as the kind of person who would be intimidated by the pastor." So then you might more easily believe that the pastor is bullying you.

It takes time and careful attention not to misrepresent our feelings, even to ourselves. Often, staying with one's own bodily sensations helps keep the mind from intruding with its own ideas of what must be happening or what it would like to believe is happening. To protect our feeling boundaries from intrusion by others can be difficult because we are such relational beings. It is very easy to simply to absorb the feelings of those around us, especially of people who are more dominant than we are. It is convenient to feel the same way they do, since then there is no conflict. But then there is also no contrast, and contrasts can enrich things for everyone.

As relational beings, we also easily pick up emotions related to alarm, fear, and anxiety. When one horse in a herd is spooked and runs, they will all get spooked and run. The same is true for birds in a flock. We can see how this might have some survival value, while there are also risks. The children's story about Chicken Little taught us not just to buy into another's anxious catastrophizing. This is an important life skill. Clergy are trained to be "a nonanxious presence" with people who are distraught.[19] All of us benefit from counteracting the tendency to pick up and adopt the feeling state of those around us, especially those feelings that sound an alarm, in order that we and the group can benefit from our own calm and maintain our own perspective on the situation. With our feelings separated and distinct from those around us, we can better

19. Richardson. *Becoming a Healthier Pastor*, chap. 5.

relate to others in a helpful manner when that is appropriate. Deliberate practice helps.

We similarly protect our *mental boundaries* when we allow ourselves to think differently from other people and even to think differently than we ever have thought before. The boundaries between thoughts and feelings are important, because one of these human functions can easily dominate the other. A common example involves how we tend to disbelieve research results when we do not like the implications of the findings. We also refuse to understand another person's point of view because we may not like the implications or we do not like the person. This is an instance of allowing our thinking to be dominated by our feelings.

With *resource boundaries* we protect our vital resources from misuse by ourselves and others. An old-fashioned but still useful way people protect their financial resources from their own misuse is by budgeting and designating certain amounts of money for certain needs. They maintain, in effect, compartments for different needs, each with their own boundaries. By doing so, for example, they can see how much money is left for food in their weekly budget. Budgeting time and energy has a similar benefit. When congregations set meetings without any established ending times, they are not keeping good resource boundaries for the participants. Members with good time boundaries will rightly insist on setting clear ending times for meetings. This practice tends to improve the discipline within the meetings themselves. Members with good financial boundaries will insist on best practices to protect their financial contributions to the congregation. All healthy relationships involve negotiating implicit if not explicit agreements about how much time and energy the interactions will take. In addition to financial, property, energy, and time resources, there are also relationship resources. When earlier we discussed stress, we mentioned that other people are a resource that can help reduce our stress. Protecting relationship resources means not overtaxing others, as well as not offering someone else's help without their consent nor allowing others to do so.

Congregation members also contribute much to their own spiritual vitality and to that of their congregations by keeping healthy *spiritual boundaries*. We will look at boundaries internal to the individual as well as at essential external boundaries. For an example of both types of spiritual boundaries, we will consider the case of Clayton, an elder of the Church of the Covenant. As Pastor Theo launched into his sermon, Clayton realized to his dismay that Pastor Theo was preaching about Jesus's pronouncement in Matt 5:21–22, which equates hatred toward one's brother with murder. Two prominent members of the congregation were brothers who had been feuding for decades. Everyone danced around the problem so as not to make an issue of it. Both were good men. No one seemed to know what had started it. Clayton tried to inconspicuously glance over to where Joshua, one of the brothers, always sat. He noticed that Joshua's face was red. After the service, Clayton rushed down to the pastor's study and was waiting there for him when he returned. Clayton asserted, "Pastor Theo, if you want to keep your position here, you will never preach on that subject again! Do I have your word on that?"

Pastor Theo later heard quietly from other members who were grateful that he had pointed out the elephant in the room. They realized how cowardly they had been and welcomed the opportunity to no longer collude in all the avoidance. Spiritually, we damage ourselves and others when we allow our ego-based feelings to dominate the spiritual part of ourselves. Part of healthy internal boundary keeping entails protecting our spiritual nature from such domination by internal forces and external forces. Likewise, we can question whether Clayton, as a lay leader, was not violating a boundary by trying to bully Pastor Theo over the content of his preaching.

Spiritual integrity may be the most important area needing our care and attention as congregation members. We too easily allow other areas of interest, such as feelings, to encroach on our spiritual well-being. We easily make the spirit subservient to other interests both individually and collectively. In the case of Covenant Church, important spiritual lessons were being avoided in order not to rock the boat and embarrass prominent members. Spiritual boundary keeping helps us not to let ego-based feelings like fear or anger violate spiritual integrity. We too easily structure our religious communities to avoid challenging issues. One device people commonly use is called "spiritual bypassing." Spiritual bypassing is the use of spiritual beliefs and practices to avoid issues rather than to deal with them. A common example is how we can use spiritual beliefs to reduce people's distress at the loss of a loved one, telling others what they want to hear rather than helping them to face the distress. Healthy spiritual boundaries can help us face directly what our feelings would have us avoid. They help us listen to the prophetic word without wanting to kill the messenger.

Healthy spiritual boundaries also help us differentiate our personal spiritual awareness from those around us. As some would say, these boundaries help us "not drink the poisoned Kool-Aid." We protect ourselves from spiritual abuse when we do not allow others to use God and Scripture against us or against others for their own selfish purposes. We also avoid employing spiritual reasoning to reinforce prejudices or to withhold deeper insights about God by attempting to control others. Who is in the driver's seat—ego-based feelings or the spirit? That is the boundary question.

With healthy spiritual boundaries we do not judge others' relationship with God or usurp their insights into their own spiritual experiences. We do not invoke God's action in relation to the other person without their consent. We do not decide for others what they should believe or practice spiritually. We do not use God to control others, such as the frustrated Vacation Bible School teacher did who demanded of a young girl, "What would Jesus think of your behavior? You should always ask yourself that!" God can be used to manipulate, correct, or condemn others, beginning with how we think about these things in our own minds. With healthy spiritual boundaries we endeavor to have the ears to hear what we do not want to hear and the eyes to see what we cannot comprehend, rather than letting habits and spiritual laziness dull our awareness. When asked what we believe about something, we answer for ourselves with integrity, even about our possible confusion, rather than deferring to some other source of authority. We can hear and respect the still, small voice within us and in others. As a consequence, with the benefit of discipline in our individual spiritual practices, we have much to contribute to the corporate spiritual practices of congregational life. We can maintain our spiritual boundaries rather than, as Clayton did, let our emotions limit and spiritually damage us and others.

Part 3 of this book has been devoted to boundary keeping in relation to the pastor as person and in relation to the shared responsibility of all church members to safeguard the church's identity and mission as together we steward the many boundaries affecting congregational life. We, all the members of the church, must give watchful attention to identity, physical, will, emotional, mental, resource, and spiritual boundaries. In our concluding chapter we gather our collective wisdom about preserving the integrity of the body of Christ in the form of best practices and try to articulate a vision for the church, which holds such practices in the highest regard.

9

Being Body of Christ with Integrity:
Toward Best Practices in Boundary Keeping

SCENARIO NINE: THE ANNUAL MEETING

The members and staff of First Church had come to dread the day of the annual congregational meeting. There were so many reasons for disregard: the meeting time was inconvenient, the agenda unclear, the preparation by the chair haphazard, the reports rambling, the business dull, the budget discussion contentious, and the elections pro forma. For years this pattern had repeated itself, to everyone's chagrin.

Two years ago a task force had been appointed to rethink and re-structure the annual meeting. A diverse group was recruited for this task, including people gifted in hospitality, worship, music, running meet-ings, finances, group dynamics, communications, and leadership. Their work began by analyzing what had gone wrong. The consensus was that the annual meeting was a prime instance of poor boundary keeping by the congregation in general. People did not respect one another's time. Many took disagreements personally. Reports often disguised problems, rather than promoting transparency. Gifts were not celebrated. People complained afterwards without making constructive suggestions. There was little sense that what they were doing had anything to do with the congregation's identity and mission as the body of Christ. The annual meeting was perfunctory and pointless. A bad time was had by all!

The task force decided to begin its work by developing a Behavior Covenant, which was adopted and implemented for all congregational gatherings, including business meetings. Today was the culmination of this project as the congregation gathered to hold its annual meeting. The results of the task force's labors were reflected in the following ways. Perhaps the biggest change was that the meeting had been moved to September, marking the beginning of the congregation's renewal of activities after the start of the school year. The meeting was now held on a Wednesday evening, starting at 6 p.m., along with a potluck supper. People of all ages were seated around tables in the fellowship hall and asked to sit with those whom they knew less well. Table conversation was to include sharing by each person about three questions: (1) How has the congregation challenged you to grow in your faith in the last year? (2) What was most effective last year in meeting the congregation's mission goals? (3) What goals should the congregation set for the coming year? One person at each table was asked to take notes on the responses, which would be collated and reviewed by the leadership team and made available to the entire congregation.

At the conclusion of the meal, forty-five minutes later, the gathered assembly sang two beloved hymns and was invited to rehearse the congregation's mission statement. The congregation was then asked to reflect on a theme Bible verse that had been selected for the coming year, Ephesians 4:15–16: "But speaking the truth in love, we must grow up in every way into him who is the head, into Christ, from whom the whole body, joined and knit together by every ligament with which it is equipped, as each part is working properly, promotes the body's growth in building itself up in love." The pastor was prepared to offer concise theological and practical reflections to the members about what this verse could mean for the next year of their life together as a church.

The congregation had received the agenda for the annual meeting at the beginning of August. Preparations had already begun in the spring for crafting a meeting that would be both energizing and efficient. The congregational president was prepared to preside according to Roberts Rules of Order and reminded the members that child care was now available for those desiring it, provided by those who were trained according to the congregation's child protection policy. The chair of the worship committee was asked to offer an opening prayer, which was taken from a resource provided by the denomination for this purpose. Written reports had been submitted in advance by all standing committees and each member of the church staff, and these had been distributed to the congregation with the agenda in early August. The reports focussed less on rehearsing past activities and more on imagining the shape of congregational life for the coming year. The chairpersons of the committees and the church staff were together invited to the front of the assembly in order to respond to comments and questions about their reports. At the conclusion of this discussion, the congregational president expressed the congregation's thanks to all those serving in leadership by offering a prayer and through the singing of a hymn of praise.

New business followed, beginning with the election of officers. Each position description was clearly presented, and at least two candidates had been nominated for each position. The candidates also had prepared brief statements in writing about their gifts and interest in serving in the prescribed role; these statements had been distributed with the other materials in advance. Elections took place by secret ballot, and all candidates were affirmed by applause after the results were announced.

For the budget presentation the finance committee now prepared a narrative budget, which both organized the line items into mission categories and provided a written explanation of how each category contributed to supporting the congregation's ministry and outreach. Special attention was given to the importance of the congregation's partnership in the work of the denomination. In this first year of the new congregational meeting format, a brief video depicted the effectiveness of the church's collective mission. (Next year instead of the video, a representative from the denomination was going to be invited to make a presentation by interactive video, in order to interpret the denomination's programs.) Congregational leaders framed discussion of the budget in terms of fulfilling the core identity and mission of the congregation as expressed in its mission statement. Other new business items had opportunities for hearings and discussion prior to the annual meeting and were presented concisely with the recommendation to approve coming from the congregation council and staff.

The highlight of the evening was a video that had been prepared by the youth group of the congregation. It consisted of video clips of interviews with many older members of the congregation sharing their best memories of their church. In the years that followed, the theme of the video changed, but it was always cross-generational and mission focussed. The meeting concluded promptly at 8:30 p.m. with the Lord's Prayer. Volunteers had signed up in advance not only for set-up and serving the meal but also for the job of cleaning up afterwards. It was understood that families with children would need to leave promptly. What had once been a meeting time filled with distaste had now been intentionally transformed into a participatory event renewing the vitality of the congregation's identity and mission. Through careful planning and implementation, this gathering was already one of the highlights of the year. These transformations occurred because the people at First Church were becoming more conscientious about good boundaries and learning to value them!

BEST PRACTICES IN PERSONAL BOUNDARY KEEPING

The tools for creating and the skills for maintaining healthy boundaries are not blunt instruments. They are more akin to dabs of color on an artist's pallet to create what is best for each particular situation. In this chapter we consolidate the best practices mentioned in earlier chapters as well as draw conclusions about other wise and ethical practices from topics we have discussed. Many of the practices we mention may seem obvious, the equivalent of "Do not text while driving" or "Look before backing up." Many of these insights are matters of due diligence that if not done constitute careless behavior toward others. If a problem occurs, the burden of proof is on the person who fails to follow such a good practice. Unfortunately, the response of many people tends to be "I was only doing what everyone else does." The purpose of this book is to raise the standard of boundary keeping in congregational life as a matter of routine practice by all members so that normal acceptable practice increases safety and well-being for all concerned.[1] Even more, such best practices will promote the capacity of congregations to fulfill their core identity and mission at a time when too many congregations are under considerable stress.

Practicing Spiritual Integrity

When our spiritual connection is strong and secure, it can vitalize and inform the rest of our being, including our ministries, both personally and

1. On the value of "interdependence" in congregational ministry, see Lehr, *Clergy Burnout*, chap. 4.

collectively.[2] Among practices to secure and enhance spiritual integrity, we highlight the following:

- Engage regularly in prayer and meditation to clear the heart and mind for receptivity to the Spirit.

- Keep safe the precious revelations that have been entrusted to you, while recognizing when you are prompted by the Holy Spirit to share them with another.[3]

- Do not let anyone get between you and God.

- Do not interpret another's spiritual experiences. If they want your help understanding them, listen to them carefully with no preconceived ideas.

- Have some way to monitor how well you are doing at living Christ's values, such as by employing of the Prayer of Examen.

- Monitor how you are treating the least important people in your day.

- Practice common daily activities, such as driving, with spiritual mindfulness, as others' lives are entrusted into your care.

- Practice the principle of charity and speaking the truth in love.

- Keep the Sabbath to restore your soul.

- In transitioning out of Sabbath, bring the benefits of Sabbath with you; do not leave them behind.

- Foster happiness for those who have what you would like.

- Foster compassion for those who are suffering. Offer a prayer of blessing to them when you become aware of their suffering.

- Watch for consumer motives in your relationship to the church; for example, watch for the feeling of simply wanting the church to fill your own needs.[4]

- Do not use God to get what you want from others.

---

2. Harbaugh et al., *Covenants and Care*, chap. 5.

3. Blodgett, *Lives Entrusted*, chap. 2.

4. Cf. Bush, *Gentle Shepherding*, 15–16.

- Remember when you have violated a boundary that forgiveness is a gift.[5] Do not expect or demand it.

- Take seriously that people in positions of responsibility need to guard against the "negligent retention" of church staff in order to protect others and the church itself. The church has suffered by retaining people who have violated boundaries, in order to give them a second chance.

- Foster self-loving, compassionate humility.

- Watch for spiritual "bypassing," which is the use of religion and religious practices to avoid unwelcome feelings.

- Remember those to whom you are gratefully indebted, but do not allow others to leverage your gratitude for their own benefit.

- Remember that unconditional love does not mean setting limits on what should be tolerated.

- On the church calendar label the pastor's day off as "Pastor's Sabbath" to encourage others to view their own practice of Sabbath in the same way.

- Welcome preaching that challenges you and holds you accountable.

Practicing Identity Integrity

Our basic and true sense of identity flows from spiritual vitality. We are called to recognize that we are caretakers of our own identity and that another's sense of identity is fragile, like ours, given the highly relational aspect of our being. Among good practices for maintaining and enhancing identity integrity, we recommend the following:

- When meeting someone, ask what name they wish you to use and abide by that.

- When meeting someone, inform them of how you wish them to refer to you. If they deviate from that, gently remind them.

- Recognize that your impression of another person is in large part the construction of your own mind. Do not hold to or make claims about others that go beyond the facts you can be certain of.

---

5. Blodgett, *Lives Entrusted*, 39.

- Recognize that when someone gives you their impression of another person, it only has the status of a hypothesis, not a fact. Try to clear your mind of preconceived ideas and to approach the person with an open mind, expecting surprises as you delight in becoming acquainted. Do not ask for impressions of other people before meeting them.

- Avoid overgeneralizing about self and others (for example, "You always . . ." or "You never . . .").

- To avoid misrepresenting people, do not label them by associating them with others or even by a category in your own mind. Examples of unhelpful labels used by some clergy for parishioners are "alligator," "clergy killer," and "clergy wannabe."[6]

- Avoid profiling, which is treating an individual as being at higher risk than others due to the group to which they belong or life circumstances beyond their control rather than evaluating each person based on their own actions or personal qualities. Call committees and internship supervisors engage in profiling when, for example, they recommend special requirements, such as counseling, to people solely because of their background. Examples include being the child of an alcoholic parent or a person who was abused as a child. In such cases, their personal identities and characteristics are bypassed and they are treated as members of a category that others have constructed and about which generalizations are made.

- When referring to more than one person, in order to not misrepresent the situation to others or in your own mind, be precise about the number of people about whom you are talking. For example, instead of referring to an opinion you are naming as belonging to "they," say "I'm getting pushback from two people on the leadership team." Lumping people together into a "they" misrepresents a situation and the people involved.

- In order not to create false impressions, avoid speculation both in your own mind and in communication with others. Stick to the facts and do not pass along another's speculation. Clarify with others the source of their information.

6. Everist and Nessan, *Transforming Leadership*, 174.

- When you wish to raise a concern, present it as your own rather than as the concern of a group of people.

- If someone raises a concern as not their own but as something that another group of people has raised, clarify whether this is their own concern as well. Explain that you are willing to address the matter with that person insofar as it is their own concern but that you are not willing to address an issue of concern raised by others who are not present.

- In order to remain true to another person's worth and to care for their feelings, only say things that meet these four criteria: 1) is it honest? 2) is it true? 3) is it helpful? 4) is it kind? Use the same four criteria for how you think about others in your own mind. This includes thoughts that objectify the other person and therefore distract from thinking about others according to their baptismal identity and congregational roles. Sexual thoughts or thoughts about what favors the other person could do for you fall into the category of not being helpful to congregational life, if not inherently harmful.

- Avoid "You" statements, even in your own mind. Instead, use "I" statements about yourself instead. This is a basic practice for clear communication.

- Do not speak as if you have special knowledge or understanding about another person. (Avoid, for example, "I can see that you are the kind of person who . . .")

- Do not let others tell you who you are.

- Recognize the influence of your "animal nature" along with the fact that you need not let it rule you.

- You are not your role. Your role is a vehicle for doing God's work.

- Identify with the principles of Christ's contrast community to keep your sense of identity from becoming defined by prevailing and conventional social standards.[7]

- Practice identifying another person in the most inclusive way, as a child of God, like all others. This helps reduce unconscious prejudice.

---

7. Bailey, *Contrast Community*.

- Resist taking it personally when following congregational policies and best practices that affect you in ways you do not like. Personalizing such policies, and fearing that others will personalize them, is a major contributor to the violation of best practices.

Practicing Will Integrity

From our true identity as those tethered to God comes the will to live in accordance with how Christ taught us to live. This recognition also gives us insight into the inherent weakness of the will and helps us affirm the need for constraints on our willpower. We also recognize the value of acting for the enhancement of the healthy will of others. Among practices that protect and strengthen the will are the following.

- Practice exercising the will as you would a muscle, even doing small unnecessary things just to give the will a workout.

- Remember that self-discipline is the ability to get yourself to do things when you do not feel like it, and the ability to get yourself not to do things you would like to do.

- Address areas of your life where you feel powerless, as exactly these areas can weaken your will.

- Recognizing the weakness of the will and the limits of self-awareness, negotiate "Behavioral Covenants" in the congregation in order to constrain one's own personal will by mutual accountability.[8] It is useful to adopt congregationwide covenants as well as covenants for each committee or sub-group, including those going on trips, in order that group behavior reflect the values, principles, and purposes of the organization.

- In your designated roles, be aware of your self-interested motives that can put the welfare of others at risk.

- Whose decision is this? is a helpful question to ask before making a decision.

- Always take no for an answer and do so as respectfully and gracefully as possible.

---

8. Cf. Rendle, *Behavioral Covenants in Congregations.*

- Whenever taking no for an answer is difficult, examine carefully why you are feeling that way.

- Get comfortable saying no. Take adequate time to reflect on a request before committing to it.

- Realize that the conventional wisdom that it is "easier to ask for forgiveness than to get permission" is unfair to others.[9]

- Watch out for entrapment so that you do not do it to others or accept it when someone is doing it to you. Physical entrapment involves blocking a person's physical exit, communicating, in effect, "You won't leave till I'm ready for you to leave." Emotional entrapment involves expressing emotional consequences or threats to another person's when ending a conversation: "If you hang up, all bets are off." Verbal entrapment also consists of asking people questions in order to trap them rather than making a statement. For example, if I am upset with someone who is regularly late to a meeting and ask, "When was the last time you were on time?" I have set a trap for the person into admitting the problem. The boundary respecting alternative is simply to say, "I want to discuss the importance to me of your being on time to our meetings." If the person acts as if it is not a problem, I may say, "I can't remember the last time you were on time." The rule is: Do not ask questions when you have a statement to make. Make the statement instead."

- Unless you are the supervisor, avoid telling others what they need to do. Avoid "You need to . . ." statements.

- Express your concern, and then respect the boundary. When expressing concern for another's personal well-being, remember that they do not have to answer to you about their personal life. Express the concern and why you have it and then respect the boundary.

- When making a request of another person, do not expect an immediate answer. Instead, invite the person to think and pray about it and get back to you. This is especially helpful for those at risk of placing the pleasing of others (perhaps of you in particular) before their own needs.

- When receiving a request from others, do not decide on the spot. Instead, tell them you will consider it and get back to them. This

9. Blodgett, *Lives Entrusted*, 82–83.

allows for more complete consideration of the implications of the decision than can be given at the moment and under the direct pressure of the other person's desire.

• Avoid giving or requesting favors that would potentially create inequality in the relationship (for example, making another person feel like something is owed to you, such as return favors). Consider instead a verbal or written expression of gratitude.

• When giving a gift or donation, mentally and emotionally release your ownership of it so that the receiving party truly is free to do with it whatever they choose, no strings attached.[10]

• "It takes three to go." Recognizing the weakness of the human will, self-discipline and sound decision making involve controlling the environment, in order not to carelessly create temptation. Based on this strategy, it is wise to avoid being alone with someone who might theoretically become sexually or emotionally attracted to you, or you to them. It is dangerously unreliable to judge that there is no risk based on self-knowledge and of one's impression of yourself and of the other person. Here we learn from the mistakes of others. When there is legitimate ministry to be done with another person one-to-one, only do it in a place where the physical behavior could be observed by others. When alone in a room, meet in a room with an interior window so others could observe, and do so when others are present. Be alert to situations that easily evoke psychological intimacy, such as car rides. To go somewhere, take three, not two. Or go separately.

• In order to avoid temptation, the perception of carelessness, and lack of due diligence, establish "Child, Youth, and Vulnerable Adult Protection Policies and Procedures." Consistently follow such policies, in order to minimize temptation and opportunity for the mistreatment of these individuals by limiting the behavioral discretion of adult participants. Conform the selection of adult participants according to such best practices.[11]

10. Hunter, *Back to the Source*, 75 reminds us of the scene in the film *Harold and Maude*, where Harold gave Maude a gift. After expressing her delight, she kissed the present and threw it into the ocean.

11. Insurance companies often have excellent model policies.

- Identify people who are highly sensitive and aware of boundary issues and learn from them. Value their perspective.

- When thinking about not following a good boundary practice, rather than believing your own reasoning, consult with someone objective who is a good boundary keeper and who is willing to tell you what you do not want to hear. Establish that the burden of proof is always on the one who seeks to violate the good boundary practice. When you discover that you are trying to second-guess normal acceptable boundary practices, beware and consult!

- Establish as routine procedure with leadership teams, staff meetings, and colleague groups that you invite awareness about and discussion from all present on boundary issues and ethical quandaries that you and they are facing in the performance of your roles.[12] Welcome mutual accountability and feedback on boundary keeping within the conduct of these groups.

- Keep track of unmet personal needs and the risks they pose, and make a plan for meeting them appropriately.[13]

- Remember to care for your future self and let that concern override current fatigue.

- Remember the value of boundaries and best practices to protect us from our weaknesses and shadow side.[14]

- Exercise having your will be made subordinate to best practices.

- Watch out for hijacking. Hijacking is the process by which a person or persons take over a process or committee to deliberately redirect it toward a different goal and against the will of those who are already involved. The process of initiating change is not hijacking when the change agent simply uses persuasion, respects differences of opinion, and takes no for an answer. The difference is not persistence but process.

- Recognize threats as power plays, as, for example, when you realize that your congregation has an important condition on its voting membership and an upcoming meeting may force you to decide how to enforce it. Do not try to influence the vote by making a threat.

---

12. Cf. Kaptein, *Workplace Morality.*

13. Olsen and Devor, *Saying No to Say Yes,* chap. 2.

14. Lehr, *Clergy Burnout,* 106–13.

- Realize that taking things personally is emotionally coercive. When your behavior is constrained by fear that another is going to take personally what you do, you are being coerced by that fear. When you take personally what others have done, you are being coercive.

- Do not conspire with others to get your own way.

- Do not engage in secret activities. Secrecy is a means to gain power over others.[15]

- Remember that human beings behave more ethically when others can know what they are doing rather than when they believe no one will know.

- Remember, love does not insist on its own way (1 Cor 13:5).

Practicing Emotional Integrity

Feelings and emotions are a big part of ministry and the way of following Christ, with generous love being the principal component. Feelings can provide us with important information about things. For example, joy conveys important truths about life, and sometimes anger accurately tells us a person or situation is threatening or harmful. Emotions move us in important ways, engaging the vitality of life. Feelings and emotions can also mislead us, however, and their power can overwhelm other important sources of information and judgment. Consequently, we need to abide by the universally recognized need for self-control in relating to our feelings and emotions.

- Listen to feelings (your own and those of others) to see if they are telling you something important. If so, take that information and release the messenger.

- Healthy relating in congregational life can include sharing burdens and difficult feelings. This helps create bonding by strengthening caring relationships for the sake of shared ministry. Since the central value is listening and being heard, do not distract from someone else's story by telling about a similar thing that happened to you. To do so undermines trust.

15. Peterson, *At Personal Risk*, 80–86.

- Practice specific techniques and methods in order compassionately to listen to another person with their feelings and emotions, neither being drawn into their feelings nor being reactive to them. Anxiety, sadness, and anger are among the feelings needing the most self-differentiation for many people. In chapters 7 and 8 we discussed some methods that can help. The central point is to keep your nervous system and brain functioning independently without being controlled by the other person's emotions. Clergy, for example, are taught to be a nonanxious presence with people who are distraught. This skill has wide application.

- Support others by affirming the feelings that they have; release any thoughts that they should feel differently than they do (for example, by experiencing anger or grief).

- Appreciate that there are times and places where people do not want attention directed at how they are doing or what they are dealing with. An alternative expression of care can be, "Good to see you," rather than "How are you doing?"

- Hearing your feelings and thoughts out loud with a witness can be helpful. To make it healthy, rather than complaining about others, express what feelings are generated in you by their behavior. For example, "I just hate it when I feel I'm being ignored." Such expression can help identify the origin of the feeling. To make it about the other person is usually avoidance. Venting about another person may feel good, but that does not make it ethically good.

- Be careful to not jump to conclusions about what someone is feeling or to speculate about how they must be feeling. Invite others to give their own expression to their feelings, and use the words most meaningful to them.

- If you want someone to understand how you feel, express your feelings in an inviting way and not as an intrusion of your feelings upon them as some people do when they are venting. Emotional dumping is intruding on another's feeling space. Moderate your intensity and language to make it as easy as possible for the other person to hear and understand.

- Saying "I know how you feel" creates distance rather than closeness for most people. While this might seem to be the opposite of what you intend, some people use this expression to stop conversation rather than to open doors.

- Sharing joys also creates an important bond that can enhance ministry relationships. The person sharing creates a bubble of joy that is easily burst if the listener detracts from it in any way rather than simply entering into the joy and expanding on it.

- Understand what "too much information" (TMI) means. The issue is not simply about the quantity of information, going on and on, while capturing another person's time. It is also about the nature of the information itself. While some personal disclosure enhances role functioning in ministry on everyone's part, such as the sharing of joys and burdens does, other personal disclosure may be unwelcome and unhelpful.

- Be aware of potential manipulation through personal sharing. It can create unhelpful bonding that takes people out of their appropriate role and crosses a boundary into personal interest. Personal sharing without clear boundaries can be the verbal equivalent of "Show me yours and I'll show you mine."

- Be aware of the false intimacy that occurs through triangulation. Avoid it by directing attention to those who are present instead of attempting to deal with the nonpresent person directly.

- Be aware of the false intimacy that can occur in counseling relationships, especially when talking about someone not present.[16] Both parties risk personalizing the care that rightly belongs to the counseling relationship.

- While some socializing is important at work, during staff meetings and in staff relations, establish a disciplined limit to socializing so that such encounters are not used to compensate for a lack of social outlets beyond the job, and so that work time is spent productively.

- Parishioners do well to monitor socializing with congregational staff so that they are not used to compensate for the lack of a social life beyond the congregation. Be open to input about this.

- Use the "Get three to go" rule, whenever you find you want to spend time alone with a church member or staff member at a church

---

16. Regarding power dynamics and relational boundaries in pastoral counseling, see Doehring, *Taking Care*, chaps. 4 and 5.

function. In situations where inappropriate feelings theoretically could occur between two people, even if they do not have those feelings at the present time, do not enter into that situation unless a third person can be there as well. A common example involves car rides, even when it is more practical for two people to go together.

- Allow others to have their own feelings about things rather than pressuring them into feeling as you do about something. Do not establish consequences for those having different feelings.

- Ministers can help maintain boundaries with parishioners who consult or confide with them by establishing a neutral meeting space, which is not filled with objects from the minister's life or work. When the latter is the case, as with many minister offices, the parishioner has to enter into the minister's psyche, which works against maintaining their own psyche boundaries in the encounter.[17]

- Routinely assess the status of your unmet personal needs with the help of an objective, outside person, insofar as these needs will press to be met inappropriately within one's congregational roles and activities.[18]

- Routinely assess the status and activity of your personal weaknesses, including weaknesses as they relate to your role, with the help of an objective, outside person. While it is not currently popular to think in terms of personal weaknesses but instead to refer to "growing edges," the latter concept does not adequately convey the peril these personal weaknesses pose for ethical behavior.

- Healthy boundary keeping and unwelcome feelings often go together. All boundary keeping and safe practices involve forgoing something that you or someone else wants. The belief that if something is good it will feel good, or, conversely, if it is not good it will not feel good, does not hold up.

- Recognize the difference between needs and wants.

- As adults we can tolerate disappointment when our desires are not met. Being willing to disappoint others facilitates easier boundary keeping for all concerned.

17. Cf. Kaptein, *Workplace Morality*, 39–41.

18. Lehr, *Clergy Burnout*, Appendix 1, 128–34, provides a useful tool for personal assessment.

- Remember that there are no cliques in the body of Christ. Relate generously with those for whom you have no natural affinity.

- Foster love over jealousy and resentment.

- Get comfortable being vulnerable.

- Remember that mutual consent does not make something right or acceptable.

Practicing Mental and Speech Integrity

Thoughts and words are basic raw materials for our relationships with others and with our selves. Our thoughts are virtually constant companions, which reflect and shape our experience. We tend to identify strongly with our own thoughts and are at risk of drawing conclusions about others based on the opinions they represent. Thoughts have both inner and outer qualities. To some degree our words express our thoughts, and to some degree our words help us discover what we think. We use thoughts and words in order to do ministry together. Thoughts and words are given high significance in corporate worship and the statement of our beliefs. In fact, differences of opinion about thoughts evoke either feelings of affinity toward others whose beliefs we share or feelings of alienation and threat when beliefs are radically different. As we have emphasized throughout this book, best practices and codes of ethics are indispensable due to the unreliability of human reasoning.[19]

- If you have not told someone something, do not expect them to know it.

- Allow others to have their own thoughts about things, rather than pressuring them into agreeing with you. Do not place consequences on differences in people's thoughts, ideas, and beliefs (for example, by saying, "If that's what you think, then . . .").

- Do not expect others to trust you personally; that is the reason for best practices.

- Do not trust your own judgment. Remember the unreliability of the human mind and the ego-driven heart as demonstrated in previous chapters.

---

19. Regarding codes of ethics, see Trull and Carter, *Ministerial Ethics*, chap. 8.

- Do not lump events together, but see each event freshly and on its own terms. When a current event reminds you of a past event, exercise the art of letting go.

- Do not speculate; stick to the facts.

- Get comfortable with not knowing.

- When in doubt, consult.

- Remember, if you are thinking about work, you are working.

- Give exercise to the Observer self, practicing mindfulness, rather than just being swept along by your thoughts.

- Remember not to label or categorize people in your own thinking or speaking.

- Practice the use of these four criteria to decide whether or not to think something or to say it to somebody else: (1) Is it honest? (2) Is it true? (3) Is it helpful? (4) Is it kind? Carelessness with our thoughts and words is the relational equivalent of careless driving. We are responsible for the damage they cause.

- Do not personally dwell upon or pass along to others what you do not know to be true.

- Do not pass along someone else's information without their consent, unless the situation is potentially harmful. The question, whose is this? informs us about the boundary.

- Practice recognizing how your thoughts and beliefs are shaped by your feelings. One exercise is to periodically contemplate how "There are things I do not like that are nonetheless true." By letting go of your "I do not like this" response to things that have happened, it is easier to recognize the truth and accept it. Otherwise we can enter into denial and avoidance.

- If you are a church member and have romantic or other personal thoughts about a minister, or if you are clergy or a staff member and have such thoughts about a church member or fellow staff member, remember that you control where you direct your attention and need to practice the "Quick Release of Thoughts" (to coin a term). Dwelling on such thoughts and feelings makes them stronger and tempts one to seek justification for acting upon them.

- Only speak about others who are not present when they have consented, or if you are certain they would consent, if you really cannot obtain consent. Ask yourself, what if the person in question was to be able to hear the conversation? Be cautious about assuming that the other person would not mind simply because you desire to talk about that person.

- Have clear agreements in the congregation about what is confidential and what is not confidential, and review these agreements regularly. For example, if for the sake of shared ministry a staff member wants it to be policy that they inform one another about what they know is going on in members' lives, all who confide must know that this is the policy in order to decide what they choose to disclose.

- When in the presence or someone who is complaining about someone not present, remind them about triangulation and help them consider talking directly to the person with whom they have the issue.

- Adopt a congregational policy not to pass along or take action on anonymous complaints.

- Monitor your stress level, and remember how stress impairs perception and judgment.

- Do not fall prey to wishful thinking. Doing no harm includes assessing what could go wrong with a potential course of action.

- If you choose to violate a best practice, accept that the burden of proof is on you.

- Work to keep your energy high. Remain calm, with your consciousness clear and expansive, in order to be at your best.

Practicing Role Integrity

Regardless of the role you have in your congregation, that role is important to the congregation's vitality and ministry. To fulfill that role according to its purpose, practice these hallmarks of faithfulness: 1) strengthening that role while not exceeding it and 2) not weakening anyone else's role or their ability to fulfill it. In healthy congregations, people help each other in setting and keeping healthy boundaries.[20] The organization itself acts on behalf of healthy boundary keeping for the sake of healthy ministry.

- Remember that the role you are in is granted to you by others. The role is in your care and stewardship for the sake of others. Again ask the question, whose is this?

- Rank all of your roles, personal and professional, in their order of importance, and evaluate how well you are filling those roles.

- There are no role boundaries without a clear definition of each role. Establish role descriptions that are as clear and complete as possible for each major role in the congregation, paid or unpaid. Regardless of the role, it is advisable not to enter a new role without clear role definition, as this can lead to unnecessary role confusion and role conflict. Routinely review the descriptions to see whether they need to be revised.

- When someone is upset with what someone is doing or not doing in a particular role and their concern is due to lack of clarity about the role definition itself, the issue is about the role definition and not about the person filling that role. The person in that role and the dissatisfied person should refer the matter to the personnel committee, which is responsible for the role description.

- Establish accountability roles. Conduct routine evaluations about how well a person is filling their role and also about how well they are doing at not going beyond that role into someone else's area of responsibility. This is done most gracefully within the context of an overall assessment of how well the congregation is meeting its ministry goals and how well each committee or subgroup is doing its job.

- Normalize mutual accountability structures. Routinely practice addressing accountability issues. Do not take these inquiries personally.

- Remember that the role is not to benefit you personally; you are to serve the role for the sake of others.

- Meet your personal needs on your personal time by keeping track of the status of those personal needs. Make a plan for addressing them.

20. Gula, *Just Ministry*, 130–33.

- If in a committed personal relationship always know when you have your next date.

- Distinguish between reasonable expectations and realistic expectations.[21] While an expectation may be reasonable given the role description, whether it is realistic depends on circumstances that not everyone will understand unless they are informed about them.

- Make peace with the realization that there is "conduct unbecoming" a person in your role. This is a standard part of professional codes of ethics that helps professionals take responsibility for the reputation and effectiveness of their profession: professionals recognize that their personal behavior can either enhance or detract from the regard people give to that role and to those who fill that role.[22]

- To avoid questions or doubts about your full mental engagement, avoid consuming alcohol or drugs during your workday.

- When considering taking on a second role with the same person or persons, for the sake of role clarity consider all possible conflicts of interest, realizing the human tendency to deny them or minimize them. Consult with an objective, outside person who is willing to tell you things you do not want to hear. When dual roles are unavoidable (or otherwise undertaken), discuss them with those concerned so that everyone can have input and be watchful.[23]

- Recognize conflicts of interest in decision making by yourself and others. Make discussion about such possible conflicts of interest commonplace. Opt out of a decision-making role or recuse yourself when you or a person close to you has a personal stake in the decision.

- Only access information about others, including Internet and other social media searches beyond what another person has revealed to you, when it is in fulfillment of your agreed-upon role toward that person and the congregation. Being a congregation member is such a role when there is a covenant about caring community, as there should be in youth work, and as there can be with adults as well.

21. Bush, *Gentle Shepherding*, 72–73.

22. For examples of constructive "statements of ministerial commitment," see Gula, *Just Ministry*, Appendix, 240–50.

23. Gula, *Ethics in Pastoral Ministry*, 80–85.

- Respect the difference between work time and personal time so that each is done most effectively. For example, do not continue addressing domestic conflict by texting at work, and do not write work e-mails while in your personal life.

- Decision-making committees and boards do well to routinely ask if anyone is aware of conflicts of interest before proceeding to deliberate and decide on an issue. Respect those who express discomfort with any dual role that you may have.

- Recognize which roles do not mix—that is, which roles are incompatible and weaken the integrity of one's primary responsibility.

- Interim positions often call for the interim pastor or interim bishop to do unpopular things for the sake of the well-being of the church. Given that, anyone wanting to be considered for the permanent position, which follows the interim, would do well not to serve as the interim. Likewise, the church would do well to keep the interim position clear of candidates for the permanent position. The reasonable risk is that the candidate would consciously or unconsciously be more risk aversive than a noncandidate who serves as an interim, to the detriment of the church.

- Parishioners do not ask clergy or staff to take personal responsibility for their affairs, such as power of attorney. If asked to take on such roles, clergy and staff refer the parishioner to other resources for such roles.

- When you are in two roles in a situation (for example, a parent chaperone on a youth trip), explain to the others involved which is primary and which is secondary.

- In dual role situations, frequently ask these questions: What hat am I wearing now? Is this the hat according to which I am thinking and acting?

- Remember that the more a member befriends the pastor or intern, the less they will see that person as their pastor, and the more difficult it is for the pastor to think and act from the pastoral role with integrity. It is the responsibility of the pastor or intern to maintain that boundary. It is not appropriate for the member to change their membership status in order to pursue a personal relationship. If the member was to do that and the relationship went badly, they would have lost both the relationship and their congregation. The cleanest thing is for the pastor or intern to respond to personal overtures by informing the member that professional ethics do not allow such dual relationships and to help the member to accept that.[24] If the parishioner asks, "What if I leave the church?" we recommend a response like, "I'm your pastor, and my responsibility is to keep that relationship strong." By the time this question would have been posed, inappropriate-feeling interactions would already have taken place.

- For clergy, interns, and other staff, keep support functions separate from evaluation functions. An example of this problem is to have internship committees expect interns to confide in them and then to negatively evaluate them on the basis of what is disclosed. These are conflicting roles.

- Avoid conflicting roles among pastoral support groups (for example, mutual ministry committees) by not having them provide evaluation or advocacy either for the pastor or for people who are disgruntled with the pastor. Such activity is triangulating.[25] The least conflicted arrangement is for the pastor to have a support group outside the congregation, possibly with people who are not clergy themselves, in order to gain perspective from those outside the profession. This addresses the need for personal support and personal accountability beyond dual roles.

- You have assumed your role based on mutual agreement between yourself and others. Either party is free to withdraw that consent. Clergy can leave their position as they wish, and congregations can decide they wish for the pastor to leave.

- One of the most difficult and damaging conflicts of interest occurs when a person's effectiveness in their role has been compromised. Personal interest generally tends toward the desire to remain in the role, while this usually conflicts with the well-being of the congregation. Honoring the tension between these two sets of interests among all responsible parties can best lead to a decision that cares for both parties.

24. Gula, *Just Ministry*, 137–43.
25. Richardson, *Becoming a Healthier Pastor*, chap. 9.

- Familiarize yourself with the concept of an "impaired professional." Various medical and psychological conditions can interfere with a person's effective performance of their role. Without adequate awareness and corrective action, a congregation's ministry can suffer. In many cases, the well-being of the congregation requires that the minister be removed in order for adequate treatment to occur and for the vital functions of the congregation to continue.

- What a congregation wants from their pastor and what the pastor wants from a position may not completely coincide. Without adequate attention to the tensions, the areas not overlapping will become neglected and may spark dissatisfaction.

- In social media contacts with church members, maintain your professional role in your content and demeanor.

- Once a year review the codes of ethics, behavioral covenants, and best practices that apply to you.[26] Treat them as your allies.

- Do not ask or expect a family member, friend, or relative who is a clergyperson to perform clergy functions for you, such as counseling, weddings, or funerals. This deprives them of being a person with the same needs and desire for ministry as anyone else in those circumstances. If they volunteer, politely decline.

- In congregational gatherings and activities, do not act based on your role in life outside the congregation, such as in a business, civic, or professional role (or even in a friendship role). Stick to being a member of the body of Christ as your assigned role.

- Do not relate to others in the congregation according to their role at work. For example, do not try to get someone's professional advice, set up a business meeting, or even arrange a personal social event since this excludes others. Help others maintain their role as congregation member.

- Suspend friendship interactions during congregational events.

Practicing Transitions to Enhance the Integrity of the Whole

Each role we assume deserves our full engagement. At the same time, it is very helpful to become skillful at moving from one role to another.

26. See the useful checklist in Lehr, *Clergy Burnout*, 114–17.

What we learn and experience in one role can better equip us for life in other roles. Effective transitions also can assist us with the process of integration.

- Practice making effective transitions from one role to another in order to be fully present and engaged in whatever you are doing. Obviously, the most important role transition is into and out of the role you play as a member of your congregation in relation to the roles you have in other parts of your life. For clergy and staff members, this also entails transitions from one function or activity to another throughout the workday in order to remain fully engaged.

- To transition from work to your personal life, do not confuse what helps you feel relaxed (like alcohol or TV) with what helps you recover your energy and enthusiasm to enter fully into your personal life and relationships (like light exercise or meditation). Aside from meditation, most practices that help us recover energy after work actually involve some expenditure of physical energy, which the stressed brain wishes to avoid.

- Sharpen your ability to quickly and effectively shift from one state of mind and heart to another. Practice making the three-part transition each day: gain temporary closure with the role you are leaving, quickly refresh, and then turn your mind and heart into the next role and activity you are entering. In the first step of closure, consider what is wise to carry forward into future activities. Clergy must practice this role transition several times a day, given the variety of activities in which they engage. Permanent role changes involve the same three components of closure, refreshment, and turning.

- When clergy leave a call, care for the integrity and effectiveness of the role means fully disengaging from the pastoral role in that setting and from all activities that involve it in order for the congregation to disengage from the clergyperson and embrace the successor.[27] Good practice involves giving notice that the minister is leaving, which includes the directive to the congregation no longer to look to this person for ministerial services but rather to utilize other pastoral services as now designated by the congregation. Notify members on social media that you will no longer be connected with them in that way as a matter of good practice, and help them not to take it per-

27. Everist and Nessan, *Transforming Leadership*, 141–42.

sonally. The new minister supports that boundary for all concerned by not making exceptions. "All concerned" includes future ministers and ministers in other congregations, who benefit from uniformity of this practice, as they may contend with requests from members for ministry from their former ministers.

- Respect that personal contact between a former pastor and church member risks adversely affecting the bond between the new pastor and church members.

- When a congregation member leaves a role, such as a leadership role, full disengagement from that role helps the successor fill the role in their own manner.

BEST PRACTICES IN COMMUNITY BOUNDARY KEEPING

Practicing Boundaries in Times of Contrast and Conflict

Amazingly, with all the social pressure we are dealing with and are placing upon others, each of us is really quite unique. Our uniqueness gives us the advantage of benefitting from a rich variety of abilities and different points of view. Creative self-discipline is required to welcome and incorporate these differences. Helpful practices include the following:

- Make the positive assumption that points of view different from your own have value. Work to be genuinely interested in other perspectives. One such practice is to develop the habit of responding, "That's interesting. That is so different from how I look at it." This will at least keep us from reflexively disagreeing; disagreement defers attention away from the other's point of view onto our own.

- Mentally practice the method that when another person is speaking, you will not be distracted by your own thoughts or reactions but instead will discipline yourself to listen and hear.

- Seek first to understand with fresh eyes, not allowing past experience to color your perception of what is happening now.

- Pray for the capacity to see the other who disagrees with you through the eyes of Christ.[28]

28. Bonhoeffer, *Life Together*, 31–35.

- Appreciate people telling you things you do not want to hear. Thank those who have done so.

- Adopt the mindset of a mediator in your own disputes so that you can see all points of view that are represented.

- Address process before content, in order to get a better outcome. Behavioral agreements at the outset establish needed boundary safeguards. An important component of such behavioral agreements is a provision for time-outs. If any party feels another is too upset to keep the agreement, they may call a time-out for themselves. However, that person also needs to state when the process is to resume so that the time-out is not just a way to avoid dealing with the issues. Per agreement, the time-out is not negotiable once the process has begun. Whoever wants a time-out gets one.

- If process cannot be agreed upon, take the matter to the next level in the organization.

- People can get good outcomes from conflict when they actively help each other out during the conflict rather than watching out for themselves. When being criticized, try to understand what the other person is saying. Practice reframing criticism as requests and then consider the validity of the request.

- Recognize that anger is often a sign that you are engaged in a power struggle.

- Familiarize yourself with principles of fair fighting and nonviolent communication.

- Clarify and communicate carefully to others these four features of a given position: (1) the what of the position, (2) why the person holds it, (3) how strongly they feel about it, and (4) why they feel so strongly about it. Only then does everyone have adequate information to know what to do with a particular point of view.

- Remember not to take things personally even when another person tries to make things personal. Help each other out. In that process, care as much for the other persons as for yourself.

Practicing Worship Integrity

Worship is the heart of congregational identity and mission, yet few are accustomed to consider the many boundaries that are involved in effective worship. Here are some examples:

- Recognize and fulfill your role as a cocreator of the worship experience for yourself and others.

- Entering into worship, suspend your likes and dislikes in order fully to participate.

- Be on time and prepared to fully engage in worship at the time the worship leader begins the service.

- Do not distract the worship leader or fellow worshipers by telling them troubling things right before worship.

- Exercise control of attention in order to stay present and not distracted by extraneous events during worship. Is it not extraneous to care for children, unless others are already caring for them.

- Turn off mobile devices before and during worship.

- When others in the worship space are preparing themselves for worship, be careful not to distract them.

- Leave state shifting to the worship leader. Allow the worship leader to lead in making the transition from one element of worship to another. It is the worship leader's role, for example, to decide whether to applaud or not after a given part of the worship service.

- Do not distract others from worship by taking photographs.

- Strive to treat all present equally without preferences based on friendship. For example, hugging some but not all during the passing of the peace shows unequal treatment .

- Keep commercialism, promotional items, and business references out of the worship space and worship materials.

- When hearing the prayers and needs of others, consider how you might help them be met. The prayers of the people provide direction to the congregation about mission opportunities.

- During communion, set aside all differences and hold everyone in your heart.

Practicing Physical Integrity

The integrity of physical things allows them to fulfill their spiritual purpose and value. The physical property owned by the congregation is in the care of all members. While a church is not a building, the property and its well-being serves the mission of the congregation. Another dimension of the physical involves the physical bodies of people involved in the congregation. By tending to our bodies, we tend to the physical aspects of ministry. Body boundaries help us feel safe and secure. When secure, people are better equipped. When people are not secure, participation is inhibited.

- Realize that caring for your physical body helps you participate fully and contribute fully to the life and ministry of the church.[29]

- Examine congregational practices, such as what is provided for snacks, as they affect health and vitality. Appreciate that others may have health reasons for not consuming the snacks that you offer. Do not take offense.

- At church potlucks, consider taking from dishes that are being neglected by others, so that all will have their contributions valued.

- Exercise "custody of the eyes" (see chapter 3), so as not to visually intrude on another's body, even when you imagine it may be welcome.

- Exercise "Quick Release of Thoughts," which are sexualizing, objectifying, or otherwise inappropriate to your role in congregational life and ministry.

- When physical contact is an integral part of ministry activity, such as in passing the peace, in greeting and parting, or in team-building exercises, give adequate time for others to make a conscious choice about how to participate. Our own practice should be exercised uniformly, so as not to reflect or express favoritism.

- Be aware of the various ways touch can be used for the self-interest of the person initiating the contact: to establish dominance, to elicit trust, to gain reassurance or comfort for the one initiating the

29. Lehr, *Clergy Burnout*, 93–97.

touching, to generate self-arousal, or to excite arousal in the other person.[30]

- If the congregation owns the residence in which the minister lives, church officials should treat access to the property according to the same rules any landlord would need to follow in your municipality.

- When considering whether to make changes to the physical aspects of the church property, make sure you have authorization to do so. The decision-making process of the congregation should be clear. If it's not clear, get it clarified before acting.

Practicing Resource Integrity

A major source of stress is the perception that our resources are over-extended, especially the resources of our time, energy, and finances. This phenomenon adversely affects congregational health insofar as people feel unable or unwilling to contribute the resources needed for congregational vitality. How the congregation respects such resources can help all members become more adept in their stewardship.

- Do not lay claim to another's resources of time, money, or property or allow others to lay claim to your personal resources.

- In order to avoid temptation and the perception of careless behavior in the handling of money, establish and follow policies and procedures.[31] In every arena of congregational life and activity, money should always be handled by two unrelated adults. Resources for such policies and procedures include the congregation's insurance carrier, accounting firm, and denomination.

- Unsolicited donations to the church of personal items one no longer wishes to have, such as used furniture, can be burdensome to those who now have to determine what to do with them without upsetting the giver. This sort of situation can be avoided if potential donors ask in advance whether the items are wanted, and if potential donors are willing to take no for an answer.

- Avoid making personal use of congregational property.

---

30. Cf. Everist and Nessan, *Transforming Leadership*, chap. 10.
31. Trull and Carter, *Ministerial Ethics*, 103.

- Respecting the resource of another person's time includes preparing adequately for activities such as meetings. In order that time is not wasted, start on time and follow a set agenda so that others are not kept waiting, and to avoid needing to brief latecomers about what happened in their absence.

- When asking for another's time, do your best to estimate the amount of time you are requesting and to articulate what it is you are wanting from them.

- In order to be generous with what is most expressive of your core values, assess and monitor how you use your resources of time, energy, and money so that you can live and serve most consistently. Living with coherence is restorative, while living inconsistently is depleting.

- Routinely participate in the gift of Sabbath.[32]

Whew! That is a lot to take in and to work on! And yet the experience that comes down through the ages is that comprehensive disciplines that have relevance for our lives are experienced more as liberating than as oppressive once we get the hang of them. The oppressive ones are the ones that are irrelevant and useless. Relevant disciplines are liberating and life-enhancing because they are expressions of care, and care leads to many wonderful things. These disciplines bring inner equanimity along with more peaceful and productive relationships. We experience more joy, inwardly and shared with others. We are more in tune with the motivations of love and compassion.

A CHURCH ALIVE WITH INTEGRITY

The triune God is a God with a mission. God's purposes in this world involve the sending of Jesus Christ by the power of the Holy Spirit to create life-giving relationships with God, among human beings, and with all of creation.[33] The Bible employs many names to talk about God's purposes for creation: "salvation," "reconciliation," "atonement," "forgiveness," "redemption," and "shalom." While each of these metaphors accents different aspects of God's work, all of them reflect God's central purposes of

32. Brueggemann, *Sabbath as Resistance*, 85–89.
33. Nessan, *Beyond Maintenance to Mission*, chap. 3.

seeking to create life-giving relationships between the triune God and all creation, including human beings made in God's own image. Life-giving relationships between God and humans are fostered through God's coming to us in worship and through the spiritual practices that immerse us in the gift of Sabbath.[34] The first boundary that human beings are called upon to honor and respect involves the worship of God. This is the first of the Ten Commandments, and the premise of the Great Commandment (Matt 22:37-38). In Luther's words, "We are to fear, love, and trust in God above all things."[35]

In order to serve God's purposes of creating life-giving relationships in this world, God in Christ by the power of the Holy Spirit has called forth a community of disciples to serve as the agents of this mission in the world. This community is the body of Christ, consisting of many members with many gifts, all of which gifts have been given for the work of ministry, to build up the body of Christ for the common good of all creation (cf. Eph 4:12). Baptism is the sacrament that mediates God's promises of love, forgiveness, and eternal life in Christ to each member, incorporating them into the body of Christ. At the same time the baptized are given the vocation to serve others for Christ's sake. They are called to serve their neighbors in thought, word, and deed. Their arenas of service include the family, the school, the workplace, the local community, and the global community.

Congregations are local communities of Christian faith called to equip members to participate in serving in God's mission for the life of the world. The core identity of the congregation is to be the body of Christ in a particular context, equipping the members to claim their baptismal promises and to live out the mission of the triune God as disciples, Christ-followers, who share the good news with others and serve the needs of their neighbors. The church has a God-given identity and mission that is its very reason for existence. Church mission statements and constitutions make clear the church's explicit purpose in relation to serving the mission of the triune God in the world. These accord with the Great Tradition of the Christian faith as witnessed in the Scriptures as God's Word and in the creeds and confessions of the church throughout the ages. The church's identity and mission belong entirely to God's purposes of bringing and restoring life-giving relationships in all creation.

---

34. Gula, *Way of Goodness and Holiness*, chaps. 1 and 3.

35. Luther, *Small Catechism*, "Explanation of the First Commandment" 1160.

BEING BODY OF CHRIST WITH INTEGRITY   195

Because of sin, however, the historical existence of the church can and does contradict God's purposes and create many scandals that discredit not only the church but even God. This occurs not only at the level of global communions and national denominations but also at the level of local congregations. There is abundant temptation to idolatry and widespread amnesia that plague local congregations in maintaining their identity in Christ Jesus and fulfilling the mission that God has entrusted to them.[36] Wherever congregations and their members fall short of following their God-given purposes, the witness to God in Christ is contradicted, and service to neighbors is undermined. As God's way of counteracting the waywardness of the church in fulfilling its core identity and mission, God instituted a rule of law to set limits on the harm human beings can do to others. This includes laws, rules, and codes of ethics to govern the functioning of the church and its members. Such measures are necessary to safeguard the church's identity and mission so that people are not harmed and God's healing purposes for the body of Christ are promoted.

This book offers wisdom and direction to the church and its leaders about the many multifaceted and complex boundaries in thought, word, and deed that need careful stewardship, in order to preserve the God-given identity and mission of the church as the body of Christ. The church's functioning is entirely predicated on building and maintaining a climate of trust both among its members and beyond them to all the people affected by its ministry.[37] Too often the church has not recognized the expansive number and variety of boundaries that need tending in order for the church to stay on focus with its central purposes. Discussion of the topic of boundaries is often reduced to consideration of sexual boundaries.[38] As important as sexual boundaries are for the well-being of the church, its members, and all those affected by its ministry, reflection on boundaries in the church needs to become much more expansive to encompass all the kinds of issues discussed in these pages. Another common way that reflecting on boundaries gets minimized is by thinking that these are matters only of concern to church leaders, especially

36. Cf. Blodgett, *Lives Entrusted*.

37. Everist and Nessan, *Transforming Ministry*, chap. 1.

38. Ending clergy sexual misconduct remains an urgent challenge. Cf. Thoburn and Baker, *Clergy Sexual Misconduct*, chap. 1. Conscientiousness about all the other types of boundaries discussed in this book can contribute to clarity also about ethical practice in maintaining sexual boundaries.

pastors.[1] While boundary keeping clearly belongs to the professional responsibility of church leaders, we intentionally have expanded the theme by describing boundaries as a shared endeavor on the part of all church members. Not only how church members act but also how they think and speak about things have great consequences for the success or failing of the church's identity and mission.

If the church is the body of Christ, then the ethical principles and best practices highlighted in this book belong to the skeleton of that body, providing the structure upon which all else depends for its healthy support. We have described a range of boundary questions and have proposed specific ways to address them, placing ethical responsibility on church leaders and members not only for how they act but also for the things that always precede actions: how we choose to think and speak about a given issue. It is our contention that it is possible to discipline not only how we speak but also how we choose to think about boundary questions in ways that foster God's life-giving purposes for creation. This contradicts much conventional wisdom, which claims we are not responsible for our thoughts but only for what we do with them. However, our approach more accords with the teachings of Jesus in the Sermon on the Mount (Matt 5:21–48) and with the apostle Paul's teaching that Jesus's disciples "have the mind of Christ" (Phil 2:5). This mind affects how we think about the world, including how we think about other persons.

The analysis of human behavior in this book is based not only on biblical and theological wisdom but on much clinical evidence about how human beings function and how they go astray. It is possible for congregations—both members and leaders—to attain a greater degree of insight into their behavior and to adopt practices that better preserve and accord with the core identity and mission of the church as the body of Christ. By naming best practices of boundary keeping in this chapter, we have aimed to synthesize the themes of the previous chapters in very concrete and usable terms. We, however, encourage readers to keep in mind that the impetus for this book is not so much to provide a how-to manual but rather to enhance the integrity of the body of Christ in fulfilling its God-given identity and mission. We enhance the body's integrity through reflecting upon and learning from the mistakes of others and through abiding by ethical practices that will strengthen the church's witness to God's love for the world in Jesus Christ.

Guide for Reflection and Discussion

PART 1: DEFINING AND PROTECTING INTEGRITY THROUGH BOUNDARIES

Chapter 1: The Necessity of Boundaries for Creating and Sustaining Identity and Effective Mission

1. Some good boundary keeping is invisible, while much is apparent. Who, over the course of your lifetime, has most impressed you as having good boundaries? How would you describe what impresses you about that person's boundary keeping?

2. How would you describe the feelings inside you that occur when you feel someone has disrespected your boundaries? Please note that feeling violated can bring forth strong emotions or shame, which are hard to share with others. Please respect this about yourself and others.

3. What elements of boundary keeping have you experienced in a tradition other than your own? What was it like for you to do something important to someone else but not to yourself? One example might be taking your shoes off to enter a place that is sacred to someone else.

4. It can be difficult and awkward for someone to stand up for themselves to enforce a boundary. Sometimes you might notice a difference in another's language use, or an edge to their voice when they are standing up for themselves. What has helped you learn to stand up for yourself gracefully under such circumstances?

5. In what ways is the identity of the church intended to be different from other organizations that have a different purpose?

6. What are the most hopeful and exciting insights for you from this chapter? What action items do you take from this chapter?

Chapter 2: Entrustment

1. People in positions of power or authority may tell you to trust them, which can mean that they are telling you to relinquish control to them. Entrustment, by contrast, does not take anything away from the other person. Entrustment means that the people God has entrusted to our care retain their power and rights over their well-being, not us. The question, who does this belong to? can help us keep that straight. Think of examples where this question is significant in your congregation.

2. Identify instances when people have mistreated or misrepresented what another person has said to them, including how you might have done that recently. Contrast this with examples of when someone acted to protect the integrity of what someone else said.

3. Consider people in your congregation whose service has recently gone unnoticed or was not adequately appreciated. How might you remedy that?

4. Think of an example of when someone thought there was a boundary violation that you did not agree with. Were you quick to disagree, or did you pause to inquire about and understand what they were pointing out? Why did you respond in this particular way?

5. Anticipate the next time you will be faced with an ethical or boundary issue. Identify whom you might consult with about it: someone who is good about boundary keeping and is willing to tell you things you might not want to hear.

6. What are the most hopeful and exciting insights for you from this chapter? What action items do you take from this chapter?

Chapter 3: Role Integrity

1. A diplomatic person can tell someone something they do not want to hear in such a way that the person is grateful and thanks them for it. Think of a time someone gave you input about yourself that was hard to hear but helpful in the long run.

2. Effective mutual accountability requires emotional maturity and skill. Otherwise we will give in to discomfort and will not engage in accountability practices. Or we might be harsh in how we speak or how we hear critical input. Think of the people you know who are graceful about giving and receiving mutual accountability. What are the particular characteristics you might learn from them?

3. List all of the separate roles you are in, and the functions you perform in your congregation. How well defined are these roles in ways that all those involved understand them? What might your congregation do to clarify those roles for yourself and others? Think of a situation in your congregation where you have more than one role with another person or other persons. What does it take for you to stay most faithful to your primary role?

4. How might you better set aside personal friendships for the sake of open and equal fellowship with other people at church with whom you are not friends? What relationships do you need to set aside, in order to relate to others in your role as a congregation member?

5. What has helped you get more comfortable with saying no to what someone wants from you? What could help you get more comfortable? What has helped you get more comfortable taking no for an answer from others? What could help you get more comfortable?

6. What are the most hopeful and exciting insights for you from this chapter? What action items do you take from this chapter?

PART 2: INTEGRITY OF COMMUNITY

Chapter 4: Integrity in Worship

1. What helps you transition your mind and heart so that you can fully participate in worship? What are the most challenging things for you to set aside in order to focus attentively on worship? What are

the most challenging distractions for you during worship? What is it like for you to put to voice parts of the service or parts of hymns that you do not believe or do not agree with? What can help you treat worship and the worship space as being more sacred?

2. If the members of your church exchange greetings with each other or pass the peace during worship, are there ways you treat people differently during that time based on your personal relationships with them?

3. Engaging with God during worship—through the words spoken in the service, heard in a sermon, or sung in the music—can express a wide variety of feelings, from remorse to joy and celebration. How fully do you let yourself feel and express those feelings?

4. Are there ways others try to relate to you while you are at church for worship according to a role that you have during the rest of the week? How might you redirect that back to your baptismal identity at worship and your roles with each other as Christians?

5. In what ways does the gospel you hear in church indict what you do in your daily life? In what ways does the gospel indict how you treat others? Who in your congregation is most challenging for you to see through the eyes of Christ?

6. What are the most hopeful and exciting insights for you from this chapter? What action items do you take from this chapter?

Chapter 5: Bearing Witness: Integrity in Interaction and Communication

1. The human mind does not like not knowing or leaving questions unanswered. For that reason we speculate a lot about the things that might happen, including about other people, which risks creating false images of them. Can you recall a recent incident when you or someone else engaged in speculation about another person? What would have been lost if you had resisted doing so?

2. In what ways is it difficult for you to show your own differences and uniqueness with others in the congregation? What are important spiritual experiences you have had that might benefit others if they

could hear about them? In what ways does the culture of your congregation bring out the best in you?

3. In what ways does the culture of your congregation encourage gossiping about others or other harmful behavior that involves speaking about others in ways that benefit the speaker at the expense of someone else? What role do you play when someone vents their feelings about others or otherwise portrays another negatively? In what ways does your congregation create values and ways of being that contrast with the community around you?

4. How we treat people in our own minds is as much an ethical matter as our outward behavior. Listening and understanding without interpreting or distorting what the other person is saying is both difficult and rare. How might you practice getting better at this, and who might help you with it?

5. Jesus said that how we treat the least important person is how we treat him. Which people in your day do you treat as least important or unimportant? If you were only to say things that you are sure are honest, true, kind and helpful, would you need to give up anything that is important to you?

6. What are the most hopeful and exciting insights for you from this chapter? What action items do you take from this chapter?

Chapter 6: Sabbath Shalom: A Day in the Kingdom

1. One impediment to meaningful Sabbath keeping is the belief that we need to spend our time with practical matters, so that time off from those concerns makes us uneasy. Walter Brueggemann thinks most of us simply "go through the motions" of keeping Sabbath without getting into it deeply. What does "going through the motions" mean for you?

2. Numbing out is one way to reduce the feeling of stress, though it clouds our awareness. What are your preferred ways of numbing out? What might be the benefit of entering into the practices of Sabbath rather than numbing out? What benefits of Sabbath practice described in this chapter are you most drawn to at this point in your life?

3. Think of a time you and another person had the freedom to go deeply into a conversation, getting to know each other and yourselves better. How can your Sabbath time regularly create the conditions for such encounters?

4. Thinking about work is work. Pastor Rob Bell and others have found that they need to get through a zone of depression or other types of discomfort before they arrive into deeper levels of Sabbath freedom. How are you doing at getting closure with thoughts about work so you can get deeply into other parts of your life? What could help you better do this?

5. Meaningful Sabbath helps us keep our bearings on the "true north" that Jesus points toward. How disruptive is true north for you at this point, given how you are living your life? If you had more courage, what changes would you make in your work or life?

6. What are the most hopeful and exciting insights for you from this chapter? What action items do you take from this chapter?

PART 3: INTEGRITY OF PERSONS

Chapter 7: The Pastor as Person

Questions for Clergy:

1. The pastor's personal life can get neglected when there is not enough time or psychological distance from pastoral responsibilities. What feelings and thoughts occur to you with the idea of receiving a Pastor-of-the-Year award? How are you doing at taking your weekly personal days and annual vacation time?

2. In what ways do you allow your personal life and personal concerns to encroach on the time designated for your pastoral role? How do your continuing education choices directly benefit your congregation rather than your personal interests?

3. What aspects of your early life led you to pastoral ministry? What unhealthy dynamics in your family of origin are you still carrying and perpetuating? Are there ways that serving as a pastor perpetuates certain roles you played in your family of origin? Are there ways that the ministry compensates for what was missing in your

childhood? In what ways are you at risk of shaping your ministry to meet your own needs?

4. How are you doing at dealing with criticism objectively? What practices can help you with this? What blind spots have others claimed that you have? How do you go about trying to solicit input on your blind spots? Who do you have available to confide in, who can help you be objective about yourself, your congregation, and pastoral ministry?

5. How are you doing at gracefully and effectively initiating conflict or contrast in your ministry? In your personal life? How are you doing at cultivating compassionate awareness of yourself rather than resorting to shaming or blaming awareness of yourself?

6. What are the most hopeful and exciting insights for you from this chapter? What action items do you take from this chapter?

Questions for Church Members:

1. As an individual, what boundary keeping helps you support the personal well-being of your pastor?

2. As a congregation, what boundary keeping helps you support the personal well-being of your pastor?

3. What are the most hopeful and exciting insights for you from this chapter? What action items do you take from this chapter?

Chapter 8: Boundaries as Shared Responsibility by Church Members

1. Do you think of your participation in the life of the congregation as a volunteer—as something you could do or not do as it suits you? Or do you consider your congregational participation as a responsibility that comes with being a part of the ministry of the congregation? How can you tell when your actions in congregational life are overly self-motivated? How might you apply the principle that the conduct you expect of your pastor is also what you expect of yourself?

2. Are there ways that your church involvement perpetuates the roles you played in the dynamics of your family of origin? Are there ways

that your church involvement is attempting to compensate for what is otherwise missing in your life? What helps you say no when that is the healthiest decision? What helps you take no for an answer from someone else?

3. How are you doing at dealing with criticism objectively? What role do you play in anonymous complaints or anonymous input? How are you doing at gracefully and effectively initiating conflict or contrast in your congregational life? In your personal life? What practices can help you with this?

4. How comfortable are you dealing with those in the congregation who insist on getting their own way? How comfortable are you taking charge in the congregation when the situation calls for it? How comfortable are you at yielding to others in the congregation when the situation calls for it?

5. How are you doing at cultivating compassionate awareness of yourself rather than resorting to shaming or blaming awareness of yourself? When and how do you most strongly feel God's love and acceptance toward you and toward everyone else? How can you connect with this more often?

6. What are the most hopeful and exciting insights for you from this chapter? What action items do you take from this chapter?

Chapter 9: Being the Body of Christ with Integrity: Toward Best Practices in Boundary Keeping

1. How do your personality and temperament relate to the recommended best practices? With which recommended best practices do you disagree? Why?

2. Which of the practices in this book do you think are most helpful for your congregation? Why?

3. Which of the practices in this book are the most important for you to adopt personally? Why?

4. What are some other practices not described in this book that can help you to keep healthy boundaries? How do they do so?

5. This book makes the case that a faithful congregation will proclaim and do things that make you and others uncomfortable. In what ways do consumer motives affect your congregation and your role in it? How do the needs of your congregation challenge you to be different than you would be if you just let your personal preferences control you?

6. What are the most hopeful and exciting insights for you from this chapter? What action items do you take from this chapter?

Bibliography

Albers, Robert H. *Shame: A Faith Perspective.* Binghamton, NY: Haworth, 1995.

Anderson, T. Carlos. *Just a Little Bit More: The Culture of Excess and the Fate of the Common Good.* Austin: Blue Ocotillo, 2014.

Armstrong, Karen. *Through the Narrow Gate: A Memoir of Spiritual Discovery.* New York: St. Martin's, 2005.

Assagioli, Roberto. *Psychosynthesis: A Collection of Basic Writings.* Amherst, MA: Synthesis Center, 2000.

Bacher, Robert N., and Michael L. Cooper-White. *Church Administration: Programs, Process, Purpose.* Minneapolis: Fortress, 2007.

Bailey, James L. *Contrast Community: Practicing the Sermon on the Mount.* Eugene, OR: Wipf & Stock, 2013.

Bash, Anthony. *Forgiveness: A Theology.* Cascade Companions 19. Eugene, OR: Cascade Books, 2015.

Batchelor, Valli Boobal, ed. *When Pastors Prey: Overcoming Clergy Sexual Abuse of Women.* Geneva: World Council of Churches Publications, 2013.

Bates, Brian, and John Cleese. *The Human Face.* New York: Dorling Kindersley, 2001.

Bazerman, Max H., and Ann E. Tenbrunsel. *Blind Spots: Why We Fail to Do What's Right and What to Do about It.* Princeton: Princeton University Press, 2011.

Bazerman, Max H. et al. "Negotiating with Yourself and Losing: Making Decisions with Competing Internal Preferences." *Academy of Management Review* 23 (1998) 225–41

Beck, Ulrich. *A God of One's Own: Religion's Capacity for Peace and Potential for Violence.* Cambridge: Polity, 2010.

Bell, Rob. *Velvet Elvis: Repainting the Christian Faith.* New York: HarperCollins, 2005.

Blodgett, Barbara J. *Lives Entrusted: An Ethic of Trust for Ministry.* Prisms. Minneapolis: Fortress, 2008.

Bonhoeffer, Dietrich. *Life Together; Prayerbook of the Bible.* Translated by Daniel W. Bloesch and James H. Burtness. Dietrich Bonhoeffer Works 5. Minneapolis: Fortress, 1996.

Borgmann, Albert. *Crossing the Postmodern Divide.* Chicago: University of Chicago, 1992.

Brown, Brené. *Daring Greatly: How the Courage to Be Vulnerable Transforms the Way We Live, Love, Parent, and Lead.* New York: Gotham, 2012.

Brown, Robert McAffe, ed. *The Essential Reinhold Niebuhr: Selected Essays and Addresses.* New Haven: Yale University Press, 1986.

Browning, Don S. *Religious Ethics and Pastoral Care.* Theology and Pastoral Care Series. Minneapolis: Fortress, 2009.

Brueggemann, Walter. *The Covenanted Self: Explorations in Law and Covenant.* Minneapolis: Fortress, 1999.

———. *Sabbath as Resistance: Saying No to the Culture of Now.* Louisville: Westminster John Knox, 2014.

Buber, Martin. *I and Thou.* Translated by Ronald Gregor Smith. 2nd ed. New York: Scribner, 1958.

Burns, David D. *The Feeling Good Handbook: Using the New Mood Therapy in Everyday Life.* New York: Morrow, 1989.

Bush, Joseph E., Jr. *Gentle Shepherding: Pastoral Ethics and Leadership.* St. Louis: Chalice, 2006.

Campbell, Troy H., and Aaron C. Kay. "Solution Aversion: On the Relation between Ideology and Motivated Disbelief." *Journal of Personality and Social Psychology* 107 (2014) 809–24.

Cannon, Katie Geneva et al., eds. *Womanist Theological Ethics: A Reader.* Louisville: Westminster John Knox, 2011.

Ched, Graham, writer and producer; with Larry Engel, dir. of photography, et al. *The Human Spark, with Alan Alda.* Originally produced in 2007. Originally broadcast as a three-part miniseries on PBS in 2009. Produced by Ched-Angier-Lewis Productions. DVD. Boston: PBS Productions, 2010.

Chopp, Rebecca S. *The Power to Speak: Feminism, Language, God.* New York: Crossroad, 1989.

Center for Faith and Giving. "Building a Narrative Budget." http://www.centerforfaithandgiving.org/Resources/AdministrativeResources/BuildingaNarrativeBudget/tabid/950/Default.aspx/

Cloud, Henry. *Boundaries for Leaders: Results, Relationships, and Being Ridiculously in Charge.* New York: HarperCollins, 2013.

Cooper-White, Pamela. *The Cry of Tamar: Violence against Women and the Church's Response.* Minneapolis: Fortress, 1995.

———. *Shared Wisdom: Use of the Self in Pastoral Care and Counseling.* Minneapolis: Fortress, 2004.

Darley, J. M., and C. D. Batson. "From Jerusalem to Jericho: A Study of Situational and Dispositional Variables in Helping Behavior." *Journal of Personality and Social Psychology* 27 (1973) 100–108.

Davidson, Donald. *The Essential Davidson.* Oxford: Clarendon, 2006.

Dickhart, Judith McWilliams. *Church-Going Insider or Gospel-Carrying Outsider? A Different View of Congregations.* Chicago: ELCA Division for Ministry, 2002.

Doblmeier, Martin, dir. *The Power of Forgiveness.* Produced by Dan Juday and Adele Schmidt. DVD. Alexandria VA: Journey Films, 2007 (New York: First Run Features, distributor).

Doehring, Carrie. *Taking Care: Monitoring Power Dynamics and Relational Boundaries in Pastoral Care and Counseling.* Nashville: Abingdon, 1995.

Epley, Nicholas, and Eugene M. Caruso. "Egocentric Ethics." *Social Justice Research* 17 (2004) 171–87.

Evangelical Lutheran Church in America. "Affirmation of Baptism." In *Evangelical Lutheran Worship,* 234–37. Minneapolis: Augsburg Fortress, 2006.

———. *Small Catechism,* by Martin Luther. In *Evangelical Lutheran Worship,* by the Evangelical Lutheran Church in America, 1160–67. Minneapolis: Augsburg Fortress, 2006.

——."A Social Statement on Sufficient, Sustainable Livelihood for All." Adopted by a more than two-thirds majority vote by the sixth Churchwide Assembly of the Evangelical Lutheran Church in America, meeting in Denver, Colorado, August 16–22, 1999. http://download.elca.org/ELCA%20Resource%20Repository/Economic_LifeSS.pdf/.

Everist, Norma Cook. *The Church as Learning Community: A Comprehensive Guide to Christian Education.* Nashville: Abingdon, 2002.

——. *Church Conflict: From Contention to Collaboration.* Nashville: Abingdon, 2004.

Everist, Norma Cook, and Craig L. Nessan. *Transforming Leadership: New Vision for a Church in Mission.* Minneapolis: Fortress, 2008.

Fortin, Jack. *The Centered Life: Awakened, Called, Set Free, Nurtured.* Minneapolis: Augsburg Fortress, 2006.

Fortune, Marie M. *Is Nothing Sacred? The Story of a Pastor, the Women He Sexually Abused, and the Congregation He Nearly Destroyed.* 1999. Reprinted, Eugene: Wipf & Stock, 2008.

——. *Love Does No Harm: Sexual Ethics for the Rest of Us.* New York: Continuum, 1998.

Foss, Michael W. *From Members to Disciples: Leadership Lessons from the Book of Acts.* Nashville: Abingdon, 2007.

Frankl, Viktor E. *Man's Search for Meaning.* 4th ed. Boston: Beacon, 1992.

Franklin, Robert M. *Crisis in the Village: Restoring Hope in African American Communities.* Minneapolis: Fortress, 2007.

Friberg, Nils C., and Mark R. Laaser. *Before the Fall: Preventing Pastoral Sexual Abuse.* Collegeville, MN: Liturgical, 1998.

Gaede, Beth Ann, ed. *When a Congregation Is Betrayed: Responding to Clergy Misconduct.* Bethesda, MD: Alban Institute, 2006.

Gentile, Mary C. *Giving Voice to Values: How to Speak Your Mind When You Know What's Right.* New Haven: Yale University, 2012.

Giere, Samuel D. *With Ears to Hear.* http://www.withearstohear.org/.

Grenz, Stanley J., and Roy D. Bell. *Betrayal of Trust: Confronting and Preventing Clergy Sexual Misconduct.* Grand Rapids: Baker, 2001.

Güggenbühl-Craig, Adolf. *Power in the Helping Professions.* Translated by Myron Gubitz. Thompson, CT: Spring, 2009.

Gula, Richard M. *Ethics in Pastoral Ministry.* Mahwah, NJ: Paulist, 1996.

——. *Just Ministry: Professional Ethics for Pastoral Ministers.* Mahwah, NJ: Paulist, 2010.

——. *The Way of Goodness and Holiness: A Spirituality for Pastoral Ministers.* Collegeville, MN: Liturgical, 2011.

Halstead, Kenneth A. *From Stuck to Unstuck: Overcoming Congregational Impasse.* Bethesda, MD: Alban Institute, 1998.

Harbaugh, Gary L. *The Pastor as Person: Maintaining Personal Integrity in the Choices and Challenges of Ministry.* Minneapolis: Augsburg, 1984.

Harbaugh, Gary L. et al. *Covenants and Care: Boundaries in Life, Faith, and Ministry.* Minneapolis: Fortress, 1998.

Hedahl, Susan K. *Listening Ministry: Rethinking Pastoral Leadership.* Minneapolis: Fortress, 2001.

Hess, Carol Lakey. *Caretakers of Our Common House: Women's Development in Communities of Faith.* Nashville: Abingdon, 1997.

Heyward, Carter. *When Boundaries Betray Us: Beyond Illusions of What Is Ethical in Therapy and Life*. San Francisco: HarperSanFrancisco, 1994.

Hinrichs, Jonathan, Jared DeFife, and Drew Westen. "Personality Subtypes in Adolescent and Adult Children of Alcoholics: A Two Part Study." *Journal of Nervous and Mental Disorders* 199 (2011) 487–98.

hooks, bell. *Killing Rage: Ending Racism*. New York: Holt, 1995.

Hopkins, Dwight N. *Being Human: Race, Culture, and Religion*. Minneapolis: Fortress, 2005.

Hopkins, Nancy Myer, and Mark Laaser, eds. *Restoring the Soul of a Church: Healing Congregations Wounded by Clergy Sexual Misconduct*. Collegeville, MN: Liturgical, 1995.

Hunter, Mic. *Back to the Source: The Spiritual Principles of Jesus*. Amazon: CreateSpace Independent Publishing, 2011.

Jameson, Frederic. *Postmodernism, or The Cultural Logic of Late Capitalism*. Durham: Duke University Press, 1991.

Jennings, Willie James. *The Christian Imagination: Theology and the Origins of Race*. New Haven: Yale University, 2010.

Jung, Patricia Beattie, and Darryl W. Stephens, eds. *Professional Sexual Ethics: A Holistic Ministry Approach*. Minneapolis: Fortress, 2013.

Kanyoro, Musimbi R. A. *Introducing Feminist Cultural Hermeneutics: An African Perspective*. Cleveland: Pilgrim, 2002.

Kaptein, Muel. *Workplace Morality: Behavioral Ethics in Organizations*. Bingly, UK: Emerald Group, 2013.

Karjala, Lynn Mary. *Understanding Trauma and Dissociation*. Atlanta: ThomasMax, 2007.

Kerns, Charles D. "Why Good Leaders Do Bad Things: Mental Gymnastics behind Unethical Behavior." *Grazaido Business Review* 6.4 (2003). <http://gbr.pepperdine.edu/2010/08/why-good-leaders-do-bad-things/>. September 8, 2015.

Kerper, Michael. "Loss of Leisure Time, Loss of Faith." <http://universespirit.org/loss-of-leisure-time-loss-of-faith> July 14, 2015.

Kierkegaard, Søren. *Concluding Unscientific Postscript*. Translated by David F. Swenson. Princeton: Princeton University Press, 1944.

Kolodiejchuk, Brian, ed. *Mother Teresa—Come Be My Light: The Private Writings of the "Saint of Calcutta."* New York: Doubleday, 2007.

LaCugna, Catherine Mowry. *God for Us: The Trinity and the Christian Life*. New York: HarperCollins, 1993.

Lathrop, Gordon W. *Holy Things: A Liturgical Theology*. Minneapolis: Fortress, 1993.

———. *The Pastor: A Spirituality*. Minneapolis: Fortress, 2006.

Law, Eric H. F. *Sacred Acts, Holy Change: Faithful Diversity and Practical Transformation*. St. Louis: Chalice, 2002.

———. *The Wolf Shall Dwell with the Lamb: A Spirituality for Leadership in a Multicultural Community*. St. Louis: Chalice, 1993.

Lebacqz, Karen. *Professional Ethics: Power and Paradox*. Nashville: Abingdon, 1985.

Lebacqz, Karen, and Joseph D. Driskill. *Ethics and Spiritual Care: A Guide for Pastors, Chaplains, and Spiritual Directors*. Nashville: Abingdon, 2000.

Lehr, Fred. *Clergy Burnout: Recovering from the 70-Hour Work Week and Other Self-Defeating Practices*. Prisms. Minneapolis: Fortress, 2006.

Levine, Robert A. *A Geography of Time: The Temporal Misadventures of a Social Psychologist.* New York: Basic Books, 1998.

Luther, Martin. *The Freedom of a Christian.* Translated and introduced by Mark D. Tranvik. Minneapolis: Fortress, 2008.

Marty, Martin. *Baptism: A User's Guide.* Minneapolis: Augsburg, 2008.

McGonigal, Kelly. *The Willpower Instinct: How Self-Control Works, Why It Matters, and What You Can Do to Get More of It.* New York: Penguin, 2012.

McLaren, Brian D. *A New Kind of Christian: A Tale of Two Friends on a Spiritual Journey.* San Francisco: Jossey-Bass, 2001.

Menking, Wayne L. *When All Else Fails: Rethinking Our Pastoral Vocation in Times of Stuck.* Eugene, OR: Wipf & Stock, 2013.

Merton, Thomas. *Conjectures of a Guilty Bystander.* New York: Doubleday, 1965.

———. *New Seeds of Contemplation.* New York: New Directions, 1961.

———. *Seeds of Contemplation.* 1949. Reprinted, New York: Dell, 1960.

Mockenhaupt, Brian. "Confessions of a Whistleblower." *AARP Bulletin* (September 2014). http://www.aarp.org/politics-society/advocacy/info-2014/dr-sam-foote-va-whistleblower.2.html/.

Nessan, Craig L. *Beyond Maintenance to Mission: A Theology of the Congregation.* 2nd ed. Minneapolis: Fortress, 2010.

———. "Sex, Aggression, and Pain: Sociobiological Implications for Theological Anthropology." *Zygon* 33 (1998) 443–54.

———. *Shalom Church: The Body of Christ as Ministering Community.* Minneapolis: Fortress, 2010.

———. "Surviving Congregational Leadership: A Theology of Family Systems," *Word and World* 20 (200) 390–99.

Nouwen, Henri J. M. *Life of the Beloved: Spiritual Living in a Secular World.* New York: Crossroad, 1992.

———. *Making All Things New: An Invitation to the Spiritual Life.* New York: Harper-Collins, 1981.

Nussbaum, Martha C. *Upheavals of Thought: The Intelligence of Emotions.* New York: Cambridge University Press, 2001.

Olsen, David C., and Nancy G. Devor. *Saying No to Say Yes: Everyday Boundaries and Pastoral Excellence.* Lanham, MD: Rowman & Littlefield, 2015.

Perrin, Norman. *Jesus and the Language of the Kingdom: Symbol and Metaphor in New Testament Interpretation.* Philadelphia: Fortress, 1976.

Peterson, Marilyn R. *At Personal Risk: Boundary Violations in Professional-Client Relationships.* New York: Norton, 1992.

Putnam, Robert D. *Bowling Alone: The Collapse and Revival of American Community.* New York: Simon & Schuster, 2000.

Ragsdale, Katherine Hancock, ed. *Boundary Wars: Intimacy and Distance in Healing Relationships.* Cleveland: Pilgrim, 1996.

Rendle, Gil. *Behavioral Covenants in Congregations: A Handbook for Honoring Differences.* Bethesda, MD: Alban, 1998.

Richardson, Ronald W. *Becoming a Healthier Pastor: Family Systems Theory and the Pastor's Own Family.* Minneapolis: Fortress, 2005.

Ridley, Matt. *The Red Queen: Sex and the Evolution of Human Nature.* New York: Perennial, 2003.

Riggs, Marcia. "Living as Religious Ethical Mediators: A Vocation for People of Faith in the Twenty-first Century." In *Womanist Theological Ethics: A Reader*, edited by Katie Geneva Cannon et al., 247–53. Louisville: Westminster John Knox, 2011.

Roberto, Michael A. *The Art of Critical Decision Making*. The Great Courses DVD. Chantilly, VA: Teaching Company, 2009.

Romero, Oscar A. *The Violence of Love: The Pastoral Wisdom of Archbishop Oscar Romero*. Compiled and translated by James R. Brockman. New York: Harper & Row, 1988.

Salter, Daniel et al. "Development of Sexually Abusive Behaviour in Sexually Victimised Males: A Longitudinal Study." *The Lancet* 361 (2003) 471–76.

Schmit, Clayton J. *Sent and Gathered: A Worship Manual for the Missional Church*. Grand Rapids: Baker Academic, 2009.

"Sensory Illusions in Aviation." https://en.wikipedia.org/wiki/Sensory_illusions_in_aviation.

Sevig, Julie B., and Michael D. Watson. "Bullying the Pastor." *The Lutheran* 24 (January 2011): <http://www.thelutheran.org/article/article.cfm?article_id=9636&key=92852494> July 26, 2015.

Snow, Luther K. *The Power of Asset Mapping: How Your Congregation Can Act on Its Gifts*. Herndon, VA: Alban Institute, 2004.

Sternberg, Robert J., and Susan T. Fiske, eds. *Ethical Challenges in the Behavioral and Brain Sciences*. New York: Cambridge University Press, 2015.

Substance Abuse and Mental Health Services Association. *Spiritual Caregiving to Help Addicted Persons and Families*. Rockville, MD: SAMHSA, 2007.

Sue, Derald Wing, ed. *Microaggressions and Marginality: Manifestation, Dynamics, and Impact*. Hoboken, NJ: Wiley, 2010.

Tanner, Kathryn. *Theories of Culture: A New Agenda for Theology*. Guides to Theological Inquiry. Minneapolis: Fortress, 1997.

Taylor, Barbara Brown. *Leaving Church: A Memoir of Faith*. New York: HarperOne, 2006.

Tenbrunsel, Ann E., and David M. Messick. "Ethical Fading: The Role of Self-Deception in Unethical Behavior." *Social Justice Research* 17 (2004) 171–87.

Tillich, Paul. *Love, Power, and Justice: Ontological Analyses and Ethical Implications*. Galaxy Book. New York: Oxford University Press, 1960.

Thoburn, John, and Rob Baker, with Maria Dal Maso, eds. *Clergy Sexual Misconduct: A Systems Approach to Prevention, Intervention, and Oversight*. Carefree, AZ: Gentle Path, 2011.

Thomas, Kim. *Even God Rested: Why It's Okay for Women to Slow Down*. Eugene, OR: Harvest House, 2003.

Trull, Joe E., and James E. Carter. *Ministerial Ethics: Moral Formation for Church Leaders*. Grand Rapids: Baker Academic, 2004.

Ubeda, Paloma. "The Consistency of Fairness Rules: An Experimental Study." *Journal of Economic Psychology* 41 (2014) 88–100.

Vaughan, Judith. *Sociality, Ethics, and Social Change: A Critical Appraisal of Reinhold Niebuhr's Ethics in the Light of Rosemary Radford Ruether's Works*. Lanham, MD: University Press of America, 1983.

Vingerhoets, A. J., M. Van Huijgevoort, and G. L. van Heck. "Leisure Sickness: A Pilot Study on Its Prevalence, Phenomenology, and Background." *Logo Psychotherapy and Psychosomatics* 71 (2002) 311–17.

Walsh, James, ed. *The Cloud of Unknowing*. Mahwah, NJ: Paulist, 1981.

Wedel, Theodore O. "Evangelism—the Mission of the Church to Those Outside Her Life." *Ecumenical Review* 6 (1953) 19–25.

Whitehead, James D., and Evelyn Eaton Whitehead. *Transforming Our Painful Emotions: Spiritual Resources in Anger, Shame, Grief, Fear, and Loneliness*. Maryknoll, NY: Orbis, 2010.

Wilson, Michael Todd, and Brad Hoffmann. *Preventing Ministry Failure: A ShepherdCare Guide for Pastors, Ministers and Other Caregivers*. Downers Grove, IL: InterVarsity, 2007.

Wingren, Gustav. *Creation and Law*. Translated by Ross MacKenzie. Philadelphia: Muhlenberg, 1961.

———. *Luther on Vocation*. Translated by Carl C. Rasmussen. Philadelphia: Muhlenberg, 1957.

Woititz, Janet Geringer. *Adult Children of Alcoholics*. Deerfield Beach, FL: Health Communications, 1983.

Woodley, Randy S. *Shalom and the Community of Creation: An Indigenous Vision*. Grand Rapids: Eerdmans, 2012.

Index of Names

Index of Subjects

wisdom, ix, 34, 37, 71, 127, 129, 162,
       172, 195–96
wishful thinking, 41, 181
whistle blowing, 113–14
worship, 19, 23–26, 34–35, 46,
       51–52, 55–56, 65–76, 81, 99,
       104, 110, 113, 118, 120, 125–
       26, 142, 150, 152, 163–64,
       179, 190, 194

zero tolerance, 6, 53

In 2007, the *Economist* published yet another special report on the American South, showing the magazine's continued fascination with the region. The weekly admitted that the South still lagged behind in education compared to the rest of the country and that its prosperity was unevenly spread but asked its readers: "What other region with such a turbulent history is now so pleasant to live in?" In the years 2004–2005 the South had attracted some 1.3 million people from other parts of the United States, including many African Americans and Mexican immigrants. "And all who come," the *Economist* emphasized, "come voluntarily." It was clear to the magazine that "the South has shed some of its bad habits, but none of its charm," and it described the region as "peaceful, pleasant and prosperous." For the *Economist* the question was no longer "will the South rise again?" but "will it one day overtake the North?"[8]

Echoing their U.S. colleagues, many European scholars of American history and culture have also developed a sustained interest in the South. Since 1988 this interest finds expression in the Southern Studies Forum, a group of historians and literary scholars from Europe and the United States who meet at workshops during the biennial conferences of the European Association for American Studies and at theme-based symposia. In 2005, for instance, the Southern Studies Forum meeting was held at the Roosevelt Study Center in Middelburg, the Netherlands, and resulted in the publication of a collection of essays entitled *Poverty and Progress in the U.S. South since 1920*.[9] In April 2011 the Roosevelt Study Center reaffirmed its commitment to southern studies when it organized a conference entitled "The U.S. South and Europe" as part of its biennial conferences on American history, which include participants from both sides of the Atlantic. The papers given at the 2011 meeting focused on various aspects of the relationship between the American South and Europe throughout the nineteenth and twentieth centuries.

As editors of the ensuing volume we believe that the scholarship presented at the 2011 Middelburg conference merits the interest of a wider audience. To begin with, the following essays demonstrate that the history of the encounter between the U.S. South and Europe is an emerging field and an excellent case in point that the study of American history—and southern history at that—benefits from a transnational perspective.[10] In the last decade a number of scholars have made an effort to study southern engagement with the world.[11] It is our aim in this volume to broaden an existing historiographical current that deals with the U.S. South in transatlantic history with more subtle and fine-grained perspectives on encounters between that region and Europe. To be sure, there is important comparative work that includes the southern experience. Obviously the American South looms large in the study of world slavery. Several books on the vicissitudes of modern nation building also include the South, such as Don H. Doyle's comparison between the American South and the Italian South and Wolfgang Schivelbusch's *Culture of Defeat,* which looks into how the former Confederates, France after the Franco-Prussian War, and Weimar Germany after World War I dealt with defeat.[12] Yet transnational history, defined as "the movement of peoples, ideas, technologies and institutions across national boundaries,"[13] has largely bypassed the American South, arguably because of Dixie's presumed cultural isolation. One recent exception is Andrew Zimmerman's book *Alabama in Africa,* which traces the attempt of German authorities to establish cotton plantations and a labor system modeled on southern agriculture in the colony of Togo with the help of African American experts from Tuskegee Institute, but the author's claim to the historical significance of this early twentieth-century episode appears vastly inflated.[14]

Surprisingly enough, there is no synthesis of the encounter between the American South and Europe. This volume seeks to lay the groundwork for future research by bringing together scholarship from a variety of perspectives. The following essays cover the time period from the antebellum era through the second half of the twentieth century, and they offer readers a multifaceted view of the political, cultural, and religious dimensions of this transatlantic relationship. Topics include mutual perceptions of the South and Europe in travel accounts, the hotly debated issues of slavery and lynching, religious fundamentalism, European reactions to representations of the South in popular films, the Jim Crow South, and the civil rights movement, as well as southern views on European decolonization.

In the seventeenth and eighteenth centuries the southern colonies of British North America were an integral part of the economic, political, and cultural networks that historians have termed the Atlantic world.[15] After the founding of the United States, the American South maintained close economic ties to Great Britain and Europe at large. After all, the South supplied Europe's textile mills with the cotton that its leaders famously declared to be "king." Secessionists were supremely confident that the European powers' dependence on southern cotton would force them to recognize the Confederacy.[16] Nevertheless, with the exception of Confederate diplomacy during the Civil War, historians have paid little attention to nineteenth- and twentieth-century relations between the American South and Europe. One main reason for this neglect was that the waves of European immigration to the United States both before and after the Civil War largely bypassed the southern states. Compared to the other sections of the United States, there were much fewer personal ties between the South and Europe. Moreover, the postbellum South lay prostrate and appeared to be cut off from the major trends of modernity—"a region at odds with the rest of the nation" and widely "perceived . . . as a national problem."[17] Southerners, it seemed, were parochial "rednecks," and southern culture was the target of ridicule. In 1917 the acerbic Baltimore journalist and cultural critic H. L. Mencken spurned the South as "almost as sterile, artistically, intellectually, culturally, as the Sahara Desert. There are single acres in Europe that house more first-rate men than all the states south of the Potomac."[18] Why should Europeans have been interested in meaningful contact with such a dreary place? And although the two world wars brought the South into closer contact with the wider world, its image as being backward and isolated did not thoroughly change as long as white southerners stubbornly and violently defended racial segregation. During the early decades of the Cold War southern racism became a major international embarrassment for the United States and its claim to lead the "Free World."[19]

The purpose of this volume is not to deny that these images existed and had a profound impact on how Europeans and southerners viewed each other. However, the following essays show the manifold ways in which southerners and Europeans encountered each other over almost two centuries. They also demonstrate that these encounters played a formative role in how southerners and Europeans conceived of their own cultures and their place in the world. In doing so, they contribute to our understanding of how regional, national, and transnational histories intersected in the globalizing world of the nineteenth and twentieth centuries.

As geographic entities both the American South and Europe are somewhat elusive. The U.S. Census Bureau designates a sixteen-state area as the "Census South," which includes the eleven ex-Confederate states (Alabama, Arkansas, Florida, Georgia, Louisiana, Mississippi, North Carolina, South Carolina, Tennessee, Texas, and Virginia) plus Oklahoma, Kentucky, West Virginia, Maryland, Delaware, and the District of Columbia (Washington, DC). While we acknowledge this definition, geography is of much less concern to our authors than the South as a cultural realm. Also our use of the term *Europe* may strike some readers as misleading and inflated since the essays refer mostly to Western Europe, especially Great Britain, Germany, France, Italy, and Sweden. We acknowledge this limitation too. Unfortunately, our call for papers did not elicit any proposals dealing with the encounter between the South and Eastern Europe. Arguably southern relations with Western Europe have been more intensive and sustained than with other parts of the "Old World."

The following essays explore four major themes: (1) the mutual perceptions and images of southerners and Europeans, (2) the ways that the encounter between Europe and the South impacted and mirrored self-images and identity formation, (3) race, and (4) ethnicity. They discuss how individuals and groups, explicitly or implicitly, triangulated identities outside the familiar dichotomies North versus South and Europe versus America. As Dutch American studies scholar Rob Kroes once observed: "There is always a triangulation going on, in the sense that the reflection on America [or the American South] as a counterpoint to European conventions functions within a larger reflection on Europe's history and destiny."[20]

Each in its own way, all the chapters here deal with people(s) whose travel or thought was transatlantic in nature. One set of essays, including those by William A. Link, Thomas Clark, Daniel Nagel, Kathleen Hilliard, Lawrence T. McDonnell, and Melvyn Stokes, is particularly interested in images and perceptions. They interrogate how connections between the South and Europe informed individuals' views about their particular time and place in history. What was the southern image of Europe, and how did Europeans imagine the South? To what extent did these images and perceptions reflect accurate observations, and to what extent did they mirror stereotypes, projections, and prejudice? How did travel and cultural contact affect such images and perceptions? How and under what circumstances did they change over time? How did their views of and encounters with Europe affect the identity of southerners? Of course, race and ethnicity are closely related to issues of identity and play a major role in nearly all chapters. Undoubtedly, privileged white male southerners dominated in establishing social and cultural contacts with Europeans, but, as the essays by William A. Link, Thomas Clark, Sarah L. Silkey, Matthias Reiss, and Clive Webb demonstrate, women and African Americans were by no means absent from the transatlantic encounter. Men and women such as Frederick Douglas, William Wells Brown, W. E. B. Du Bois, Ida B. Wells, Martin Luther King Jr., and Bayard Rustin must also be included in the story of the American South and Europe. In addition to race, ethnicity figures into the picture, especially in the essays by Thomas Clark, Daniel Nagel, and Stefano Luconi. A brief summary of the individual chapters may be helpful to sketch out the scope of this book.

In his essay "Southerners Abroad: Europe and the Cultural Encounter, 1830–1895," William A. Link urges us to take a closer look at how travel and tourism shaped southern identity and self-images. Experiences varied greatly, Link finds, depending on race and gender. While travel to Europe reinforced idealized notions about the South as a hierarchical yet harmonious society, white women sometimes cherished travel as a liberation from the constraints of patriarchy. African Americans experienced travel to Europe as a temporary respite from slavery and racial oppression at home and therefore developed romanticized notions of Europe that ignored racism as a common transatlantic ideology.

Thomas Clark's essay reverses the lens by examining the travel accounts of four European travelers to the antebellum South and to the city of New Orleans in particular. In addition to the famed Alexis de Tocqueville, the author looks at three German-speaking travelers: Julius Fröbel, a German liberal of the Forty-Eighter generation; Samuel Ludvigh, an Austro-Hungarian radical freethinker; and Louise Weil, a middle-class Protestant woman from Swabia. Their views of the South, the author argues, were strongly influenced by the North-South dichotomy, albeit in quite different ways. While Tocqueville and Fröbel considered the slaveholding South as dull and backward compared to the democratic and entrepreneurial Yankee North, Ludvigh, who had become frustrated with Yankee capitalism, embraced southern culture as striking just the right balance between republicanism and progress on the one hand and European-style culture and personal freedom on the other hand. Louise Weil's travel account, though not explicitly political, was critical of both the northern and the southern versions of American culture and ultimately rejected them both. Clark's essay exemplifies how images were constructed in an implicit process of comparative triangulation among the North, the South, and the observers' culture.

In his essay "The German Forty-Eighters' Critique of the U.S. South, 1850–1861," Daniel Nagel focuses on the small yet influential group of "revolutionary refugees" who had participated in the Revolution of 1848–49 and subsequently fled to the United States. As his research of German American newspapers and periodicals demonstrates, the Forty-Eighters eagerly embraced American republicanism but considered southern slavery a cancer that threatened the American republic. German immigrants, they believed, had a special role to play in saving the United States from slavery, not the least because Germans represented a superior culture. Nagel argues that republicanism was central to the transatlantic political discourse and that the Forty-Eighters' brand of republicanism made a major contribution to the fledgling Republican Party. When the Civil War broke out, the Forty-Eighters welcomed the conflict and vigorously supported the cause of the Union, because they were convinced that the military contest would lead to the abolition of slavery and inch them one step closer to implementing their republicanism of freedom and equality.

Based on fiction, travel journals, newspapers, and personal papers, Kathleen Hilliard explores how antebellum residents of Charleston, South Carolina, situated themselves in world history by comparing their city to Venice, the once powerful and prosperous maritime republic of the Mediterranean. Their meditations on Venice's "Days of Power and Glory," Hilliard argues, reflected deep-seated anxieties about Charleston's future and the desire to stem their city's decline, ignoring that Venice itself had long since declined. Ironically, Charleston found common ground with Venice in the decades after the Civil War, when Charlestonians used the moniker "Venice of America" for commercial gain. Like Venice, Charleston trades on its history and myths.

Lawrence T. McDonnell's essay also deals with the antebellum elites of South Carolina and their use of European history, in this case medieval England, to reassert their own historical and cultural identity. Appalled by the modernizing forces of industrialization and capitalism in Victorian England, elite Carolinians turned to Elizabethan chivalry as a redeeming social ideal, staging elaborate jousts and tilting matches and emulating the lifestyles of heroic knights. McDonnell cautions against dismissing antebellum chivalry as a charade. Rather, the author views it as a search for a paternalist utopia insulated from the depravations of modern capitalism. When war broke out in 1861, McDonnell concludes, South Carolina's slaveholding elite rode forth to battle, not simply as slavery's defenders, but in pursuit of their chivalrous dreams.

In "Slavery or Independence: The Confederate Dilemma in Europe," Don H. Doyle discusses the reasons why the Confederacy failed to secure full diplomatic recognition from the European powers during the Civil War, despite Europe's dependence on southern cotton, which, Confederate leaders firmly believed, should have forced Britain and France to recognize southern independence. Overbearing "King Cotton diplomacy," Doyle shows, was not the only miscalculation on the part of the Confederate leadership. Equally important, Confederate diplomats and statesmen never understood that slavery shaped British and European public opinion of the American Civil War. Caught up in their own delusions, they were completely unable to devise a propaganda strategy vis-à-vis European audiences who were strongly antislavery.

Stefano Luconi's essay on the lynching of Italian immigrants in the New South complicates recent interpretations that hold that their uncertain racial status explains anti-Italian mob violence. While it is true that southern "Anglo-Saxons" questioned the whiteness of Italians, many of whom came from Sicily and had a darkish complexion, the author argues that race often served as a pretext for other motivations, such as economic, political, and labor conflicts between local elites and Italian immigrants. Luconi's essay emphasizes the volatility of race and ethnicity in a society that was supposedly built on a strict racial dichotomy of black and white.

Sarah L. Silkey also looks at southern lynch law from a transnational perspective. Her topic is the transatlantic antilynching campaign that the African American journalist and social reformer Ida B. Wells launched in Great Britain in 1893–94. Wells and other antilynching activists denounced racist mob violence as a disgrace that singled out the United States and the South among the "civilized nations" of the world. Most important, Wells enlightened British audiences that southern lynchings were not wholesome "frontier justice" to fight brazen outlaws, but a brutal instrument of racist oppression. Craving foreign capital and international respectability, southern leaders had to respond to British criticism of lynch law. At the same time, however, they remained committed to white supremacy and could not afford to appear soft on foreign meddling. The results of Wells's campaign were mixed. She succeeded in arousing the outrage of British social reformers, but international protests provoked a backlash among white southerners. Still, Silkey concludes, the campaign made southern racism and mob violence an international issue and helped raise the costs of lynching in terms of the white South's prestige.

In his essay "Transatlantic Fundamentalism: Southern Preachers in London's Pulpits," William R. Glass explores the transatlantic dimensions of southern Protestant fundamentalism by focusing on two pastors, A. C. Dixon and Leonard G. Broughton, who moved before World War I to London, where they ministered for several years. Both Dixon and

Broughton were salient figures in the American fundamentalist movement. Their sojourn to London, Glass shows, contributed to a fruitful exchange between conservative Protestants in Great Britain and the United States. Yet Glass also points to the limits of transnationalism. Ironically, the two London churches that appointed Dixon and Broughton as their new pastors, respectively, had a tradition of antislavery activity that the southern white clergymen found difficult to accommodate. Eventually, the author concludes, neither Dixon nor Broughton had much impact on the development of British evangelicalism.

Film historian Melvyn Stokes examines the response of British and French critics to *The Birth of a Nation* (1915) and *Gone With the Wind* (1939), arguably the two most popular and commercially successful movies on southern history during the first half of the twentieth century.[21] Stokes is interested in how these critics read the two movies against the backdrop of World War I and World War II, respectively, and how they related the films to their own national experiences and identities. Unlike in the United States, *The Birth of a Nation* did not provoke controversy in Britain, seemingly because British critics and viewers did not question the movie's version of Reconstruction and its white supremacist message. Several French critics, however, insisted that the South fought not for states' rights, but to preserve slavery. When *Gone With the Wind* came to Britain in 1940 and to France after World War II, critics interpreted the movie as a war drama to which viewers could relate from their own experiences. Despite some criticism of the film's romantic images of the plantation South, most reviewers failed to address the political and historical subtexts of *Gone With the Wind*.

Yet the author argues that British and French critics could hardly have done so, given that in America both popular images of and academic historiography on the Civil War and Reconstruction were still dominated by stereotypes of "Negro rule" and corrupt carpetbaggers.

Gunnar Myrdal's *An American Dilemma* has enjoyed the status of a "classic" almost since its publication in 1944. Louis Mazzari's essay on Myrdal's cooperation with the Chapel Hill–educated sociologist Arthur Raper reminds us that the book was the result of an encounter between Europe and the South. In discussing race relations with white southerners, Myrdal shrewdly used his seemingly innocent "outsider's perspective" to elicit candid statements his interviewees might not have given to American researchers. Their cooperation on *An American Dilemma,* Mazzari holds, had a formative impact on both Myrdal's and Raper's subsequent careers and their belief that cutting-edge social science was a key instrument to effect social change. The extent to which *An American Dilemma* actually paved the way for the civil rights movement remains controversial, however. Critics have pointed out that Myrdal "underestimated the strength of African American culture and its central institutions in the struggle for black social, economic and political equality."[22]

Matthias Reiss explores a very special dimension of the relationship between the South and Europe by looking at the experiences and perceptions of German prisoners of war who were interned in southern POW camps from 1943 through 1946. Again, race provides the lens for reconstructing the views of these involuntary visitors. How did German soldiers, who had been indoctrinated by Nazi racism, react to the Jim Crow South? How did firsthand observations of American racism affect their responsiveness to U.S. reeducation programs aimed at teaching the prisoners the superiority of American democracy? Reiss shows that the Germans came into close contact with African Americans and that they were keenly aware of the discrimination and exploitation blacks suffered under Jim Crow. Apart from criticizing American hypocrisy on race, the German soldiers developed a sense of solidarity with their black fellow laborers that involved a peculiar cultural dimension. African Americans appeared to be the antithesis to the soulless American materialism that Germans, believing in the superiority of their own sophisticated *Kultur,* had long feared and despised. The experience of antiblack racism in the South, according to Reiss, enabled German POWs to resist the official reeducation programs.

In his essay "Britain, the American South, and the Wide Civil Rights Movement," Clive Webb investigates the transatlantic connections between the struggles for racial equality in Britain and the American South in the 1950s and 1960s. The arrival of unprecedented numbers of Caribbean migrants caused racist reactions and a series of racial disorders in Britain in the late 1950s and early 1960s that showed that the nation was not immune to the racial bigotry and brutality that was so characteristic of the U.S. South. The southern civil rights struggle, Webb demonstrates, had a significant influence in shaping public policy on race relations in Britain during these years. It influenced the growth of organized protest by both liberal reformers and racist reactionaries and helped shape the British government's legislative reforms aimed at improving conditions for the migrant population. Yet, as the author points out, there were also limitations to the diffusion of American influences in the United Kingdom due to smaller numbers and the cultural heterogeneity of the black immigrant population. Britain's racial problems did not resemble those in the Jim Crow South but had much more in common with those in the urban North.

The last essay, by Daniel Geary and Jennifer Sutton, brings the relationship between Europe and the U.S. South into the 1970s and 1980s. Noting that historians have often reduced the agendas of white supremacists to local concerns, such as school integration, the authors focus on how southern white supremacists conceived of European decolonization in Africa. Southern defenders of Jim Crow strongly identified with whites in Rhodesia and South Africa and were fiercely critical of British policies, in particular, that indicated support for majority rule. In their view "White Africa" and the American South were the last holdouts of "white civilization." Southern segregationists lobbied for U.S. diplomatic recognition of Rhodesia and later against imposing sanctions on South Africa. Before long, however, the cause of white supremacy was doomed both in Africa and in the American South.

Taken together, the fourteen essays in this volume reveal a breadth and variety of cultural contacts and mutual engagements between Europe and the U.S. South that defy old clichés of southern parochialism and isolation. Indeed, as more historians have come to understand, the South has always belonged to a broader transnational culture, and its relationship with Europe has been one important aspect of its global connections. We hope that students of southern history and of American, European, and transnational history will find this book challenging and that its publication will stimulate further research into the South's manifold entanglements with the wider world.

Notes

1. FDR, letter, July 5, 1938, in National Emergency Council, *Report on Economic Conditions of the South* (Washington, DC, 1938), 1; Peter Applebome, "A Sweetness Tempers South's Bitter Past," *New York Times,* July 31, 1994, 1 and 20. See also Peter Applebome, *Dixie Rising: How the South Is Shaping American Values, Politics, and Culture* (New York: Times Books, 1996).

2. Earl Black and Merle Black, *The Rise of Southern Republicans* (Cambridge: Belknap Press of Harvard University Press, 2002); see also Joseph E. Lowndes, *From the New Deal to the New Right: Race and the Southern Origins of Modern Conservatism* (New Haven and London: Yale University Press, 2008). On the South and evangelical conservatism, see Darren Dochuk, *From Bible Belt to Sun-*

belt: Plain-Folk Religion, Grassroots Politics, and the Rise of Evangelical Conservatism (New York: W. W. Norton, 2011); Bethany Moreton, *To Serve God and Wal-Mart: The Making of Christian Free Enterprise* (Cambridge: Harvard University Press, 2009).

3. Naipaul and Berendt are quoted in Helen Taylor, *Circling Dixie: Contemporary Southern Culture through a Transatlantic Lens* (New Brunswick and London: Rutgers University Press, 2001), 10.

4. Paul Harvey, "'Sweet Home Alabama': Southern Culture and the American Search for Community," *Southern Cultures* 1.3 (Spring 1995): 321–34.

5. Charles Reagan Wilson and William Ferris, eds., *Encyclopedia of Southern Culture* (Chapel Hill: University of North Carolina Press, 1989); Charles Reagan Wilson, ed., *The New Encyclopedia of Southern Culture,* 24 vols. (Chapel Hill: University of North Carolina Press, 2006–13).

6. See John Boles, ed., *A Companion to the American South* (Malden, MA: Blackwell Publishers, 2002).

7. "Survey the American South," *Economist,* Dec. 10, 1994, 3, 5, 17–18; Jonathan Freedland, "Everyone's Whistling Dixie," *Guardian,* Mar. 2, 1996, 1.

8. "A Special Report on the American South," *Economist,* Mar. 3, 2007, 3–12, quotations on 4 and 12.

9. On the Southern Studies Forum, see www.eaas.eu/eaas-networks/southern-studies-forum (accessed May 22, 2013); Suzanne W. Jones and Mark Newman, eds., *Poverty and Progress in the U.S. South since 1920* (Amsterdam: VU University Press, 2006).

10. Thomas Bender, *A Nation among Nations: America's Place in World History* (New York: Hill and Wang, 2006); Ian Tyrrell, *Transnational Nation: United States History in Global Perspective since 1789* (New York: Palgrave Macmillan, 2007).

11. See, for instance, Joseph A. Fry, *Dixie Looks Abroad: The South and U.S. Foreign Relations, 1789–1973* (Baton Rouge: Louisiana State University Press, 2002); Michael O'Brien, *Conjectures of Order: Intellectual Life and the American South, 1810–1860,* 2 vols. (Chapel Hill: University of North Carolina Press, 2003); James C. Cobb and William Stueck, eds., *Globalization and the American South* (Athens and London: University of Georgia Press, 2005); James L. Peacock, Harry L. Watson, and Carrie R. Matthews, eds., *The American South in a Global World* (Chapel Hill and London: University of North Carolina Press, 2005); James L. Peacock, *Grounded Globalism: How the U.S. South Embraces the World* (Athens and London: University of Georgia Press, 2007); Richard Grey and Waldemar Zacharasiewicz, eds., *Transatlantic Exchanges: The American South in Europe—Europe in the American South* (Vienna: Austrian Academy of Sciences Press, 2007); Brian D. Schoen, *The Fragile Fabric of Union: Cotton, Federal Politics, and the Global Origins of the Civil War* (Baltimore: Johns Hopkins University Press, 2009).

12. Don H. Doyle, *Nations Divided: America, Italy, and the Southern Question* (Athens: University of Georgia Press, 2002). See also Don H. Doyle, ed., *Seces-*

sion as an International Phenomenon: From America's Civil War to Contemporary Separatist Movements (Athens: University of Georgia Press, 2010); and Wolfgang Schivelbusch, *The Culture of Defeat: On National Trauma, Mourning, and Recovery* (New York: Metropolitan Books, 2003). Paul Quigley, *Shifting Grounds: Nationalism and the American South, 1848–1865* (New York: Oxford University Press, 2012), also includes a comparative perspective.

13. Tyrrell, *Transnational Nation,* 3.

14. Andrew Zimmerman, *Alabama in Africa: Booker T. Washington, the German Empire and the Globalization of the New South* (Princeton and Oxford: Princeton University Press, 2010); see Manfred Berg's critical review in *Historische Zeitschrift* 293 (2011): 236–38.

15. See David Armitage and M. J. Braddick, eds., *The British Atlantic World 1500–1800,* 2nd ed. (New York: Palgrave, 2009); Timothy H. Breen, *Colonial America in an Atlantic World* (New York: Pearson and Longman, 2004).

16. The classic account is Frank Lawrence Owsley, *King Cotton Diplomacy: Foreign Relations of the Confederate States of America,* 2nd ed. (Chicago: University of Chicago Press, 1959); see also Don H. Doyle's essay in this volume. For a comprehensive new study that places Confederate diplomacy into the cultural context of how southerners viewed England, see Holger Löttel, *Um Ehre und Anerkennung: Englandbilder im amerikanischen Süden und die Außenpolitik der Konföderation* (Stuttgart: Steiner, 2009).

17. Dewey Grantham, *The South in Modern America: A Region at Odds* (New York: HarperCollins, 1994), xv–xvi.

18. H. L. Mencken, "The Sahara of the Bozart," in H. L. Mencken, *Prejudices: Second Series* (1920; New York: Octagon Books, 1977), 136.

19. See Thomas Borstelman, *The Cold War and the Color Line: American Race Relations in the Global Arena* (Cambridge: Harvard University Press, 2001); Mary L. Dudziak, *Cold War Civil Rights: Race and the Image of American Democracy* (Princeton: Princeton University Press, 2001).

20. Rob Kroes, "America and the European Sense of History," in Günter H. Lenz and Peter J. Ling, eds., *Transatlantic Encounters: Multiculturalism, National Identity and the Uses of the Past* (Amsterdam: VU University Press, 2000), 107.

21. On the ongoing popularity of the novel-made-film *Gone With the Wind* in its many manifestations and the flops of the sequels, see Taylor, *Circling Dixie,* chap. 2.

22. Richard H. King, "The Ambiguities of Enlightenment: Gunnar Myrdal and African American Culture," in Lenz and Ling, *Transatlantic Encounters,* 167–83, quotation on 169.

1

Southerners Abroad

Europe and the Cultural Encounter, 1830–1895

William A. Link

Old England! old England! thrice blessed and free,
The poor hunted slave finds a shelter in thee;
Where no blood-thirsty hound ever dares on his track:
At thy voice, old England, the monster falls back.
Go back, then, ye blood-hounds, that howl in my path;
In the land of old England I'm free from your wrath.
And the sons of Great Britain my deep scars shall see.
Till they cry, with one voice, "Let the bondman be free!"[1]

With the transportation revolution rendering world travel a more common experience, during the last half of the nineteenth century greater numbers of Americans, southerners among them, visited Europe. Tourism by southerners was not new, but by the late 1840s, the economics and technology of travel had changed significantly. Steam-powered paddleboats, which also relied on sail power, were followed by the advent of screw propulsion after the Civil War, offering relatively cheap, safe, and fast service across the Atlantic. The Grand Tour became no longer the exclusive domain of southern white males. As travel became faster and more accessible, a greater diversity of people—women and African Americans, as well as wealthier whites—participated in the cultural experience of tourism. The Civil War offered only a brief interruption in the transatlantic currents of humanity and emancipation. With the end of the Civil War, the South became more consciously globally oriented toward a new emphasis on industrialization and the development of overseas materials for a variety of southern goods.

Whether the increased levels of travel shaped southerners' sense of self, their cultural and political identities, and their awareness of their region in a global context remain important matters for historians to consider.[2] During the first half of the nineteenth century, Romanticism at various levels emphasized individual self-realization through travel. Leaving home forced white and black southerners to think about themselves in a new light. "That something can be learned from those who leave home," writes Michael O'Brien, "is a truism of cultural criticism, the more so when one considers the early nineteenth century, because then Romanticism was redefining the meaning of home."[3]

Despite a growing call among historians to understand the South globally, few scholars have examined transnational experiences, how travel shaped southerners' cultural and political identities. Michael O'Brien's magisterial *Conjectures of Order* portrays a robust cosmopolitanism among southern intellectuals, but little scholarship has explored how travel and tourism more generally shaped southerners.[4] Other scholars have ignored the subject from essential critical perspectives. Although we know a great deal generally about southerners' consciousness of race and gender, we know less about these as globalized phenomena. More generally, there is an abundant literature about the self and the fashioning of identity, but little of it explores how the self emerged out of the experience of travel. Travel provided an idiom for self-discovery, and Europe became a place where the conditions of the South could be refracted and interpreted.

Southerners' cultural encounter with Europe, and the world at large, had roots in the nineteenth century and reached a fuller fruition after 1900.[5] Overseas travel increasingly became a way for southerners to understand themselves and to sharpen their regional identity. This essay explores how southerners encountered Europe during the nineteenth century by examining the different ways in which whites and blacks, men and women, learned more about themselves abroad.[6] Those experiences were fundamentally different. Travel for white males enabled them to recreate their home, if often to fantasize about it. Some white women experienced travel as offering some escape from the constraints of patriarchy. African Americans, confronting harsher realities, found that travel usually represented

freedom from slavery and racial oppression at home. Race, along with gender, thus offers an interesting prism to examine how southerners perceived
themselves in a global context.

Before the Civil War, it was not uncommon for southern white males from
the planter class to travel to Europe. No "young American of large intellect,"
wrote South Carolinian William Henry Trescot—who was undoubtedly
referring to young planters—"could have been properly educated without
some experience of the old world." Even superficial foreign travel had a
refining effect. Those southerners who actually lived abroad found it transformative. Primarily, overseas travel made Americans understand, Trescot
observed, "what history really is." There was a "vitality, a reality in the
past entirely new to his experience." At home the future seemed free, but
in Europe it appeared "bound irrevocably" to the past. White southerners
returning from European experiences returned different people, according
to Trescot. They now possessed an "intense consciousness of the sacred
unity of the whole history of humanity" and an "earnestness of purpose."[7]

Prior to the 1850s, many southern travelers were transported the old-
fashioned way, by sailing ship, a voyage that took as long as a month's time
and was often precarious and unpleasant. Christopher Happoldt, a young
South Carolinian, visited England and the European Continent between
June and December 1838, leaving from Charleston on a sailing schooner
loaded with a cargo of cotton. The trip to Liverpool, lasting about a month,
brought boredom and seasickness. Two weeks into it, the schooner encountered high winds and rough seas that drove the vessel off course. The rolling of the ship on rough seas confined Happoldt to his berth all day. The
appearance of the Irish coast was a relief to crew and passengers alike.[8]

Ten years later, another South Carolinian, Wyatt Aiken, traveled
aboard the cotton schooner *Java* from Charleston to Liverpool. Having just
finished his junior year at South Carolina College, Aiken craved adventure.
The *Java,* carrying twenty-four hundred bales of cotton, left Charleston
on June 28, 1848. Aiken was the only passenger, with a crew consisting of
the captain, first and second mates, steward, boatswain, thirteen common
sailors, and a sailor boy. Before weighing anchor, the crew was gathered up
from Charleston haunts and dives; two of them, too drunk to walk, were
loaded on wheelbarrows. Aiken became sick "before the spires of the city
had receded from view," and for eight days he "ate not a mouthfull, nor
drank a drop of any kind of liquid." On July 4, the captain forced him to

drink a glass of champagne, but it was "vomited with as much ease as it had been drunk." The voyage took thirty-five "miserable and lonely" days.

Aiken's tour evoked a cultural alienation that many Americans experienced in the Atlantic crossing. Arriving at the Liverpool docks, Aiken spent a week in London, where he heard the popular Swedish singer Jenny Lind. He reported that her "enchanting voice" had "but little music in it to my ear" because seated next to him was a "burly black negro." Already attuned to differences of race, Aiken also became acutely aware of class divisions when he rode in a third-class railroad car. The cars were crammed with lower-class English; the carriage, he wrote, was "like a large waggonboy put upon the wheels, no seats and no cover." The railroad agent reminded Aiken that no true gentleman ever traveled in the third-class car.[9]

During the nineteenth century, growing numbers of southerners moved across the Atlantic for business, leisure, and education. The exploration of the self and character development became increasingly a more essential consequence of travel abroad. James Johnston Pettigrew, born to a planter family in eastern North Carolina's Tyrrell County, possessed a prodigious intellect. Entering the University of North Carolina at the age of fifteen, he graduated first in his class. President James K. Polk, who attended Pettigrew's commencement exercises in 1847 and heard his valedictory address, was so impressed that he appointed him to the faculty of the Naval Observatory in Washington. Remaining there only a few months, Pettigrew moved to Charleston to study for the bar. In January 1850, he traveled for the first time aboard the Cunard steamer *Cambria,* arriving in Liverpool.

By the end of the antebellum period, because of steamships, travel by elite whites such as Pettigrew had assumed a different character than that experienced by Happoldt and Aiken. The crossing became shorter, schedules more predictable, and travel less ardous. Pettigrew wrote in his travel diary how steamships' sailings from Boston harbor had become routine events. Though there was a "pleasing melancholy" to his departure, travel had become ordinary, though he was in search of the exotic and authentic. About a week after the *Cambria's* departure, Pettigrew awoke one morning to see the famous Liverpool docks; the ship lay next to five other vessels. He immediately noted the presence of customs officials, and for the first time in his life, he felt the "restraint of the Police." His first experience with a customs house exposed Pettigrew to a more intrusive government and a differently organized social system—and the tension between invasive state power and the need for social order. Customs officers were "exceedingly polite, and the mob exceedingly rough," a racial characteristic, he believed, of Anglo-Saxons. He found especially offensive the invasion of personal space. Despite the experience of having customs officials search passengers' luggage, Pettigrew admitted the advantage of having a strong police force to keep order.

Pettigrew was an acute social observer who drew connections between life in the slave South and life abroad. The English working class, he noted, exhibited a "rascally appearance" that was worse than existed in New York City. Business was bustling, with fortunes made and lost.[10] The abject condition of poor people in "Anglo-Saxon" countries, he observed, reflected their proclivity toward marriage and a high rate of reproduction, which resulted in a Malthusian overpopulation. He compared the English countryside's smaller, well-cultivated farms with the landscape of the Carolinas' larger rice and cotton plantations. But he also noted poverty "as I never before beheld." The comparison between slaveholding and free societies was hard to ignore.[11]

Perhaps the most cosmopolitan white southerner of his generation, Johnston Pettigrew lived most of the decade before the Civil War in Europe. During the 1850s, he spent seven years in Europe, off and on in Germany and Spain, touring the Continent, mastering four languages, and gaining the ability to read Arabic, Greek, and Hebrew. In July 1859, Pettigrew traveled to Italy to join the early stages of il Risorgimento, a political movement to unify Italy that became a model for cultural nationalists everywhere. Crossing Mount Cenis at the French-Italian border on his birthday—which was July 4—Pettigrew wanted to participate in Italy's national fulfillment. Every people, Pettigrew declared, possessed "an inalienable right of self-government, without responsibility to aught on earth, save such as may be imposed by a due respect for the opinions of mankind."

Pettigrew believed that Italian nationalists had history on their side, with "all the fervor of youth" and the inspiration of the American Revolution. No emotion in his life was "ever so pure, so free from every shade of conscientious doubt or selfish consideration." The struggle for Italian nationhood resisted tyranny and oppression. In Pettigrew's romantic conceptualization, Italy served as a vessel of culture that was "renowned through all ages, and rendered sacred by recollections of intellect, art, and religion."[12] In the final analysis, however, Pettigrew's attempt to participate in il Risorgimento amounted to nothing. Before he joined the fight, a peace with Austria was negotiated—"entirely frustrating," he wrote, "the object of my journey." But Pettigrew continued his odyssey by spending the next months traveling around Italy and Spain.

Pettigrew's romantic nationalism, and his experience with the Confederacy, flowed from his European experiences. An eager secessionist, he joined the Confederate army after the outbreak of the Civil War, serving as brigadier general. Commanding a division in the disastrous Pickett's Charge at Gettysburg, he was killed during the Confederate retreat following that battle. During his 1859 tour, Pettigrew described the aspiring nationalities of southern Europe as models of national independence and identity. "Noble, romantic Spain!" he wrote enthusiastically. Spain, like the U.S. South, lay outside of the rushing stream of modern life. "Adieu to a civilization which reduces men to machines," he wrote, which sacrificed "half that is stalwart and individual in humanity to the false glitter of centralization, and to the luxurious enjoyments of a manufacturing, money age!"[13]

Spain became especially attractive to Pettigrew because of what that country said about the South. Especially in Spain, he wrote, a conflict raged between two ideals: "The one, that mankind are made for government, the other, that government is made for mankind." The French Revolution introduced the political and social principle of the unified state and the "great central power" that prescribed what a citizen "shall do, and what he shall not do." The "great central power" in Spain, as in the South, remained something alien. The principles of states' rights and local control, Pettigrew believed, were "profoundly ingrained in the Spanish heart." Spaniards, Pettigrew believed, possessed "most happily the combination of national, local and personal pride, which fits men for living in an organized community, with the advantages of self-government."[14]

To some extent, travel abroad served to reinforce ideas about an idealized South that was predicated on unfree labor and harmonious social relationships. In other words, in the case of Pettigrew and others, what appeared to be self-reflective were in reality profoundly conservative ideas that were organized around traditional notions of social organization. For this reason, perhaps, Spain especially intrigued Pettigrew in what it implicitly said about the U.S. South. Experiences as a tourist and visitor to Europe helped Pettigrew to define the South against a backdrop of qualities of social structure, national identity, and culture that appealed to him while abroad.[15]

With greatly expanded access, travel became a more common form of self-discovery for women. Tourism provided a way for white males and females to comprehend their home region; in this sense, gender did not divide white southerners. At the same time, more women traveled in the late nineteenth century—certainly many more women than for most of the antebellum period. Travel by women reflected cheaper and more widespread transatlantic travel, but it also resulted from an expanded public presence of middle-class women. On some occasions, gender provided a different lens for travelers. Travel for women reinforced the mores and taboos of home but provided space for a degree of freedom.

Leaving in 1851 from a northern port aboard the *Arctic,* a three-thousand-ton paddle steamer on the Collins Line, Georgian Kate Jones wrote she "could not suppress a feeling of sadness" to realize that her loved ones were providing a "parting kiss and a grasping hand" as she and her family sailed away. She consoled herself in the knowledge that her friends at home prayed and thought about her.[16] Jones's experiences resembled those of her counterparts. During the voyage, she complained about seasickness that "beggars description." Jones was so sick that for several days she could not lift her head from her pillow "without feeling as I should tilt over."[17]

Jones, a Georgia slaveholder, traveled with her family to visit the Crystal Palace Exposition in London. Like most southern white women, she accepted her home region's racial attitudes unquestioningly. Jones claimed a strong sense of American nationality, though she made a point of telling fellow passengers that she was "not only an American, but from *the South too.*"[18] Jones befriended Archibald Alexander, a native Virginian who helped to found the Presbyterian Princeton Theological Seminary. Alexander became a dinner companion; Jones and her husband discovered a common worldview. Joined by another passenger from Virginia, she described how the group exalted their "beloved southern homes" and "our peculiar institutions, &c." They shared "anecdotes & incidents of our negroes," including "their sayings, superstitions, &c." In the condescending, patronizing way that slaveholders liked to describe "our negroes," the group exchanged "apt quotations" of their slaves. One of Jones's slaves, "Long Mary," committed "exquisite blunders" that "came in for a full share of admiration." Alexander in particular "laughed immoderately" and declared "that if we could only change the purpose of the tour & give Soirees a la Ethiopian they would guaranty us a rich harvest."[19]

Jones's visit to the Crystal Palace Exposition, where she observed a combination of the fantastic and the practical, became a startling cultural experience. The exhibition displayed, for Jones, European luxury and American simplicity. Entering the exposition hall, she encountered a "magnificent interior—the most labor'd description would fail to impress a shadow of the reality." Sculpture, statuary, and paintings adorned the walls; the largest diamond in the world was on display; carpets and furniture came from around the world. The value of these luxuries, she wrote, was "*beyond* our *republican* comprehension." This collection of "brilliant magnificence" evoked feelings of wonder. Wandering into an "enchanted room" made her feel that the stories of Aladdin might be realized. For Jones, the exhibition seemed to combine European decadence with an implicit comparison with southern society.[20]

Other southern white women recognized travel as a flight from the travails of home. Laura Beecher Comer, who visited Europe during the summer of 1872, was born in Connecticut, the niece of the famed Congregationalist evangelical Lyman Beecher. Moving to Georgia, she was unhappily married to cotton planter James Comer and lived in Columbus during the Civil War. After James died in 1864, Laura entered a dark depression. She sought release by traveling abroad. In July 1872, she boarded the *Cuba*, a Cunard steamer, in New York and sailed to England. "Is the dream of my life to be realized?" she wrote in her diary before leaving Georgia. "Am I to start for Europe to-morrow? How wonderfully mysterious are God's dealings with us, his frail, finite beings!" After a week aboard the *Cuba*, her enthusiasm dampened, and she reported becoming "very weary of 'ship life,' a little sick all the time."[21] Traveling to Europe and the Continent over the next three months, she felt loss, anxiety, and depression; the trip came to embody her own unhappiness. Her enthusiasm for travel became transformed. "O, how glad I shall be when this long and weary trip is over and if God so will I again reach my home," she wrote.[22]

Comer's unhappiness became enveloped in religious language. Experiencing alienation and separation from traveling, she considered her loneliness. "I am alone and not well but I really cannot be unhappy; since God the Father and God the Son have in their Infinite Wisdom blessed me beyond my deservings," she wrote during the third month of her trip. "What am I? Nothing and fading—fading—fading! Soon shall be in eternity! . . . To believe and trust as a child is all we can do since our plans are futile and vain unaided by Divine Grace do we not grope in darkness? Lord have mercy upon us & keep us daily from running against thee!"[23]

Traveling women, like men, frequently commented that the European tour forced them to reconsider life at home. "Being removed to a new land from your own," wrote North Carolinian June Spencer in August 1884, had the "effect of making your own country and all your past life seem but a misty dream." The daughter of the famed writer, historian, poet, and anti-Reconstruction activist Cornelia Phillips Spencer, June Spencer graduated from Peace Institute in Raleigh, North Carolina, then studied art at Cooper Union in New York City. In 1884, at the age of twenty-two, she toured England and Germany for six months. While traveling, Spencer wrote, she was sometimes "hardly sure of my own identity, or that I have not severed forever all connection with my past." Her letters to her mother were later published in serialized form in the *North Carolina Presbyterian*.

The cultural experience became for Spencer especially vivid when she considered matters of race. Visiting the zoological garden in Dresden, Germany, she watched an exhibition of black South Africans who were clothed in "native dress" and "profusely adorned" in beads. The exhibition, set in a mock landscape of huts and featuring faux animals, emphasized the barbarity of the Africans, who showed off "some barbarous, uncouth motions which they call dancing, to the barbarous sounds of their 'Tum-tums.'" Inevitably, however, this experience of travel led to a consideration of race across national boundaries. The Africans were, June thought, "a superior looking race, physically, to be sure," with good features, "their hair perfectly straight." They were, however, "very black." More important, even June recognized the ridiculous nature of the exhibition. There was "something piteous in the spectacle of their wretched mummeries, and something unpleasing in the sight of these civilized people amusing themselves, looking on precisely as if at a pack of trained monkeys." The Africans, "poor creatures," seemed chilled and "withered" by the cool Dresden summer.[24]

Born a slave in eastern Maryland in 1817, Samuel Ringgold Ward escaped at the age of three with his parents to New Jersey and New York and, eventually, Canada. Educated by Quakers and licensed as a Congregational minister, Ward studied medicine and law and, in the 1840s, became an abolitionist organizer. In April 1853, he traveled to England aboard the Cunard liner *Europa* to conduct a speaking tour in the British Isles. As an African American traveler, Ward, unlike white tourists, did not visit Europe for private leisure or cultural uplift. Instead, he visited the British Isles as a part of a stream of black abolitionists who looked to Europe for support in the fight against slavery. On the *Europa,* Ward was told that he could not take his meals with fellow white passengers because Cunard officials feared southern white passengers' reaction. He noted a bitter contradiction that, as a Canadian, he was a British subject, yet his rights as an Englishman did not exist aboard the *Europa.* The "abominable system" of slavery trumped everything else.[25]

For black people travel abroad was accompanied by white contempt and the common humiliations and insulting experiences of second-class status. Prior to the Civil War, African Americans' intellectual culture, as Michael O'Brien points out, was entirely expatriate, and the only place in which black people could be educated, read, and write lay outside the South and, to an extent, outside the United States.[26] The most famous nineteenth-century African American, Frederick Douglass, escaped from enslavement in Baltimore in 1838 by disguising himself and riding a railroad passenger train to freedom in New York City. In every sense, for him travel meant escape from oppression. In 1845, Douglass published his *Narrative,* which became a success story of how a slave freed himself from the physical and psychological shackles of enslavement, and at the center of that story was flight and travel across borders. Fearful that the celebrity that accompanied the *Narrative* might bring his reenslavement, in 1848 Douglass took flight again—in an extended tour of the British Isles. By the time he left, two years later, British supporters had raised enough money to purchase his freedom.

In 1845, Douglass sailed to Ireland and England on the Cunard's *Cambria*—five years before Johnston Pettigrew crossed the Atlantic on the same ship. His expatriation, Douglass later wrote, "proved to be a necessary step in the path of knowledge and usefulness." Some of the happiest moments of his life were spent in Britain, he wrote. Douglass ironically noted how he experienced his Grand Tour, which paralleled the journey of white tourists. A "rude, uncultivated fugitive slave was driven, by stern necessity," Douglass later wrote, "to that country to which young American gentlemen go to increase their stock of knowledge, to seek pleasure, to have their rough, democratic manners softened by contact with English aristocratic refinement."[27]

Douglass's frame of reference was unquestionably southern—the place of his birth—but he considered matters of freedom in global terms. The two years abroad accentuated Douglass's awareness of white supremacy. "In thinking of America," he wrote to his mentor William Lloyd Garrison, "I sometimes find myself admiring her bright blue sky, her grand old woods, her fertile fields, her beautiful rivers, her mighty lakes, and star-crowned mountains." Living abroad validated the reality that his home country was "cursed with the infernal spirit of slaveholding, robbery, and wrong." America, Douglass said, would "not allow her children to love her." In contrast, the experience abroad opened up new possibilities. During speaking tours, British audiences exhibited a "deep sympathy for the slave, and the strong abhorrence of the slaveholder," along with an "entire absence of everything that looked like prejudice against me, on account of the color of my skin."

Douglass's overseas experiences contrasted with his bitter struggle at home. In the South, he was nothing but a slave; freedom in the North meant facing "inveterate prejudice against color." On numerous occasions, while living in the North, Douglass was told: "We don't allow niggers here." Even when he visited a church service in New Bedford, Massachusetts, a deacon greeted him by telling him that black people were not permitted in the church. When he attempted to attend a Lyceum in the same town, he was banned because of his skin color; while traveling on a cold night in December 1843 aboard a steamer from New York to Boston, he was again told, "We don't allow niggers in here." In Boston, following a strenuous speaking tour, a local eating house refused him service. An omnibus driver in Weymouth, Massachusetts, refused, with "fiendish hate," to seat him.

Only days into his first trip to the British Isles, three thousand miles distant from home, Douglass's status was transformed. "Thank heaven for the respite I now enjoy," he declared. There was little to remind him of his skin color, and he was treated with the same respect paid to white people. There was no "American democratic christian," Douglass wrote sarcastically, barring him from buildings and public establishments with the insult, "They don't allow niggers in here!" Britons knew little of mass racism, what Douglass called "the republican negro hate prevalent in our glorious land." Instead, they measured people according to their moral and intellectual worth. Whatever bad that was said of the British class system, there was "none based on the color of a man's skin." A race-based "aristocracy" belonged instead "preeminently to 'the land of the free, and the home of the brave.'" Such widespread popular racism existed nowhere, "in any but Americans," and it "sticks to them wherever they go. They find it almost as hard to get rid of, as to get rid of their skins."[28]

Travel abroad provided, in many respects, ways to fantasize about home. While whites often exalted American traits while abroad, African Americans exaggerated their freedom from racial oppression in Europe. In particular, black travelers often projected romanticized notions about what Europe represented that ignored values of race that permeated the West and drove its domination of the nonwhite world. William Wells Brown, author of one of the best-known slave narratives, escaped from slavery in St. Louis as a young man. He eventually settled in Buffalo, becoming one of the better known of a group of transatlantic black abolitionists.

In July 1849, Brown took his first tour of England, traveling from Boston across the Atlantic in a nine-day journey aboard the Cunard's *Canada*. When he arrived at the Liverpool docks, he declared that nothing could "convey . . . the feelings which came over him when he landed." He felt liberated.[29] No one having his skin color, he later wrote, could visit Britain "without being struck with the marked difference between the English and the Americans." The racial prejudice existing throughout the United States, and to some extent aboard the *Canada*, "vanished as soon as a I set foot on the soil of Britain." In the South, he was chattel property; in the North, he remained "one born to occupy an inferior position." On ships, he was forced to ride in inferior quarters; in hotels, he could only eat in kitchens. Jim Crow transportation humiliated him, while northern churches required that he sit in a segregated pew.

All this changed, Brown maintained, after he crossed the Atlantic. In England, Brown became "a man, and an equal." The dogs in the street "appeared conscious of my manhood."[30] Proslavery polemicists' comparison between American slaves and the English working class was, according to Brown, fallacious. Whatever oppression English workers suffered, they freely chose their employers. They also enjoyed access to education, and, though class obstructed social mobility, rich and poor enjoyed at least some access to the legal system. Enslaved Americans possessed no such rights, lacking the ability to protect their families and themselves. For the enslaved, the past was "as yesterday, and the future scarcely more than to-morrow."[31]

In August 1849, Brown traveled to Paris as an American delegate to the International Peace Congress, which met in various European capitals from 1848 to 1853. Brown heard luminaries such as Victor Hugo, who was elected president of the congress, and the British reformer and internationalist Richard Cobden. Brown, while in Paris, attended a reception hosted by the French foreign minister, Alexis de Tocqueville, whose *Democracy in America* remains one of the best-known travel accounts of nineteenth-century America. "Had I been in America, where colour is considered a crime," he noted, "I would not have been seen at such a gathering, unless as a servant." When he was introduced to de Tocqueville's wife as a former slave, she told him: "I hope you feel yourself free in Paris."[32]

While traveling across the Atlantic on the *Canada,* Brown was insulted by several fellow American passengers. He often heard the comments: "That nigger had better be on his master's farm," and "What could the American Peace Society be thinking about to send a black man as a delegate to Paris?" Later, one of these same passengers approached him at the Peace Congress, asking for an introduction to Hugo and Cobden. Brown flatly refused. "What a change comes over the dreams of my white American brother, by crossing the ocean," Brown noted. "The man who would not have been seen walking with me in the streets of New York, and who would not have shaken hands with me with a pair of tongs while on the passage from the United States, could come with hat in hand in Paris, and say, 'I was your fellow-passenger.'"[33]

Travel, for African Americans, amplified the global qualities of race. With the end of slavery, the black experience became, more and more, diasporic, as black people sought refuge from postemancipation oppression by leaving the South. The experience of race became a matter that transcended region, though most black people remained southern. W. E. B. Du Bois, born in the North, adopted the South as a student at Fisk University in Nashville and a long-time resident of Atlanta, where he later reflected that he began his "real life work" and "found myself" in the "real condition of my people." Along with frequent travel throughout the South, Du Bois traveled to Europe, where he studied two years at the University of Berlin.[34]

In his autobiography, W. E. B. Du Bois described how his time in Europe profoundly changed his "outlook on life and my thought and feeling toward it." Nearly fifty years after Douglass first crossed the Atlantic, Du Bois, twenty-four years old and completing a Harvard doctorate, traveled to the University of Berlin. In 1892, he crossed the Atlantic, "in a trance," always telling himself: "It is not real; I must be dreaming!" For Du Bois, departing America was liberating. The "possible beauty and elegance of life permeated my soul; I gained a respect for manners." He was a person who wanted a world that was "hard, smooth and swift," and he had little time for "rounded corners and ornament, for unhurried thought and slow contemplation." In Europe, he sat still and discovered the world. He learned about Beethoven, Richard Wagner's *Ring Cycle,* the art of Rembrandt and Titian. He realized, Du Bois later said, the "history and striving of men and also their taste and expression."[35]

Du Bois's experiences overseas, like those of Douglass, were connected to the broadening and deepening of his racial consciousness. Traveling through Europe, he learned more about himself. For Du Bois, Europeans slowly became "not white folks, but folks." He became "not less fanatically a Negro, but 'Negro' meant a greater, broader sense of humanity and world fellow-ship." Globalizing his perspective, Du Bois recognized his struggle as "not against the world, but simply against American narrowness and color prejudice, with the greater, finer world at my back." For white Europeans, he was no longer, as he was at home, a "curiosity, or something sub-human." Du Bois gained a new point of view about white America. He took particular satisfaction that the University of Berlin did not recognize a Harvard degree—just as Harvard did not recognize his degree from Fisk University.

Du Bois described an especially illustrative instance of the sharpening of his racial consciousness. In August 1892, boarding a passenger steamer to travel from Rotterdam to Germany, up the Rhine, he befriended a Dutch woman and her three daughters. Although he instinctively "put as much space between us as the small vessel allowed," it did not "allow much, and the lady's innate breeding allowed less." The woman's twelve-year-old daughter befriended him, and they became "happy companions, laughing, eating and singing together, talking English, French and German and viewing the lovely castled German towns." Eventually, Du Bois joined the Dutch family in touring the Rhine towns. Out of this experience of free social interaction with white Europeans—sharply in contrast with American racial etiquette—he freed himself from the "extremes of my racial provincialism." In Berlin, he lived with a German family, the Marbachs, who included a mother and four daughters. In this setting, the veil of racial prejudice fell. "I ceased to hate or suspect people simply because they belonged to one race or color," he recalled, and they became "a happy group closely bound to each other," attending church and concerts together, taking excursions, reading poetry, and lunching in country inns.[36]

Du Bois at some point fell in love with the one of the Marbach daughters, Dora. Attending the town's annual ball, he danced with all of the Marbach girls. At the *Damen Wahl* (ladies' choice), Dora Marbach asked him to dance. He changed the words of the German folk song "Die Lora am Thore" (Lora at the gate) to "Dora at the gate." Du Bois and Dora confessed love for each other; she promised to marry him immediately. But he drew back, explaining later that he "knew this would be unfair to her and fatal for my work at home, where I had neither property nor social standing for this blue-eyed stranger." But Dora could not understand Du Bois's reluctance. An American woman boarding for a month at the Marbachs', horrified at this interracial contact, tried to thwart the relationship. The American woman, a "nervous gossip," was astonished to see that Du Bois was "so well received in this household." "What she told Frau Marbach about American Negroes I do not know," Du Bois, recalled, "but I can imagine." Although the Marbachs ignored the Americans, Du Bois was emotionally bruised, in this painful reminder of the power of racial mores back home.[37]

Du Bois, an outsider and an insider regarding the U.S. South, became the most articulate interpreter of how travel and the intercourse of culture and ideas across national borders shaped perceptions of race. His experiences during the 1890s surely had much to do with his realization that the problem of race was a global problem, a view running contrary to the assumption that racial oppression was something peculiar to the South and to the United States. Subsequently, his pan-Africanism reflected his concept of a "double consciousness" in which black people were connected to their heritage in the western hemisphere, Africa, and the world writ large.[38] In many respects, nonetheless, Du Bois shared something in common with the experiences of Johnston Pettigrew, one of the few nineteenth-century southerners who could match his intellect. Pettigrew's immersion in European culture, years earlier, helped him to refine his own sense of self through an understanding of the particular position of the slaveholding South. His region's differentness, he realized, possessed global qualities. Pettigrew's conclusions reinforced his own sense of priorities and led him to die on the battlefield. Three decades after Pettigrew's death, Du Bois's visit to Europe reinforced, broadened, and clarified his understanding of the power of race and nationhood. Du Bois recognized, through the European experience, the centrality of race to his own intellectual development and the power that race had on a global level.

Notes

1. William Wells Brown, speech, Sept. 5, 1849, Lecture Hall, Croydon, England, in C. Peter Ripley et al., eds., *The Black Abolitionist Papers, Vol. I: The British Isles, 1830–1865* (Chapel Hill: University of North Carolina Press, 1985), 172.

2. Historians have focused especially on how and to what extent antebellum southern white travelers engaged in proslavery analyses that reflected their views of European society. Travelers, according to this view, perceived Europe through a limited lens that offered an obstructed view of their home region. See

Daniel Kilbride, "Slavery, Nation, and Ideology: Virginians on the Grand Tour in the 1850s," in Peter Wallenstein and Bertram Wyatt-Brown, eds., *Virginia's Civil War* (Charlottesville: University Press of Virginia, 2005), 62–71. See also Daniel Kilbride, "Travel, Ritual, and National Identity: Planters on the European Tour, 1820–1860," *Journal of Southern History* 69 (Aug. 2003): 549–84; Michael O'Brien, "Italy and the Southern Romantics," in Michael O'Brien, *Rethinking the South* (Baltimore: Johns Hopkins University Press, 1988), 84–111.

3. O'Brien, "Italy and the Southern Romantics," 90.

4. Michael O'Brien, *Conjectures of Order: Intellectual Life and the American South, 1810–1860,* 2 vols. (Chapel Hill: University of North Carolina Press, 2004).

5. Benjamin E. Wise, *William Alexander Percy: The Curious Life of a Mississippi Planter and Sexual Freethinker* (Chapel Hill: University of North Carolina Press, 2012).

6. Mechal Sobel, "The Revolution in Selves: Black and White Inner Aliens," in Ronald Hoffman, Mechal Sobel, and Fredrika Teute, eds., *Through a Glass Darkly: Reflections on Personal Identity in Early America* (Chapel Hill: University of North Carolina Press, 1997), 163–205.

7. William Henry Trescot, *Memorial of the Life of J. Johnston Pettigrew* (Charleston: John Russell, 1870), 21–24.

8. Christopher Happoldt Diary, 1838, Southern Historical Collection, University of North Carolina, Chapel Hill (hereafter SHC).

9. Wyatt Aiken autobiography, SHC.

10. James Johnston Pettigrew, travel diary, June 22, 1850, subseries 3.3, folder 525, Pettigrew Family Papers, SHC.

11. Pettigrew, travel diary, Jan. 9, 1850–Sept. 28, 1852.

12. James Johnston Pettigrew, *Notes on Spain and the Spaniards, in the Summer of 1859, with a Glance at Sardinia,* ed. Clyde N. Wilson (Columbia: University of South Carolina Press, 2010), 1–2.

13. Ibid., 51.

14. Ibid., 374–76.

15. Ibid.

16. Anne Boykin (Kate) Jones Diary, May 26, 1851, SHC.

17. Jones Diary, May 30, 1851.

18. Jones Diary, July 1, 1851.

19. Jones Diary, May 30, 1851.

20. Jones Diary, June 14, 1851.

21. Laura Beecher Comer Diary, June 16, July 18, 1872, SHC.

22. Comer Diary, Sept. 18, 1872.

23. Comer Diary, Oct. 27, 1872.

24. "Letters of a Young Lady," Aug. 1884, folder 93, Papers of Cornelia Phillips Spencer, SHC.

25. Samuel Ringgold Ward, speech, May 16, 1853, Exeter Hall, London, in Ripley et al., *Black Abolitionist Papers,* 1: 341–42. On transatlantic black

abolitionists, see R. J. M. Blackett, *Building an Antislavery Wall: Black Americans in the Atlantic Abolitionist Movement, 1830–1860* (Baton Rouge: Louisiana State University Press, 1983).

26. O'Brien, *Conjectures of Order,* 1: 13.

27. Frederick Douglass, *My Bondage and My Freedom* (New York and Auburn: Miller, Orton and Mulligan, 1855), chap. 24.

28. Ibid.

29. William Wells Brown, speech, Sept. 5, 1849, 172.

30. William Wells Brown*, Three Years in Europe: Places I Have Seen and People I Have Met* (London: Charles Gilpin, 1852), 8–9.

31. Ibid., 139–41.

32. Ibid., 50–51.

33. Ibid., 34–35.

34. W. E. B. Du Bois, *The Autobiography of W. E. B. Du Bois: A Soliloquy on Viewing My Life from the Last Decade of Its First Century* (New York: International Publishers, 1968), 212–13.

35. Ibid., 156.

36. Ibid., 159–62.

37. Ibid.

38. Paul Gilroy, *The Black Atlantic: Modernity and Double Consciousness* (Cambridge: Harvard University Press, 1993), chap. 4.

2

Alexis de Tocqueville and Three German Travel Accounts on the Antebellum South and New Orleans

Thomas Clark

The scene changes so suddenly that you think yourself on the other side of the world.
> —Alexis de Tocqueville on crossing the Ohio into Kentucky

The Mason-Dixon Line from across the Atlantic

In the German author Thomas Meinecke's 1996 novel *The Church of John F. Kennedy,* a feverish Pynchonesque German American pastiche set in the Deep South, one finds the following paragraph:

> On the trip across country roads Assmann recalled scenes from a number of movies, in which deviously planted traffic diversion signs hinted at evil chainsaws and troughs of blood. Alligator heads, which were occasionally seen rising above murky waters, dragged the travelers' imagination into the innermost, most impenetrable of swamps, where they saw their own bodies dangling from giant cypresses. In the mudholes of Louisiana, Wenzel began to explain, behind ghostly veils of Spanish moss, Hollywood had, in a way, found its eternal Vietnam.[1]

In this brief passage, Meinecke manages to summarize some of the key elements that have consistently defined European (and American) perceptions of the South. There is, first and foremost, the recurrent trope of southernness as the embodiment of the irrational, uncanny, tropically foreign, and archaically violent, a heartland of darkness so removed from other conventions of U.S. Americanness, both as space and as psychological state, that it becomes part of a different realm. There is the mediated nature of this South, where travelers' impressions are inevitably prestructured by films, novels, and their antecedents' accounts, which frequently serve to reinforce the southern imaginary at the cost of empirical observation. Finally, Meinecke reminds us that European perceptions and descriptions of the South are inevitably informed by and entangled with American images that evolved from the ongoing national debate on the nature and boundaries of U.S. identity, or rather identities.

If we move backward past Hollywood, TV images of the civil rights struggle, Faulkner, Mitchell, and Dixon into the antebellum era, we will find that the idea of "Dixie" principally emerged as one half of a mutual identity construction process between northern Yankees and southern Cavaliers.[2] As early as 1787 the Antifederalist James Winthrop had argued in the debate over the Federal Constitution that "it is impossible for one code of laws to suit Georgia and Massachusetts. . . . The inhabitants of warmer climates are more dissolute in their manners, and less industrious, than in colder countries. A degree of severity is, therefore, necessary with one which would cramp the spirit of the other."[3] This juxtaposition between a stern, rational, and sober North and a tropically lascivious, emotion-driven South, whether expressed in climatological, ethnocultural, or economic terms, became a staple of intra-U.S. discourse. As late as 2001 a Louisiana scholar could affirm that his state was representative "of everything that the New England tradition in American literature and culture and thought is not. Louisiana represents the heart over the intellect, spontaneity over calculation, instinct over reason, music over the word, forgiveness over judgment, impermanence over permanence, and community over the isolated and alienated individual."[4]

An overarching southern identity congealed during the nineteenth century, as Americans became obsessed with questions of national character, and the South attempted to negotiate its internal contradictions concerning slavery, democracy, capitalism, and expansion by forging a homogenous "non-Yankee" sectional identity based more on myth than fact. Thus a patchwork of Souths—Piedmont and Tidewater, slaveholding and nonslaveholding, upper and lower, urban, rural, and frontier, Anglo, Franco, and Hispanic—could begin imagining itself as a nation defined by the peculiar institution, white states-rights republicanism, a genteel plantation culture, and the set of traits cataloged above.[5] The North, in turn, ambivalently chastised its strange sibling for its supposed feudal backwardness while wistfully yearning for aspects of its genteel lifestyle and imagined organic cohesion in the wake of anxieties over growing into an amoral society of soulless and pragmatic materialists.[6]

It seems banal to point out the ubiquity of this North-South divide in American society both as a source of political conflict and as a topic of cultural discourse between 1830 and the outbreak of the Civil War. And yet studies of European perceptions of America during this era tend to focus on the well-established bipolarity between "Old" and "New World"[7] or to emphasize a specifically binational framework of comparison, in which the fundamental intranational alterity of North and South is reduced to observing commentaries on the slavery debate, nullification, or the effect of different climates. By contrast, this essay will argue for the importance of the North-South divide as a conceptual frame for European observers and scholars alike, focusing on the way it disrupted or determined the construction of an American national image from an external vantage point.

Taking some cues from Werner and Zimmermann's programmatic article on the concept of *histoire croisée*,[8] we must first consider that the European traveler's act of *comparison* between America and Europe always also involved a *transfer* of conceptions from American to European observers. For our case this means that Old World travelers of the antebellum nineteenth-century United States were confronted in both their preparatory readings and their en-route conversations with a firmly established cultural Mason-Dixon dividing line confirmed by northerners and southerners alike. It was on this fixed template that they inevitably grafted their own perceptions as political and social commentators, businessmen seeking opportunities, or advisors to immigrants.

Second, the key matrix of mutual transatlantic perceptions so skillfully conceptualized by Rob Kroes[9] as a metaphorical juxtaposition of a horizontal, new, plural, atomistic America against a vertical, old, homogenous, organic Europe fused with the North-South paradigm into a complex triangular model in which the North, viewed by Europeans (and Americans) as a supposedly democratic-egalitarian, materialistic, and hyperdynamic Yankee culture, remained the true antipode to their own world, whether as an inspirational model or as an object of derision, while the South presented a vexing multiplicity of American, European, African, and even oriental traits. Old World chivalry coexisted with frontier anarchy and materialist dollar worship, African "savagery" with forms of oriental decadence and despotism engendered by the practice of slavery that turned masters into whimsical tyrants and harem keepers. The South thus emerged as an antithesis to what the United States was understood to embody, yet also as its perverse supplement that magnified its contradictions, displaying American depravity, harboring its remaining European virtues, and exuding the mystery of an incomprehensibly exotic foreign "other."

In the following essay, which should be considered an exploration into a potentially vast body of material, I would like to present some evidence for this thesis by discussing Alexis de Tocqueville's view of the South and comparing it with accounts by German-speaking travelers of diverse backgrounds: Julius Fröbel, a well-known German liberal of the Forty-Eighter generation; Samuel Ludvigh, a radical freethinker from Austro-Hungary who had long since settled in the North; and Louise Weil, a middle-class Protestant woman from Swabia, who spent several years in the United States. Pending the analysis of a much larger corpus of sources, this juxtaposition already clearly shows how quite distinctive perceptions of the South resulting from the travelers' highly divergent European backgrounds and agendas concerning the United States nonetheless converged in their dependence on conventional American Yankee/Dixie dichotomies in which opinions on the South were strongly influenced by those held of the North or of the United States as a whole and vice versa and that led some observers to bracket the South as an essentially un-American part of America. A further complication in three of these accounts is the preeminent role played by New Orleans, a place of particular distinction within the South due to its urbanity, Franco-Spanish heritage, and complex racial culture. In all of the present accounts perceptions of "the Big Easy" served to further amplify both the distance of southern identity from Yankeedom and its exotic multiplicity.

Tocqueville and Fröbel: The Un-American South

Alexis de Tocqueville has been celebrated as the keenest and most detached observer of America, but as I have argued elsewhere,[10] his unusually non-judgmental perspective by no means implies he was closer to recognizing some "true," "real" America than a deeply resentful observer such as Frances Trollope. Tocqueville's purpose was to study a working democracy, that is, a society in which traditional hierarchies had dissolved into complete social and increasingly economic equality and where the people at large constituted the supreme sovereign. This project he considered essential to finding ways and means of dealing with the inevitable coming of democracy to France, which, in contrast to the United States, had remained politically unstable ever since the revolution of 1789. Not surprisingly, he spent most of his time in New England and talking to New England Whigs, and many of his ideas about American democracy were shaped by the township tradition and distinctly northeastern perspectives on government and constitution. Of his nine months in the United States, Tocqueville spent only about one and a half months in the South, traveling from Cincinnati to Tennessee; down the Mississippi to New Orleans; and then hurriedly back to Washington, DC, via Mississippi, Alabama, Georgia, the two Carolinas, and Virginia.[11] He saw virtually nothing of the Old South, skirting Charleston, and had no interest in visiting a plantation. Moreover, in his completed work *De la démocratie en Amérique* he sequestered most of his sparse observations on the South, many of which concerned slavery, into an addendum to the first 1835 volume and left its exhaustive treatment to his companion Beaumont, who produced the novel *Marie; or, Slavery in the United States.*[12]

Tocqueville's relative disinterest is not surprising, for as we can read in his journal, the South to him was simply not part of America, or at least not the democratic America that interested him: "As far as I can judge a republic does not seem to be as natural and appropriate a social state for the South as for the North of the United States. . . . The North presents me, externally at least, with the picture of a strong, regular, durable government, perfectly suited to the physical and moral state of things. In the South there is in the way things are run something feverish, disordered, revolutionary and passionate, which does not give the same sense of strength and durability."[13] With a string of suggestive adjectives Tocqueville embraced the tropical paradigm of the South, demoting it to an unstable banana republic sharply countervailed by the North's image of an ideal polity. Notably, this impression was penned in Baltimore before Tocqueville had even seen the South, except for a bit of Maryland. It was based on reading and on conversations with Americans, including southerners, he had met while traveling the North and thus exemplifies the mediated and preemptive quality of many European pronouncements on the South.

Tocqueville, like most Europeans and Americans, came to believe that the major difference between the sections was slavery and its creation of a labor-adverse white leisure class.[14] He mistakenly assumed that even the poorest farmers owned a slave or two[15] (when, in fact, roughly one-third of southern families owned slaves) and described the white inhabitants of Kentucky and Tennessee as a strange blend of savagely living violent frontiersmen and patriarchal "country gentlemen of old Europe," all of the same Virginian migrant stock.[16] His binary conception of the U.S. vision crystallized into a highly stylized account of his crossing of the border from free Ohio into slave Kentucky on December 20, 1831:

> For the first time we have had the chance to examine there the effect that slavery produces on society. On the right bank of the Ohio everything is activity, industry, labor is honored; there are no slaves. Pass to the left bank and the scene changes so suddenly that you think yourself on the other side of the world; the enterprising spirit is gone. There, work is not only painful: it's shameful, and you degrade yourself in submitting yourself to it. To ride, to hunt, to smoke like a Turk in the sunshine: there is the destiny of the white. To do any other kind of manual labor is to act like a slave. The whites, to the South of Ohio, form a veritable aristocracy which, like the others, combines many prejudices with high sentiments and instincts.[17]

The "Turkish" manner of leisured despots over a slave population, together with the effects of the warm, passion-inducing climate, defined all southerners as a bewildering hybrid of decadent oriental, European nobleman, and American savage. They were "brave, comparatively ignorant, hospitable, generous, easy to irritate, violent in their resentments, without industry or the spirit of enterprise." In the frontier areas of the South, among which Tocqueville counted Kentucky, Tennessee, and most other thinly populated areas, where men "must fight daily against all the miseries of life," their passions were "still more irritable and violent and further removed from society. The slightest tiresome contact with it will be painful to them; less civilized, they will have learnt even less to master themselves. . . . They are men of the South, masters of slaves, but rendered half savage by solitude and hardened by the miseries of life."[18] A lawyer in Alabama confirmed to Tocqueville that "there is no one here but carries arms under his clothes. At the slightest quarrel, knife or pistol comes to hand. These things happen continually; it is a semibarbarous state of society."[19]

Since Tocqueville believed that the "moeurs," that is, "the whole moral and intellectual condition of a people," determined their civic and political fate,[20] U.S. institutions that blossomed in the North seemed bound to fail in Dixie. He observed the "bad state of the judiciary in Kentucky, Tennessee, Mississippi, Alabama and Georgia. Bar slight exceptions the same institutions as in the North, but bad choice of men. . . . Coterie of petty political leaders; civil commotions due to bad state of justice; first cause of brutish manners in this part of the Union. No confidence in right."[21]

Not only were southerners not as level-headed as Yankees, but they were also "poorer, less persevering, less well educated. No schools. Half or two-thirds cannot read. Religious feeling not only certainly less strong, but runs more to fanaticism."[22] Thus, further key elements that defined the democratic culture of New England, education and an enlightened faith, were absent. Yet while Tocqueville the scholar of democracy dismissed the South as a failure, Tocqueville the aristocrat recognized his kinship with southerners, who embodied certain "Old World" qualities that Tocqueville associated with his own class and in other contexts yearned for nostalgically: "They say, and I am very much inclined to believe, that in the matter of honour these men practice delicacies and refinements unknown in the North. They are frank, hospitable and put many things before money." Yet he knew "they will end, nevertheless, by being dominated by the North. Every day the latter grows more wealthy and densely populated while the South is stationary or growing poor."[23]

New Orleans, in some respects, appeared decidedly different from the "savage South." Like numerous other travelers Tocqueville juxtaposed the eerie wilderness and isolation of the Mississippi River with the bustling metropolis it led to, the most striking characteristic of which was a bewildering multiplicity: "Beautiful houses. Huts. Muddy, unpaved streets. Spanish architecture: flat roofs; English: bricks, little doors; French: massive carriage entrances. Population just as mixed. Faces with every shade of color. Language French, English, Spanish, Creole. General French look, but all the same notices and commercial announcements mostly in English. Industrial and commercial world American."[24] Ultimately, however, New Orleans simply confirmed and amplified the principal dichotomy between Yankees and Cavaliers. In New Orleans, the French took on the role of the southerners, in that they were leisurely, honorable, conservative, aristocratically minded landholders. As the French consul Guiellemin told Tocqueville, it was enterprising Americans, "who descend on us every year from the North," who fueled commerce with their obsessive "longing for wealth; they have long given up everything else for that; they come with little to lose and very few of the honorable scruples the French feel about paying their debts."[25] At times Tocqueville felt he was in France, but it was a strangely creolized version of his fatherland. As elsewhere in the South, racism and slavery, by virtue of the de facto concubinage of mulatto women to white men, which he observed at a Quadroon ball, created an "incredible laxity of morals."[26]

Indeed, besides its unfitness for democracy, the moral perversion of slavery paired with miscegenation was one of the most lasting impressions Tocqueville took home from the South. In a forceful anecdote he recounted the agonies of a dying slaveholder who could not bring himself to manumit his mulatto offspring yet shuddered at the idea of his own children being sold to a less—literally—paternal master.[27] Volume 1 of *Democracy in America* concludes with a sinister vision of an almost inevitable race war, which would possibly lead to an exodus of whites from the Deep South and the establishment of a separate black state. Secession and possibly civil war with the free states seemed likely also.[28] One way or another, the South as it presently existed was doomed in Tocqueville's eyes. Candid as he was, he admitted to having spent too little time there to gain a deep appreciation of it,[29] but since his project was about understanding "democracy in America" rather than the sectional intricacies of the United States, he never returned to a further examination of a South lacking so dearly what fascinated him about America in the first place.

Bereft of a sound empirical foundation and feeding heavily upon native narratives, Tocqueville's South refracted American Yankee/Dixie stereotypes through the lens of a European aristocrat seeking to understand democratic modernity. His ambivalent impressions of an (un)-American South of frontier savagery and aristocratic ideals, immoral slavery and high-minded gentility, of commercial dependency upon the North and fierce sectional pride, mediated as they themselves were, echoed through numerous later depictions of the antebellum South. A German contemporary of Tocqueville's took his notion of the South's un-Americanness to its logical conclusion.

The German natural scientist and liberal democrat Julius Fröbel was a key figure of the German *Vormärz* and participated in the Austrian and German revolutions of 1848. Having worked as a professor of mineralogy and a radical publisher in Zurich since 1836, he joined the failed Vienna uprising of 1848 and subsequently emigrated to the United States, traveling the Upper South, the West, Mexico, and Central America. Contrary to his ideological kinsman Samuel Ludvigh, discussed below, he returned to Europe in 1857 and published a two-volume account of his American experiences, discussing politics, the economy, slavery, and culture in great detail.[30] Fröbel found the United States to be best understood through Swiss republican and British eyes, finding many supposedly American traits to be English in origin, and he viewed its particularities with sympathy. He resembled his French precursor Tocqueville in perceiving individualism, egalitarianism, and restless ambition as key characteristics of U.S. society, noting that American equality was aristocratic in that people struggled to pull even with their economic betters rather than settling for the lowest common denominator.[31] Emerging from his American sojourn as a pragmatic market liberal and (avidly racist) free-soil enemy of slavery, who had shed any traces of pre-Marxian socialist thought he may have previously entertained, Fröbel, like so many Forty-Eighters, became a staunch supporter of the Republican Party and, in stark contrast to Ludvigh, greatly admired the entrepreneurial Yankee spirit.[32] It was from this perspective that he came to the harsh and bold conclusion that economically, socially, and culturally Virginia and the whole American South were more akin to the backward, stagnating realm of Latin America, which he had studied and traveled with such great interest, than to the North. Observing that even the Virginian press was lamenting the decline of the once great state, he stated:

> But where the fault for this actually lies will not be admitted here nor there. The most one rises to, is to operate against a symptom of the disease, rather than attacking it at its root, which in the southern states of the Union is slavery, in the Spanish-American countries the rule of the clergy and the military, in both—which is entwined therewith—the lack or the insufficient development of a self-reliant middle class, whose industrious manner constitutes the strength and growth of today's civilized world and whose extraordinary dominance in the northern states of the Union are their equally extraordinary source of power.[33]

In Fröbel's mind, the only option left to Virginia (and the other southern states), as well as to Central America, was to invite massive numbers of enterprising migrants from the North, who could and would transform both the Old Dominion and Spanish America from failing states governed by self-interested oligarchies into a second Ohio or Pennsylvania.[34] Much as he was impressed with the romantic beauty of Virginia and Nicaragua, the hospitality of their inhabitants and their potential,[35] Fröbel saw no future for these southern cultures, if they were not dramatically "Yankeefied." As Tocqueville had predicted earlier, Dixie as it was, or seemed to be, would either embrace the North or disappear for good behind thick veils of Spanish moss.

Ludvigh and Weil: The Tropical South as Republican Alternative and Bewildering Babylon

A different and somewhat surprising evaluation of the South's tropical otherness, which Tocqueville and Fröbel viewed as highly problematic, was provided by the Austro-Hungarian newspaper editor, publisher, and freethinker Samuel Ludvigh, who had emigrated to the northern United States in 1837, after travels and political activity in Europe and Turkey, living there until his death near Cincinnati in 1869. Whereas Tocqueville was a preinformed visitor and Fröbel a temporary exile, Ludvigh had spent nearly a decade in Pennsylvania and New York as a writer and publisher of anticlerical and republican magazines and books catering to German immigrant communities when he headed South in 1846. While Ludvigh idolized the U.S. Constitution and political system as harbingers of freedom and equality, he was quite critical of northern society's moral prudery coupled with its relentless materialism. To the sensibility of an egalitarian freethinker socialized in a multiethnic catholic empire, the tropically lax slaveholding South seemed both enticing and problematic.

Like Tocqueville, Ludvigh, descending the Mississippi, almost ritually described the transition into a distinct southern realm as entering a "Heart of Darkness." He observed that "people and vegetation are beginning to take on a different character. Around the liberty tree of white *grandezza* creep the weeds of slavery, and the cotton trees are strangled by Spanish moss."[36] On viewing Baton Rouge he observed that republican institutions had turned the Spanish and French colonial wilderness of isolated fur-trading outposts and roaming savages into a prosperous land. At the same time the perverse inequality of slavery was mirrored in the plantation architecture of mansions surrounded by squalid huts, which reminded him of

Hungarian feudal estates.[37] However, by the "southern skies, where golden orange trees blossom in the open," he felt transported "with a stroke of magic . . . from the wilderness forests to Treviso in Italy."[38] The South thus appeared to the cosmopolitan Ludvigh, as to the provincial Weil discussed below, as a bewildering collage of republican vitality, feudal inequality, foreboding American wilderness, and Renaissance pastoral. This multiplicity intensified in New Orleans. Despite his misgivings about slavery, the freethinking Ludvigh, after successfully lecturing and selling his papers in the city, reveled in the secular atmosphere of the bustling port, which he called "the only free city in America," free, that is, of the stern moralism of his northern home.[39] "Spanish grandezza, French ease, German stolidness and Yankee hucksterism meet as extremes and the former three neutralize the dark spirit of English Puritanism," Ludvigh fawned. Southern culture had also shaped German immigrants for the better: "The Germans here are marked by greater freedom of thought and there is less envy and miserliness. . . . Generally, money in the South is viewed more as a means to afford pleasures, in the North as a means of holding property." Ludvigh hastened to add that he preferred the "chivalresque character" of southerners to the "gold-greedy" mindset of the Yankees among which he lived.[40]

New Orleans played a central part in Ludvigh's enthusiastic endorsement of southern culture. Although the city lacked restrictive Sabbath laws and other Boston-style instruments of social control, Ludvigh nonetheless claimed that "honesty, morality and safety are better in New Orleans than in any other city of the Union!" since there were no unruly mobs as in New York or Philadelphia.[41] While the baffling heterogeneity and inequality of a city peopled by all sorts of religious sects, the dismally poor and super-rich, Indians, blacks, gruff sailors, and refined dandies indicated to him that humanity would be unable to realize European communist ideals for centuries to come, he imagined New Orleans as a cosmopolitan, worldly, prosperous, technologically advanced, and socially stable republican alternative to the tight-lipped Calvinist democratic capitalism of the North.[42] He made much of the myth of Andrew Jackson's victory in the War of 1812 having been won by common patriotic backwoodsmen and marveled at the size and quantity of the city's modern cotton presses, as well as its gas- and waterworks, adding a democratic and techno-industrial perspective to the traditional picture of an aristocratic-agrarian South.[43] Moreover, he found New Orleans to be a worthy cultural rival to Europe, as exemplified by the magnificent St. Charles and Orleans theatres.[44]

The freethinking reformer Ludvigh, evidently frustrated by the Yankee culture of New York and Ohio, discovered in the South a liberating otherness that he employed to recast Jefferson's vision of a resplendent republican empire on the Mississippi in a globalized, multicultural frame. The South, or rather New Orleans, as a pars pro toto, was judged to be no feudal backwater, but rather the more genuinely advanced section of the United States, which had effectively absorbed the best aspects of aristocratic, democratic, traditional, and modern American and European societies, and whose Cain's mark of slavery had to be viewed in perspective, considering the dramatic socioeconomic inequality in the supposedly egalitarian North.[45] While Ludvigh, like many German liberals, haughtily believed that a morally and politically far superior republic would eventually arise in Germany to dwarf the "heterogeneous Chaos of people and races" that was the United States,[46] the South, for all of its shortcomings, seemed to be the true asylum of an individual liberty Ludvigh pined for in the morally uptight North. His enchantment with New Orleans, and to a lesser extent Charleston and Savannah, as well as his callously ironic commentaries on the fate of slaves,[47] indicate how strongly his perception of the South was driven by self-indulgent exotic fantasies feeding on Yankee frustration. To the liberal cosmopolitan atheist and social democrat Ludvigh, the triangulated comparison of Europe, North, and South revealed the first to be deficient as backwardly feudal economically and illiberal politically, while the second was politically democratic, culturally illiberal, and economically too liberal in its nakedly reductive capitalist ways. The South, on the other hand, struck an effective balance between American republicanism and technological progress, European cultured urbanity and indulgent "oriental" laissez-faire in terms of social freedom, if only for whites.

From the perspective of a bourgeois Swabian Protestant minister's daughter, those very qualities made the South appear like the gates of Hell. Louise Weil's critical emigration narrative, *Aus dem schwäbischen Pfarrhaus nach Amerika,* lacks the explicitly political dimension of analysis central to those of the male intellectuals discussed here. Weil traveled to the United States in 1854 at age seventeen, spending five years mainly in the North and working for eighteen months as a teacher at the Harmonist utopian community of Economy, Pennsylvania, founded by fellow Swabians. Toward the end of her American sojourn she traveled to New Orleans to visit two of her brothers, who had settled there as entrepreneurs. Weil's book was written as a warning to potential female emigrants in Germany hoping for careers in the United States as self-sufficient domestics, governesses, or teachers. The egalitarianism that fascinated Tocqueville she perceived as a threat to bourgeois norms by the unrestrained reign of the hoi polloi. However, she came to admit that American women's education and training were so far superior to her own that she, and by extension any German middle-class woman, was unable to compete successfully on the job market except on the lowest rungs. Her central conclusion was that, contrary to popular myth, only marriage could provide economic security for female immigrants, and thus America was no promised land but merely a dangerous game of chance.[48] On this argumentative axis Weil did not observe a practical difference between North and South. While the latter's planter class created a distinctive and highly lucrative job market for well-paid governesses, who lived in comfort and ease, these positions were traditionally occupied by French women whose qualifications in music and languages were once again beyond the reach of middle-class Germans.[49] Nonetheless, Weil clearly distinguished between North and South by adopting conventional discourses on southern orientalism and multiplicity and filtering them through her German Protestant sensibility. Her ambivalence about the South, and particularly New Orleans, was strongly biographical: after failing professionally in the North and resisting assimilation, it became a realm of security and familiarity in the form of her prosperous and caring brothers and the German immigrant community there. Yet the perverse, exotically sinful culture of the city and its impact on her siblings precluded any identification with southern culture, and Weil ultimately rejected both versions of the United States, excepting only the utopian community of Economy, Pennsylvania, from condemnation.

As in Tocqueville's and Ludvigh's accounts, the Mississippi occupied a space taken in later decades by the Kongo: a slithering primeval giant, both sublime and uncanny, in Weil's words a "genuine jungle as it sprang from the hand of God Almighty on the third day of the creation." Out of this virgin land popped isles of cultivation and occasionally small towns, in which she found "magnificent houses, factories, churches," and to her particular surprise in this "remote wild region" refined ladies who "develop a luxury which can compete with the greatest cities of the North." Such pleasantries harshly contrasted with less pleasant episodes, such as an encounter aboard a steamship with backwoods folk, depicted as hideous beasts, and a near drowning, which, together with tales of other river tragedies, conveyed the message that "life counts little in these parts."[50] Where Tocqueville observed an amalgam of violence and gentility in the western South, Weil was similarly surprised by the coexistence of a brute male-dominated frontier of "poisonous swamps" and "dark jungle" and a domesticated civilization satisfying northern and even European standards.[51]

As the wilderness gave way to plantation culture, Weil's Protestant sensibility was overwhelmed by the tropical exoticity of Louisiana and New Orleans, which she ambivalently framed with classical orientalist tropes of Edenic beauty and lushness, as well as moral depravity and bigotry, such as she never employed in her observations of the North. Like Ludvigh, she marveled at the ostentatious sugar plantations of Baton Rouge, as well as the exotic fruits and foods of the New Orleans market and the city's rich gardens, while observing the sadness of the slaves and the brutality of the slave system.[52] Weil explicitly commented on the depravity of slave sales, the sexual abuse of female slaves, and the Calabouse, a system of outsourcing corporeal punishment of slaves to professional torturers.[53] To her surprise, she found her once staunchly abolitionist brother considering the purchase of a slave over employing another hard-drinking German servant, one of the many markers of cultural cross-fertilization with which she was uncomfortable.[54]

Indeed, Weil, like all visitors, found the multiplicity of the city, featuring "a contribution from each corner of the globe," both astounding and unsettling. Bigoted Creole Catholicism, which she juxtaposed with the innocent purity of Native Americans, coexisted with the sober Lutheranism of German immigrants and strange new cults such as spiritualism, of which Weil's brother had become an adherent.[55] Murder and crime were ubiquitous, and she witnessed the unbridled passion and emotional instability of the South firsthand when a gentleman from the "Higher South" nearly went mad over the death of his Creole wife, only to elope with a German immigrant's newlywed six days later.[56] For Tocqueville the tropical passion of southerners undermined democratic institutions; for Weil it corroded the bourgeois social fabric of stable family structures and civil intercourse. Weil summarized her ambivalence in the words of others: while her brother announced to her before her arrival that she would find New Orleans to be a stop en route to Paradise, a friend of her brother's told her: "here in New Orleans, which is probably the worst city on earth, one actually stands in the antechamber of hell."[57]

For all the depravity of the city, Weil found solace and pleasure in European high and German immigrant culture, as well as among the elegance and refinement of the better circles her merchant brother introduced her to. While nearly a second home to Weil due to her strong attachment to her brothers, New Orleans's ultimate foreignness and danger were expressed symbolically by the looming threat of the yellow fever, which necessitated her departure after two months, upon which she returned to Germany via New York.[58] The destructive climate of the city is confirmed by the narrative's conclusion, the receipt and reproduction of a letter recounting the death of her brother Adolph from the yellow fever.

Weil never attempted an explicit juxtaposition of North and South, and neither section was judged by her as unequivocally superior to the other. Neither was suitable for female immigrants. Her narrative stood as a warning against the false promise of equality and prosperity through work in the North, yet the depravity of the slaveholding South and the immorality of New Orleans provided no alternative.[59] The true alternative to the shoddy materialism of the dire North and the tropical corruption of the South was the utopian project of Economy, Pennsylvania, which Weil eulogized in a poem at the outset of her narrative. A homogenous community of devout Christians, it appeared to her as an abundant paradise, not of a tropical nature, but rather built upon the Calvinist industriousness of its inhabitants, who were technical pioneers employing steam-driven machinery and who amassed considerable wealth, but without succumbing to the restless materialism and divisive individualism that so many Europeans considered a Yankee pathology. Yet Economy was a dying community due to its celibacy rules, whereas the multiplicitous South richly pulsed with life, disgusting and brief as that life may have been for less fortunate individuals. In sum, Weil both demystified and complicated the supposed land of "opportunity" for her audience, with the South emerging from her critical portrait as a confusingly plural salad bowl of familiar, transformed, and utterly alien cultures, a far stranger otherness than the North, in which Weil's orientation depended on the guidance of her acculturated brothers.

Tocqueville and the three German travelers discussed here all agreed that the North and the South were fundamentally distinct societies and built their argument upon the native U.S. discourse concerning these distinctions, while filtering it through perspectives that betrayed their own agendas and their origins in different European political cultures and social milieus. We can only gain a deeper appreciation of how such travelers constructed their images of the South—and of the United States—if we pursue the study of Atlantic image transfers; take into account the implicit process of comparative triangulation among North, South, and observer culture; and resist the enticing simplicity of national reference frames. A *croisée* approach to transnational travel literature will reveal the submerged mechanisms of national identity construction and does greater justice to the complexity of the American South and its Spanish mosses.

Notes

1. Thomas Meinecke, *The Church of John F. Kennedy,* 2nd ed., Edition Suhrkamp (Frankfurt: Suhrkamp, 1997), 52.

2. William Robert Taylor, *Cavalier and Yankee: The Old South and American National Character* (New York: Harper Torchbooks, 1969).

3. James Winthrop, "Agrippa," Dec. 3, 1787, http://teachingamericanhistory .org/library/index.asp?document=1634.

4. Lafcadio Hearn, *Inventing New Orleans: Writings of Lafcadio Hearn,* ed. S. Frederick Starr, (Jackson: University Press of Mississippi, 2001), xii, http://www .questia.com/PM.qst?a=o&d=113399566.

5. For the actual heterogeneity of the South, see William W. Freehling, *The Road to Disunion* (New York: Oxford University Press, 1990).

6. Taylor, *Cavalier and Yankee,* 18.

7. See, e.g., Robert H. Wiebe, *Self-Rule: A Cultural History of American Democracy* (Chicago: University of Chicago Press, 1995), 41–60.

8. Michael Werner and Bénédicte Zimmermann, "Histoire Croisée and the Challenge of Reflexivity," *History and Theory* 45.1 (2006): 30–50.

9. Rob Kroes, "America and Europe—A Clash of Imagined Communities," in John Dean and Jean Paul Gabilliet, eds., *European Readings of American Popular Culture* (Westport, CT: Greenwood Press, 1996), xxv–lii; Rob Kroes, *If You've Seen One, You've Seen the Mall: Europeans and American Mass Culture* (Urbana: University of Illinois Press, 1996).

10. Thomas Clark, "'The American Democrat' Reads *Democracy in America:* Cooper and Tocqueville in the Transatlantic Hall of Mirrors," *Amerikastudien/American Studies* [Germany] 52.2 (2007): 187–208; Thomas Clark, "Die Démocratie in Amerika: Zur Wirkungsgeschichte Tocquevilles in Den Vereinigten Staaten," in Karlfriedrich Herb and Oliver Hidalgo, eds., *Alter Staat—Neue Politik. Tocqueville's Entdeckung der modernen Demokratie* (Baden Baden: Nomos, 2004), 155–75.

11. The complete itinerary is given at http://www.tocqueville.org/chap4b.htm (accessed June 2, 2009). This is compiled from the two key works concerning Tocqueville's trip: George Wilson Pierson, *Tocqueville in America,* Johns Hopkins paperback ed. (Baltimore: Johns Hopkins University Press, 1996); and Alexis de Tocqueville, J. P. Mayer, and A. P. Kerr, *Journey to America,* rev. and augmented ed. (Garden City, NY: Anchor, 1971).

12. Cf. James L. Crouthamel, "Tocqueville's South," *Journal of the Early Republic* 2.4 (1982): 381–401. This is the most significant study on Tocqueville and the South, but while it is descriptively exhaustive, it falls short of analyzing the reasons for Tocqueville's view of the South as addressed in the present essay.

13. Tocqueville, Mayer, and Kerr, *Journey to America*, 160–61.

14. Ibid., 284.

15. Ibid., 282.

16. Ibid., 282.

17. Pierson, *Tocqueville in America*, 581.

18. Tocqueville, Mayer, and Kerr, *Journey to America*, 280–85.

19. Ibid., 103.

20. Alexis de Tocqueville, *Democracy in America,* 2 vols., ed. Phillips Bradley (New York: A. A. Knopf, 1945), 1: 310.

21. Tocqueville, Mayer, and Kerr, *Journey to America*, 169.

22. Ibid.

23. Pierson, *Tocqueville in America*, 582.

24. Tocqueville, Mayer, and Kerr, *Journey to America*, 165.

25. Ibid., 98.

26. Ibid., 165.

27. Tocqueville, *Democracy in America,* 1: 396.

28. Ibid., 1: 390–92, 418ff.

29. "It would be absurd to want to pass judgment on a whole people after spending a week or ten days among them. So I can only trust to hearsay" (Tocqueville, Mayer, and Kerr, *Journey to America*, 284).

30. Julius Fröbel, *Aus Amerika. Erfahrungen, Reisen und Studien,* 2 vols. (Leipzig: Weber, 1857).

31. Fröbel, *Aus Amerika,* 1: 18–20, 108, 117, 2: 605.

32. Wilhelm Mommsen, "Julius Fröbel, Wirrniss und Weitsicht," *Historische Zeitschrift* 181.3 (1956): 510–11.

33. Fröbel, *Aus Amerika,* 1: 118 (translation by the author).

34. Ibid., 1: 120, 2: 606–7.

35. Ibid., 1: 71–106, 2: 608–10.

36. Samuel Ludvigh, *Licht-Und Schattenbilder Republikanischer Zustände. Skizzirt Von Samuel Ludvigh Während Seiner Reise in Den Vereinigten Staaten Von Nord-Amerika 1846* (Leipzig: Wilhelm Jurany, 1848), 269.

37. Ibid., 274.

38. Ibid., 275.

39. Ibid., 276.

40. Ibid., 276–77, 311.

41. Ibid., 278.

42. Ibid., 279.

43. Ibid., 281, 306, 309–10.

44. Ibid., 288, 305.

45. Ibid., 278.

46. Ibid., 315.

47. Ibid., 311–12.

48. Anabel Aliaga-Buchenau, "Erfahrungen einer deutschen Auswanderin im Amerika des neunzehnten Jahrhunderts. Louise Weil, Aus dem Schwäbischen Pfarrhaus nach Amerika," in Hartmut Fischer, ed., *Winnetou lebt . . . ? & Amerika liegt am Dümmer. Amerika in deutscher Literatur* (Northeim: Gymnasium Corvinianum, 2009), 68–81.

49. Louise Weil, *Aus Dem Schwäbischen Pfarrhaus Nach Amerika* (Stuttgart: Franckh, 1860), 255.

50. Ibid., 225.

51. Ibid., 262–63.

52. Ibid., 227, 240.

53. Ibid., 253.

54. Ibid., 251.

55. Ibid., 238.

56. Ibid., 233–34.

57. Ibid., 236.

58. Ibid., 258.

59. Ibid., 124, 140, 172.

3

The German Forty-Eighters' Critique of the U.S. South, 1850–1861

Daniel Nagel

The history of immigrants is often complex, confusing, and even contradictory. Groups that may seem to be united by a single language and culture are often divided along regional, religious, cultural, or political lines. This was certainly the case with the one million German immigrants who came to the United States during the 1850s. They varied in many ways, not the least of which was their attitude toward slavery and southern slaveholders.

As Andrea Mehrländer has recently pointed out, many German immigrants who settled in the South fully embraced its distinctive culture, including the "peculiar institution."[1] However, not all German immigrants were so fond of the South. In particular, the German Forty-Eighters viewed southern slavery as an abomination, a cancer that threatened the American republic.[2] Their conviction was fueled by Republicanism, an ideology that fused American and French Republicanism of the eighteenth century with German idealism and stressed the importance of virtuous citizens. The Forty-Eighters went so far as to suggest that German immigrants had a special role to play in saving the United States from the southern threat. At the same time, they portrayed their mission as a distinctly American one: they hoped for German virtues to transform American society and ensure that freedom would triumph—not only in America but all over the world. The Forty-Eighters' critique of the South formed the basis of the enduring political alliance between the Forty-Eighters and the Republican Party, which allowed Forty-Eighters such as Carl Schurz to shape the United States in profound ways.

The German Forty-Eighters were a group of radical revolutionaries who tried to create a German republic during the Revolution of 1848–49. After a revolutionary uprising in Baden and the neighboring Palatinate was crushed by the Prussian military in May 1849, they fled to Switzerland.[3] Many returned home to face prosecution from the reinstated authorities, but others, including most of the intellectual, political, and military leaders, left Europe and settled in the United States.[4] By the 1850s they were known as the "Forty-Eighters." They shared the common experiences of the failed revolution and a life in exile. Despite frequent personal conflicts between them, they shared a political ideology that justifies speaking of "the" Forty-Eighters.

This small group of "revolutionary refugees," a few thousand people at most, must be separated from the much larger group of more than a million "ordinary" Germans who immigrated to the United States during the 1850s. The majority of these immigrants were not political refugees, but people who sought a better standard of living. Forty-Eighters and ordinary Germans mostly settled in the Mid-Atlantic, the Old Northwest, and the West, avoiding New England and the South. There are a few exceptions to this rule, such as the German settlements in Texas and various cities in slaveholding Border States like Baltimore, St. Louis, and Louisville.[5]

Many Forty-Eighters fell into obscurity; others refrained from political activities. A considerable number, however, continued their political struggle, hoping in vain for renewed revolution in Germany. This revolution never came, and so the Forty-Eighters had to face the challenge of not only making a livelihood but also finding a political goal worth fighting for in the United States. Many Forty-Eighters, determined to continue their political work, joined existing German American newspapers or founded new ones. These newspapers are the main sources of the research presented in this article.[6] Based on their talents, number, and commitment to liberal causes, the Forty-Eighters soon became ethnic leaders within German American communities.

However, the leadership of the Forty-Eighters was constantly under attack by more conservative German Americans, who were aligned with the Democratic Party. The conservatives' most prominent and influential voice was the widely circulating *New Yorker Staatszeitung.* The Forty-Eighters generally found it easier to appeal to Protestant Germans due to their hostility toward the Catholic Church—a result of the church's opposition to the liberal agenda of the Revolution of 1848–49.[7] In this way, the Forty-Eighters were similar to many other Americans who were concerned by the growing influence of the Catholic Church in the United States, which they considered to be a threat to Republicanism. However, the Forty-Eighters rejected all attempts to make German immigrants comply with nativists' understanding of American values.[8] Instead, they constantly stressed their determination to retain their ethnic traditions, especially the German language, which they considered to be the core of their cultural identity.

Several recent studies, by Mischa Honeck, Christian B. Keller, and Alison Efford, have shed new light on the complex process of cooperation and confrontation between German and Anglo Americans.[9] In doing so, they have largely supplanted Bruce Levine's interpretation, which places the Forty-Eighters in the context of the emerging labor movement.[10] The view provided by this essay is largely compatible with these more recent works, but in addition it portrays the Forty-Eighters as exponents of the political ideology of Republicanism. Republicanism in Germany and the United States during the nineteenth century has not been well researched.[11] Many historians seem to assume that it had vanished or been replaced by either liberalism or nationalism. Moreover, scholarship on nineteenth-century Republicanism as a transatlantic phenomenon is virtually nonexistent. This essay aims to show that Republicanism remained central to transatlantic political discourse until at least 1860. In fact, Republicanism served as the basis of political cooperation between the Forty-Eighters and the Republican Party.

To the Forty-Eighters Republicanism meant the absence of monarchical rule and government by the people or their representatives. Citizens of a republic had to be virtuous and act according to the common weal, in order for the republic to survive. Virtue rested in the people, if they were not corrupted by wealthy or powerful interests. Immoral behavior, like selfishness, threatened the survival of the republic, because it corrupted republican institutions and destroyed the republic from inside. The Forty-Eighters advocated a democratic society that guaranteed the human rights of all people. If people in a republic were truly free and equal, these independent citizens could participate in the democratic political process and engage in an open discourse on any given matter. Freedom and equality therefore were fundamental principles of republican government, because open debates among citizens enabled them to make the right decisions, that is, to act according to the common good.

The Forty-Eighters regarded the United States as a model of Republicanism in a world of monarchies. They admired the U.S. Constitution, the

Declaration of Independence, and the Founding Fathers, whom they considered to be exemplary embodiments of Republican virtue. The reality of the United States that they encountered during the early 1850s, however, did not live up to their ideal. They criticized American materialism and the excessive influence of religion in the public sphere. They also attacked the political parties, which they thought suffered from a lack of principled positions.[12]

For their critique of the United States they applied a philosophy that built on the work of Georg Wilhelm Friedrich Hegel, known as Young Hegelianism. Young Hegelians turned Hegel's dialectic into a method of criticizing reality, using reason to compare it to the demands of an ideal theory and defining progress as the resolution of the difference.[13] An ideal theory was, for example, Republicanism, which provided the goal of a truly republican society based on virtue. The Young Hegelian critique of reality led to a dialectical interpretation of politics. The Forty-Eighters expected political parties to represent either the imperfect reality (slavery) or the ideal theory (freedom). The resulting conflict had to be resolved in a synthesis, and to the Forty-Eighters the only acceptable synthesis was freedom, because compromise between freedom and slavery was impossible.[14] In their first confrontation with American politics, however, they had to face the fact that both dominant political parties, Democrats and Whigs, supported the Compromise of 1850. The compromise included provisions such as the Fugitive Slave Law, which the Forty-Eighters considered to be a perversion of justice.[15]

Instead of heeding the Forty-Eighters' demand to repeal the law, both major parties avoided making it a campaign issue.[16] The Democratic platform of 1852, for instance, expressed the party's determination "to resist all attempts at renewing . . . the agitation of the slavery question."[17] To the Forty-Eighters, this position was untenable. They believed that parties should provide voters with a clear choice between *freedom* and *slavery*. In a republican society that was based on free speech and free exchange of political ideas, virtuous citizens would always side with freedom, thereby paving the way for progress.

With both major parties clinging to the Compromise of 1850, many Forty-Eighters abandoned the existing political parties and focused their hopes on the emergence of a "party of general freedom" (*allgemeine Freiheitspartei*).[18] This party was supposed to not only fight slavery and the Democratic Party but also promote the principles of the Declaration of

Independence, freedom and equality. In the opinion of the Forty-Eighters, the necessary reforms could be initiated within the current political system because the United States had already rejected monarchical rule during the American Revolution and offered its male citizens (and immigrants) free participation in a republican system of government.[19]

The Forty-Eighters were convinced that German Americans were destined to play an important role in this reform movement; some even thought that they would be able to initiate it. They ignored the religious and regional fragmentation of the German American community and constructed a German American identity based on belief in the progressive, freedom-loving "German spirit" (*deutscher Geist*), which was destined to save the American republic by preserving republican freedom and equality.[20]

When the Kansas-Nebraska Act of 1854 repealed the Missouri Compromise of 1820 and opened up the remaining parts of the Louisiana Purchase for slavery, the Forty-Eighters were enraged. In their opinion, slavery should be confined to a steadily decreasing area. The Forty-Eighters were willing to accept slavery as an aberration in retreat, but not as an expanding institution: slavery on the march was worse than existing slavery. The passage of the Kansas-Nebraska Act signaled that slaveholders were using Congress to extend their corrupting influence on republican government, thereby threatening the foundations of the American republic.[21]

The Forty-Eighters' critique of slavery rested on the assertion that slavery corrupted the virtuous republican citizen and was therefore unrepublican. Instead of enabling people to participate in a free republican society as equals, it denied slaves basic human rights and treated them as property, although they were undoubtedly human.[22] "The root of slavery is the denial of human rights," declared Christian Essellen, editor of the German American monthly *Atlantis*. The human rights enshrined in the Declaration of Independence and the French Déclaration des Droits de l'Homme et du Citoyen constituted "the foundation of any political freedom, of any civilization of the present century." All people had the right to enjoy these rights; they could not be denied on the basis of "cultural considerations" or race. Therefore, Essellen concluded, "we must demand equal rights for the Negro, as for ourselves, not for the sake of the Negro, but for our own sake, for the sake of our own civilization."[23]

When they applied these standards to the South, the Forty-Eighters saw not a republican but a despotic southern society. In the words of Friedrich Kapp, it was based on the "unaccountable violence" of the slaveholders, who not only owned the labor but also ruled the bodies and minds of the slaves without their consent.[24] Laws that prohibited teaching slaves to read or write served as an example. By preventing slaves from educating themselves, the slaveholders inhibited individual progress, which the Forty-Eighters considered crucial to progress itself.[25]

The Forty-Eighters were also appalled by the practice of slave breeding in the Border South, as well as by the fact that slaves were sold like cattle.[26] The German term *Sklavenzüchter* (slave breeder) soon became a derogatory term for all slaveholders.[27] However, the most powerful indictment rested on the effects of slavery on black and white families. The Forty-Eighters considered the family to be the foundation of a republican society.[28] Southern slaveholders not only broke up black families for financial gain or out of financial necessity but also exploited female slaves sexually, thereby contradicting their claim of the "superiority of the white race" and their rejection of the amalgamation of the races.[29]

To the Forty-Eighters this was immoral behavior of the worst kind. August Willich wrote: "It is the most diabolic [aspect of slavery] that the slaveholders do not respect any rights of the human beings, who are at their mercy. Instead they sacrifice them to their passions."[30] Wilhelm Rothacker added: "If the impressionable hearts of children have to observe such outrageous brutality from an early age on, the beautiful, but delicate seed of morality cannot thrive." And he predicted that a society that allowed such conditions would suffer "terrible consequences."[31]

The violent rule of the slaveholders brutalized and demoralized both the oppressor and the oppressed.[32] As a result the Forty-Eighters considered morality in the South to be all but destroyed.[33] Consequently, slavery's degradation of southern morality had a direct impact on the political sphere, because it destroyed republican institutions in the slave states by undermining virtue. The result was the undemocratic rule of a small "slaveholding-aristocracy."[34]

In the opinion of the Forty-Eighters, it was not only slaves who suffered as a result but also poor, nonslaveholding whites. The absence of a public school system in the South resulted in widespread illiteracy.[35] It also enabled slaveholders to use the ignorance of poor whites to strengthen their political and economic dominance by "exploiting the prejudices against the Negro" and the "racial pride" of poor whites.[36]

Some Forty-Eighters considered poor whites to be just as oppressed as slaves.[37] Friedrich Kapp even stated that the slavery question was not a Negro question, but "a conflict between two classes of white people," between a small privileged group of slaveholders and a large group of non-privileged nonslaveholders. With slaves removed from the equation, Kapp was able to interpret the slavery question as a conflict between aristocratic rule and government by the people (*Adelsherrschaft* and *Volksherrschaft*), an interpretation that resembled the Forty-Eighters' struggle against aristocratic privileges and monarchical rule in the Revolution of 1848–49.[38] Most Forty-Eighters were not willing to minimize the effects of slavery on slaves but aimed to show how the institution affected the whole society, black and white. This position also built on their experiences in the Revolution of 1848–49, when they had fought for the interests of the economic underclass by demanding a democratic society that allowed everyone to acquire property and participate in the political process.

All Forty-Eighters were equally concerned that this republican freedom did not exist in the South. Even the U.S. Constitution seemed only to apply to the South, if it served the interests of the slaveholders.[39] For instance, abolitionist literature was de facto banned from most of the South, even though the Constitution guaranteed freedom of the press. For many Forty-Eighters, this was not just an abstract issue, because it affected those who lived in the slave states, especially journalists. One prominent Forty-Eighter, Adolph Douai, published an antislavery newspaper in San Antonio, Texas. After awhile his position with his American neighbors, as well as with the German American community, deteriorated, and he had to sell the press and leave Texas.[40] His example showed that the freedom that constituted an open society was absent from many parts of the South. Even in the Border South a German American newspaper had to tread carefully or risk being faced with mob violence.[41]

In economic terms, the effects of slavery were no less unfavorable. The Forty-Eighters analyzed the economic condition of the South and found that while slaveholders benefited from the existence of slavery, southern society as a whole suffered from it. To illustrate their point, they used the example of Virginia, whose decline compared to the revolutionary period was obvious. Despite the fact that the state had ample natural resources, it had fallen behind neighboring Pennsylvania in terms of density of population, population growth, value of the land, and development of manufacturing and infrastructure.[42]

In their opinion slave labor itself was slow and crude and lacked intelligent planning. Slaves had no motivation to work efficiently, because they had nothing to gain from their labor.[43] The lesson was clear: slavery inhibited economic progress, because it could only be used to produce staple crops such as cotton, tobacco, and sugar. The primitive state of agricultural methods reduced many regions to barren wastelands, so that slaveholders, like locusts, had to take their slaves to new places, where the process would start all over again.[44] "Modern, rational and industrial methods of agriculture," necessary to develop the agricultural resources of states like Missouri, were incompatible with slave labor; only "free labor" (*freie Arbeit*) was able "to turn the land from its primitive state into domiciles for intelligent families."[45]

The only solution to these problems was the large-scale immigration of farmers and artisans who could supplant slavery by showing the superiority of free labor. Free labor, which enabled all citizens to use their intelligence and industry in the free marketplace, was the only way to create prosperity for all people. The Forty-Eighters envisioned a society based on a strong middle class, consisting of independent farmers, artisans, manufacturers, tradesmen, and artists. Southern leaders acknowledged the need for economic development but feared at the same time that large-scale immigration and economic diversification would undermine slavery.[46] These conflicting goals could not be reconciled, and the inevitable result was stagnation, which proved, in the opinion of Friedrich Kapp, that an unfree society was always inferior to a free society. The slaveholders' claim that cotton was king was nothing more than a delusion. In fact the South suffered from dependency on northern manufacturers, traders, and capital. Compared to the rapidly emerging industrial society in the North, the southern economy appeared static, underdeveloped, and backward, resembling the declining agrarian empires of earlier times.[47] In the opinion of the Forty-Eighters, the progress of civilization in the nineteenth century consisted partly of liberating people from ancient forms of oppression, such as slavery and European feudalism. In modern societies, built on human rights of freedom and equality, there was no place for slavery. Indeed, it was the duty of mankind to ensure that all men enjoyed the human rights enshrined in the Declaration of Independence.

The most dangerous aspect of southern slavery was that it allowed the South to impose its will on the North because of its dominant position within the Democratic Party. Southern slaveholders were able to find a sufficient number of "office hunters" (*Ämterjäger*) within their ranks who were willing to support the slaveholders' interest in exchange for public offices.

This corruption of republican virtue threatened the very foundation of the United States. To the Forty-Eighters it was clear that slavery had to be abolished, because—in the words of Karl Heinzen—it destroyed Republicanism.[48] Although they realized how difficult this undertaking would be, even moderate Forty-Eighters like Carl Schurz declared that principled opposition to slavery was the only course that he was willing to take.[49]

In the opinion of the Forty-Eighters, American slavery posed a great threat to the extension of human rights and the establishment and expansion of a truly republican society on the American continent. As a result, if American slavery thrived, the cause of freedom suffered worldwide. The Forty-Eighters were absolutely adamant that the progress of civilization in the nineteenth century demanded the abolition of slavery not at some distant point in the future, but in the near future, the sooner the better. However, the Forty-Eighters never became "immediatists," because they realized the magnitude of the task of liberating four million slaves. Wilhelm Rothacker summed up the conviction of most Forty-Eighters when he wrote: "Slavery was transplanted here in the most painful way and it will probably take a dangerous operation to cut it out again."[50] The best solution to the slavery question, they felt, was the gradual emancipation of slaves: the Louisville Platform even advised that the "sudden abolition" of slavery was "neither possible nor advisable."[51]

Instead, many Forty-Eighters proposed measures to mitigate the conditions of slavery, such as protecting slave families by preventing the sale of children or spouses, granting personal and economic independence to slaves, and liberating slaves born after a certain date. Due to the importance of education to their political ideology, they also wanted to prepare slaves for freedom through education paid for by the government or slaveholders.[52] Their approach to abolishing slavery built on their experiences in the fight to abolish the last remnants of feudalism during the European revolutions of 1848. Friedrich Kapp, for instance, linked the liberation of slaves to the gradual liberation of European peasants from "serfdom."[53] Even Karl Heinzen, who occasionally threatened slaveholders with the violent abolition of slavery, advocated gradual emancipation as late as November 1860.[54]

These broad and abstract plans, which lacked specifics, did not satisfy the urgency that the Forty-Eighters felt in reversing the advance of slavery. In order to change momentum and turn public opinion against it, they aimed at undermining the "peculiar institution" where it was weakest: in the Border South. They attempted to initiate an open debate in the slave states on the dangers of slavery and the merits of free labor, in which, they thought, freedom would prevail.[55]

The Forty-Eighters considered poor, nonslaveholding whites to be possible allies in their fight against the oppression of the slaveholder aristocracy. An organized opposition would enable the great mass of whites to assert their interests and break the slaveholders' grip on power. To avoid dangerous conflicts with proslavery forces, some Forty-Eighters like Heinrich Börnstein, owner of the *St. Louis Anzeiger des Westens,* avoided discussing the fate of slaves at all. Instead, he stated that emancipation meant the emancipation of the "free white population" from the rule of the slaveholders.[56] The Forty-Eighters envisioned a special role for German immigrants, who should prove the superiority of free labor by making more productive use of the land than slave labor was able to achieve. Leading by example could lead to the elimination of slavery, for instance, in West Texas, where German immigrants served as the "avant-garde of freedom."[57]

Most Forty-Eighters did not consider the speed of emancipation to be crucial, as long as there was obvious progress. As long as freedom was on the march and slavery retreated, development followed their belief in the steady progress of mankind. They hoped in vain to witness the emergence of an "antislavery mood" in the Border South, however, because they underestimated the power of white racism to overcome class differences in southern society. The only real success came in the city of St. Louis, where German Forty-Eighters succeeded in organizing the German vote to elect Francis P. Blair to the House of Representatives. They also overwhelmingly voted for Abraham Lincoln in the presidential election of 1860, thereby giving Lincoln more votes than he received from all other slave states combined.[58]

Although the Forty-Eighters did not advocate immediate abolition, they felt a great urgency that concrete steps had to be taken to start the process of emancipation. As a result of the lack of progress in containing and abolishing slavery during the 1850s, the opposition of the Forty-Eighters to slavery became more and more pronounced. They warned slaveholders that if progress was not forthcoming, slaves could be emancipated by force, for instance, if the South seceded. Secession, the Forty-Eighters believed, would only hasten the demise of slavery. The poorer, less industrialized, and less populous South would be no match for the much more advanced North.[59]

The similarity between the Forty-Eighters' critique of the U.S. South and the antislavery argument of liberal northerners should not be taken for granted. A large and influential group of conservative German Americans was closely aligned with the Democratic Party and did not share this negative view of the South at all. Instead they blamed antislavery northerners for the growing sectional tension and denounced "Negro sympathy, hypocritical philanthropy or antislavery, nativism and temperance nonsense." They also rejected the view that German Americans had the right to maintain a separate German American identity.[60]

As the basis for their political activities in the United States, the Forty-Eighters had constructed a German American identity. It called for all German Americans to fight slavery and promote freedom and equality of all people. According to their Young Hegelian worldview, a conflict between the diametrically opposed principles of freedom and slavery was unavoidable. The emergence of the antislavery Republican Party in the mid-1850s signaled that the conflict between freedom and slavery was drawing closer, enabling the Forty-Eighters to align themselves with the long-awaited "party of freedom." The fact that Forty-Eighters and Republicans shared a broadly similar interpretation of the South and the dangers it posed to republican government facilitated cooperation in the presidential campaign of 1856 and beyond.

In 1856, the Republican Party enjoyed a large amount of enthusiastic support among the Forty-Eighters, because it aggressively denounced slavery and the Democratic Party. The uncompromising language of the Philadelphia Platform of 1856 appealed even to the radical Karl Heinzen, because it condemned slavery as "barbarism" and contained statements that could be understood as endorsing federal intervention to secure the rights of the Declaration of Independence for all people.[61] While the platform used this language to fight the introduction of slavery into the territories, Karl Heinzen concluded that it enabled government to intervene on the side of freedom and equality against slavery, where it already existed. The Philadelphia Platform provided a blueprint for a revolutionary federal antislavery policy, even if it was not intended as such.[62] As Christian Essellen had demanded, the platform did not merely condemn slavery but also offered a positive justification by referring to human rights as the basis of the fight against slavery.[63] For these reasons the Forty-Eighters were willing to overlook or downplay the presence of nativists in the ranks of the Republican Party: the real danger to republican freedom was posed by southern slaveholders.

The Forty-Eighters rejected warnings that this policy endangered the

Union. Even though they admired the Constitution, the Union was only worth fighting for if it was a Union based on freedom and Republicanism—and Republicanism depended on the dominance of free labor and a virtuous citizenry.[64] Preservation of the Union was not a goal in itself; if the Union was not freed from slavery, it would perish anyway. The only possible way to save it was to abolish slavery, not to maintain the status quo or to tolerate the continuing advance of slavery.[65] Christian Essellen was certain that the outcome of this conflict had world-historic consequences: "The fight for containment or expansion of slavery exceeds all political questions that are at risk in Europe in terms of cultural-historical, purely humane significance. The problem that world history has dealt the American nation is the greatest and most universal problem history has ever assigned to a nation or an era, and it irrevocably puts the Union at the forefront of the civilized world. The American nation has to build a state that exclusively rests on absolute adherence to the law [*Rechtsbewusstsein*], a state that has no religious, dynastic, military, bureaucratic, or national foundation."[66]

In the opinion of the Forty-Eighters, the emergence of the Republican Party signaled the beginning of the end for the institution of slavery in the United States. Due to their Young Hegelian philosophy, the Forty-Eighters not only expected but welcomed a final battle between the diametrically opposed principles of freedom (thesis) and slavery (antithesis). To them, thesis and antithesis could only be reconciled in the emergence of an American republic that was entirely free of slavery.[67]

With the debate among the Forty-Eighters on slavery all but settled, they waited for the wind of public opinion to shift against slavery. Many campaigned hard for the Republican Party and succeeded in winning a substantial part of the "German vote" for it. This signaled a marked change, because in the past German Americans had collectively supported the Democratic Party. Nevertheless, the Forty-Eighters were not satisfied with their success: Karl Heinzen expected a southern revolt in the wake of a Republican victory in the presidential elections and was disappointed when the Republican candidate John C. Fremont lost to the Democrat James Buchanan. Others, including Carl Schurz, took confidence in the unexpected strength of the Republican Party.

Soon after 1856 new conflicts threatened to destroy the alliance between the Forty-Eighters and the Republican Party. With the unifying cause of fighting slavery gone, Republicans in several states attempted to impose new limits on the rights of immigrants. In Massachusetts, voters approved the so-called Two Year Amendment in May 1859, which imposed a two-year waiting period until a naturalized citizen could vote.[68] The Forty-Eighters were enraged, because they considered it absurd that the Republican Party claimed to fight for the freedom and equality of enslaved African Americans while it denied certain rights to immigrants at the same time.[69] The result was a long and bitter conflict among the Forty-Eighters, who debated whether they should break with the Republican Party altogether to form a "German Party" or remain within the ranks of the Republican Party in order to force it to renounce nativism. In the end the latter group won the argument, because the Forty-Eighters realized that the Republican Party was the only option to defeat the Democratic Party and the hated "slaveholder aristocracy."[70] However, the relationship between Anglo American and German American Republicans would never be the same again.

Despite these conflicts, the Forty-Eighters' insistence that the slavery question had to be dealt with grew more urgent. Their continuing radicalization can be observed in their positive reaction to John Brown's attempt to instigate a slave insurrection in the South. Although they considered the revolt to be badly planned and executed, they nevertheless approved of Brown's motives. His appearance signaled that the country was heading for a violent conflict between freedom and slavery.[71] Carl Schurz even predicted a sectional conflict of "colossal magnitude." In his estimation "the principles" embodied by the sectional parties, freedom and slavery, would directly confront each other. Welcoming a final, decisive crisis as a measure that would solve the antagonism between South and North, he argued that delay and indecisiveness were the greater danger. Schurz was convinced that the strength of "progressive principles" guaranteed the future of the Union. He did not consider it impossible that bloodshed could be avoided, if the North acted resolutely and displayed unity in the moment of crisis. He even thought that "progressive elements" showed renewed strength in the South and predicted that they were strong enough to contain the "oligarchy."[72]

Aiming to strengthen these progressive forces, Schurz in August 1860 voiced a final appeal to slaveholders that the day of reckoning drew closer: "Slaveholders of America, I appeal to you. Are you really in earnest when you speak of perpetuating slavery? Shall it never cease? Never? Stop and consider where you are and in what day you live. . . . This is the world of the nineteenth century. The last remnants of feudalism in the old world are fast disappearing. . . . And you, citizens of a Republic, you can arrest the wheel of progress with your Dred Scott decisions and Democratic platforms? Look around and see how lonesome you are in this wide world of ours. As far as modern civilization throws its rays, what people what class of society is there like you? . . . There is no human heart that sympathizes with your cause, unless it sympathizes with the cause of despotism in every form. . . . And in this appalling solitude you stand alone against a hopeful world, alone against a great century, fighting your hopeless fight—hopeless as the struggle of the Indians against the onward march of civilization. . . . And in the face of all this you insist upon hugging, with dogged stubbornness, your fatal institution? Why not manfully swing round into the grand march of progressive humanity? . . . The final crisis, unless prevented by timely reform, will come with the inexorable certainty of fate, the more terrible the longer it is delayed."[73]

In comparison, the slaveholders' views were the perfect opposite of the Forty-Eighters'. Slaveholders were firmly convinced that the republican institutions of the South depended on the existence of slavery. In fact, southern slaveholders promoted a diametrically opposed form of Republicanism, a Republicanism of slavery, which could not be reconciled with the Forty-Eighters' Republicanism of freedom. While slaveholders demanded that the federal government protect slavery, Forty-Eighters demanded the extension of free-labor Republicanism to the South. It was again Carl Schurz who summed up the "standard of Republicanism" that formed the basis of the alliance between Forty-Eighters and the Republican Party. He declared that it was the goal of the Republican Platform of 1860 "to lift the creed of the party far above the level of mere oppositional policy. The platform gives it a positive character. The Republicans stand before the country, not only as the anti-slavery party, but emphatically as the party of free labor. While penning up slave labor within the limits which the legislation of States has assigned to it, we propose to plant free labor in the Territories by the Homestead Bill, and to promote free labor all over the land by the encouragement of home industry. In throwing its shield over the eternal principles of human rights, the platform presents the anti-slavery policy of the party in its logical connection with the great material interests of the country. To man, his birthright; to labor, freedom; to him that wants to labor, work and independence; to him that works, his dues. This is the Republican platform."[74]

The Forty-Eighters considered themselves to be "men of action," who aimed to build a perfect republican society based on reason and virtue through concrete action such as the expansion of free labor. Eric Foner has rightly stressed the importance of free labor for the ideology of the Republican Party. He points out that the concept of free labor included belief in progress, social mobility, economic independence, and the expansion of democratic institutions. Free labor, in his words, represented "a model of good society."[75]

This was especially the case for the Forty-Eighters. In their opinion, free labor formed the foundation of a true republican society. By enabling all members of a republican society to become economically independent, free labor allowed them to act as virtuous citizens, ensured the expansion of freedom and equality, and ultimately permitted republican government to function.[76] Free labor must not be confused with wage labor or white labor. The Forty-Eighters' concept of free labor was inclusive and allowed men of all races to participate in the resulting capitalist society, as long as they placed work at the center of their lives. Their economic ideal was the small independent farmer, shopkeeper, or artisan, not the wage laborer who worked in a large factory. The Forty-Eighters remained beholden to Jeffersonian democracy and only rarely glimpsed the changes that would make the United States the leading industrial power in the world.

The Forty-Eighters regarded southern slaveholders as mortal enemies of free labor. The economic power of slaveholders was the result of their exploiting the unfree labor of their African American slaves. Even their political careers and their status as gentlemen depended on a privileged status that enabled them to leave work to their slaves and overseers. In the eyes of the Forty-Eighters, slaveholders despised not only free labor but labor altogether. Slaveholders who rejected this crucial element of Republicanism could hardly claim to be virtuous members of republican society.[77]

The Forty-Eighters shared these convictions with leading figures of the Republican Party. For instance, Abraham Lincoln declared unequivocally that the "negro" was not equal "in color, perhaps not in moral or intellectual endowment. But in the right to eat the bread, without leave of anybody else, which his own hand earns, he is my equal . . . and the equal of every living man."[78] Lincoln's statement can be understood as a display of Republicanism that tried to fulfill the promise of the Declaration of Independence, which he thought set a "standard maxim for free society."[79] The Forty-Eighters were much more radical in their demands and their language, but they found common ground with leading figures of the Republican Party in promoting a Republicanism of freedom and equality. They also agreed that it was the duty of the federal government to implement this ideal of a republican society against the interests of slaveholders. Republicanism went further than a purely liberal ideology by calling for active intervention by the government in order to promote the general welfare of all people, especially those of a lower social rank. The land-reform movement can serve as an example of a governmental intervention that not only aimed at distributing federal land to settlers but also tried to evenly distribute land and avoid its concentration in the hands of a few wealthy individuals.[80]

The presidential campaign of 1860 lacked the enthusiasm that had characterized the Forty-Eighters' campaign for Frémont in 1856. Due to the support of nativist laws by several Republican state parties, the Forty-Eighters demanded protections against nativist measures and stressed that the fight against slavery must remain the primary goal of the Republican Party. The Chicago Convention of 1860 approved most of their demands, because the delegates wanted to ensure the support of the Forty-Eighters in the upcoming elections.[81] The twin goals of fighting slavery and defeating the Democratic Party served as the basis for cooperation between German Forty-Eighters and Republicans. The danger of slavery destroying the American republic led the Forty-Eighters to support the Republican Party, which undoubtedly was more nativist than the Democratic Party. Similarly, it made Republicans willing to compromise with immigrants of whom they were not too fond.

To the South it was unacceptable to have a president who openly declared that slavery had eventually to be abolished. It mattered little that Lincoln promised not to touch slavery where it existed, because he considered blacks and whites equal—at least in the realm of economics. Whatever this meant in practice, it was a direct attack on "the cornerstone" of southern Republicanism. The escalation of this conflict between different, incompatible Republicanisms provides an explanation as to why the conflict between North and South resulted in the violent military struggle that is known as the Civil War.

By constantly stressing the need for American society to confront and eventually eliminate slavery, the Forty-Eighters participated in a major realignment of American parties along sectional lines. Their German American followers added crucial votes to the Republican Party, which enabled the Forty-Eighters to gain influence and promote their belief that southern slavery posed the greatest challenge to the perfection of Republicanism. When the Civil War broke out, the Forty-Eighters welcomed the conflict

and vigorously supported the cause of the Union, because they were convinced that a military struggle between North and South would lead to the
abolition of slavery and inch them one step closer to implementing their
Republicanism of freedom and equality. It was the duty of German Americans as freedom fighters, they declared, to rid the American republic of the
stain of slavery.[82] In the opinion of the Forty-Eighters, the victory of the
North would ensure that the American republic would fulfill its world-
historic mission of promoting freedom and equality worldwide. In a not too
distant future, people all over the world would emulate this example and
turn a world of monarchies into a world of republics. In this worldview, the
South had no right to stand in the way of progress. Its outdated social, economic, and political structure had to be destroyed to pave the way for a better future for all mankind. Out of the ruins of the southern Republicanism
of slavery, a new southern society would emerge, adhering to free labor and
republican principles of freedom and equality. For this reason, the Forty-
Eighters welcomed the Civil War and rejected all attempts at a last-minute
compromise. According to their Young Hegelian worldview, the sooner the
decisive battle between freedom and slavery came, the earlier the Republicanism of freedom and equality would emerge triumphant.[83]

Notes

1. Andrea Mehrländer, *The Germans of Charleston, Richmond and New
Orleans during the Civil War Period, 1850–1870* (Berlin: De Gruyter, 2011).

2. There are numerous statements by Forty-Eighters describing slavery as a
cancer. See, e.g., *Der Pionier*, May 13, 1854.

3. For detailed accounts of the Revolution of 1848–49 in Baden and the
Palatinate, see Wolfgang von Hippel, *Revolution im deutschen Südwesten. Das
Großherzogtum Baden 1848/49* (Stuttgart: Kohlhammer, 1998); and Hans Fen-
ske et al., eds., *Die Pfalz und die Revolution 1848/49* (Kaiserslautern: Institut für
Pfälzische Geschichte, 2000).

4. For details see Herbert Reiter, *Politisches Asyl im 19. Jahrhundert. Die
deutschen politischen Flüchtlinge des Vormärz und der Revolution von 1848/49 in
Europa und den USA* (Berlin: Duncker & Humblot, 1992).

5. Bruce Levine, *The Spirit of 1848: German Immigrants, Labor Conflict, and
the Coming of the Civil War* (Urbana: University of Illinois Press, 1992), 15–34,
53–60.

6. All quotes have been translated from the original German by the author,
except where noted.

7. See Michael Hochgeschwender, *Wahrheit, Einheit, Ordnung. Der ameri-*

kanische Katholizismus und die Sklavenfrage 1835–1870 (Paderborn: Ferdinand Schöningh, 2006).

8. Ray Allen Billington, *The Protestant Crusade 1800–1860: A Study of the Origins of American Nativism* (New York: Peter Smith, 1938).

9. See Mischa Honeck, *We Are the Revolutionists: German-Speaking Immigrants and American Abolitionists after 1848* (Athens: University of Georgia Press, 2010); Christian B. Keller, *Chancellorsville and the Germans: Nativism, Ethnicity, and Civil War Memory* (New York: Fordham University Press, 2007); and Alison Efford, "New Citizens: German Immigrants, African Americans, and the Reconstruction of Citizenship, 1865–1877" (PhD diss., Ohio State University, 2008).

10. Levine, *Spirit of 1848.*

11. An exception for Germany is Paul Nolte, *Gemeindebürgertum und Liberalismus in Baden 1800–1850. Tradition—Radikalismus—Republik* (Göttingen: Vandenhoeck & Ruprecht, 1992).

12. *Atlantische Studien* 2 (1853): 16–30; Hans-Ulrich Wehler, *Friedrich Kapp. Vom radikalen Frühsozialisten des Vormärz zum liberalen Parteipolitiker des Bismarckreichs. Briefe 1843–1884* (Frankfurt am Main: Insel Verlag, 1969), 66–70.

13. Elmar Treptow, "Theorie und Praxis bei Hegel und den Junghegelianern" (habilitation treatise, University of Munich, 1971).

14. *Atlantis*, n.s, 5.1 (July 1856): 44–54.

15. Friedrich Kapp, *Geschichte der Sklaverei in den Vereinigten Staaten von Amerika* (New York: L. Hauser, 1860); Fr[iedrich] K[app], "Die politischen Parteien in den Vereinigten Staaten," *Atlantische Studien* 1 (1853): 92–93; *Hochwächter,* June 9, 1852; *Wächter vom Erie,* Aug. 9, 1852; *Herold des Westens,* Sept. 22, 1853; and Wilhelm Rothacker, "Sklaverei," *Hochwächter,* Feb. 23, 1853.

16. Karl Heinzen was the first Forty-Eighter to demand outright repeal of the Fugitive Slave Law. See *Deutsche Schnellpost,* Feb. 8, Apr. 28, Aug. 25, 1851. He was joined by Friedrich Kapp, "Die Präsidentschaftswahl in Frankreich und den Vereinigten Staaten," in *Deutscher Zuschauer,* July 16, 1851; and Friedrich Hassausrek's *Hochwächter,* Dec. 15, 1852. The call for repeal became a staple of all German American political platforms, like the influential *Louisville Platform* (*Anzeiger des Westens,* Mar. 11, 1854). For an English translation, see Don Heinrich Tolzmann, "A German-American Position Statement: The Louisville Platform," in Don Heinrich Tolzmann, *The German-American Forty-Eighters 1848–1998* (Nashville: Max Kade German-American Center et al., 1998), 96–105.

17. Arthur M. Schlesinger Jr., ed., *History of American Presidential Elections, Vol. 3, 1848–1868* (New York: Chelsea House, 1985), 952.

18. The Forty-Eighters did not consider the Free Soil Party, already in decline in the early 1850s, to be a serious alternative to the major parties, Democrats and Whigs.

19. *Deutsche Schnellpost,* Jan. 31, 1851; *Hochwächter,* Jan. 7, 14, 1852.

20. Crucial for the development of a hybrid German American identity were Karl Heinzen's writings; see *Deutsche Schnellpost,* Feb. 14, Aug. 7, 25, 28, 1851.

21. *San Antonio Zeitung,* Feb. 18, June 10, 1854.

22. Karl Heinzen, *Teutscher Radikalismus in Amerika. Ausgewählte Vorträge und Flugschriften* (Boston: Verein zur Verbreitung radikaler Prinzipien, 1875), 3: 154–55; Wilhelm Rothacker, "Sklaverei," *Hochwächter,* Feb. 19, 1853; *Herold des Westens,* Sept. 22, 1853; Julius Fröbel, *Aus Amerika. Erfahrungen, Reisen und Studien* (Leipzig: J. J. Weber, 1857), 1: 130–31; *Sociale Republik,* Jan. 14, 1860; *New Yorker Demokrat,* Mar. 30, 1861.

23. *Atlantis,* n.s., 2.5 (May 1855): 204–19; 2.1 (Jan. 1855): 8–21; 3.3 (Sept. 1855): 204–19. See also *San Antonio Zeitung,* Sept. 10, 1853.

24. Friedrich Kapp, *Aus und über Amerika. Thatsachen und Erlebnisse* (Berlin: J. Springer, 1876), 2: 130.

25. Wilhelm Rothacker, "Sklaverei," *Hochwächter,* Jan. 26, 1853; Fr[iedrich] K[app], "Zur Sklavenfrage in den Vereinigten Staaten," *Atlantische Studien* 8 (1856): 123; Gustav Struve, *Die Union vor dem Richterstuhle des gesunden Menschenverstandes* (New York: Gustav Struve/Expedition der New Yorker Staatszeitung, 1855), 42–43.

26. Adolf Douai, *Land und Leute in der Union* (Berlin: O. Janke, 1864), 51–52; Theodor Griesinger, *Land und Leute in Amerika. Skizzen aus dem amerikanischen Leben* (Stuttgart: A. Kröner 1863), 1: 425–36; Fröbel, *Aus Amerika* 1: 103–5; *Hochwächter,* Dec. 1, 1852; *New Yorker Demokrat,* Sept. 1, 1860.

27. Struve, *Die Union,* 124; Kapp, "Die Präsidentschaftswahl in Frankreich und den Vereinigten Staaten"; *Republik der Arbeiter,* Oct. 29, 1853; *San Antonio Zeitung,* June 10, 1854; *New Yorker Criminal-Zeitung,* Mar. 7, 1856; *Cincinnati Republikaner,* Oct. 10, 1859.

28. *New Yorker Criminal-Zeitung,* Mar. 28, 1856; Douai, *Land und Leute,* 287; Struve, *Die Union,* 42; *Der Pionier,* June 8, 1856.

29. *Atlantis,* n.s., 8.2 (Feb. 1858): 109–17; Struve, *Die Union,* 42–43; Griesinger, *Land und Leute,* 1: 433–36; *Der Pionier,* Feb. 2, 1860; *Cincinnati Republikaner,* July 5, 1860.

30. *Cincinnati Republikaner,* July 5, 1860.

31. Wilhelm Rothacker, "Sklaverei," *Hochwächter,* Feb. 2, 1853.

32. *New Yorker Criminal-Zeitung,* Nov. 16, 1860.

33. Struve, *Die Union,* 41.

34. *San Antonio Zeitung,* June 10, 1854.

35. Fr[iedrich] K[app], "Zur Sklavenfrage in den Vereinigten Staaten," *Atlantische Studien* 7 (1855): 82.

36. Daniel Hertle, *Die Deutschen in Nordamerika und der Freiheitskampf in Missouri* (Chicago: Daniel Hertle, 1865), 46.

37. *Atlantis,* n.s., 7.3 (Sept. 1857): 227–37.

38. Kapp, *Geschichte der Sklaverei,* 515–16.

39. Fr[iedrich] K[app], "Zur Sklavenfrage in den Vereinigten Staaten," *Atlantische Studien* 8 (1856): 116–25.

40. Honeck, *We Are the Revolutionists,* 38–70.

41. Hertle, *Die Deutschen in Nordamerika*, 46–47.

42. Fröbel, *Aus Amerika*, 1: 107–23. Fröbel had firsthand experience of Virginia, because he had traveled the South extensively. He was also familiar with Frederick Law Olmstead's *Journey to the Seaboard Slave States* and borrowed frequently from it, as he acknowledged.

43. *Atlantis*, n.s., 3.6 (Dec. 1855): 469–72.

44. Douai, *Land und Leute*, 269–73.

45. *Anzeiger des Westens*, June 13, 1858.

46. Fröbel, *Aus Amerika*, 1: 107–23, *San Antonio Zeitung*, Jan. 6, 1855.

47. Cf. Bayly, *The Birth of the Modern World, 1780–1914* (Oxford: Blackwell, 2004), 27–29.

48. *Der Pionier*, May 13, 1854, Dec. 14, 1860. See also Bayly, *Birth of the Modern World*, 285–87, which uses the phrase "corruption of the righteous republic" in a much broader context.

49. Eberhard Kessel, ed., *Die Briefe von Carl Schurz an Gottfried Kinkel* (Heidelberg: Carl Winter, 1965), 120.

50. Wilhelm Rothacker, "Sklaverei," *Hochwächter*, Mar. 16, 1853.

51. *Anzeiger des Westens*, Mar. 11, 1854.

52. *New Yorker Deutsche Zeitung*, Oct. 15, 1851; *Der Pionier*, July 5, 1857; *Atlantis*, n.s., 8.6 (June 1858): 436–37; Fröbel, *Aus Amerika*, 1: 170–88.

53. Kapp, *Geschichte der Sklaverei*, 512–14. See also *Atlantis*, n.s., 3.1 (July 1855): 30–32.

54. *Der Pionier*, Nov. 1, 1860.

55. Struve, *Die Union*, 46; Fröbel, *Aus Amerika*, 3: 481–83; Wilhelm Rothacker, "Sklaverei," *Hochwächter*, Mar. 16, 1853; *San Antonio Zeitung*, Sept. 10, 1853, Apr. 15, May 27, 1854; *Cincinnati Republikaner*, Feb. 21, 1860; *New Yorker Demokrat*, Nov. 23, 1860.

56. *Anzeiger des Westens*, June 13, 1858.

57. Friedrich Kapp, "Die Geschichte der deutschen Ansiedlungen des westlichen Texas und deren Bedeutung für die Vereinigten Staaten," *Atlantische Studien* 8 (1857): 185–86.

58. Walter D. Kamphoefner, "St. Louis Germans and the Republican Party 1848–1860," *Mid-America* 57 (1975): 69–88.

59. Fröbel, *Aus Amerika*, 1: 172–73; *Deutscher Zuschauer*, July 23, 1851; *New Yorker Deutsche Zeitung*, Sept. 24, 1851; *Der Pionier*, June 29, 1856; *Atlantis*, n.s., 4.5 (Sept. 1856): 386–87, 7.3 (Sept. 1857): 234–36.

60. *New Yorker Staatszeitung*, Oct. 17, 1855.

61. Schlesinger, *History of American Presidential Elections, Vol. 3, 1848–1868*, 1040.

62. *Der Pionier*, June 22, 1856.

63. *Atlantis*, n.s., 4.3 (Mar. 1856): 212–13.

64. *Atlantis*, n.s., 5.1 (July 1856): 44–54.

65. "Gustav Struve's Aufruf an die Deutschen," *New Yorker Staatszeitung*, July 26, 1856; *Atlantis*, n.s., 4.6 (June 1856): 465; Friedrich Hecker, "Ansprache an die

deutsch-amerikanische Bevölkerung der Vereinigten Staaten," *Belleviller Volksblatt,* Sept. 13, 1856.

66. *Atlantis,* n.s., 5.1 (July 1856): 63–64.

67. *Atlantis,* n.s., 5.1 (July 1856): 46–47; *Der Pionier,* June 29, 1856. Cf. *Anzeiger des Westens,* Oct. 2, 1856; *New Yorker Criminal-Zeitung,* Aug. 22, 1856.

68. Cf. Tyler Anbinder, *Nativism and Slavery: The Northern Know Nothings and the Politics of the 1850s* (Oxford: Oxford University Press, 1992), 247–53.

69. Cf. the eloquent speech by Carl Schurz on "True Americanism" in Boston's Faneuil Hall, Apr. 18, 1859, in Carl Schurz, *Correspondence and Political Papers of Carl Schurz* (New York: G. P. Putnam's Sons, 1913), 1: 48–72.

70. As an example, see *Baltimore Wecker,* Oct. 22, 1858.

71. *New Yorker Criminal-Zeitung,* Oct. 28, 1859; *Der Pionier,* Oct. 29, 1859; Kapp, *Aus und über Amerika,* 1: 120–37.

72. Kessel, *Die Briefe von Carl Schurz an Gottfried Kinkel,* 137.

73. Schurz, *Correspondence and Political Papers,* 1: 156–59. The original speech is in English.

74. Carl Schurz, *Speeches of Carl Schurz: Collected and Revised by the Author* (Philadelphia: J. B. Lippincott, 1865), 107. The original speech is in English.

75. Eric Foner, *Free Soil, Free Labor, Free Men: The Ideology of the Republican Party before the Civil War* (New York: Oxford University Press, 1970), 11–39.

76. Of course, free labor also enabled German immigrants to participate in American society, providing opportunities that a slaveholding society could not offer. The Forty-Eighters' outlook was not totally idealistic and altruistic, although they considered it to be that way, but it also was not solely based on the interests of German immigrants. Interests and idealism worked together to create a powerful argument for an American society without slavery that allowed everyone to prosper. If slavery corrupted and destroyed the American republic, it would hurt not only German immigrants but the cause of freedom worldwide.

77. *Atlantis,* n.s., 5.1 (July 1856): 44–54.

78. Abraham Lincoln, *The Collected Works of Abraham Lincoln,* 9 vols., ed. Roy Basler (New Brunswick: Rutgers University Press, 1953), 3: 16. See also Eric Foner, *The Fiery Trial: Abraham Lincoln and American Slavery* (New York: W. W. Norton, 2010), 67–68, 96–98, 103–17.

79. Lincoln, *Collected Works,* 2: 406.

80. *Deutscher Zuschauer,* July 23, Aug. 20, Sept. 24, Oct. 1, 1851; *Hochwächter,* Dec. 1, 1852; *Herold des Westens,* Sept. 25, 1853.

81. James M. Bergquist, "The Forty-Eighters and the Republican Convention of 1860," in Charlotte Lang Brancaforte, ed., *The German Forty-Eighters in the United States* (New York: Peter Lang, 1989), 141–56.

82. *Westliche Post,* Feb. 13, 1861.

83. *Anzeiger des Westens,* Dec. 17, 1860; *Der Pionier,* Feb. 14, 1861; *Cincinnati Republikaner,* Jan. 26, Mar. 5, 6, 1861; *New Yorker Criminal-Zeitung,* Apr. 26, 1861.

4

"In the Days of Her Power and Glory"

Visions of Venice in Antebellum Charleston

Kathleen Hilliard

On the last morning of his visit to Venice in 1837, James Hammond climbed the steps of the campanile in Piazza San Marco. Looking over the "ancient" city, the South Carolina politician and slaveholder recalled all he had seen over the past four days—the Rialto Bridge, the Ducal Place, the Arsenal, the Bridge of Sighs, the tombs of Canova and Titian, splendid St. Mark's itself. He found the city "unique and interesting," "old and cultured." Yet the arresting vista vexed him. Venice's "fall," he noted, "like that of Tyre does indeed stain the pride of glory and bring into contempt the honorable of the earth." In Venice, Hammond, true Carolinian that he was, found a cautionary tale.[1]

Politically, economically, culturally, Hammond, his class, and his state rarely heeded such warnings. When in 1861 the richest, most powerful ruling class the United States had ever seen leaped to its doom, few should have been surprised. A good bit of the brooding—and scheming—Carolinians had done in the lead-up to the self-destruction of secession had focused on the rise and collapse of a "sea-drinking"[2] city much like their own. Comparing Charleston—the "Queen City of the South," their "Holy City"—to the "Queen City of the Adriatic" aimed to rally citizens to the cause of southern political and economic independence. But to Carolinians who traveled Venice's canals, stealing "along noiselessly through the silent streets—and gloomy watery alleys," the metaphor was more troubling. Nineteenth-century Carolinians could not but wonder: Did Venice's decrepit condition augur Charleston's own precipitous decline?[3]

Carolina travelers and writers—among them Charleston lawyer Henry Cruger—sought to answer that question. He did so with some wariness, however. There was vanity, he recognized, in "seek[ing] analogies between our institutions and those of Europe." Still, he explained in an 1832 review of James Fenimore Cooper's novel *The Bravo,* "there are causes, political, commercial, and physical that must produce like results, though in different hemispheres, and under various influences; and local similitudes, however slight, readily bring about an association." In reading Cooper's tale of power and corruption in fifteenth-century Venice, Cruger could not help but think of Charleston.[4]

The "similitudes" found in examining American and European politics, economy, and culture have proven intellectually and analytically profitable for historians of the American South. Along with Peter Kolchin's work on southern slavery and Russian serfdom, Shearer Davis Bowman's assessment of southern landed elites and Prussian Junkers, and the wealth of scholarship on slave systems throughout the Atlantic, a vibrant literature comparing southern economic and political development to that of Italy has emerged in recent years.[5] Raimondo Luraghi and Susanna Delfino have employed the comparison to understand and gauge modernity or premodernity in southern Italy and the southern United States. More recently, Enrico dal Lago has deepened this analysis, weighing not just elite agrarian economies but the worldviews of antebellum southern plantation holders and preunification Italian landowners more broadly. Finally, Don Doyle has spearheaded consideration of comparative nationalism movements, and his work on the American South and the Italian Mezzogiorno is among the most important in the field.[6]

But if historians have been eager to make the connection, "very few antebellum southerners," Michael O'Brien argues, drew the parallel.[7] In his comprehensive set of volumes on southern intellectual life, he notes Cruger's analogy but explains it away as the grumbling complaint of a Yankee-bound critic of southern industrial ineptitude. As one Virginia poet wrote, southerners found Italy "uselessly delightful," and O'Brien argues that they looked to it as a "refuge from vulgar America." They found no semblance of themselves, he suggests, in the faces of their Italian brothers.[8]

Broadly speaking, O'Brien may be right, but with regard to the Cruger review in particular, he errs in using proud Venice as a stand-in for

Italy and self-referring Charleston as a proxy for the antebellum South. Indeed, denizens of both cities would scorn such sweeping generalizations, pointing to the uniqueness of their respective histories, cultures, peoples, and locales. This essay, then, begins where O'Brien leaves off, probing the Venetian metaphor specifically and exploring the ways Charlestonians situated themselves historically and globally in the antebellum period. Their meditations on the once-prosperous city-state reflect the ambivalent, uncertain, and often contradictory feelings of aspiration and dread that marked Charlestonians' consideration of their city's future.

Certainly the low, marshy landscapes of the two queen cities invited comparison. Charleston poet William Gilmore Simms was fond of the simile, deploying it in nostalgic hymns to his city home. In *Father Abbott* (1849), Simms called to readers: "see the noble City, with its spires, rising, almost like another Venice, from the bosom of the deep." Again, Charleston sprang, "sudden, like another Venice," from "the waters of the great deep, rolling into the doors of her habitations" in a series of articles for the *Southern Patriot* in 1845. Finally, in *Harper's New Monthly Magazine* in 1857, he took Yankee readers on a voyage into his city: "As you enter from the sea, between the Islands of Sullivan and Morris, the city opens before you in the foreground, five miles distant—rising, like another Venice, from the ocean."[9]

Such allusions are worth examining for what they say about both seaside queens. Simms's affair with the Palmetto City was fraught with pride and disappointment both. A reverent raconteur of Charleston's chivalric past and a critic chary of King Street commercialism, Simms was a keen outsider who never found his way into the city's most influential cliques. He never found his way to Venice either. The vision he imagined rising from the marshy lagoon emerged, as it did with most antebellum Americans, from his reading of William Shakespeare's sixteenth-century *Othello* and *Merchant of Venice*, Thomas Otway's seventeenth-century *Venice Preserved*, and Cooper's *The Bravo*. Charlestonians took advantage of a wide variety of theatrical offerings too—Venetian waterscapes and merchant machinations played out before their eyes at the Charleston Theater, and, we can imagine, performances consumed conversation in city streets from the late eighteenth century onward. Accounts of the history of Venice, discussion of its contemporary politics and condition, and travelers' notes and correspondence animated local papers. Charlestonians—prating poets and tradesmen alike—found fodder for dreamy imagination in both the high and the low of Charleston commerce and culture.[10]

Pride and nostalgia both animated Simms's writing, and for that reason, Venice held appeal. Simms wrote his 1857 *Harper's* essay in flinching
response to a nasty and widely circulated description of Charleston by traveler and author Léon Beauvallet as "dreadfully filthy; besides it is very ugly,
and outrageously built." The "most comical of all ridiculous books," Simms
ranted, Beauvallet's *Rachel in the New World* saw Charleston through "the
false medium" of the author's failed attempts to profit from a U.S. tour.[11]
Simms's hackles were already raised, it would seem, from his own poorly
received—and dismally unprofitable—lecture tour of northern states in
1856. His ode to the "Palmetto City" refuted "malignant misrepresen-
tations" of Charleston, indeed of the South as a whole.[12] Venice, at least
the Venice of Shakespeare and Otway, served as a logical counter. Simms
emphasized the landscape but, more importantly, highlighted both cities' intimate relation with the sea—the bounty from which each had been
blessed in years past and from which both might profit in the future.

The Venetian analogy that Simms, Cruger, and others employed
emerged amid growing sectional division, propagated by partisans wary
of the agricultural South's dependence on northern manufacturing and
shipping and resentful of onerous tariff burdens. Simms's writing reflected
more than *southern* partisanship, however. His civic chauvinism burst forth
at a time when Charleston's economic fortunes were on the wane. Charleston, Simms and others reminded all who would listen, had once been great.
Founded as a port city on the marshy peninsula between the Ashley and
Cooper rivers in 1670, Charlestown had developed into a prosperous city of
domestic and international trade. Favorable winds helped create a market
for the rice, indigo, and—after 1800—cotton that served as the economic
base for the growing city. Tremendous volumes of merchant and plantation
capital poured into Charleston, and a wealthy citizenry developed a vibrant
social and political culture, flourishing across the colonial and revolutionary periods and culminating in the opening years of the nineteenth century.

By the 1830s, political power's shift to the midlands of South Carolina,
the decline of sea-island cotton, and the rise of New York as the chief port
on the Atlantic coast put paid to that golden age, and Charlestonians were
left with little more than its memory. As historian George Rogers Jr. has
eloquently argued, Charlestonians turned inward, looking "to their historic
past for reassurance" that this era of prosperity might be reclaimed. This
conscious "search for the past" took any number of forms. Charlestonians
elevated to the status of idols the city's revolutionary heroes. They assumed

new family names, claiming or reclaiming prosperous, respected, and honorable bloodlines as their own. They promoted classical learning and spearheaded efforts to collect documents sacred to the city's and the state's eighteenth-century heritage. Refashioned and recast to display Charleston's golden age in shimmering glory, this "usable past" acquired almost talismanic value, a "mythological importance," that, Maurie McInnis argues, "guided them in shaping their society as they believed it had been not as it truly was."[13] Such selective and consciously collected and cultivated memory was persistent and evident to even first-time visitors to the city. Writing in 1836, the Irish actor Tyrone Power noted that an "air of greater antiquity prevails throughout this city than may be discovered in any other I have visited in the States; I should conceive it to be just in the condition the English Army left it." As late as 1861, Dickens saw it, too. There is "no want of memories in this city to keep awake remembrances of the War of Independence," he declared; even "the poorest negro" was quick to point out its landmarks. Everywhere, those memories spoke of glory fled. Once, "no city on the Atlantic had more Commerce than Charleston," but it had undergone "many fluctuations," and the good times were gone.[14]

That the city yearned to recapture trade was evident to all. And while some hailed increased domestic manufacturing as the most sensible solution, Charleston's chief advocates had far grander expectations. Sooty, grubby, disorderly, mobocratic London and Manchester held no appeal. Only a Yankee would stoop so low. Charleston aspired to empire. "Like Venice in the days of her power and glory," Christopher Memminger urged Charlestonians in 1858, "Charleston must have a sphere of operations in many important interests, exclusively her own." The *Mercury* issued a similar message in 1856: "The glory of the South is dependent upon the education of her merchants," the paper declared, calling on citizens to imagine and make possible "the almost incomprehensible dreams which are related of the past splendor and fame and riches of the merchant princes of Tyre, of Venice, and Genoa."[15] Throughout the 1850s, the *Mercury* echoed such retrospective calls to economic arms. And though Venice was not always the sole object of proponents' plans, it was among the most common. Charlestonians saw similarities in the two cities' founding, geography, and even ancestry, proudly boasting that one of the city's founding families, the Prioleaus, were descended from the seventeenth-century Venetian doge Antonin Prioli.[16] It made sense, then, to build Charleston's future on the cities' common past.

But retrospective Charleston found that it could not recapture greatness by simply wishing it so. Commercial proponents reminded tight-fisted
neighbors that "the golden age of Venice, of Genoa, of Leghorn, and other
large cities on the Mediterranean, all . . . flourished by their foreign commerce." To obtain such preeminence, merchants hectored, "almost incredible sums of money were expended to make these ports receptacles of a
commerce which they then monopolized." They faced down Yankee doubt-
ers too. Confronting accusations that the South lacked commercial energy
and that slavery retarded the regional economy, southerners launched efforts
to develop direct trade with Europe. Charlestonians, in particular, chafed
at the suggestion that their port and low-country climate were unsuited to
thrive. "[They] complain of produce and costly goods corrupting or dete-
riorating in Southern climes!" partisans exclaimed in exasperation. Such
accusations ignored history, for "Venice, a southern city, conducted the
trade of all the East, and was the entrepot of the world's commerce for the
main period of her history!"[17]

In the late antebellum era, it was not the sea that held the key to Charleston's fortune, however, but the railroad. Here, one might imagine, the
Venetian analogy broke down. After all, it was the "the waters of the
great deep, rolling into the doors of its habitations," that bonded the two
cities. Not so. In April 1857, the *Mercury* regaled readers with descriptions
of festivities attending completion of the Charleston-Memphis railroad. A
"gentleman," it reported, "at his own expense, has ordered a large, finely
finished and well bound cask to be filled at Charleston with ocean water."
The city's delegation planned to carry the cask by rail and solemnly pour
the water into the Mississippi, thereby consummating the "grand marriage
of the Atlantic to the Mississippi." Lest readers miss the allusion, the paper
explained that the ceremony was meant to "serve the same purpose in the
marriage ceremonies between Old Ocean and Mississippi that the Doge's
ring anciently did in the marriage of Venice to the Adriatic." Since the
twelfth century, in that annual Ascension Day celebration, the Venetian
oligarch cast a gold ring into the waters while intoning, "O Sea, we wed
thee, in sign of our true and everlasting dominion!" Festivities marked celebrations back in Charleston, too. Lawrence Keitt's long-winded toast to
the railroad's completion welcomed the "splendid commerce" that enriched
the great empires of history—Thebes, Genoa, and, of course, Venice. Such
riches, he proclaimed to the newly linked merchants of "South and West,"
will "come to you a bidden guest."[18]

The *Mercury* extended the Venice metaphor in 1858. Imagining the city's low-country environs a "fairy vision . . . a modern Venice," it celebrated the "indomitable energies of a few far-seeing practical men" who had done so much "to establish the city of Charleston on a firm commercial basis" and would shortly "render her the 'Empire City of the South.'" Soon, the paper predicted, Charleston would be free from "interruptions of trade or desponding forebodings" for the future. To achieve such success, the paper exhorted, civic leaders must reject "Old Fogyism" and embrace the "Goddess Enterprise." Most important, the city must invest further in railroads. These, the *Mercury* imagined, would "contribute MILLIONS OF WEALTH to the city" and its hinterlands. The path from Charleston to Venice, ironically, would be traversed by locomotive.[19]

These predictions would not come to pass. Secession and Civil War intervened, and we need not waste time in wondering whether Charleston's Venetian dreams could ever have risen out of the muck of fantasy. City partisans—hard-driven merchants and dreaming romantics alike—might have foreseen the vanity of such aspirations had they studied Venice more closely. Back in their offices or breezy ocean-side parlors, it was easy to dream of Venice—to read of the bustle that marked the world of Antonio and Shylock, to bask in Cooper's vivid description of the seaside queen, or to take in the commercial color of Canaletto's landscape paintings. But the Venice of their dreams was not Venice at all. Rather, Charlestonians greedily consumed the so-called myth of Venice, a consciously constructed past *sui generis*.

Promoting their city as an exceptional place, Venetians regarded it as divinely sanctioned, commercially blessed, and politically enlightened. Historian James Grubb has argued that the "many-layered confection known as the myth of Venice is no single myth but an accumulation of historical explanation and contingent propaganda."[20] That self-propagated myth was indeed alluring to both retrospective and prospective purveyors of Carolina's own "holy city." As we have seen, in the midst of economic decline, antebellum Charlestonians created and valorized a "usable past," celebrating seventeenth-century heroes, smoothing over internecine rancor, and flaunting the city's once-proud prosperity. It was at once both a past that provided solace and a base on which to build for the future. They girded this foundation with stories—indeed, myths—of Venice, whose history, they imagined, mirrored their own.

But more important than what Charlestonians chose to see in Venice's past was what they opted not to consider. Those Carolinians who traveled to Venice encountered a city that, like Charleston in the nineteenth century, had fallen into steep decline. This was the Venice—and Charleston—that Henry Cruger portrayed in his review of Cooper's *The Bravo*. In describing Venice, he emphasized its "prostrate and torpid condition," seeing in certain resemblances of situation and history commonalities between this "once flourishing city" and his own. "When the moon has thrown its light around," he declared, "as the solitary passenger, through the deserted and sepulchral street of Charleston, meditates upon her time-worn, rusty and mouldering edifices, he is reminded gloomily of the blank, icy, and desolate aspect of that other city afar; now manifestly 'expiring before the eyes' of her inhabitants, and fast 'sinking into the slime of her own canals.'"[21]

In their studies of southern intellectual life and antebellum travelers, Michael O'Brien and Daniel Kilbride have each observed an absence of "reflections upon the meaning of the American South," with Kilbride noting that elite southerners preferred to seek a common class bond with wealthy Yankees under a nationalist banner rather than any sort of sectional partisanship.[22] And though most Carolina travelers hewed to this script, and few made the connection between Venice and Charleston specifically, it is worth noting the taut interplay of retrospective attraction and contemporary revulsion that held sway in their antebellum accounts. Almost universal was the sentiment most bluntly noted by James Hammond. "Every thing bespeaks a noble people *that have been!*" he exclaimed, his excitement tempered with recognition of greatness lost. Robert Barnwell was struck by Venice's "torpid condition" as he reached the city for the first time in 1854. His "Rail Car shot puffing and blowing away all the Romance of former days"; his entrance via a "grim official guardhouse was [his] first salutation and significant emblem of her humbled state." Though greeted with "water streets and gondola," he was "disappointed." It was, he explained, "like recognizing and greeting a loved face yet finding it somewhat faded." Carolina traveler Joseph Daniel Aiken likewise found little to admire in 1849. He made the usual tour of palaces and churches and was impressed by Canova's tomb and Tiziano's great works but found Venice's streets and canals "narrow and unpleasant." Admittedly, Aiken timed his trip poorly, seeing the city under "unfavourable circumstances." He arrived just in time to witness "the entry, by boats, up the grand canal of General Gorskowski & the Austrians." Daniele Manin's attempt to throw off the city's oppressors had been squelched only days earlier, and the city bore devastating marks of defeat. Aiken reported that sixty thousand balls had been "thrown into the city," and everywhere he saw their "injurious" scars. "Everything was in a State of Confusion, the citizens nearly starved," churches pocked, and the new railway to the city "seriously damaged." Aiken expressed little sympathy for Venetians' plight, however. This place was a "city of the dead," he remarked, "a den of thieves at best & no place for a decent man to live any time."[23]

Charleston painter James De Veaux could countenance the Austrians—romanticizing the "splendid soldiery" that kept Venetians and the artist himself "awed into subjection." More tragic, De Veaux believed, were the "last of that noble race," the few remaining families of the Venetian mercantile elite. De Veaux spent his final evening in Venice in the company of an elderly matriarch of the Foscari family. Casting his eyes around the palace, he noted ruefully that all the other apartments of the once-grand palazzo were "now occupied by tradesmen and their families." "Thus passeth the glory of the world," he sighed.[24]

Indeed, the trade and bustle Charleston coveted had fallen into petty, messy, common barter. "Many of [the palazzi] are uninhabited now," Robert Barnwell reported, "and in the possession of Austrian families." He mourned the precipitous decline of "Venetian nobility," a class "fast dying out," hundreds of years of "wealth and glory turned to dust." The "Hebrew," he noted disdainfully, "is in her Palaces," and "the Tradesman walks over her marble." Cruger summed up this sentiment best, echoing Cooper's protagonists in *The Bravo:* "I have seen faces on the Rialto of late, Signore, that look empty purses." The grubby beggaring that passed for trade in Venice in the first half of the nineteenth century was a far cry from the vast exchanges of commercial capital that sustained the city in its "palmiest days." And while visitors might still find romance in the silent slip of "funeral like gondolas," sympathy and, with some, outright scorn marked their reactions. How could the jewel city whose domain had reached so far, whose ships had ruled the sea, whose families had ranked with the wealthiest and most powerful in the world, have sunk so low?[25]

In the years after Appomattox, Charlestonians asked the same questions about their own fallen city. Others walked its ruined streets; sighed over its faded glory; drew sad morals to pass along in other, lesser struggling towns. The Venetian metaphor, indeed most mentions of Venice at all, fell from Carolina papers. The city looked inward, seeking to sort out the mess it had made of its prospects. With Italian unification complete in

1866, however, Venice once again made the news. "Mournful Condition of the Grand Old City of Venice 1866," the article in a November 1866 issue of the *Greenville Mountaineer* read. "The Star of Venice has set forever, and nothing can bring it again above the horizon. Her prosperity belongs to another age and race. The glory of the past may gild her present aspect, but will no more warm it into life." The article described the grand plans of its citizens, its hopes and dreams for recovery and rebuilding all that was lost. "But it certainly seems all in vain," the paper editorialized. "Her old trade has left her, and what manufacturers could now be established with any prospect of success? The most Venice can hope for is a comfortable old age as a provincial town." Any Carolinian would have read these words, of course, and thought of their own disgraced ocean queen.[26]

    With secession and Civil War, Charleston realized its Venetian dreams all too well. In the half century after Confederate defeat, as Yankee travelers came to embrace what Nina Silber has called the "romance of reunion," and Charleston came to pursue—or resign itself to—the tourist trade, the Venetian metaphor reemerged once again.[27] Guides to and narrative descriptions of the United States deployed and discussed the metaphor, while Charleston itself flaunted the moniker "the Venice of America" for commercial gain.[28] Travelers made more direct comparisons. Complaining to his cousin in 1896 about Venetian weather, Langdon Cheves thought of home: "It is so hot and enervating just like Charleston which it resembles in many more agreeable particulars." Pondering the comparison further, he added, "I wish it would inspire Charleston with some of its animation." Other travelers' diaries detail mornings spent sightseeing and afternoons perusing the shops, most of which catered to the tourist trade, hawking all manner of "glass beads" and "lace." Taken together, they hint at the new buy-cheap/sell-dear moral Charlestonians might draw for their own beloved city. Writing back to the *Charleston Courier* in 1913, August Kohn regaled readers with images of St. Mark's Square: the "gilt clock" atop the campanile, the "glories of the Doge's Palace," and another eye-catching sight. "Ranged around," he described, "are the principal stores, generally two stories in height, and there you may spend all your money on laces, jewelry and bric-a-brac." Everywhere, he noted, the "lion with wings" attracted tourist cash, "the design . . . offered as paper weights in the curio shops, at fancy prices." This proud emblem of Venice marked all manner of goods purveyed, just as the ubiquitous palmetto tree now stamps every hat, t-shirt, or whatnot Charleston visitors consume. Proud pasts became cheap brands.[29]

Here, then, Charleston found at last indisputable common ground with her fellow sea-drinking queen. Both still trade on their history—or, more specifically, the soothing sui generis myths that natives told themselves and their kin. This ironic convergence of civic development was perhaps presaged by antebellum Charleston mythmakers' conflicted consideration of contemporary Venice and its history. As "America's Most Historic City" and a "tourist theater," Charleston relives daily the "days of its glory" at the expense of the grubby trade it so desperately tried to avoid. Civic narrative here vanquishes history endlessly and so too the very future its citizens once held dear.[30]

Notes

1. Entries, Oct. 16, 20, 1837, Diary of a European Tour, James Henry Hammond Papers, South Caroliniana Library, University of South Carolina, Columbia (hereafter SCL).

2. Josephine Pinckney, *Sea-Drinking Cities: Poems* (New York: Harper & Brothers, 1927).

3. Entries, Aug.–Oct. 1854, Leaves from Italy and Tyrol, 103–4, Robert Woodward Barnwell Papers, SCL. For further analysis of the Charleston-Venice metaphor, see Kenneth Severens, "'Rising like Another Venice from the Sea': Imagery, Invention, and Architectural Style in Antebellum Charleston," and John P. Radford, "Symbolic Landscape and Geographical Determinism: Charleston and the Myth of Venice, 1820–1860" (both papers presented at "From Revolution to Revolution: New Directions in Antebellum Lowcountry Studies, 1775–1869," College of Charleston, May 9–11, 1996).

4. [Henry Cruger], review of *The Bravo,* by James Fenimore Cooper, *Southern Review* 8 (1832): 398. There is some dispute over the author of this review. Michael O'Brien makes a strong case for Cruger, a Charleston lawyer who would abandon "Charleston for New York, because he felt that Charleston was failing to match the insistent demands of American progress and vitality." See Michael O'Brien, *Conjectures of Order: Intellectual Life and the American South, 1810–1860,* 2 vols. (Chapel Hill: University of North Carolina Press, 2004), 1: 158. In his own study of the city, Walter J. Fraser attributes the review to Hugh Swinton Legaré. See Walter J. Fraser, *Charleston! Charleston! The History of a Southern City* (Columbia: University of South Carolina Press, 1989), 206.

5. For an excellent overview of the potential and pitfalls of comparative history for the Old South and the utility of the Italian comparison in particular, see Peter Kolchin, "The American South in Comparative Perspective," in Rick Halpern and Enrico dal Lago, eds., *The American South and the Italian Mezzogiorno: Essays in Comparative History* (New York: Palgrave, 2002), 26–59; Peter Kolchin,

Unfree Labor: American Slavery and Russian Serfdom (Cambridge: Harvard University Press, 1987); Shearer Davis Bowman, *Masters and Lords: Mid-19th Century U.S. Planters and Prussian Junkers* (New York: Oxford University Press, 1993). Frank Tannenbaum's flawed but seminal *Slave and Citizen* ranks among the most important early works on comparative slavery and introduced a vibrant and extensive historiography that has flourished in years since. See Frank Tannenbaum, *Slave and Citizen: The Negro in the Americas* (New York: Knopf, 1946).

6. Raimondo Luraghi, *The Rise and Fall of the Plantation South* (New York: Franklin Watts, 1978); Susanna Delfino, "The Idea of Southern Backwardness," in Susanna Delfino and Michelle Gillespie, eds., *Global Perspectives on Industrial Transformation in the American South* (Columbia: University of Missouri Press, 2005), 105–30; Enrico Dal Lago, *Agrarian Elites: American Slaveholders and Southern Italian Landowners, 1815–1861* (Baton Rouge: Louisiana State University Press, 2005); Don Doyle, *Nations Divided: America, Italy, and the Southern Question* (Athens: University of Georgia Press, 2002).

7. O'Brien, *Conjectures of Order*, 1: 158. Recent work challenges O'Brien on this point, particularly with regard to secession-minded southerners' understanding and interpretation of Italian political movements. See, in particular, Ann L. Tucker, "Internationalizing the Confederacy: Italy and the Creation of Southern Nationalism" (master's thesis, University of South Carolina, 2008).

8. O'Brien, *Conjectures of Order*, 1: 154.

9. William Gilmore Simms, *Father Abbott; or, The Home Tourist* (Charleston: Miller & Browne, 1849), 13; William Gilmore Simms, "From Our Correspondent. En Route, Aug. 24, 1845," *Southern Patriot*, Sept. 22, 1845; William Gilmore Simms, "Charleston: The Palmetto City," *Harper's New Monthly Magazine* 85 (1857): 2.

10. Charles S. Watson, *The History of Southern Drama* (Lexington: University Press of Kentucky, 1997), 25–47. Local papers included occasional discussions of Otway's and Shakespeare's works and ran advertisements for local productions. For examples, see *Charleston City Gazette*, Mar. 22, 1824; *Charleston Courier*, Feb. 27, 1843; *Charleston Courier*, Jan. 18, 1853; *Charleston Courier*, Mar. 22, 1826.

11. Léon Beauvallet, *Rachel and the New World: A Trip to the United States and Cuba* (New York: Dix, Edwards, and Company, 1856), 306; Simms, "Charleston: The Palmetto City," 3–5.

12. Miriam J. Shillingsburg, "Simms's Failed Lecture Tour of 1856: The Mind of the North," in John C. Guilds, ed., *"Long Years of Neglect": The Work and Reputation of William Gilmore Simms* (Fayetteville: University of Arkansas Press, 1988), 183–201.

13. George Rogers Jr., *Charleston in the Age of the Pinckneys* (Norman: University of Oklahoma Press, 1969), 150–55; O'Brien, *Conjectures of Order*, 2: 628–29; Van Wyck Brooks, "On Creating a Usable Past," *Dial* 64 (Apr. 11, 1918): 337–41; Maurie D. McInnis, *The Politics of Taste in Antebellum Charleston* (Chapel Hill: University of North Carolina Press, 2005), 8. The crowded field of memory studies merits more attention than a single footnote can offer. Readers interested in the

field might consider: Pierre Nora, "Between Memory and History: Les Lieuxs de Memoire," *Representations* 26 (Spring 1989): 7–25; David Lowenthal, *The Past Is a Foreign Country* (New York: Cambridge University Press, 1985); Michael Kammen, *Mystic Chords of Memory: The Transformation of Tradition in American Culture* (New York: Vintage, 1993); John Bodnar, *Remaking America: Public Memory, Commemoration, and Patriotism in the Twentieth Century* (Princeton: Princeton University Press, 1992); Roy Rosenzweig and David Thelen, *The Presence of the Past: Popular Uses of History in American Life* (New York: Columbia University Press, 1998). For the South in particular, see W. Fitzhugh Brundage's excellent *The Southern Past: A Clash of Race and Memory* (Cambridge: Harvard University Press, 2005).

14. Tyrone Power, *Impressions of America during the years 1833, 1834, and 1835* (London: Samuel Bentley, 1836), 2: 97–98; Charles Dickens, "Charleston City," *All the Year Round* 4 (Feb. 23, 1861): 463.

15. "The Public Schools of Charleston," *De Bow's Review* 25 (1858): 370; "Direct Trade," *Charleston Mercury,* Dec. 29, 1856. See also "Direct Trade," *Charleston Mercury,* Dec. 15, 1856.

16. For discussion of Charleston's ancestral connection to Antonin Prioli, see David Ramsay, *History of South Carolina: From Its First Settlement in 1670 to the Year 1808* (Newberry, SC: W. J. Duffie, 1858), 4; James De Bow, "The Huguenots of the South," *De Bow's Review* 5 (1861): 521; John Warner Barber and Henry Howe, *Our Whole Country; or, The Past and Present of the United States* (Cincinnati: Henry Howe, 1861), 1: 734.

17. "Commercial Facilities and Burdens," *Charleston Mercury,* Apr. 10, 1856; "Direct Trade of Southern States with Europe," *De Bow's Review* 4 (1847): 210; "Statistical Bureaus in the States," *De Bow's Review* 8 (1850): 439.

18. "Charleston and Memphis RR," *Charleston Mercury,* Apr. 1, 1857; Jan Morris, *The World of Venice,* rev. ed. (New York: Harcourt Brace & Company, 1993), 287; "Dinner at the Military Hall," *Charleston Mercury,* June 1, 1857. See also "Rail Road Frolics Ahead—Grand Marriage in High Life," *Charleston Courier,* Apr. 2, 1857.

19. "A Vision of Mount Pleasant in 1870," *Charleston Mercury,* Dec. 27, 1858. Here and following, all emphasis is taken from original documents.

20. See James S. Grubb, "When Myths Lose Power: Four Decades of Venetian Historiography," *Journal of Modern History* 58 (1986): 43.

21. Cruger, review of *The Bravo,* 398.

22. Michael O'Brien, *Rethinking the South: Essays in Intellectual History* (Athens: University of Georgia Press, 1993), 109; Daniel Kilbride, "Travel, Ritual, and National Identity: Planters on the European Tour, 1820–1860," *Journal of Southern History* 69 (2003): 549–84. For a lengthier discussion of Charlestonians as "cultural tourists" on the "Grand Tour" and the art collected on their journeys, see Maurie D. McInnis, ed., *In Pursuit of Refinement: Charlestonians Abroad, 1780–1865* (Columbia: University of South Carolina Press, 1999).

23. Cruger, review of *The Bravo*, 398; entry, Oct. 16, 1837, Diary of a European Tour, Hammond Papers, SCL; entries, Aug.–Oct. 1854, Leaves from Italy and Tyrol, 99–100, Barnwell Papers, SCL; entry, Aug. 27, 1849, Joseph Daniel Aiken Travel Diary, South Carolina Historical Society (hereafter SCHS).

24. Robert W. Gibbes, *A Memoir of James De Veaux, of Charleston, S.C.* (Columbia: I. C. Morgan's Letter Press Print, 1846), 186, 189–90.

25. Entries, Aug.–Oct. 1854, Leaves from Italy and Tyrol, 138–39, Barnwell Papers, SCL; Cruger, review of *The Bravo*, 390; entries, Aug.–Oct. 1854, Leaves from Italy and Tyrol, 126, Barnwell Papers, SCL.

26. "Mournful Condition of the Grand Old City of Venice," *Greenville Mountaineer*, Nov. 29, 1866.

27. Nina Silber, *The Romance of Reunion: Northerners and the South, 1865–1900* (Chapel Hill: University of North Carolina Press, 1997), 66–92. Recent scholarship has examined the ways in which southerners have molded their past to attract tourists. For a thoughtful discussion of the ways in which southern city leaders and chambers of commerce "created" distinct civic identities, especially for the tourist trade, see Karen Cox, *Dreaming of Dixie: How the South was Created in American Popular Culture* (Chapel Hill: University of North Carolina Press, 2011), 130–62. More specific to Charleston, Stephanie Yuhl offers an assessment of the efforts of the city's elite white "cultural producers" to imagine "their city as the last enclave of genteel white aristocrats and subservient African American folk in an otherwise tumultuous nation." Mythmaking and the creation of a usable past, she argues, was and is central to the success of Charleston's tourist trade. See Stephanie Yuhl, *A Golden Haze of Memory: The Making of Historic Charleston* (Chapel Hill: University of North Carolina Press, 2005), 6. Fitzhugh Brundage makes a similar case, arguing that city leaders transformed Charleston into a "theater of the Old South" in the 1920s and 1930s (*Southern Past*, 225). Both Brundage and Yuhl offer an important assessment of the relationship between memory making and increasing racial oppression. While this essay does not address this theme with regard to the Venetian metaphor, it is important to remember the important broader context they describe.

28. Advertisement for the Annual Meeting of the National Educational Association, *School Journal*, May 12, 1900, 523. For other late–nineteenth century comparisons to Venice, see *Appleton's Illustrated Hand-Book of American Winter Resorts* (New York: D. Appleton & Company, 1884), 43; Edward King, *The Great South* (Hartford, CT: American Publishing Company, 1875), 444; *Our Native Land; or, Glances at American Scenery and Places* (New York: D. Appleton & Company, 1882), 480; C. H. Glidden, "Yachting in the Sunny South," *Outing* 32 (1898): 136; Willard Glazier, *Peculiarities of American Cities* (Philadelphia: Hubbard Brothers Publishers, 1884), 115.

29. Langdon Cheves to Alice, May 14, 1896, Langdon Cheves Papers, SCHS; Anne A. Porcher, Diary of a European Trip, Aug. 4, 1897, Porcher Family Papers, SCHS; Mary Jane Ross, Travel Diary, Nov. 10–15, 1892, SCL; August Kohn, *Diary of a European Trip* (Charleston: Daggett, 1913), 44–45.

30. Brundage, *Southern Past*, 194.

5

Elizabethan Dreams, Victorian Nightmares

Antebellum South Carolina's Future through an English Looking Glass

Lawrence T. McDonnell

Galloping horsemen, gleaming armor, a pale moon rising over a distant castle: such symbols seemingly befit the midlands of medieval Britain better than those of antebellum South Carolina. But when "Black Hawk," "Grey Eagle," "Red Rover," "Blue Ranger," "Thundergust," and "Wildfire" welcomed their friends to a Christmas Eve gathering of the "Nighthawks of the Congaree" at their "Hole in the Wall" haunt in 1847, this was the imagery they adopted.[1] The Nighthawks promised carnival—"The first shall be last, and the last shall be first!"—but whether they were college students or rural planters' sons, a regular club where young men might drink and carouse apart from disapproving women and clerics, or simply a small set of playful fellows out to advertise a holiday dance, we cannot say. Were they an unlucky slave patrol, comically escalating the duty to ride the roads during the season of celebration into a dream of ancient chivalry? Or did they actually play out fantasy just as their invitation depicted, donning armor, mounting thoroughbreds, and jousting under the stars? Certainly others did, across the state and further afield, during the decade and a half before secession. Myths of moonlight and magnolias flourished from such weird and twisted roots and more dangerous dreams besides.

For many southerners, chivalry was pure pretend: a fashionable style, a Romantic conceit, well deserving the derision outsiders heaped upon it.[2] "The age of Chivalry is gone," they admitted, and all "whin[ing] over the want of Knights, and tournaments, and of scarfs waved by ladies' fair hands" and all other such "tomfooleries" was simply sickly sentimentality.[3] To northerners, it seemed "inexplicable" that "men, grown men . . . should make such Jack Puddings of themselves" as did Arkansas's "knights of the coonskin cap," Virginia's "Baron de Corncob," and the "Champion of Skunk's Misery," decked out in "pasteboard bucklers and helmets of the same material," pretending to a nobility of the most ludicrous sort.[4] Jousting was just "an expensive, dangerous amusement which the masses cannot imitate, and in which they cannot participate," the *Boston Investigator* charged, a symbol of the "barbaric pride, venality, and ignorance" that typified southern culture.[5] Circuses mocked such exercises.[6] Poets parodied them. Knightly self-portrayal became the acme of ridiculous self-importance or worse.[7] "O his armour is bright, his steed is strong / And his housings are rich and rare," sneered abolitionist Jane Swisshelm. "He *sold a baby* to buy him his horse / And another his trappings fair."[8]

Critics found it especially easy to disparage the self-admiring "*chivãl'ry* (do not pronounce *chiv'alry;* no one here says so, and surely we must know; who else should?) of South Caarol-i-nar."[9] Yet in Charleston and across much of the low country, few questioned the sincerity of would-be Galahads. There, men believed themselves the splendid seed of a slaveholding aristocracy rooted in knightly tradition, legitimate descendants of "the Hugonot & the Cavalier."[10] To Alfred Huger, the social characteristics of this honorable offspring were unmistakable: "their granite-integrity—their fixed & Enduring friendships—their dauntless courage & the softness of their affections" presented the most "brilliant combination of Materials & of Character which have influenced mankind from their earliest history."[11]

"The age of chivalry indeed is past," Virginian Beverly Tucker declared, "but does not the spirit of chivalry still live?"[12] Elite Carolinians refused to content themselves with such vague sentiments. Instead, they sought to seize their imagined birthright and improve upon it, too.[13] Through such endeavors of recreation, historian Ted Ownby reminds us, "people express not only who they are, but, very often, who they are not."[14] Increasingly appalled by the brutal age of iron and steam in which they lived, disgusted by the market-driven values of Victorian culture, they embraced a different code, pursued a different future. They admired the history of noble deeds, cultivated the manners of courtliness, aspired to embody gallantry in daily life. They played out chivalry's rituals with deep earnestness in feast and dance, race and joust. They itched to do more. At the very least, we may say, chivalry's devotees in South Carolina partook of the same earnest fantasies that inspired Congressman Lawrence Keitt to declare in 1857 that beset slaveholders would defend their honor, heritage, hierarchy, and households at sword's point against lowborn, meddlesome Yankees: "lance couched, helmet on, visor down!"[15]

Knightly reveries meshed seamlessly for southerners with come-what-may political bombast in these years, but historians have mostly minimized its importance, trivializing talk of chivalric war as hyperbolic metaphor, dismissing the tournaments, feasts, and balls planters recreated as quaint, failed, silly.[16] The problem is that such performances abounded, spreading in size, popularity, and reputation across the 1850s—especially in South Carolina. And when the tilting stopped, the shooting started. It was precisely here in just these years that the cutting edge of the South's slaveocracy worked out what they were willing to live and die for, and when crisis came in 1860, they downed their lances, donned the gray, sang "Dixie," and went off to kill for their doomed world.

More than this, they provoked the war.[17] However odd their words and deeds may seem a century and a half later, Keitt and his kind were not kidding. Admitting the truth of Lincoln's biblical quotation, they fought to build a house undivided according to their own precapitalist visions and—sooner or later—to burn down their northern neighbor's offendingly Victorian home, making war upon the whole egalitarian, capitalist world.[18] They deserve our respect—I do not mean admiration here—and close analysis.

For elite Carolinians, chivalry was no charade. Though politicians spoke of social order resting on labor's stinking mudsill, though reformers focused on the warmth of the family circle, gallants knew better. In claiming the name of gentleman, strong, principled fellows established ties of mutuality and courtesy between them, upholding a respectful code of conduct, balancing claims of rank and merit, vivifying a rigorous masculine ideal. That manly bond was the true social bedrock. Decent standards of behavior, defined by custom, force, faith, and blood, rose upon it: prescribed, displayed, enforced.[19] Not that chivalry's advocates aimed to recreate a lost world of knights and castles, as European eccentrics hoped.[20] Arthurian England was too bleak, divided, and unstable to go questing after, a world too much like their own. They aimed higher than that.

Even at their most fanciful, chivalry's performances in South Carolina demonstrated the deep play of political conservatism.[21] Consider the great tournament held in April 1851 at Pineville, the low country planter elite's summer residence in the rice swamp of Colleton District. Commanded by a "King at Arms," "Master of Horse," and various heralds, attended by appropriately decked-out "Moors," and watched by dozens of fair damsels hoping to be crowned the Queen of Love, twenty-one knights and a "sultan" named Augustin Taveau tried their prowess in "riding at the rings"—approaching a wooden frame at a gallop and snaring a dangling ring with the tips of their lances. Honor itself was at stake here. "You must brave danger," an elder warned, "but also fear shame!"[22] Since the first major tournament of this type had been held at White Sulphur Springs, Virginia, a decade before, not much in the way of danger had befallen any rider; still there was the worry that they might be badly outclassed at their game or unhorsed entirely.[23] More than this, Carolinians showed an earnestness and sense of larger purpose that Virginian contests seemed to lack. "Of noble name and knightly," the *Charleston Courier* declared, "they burn to claim the gilded spurs."[24] Burn they must have, sweating in the Carolina sun in the fancy garb of the Knight of This and the Lady of That. What was the point of all this overwrought, fanciful play?

The whole effort aimed at succeeding where conservative Britons had failed a decade before. In 1839, Archibald Montgomerie, the Thirteenth Earl of Eglinton, had invited England's aristocracy to his lowland Scottish estate as participants in a grand chivalric tournament.[25] Eglinton staged the strange spectacle not merely to win social influence and a handsome profit besides. He intended the display of prowess and bearing to revive the fortunes of Britain's marginalized conservative landed elite. Shunted aside as a moral force and a political class by the rude dynamism of a rising bourgeoisie, and thoroughly undermined by its own cultural excesses and intellectual torpor, the gentry might ride back to prominence and power, Eglinton hoped, by pointing to the ancient deeds and chivalric qualities that gave titled claims to national leadership undeniable substance. This was what had made England great; this was what would keep her great.

In the event, unfortunately, all the pomp and circumstance went comically wrong, entirely ruining the effect. Train and carriage schedules got botched. Unanticipated crowds went unsheltered and unfed. Persistent rains turned the field of honor into a sea of mud, rendering onlookers and participants in decidedly unchivalric shades of brown. Strong winds swept down from the highlands, carrying away bunting, tents, banners, hats. Just about anything that might take flight, did. Denuded of medieval fantasy, Eglinton's tournament wound up decidedly Victorian, soggy, and disappointing.

The earl was ruined, and so, it seemed, was his conservative vision: if the squires could so badly bungle a local festival, who dared pass the reins of national power into their hands? Across the 1840s, the liberal sentiment of Dickens displaced the conservative romance of Sir Walter Scott; demands for a Great Charter drowned out calls for government by bluebloods, and cotton mills, imperial profits, and technological prowess ushered chivalry's advocates—ignominiously dubbed the "Eglinton Patent Emasculated Mopstick Middle Age Recovery Society"—steadily toward oblivion.[26] A generation later, a well-heeled folk not gentle but genteel would recast medievalism as dreamy nostalgia and rural fashion, attractively unthreatening to a class that had made its money and longed now desperately to deny grubby origins.[27]

That is one way, too, of looking at what went on in South Carolina and in more limited ways across the American South in the years after Eglinton's fiasco. For the British journalist William Howard Russell, Carolinians' "profession of faith in the cavaliers and their cause," their "agricultural faith and the belief of a landed gentry," was simply a matter of fashion and baseless snobbery. Russell had witnessed the Charge of the Light Brigade, and he thought he knew chivalry and its dreadful ironies when he saw them. "I see no trace of cavalier descent in the names of Huger, Rose, Manning, Chesnut, Pickens," he protested.[28] But that view misread the central aim of all of Eglinton's ambitions and the slaveholders' disastrous course, too. These men were not simply looking for the alibi later Victorians sought, seeking to shape sensibility for defensive purposes, or whistling past the graveyard. In South Carolina, as in rural Britain, privilege rested ultimately upon potency, not pedigree. "We are all *parvenus,* pretenders or snobs," the low-country planter-politician William J. Grayson conceded, but some had the power to make claims of higher status stick.[29] That was the kernel of rough wisdom at honor's core. From the beginning, the earl's plan had been aggressively political, and so it was for jousting Carolinians who followed his unfortunate example.

It was, moreover, hardly the brutal, factionalized, impoverished, priest-ridden world of the Middle Ages English conservatives had hoped to recover in the early days of Victoria's reign. Who would have imagined that the elbows-out elite surrounding the young queen would have countenanced that goal?[30] Rather, it was the imagined rebirth of medieval chivalry they longed to create: all the heraldry and self-aggrandizement without the intramural bloodshed and pious dogma, of just the sort that had flourished in the Elizabethan age. Under that last great queen, the nation's power had been unified and magnified, launching a truly Great Britain on a proud course of empire. Celebrations of feast and joust, the knighting of pirates and entrepreneurs, nouveau heraldry and castle building, and the transmutation of chivalry into a code of honor had been part and parcel of that rise. Now, with noble, tried, conservative hands steadying the helm, Victoria might claim legitimate political descent from the triumphantly illegitimate virgin Elizabeth—magnificent alchemy—leading England to greater heights still.[31]

Though British Romantics abandoned Eglinton's idyll for the carping of Thomas Carlyle, Carolinians eagerly took up the quest. Thoroughly steeped in British culture (or Americanized imitations of it), many came to see Elizabethan recreations of medieval social relations as the sum of all they hoped for. Initially, of course, they swooned over the novels of Scott and his imitators, who comingled the rugged twelfth and rosy sixteenth centuries so shamelessly.[32] But most dug deeper, ransacking history and literature for themes, qualities, and heroic examples that might link their own lives with the knightly champions who made their blood race.[33]

Ultimately, it was not some legendary Galahad, Norman invader, or Christian crusader they focused upon, but a small set of early modern soldier-scribblers at the heart of medievalism's revival. A Drake or Hawkins, charming the queen with gentle manners and terrifying the nation's foes with daring deeds, was worth emulating. In Essex, Raleigh, Walsingham, and their circles, the code of honor reached its acme. Those heroes had launched the first plantations, made England a world power, and left a rich legacy of letters besides.

More satisfying still, the French chevalier Bayard, fighting "sans peur et sans reproche," demonstrated that a man might hold fast to chivalry's tenets while others went chasing after money, fame, and power. No wonder Carolina ideologues from Will Taber to William Gilmore Simms sang his praises.[34] Best of all for planters in search of a role model was that "flower of English manhood" Sir Philip Sidney: devout, cultured, brave, honorable, self-sacrificing.[35] To liberal Victorians, Sidney was nobody, the dilettante who missed his chance to make his mark. To chivalry's admirers, he embodied all a true man once was, and yet might be again.

For a gentleman is not an idler, a trifler, a dandy; he is not a scholar only, a soldier, a mechanic, a merchant; he is the flower of men, in whom the accomplishment of the soldier, the skill of the mechanic, the sagacity of the merchant, all have their part and appreciation. A sense of duty is his main-spring, and like a watch crusted with precious stones, his function is not to look prettily, but to tell the time of day. Philip Sidney was not a gentleman because his grandfather was the Duke of Northumberland and his father lord-deputy of Ireland, but because he was himself generous, simple, truthful, noble, refined.[36]

For South Carolinians coming of age in the late 1840s, Sidney was the sum of all the masculine values drummed into them since birth.[37] No one drank more deeply—or disastrously—from chivalry's cup than William R. Taber Jr., black sheep of the politically prominent Rhett clan and editor of the *Charleston Mercury*. Portraits depict him as dashingly handsome, recklessly Romantic, a cavalier reborn. On his best days, he personified that ideal; on his worst, he died for it, taking a bullet to the brain in a duel that tested the limits of manhood and duty to the breaking point.[38] Taber dead made chivalry alive—immortal, some said—as never before in the South's Holy City. Tributes to his memory poured in, linking chivalry to secession more effectively than any other propaganda could have achieved. "He believed that the continuance of the race of gentlemen (in the Bayard, Roland, or Philip Sidney meaning of the word) was more important than the existence of the Union, and he labored with pen and tongue to hedge South Carolina with barriers against the terrible invasion of Northern vulgarity, which has done so much to debauch our press and disgrace our people. This was a noble mission, well understood and manfully worked out to the close."[39] In case anyone missed the meaning of this political parable, short days after Will Taber was laid to rest, the *Mercury* mourned the loss of "so fine a flower / Untimely cropt" with the poem "A Lament for Sir Philip Sidney."[40] Others dropped hints of devotion to chivalry's cult in more subtle ways. They styled their hair, beards, and mustaches after knightly heroes. They renamed their plantations in the grand style of Elizabethan manor houses and medievalist imagination: Bolan Hall and Castle Hill, Richmond, Kensington, Twickenham Place, Bonny Doone, Rosdhu, Waverly.[41] They built overwrought homes with outlandish great halls, erected houses, churches, even slave cabins in a consciously gothic style.[42] They searched out proud lineages for present status or, like James Hammond, drew up their own heraldic coats of arms when all trace of noble ancestry was lacking.[43] At least one master had his slaves dig a moat around his mansion. In Charleston, the new arsenal became the Citadel, ecclesiological gothic churches flourished,[44] and crenellation etched the tops of the most unmilitary buildings.[45]

More commonly, men of means aimed to demonstrate virtues of honor and chivalry without all the hammering and subterfuge, dealing justly and generously with neighbors, raising sons up in the paths of duty, maintaining a prickly sense of independence, and leaving others to draw knightly comparisons.[46] Who would call John Townsend self-interested or narrow when every year he crowned the seaside feasts he held with a dish of palmetto cabbage, one for each of the dozens of his honored guests? The boiled sprout itself was not so tasty, but all knew that each portion signified the death of a tree on Townsend's plantation, slow growing and essential to long-term economic success—an act of almost reckless largesse on a soil so easily ruined by wind and tide. When a hurricane finally washed away Townsend's world a generation after Appomattox—house, island, and all went beneath the waves—none could have been much surprised. Nor, by that stage, did it matter much by his own lights: the old man's memory would live on regardless, like the rumbling of ancient chariot wheels.[47]

In the last years before Lincoln's election, such apparently hyperbolic acts of self-performance escalated into full-blown medieval tournaments, jousts, and tilting matches of all sorts. Sometimes these were associated with the annual festivities of volunteer militia companies, but more commonly wealthy planters organized them for the local community.[48] Across the low country, from Georgetown to Beaufort Districts; in the midlands near Augusta; in lower Richland District, near Camden; and less frequently above the fall line, such celebrations became annual events. By 1859, Charleston even boasted a tilting club that attracted would-be knights of mixed pedigree and prospects. "Perfectly free from those evils which would render it expensive," the group enlisted clerks and bank tellers, storekeepers and wharfingers, as scions of chivalry.[49]

Why "the inspiriting sport of this gay hour?—these knightly and gallant darings?" One supporter explained tilting's attraction to Charleston's youth: beyond perfecting skill in the rites of chivalry, club members relished the chance to present manly character in its "truest and happiest light." Sporting success reflected competitors' "virtues as men," promoting the goal of "true social and virtuous intercourse." Having demonstrated the "purity of [their] entire lives" and dedication to the cause "of right, of justice, of virtue, and of honour," tilters were ready at last for "an ordeal before [the] battery of beauty" and their male relatives, too.[50] Could Balaclava have been more daunting than sallying forth among Charleston's belles?

Moderns may snicker at such overwrought sentiment, but it is exactly the sincerity of exaggeration here we need to focus upon. For elite Carolinians, melodrama was not merely a mode of theater: it was a way of life.[51] Lacking any well-defined tradition of how men were expected to comport themselves on the tilting ground, men simply created one, assuming alternate identities and performing social drama from the merest scraps of script.[52] Participants arrayed themselves in astonishing examples of "man-millinery," portrayed themselves as bearers of noble titles, from the Knight of Walworth or the Palmetto Knight to the more exotic Knight of Norway, Mexican Lancer, or Knight of the Ocean.[53] All of this suggests that enthusiasm for tournaments in South Carolina was more a celebration of ritual than a type of game. Elements of melodrama are evident in the theatrical costuming and stylized behavior of participants, the rigidity of narrative form, and the unimportance of scoring participants. Tilting was a game or sport only in that it partook of liminality, temporarily suspending the rules of social reality. That escape into fantasy was all important, and in this sense the tournament is best understood as a ritual invocation, an opportunity for celebrants to be released from the mask of prosaic everyday existence, standing forth as the chivalrous heroes they aimed to emulate. Within that charmed circle of blood, taste, and merit where men had the wit to see, interpret, and mirror each other's chivalrous behavior, honorable status was claimed and mutually affirmed. Those beyond were relegated to a lower level. How well one rode, whether one hit one's target, was almost irrelevant to the story participants enacted in the course of play. The French scholar Roland Barthes made the same point in his famous analysis of wrestling: "The public is completely uninterested in knowing whether the contest is rigged or not, and rightly so. . . . What is expected is the intelligible representation of moral situations which are usually private. This emptying out of interiority to the benefit of its external signs, this exhaustion of the content by the form, is the very principle of triumphant classical art."[54] Tournaments functioned as a melodramatic tale Carolinians told about who they were—or might be—and what values truly mattered in their world. By linking a lost dream of Elizabethan chivalry to their besieged, slave-based honor culture, they sought to realize an ethos of revolutionary power: the advent of a paternalist utopia where the liberal excesses of Victorian reform might be rolled back; the degrading folly of capitalist exploitation denied; and the planters' conservatism affirmed, purified, and celebrated.[55]

Realizing those world-changing ambitions, however, meant balancing Tudor and Victorian ideals more perfectly than any mortal could have done. The fortunes of the Charleston Tilting Club display this difficulty in microcosm. Elsewhere it was the confluence—not to say confusion—of chivalry and paternalism that attracted supporters. Here, respectable meetings and a sober constitution replaced gay costumes and courtly bearing. Riders actually practiced tilting, and in bland blue uniforms, no less. Predictably, membership never exceeded twenty knights. In 1860, as laborious ritual displaced melodramatic play, the club was barely struggling along.[56] Most men confined themselves to "intellectual jousts" to affirm manhood and fend off the South's foes.[57]

Most telling of all perhaps, from 1857 onward, Carolinians embraced the remarkable "Chess Mania" that swept across the nation. Celebrating the exploits of Paul Morphy, the New Orleans prodigy who electrified America and Europe with his brilliant play, ordinary men by the hundreds formed local chess clubs, enacting honor and chivalry across the game board in emulation of their "Southern Bayard."[58] For those who lacked horse or lance or the social capital necessary to take up jousting, chess proved the next best thing. Illustrating coolness and bravery, testing the character of one's opponent, then resetting the pieces with a handshake after each bloody battle, southerners here played out in miniature social dramas that dragooned and galvanized secession sentiment on the march to war.

By the late 1850s, elite Carolinians came to believe, there was no other choice. The growth of cities and factories, the breakdown of face-to-face social ties, the eclipse of masculine control over women and inferiors—and the disappearance of slavery—summed up a world steadily encroaching upon the borders of the South they saw as simply "devilish." Confronting the political economy of Smith and Ricardo, the utilitarianism of Mill, and the democratizing demands of British abolitionists and Chartists, Carolina planters and intellectuals came to view Victorian England as everything their precapitalist civilization stood in opposition to. In Europe and the North, as they saw it, the Victorian "love of gain" had "nearly effected the conquest of Christendom." Worse still, on the eve of Lincoln's election, that "offspring of the devil," capitalism seemed set to besiege their

Holy City itself. "It cannot be the will of God," protested Frederick Porcher, "that his creatures shall exist in hopeless degradation, toiling harder than slaves, with none of the slaves' security."[59] At a time when capitalist "Utility," the "Earth-born God," threatened "to convert the world into one great workhouse, or Panopticon," crushing every independent moral impulse, slavery's chivalry rode forward in defense of "Genius, Virtue and Heroism."[60] Manfully defending their peculiar institution meant holding the solid mudsill upon which the towers of Christian civilization must arise. "The interests of labour and capital can never be permanently or properly reconciled," explained William Henry Trescot, "except under the institution of slavery."[61]

In saying that, for this folk, slavery was "less a business than a way of life," we must recognize the vast aggression of their conservative ambition.[62] Only chattel bondage, they believed, could provide the secure foundation to recreate the Elizabethan vision of a medieval world of lords and vassals, where honor prevailed among men, men ruled over women and chattels, and labor tied to land produced wondrous profits and social harmony. Ultimately, the play and ritual that enlisted men to the cult of chivalry was only the most melodramatic aspect of a movement that aimed toward world-saving action. In their desperate quest to live sincerely, to root out falsehood and defend the values of honor they took so seriously, Carolinians embraced dueling with a fervent passion, murdering each other—or patching up what we might see as irremediable differences—with an ease and impersonality that pervades the theater of chivalry.[63]

Understanding that melodramatic vision as central to manly action is crucial, too, if we hope to make sense of South Carolina's rashest act before secession: the caning of Massachusetts senator Charles Sumner. What drove Congressman Preston Brooks, moderate and mild, to do that very foolish thing, wearing out his cane on the abolitionist's head and shoulders, propelling the Republican Party to electoral victory across the North in the fall of 1856, and putting the "slave power" problem so disastrously in the center of the national conversation?[64]

Sumner had sneered that the aging Carolina senator Andrew Pickens Butler had read too many romantic novels and now fancied himself a chivalrous knight. Rather, the Yankee taunted, quixotic Butler was a pompous, slobbering, doddering slave driver; the fair maid he defended was the repulsive "harlot, Slavery."[65] That jab hit home on too many levels for Butler's nephew Brooks to keep silent. "My colleague redressed a wrong to his blood and his state," Brooks's accomplice Lawrence Keitt explained, "and he did it in a fair and manly way. Sir, in the feudal code of chivalry—the only code the wit of man has ever constructed—the churl was never touched with the knight's sword; his person was mulcted by the quarter-staff."[66] Hence the assault: Brooks was above suing; Sumner was below dueling. "The rapier or pistol for gentlemen," agreed another young gallant, "& the cudgel for dogs."[67]

And so, come 1861, play became revolution. The great Romantics of the nineteenth-century West, South Carolina's slaveholding elite rode forth to battle, where most never did imagine, never could have imagined, they would go. They were never simply slavery's defenders, but crusaders in its name, tilting against the world. Compelled by an idealized vision of England's past, repelled by dreadful imaginings of a Victorian capitalist, egalitarian future springing up on their soil, planters translated hopes and fears into political action, breaking up the American Union. Southern chivalry would vanquish abolition's forces at the first charge, Congressman Keitt promised. But by the summer of 1864, when the Carolina colonel finally met Grant's army at Cold Harbor, there was nothing gallant or knightly about the passage of arms.[68] Ordered forward to probe for enemy skirmishers, Keitt instead launched the raw recruits of his brigade against seasoned troopers, well entrenched and armed with seven-shot repeating Spencer rifles. Riding ahead on a splendid gray charger, the "true chevalier" Keitt made a splendid target. A bullet in the liver toppled him from his horse, and the onrushing Confederates "went to pieces in abject rout." "They actually groveled upon the ground," one stunned Rebel wondered. No threats or commands could rouse the green troops to stand and fight: "if compelled to wriggle out of one hole they wriggled into another." As for Keitt, he lingered on painfully for hours, passing with the pitifully melodramatic judgment, "Such is the fate of war."[69] And of chivalry, we might add—respectfully if not gladly—and all ruling classes once their hour has passed.

Notes

1. "Nighthawks of the Congaree" invitation, Dec. 24, 18[47?], Glass Family Papers, South Caroliniana Library, University of South Carolina (hereafter SCL).

2. Isaac Hayne to Charles C. Pinckney, Apr. 23, 1860, Charles Cotesworth Pinckney Jr. Papers, SCL; "An Affair of Honor," *Harper's Magazine* 17 (1858): 861. More than one joust attracted some wag dressed as Don Quixote, appearing unannounced to spoil the dramatic effect. See *Chillicothe Scioto Gazette*, Sept. 18, 1845.

3. M., "Fields of Heroism," *Southern Literary Messenger* 9 (1843): 190.

4. *Pensacola Gazette,* Mar. 11, 1843; *Mississippi Free Trader and Natchez Gazette,* Sept. 25, 1845; *Milwaukee Sentinel,* Nov. 9, 1844.

5. *Boston Investigator,* Oct. 25, 1843.

6. See, e.g., *Boston Daily Atlas,* Dec. 4, 1844; *Raleigh Daily Register,* May 11, 1853; *Daily Cleveland Herald,* July 28, 1853, Sept. 11, 1856.

7. *Philadelphia North American and United States Gazette,* Oct. 17, 1849.

8. Jane G. Swisshelm, "Chivalry," *Emancipator and Weekly Chronicle,* Feb. 26, 1845.

9. Thomas S. Perry, *The Life and Letters of Francis Lieber* (Boston: James R. Osgood, 1882), 254.

10. William J. Grayson, "The Character of a Gentleman," *Southern Quarterly Review* 8 (1853): 68 (quote); Nathaniel R. Middleton, *Moral Courage. An Address before the Society of the Alumni of the College of Charleston* (Charleston: Burges, James, and Paxton, 1848); Iveson L. Brookes, *A Defence of the South against the Reproaches and Incroachments of the North: In Which Slavery Is Shown to Be an Institution of God Intended to Form the Best Social State and the Only Safeguard to the Permanence of a Republican Government* (Hamburg, SC: Republican Office, 1850), esp. 32; J. Milton Mackie, *From Cape Cod to Dixie and the Tropics* (New York: G. P Putnam, 1864), 112.

11. Alfred Huger to Robert N. Gourdin, Aug. 23, 18[59?], Robert Newman Gourdin Papers, Emory University, Atlanta, GA.

12. *Washington Daily National Intelligencer,* Sept. 13, 1844.

13. A Bachelor Knight [William G. Simms], *The Book of My Lady: A Melange* (Boston: Allen and Ticknor, 1833), esp. 12, 150–54.

14. Ted Ownby, *Subduing Satan: Religion, Recreation, and Manhood in the Rural South, 1865–1920* (Chapel Hill: University of North Carolina Press, 1990), 2.

15. John H. Merchant Jr., "Lawrence M. Keitt: South Carolina Fire-Eater" (PhD diss., University of Virginia, 1976), 209.

16. See, e.g., Rollin G. Osterweis, *Romanticism and Nationalism in the Old South* (Baton Rouge: Louisiana State University Press, 1949); William R. Taylor, *Cavalier and Yankee: The Old South and American National Character* (New York: Harper & Row, 1961).

17. Explaining that disastrous choice—what Eugene Genovese correctly terms "a self-inflicted beheading"—is still the heart of the problem for scholars of Civil War causation. See Eugene D. Genovese, *The Political Economy of Slavery: Studies in the Economy and Society of the Slave South* (New York: Vintage Books, 1965), 266; Eugene D. Genovese, *The Slaveholders' Dilemma: Freedom and Progress in Southern Conservative Thought, 1820–1860* (Columbia: University of South Carolina Press, 1992).

18. Peter Della Torre, *Is Southern Civilization Worth Preserving?* (Charleston: Southern Rights Association, 1851); William P. Miles, *Republican Government Not*

Everywhere and Always the Best; and Liberty Not the Birth Right of Mankind: An Address Delivered before the Alumni Society of the College of Charleston, March 20, 1852 (Charleston: Walker and James, 1852); William J. Grayson, *The Hireling and the Slave, Chicora, and Other Poems* (Charleston: McCarter and Company, 1856); [Frederick A. Porcher], "Southern and Northern Civilizations Contrasted," *Russell's Magazine* 1 (1857): 97–107; [Frederick A. Porcher], "The Conflict of Capital and Labour," *Russell's Magazine* 3 (1858): 289–98. This is not the place to consider whether economic and social relations in the Old South were objectively pre-capitalist. For a discussion of the crisis of primitive accumulation sweeping over South Carolina in the 1850s and the economic contradictions that helped generate secession, see Lawrence T. McDonnell, "Politics, Chess, Hats: The Microhistory of Disunion in Charleston, South Carolina" (PhD diss., University of Illinois at Urbana-Champaign, 2013), chap. 11. Here, my point is that leading Carolinians understood their world as beset by a rapacious, ungodly, ruinous capitalism.

19. E. P. Rogers, *Earnest Words to Young Men, in a Series of Discourses* (Charleston: Walker and James, 1851); Charles Butler, *The American Gentleman* (Philadelphia: Hogan and Thompson, 1836); Michael Brander, *The Victorian Gentleman* (London: Gordon Cremonis, 1975); David Castronomo, *The English Gentleman: Images and Ideals in Literature and Society* (New York: Unger, 1987); Robert L. Rainard, "The Gentlemanly Ideal in the South, 1660–1860: An Overview," *Southern Studies* 25 (1986): 295–304; Elizabeth Fox-Genovese and Eugene D. Genovese, *The Mind of the Master Class: History and Faith in the Southern Slaveholders' Worldview* (New York: Cambridge University Press, 2005), 337–42.

20. Charles Dellheim, *The Face of the Past: The Preservation of the Medieval Inheritance in Victorian England* (Cambridge: Cambridge University Press, 1982); Alice P. Kenney and Leslie J. Workman, "Ruins, Romance, and Reality: Medievalism in Anglo-American Imagination and Taste, 1750–1840," *Winterthur Portfolio* 10 (1975): 131–64; Mark Girouard, *The Return to Camelot: Chivalry and the English Gentleman* (New Haven: Yale University Press, 1981).

21. Cf. Timothy H. Breen, "Horses and Gentlemen: The Cultural Significance of Gambling among the Gentry of Virginia," *William and Mary Quarterly* 34 (1977): 239–57.

22. "Extracts from a letter from Mrs. Charles Sinkler to her father Mr. Wharton in Philadelphia," Apr. 25, 1851, and "Order of Review," n.d., both in St. John's Berkeley Papers, SCL; "On Running at the Ring," n.d., William Mazyck Porcher Papers, SCL; *Charleston Mercury*, May 12, 1851; Anne S. Fishburne, *Belvidere: A Plantation Memory* (Columbia: University of South Carolina Press, 1950), 14–18. In this sense, tilting trained Carolinians in the masculine values set forth in works such as Middleton, *Moral Courage;* and Abner A. Porter, *Our Danger and Duty: A Discourse Delivered in the Glebe-Street Presbyterian Church, on Friday, December 6th, 1850* (Charleston: E. C. Councell, 1850). On honor in the Old South, the crucial text remains Bertram Wyatt-Brown, *Southern Honor: Ethics and Behavior in the Old South* (New York: Oxford University Press, 1982).

23. For accounts of tournaments in other areas of the South, see *New York Herald,* July 26, 1842, Aug. 19, 1843, Sept. 13, 22, 1848, Oct. 27, 1849, Aug. 11, Sept. 17, 22, 1856, June 7, 1857; *New York Weekly Herald,* Sept. 23, 1854; *Washington National Daily Intelligencer,* July 22, 1843, Aug. 14, 1845; *Pensacola Gazette,* Oct. 12, 1844; *Mississippi Free Trader and Natchez Gazette,* Oct. 3, 1849; *Boston Daily Atlas,* Sept. 18, 1851; *Savannah Daily Morning News,* Feb. 26, 1852; *Richmond Daily Whig,* Oct. 28, 1854; *Charlestown Virginia Free Press,* Aug. 21, Sept. 4, 11, 25, 1856, Aug. 6, Dec. 3, 1857, Aug. 4, 1859; *Columbia Daily South Carolinian,* Oct. 24, 1856; *Weekly Raleigh Register,* Nov. 12, 1856, Sept. 23, 1857, July 28, Sept. 29, 1858; *Charleston Mercury,* June 5, 1857, Oct. 26, 1858; Hansen Hiss, "The Knights of the Lance in the South," *Outing* 31 (1898): 338–43; Susan B. Eppes, *Through Some Eventful Years* (Macon, GA: J. W. Burke, 1926), 74; Esther J. Crooks and Ruth W. Crooks, *The Ring Tournament in the United States* (Richmond: Garrett and Massie, 1936); Osterweis, *Romanticism and Nationalism,* 3–5, 98–99; Harnett T. Kane, *The Romantic South* (New York: Coward-McCann, 1961), 182–85; Wayne Austerman, "Ancient Weapons in a Modern War: The South's Legions of Lancers," *Civil War Times Illustrated* 24 (1985): 20–25; Charlene Boyer Lewis, *Ladies and Gentlemen on Display: Planter Society at the Virginia Springs, 1790–1860* (Charlottesville: University of Virginia Press, 2001), 201–5; Kelley N. Seay, "Jousting and the Evolution of Southernness in Maryland," *Maryland Historical Magazine* 99 (2004): 50–79; Fox-Genovese and Genovese, *Mind of the Master Class,* 353–58.

24. *Charleston Daily Courier,* Apr. 25, 1851. The quotation paraphrases Sir Walter Scott, *Marmion; A Tale of Flodden Field* (Edinburgh: J. Ballantyne, 1808), 28–29.

25. Eglinton's misfortunes, summarized here, are examined fully in Ian Anstruther, *The Knight and the Umbrella: An Account of the Eglinton Tournament, 1839* (London: Geoffrey Blis, 1963). For representative American newspaper commentary, see *New York Morning Herald,* May 4, Oct. 11, 1839; *Washington Daily National Intelligencer,* May 8, Sept. 19, 26, Oct. 8, 1839; *Cleveland Daily Herald and Gazette,* May 9, July 30, Oct. 4, 1839; *Indianapolis Indiana Journal,* May 11, Aug. 17, Sept. 21, Oct. 5, 12, 1839; *Little Rock Arkansas State Gazette,* July 31, 1839; *New York Spectator,* Sept. 26, 1839; *Boston Courier,* Sept. 30, 1839.

26. *Boston Courier,* Oct. 24, 1839. Compounding the mockery, by 1842, rubberized raincoats were being marketed in a popular "Tournament" style. See *New York Herald,* Dec. 17, 1842. For other samples of the humiliation chivalry's proponents in Victorian Britain endured, see *Philadelphia North American,* Oct. 23, 1839; *Philadelphia Pennsylvania Inquirer and National Gazette,* May 15, 1843; *The Comic Almanack: An Ephemeris in Jest and Earnest, Containing Merry Tales, Humorous Poetry, Quips, and Oddities,* 2 vols. (London: Chatto and Windus, n.d. [1854?]).

27. Geoffrey F. A. Best, *Mid-Victorian Britain, 1851–1875* (London: Weidenfeld and Nicholson, 1971); Morse Peckham, "Victorian Counterculture," *Victorian*

Studies 18 (1975): 257–76; Peter Bailey, *Leisure and Class in Victorian England: Rational Recreation and the Contest for Control, 1830–1885* (London: Methuen, 1987); David Newsome, *The Victorian World Picture: Perceptions and Introspections in an Age of Change* (New Brunswick, NJ: Rutgers University Press, 1997).

28. William H. Russell, *My Diary North and South,* 2 vols. (London: Bradbury and Evans, 1863), 1: 171–72.

29. Grayson, "Character of a Gentleman," 68.

30. For examples of these attitudes, see Newsome, *Victorian World Picture;* Christopher L. Brown, *Moral Capital: Foundations of British Abolitionism* (Chapel Hill: University of North Carolina Press, 2006).

31. On Elizabethan chivalry, see Frances A. Yates, *Elizabethan Chivalry: The Romance of the Accession Day Tilts* (London: Trinity Press, 1957); Richard C. McCoy, *The Rites of Knighthood: The Literature and Politics of Elizabethan Chivalry* (Berkeley: University of California Press, 1989); Alan R. Young, "'In Gallant Course before Ten Thousand Eyes': The Tournament in the 1580s," in A. L. Magnusson and C. E. McGee, eds., *The Elizabethan Theatre XI: Papers Given at the Eleventh International Conference on Elizabethan Theatre Held at the University of Waterloo, Waterloo, Ontario, in July 1985* (Port Credit, Ont.: P. D. Meany, 1990), 33–53; A. L. Rowse, *The Elizabethan Renaissance: The Life of the Society* (New York: Penguin, 2000); Rory Rapple, *Martial Power and Elizabethan Political Culture: Military Men in England and Ireland, 1558–1594* (Cambridge: Cambridge University Press, 2009). On chivalry's development more generally, see Maurice Keen, *Chivalry* (New Haven: Yale University Press, 1984); Richard Barber, *The Knight and Chivalry* (Woodbridge: Boydell Press, 1995).

32. Hamilton J. Eckenrode, "Sir Walter Scott and the South," *North American Review* 206 (1917): 595–603; Grace W. Landrum, "Notes on the Reading of the Old South," *American Literature* 3 (1931): 60–71; Grace W. Landrum, "Sir Walter Scott and His Literary Rivals in the Old South," *American Literature* 2 (1930): 256–76.

33. See, e.g., William G. Simms, *The Life of Chevalier Bayard: "The Good Knight," "Sans peur et sans reproche"* (New York: Harper & Brothers, 1847); Mary E. Lee, "Bertrand du Guesclin: A Historical Ballad," *Southern Literary Messenger* 13 (1847): 636–37; David F. Jamison, *The Life and Times of Bertrand du Guesclin* (Charleston: John Russell, 1864).

34. In private correspondence, Charlestonians frequently ascribed chivalrous titles to members of their circles, esp. James Hamilton Jr., "The Bayard of the South." See Robert Tinkler, *James Hamilton of South Carolina* (Baton Rouge: Louisiana State University Press, 2004). To others, less impressed, he was the original "Jim Dandy."

35. On Sidney, see esp. H. R. Fox Bourne, *Sir Philip Sidney: Type of English Chivalry in the Elizabethan Age* (New York: G. P. Putnam's Sons, 1891); Alan Stewart, *Philip Sidney: A Double Life* (London: Chatto and Windus, 2000).

36. George W. Curtis, *Literary and Social Essays* (New York: Harper & Brothers, 1895), 174.

37. Michael P. Johnson, "Planters and Patriarchy: Charleston, 1800–1860," *Journal of Southern History* 46 (1980): 45–72.

38. Will Taber, a figure of importance in the Old South of whom we have known too little, is discussed at length in McDonnell, "Politics, Chess, Hats," chap. 7.

39. "W. R. Taber," *New Orleans Delta,* undated clipping [1856], J. Ward Hopkins Scrapbook, SCL.

40. *Charleston Mercury,* Oct. 11, 1856.

41. Chalmers G. Davidson, *The Last Foray: The South Carolina Planters of 1860: A Sociological Study* (Columbia: University of South Carolina Press, 1971).

42. John M. Vlach, *Back of the Big House: The Architecture of Plantation Slavery* (Chapel Hill: University of North Carolina Press, 1993), 22–23. For earlier examples, see Henry C. Forman, *The Architecture of the Old South: The Medieval Style, 1585–1850* (Cambridge: Harvard University Press, 1948), 177–78.

43. "Untitled Thoughts," n.d., James Henry Hammond Papers, SCL; Henry E. Ravenel, *Ravenel Records: A History and Genealogy of the Huguenot Family of Ravenel, of South Carolina; with Some Incidental Account of the Parish of St. John's Berkeley, Which Was Their Principal Location* (Atlanta: Franklin, 1898), esp. 26–27.

44. James M. Patrick, "Ecclesiological Gothic in the Old South," *Winterthur Portfolio* 15 (1980): 117–38.

45. Gene Waddell, *Charleston Architecture, 1670–1860,* 2 vols. (Charleston: Gibbs Smith, 2003), 1: 272–73; Kenneth Severens, *Southern Architecture: 350 Years of Distinctive American Buildings* (New York: E. P. Dutton, 1981); Mills Lane, *Architecture of the Old South: South Carolina* (Savannah: Beehive Press, 1984), 223–33; Albert Simons and Samuel Lapham Jr., eds., *The Early Architecture of Charleston* (Columbia: University of South Carolina Press, 1970), 181, 183.

46. Cf., Maurie D. McInnis, *The Politics of Taste in Antebellum Charleston* (Chapel Hill: University of North Carolina Press, 2005).

47. I. Jenkins Mikell, *The Rumbling of the Chariot Wheels* (Columbia: State Company, 1923), 169–79.

48. See, e.g., *Charleston Daily Courier,* Oct. 4, 1860; *Charleston Tri-Weekly Courier,* June 9, 1860; *Charleston Mercury,* Nov. 21, 1860.

49. *Charleston Daily Courier,* Sept. 17–18, Oct. 12, 1860; *Charleston Mercury,* Sept. 18, 1860.

50. *Charleston Daily Courier,* Oct. 12, 1860.

51. Nina Auerbach, *Private Theatricals: The Lives of the Victorians* (Cambridge: Harvard University Press, 1990).

52. For representative examples of these tournaments, see *Charleston Mercury,* Apr. 16, July 1, 1857, May 6, 14, 1859; *Charleston Tri-Weekly Courier,* May 19, 1859; "Columbia Tournament," May 8, 1860, Crawford Family Papers, SCL.

53. "The Tournament," undated clipping [1857?], 120–21, Frederick Fraser Scrapbook, Perkins Library, Duke University.

54. Roland Barthes, *Mythologies* (New York: Hill & Wang, 1972), 15, 18.

55. Gregory Bateson, *Steps to an Ecology of Mind: Collected Essays in Anthropology, Psychiatry, Evolution, and Epistemology* (New York: Ballantine, 1972), 177–93.

56. *Charleston Mercury,* Apr. 16, 1857; *Charleston Daily Courier,* Sept. 18, 1860.

57. Robert B. Rhett to Robert B. Rhett Jr., undated letter [1846], Robert Barnwell Rhett Papers, SCL.

58. *Charleston Tri-Weekly Courier,* May 5, 1859; "Paul Morphy," *Chess Monthly* 3 (1859): 194; Moncure D. Conway, *Autobiography, Memories, and Experiences,* 2 vols. (London: Cassell and Company, 1904), 1: 257–58. "Chess fever" in Charleston is examined at length in McDonnell, "Politics, Chess, Hats," chaps. 9-10.

59. [Porcher], "Conflict of Capital and Labour," esp. 293–95.

60. S*****s, "Modern Improvements," *Magnolia: Or Southern Monthly* 3 (1841): 219.

61. William H. Trescot, *The Position and Course of the South* (Charleston: Walker and James, 1850), 9; Elizabeth Fox-Genovese and Eugene D. Genovese, *Slavery in White and Black: Class and Race in the Southern Slaveholders' New World Order* (New York: Cambridge University Press, 2008).

62. Ulrich B. Phillips, *American Negro Slavery: A Survey of the Supply, Employment, and Control of Negro Labor as Determined by the Plantation Regime* (New York: D. Appleton, 1918), 401.

63. On dueling as theater, see esp. John L. Wilson, *The Code of Honor; or, Rules for the Government of Principals and Seconds in Duelling* (Charleston: J. Phynney, 1838).

64. *Alleged Assault upon Senator Sumner,* 34th Congress, 1st Session, House Report No. 182 (Washington, DC, 1856), esp. 33–34; Preston S. Brooks to Joel H. Brooks, May 23, June 21, 1856, and J. H. Brooks to Yates Snowden, Aug. 16, 1893, all in Preston Smith Brooks Papers, SCL; David Donald, *Charles Sumner and the Coming of the Civil War* (New York: Alfred A. Knopf, 1960), 278–311.

65. *Congressional Globe,* 34th Congress, 1st Session, 530 (May 19, 1856). Cf. Kenneth Greenberg, *Masters and Statesmen: The Political Culture of American Slavery* (Baltimore: Johns Hopkins University Press, 1986), 144–46.

66. *Congressional Globe,* 34th Congress, 1st Session, 838 (July 16, 1856).

67. William Whaley to James D. Allen, July 21, 1856, William Whaley Papers, SCL.

68. On the charge as central to the performance of courage in the Civil War, see Gerald F. Linderman, *Embattled Courage: The Experience of Combat in the American Civil War* (New York: Free Press, 1987), 21–25. Cf. the variant opinions in Grady McWhiney and Perry D. Jamieson, *Attack and Die: Civil War Military Tactics and the Southern Heritage* (Tuscaloosa: University of Alabama Press, 1982); Fox-Genovese and Genovese, *Mind of the Master Class,* 330.

69. Ernest B. Furgerson, *Not War but Murder: Cold Harbor 1864* (New York: Vintage Books, 2001), 89–92.

6

Slavery or Independence

The Confederate Dilemma in Europe

Don H. Doyle

Henry Adams had observed the Confederate agents at work in London throughout America's Civil War while he served as personal secretary to his father, the U.S. minister to Britain. "The Southern secessionists were certainly unbalanced in mind," he wrote in his autobiography; they were "haunted by suspicion, by *idées fixes,* by violent morbid excitement; but that was not all. They were stupendously ignorant of the world."[1] Adams was a bit unfair, but there was an unusual strain of delusion, even madness, that ran through southern diplomacy from beginning to end, a stubbornness of mind and a certain petulance that did not permit learning from failure and gave little room for reflection and reassessment of policy.

The novelist William Faulkner once compared the spirit of secession in 1861 to people running madly off the edge of a cliff and, for a moment, suspended in air, feeling as though they were flying, not yet aware that the rocky chasm below was rushing toward them: "At which moment the destiny of the land, the nation, the South, the State, the County, was already whirling into the plunge of its precipice, not that the State and the South knew it, because the first seconds of fall always seem like soar: a weightless deliberation preliminary to a rush not downward but upward, the falling body reversed during that second by transubstantiation into the upward rush of earth; a soar, an apex, the South's own apotheosis of its destiny and its pride."[2]

They must have thought they were soaring that night in December 1860 when South Carolina led the parade of Deep South states that declared separation from the Union. People filled the streets of Charleston, their torches illuminating the crowds on Meeting Street, bonfires blazing, young boys setting off rockets, cannons fired in salute, and militias parading as the crowd cheered.[3] In rapid order six Deep South states followed: Mississippi, Florida, Alabama, Georgia, Louisiana, and Texas—all declaring their states out of the Union by early February when their delegates met in Montgomery to create a new union of their own.

The new constitution unblinkingly proclaimed that it was designed to form "a permanent federal government." Almost overnight the delegates in Montgomery assembled the machinery of nationhood: a constitution; a government with president, vice president, and congress; an army and navy; postal system, flag, uniforms, paper money, even an official seal with the national motto—"Deo Vindice" (God Will Vindicate). Styled as the Confederate States of America, this self-declared new nation presented itself to the world as a fait accompli and sent forth envoys to be recognized "among the nations of the world."

The haste in creating the Confederate nation was driven by international as well as internal concerns. Besides convincing their own people and those in the North that this was not a bluff intended to extract concessions within the existing Union, the Confederacy had to create a national government in order to win international recognition.[4] Among its first orders of business the new government sent commissioners to key foreign capitals with instructions to arrange for treaties of friendship and commerce; formal recognition would follow in due time.

International recognition was more than just an honor or legal technicality. It meant a nation existed as a sovereign government in the eyes of other nations. More practically, it meant that diplomats could be officially received by those of other nations and that they could negotiate binding treaties, financial loans, or military defense compacts. Once recognized as a sovereign nation, instead of an insurgency within an established nation, the Confederacy would enjoy all the rights accorded other nations under international law.[5] This would transform the nature of the war itself. So long as the conflict was defined as a civil war in which the United States was fighting to suppress a domestic insurrection, any form of aid or recognition of the rebels by foreign powers would be considered an act of war against the United States. With recognition, it would become an international conflict in which third parties could legitimately intervene, whether to break the blockade, create military alliances, provide loans, or offer their good offices in mediating a peace. International recognition would transform the Confederate States of America from a putative de facto nation to a legitimate de jure sovereignty. Recognition meant that the Confederate States of America would join the family of nations—it meant victory for the South.[6]

It appeared to everyone the Confederacy was on its way to early recognition in May 1861, when the British government declared its neutrality and recognized both sides as belligerents. France and several other countries followed suit. Recognition as a belligerent did not carry the same weight as the recognition of sovereignty and independence, but it contradicted the official position of the United States that the southern rebellion was nothing more than a treasonous insurrection led by criminals. The British were declaring that the American conflict was a genuine war, not just a domestic rebellion, and they were declaring their neutrality between the two belligerent parties. According to the prevailing interpretation of international law, such recognition was justified whenever an insurgency appeared to be in control of a defined territory under a stable system of government, capable of fielding an organized military force. European powers were recognizing the war as more than a civil uprising but not yet recognizing the nation that was its purpose.[7]

Secessionist leaders went into war fully confident that Europe's great powers would have to recognize their new nation out of sheer economic necessity. They never would have risked war if they had not expected this, and it proved to be their gravest miscalculation. Their overconfidence stemmed from a conviction that "Cotton was King," that the South was the dominant supplier of the world's cotton, and that the great powers of Europe would simply have no choice but to do business with an independent South.[8]

"Without firing a gun, without drawing a sword, should they make war on us we could bring the whole world to our feet," James Henry Hammond boasted in a speech before the U.S. Senate in 1858. "The South is perfectly competent to go on, one, two, or even three years without planting a seed of cotton. . . . What would happen if no cotton was furnished for three years? . . . England would topple headlong and carry the whole civilized world with her, save the South. No, you dare not make war on cotton. No power on earth dares to make war upon it. Cotton is king!"[9]

The failure of King Cotton diplomacy is by now a familiar story. The bumper crop of 1860 ameliorated early threats of the predicted "cotton famine," and the shift toward other suppliers in India and Egypt weakened the leverage the South hoped would purchase intervention. The failure of Confederate diplomacy cannot be fully explained by the exaggerated reliance on King Cotton. Nor can it be said to have failed for want of military success, insofar as it was able to field an army and defend most of its territory until the end of 1864, when Sherman's army took Atlanta, from which it would launch its demoralizing march to the sea. To understand the failure of Confederate diplomacy we must turn to the moral and political issues that lay at the heart of the South's claim to independence.[10]

Jefferson Davis was convinced the Confederacy was going to win its independence on the field of battle and was indifferent toward foreign policy at the beginning of the war. He used diplomatic appointments with an eye to getting rid of political rivals and generally made terrible choices of men to represent the Confederacy abroad. Leading the European commission was William Yancey, a fire-eating proslavery secessionist with no diplomatic experience.

Notwithstanding, the Confederacy began with great advantages and appeared to be on the verge of triumph even before Yancey and his commission arrived in London. It was Union policies rather than Confederate diplomacy that shifted European support in their favor. In March 1861 the new Republican Congress passed a high protective tariff, which seemed to vindicate the South's charge that northern manufacturers planned to exploit the South and harm European trade with America. In April Lincoln declared a blockade of southern ports, which threatened to shut off European access to cotton. By implication the blockade, usually an instrument of international war, seemed to concede that this was something more than just a nation suppressing a domestic insurrection.

One other Union policy that gave advantage to the South was Lincoln's emphatic assurance in his March 4 inaugural address that he had neither the constitutional authority nor the "inclination" to interfere with slavery in the states where it existed. Suddenly, what antislavery advocates abroad were heralding as the triumph of the Republican Party over the "slave power" collapsed. Lincoln's aim was to show the South had no legitimate cause for rebellion, but it left the Union cause with no moral purpose beyond the perpetuation of federal power. Both sides were denying slavery to be at the heart of the conflict. For European onlookers it seemed to confirm that this was just another quarrel in a fractious democracy, of no consequence to the world at large.

All these Union policies represented gifts to the Confederate diplomatic mission in Europe. Not only did the tariff and blockade help reify the Confederate narrative of northern tyranny, but they also exerted tremendous economic pressure on Europe to recognize the South, which of course trumpeted its devotion to the principles of free trade.[11]

Apart from economic inducements to recognize an independent South, there were powerful ideological biases and geopolitical designs that favored Confederate success among the Great Powers of Europe. The aristocratic governing classes ensconced in European courts were generally happy to see the United States weakened and fragmented. They feared the rising commercial prowess of America, its expansionist ambitions in North America and the Caribbean, and the encouragement it gave to European republicans who wanted to democratize European society.

"Every friend of despotism rejoices at your misfortune," William Howard Russell of the *London Times* wrote to his American friend John Bigelow in April 1861. "I fear my friend you are going to immortal smash. . . . The world will only see in it all, the failure of republican institutions in time of pressure as demonstrated by all history—that history which America vainly thought she was going to set right and re-establish on new grounds and principles."[12]

Conservatives and liberals, monarchists and republicans, all came to see in the American imbroglio a crisis for the "experiment" in democratic self-rule. Sir John Ramsden, Tory member of Parliament, announced to his colleagues that what they were witnessing in America was nothing less than "the bursting of the great republican bubble which had been so often held up to us as the model on which to recast our own English Constitution." To those reformers advocating American-style "universal suffrage," Ramsden advised that they give careful consideration instead to "the great distinction between the safe and rational, and tempered liberties of England, and the wild and unreflecting excesses of mob-rule which had too often desecrated freedom and outraged humanity in America."[13]

For many in Europe's aristocratic governing classes the American crisis confirmed a long-held bias that self-government worked only for small, compact populations, towns, or city states and that large countries given over to democracy would, sooner or later, lapse into anarchy or despotism. The idea that democratic self-rule and equality would lead to its own manner of despotism was articulated famously by Alexis de Tocqueville, whose widely read account *Democracy in America* (1835) warned of the "tyranny of the majority." When Lincoln suspended the right of habeas corpus and imprisoned suspected enemies of the Union, Confederate sympathizers at home and abroad took glee in referring to the "American Bastille."[14]

Many Europeans regarded the United States as simply too vast and diverse to ever constitute a viable nation and too immature and quarrelsome to sustain a viable government. Lacking a mature governing class bred by generations of inherited experience, democracy was naturally inclined toward factionalism and disorder. Now the "mobocracy" had seized control of the U.S. government, southern sympathizers argued. Among the most disturbing signs of "extreme democracy" were the "hordes" of immigrants coming out of the most impoverished and revolutionary elements of European society to influence American politics.

In contrast, Confederate advocates depicted the South as a society modeled on the European aristocratic order, with a pure Anglo-Saxon ruling class whose learning and cultivation rested on the subjugated labor of the lower classes. The American political system, sniffed Alexander Beresford Hope, an English sympathizer with the South, "makes it impossible that a really great man can become President" and allows an unknown like Lincoln, "a clever woodcutter . . . who could navigate a barge down the Mississippi better than most men, and . . . talk glibly enough," to be swept to the highest office in the land on nothing more than his popular appeal.[15]

There was also a growing disposition among Europeans of varying political persuasions to view the American Civil War as yet another example of a senseless fratricidal war with no real purpose. Cynicism toward war had been cultivated in Britain during its army's unfortunate participation in the Crimean War (1853–56). London *Times* reporter William Howard Russell issued disturbing reports from the field, including an account of the disastrous charge of the Light Brigade, as well as descriptions of Florence Nightingale's heroic service to the wounded.[16] In 1859 the Battle of Solferino, part of the Second War of Italian Independence, inspired Jean Henri Dunant to write a moving humanitarian plea against senseless slaughter, which was widely distributed and was credited with the beginnings of the International Red Cross and the Geneva Conventions.[17]

Confederate agents and their sympathizers abroad introduced humanitarian appeals increasingly as the war continued without any end in sight. We "do not place ourselves before the bar of nations to ask for favors," Secretary of State Robert Hunter instructed his envoys in September 1861; "we seek for what we believe to be justice not only to ourselves, but justice to the great interests of peace and humanity." It "seems to be the duty of each of the nations of the earth to throw the moral weight of its recognition into the scale of peace as soon as possible. For to delay will only be to prolong unnecessarily the sufferings of war."[18]

In April 1862, Judah P. Benjamin, the newly appointed Confederate secretary of state, instructed agents abroad to make a humanitarian plea for European intervention as the only means of ending a senseless war that had brought so much bloodshed to America and starvation to the cotton mill workers of Europe.[19] John Slidell in Paris learned to put such humanitarian arguments to good use. In his first interview with Napoleon III, Slidell flattered him as a leader "who exercised so potent an influence over the destinies of the world to put an end to a strife which was not only devastating the South and exhausting the North, but paralyzed the commerce and industry of Europe."[20] Similar language was employed by British MP William Lindsay, a tireless advocate of southern recognition, who pleaded that "every principle of humanity demanded prompt intervention to stop so dreadful an effusion of blood and the mutual exhaustion of both parties."[21]

Confederate agents decried the atrocities of the Union against its former countrymen, begging the British foreign secretary to see that "the moral weight of this great and Christian people" be "thrown into the scale to prevent the barbarous and inhuman spectacle of war between citizens so lately claiming a common country conducted upon principles which would have been a disgrace to the age in which we live."[22] "The continuance of the desolating warfare which is now ravaging this country," Judah P. Benjamin instructed his envoys to convey to Britain and France, "is attributable in no small degree to the attitude of neutral nations in abstaining from the acknowledgment of our independent existence as a nation of the earth." "The heat of popular passion, which in the Northern Government controls public policy," Benjamin went on, "will not permit their rulers to entertain for a moment the idea of separation, so long as foreign nations tacitly assert the belief that it is in the power of the United States to subjugate the South. National pride, the hatred engendered by this war, the exasperation of defeat in their cherished hope of subduing the South, all combine to render the Administration of Mr. Lincoln powerless to accept the accomplished fact [of] our independence, unless Sustained by the aid of neutral nations."[23] Slidell complied by telling the French that recognition would "prevent the further continuance of an unnecessary war and the useless effusion of blood."

William Gladstone played to the same humanitarian concern for ending this "horrible war" in his famous Newcastle speech in which he proclaimed that Jefferson Davis had made a nation.[24] Benjamin also instructed his agents to emphasize the barbarous nature of a war that sought to arm slaves to rise against their masters, "a servile war of whose horrors mankind has had a shocking example within the memory of many now living," alluding to any of a number of unforgettable uprisings against whites. "The perfidy, vindictiveness, and savage cruelty with which the war is waged against us have had but few parallels in the annals of nations."[25]

Economic interest in resuming the cotton trade, ideological opposition to democracy, and humanitarian appeals to peace all tilted in favor of Confederate success in winning recognition abroad. Why then did the Confederate mission to Europe fail? The stock answer usually gives much weight to the popular opposition in Europe to slavery and the eventual role of Lincoln's Emancipation Proclamation in overcoming earlier outrage over his guarantees for slavery. There is no question that European antipathy toward slavery played a vital role in upsetting Confederate plans for independence.

But to say this raises another question: Why was slavery an obstacle to international recognition in 1861 when it had not been for other countries earlier? The United States, after all, was welcomed into the family of nations after the American Revolution, when slavery existed in nearly all its states. Brazil, with its large slave-based economy, won recognition without a problem after declaring its independence in 1822. Mexico and the other Spanish American republics abolished slavery sometime after independence, and not as a condition for recognition. Spain continued slavery in its Caribbean colonies, Cuba and Puerto Rico, without suffering any international repercussions. Britain had ended slavery in its imperial possessions as recently as 1833, and there had been no international sanctions or protests against it prior to that. The Second Republic of France won swift recognition among the nations of the world, the United States first among them, though slavery in French territories was not abolished until later that year.[26]

What had changed in the European mind that made slavery a problem for the Confederacy when it had not been for other nations earlier? Certainly the cumulative effect of abolitionist edicts created a majority of powerful nations that by renouncing slavery as an evil left the remaining sanctuaries of slavery, Brazil, Spain, and the American South, standing against the moral tide of international public opinion. William Yancey, writing from

London after months of futile lobbying for recognition, may have put his finger on it when he complained to his brother: "Anti-slavery sentiment is universal. Uncle Tom's Cabin has been read and believed."²⁷ The Paris correspondent to the *Charleston Mercury* noted in similar language that public opinion there had been "entirely Uncle Tommied for the present."²⁸

The impact of Harriet Beecher Stowe's book *Uncle Tom's Cabin* (1852) on American politics and public opinion is well known, but its impact abroad was no less astonishing. The book had colossal sales in Europe; an estimated one and a half million copies were purchased in Britain alone— far more than in the United States. Uncle Tom shows were performed in West End theaters in London, often as a Victorian melodrama or as a musical minstrel show. The story was adapted to local cultures across Europe and performed in a great variety of styles. Giuseppe Rota's musical opera *Bianchi e Negri* enjoyed a successful run at La Scala in Milan before coming to the London stage. Uncle Tom mania in Europe during the 1850s created a market for "paintings, puzzles, cards, board games, plates, spoons, china figurines, bronze ornaments, dolls, and wallpaper," all depicting images and characters from the book.²⁹

The plot of *Uncle Tom's Cabin* was melodramatic, the characters stereotypes of good and evil, and the whole story was drenched in sentimentality of a sort that often strikes contemporary readers as maudlin. Readers at the time, however, were genuinely moved by the book, and both men and women confessed to openly weeping in response. Even Lord Palmerston, the crusty prime minister of Britain, reported reading the book three times, supposedly while he was mulling over the decision to intervene in the war.³⁰

The popularity of Stowe's book may be an indicator, as much as a cause, of the shift in public sentiment against slavery in Europe, for there had been deep religious and political currents at work beneath the rise of antislavery sentiment in the Atlantic world for some time. Slavery had come to be seen by a growing number as a barbaric relic of the past that contradicted both Christian morality and liberal ideals of human equality. A system of labor that had been integral to the development of the New World and remained a robust source of profit in the mid-nineteenth century was abolished in one nation after another, notwithstanding powerful economic interests in its favor. Abolitionism was a moral and ideological force above all, and it led people to view the end of the African slave trade and the emancipation of slave labor as proud marks of human progress.³¹

The British took special pride in their role in ending the international slave trade and abolishing slavery throughout the British Empire in 1833. France had abolished slavery in 1794, but Napoleon restored it in its Caribbean sugar colonies in 1802. In 1848 the Second Republic brought slavery to a complete end. The Spanish American republics, one by one, issued emancipation acts during or after their wars for independence. In the United States all the northern states with slavery introduced some form of gradual emancipation, and the federal government had restricted slavery in much of the nation's western territories. In the American hemisphere, where African slavery had expanded for more than three centuries, the only significant sanctuaries remaining in 1860 were the Empire of Brazil, the Spanish Empire (Cuba and Puerto Rico), and fifteen states in the American South.[32]

The South's problem with international diplomacy and public opinion abroad was not the existence of slavery per se, but that its very reason for seeking independence was to perpetuate slavery, forever, according to its constitution, and possibly expand its domain into the Caribbean and parts of Latin America. The foreign public understood clearly that it was the Republican Party's promise to limit the expansion of slavery and, the South feared, put it on the road to eventual extinction that ignited secession after Lincoln's election. No amount of obfuscation about the protective tariff as the underlying cause of the conflict could hide the simple truth that what the southern rebels feared was living under a national government that was hostile to slavery.

Nor did Confederates abroad grasp how poorly their defense of slavery as a benign "domestic institution" resonated in the age of *Uncle Tom's Cabin*. The American South was distinct among slave societies in the New World in that it incubated an elaborate paternalistic ideology that defended slavery as a positive good that should be perpetuated forever.[33] Europeans were accustomed to hearing slavery defended as a necessary evil, a profitable system of labor essential to economic prosperity, but claims that it was beneficial for all, or that slaves were happy in their work, failed to resonate with public opinion in the 1860s. Nor did the South's claims for its contented slaves jibe with its dire warnings of slave revolts and racial mayhem should meddling abolitionists gain control of the national government.

Elsewhere the end of slavery during the nineteenth century met with stiff resistance, debate, and considerable public uproar, but not with organized armed rebellion—except in the American South. Slave revolts played a powerful role in undermining support for slavery, not least by damaging the image of slaves happy in their bondage. As a general rule, however, the nations of Europe and Latin America ended slavery by peaceful legislation rather than by violent warfare.[34]

One of the unusual features of the American South was the refusal of the slaveholding elite to even debate the future of slavery and its heedless determination to take up arms rather than accept the verdict of the election in 1860. Alongside its proslavery ideology the South had created an effective system to silence dissent and close off serious debate on slavery. Anyone who probed the morality of slavery or even questioned its impact on the safety and welfare of whites was censored, attacked, and driven out of the South. The proslavery South saw abolitionism as the imported idea of fanatical zealots from outside the South, those who were ignorant of the actual conditions of slavery or, alternately, hypocrites who had no genuine philanthropic concern for the slave and were intent on fomenting slave uprisings.

Confederate agents abroad were quick to realize that Europeans had serious concerns about slavery but remarkably slow to respond with any effective policy or propaganda. In their very first dispatch from London in May 1861, William Yancey and Ambrose Dudley Mann warned of the obstacle that slavery posed to Confederate recognition abroad: "We are satisfied that the public mind here is entirely opposed . . . on the question of slavery, and that the sincerity and universality of this feeling embarrass the Government in dealing with the question of our recognition."[35] They were under instructions from Richmond not to engage discussions of slavery as a cause of secession and to emphasize instead differences between agrarian and industrial interests and sentiments, paying particular attention to the protective tariff and reminding Europeans of their desire for free trade.[36]

The American Civil War witnessed the birth of what would later be known as public diplomacy, organized campaigns to influence the "public mind" abroad. The Union jumped into this early with a group of prominent religious and political figures—Thurlow Weed, Catholic archbishop John Hughes, and others—who were sent over to Britain and France primarily on public speaking tours. But modern print technology and the need for anonymity made published tracts, newspaper articles, and books the most effective means of shaping public opinion abroad. Such campaigns in "public diplomacy" often involved enlisting native journalists and publishers and paying, as was often necessary, to buy favorable press. Confederate and Union agents also penned their pamphlets, letters to the editor, and other publications, often adopting fictitious noms de plume.

Effective propaganda campaigns involved a marriage between journalism and diplomacy, and Edwin De Leon seemed to be born to the task. A smooth-talking journalist from Columbia, South Carolina, he was the son of Sephardic Jews who had migrated to South Carolina from Leon, Spain. He began his career as a journalist promoting the voice of "Young America," a nationalist movement of the 1840s modeled on Giuseppe Mazzini's Giovane Italia. He went on to become an outspoken proponent of southern rights as editor of a prosecessionist newspaper in Washington. It may have been to get him out of town that President Franklin Pierce appointed him consul general to Alexandria, Egypt, in 1854. De Leon stayed in Egypt until 1861, when he resigned in solidarity with the Confederacy and made his way to Paris to offer his services as an unaccredited agent to the first Confederate European commission. He helped Pierre Rost arrange meetings with French government officials and wrote numerous letters to leading newspapers in London and Paris.[37]

De Leon soon became convinced that the Confederacy needed a fully funded, well-organized campaign to educate the public regarding the South, and early the next year he returned to Richmond to persuade Jefferson Davis. In April 1862, more than a year after the first European commission had been sent over, De Leon was appointed, unofficially of course, special agent in charge of Confederate propaganda in Europe and was issued a handsome fund of twenty-five thousand dollars to be dispensed as he saw fit.

De Leon was charming, glib, and energetic in his self-described role as "ambassador to public opinion." He became convinced early in the game that the British government was too cowardly to do anything to risk war with the United States and the British public too prejudiced against slavery to open their minds to the cause of the South. France was the key to Confederate success, and Emperor Napoleon III would be less restrained by popular pressure. Furthermore, Napoleon's ambitions to expand French influence in Mexico and across Latin America would require an independent Confederacy, both to check U.S. expansion and to stem the influence of democratic ideas.

De Leon set up offices in Paris and began spending money freely to enlist, or more accurately bribe, a legion of French journalists and editors who lent their pens to the southern cause. Instead of wasting money on

Parisian journals, where liberal opinion ran strong among the public, De Leon concentrated his influence on the provincial press, which was more important to Napoleon III's base of power.

While De Leon's "bought opinions" did their work to build support for the Confederacy in the press and inside Napoleon's court, he decided to launch his own education program by writing a thirty-two-page pamphlet in French, *La vérité sur les États Confédérés d'Amérique*. Its appearance in August 1862 was timely, as France and all of Europe approached another season of cotton shortages, and as Confederate armed forces began to advance toward Washington and Maryland. De Leon presented himself to French readers as a knowing witness to the actual conditions of slavery and the South's struggle for independence. He dismissed recent Union victories, including the capture of New Orleans, by arguing that they would only inflame the South, "which battles for its homes and lands, for its liberty and [the] honor of its women." The alleged superiority of soldiers and resources in the North, he added, depended mostly on "foreign mercenaries commanded by the refuse of the old world." Then he turned to ridiculing "Madam Stowe's novel," which "represents the slave's goal to be to massacre one's master." "We have paid special attention to this interesting class while staying in the South," he confided to readers. "Instead of being a weak source, the slaves have contributed greatly to the South's strength by their resistance to the false 'friends of the blacks.'" He predicted the slaves would stand by their masters. "The negro knows very well by experience that the Yankee has no real sympathy for its race." Blacks were despised and segregated in the northern cities, he testified, and instead of being liberated by the Union Army had been put to hard labor as "contraband" of war.

De Leon went on to draw a flattering portrait of Jefferson Davis, comparing him to George Washington in his military valor and statesmanlike character. Pamphlet readers were treated to a noble-looking portrait of Jefferson Davis as a frontispiece in the booklet. De Leon made it a practice to hand out copies of this portrait to European government officials and diplomats, never failing to contrast the aristocratic appearance of Davis with the homely visage of Abraham Lincoln, which alone spoke volumes for the southern cause to De Leon's mind.

The pamphlet turned to a remarkable ethnographic argument intended to pander to his French readers. The real source of discord between North and South, he explained, was rooted in fundamental ethnic and cultural differences comparable to those between France and England. The North descended from "the races of Anglo-Saxon origin," whereas "the South was principally populated by a Latin race." Unable to conquer the South on its own, De Leon argued, the North had "attracted all the famished revolutionaries and malcontents of Germany, all the Red republicans, and almost all the Irish emigrants to sustain its army." He closed by comparing the North to the Puritans under Cromwell, fired by self-righteous zealotry against the enemies of the true faith.[38]

De Leon was highly satisfied with his effort to educate the French, and his dispatch to Richmond the following October detailed his triumphs. To counteract the efforts of the North to "the manufacture of public opinion" in Europe, he reported, "I have been compelled to use extraordinary exertions, which I am happy to say, have wrought great results within the last two months." "To my surprise, the slavery question, which has been dropped in England, was made the great bugbear in France, and our advocates were pleading piteously in extenuation of our sins in that respect, and shuddering at the epithet *esclavagiste,* with which the partisans of the North were pelting them. Strange as it may seem, there is really more feeling for the black on this side of the channel than on the other, as the sentimental side of the French character has been enlisted by the supposed sufferings of that race." Referring to this recent pamphlet as a "text book for our friends in the press," De Leon summarized the most brilliant points of his argument by underscoring that "the South is able to vindicate her independence without foreign assistance, and is rapidly doing so; that her resources are ample for her needs; that she has nothing to apologize for in her peculiar institution but has ever been the best friend of the black race."[39]

De Leon's pamphlet, in truth, went largely unnoticed by the French public. Paul Pecquet du Bellet, a Louisiana Creole who had lived in Paris for years, was fully sympathetic to the southern cause, but he mocked De Leon's education campaign. With but one exception, Pecquet du Bellet observed, French journals maintained a "disdainful silence" toward the pamphlet. De Leon, he judged, was not quite au fait with the conversation current in France on the American Question. Then there was the problem of De Leon's "peculiar style" of French, which he thought a bit too "Americanized" for the tastes of French editors.

Pecquet recognized that the problem went much deeper than style, for he knew that no amount of testimony about the benign paternalism of American slavery was going to sustain sympathy among the French public. All informed French readers understood that slavery lay at the heart of the

American conflict, and De Leon's efforts to deny that or, worse, to educate the French as to the "true" nature of the South's gentle brand of slavery only served to bring attention to the issue.[40]

In France, another Confederate agent observed, the prejudice against slavery had "passed into . . . one of those fixed principles, which neither individuals nor nations permit to be called in question."[41] French liberals saw themselves as the European champions of liberty, equality, and fraternity, and they could not help but see the Confederacy as the enemy of these ideals. As Pecquet expressed it, even those editors who were sympathetic to the South did not dare defend those "'Southern Cannibals' who breakfasted every morning upon a new born infant negro."[42]

So long as Lincoln denied emancipation as the Union cause, Confederate agents abroad could safely ignore the entire slavery debate or plausibly deny it to be the issue. Even after Lincoln announced his emancipation policy in September 1862, Confederate sympathizers in Europe found traction by denouncing it as a cynical ploy that was intended to foment "servile insurrection" against southern whites. After January 1863 when the Emancipation Proclamation became law and after it became clear that slaves were not rising in violence, hundreds of public meetings in support of the Union erupted across Britain while more discreet signals of Union support rippled across the Continent.[43]

Jefferson Davis had never been optimistic about the Confederate diplomatic campaign abroad, and in a public speech of December 1862 he said, "We have expected sometimes recognition and sometimes intervention at the hands of foreign nations, and we have had a right to expect it. Never before in the history of the world had a people for so long a time maintained their ground, and showed themselves capable of maintaining their national existence, without securing the recognition of commercial nations. I know not why this has been so, but this I say, 'put not your trust in princes,' and rest not your hopes in foreign nations. This war is ours; we must fight it out ourselves."[44]

Instead of formulating a revised strategy to answer the Union's emancipation policy, Davis continued under the delusion that Europe needed the South more than the South needed Europe. He reissued warnings that the Confederacy would recall its envoys, who, he complained, were "now waiting in servants' halls and on the back stairs" of foreign ministries. Europe would have to send its emissaries to Richmond if they wanted to do business with the South. There were others, including Confederate vice president Alexander Stephens, who were calling for a full withdrawal of the entire diplomatic corps, and in April 1863, a motion in the Confederate Congress to force recall of all foreign commissioners nearly passed.[45]

By June 1863 even De Leon's irrepressible confidence was wobbling. The European public's prejudice against slavery, he wrote to Richmond, presented an insuperable obstacle to Confederate recognition. The only strategy left would be to nullify the moral force of Union emancipation policy with the Confederacy's own plan for voluntary, gradual emancipation. But even as he recommended emancipation as the last viable solution, De Leon realized the insoluble Confederate dilemma: the sole way for the South to achieve independence was to abandon the very reason it wanted independence in the first place—to guarantee the future of slavery. Even De Leon had no stomach for emancipation, and he fully understood that it would be political suicide for Confederate leaders to publicly embrace such a policy. In June 1863 De Leon advised Davis to recall all overseas commissions, channel all monies spent on diplomacy into the war effort, and stand on their dignity until Europe begged the South for recognition.[46]

Later in the same year De Leon got his wish, though not in the manner he preferred. In December he was summarily fired after his dispatches, containing scurrilous comments about the French being an amoral "mercenary race," along with intemperate remarks about his fellow diplomats, were intercepted by the Union Navy and published in New York newspapers.[47]

The South's insoluble problem of slavery took an unexpected turn at the eleventh hour. The Confederate high command met in secret to concoct a last-ditch scheme to send a secret mission to London and Paris with instructions to promise eventual emancipation of the slaves in exchange for international recognition and support. The Confederate constitution expressly prohibited any law to abolish slavery, but Davis was betting that southern whites would be willing to sacrifice slavery in order to achieve independence. He could not ask any of the Confederate envoys then in Europe to betray all they had defended to offer emancipation. He called on Duncan Kenner, a wealthy Louisiana slaveholder, who had been an early advocate of just such a plan. Coming from such an eminent member of the slaveholding elite, the offer of emancipation would seem unimpeachable. By the time Kenner finally reached Europe in February 1865 the verdict of the battlefield had already decided the end of the Confederacy. It would be superfluous to add that the entire idea of Confederate emancipation was forbidden by the very constitution on which the putative nation had been founded. It would be equally unnecessary to observe that such a plan was politically untenable. The abolition of southern slavery had to come from without.[48]

Robert Toombs, who played a key role as the first Confederate secretary of state in 1861, looked back with regret that the South had not "made abolition of slavery a part of its policy." If it had, he mused, "the Confederacy would have succeeded." "If the South had made the abolition of slavery a part of its policy," John Bigelow answered, "there would have been no war, and the Confederate maggot would never have been hatched."[49]

Notes

1. Henry Adams, *The Education of Henry Adams: An Autobiography* (Boston: Houghton Mifflin, 1918), 100.

2. William Faulkner, *Novels, 1942–1954: Go Down, Moses; Intruder in the Dust; Requiem for a Nun; A Fable* (New York: The Library of America, 1994), *Requiem for a Nun,* Act III, "The Jail," 627.

3. William Freehling, *The Road to Disunion: Secessionists Triumphant, 1854–1861,* 2 vols. (New York: Oxford University Press, 1990), 2: 422–23.

4. Paolo E. Coletta, "Recognition Policy," in Alexander DeConde, ed., *Encyclopedia of American Foreign Policy: Studies of the Principal Movements and Ideas* (New York: Scribner, 1978), 882–92.

5. Ibid.; Stephen C. Neff, *War and the Law of Nations: A General History* (Cambridge: Cambridge University Press, 2005), 256–75; Stephen C. Neff, *Justice in Blue and Gray: A Legal History of the Civil War* (Cambridge: Harvard University Press, 2010), 167–69.

6. Howard Jones, *Blue and Gray Diplomacy: A History of Union and Confederate Foreign Relations* (Chapel Hill: University of North Carolina Press, 2010); Neff, *Justice in Blue and Gray;* Neff, *War and the Law of Nations.*

7. Neff, *War and the Law of Nations,* 168.

8. David Christy et al., *Cotton Is King, and Pro-slavery Arguments . . .* (Pritchard, Abbott & Loomis, 1860); Frank Lawrence Owsley, *King Cotton Diplomacy: Foreign Relations of the Confederate States of America,* 2nd ed. (1931; Chicago: University of Chicago Press, 1959).

9. Owsley, *King Cotton Diplomacy,* 16.

10. Charles M. Hubbard, *The Burden of Confederate Diplomacy* (Knoxville: University of Tennessee Press, 1998); Gregory Mattson, "Pariah Diplomacy: The Slavery Issue in Confederate Foreign Relations" (PhD diss., University of Southern Mississippi, 1999); Jones, *Blue and Gray Diplomacy.*

11. James D. Richardson, *A Compilation of the Messages and Papers of the Con-*

federacy: Including the Diplomatic Correspondence, 1861–1865, 2 vols. (Nashville: United States Pub. Co., 1904), 2: 3–8.

12. John Bigelow, *Retrospections of an Active Life: 1817–1863* (New York: Baker & Taylor, 1909), 1: 346.

13. Ramsden, Committee, First Night, HC Deb 27 May 1861 vol. 163, 134, http://hansard.millbanksystems.com/commons/1861/may/27/committee-first-night#S3V0163P0_18610527_HOC_57 (accessed Apr. 17, 2011).

14. Eye Witness, *The Bastille in America; or, Democratic Absolutism* (London: R. Hardwicke, 1861); [W. H. Winder], *Secrets of the American Bastille* (Philadelphia: J. Campbell, 1863).

15. A. J. B. Beresford Hope, *A Popular View of the American Civil War*, 3rd ed. (London: J. Ridgway, 1861), 18.

16. William Howard Russell, *Despatches from the Crimea* (Annapolis, MD: Naval Institute Press, 2007).

17. Jean Henry Dunant, *Un souvenir de Solferino* (Geneva: Fick, 1862).

18. Hunter to Slidell, Richmond, Sept. 23, 1861, *Official Records of the Union and Confederate Navies in the War of the Rebellion*, 30 vols. (Washington, DC: Government Printing Office, 1922) (hereafter *ORN*), ser. 2, 3: 272.

19. Benjamin to Slidell, Apr. 12, 1862, *ORN*, ser. 2, 3: 386–90.

20. Beckles Willson, *John Slidell and the Confederates in Paris (1862–65)* (New York: Minton, Balch & Company, 1932), 79–89; Slidell to Benjamin, July 25, 1862, *ORN*, ser. 2, 3: 481.

21. Slidell to Benjamin, Paris, Apr. 14, 1862, "Memorandum of Dispatch No. 5," *ORN*, ser. 2, 3: 394.

22. William Yancey, Pierre Rost, and Ambrose Dudley Mann to John Russell, London, Aug. 14, 1861, *ORN*, ser. 2, 3: 240.

23. Benjamin to Mason and Slidell, Apr. 12, 1862, and Slidell to Thouvenel, July 21, 1862, both *ORN*, ser. 2, 3: 385–90, 471.

24. Slidell to Thouvenel, July 21, 1862, *ORN*, ser. 2, 3: 471.

25. Benjamin to Mann, Aug. 14, 1862, *ORN*, ser. 2, 3: 513.

26. Julius Goebel, "The Recognition Policy of the United States" (PhD diss., Columbia University, 1915).

27. Eric H. Walther, *William Lowndes Yancey and the Coming of the Civil War* (Chapel Hill: University of North Carolina Press, 2006), 315.

28. *Charleston Mercury*, Dec. 20, 1860.

29. Denise Kohn, Sarah Meer, and Emily Bishop Todd, *Transatlantic Stowe: Harriet Beecher Stowe and European Culture* (Iowa City: University of Iowa Press, 2006); Sarah Meer, *Uncle Tom Mania: Slavery, Minstrelsy, and Transatlantic Culture in the 1850s* (Athens: University of Georgia Press, 2005); "Victorian Literature: The Reception of Uncle Tom's Cabin in Victorian Europe," *Victorian Literature* 15 (2011): http://victoriancircle.blogspot.com/2011/03/reception-of-uncle-toms-cabin-in.html; "The National and International Impact of Uncle Tom's Cabin," Harriet Beecher Stowe Center, Nov. 15, 2011, http://www.harrietbeecherstowecenter

.org/utc/impact.shtml; Giuseppe Rota, *Bianchi e Negri* . . . (Naples: Cosmopolita, 1862); *The Musical World* (London: Duncan Davison & Co., 1863), 516.

30. Stephen B. Oates, *The Approaching Fury: Voices of the Storm, 1820–1861* (New York: HarperCollins, 1998), 125.

31. David Brion Davis, *Inhuman Bondage: The Rise and Fall of Slavery in the New World* (New York: Oxford University Press, 2006); Seymour Drescher, *Abolition: A History of Slavery and Antislavery* (New York: Cambridge University Press, 2009).

32. Davis, *Inhuman Bondage;* Drescher, *Abolition.*

33. Lacy K. Ford, *Deliver Us from Evil: The Slavery Question in the Old South* (New York: Oxford University Press, 2009); Barbara Weinstein, "Slavery, Citizenship, and National Identity in Brazil and the U.S. South," in Don Harrison Doyle and Marco Antonio Villela Pamplona, eds., *Nationalism in the New World* (Athens: University of Georgia Press, 2006), 248–71.

34. Davis, *Inhuman Bondage;* Drescher, *Abolition.*

35. Richardson, *Compilation,* 2: 37.

36. Robert Toombs to William Yancey, Pierre A. Rost, and A. Dudley Mann, Montgomery, Mar. 16, 1861, *ORN,* ser. 2, 3: 91–195.

37. Edwin De Leon, *Secret History of Confederate Diplomacy Abroad,* ed. William C. Davis (Lawrence: University Press of Kansas, 2005).

38. Edwin De Leon, *La vérité sur Les États Confédérés d'amérique* (Paris: E. Dentu, 1862); De Leon, *Secret History,* app. 3, English translation of "The Truth about the Confederate States of America."

39. De Leon, *Secret History,* 141–43; for the full dispatch, see De Leon to Judah P. Benjamin, Paris, Sept. 30, 1862, in *Official Records of the War of the Rebellion* (Washington, DC: Government Printing Office, 1900), ser. 4, 2: 99–105.

40. Paul Pecquet du Bellet, *The Diplomacy of the Confederate Cabinet of Richmond and Its Agents Abroad,* ed. William Stanley Hoole (Tuscaloosa, AL: Confederate Pub. Co, 1963), 65–66, 28–29.

41. Hotze to Benjamin, London, Sept. 26, 1863, *ORN,* ser. 2, 3: 914–918, quoted in Owsley, *King Cotton Diplomacy,* 531.

42. Pecquet du Bellet, *Diplomacy of the Confederate Cabinet,* 29.

43. *Address of the French Protestant Pastors to Ministers and Pastors of All Denominations in Great Britain, on American Slavery* . . . (Manchester: J. F. Wilkinson, 1863).

44. Jefferson Davis, speech, House Chamber, Mississippi Capitol, Jackson, Dec. 26, 1862, Papers of Jefferson Davis, Oct. 21, 2011, http://jeffersondavis.rice.edu/Content.aspx?id=113.

45. James Morton Callahan, *The Diplomatic History of the Southern Confederacy* (Baltimore: Johns Hopkins University Press, 1901), 95–96.

46. De Leon, *Secret History,* xx.

47. Ibid., xxii.

48. Bruce Levine, *Confederate Emancipation: Southern Plans to Free and Arm Slaves during the Civil War* (New York: Oxford University Press, 2006).

49. John Bigelow, "The Confederate Diplomatists and Their Shirt of Nessus: A Chapter of Secret History," *Century* 42 (1891): 126n. Bigelow was quoting an interview with Toombs in the *New York Times,* July 24, 1890.

The Lynching of Southern Europeans in the Southern United States

The Plight of Italian Immigrants in Dixie

Stefano Luconi

The literature on lynchings in the U.S. South has developed significantly in the last couple of decades. As studies in this field have grown in number, in the efforts to overcome the black-versus-white divide underlying U.S. history, scholarly attention has focused not only on African Americans but also on members of other minorities, like Hispanics and Syrian Americans, who fell victim to the same excruciations.[1]

Against such a backdrop, the following pages revisit the case of Italian Americans' lynchings in the South and reassess in particular to what extent the perception of this immigrant group as ethnically and even racially alien to the U.S. Anglo-Saxon mainstream affected the resort to summary justice against the newcomers from Italy. Unlike current scholarship, this essay concludes that, although the challenge to Italians' white identity in the eyes of the broader adoptive society generally offered the rationale for mob violence, it actually accounted only in part for the lynchings and that extrajudicial killings more often stemmed from competition and clashes in the fields of economy, politics, and labor relations.

According to historian Patrizia Salvetti, at least thirty-four Italian immigrants—mainly Sicilians—were lynched in the United States between 1886 and 1910.[2] These crimes were committed primarily in the South. The most infamous occurred in 1891 in New Orleans, where a bloodthirsty mob killed eleven defendants of Sicilian extraction who had just been found not guilty of murdering the local police superintendent, David Hennessey. Asked who had shot him, the dying Hennessey had answered "Dagoes," a notorious ethnic slur to refer to Italians, and the native citizens of New Orleans took revenge on this immigrant group regardless of the court verdict. As the police forces remained idle, the acquitted men were dragged out of their hideouts in the jail building and shot. A few corpses and half-dead bodies were later hanged from the lampposts of the square that the jail overlooked.[3] The last instance of summary justice against people of Italian origin took place in Tampa, Florida, in 1910. There, on September 20, law-enforcement officers arrested two Sicilians, Angelo Albano and Castenge (alias Castenzio and Costanzo) Ficarotta, on charges of complicity in the shooting of Frank Esterling, an accountant for a cigar manufacturer. While Albano and Ficarotta were being taken to the county jail, a crowd seized the two prisoners and hanged them.[4]

Commenting on the latter incident, the New York City–based Italian-language daily *Il Progresso Italo-Americano* remarked that "those who know statistics about lynching are aware that the victims are black people. Europeans have not been lynched except for Italians only. In fact, a white person—probably a Bulgarian—was lynched in Baton Rouge in 1907. Yet it was a misunderstanding. The thugs there attacked a group of workers from Macedonia. But they actually intended to give chase to Italian laborers living nearby."[5] This statement was incorrect. William Fitzhugh Brundage has documented that 723 whites were lynched in the United States from 1880 to 1930.[6] In Louisiana alone 46 whites had been subjected to summary justice in the decade between 1866 and 1876 before a single Italian immigrant was killed by a crowd.[7] Salvetti, who drew her data exclusively from research into the records of Italy's Ministry of Foreign Affairs and did not use U.S. sources, is likely to have underestimated the real number of Italian American victims. Italian diplomats may have overlooked those immigrants who had become U.S. citizens, as well as the U.S.-born children of the newcomers, because the Italian government had no jurisdiction over these people.[8] In addition, it is possible that killings in small centers without Italian consular agents sometimes went unreported and left no evidence in the archives of the Ministry of Foreign Affairs. An article by Clive Webb, who relied on unspecified sources in the records of the Tuskegee Institute and the National Association for the Advancement of Colored People, mentions additional lynchings of Sicilian immigrants in Shelby Depot, Mississippi, in 1887; in Marion, North Carolina, in 1906; and in Chathamville, Louisiana, in 1907.[9]

Even assuming that Salvetti's list is shorter than the actual number of casualties, Italian Americans were only a small minority among them. Yet the mistake of *Il Progresso Italo-Americano* reveals Italian Americans' insecurity regarding their racial standing in the United States. While explaining the lynching of the Italian newcomers, the daily pointed out that "only racial hatred can explain it."[10] At that time the word *race* was an ambiguous term in the Italian-language press in the United States. Many newspapers used it as a synonym for what today could more aptly be called "ethnicity."[11] In this instance, however, we can take the meaning of such an expression at face value.

Indeed, at the turn of the twentieth century, Italian immigrants—especially those from Sicily—were placed between whites and blacks in the racial hierarchy. On the one hand, in the eyes of the broader U.S. society, the generally dark-skinned newcomers from southern Italy looked more similar to African Americans than to white Europeans. On the other, the pseudo-scientific theories of eugenics overemphasized the African biological "contamination" of the Italian population over the centuries. Ironically enough, this misrepresentation of immigrants from Italy drew in part upon the transnational spread of the findings of such Italian positivists as anthropologists Giuseppe Sergi and Luigi Pigorini, criminologists Cesare Lombroso and Enrico Ferri, and sociologist Alfredo Niceforo. Their writings found a prompt echo on the other shore of the Atlantic in xenophobic essays by, among others, Edward Alsworth Ross and Madison Grant. Reflecting national stereotypes in their homeland, these Italian scholars contrasted northern Italians, who allegedly belonged to an Alpine race, with southern Italians, who were supposedly inferior to the former because they were part of a Mediterranean race that presumably shared a significant number of distinctive features with the African race. Since the great bulk of Italian newcomers to the United States had been born in southern Italy, it was almost unavoidable that the characteristics of the people from this specific region were ascribed to all individuals from the nation.[12]

Italian travelers to the U.S. South often complained that their fellow countrymen who had settled there were treated as if they were blacks.[13] Common conditions of peonage and agricultural work back to back with African Americans on the sugar cane, cotton, and rice plantations, as well as life in the same quarters as blacks, ended up blurring the difference between

Italian Americans and people of color.[14] Especially in the flood plain of the lower Mississippi Valley, Italian immigrants were initially recruited as a more reliable and less indolent alternative to the black labor force after the abolition of slavery had induced many former slaves to leave the fields, to drift from one plantation to the other almost at their own pleasure, or to migrate to the North.[15] The performance of African Americans' traditional jobs in agriculture eventually caused Italian newcomers to lose their Caucasian characterization in the eyes of native whites. As historian Robert L. Brandfon has argued, "by replacing the Negro in the same type of work and under the same conditions, the Italians assumed the status of Negroes."[16] For instance, testifying before a congressional committee on immigration in 1890, a railroad construction boss contended that an Italian was not a white man but a "Dago."[17] In 1911, even several members of the Committee on Immigration and Naturalization of the U.S. House of Representatives doubted that southern Italians were "full-blooded Caucasian," and the report of a senatorial commission investigating immigration pointed to a likely "infusion of African blood" among Sicilians.[18] Remarkably, in 1905, in one of the first academic studies about lynching that included a racial breakdown of the victims, James Elbert Cutler listed the data about Italian casualties under the category grouping people who were neither "negroes" nor "whites."[19] On the eve of World War I, even the Italian ambassador in Washington himself, Edmondo Mayor des Planches, acknowledged that newcomers from Italy "hold a racial middle ground between whites and blacks."[20] Italian immigrants' in-betweenness long survived in southern states. Significantly, as late as 1922, a court in Alabama cleared an African American man of miscegenation charges on the grounds that it could not be demonstrated that his Sicilian partner was white.[21]

While Italian Americans' full "whiteness" was generally denied and members of this immigrant minority were often associated with blacks, it could be easily suggested that their ambiguous racial status accounted for the fact that they became victims of the same violence and brutality that were usually reserved for African Americans as retribution and punishment for actual crimes or alleged felonies.[22] As was the case for blacks, there was at least one incident in which the rape of a white woman was the cause for the lynching of an Italian American. This very charge resulted in the first mob killing of an Italian immigrant, Federico Villarosa, in Vicksburg, Mississippi, in 1886. Accused of assault on a thirteen-year-old white girl, who was the daughter of the local postmaster, Villarosa was hanged by an angry throng while he was still waiting for a hearing in court.[23]

Coeval sources argued that the failure to ascribe a white identity to Italian immigrants caused the resort to summary justice against them. Newspaper accounts about the lynching of five Sicilians in Tallulah, Louisiana, in 1899 offered a case in point. The victims were killed after they had tried to assassinate—but only managed to wound—the local coroner following an argument over a goat.[24] The incident had all the ingredients to give good reason for the stigmatization of the Italians' tendency to overreact and employ violence to settle disputes. Yet press reports focused on the racial perception of the newcomers. For instance, *Harper's Weekly* commented that, in the minds of the local residents, the Italian newcomers deserved the same treatment as an African American who shot at or murdered a white man— namely lynching without trial—because they could be hardly classified as white people.[25] Likewise, the *New Orleans Times-Democrat* stressed that "the people [in Tallulah] believe that they were justified in the action they took" because the "maintenance of white supremacy at any cost" was at stake.[26]

Reflecting what Richard Hofstadter has called a "mystique" of white Anglo-Saxon superiority over southern and eastern European immigrant groups, even the reputable *New York Times* contended, with reference to the Sicilian newcomers who had been charged with the killing of police chief Hennessey in New Orleans, that "our rattlesnakes are as good citizens as they; our own murderers are men of feeling and nobility compared to them."[27] Likewise, a report to the Second Congress of Italians Abroad, held in Rome in 1911, contended that the lynchings of immigrants in the United States in general and in Louisiana in particular were in part the consequence of both the newcomers' failure to distance themselves from people of color and their tendency to treat blacks as equals.[28]

Scholars have followed suit. For instance, to historian George Cunningham, social intimacy and familiarity with African Americans was "a hindrance to white solidarity" in southern states, challenged the racial order of a society that was not only unprepared for interracial relations but even antagonized by them, and was responsible for hostility toward Italian immigrants that could eventually result in lynchings.[29] By the same token, John Higham has contended that summary justice against Italian newcomers arose from the fact that they "violated the white man's code" because they associated themselves with African Americans "nearly on terms of equality."[30]

Explaining mob justice against Italian Americans on the grounds of ethnically motivated intolerance, because of their hazy racial classification between blacks and whites, matches scholarly interpretations that have stressed the marginality of Italian immigrants and their progeny in a society dominated by people of Anglo-Saxon extraction.[31] Yet even prior to World War II—which, according to conventional scholarly wisdom, marked the beginning of Italian Americans' whitening[32]—not everybody agreed that Italians did not belong to the Caucasian race and thereby deserved lynching if they committed crimes. For instance, while intraracial violence among people of color did not result in summary justice, a crowd of white residents of Brazos County, Louisiana, killed a black farmer who had raped a Sicilian woman in 1896.[33] Likewise, in 1913, in Jennings, Louisiana, a mob lynched an African American because he had struck a Sicilian merchant who swept dirt on the former's shoes while he was cleaning his store.[34] These episodes and, specifically, the kind of punishment that the local communities reserved for the African American assailants implicitly placed Italian immigrants on the white side of the racial divide. An incident that occurred during a 1934 riot in Harlem offers a similar case in point for the establishment of Italian Americans in the Caucasian race in public perception. After an African American mob made a fruitless attempt to lynch an Italian American baker who had been accused of short-changing a woman of color, the *Amsterdam News*—a local newspaper for black readers—commented that it was "unbelievable that Negroes should threaten to lynch a white man."[35]

Against this backdrop, one could similarly reassess the reasons for the lynching of Italian Americans and argue that racial hatred was often a pretext concealing other motivations. A reexamination of some of the cases already surveyed will help demonstrate such a point.

The five Italians lynched in Tallulah in 1899 were grocers who had been held up to public scorn because they had given their black and white employees equal pay. They had therefore violated the cornerstone of the southern economy after the Civil War, namely the principle that African American workers were to provide a cheap labor force by receiving lower wages than their Caucasian companions. The Italians' success in business also provoked the antagonism of local competitors of Anglo-Saxon ancestry.[36] A report by Italy's consular agent in New Orleans confirmed that ethnic hostility did not account for the murder of the five immigrants by itself. While he did not rule out that "racial hatred" had played a role in the lynching, he listed two additional causes that had made a significant contribution to it. On the one hand, he emphasized the jealousy of the native merchants for the victims' economic achievements, pointing to a conspiracy "among rival storekeepers . . . from a spirit of rivalry in trade." On the other, he stressed the "desire to prevent the Italians from voting" because of their growing influence in local politics as a swing constituency that—albeit very small—could decide the outcome of elections in a township where registered voters usually numbered fewer than 150.[37]

Indeed, if lynching was among the means of intimidating and disenfranchising African American voters in the post-Reconstruction South, one can reasonably envisage that the same strategy was used to interfere with Italian Americans' suffrage, too.[38] As Kate McCullough has pointed out in much broader terms, "the lynching of the Italians produces an effect similar to the lynching of African Americans: it terrorizes the community under attack and reinforces the white population's sense of power."[39]

Business and politics intertwined in the New Orleans 1891 lynching, too. Hennessey was killed during a conflict between rival Sicilian crime organizations, the Matrangas and the Provenzanos. The police chief, however, was hardly an innocent victim who was assassinated while performing his duties. He, too, was probably involved in illegal activities and was perhaps so corrupt that both gangs had him on their own payrolls.[40] In any case, his assassination triggered a moral crusade to sweep away the allegedly Italian-dominated criminal activities from New Orleans by means of bloodshed, notwithstanding the not-guilty verdict. Remarkably, the most authoritative local daily—the *Times-Picayune*—praised mob justice by arguing that "desperate diseases require desperate measures."[41] Likewise, in response to the complaints of the Italian government, which had recalled its ambassador from Washington and had even come close to threatening war against the United States in protest over the failure of local authorities to protect the lives of its own citizens on American soil, Republican senator Henry Cabot Lodge of Massachusetts advocated immigration restrictions to prevent alien criminals from entering the United States and, thereby, from igniting the natives' supposedly legitimate retaliatory violence that had struck the eleven Sicilians in New Orleans.[42]

Actually, in a city where Italian immigrants' involvement in the underworld dated back to the late 1860s in the eyes of numerous local residents, the Sicilians' alleged criminal activities did contribute to the carnage.[43] Yet the resort to lynching in the struggle to uproot the supposed presence of the Mafia from New Orleans was also exploited to intimidate Italian Americans in order to break their monopoly over the importation of tropical fruits, to snatch the control of the city's French Market from their hands, to curb their inroads into the lucrative fishing and oyster trade, to force them out of longshoremen activities on the harbor's docks, and to hamper their rise in local politics. Italian Americans' economic success and early stages of involvement in civic affairs had caused envy and fear among numerous native residents. By the time Hennesey was assassinated, the Sicilian immigrants allegedly operated more than three thousand fruit and other food retail outlets in New Orleans. Moreover, the rivalry between the Matrangas and the Provenzanos included a fight over the control of both the waterfront and ward politics in the Sicilian community.[44]

It was hardly by chance that the defendants in the case resulting from Hennessey's murder included such a prominent leader of the local Little Italy as Joseph Macheca. A wealthy Sicilian businessman with large interests in fruit commerce, as well as in the seafood industries, Macheca had also organized many of his fellow ethnics into an association that opposed the Democratic political machine of Mayor Joseph A. Shakspeare in the elections of 1888.[45] As historian Richard Gambino has concluded, the 1891 lynching was part of a much larger struggle that the antebellum commercial and professional establishment of Anglo-Saxon and French ancestries had orchestrated to retain its economic, political, and social power in the face of the rise of recent newcomers such as the Italians in the late nineteenth century.[46]

Indeed, for example, in the aftermath of the lynching, the City Council granted the business of unloading ships to the recently established Louisiana Construction and Improvement Corporation, whose president was James D. Houston, one of the leaders of the mob that had lynched Hennessey's supposed murderers. Moreover, the Louisiana Construction and Improvement Corporation yielded to the request of the New Orleans Longshoremen's and Screwmen's Association that only the latter's members be employed on the waterfront. Remarkably, this union barred Sicilian immigrants from its ranks.[47] By the same token, Italian Americans were kept at the margins of politics until the late senator Huey Long's Democratic machine handpicked Conservation Commissioner Robert S. Maestri—a wealthy businessman involved in shady deals, the son of a poultry peddler, and the financial backbone of the party's state organization—for the position of mayor of New Orleans in 1936.[48]

Business rivalries and political antagonism were also connected to the summary execution of three Sicilian immigrants in Hahnville, Louisiana, in 1896, while they were in jail on charges of murder in two unrelated killings. The evidence against the detainees was rather flimsy and circumstantial. Yet the suspicions of the community where they lived fell on the Italian newcomers because the victims of two distinct assassinations had had quarrels with the three Sicilians about competition in their respective trades a short time before being murdered.[49] Moreover, this episode of summary justice occurred a few months after Louisiana's Italian Americans had come out against a state law aiming at the disfranchisement of immigrants and African Americans by introducing several literacy and property restrictions on suffrage for prospective voters whose parents or grandparents had not cast their ballots prior to January 1, 1867. Italian Americans had sided with blacks and staged a parade in New Orleans to protest the changes in the legal requirements to exercise the right to vote. Their action met with strong criticism because "they interfere in American politics, and tell us what kind of constitution, what system of laws, and what suffrage is acceptable to them as Italians."[50] While the memory of the 1891 lynching was still alive throughout the state, the mob killings of their fellow countrymen in Hahnville contributed to reminding Italian Americans of the vulnerability of their lives in Louisiana and, consequently, to suffocating their opposition to the amendments to the election rules. In return for their new attitude toward the white establishment, however, when the changes became part of the Louisiana Constitution in 1898, Italian Americans were rewarded with the so-called dago clause, by which immigrants who had been naturalized before January 1 of that year were exempted from literacy and property requirement to vote.[51]

Threats of lynching, rather than actual mob killings, sometimes were sufficient by themselves to sweep away the economic competition from Italian immigrants. For instance, when the consequences of the 1907 recession struck the lumber industry in Kentwood, Louisiana, the following year and caused a significant rise in unemployment, Italian newcomers and their families were threatened with death unless they left town, so that jobs for U.S.-born residents could be secured. Lumber mills tended to retain their Italian American employees because they were more dedicated to their trade than were native workers. Therefore, it seemed that the only way to get employment for the latter was to scare the former into moving away.[52] Likewise, a few months earlier, a mob had beaten an Italian shoemaker almost to death because of an apparent quarrel over school segregation in Samrall,

Mississippi. In fact, the assault had resulted from the efforts of U.S.-born laid-off workers to frighten the members of the Italian American community and get rid of them as competitors for positions in local sawmills.[53]

The Tampa incident added a further element, namely labor disputes, to the causes for the lynching of Italian Americans. Albano and Ficarotta were killed during a six-month walkout of roughly ten thousand cigar workers who had gone on strike to push their employers into recognizing the Cigar Makers International Union, discontinuing the entrepreneurs' open shop policy, and complying with a plan of equalization that aimed at preventing plant owners from cutting wage rates.[54] Although the victims were not labor activists, rumors circulated that they were professional murderers whom the strikers' committee had engaged to retaliate against Esterling because he was involved in the hiring of scabs.[55]

Tampa's cigar-making entrepreneurs had relied on vigilantism to quell labor controversies since the turn of the twentieth century. For instance, in order to speed up the end of a previous strike in 1901, a self-proclaimed Citizens' Committee abducted thirteen union leaders and placed them on a boat heading for Honduras after threatening them with death in case they dared return to Tampa. The following year, something similar happened to Francisco Milián, the mayor of West Tampa and a revered *lector* at the Bustillo Brothers and Diaz Cigar Company. A peculiar institution in cigar factories, the *lector* was paid by workers to read to them and was an instrument for the latter's politicization. Accused of reading inflammatory materials aiming to pit the cigar makers against the plant management and owners, Milián was kidnapped with the complicity of the police, beaten, and forced to leave Tampa on a steamer on its way to Cuba. Both the union leaders and Milián eventually managed to return to Tampa, but their experiences offered evidence of the manufacturers' resort to violence in fighting radicalism and workers' organizations.[56] The 1910 strike was no exception. Plant owners recruited squads to patrol the streets, to protect the strikebreakers, to assault the union members on the picket lines, and to disrupt any other activity in support of the walkout.[57]

According to *La Parola dei Socialisti,* the mouthpiece of the Socialist Party of America for Italian immigrants, it was one of those groups of vigilantes that lynched Albano and Ficarotta.[58] Their murderers' purpose was less retaliation against the two Italians for the shooting of Esterling than threatening the dark-skinned Cuban and Italian cigar makers, who had been on strike for roughly three months, and thus coercing them into going back to work. Especially Albano seemed to be tailor-made for the role of the designated victim. Before turning to selling insurance, he had been a tobacco worker and a member of Local 462 of the Cigar Makers International Union.[59] He therefore became the unintentional scapegoat for a warning to the strikers' most belligerent faction. It was hardly by chance that a notice was pinned to Albano's belt while his corpse was still hanging from the rope. Written in black ink, it read, "Beware! Others take note or go the same way. We know seven more. We are watching you. If any more citizens are molested, look out—Justice."[60]

Not even the Italian vice-consul in New Orleans, Gerolamo Moroni, failed to realize that intimidation of the striking workers was the main purpose of Albano's and Ficarotta's lynchings. Although he criticized the walk-out from a conservative standpoint, in his report to the Italian ambassador in Washington about the killing of the two Sicilian immigrants, Moroni pointed out that the aim of the double hanging was "teaching an awful lesson to the strikers of the cigar factories who had passed from quiet protest to acts of violence against the manufacturers."[61] After all, a few postcards made out of the photographs of Albano's and Ficarotta's hanging corpses had captions reading, "labor agitators lynched during the cigar makers' strike."[62]

The labor connection of the lynching was so strong and undeniable that both commercial and radical Italian-language periodicals agreed on it. For instance, *L'Italia*—a conservative weekly published in Chicago—and *La Parola dei Socialisti* stated in the aftermath of the killing that both Albano and Ficarotta were labor activists involved in the walkout.[63] So did Milan's *Corriere della Sera,* the most authoritative daily in Italy, which even contended incorrectly that Albano and Ficarotta were "the leaders of the strike."[64]

The Italian immigrants' cult of Black Madonnas and saints of color such as Benedict the Moor—a legacy of the preemigration experience in the southern regions of their mother country, long controlled by Arabs in the early Middle Ages, leading to syncretic religious cults—further contributed to blurring the difference between people of Italian and African ancestries.[65] Patrick Q. Mason has observed that "more Catholics were lynched in the late nineteenth-century South than any other religious group (excepting black Christians), more than Mormons and Jews combined."[66] Yet Catholicism was not an issue in the lynchings of Italian Americans. The 1891 mass killings in New Orleans offer a case in point because Police Chief Hennessey was Catholic, as well, and a few Irish Catholics participated in the lynching, following the strained relations between these two immigrant groups.[67]

As happened in the Hahnville lynchings, cries of "kill the Dago" or "hang the Dago" usually mobilized the mobs that inflicted summary justice on Italian immigrants, and the latter's murder by enraged throngs often occurred against the backdrop of white supremacists' backlash not only against blacks but also against newcomers who were not of Anglo-Saxon stock.[68] Yet one cannot conclude that all the lynchings of people from an Italian background resulted only from ethnic hatred and the victims' racial in-betweenness. As in the case of African Americans, summary justice was a means of social control of Italian Americans, too. At least the dynamics of retribution in New Orleans and Tampa demonstrate that the racialized perception of Italian Americans was sometimes a smokescreen that masked other kinds of rivalries and antagonism. The fact that the dark-skinned Italian immigrants and their children looked more similar to African Americans than to white people did contribute to lynching violence, in order to murder single Italian Americans and to intimidate their ethnic communities. Nonetheless, lynchings also resulted from economic, political, and labor conflicts between the local establishment and Italian Americans and exploited the latter's alleged crimes as an excuse for bloody punishment that intended to sweep away competition and challenges in different spheres of public life.

Furthermore, this essay points to the inconsistent perception of Italian Americans on the part of southerners from an Anglo-Saxon background. Summary justice against Italian immigrants drew in part upon other-than-ethnic differences in response to the fact that, almost by definition, the construction of race serves economic, political, and labor interests, too.[69] Therefore, the racial categorization of the members of this national minority turned out to be rather volatile and contingent, if not even fortuitous. Indeed, the in-betweenness of Italian Americans shifted toward blackness at certain times and places as well as toward whiteness at others, depending on the circumstances. For instance, to mention cases from Louisiana only, if Sicilians were not regarded as full-fledged white people both in New Orleans in 1891 and in Tallulah in 1899, which resulted in their lynching, their fellow ethnics looked Caucasian enough to be initially employed on plantations as an alternative to the black workforce and to be protected by the mob killing of their rapists of African descent in Brazos County in

1896. In turn, this indetermination suggests that anti-Italian racism and nativism were less systematic and unswerving than scholars—especially those of Italian ancestry—have usually acknowledged.[70]

Finally, broadening the perspective beyond the conventional white-versus-black divide to include the diverse shade that was usually attributed to the Italian immigrants, this chapter makes an additional contribution to an understanding of southern history against the backdrop of the strengthening of white supremacy in the decades that followed the end of the Reconstruction. Reflecting in part the findings of previous studies—which, however, have not addressed the specific plight of Italian Americans at all and have been primarily interested in assessing issues of historical continuity and discontinuity in postbellum southern society—it helps offer some insights to further corroborate the thesis that in the so-called New South race, political, and class relations could be hardly separated, while the resort to lynching was also related to rivalries in settings that were being shaped by a rapid economic expansion and the fast-paced emergence of an other-than-Anglo-Saxon middle class.[71] The 1891 incident in New Orleans—where, as Dennis C. Rousey has emphasized, it was the very "leadership class" that took revenge on the Sicilian defendants[72]—and labor disputes such as the 1910 strike in Tampa's cigar factories exemplified the former case. The developments along New Orleans' waterfront and in its French Market, as well as, though to a lesser extent, the experience of Tallulah's storekeepers, highlighted the latter. In other words, the lynchings of Italian Americans are an example of the harsh reactions of the entrenched establishment of Anglo-Saxon descent, struggling to retain its own primacy, to the challenges of outsiders at the local level and support the view that those regarded as being alien to any community were more likely to provoke suspicion, hostility, and mob justice in the postbellum South.[73]

Notes

1. Stewart E. Tolnay and E. M. Beck, *A Festival of Violence: An Analysis of Southern Lynchings, 1882–1930* (Urbana: University of Illinois Press, 1995); William Fitzhugh Brundage, ed., *Under the Sentence of Death: Lynching in the South* (Chapel Hill: University of North Carolina Press, 1997); Margaret Vandiver, *Lynchings and Legal Executions in the South* (New Brunswick, NJ: Rutgers University Press, 2006); William D. Carrigan, *The Making of a Lynching Culture: Violence and Vigilantism in Central Texas, 1836–1916* (Urbana: University of Illinois Press, 2006); Vann R. Newkirk, *Lynching in North Carolina: A History, 1865–1941* (Jef-

ferson, NC: McFarland, 2009); Manfred Berg, *Popular Justice: A History of Lynching in America* (Chicago: Ivan R. Dee, 2011); Michael J. Pfeifer, *The Roots of Rough Justice: Origins of American Lynching* (Urbana: University of Illinois Press, 2011); William D. Carrigan and Clive Webb, "Muerto por unos desconocidos (Killed by Persons Unknown): Mob Violence against African Americans and Mexican Americans," in Stephanie Cole and Alison Parker, eds., *Beyond Black and White: Race, Ethnicity, and Gender in the U.S. South and Southwest* (College Station: Texas A&M University Press, 2004), 35–74; Sarah M. A. Gualtieri, *Between Arab and White: Race and Ethnicity in the Early Syrian Diaspora* (Berkeley: University of California Press, 2009), 113–34.

2. Patrizia Salvetti, *Corda e sapone: Storie di linciaggi degli italiani negli Stati Uniti* (Rome: Donzelli, 2003).

3. Herbert Asbury, *The French Quarter: An Informal History of the New Orleans Underworld* (New York: Knopf, 1936), 403–16; Frank Shay, *Judge Lynch, His First Hundred Years* (New York: Washburn, 1938), 161–68; John S. Kendall, "Who Killa De Chief?" *Louisiana Historical Quarterly* 22 (1939): 492–530; Richard Gambino, *Vendetta: The True Story of the Largest Lynching in U.S. History* (Garden City, NY: Doubleday, 1977); Liborio Casilli, "Un drammatico episodio dell'emigrazione italiana: Il linciaggio di New Orleans del 14 marzo 1891," *Studi Storici Meridionali* 11 (1991): 125–39; Jerre Mangione and Ben Morreale, *La Storia: Five Centuries of the Italian-American Experience* (New York: HarperCollins, 1992), 202–13; Joseph Gentile, *The Innocent Lynched: The Story of Eleven Italians Lynched in New Orleans* (Bloomington, IN: iUniverse, 2000). For anti-Italian ethnic epithets, see Donald Tricarico, "Labels and Stereotypes," in Salvatore J. LaGumina et al., eds., *The Italian American Experience: An Encyclopedia* (New York: Garland, 2000), 319–21.

4. "Two Men Taken from Officers and Hanged," *Tampa Morning Tribune*, Sept. 21, 1910, 10; Laura Pilotti, "La serie 'Z-Contenzioso' dell'Archivio Storico-diplomatico del Ministero degli Affari Esteri," *Il Veltro: Rivista della Civiltà Italiana* 34 (1990): 104–8.

5. "All'indomani dell'eccidio di Tampa," *Il Progresso Italo-Americano*, Sept. 25, 1910, 1.

6. William Fitzhugh Brundage, *Lynching in the New South: Georgia and Virginia, 1880–1930* (Urbana: University of Illinois Press, 1993), 259.

7. Gilles Vandal, *Rethinking Southern Violence: Homicides in Post-Civil War Louisiana, 1866–1884* (Columbus: Ohio State University Press, 2000), 67–93.

8. Salvetti, *Corda e sapone*, ix. In a recent study of anti-Italian prejudice worldwide, Matteo Sanfilippo has listed a total of twenty-six lynchings of Italian immigrants in the United States, matching Salvetti's findings. However, he has focused on the nineteenth century only and has not included any twentieth-century cases of mob killings. See Matteo Sanfilippo, *Faccia da italiano* (Rome: Salerno, 2011), 46.

9. Clive Webb, "The Lynching of Sicilian Immigrants in the American South,

1886–1910," *American Nineteenth Century History* 3 (2002): 45–76. The lynching of two Italians in Marion is also mentioned—albeit cursorily—in Luciano J. Iorizzo, *Italian Immigration and the Impact of the Padrone System* (New York: Arno Press, 1980), 212.

10. "All'indomani dell'eccidio di Tampa."

11. For an in-depth and extensive study of the Italian-language press in the United States at the time of mass immigration, see Bénédicte Deschamps, "De la presse 'coloniale' à la presse italo-américaine: Le parcours de six périodiques italiens aux États-Unis" (PhD diss., University of Paris 7—Denis Diderot, 1996).

12. Bénédicte Deschamps, "Le racisme anti-italien aux États-Unis (1880–1940)," in Michel Prum, ed., *Exclure au nom de la race (États-Unis, Irlande, Grande-Bretagne)* (Paris: Syllepse, 2000), 61–66; David R. Roediger, *Colored White: Transcending the Racial Past* (Berkeley: University of California Press, 2002), 34–37, 142–44, 163, 167; Peter R. D'Agostino, "Craniums, Criminals, and the 'Cursed Race': Italian Anthropology in U.S. Racial Thought," *Comparative Studies in Society and History* 72 (2002): 319–43; Ferdinando Fasce, "Gente di mezzo: Gli italiani e gli altri," in Piero Bevilacqua, Andreina De Clementi, and Emilio Franzina, eds., *Storia dell'emigrazione italiana: Arrivi* (Rome: Donzelli, 2002), 235–43; Edward Alsworth Ross, *The Old World in the New: The Significance of Past and Present Immigration to the American People* (New York: Century, 1914), 97–119, 293–95; Madison Grant, *The Passing of the Great Race* (New York: Charles Scribner's Sons, 1921), 71.

13. Matteo Sanfilippo, *Problemi di storiografia dell'emigrazione italiana* (Viterbo: Sette Città, 2002), 69–70.

14. Pete Daniel, *The Shadow of Slavery: Peonage in the South, 1901–1969* (Urbana: University of Illinois Press, 1972), 94, 103, 152; Jean Ann Scarpaci, *Italian Immigrants in Louisiana Sugar Parishes: Recruitment, Labor Conditions, and Community Relations, 1880–1910* (New York: Arno Press, 1980), 148–49; Ernesto R. Milani, "Peonage at Sunny Side and the Reaction of the Italian Government," *Arkansas Historical Quarterly* 45 (1991): 30–39.

15. Alfred H. Stone, *Studies in the American Race Problem* (New York: Doubleday, 1908), 115–23, 188–208; Ernesto R. Milani, "Marchigiani and Veneti on Sunny Side Plantation," in Rudolph J. Vecoli, ed., *Italian Immigrants in Rural and Small Town America* (Staten Island, NY: American Italian Historical Association, 1987), 18–30.

16. Robert L. Brandfon, "The End of Immigration to the Cotton Fields," *Mississippi Valley Historical Review* 50 (1964): 610.

17. As quoted in George J. Manson, "The 'Foreign Element' in New York City," *Harper's Weekly,* Oct. 18, 1890, 817.

18. U.S. House of Representatives, 62nd Congress, 2nd Session, Committee on Immigration and Naturalization, *Hearings Relative to the Further Restriction of Immigration* (Washington, DC: U.S. Government Printing Office, 1912), 77–78; U.S. Senate, 61st Congress, 3rd Session, *Abstracts of the Reports of the Immigration*

Commission: With Conclusions and Recommendations, and Views of the Minority, 2 vols. (Washington, DC: U.S. Government Printing Office, 1911), 1: 250.

19. James Elbert Cutler, *Lynch-Law: An Investigation into the History of Lynching in the United States* (New York: Longman, Green, 1905), 181.

20. Edmondo Mayor des Planches, *Attraverso gli Stati Uniti: Per l'emigrazione italiana* (Turin: Unione Tipografico-Editrice Torinese, 1913), 144.

21. Matthew Frye Jacobson, *Whiteness of a Different Color: European Immigrants and the Alchemy of Race* (Cambridge: Harvard University Press, 1998), 4.

22. Joseph P. Cosco, *Imaging Italians: The Clash of Romance and Race in American Perceptions, 1880–1910* (Albany: State University of New York Press, 2003), 155.

23. "Lynched by a Mob," *New York Times,* Mar. 30, 1886, 5.

24. "The Italian Lynchings," *Outlook,* Aug. 5, 1899, 735; "The Lynching Affair at Tallulah," *Christian Advocate,* Aug. 17, 1899, 1294; Edward F. Haas, "Guns, Goats, and Italians: The Tallulah Lynching of 1899," *North Louisiana Historical Association Journal* 13.2–3 (1982): 45–58; Salvetti, *Corda e sapone,* 55–58.

25. Norman Walker, "Tallulah's Shame," *Harper's Weekly,* Aug. 5, 1899, 779.

26. *New Orleans Times-Democrat,* July 25, 1899, as quoted in Haas, "Guns, Goats, and Italians," 52.

27. Richard Hofstadter, *Social Darwinism in American Thought* (New York: Braziller, 1959), 172; "The New-Orleans Affair," *New York Times,* Mar. 16, 1891, 4.

28. Luigi Scala, "Poche considerazioni giuridiche e sociali su l'emigrazione italiana negli Stati Uniti e particolarmente in Louisiana," in *Atti del Congresso degli italiani all'estero* (Rome: Tipografia Editrice Nazionale, 1913), 17–23.

29. George E. Cunningham, "The Italian: A Hindrance to White Solidarity in Louisiana, 1890–1898," *Journal of Negro History* 50 (1965): 22–36.

30. John Higham, *Strangers in the Land: Patterns of American Nativism, 1860–1925* (New York: Atheneum, 1981), 169.

31. Peter Vellon, "'Between White Men and Negroes': The Perception of Southern Italian Immigrants through the Lens of Italian Lynchings," in William J. Connell and Fred Gardaphé, eds., *Anti-Italianism: Essays on a Prejudice* (New York: Palgrave Macmillan, 2010), 23–32.

32. David A. J. Richards, *Italian American: The Racializing of an Ethnic Identity* (New York: New York University Press, 1999); Rudolph J. Vecoli, "Italian Americans and Race: To Be or Not To Be White," in Aldo Bove and Giuseppe Massara, eds., *'Merica* (Stony Brook: Forum Italicum, 2006), 102.

33. Cynthia Skove Nevels, *Lynching to Belong: Claiming Whiteness through Racial Violence* (College Station: Texas A&M University Press, 2007), 71–73, 85–94.

34. Ralph Ginzburg, *100 Years of Lynchings* (Baltimore: Black Classic Press, 1988), 88.

35. As quoted in Isabel Boiko Price, "Black Response to Anti-Semitism:

Negroes and Jews in New York, 1880 to World War II" (PhD diss., University of New Mexico, 1973), 253–54.

36. Haas, "Guns, Goats, and Italians," 45–46, 52; Vincent J. Marsala, "Italian Settlement in North Louisiana: A Preliminary Study," 1990, 3, unpublished typescript, Noel Memorial Library, Archives and Special Collections, Louisiana State University, Shreveport.

37. Natale Piazza to Emilio Visconti Venosta, New Orleans, July 26, 1899, Records of the Ministry of Foreign Affairs, Series P—Contenzioso, box 656, Archivio Storico del Ministero degli Affari Esteri, Rome, Italy.

38. Terence Finnegan, "Lynching and Political Power in Mississippi and South Carolina," in Brundage, *Under the Sentence of Death*, 189–218.

39. Kate McCullough, *Regions of Identity: The Construction of America in Women's Fiction, 1885–1914* (Stanford: Stanford University Press, 1999), 77.

40. John V. Baiamonte Jr., "'Who Killa de Chief' Revisited: The Hennessey Assassination and Its Aftermath, 1890–1991," *Louisiana History* 33 (1992): 117–46.

41. *Times-Picayune*, Mar. 15, 1891, as quoted in Andrew F. Rolle, *The Immigrant Upraised: Italian Adventurers and Colonists in an Expanding America* (Norman: University of Oklahoma Press, 1968), 103.

42. "Correspondence in Relation to the Killing of Prisoners in New Orleans, March 14, 1891," in *Foreign Relations of the United States, 1891–1892* (Washington, DC: U.S. Government Printing Office, 1892), 658–728; Marco Rimanelli, "The New Orleans Lynching and U.S.-Italian Relations from Harmony to War-Scare: Immigration, Mafia, Diplomacy," in Marco Rimanelli and Sheryl Lynn Postman, eds., *The 1891 Lynching and US-Italian Relations: A Look Back* (New York: Peter Lang, 1992), 106–82; David A. Smith, "From Mississippi to the Mediterranean: The 1891 New Orleans Lynching and Its Effects on the United States Diplomacy and the American Navy," *Southern Exposure* 19 (1998): 60–95; Henry Cabot Lodge, "Lynch Law and Unrestricted Immigration," *North American Review* 152 (1891): 602–12.

43. John N. Coxe, "The New Orleans Mafia Incident," *Louisiana Historical Quarterly* 20 (1937): 1067–1110; Joy Jackson, "Crime and the Conscience of a City," *Louisiana History* 9 (1968): 235–44; Damon R. Barbat, "The Illegitimate Birth of the Mafia in New Orleans," *Southern Studies* 24 (1985): 343–51.

44. Humbert S. Nelli, *The Business of Crime: Italians and Syndicate Crime in the United States* (New York: Oxford University Press, 1976), 37–38, 61–62; Baiamonte, "'Who Killa de Chief' Revisited," 128–29; Michael Kurtz, "Organized Crime in Louisiana History," *Louisiana History* 24 (1983): 362–64.

45. Melinda Meek Hennessey, "Race and Violence in Reconstruction New Orleans: The 1868 Riot," *Louisiana History* 20 (1979): 77–91. For Macheca, see also the rather anecdotal account by Thomas Hunt and Martha Macheca Sheldon, *Deep Water: Joseph P. Macheca and the Birth of the American Mafia* (Bloomington, IN: iUniverse, 2007).

46. Gambino, *Vendetta*, 130.

47. Baiamonte, "'Who Killa de Chief' Revisited," 137.

48. Roger Biles, *The South and the New Deal* (Lexington: University Press of Kentucky, 2006), 132. For Maestri, see Edward F. Haas, "New Orleans on the Half-Shell: The Maestri Era, 1936–1946," *Louisiana History* 13 (1972): 283–310.

49. "Trio Lynched in St. Charles," *Daily Picayune,* Aug. 8, 1896, 2; "Hanged and Shot Three," *New York Times,* Aug. 10, 1896, 1; Anthony V. Margavio and Jerome J. Salomone, *Bread and Respect: The Italians of Louisiana* (Gretna, LA: Pelican, 2002), 200–202; Salvetti, *Corda e sapone,* 49–55.

50. "The Italian Parade," *Daily Picayune,* Mar. 25, 1896, 4.

51. Alan G. Gauthreaux, "An Inhospitable Land: Anti-Italian Sentiment and Violence in Louisiana, 1891–1924," *Louisiana History* 51 (2010): 52–58.

52. "Soldiers Now on Duty in Kentwood," *Times Democrat,* Mar. 29, 1908, 1; Ministero degli Affari Esteri, Commissariato Generale dell'Emigrazione, "Gli Stati Uniti e l'emigrazione italiana," in *Emigrazione e colonie: Raccolta di rapporti dei RR. Agenti diplomatici e consolari: Vol. III: America* (Rome: Tipografia dell'Unione Editrice, 1909), 125; John V. Baiamonte Jr., *Spirit of Vengeance: Nativism and Louisiana Justice, 1921–1924* (Baton Rouge: Louisiana State University Press, 1986), 12.

53. "Italians in the South," *Outlook,* Nov. 16, 1907, 557–58.

54. George E. Pozzetta, "Italians and the Tampa General Strike of 1910," in George E. Pozzetta, ed., *Pane e Lavoro: The Italian-American Working Class* (Toronto: Multicultural History Society of Ontario, 1980), 29–46.

55. "A Lynching and a Lesson," *Tampa Morning Tribune,* Sept. 22, 1910, 6; "Il linciaggio di Tampa," *Il Progresso Italo-Americano,* Sept. 27, 1910, 1.

56. Gary Ross Mormino and George E. Pozzetta, *The Immigrant World of Ybor City: Italians and Their Latin Neighbors in Tampa, 1885–1985* (Urbana: University of Illinois Press, 1987), 98, 117; Armando Mendez, *Ciutad de Cigars, West Tampa* (Tampa: Florida Historical Society, 1994), 49, 93–94.

57. Robert P. Ingalls, *Urban Vigilantes in the New South: Tampa, 1882–1936* (Knoxville: University of Tennessee Press, 1988), 55–115.

58. Giovanni Vaccaro, "Due operai linciati," *La Parola dei Socialisti,* Oct. 1, 1910, 3. For *La Parola dei Socialisti,* see Annamaria Tasca, "Italians," in Dirk Hoerder, ed., *The Immigrant Labor Press in North America, 1840s–1970s: An Annotated Bibliography,* 3 vols. (Westport, CT: Greenwood, 1987), 3: 97.

59. C. Pugliesi, "Una lettera dal luogo del massacro," *Il Progresso Italo-Americano,* Sept. 30, 1910, 2.

60. "Il linciaggio di due italiani a Tampa, Fla.," *La Tribuna Italiana d'America,* Oct. 1, 1910, 1, 5.

61. Gaetano Moroni to Luigi Girolamo Cusani Confalonieri, Oct. 11, 1910, as quoted in Mormino and Pozzetta, *The Immigrant World of Ybor City,* 120.

62. James Allen et al., *Without Sanctuary: Lynching Photography in America* (Santa Fe: Twin Palms, 2000), 76.

63. "Due Italiani linciati da una folla sanguinaria," *L'Italia,* Sept. 24, 1910, 1; "Per i linciati di Tampa," *La Parola dei Socialisti,* Oct. 15, 1910, 3.

64. "Il linciaggio di due italiani strappati in un agguato alla polizia," *Corriere della Sera,* Sept. 22, 1910, 2. In this article the *Corriere della Sera* mistakenly renamed Ficarotta as "Picarotta."

65. Lucia Chiavola Birbaum, *Black Madonnas: Feminism, Religion and Politics in Italy* (Boston: Northeastern University Press, 1993); Anthony D'Angelo, "Italian Harlem's Saint Benedict the Moor," in Mary Jo Bona and Anthony Julian Tamburri, eds., *Through the Looking Glass: Italian and Italian/American Images in the Media* (Staten Island, NY: American Italian Historical Association, 1996), 235–40.

66. Patrick Q. Mason, "Sinners in the Hands of an Angry Mob: Violence against Religious Outsiders in the U.S. South, 1865–1910" (PhD diss., University of Notre Dame, 2005), 252.

67. Liz Burke, "Ethnic and Race Relations, Irish and Italians," in James P. Byrne, Philip Coleman, and Jason King, eds., *Ireland and the Americas: Culture, Politics, and History* (Santa Barbara, CA: ABC-Clio, 2008), 307.

68. "The Triple Lynching in St. Charles Parish," *Daily Picayune,* Aug. 10, 1896, 1.

69. Joan Ferrante and Prince Brown Jr., eds., *The Social Construction of Race and Ethnicity in the United States* (Upper Saddle River, NJ: Prentice Hall, 2001).

70. Salvatore J. LaGumina, "Introduction," in Salvatore J. LaGumina, ed., *Wop! A Documentary History of Anti-Italian Discrimination in the United States* (San Francisco: Straight Arrow Books, 1973), 9–19; Rudolph J. Vecoli, "Razza, razzismo e italo-americani," in Marcello Saija, ed., *L'emigrazione italiana transoceanica tra Otto e Novecento e la storia delle comunità derivate* (Messina: Trisform, 2003), 325–39; Fred Gardaphé, "Invisible People: Shadows and Light in Italian American Culture," in Connell and Gardaphé, *Anti-Italianism,* 1–10. For a more balanced view, see Jennifer Guglielmo and Salvatore Salerno, eds., *Are Italians White? How Race Is Made in America* (New York: Routledge, 2003).

71. C. Vann Woodward, *Origins of the New South, 1877–1913* (Baton Rouge: Louisiana State University Press, 1951); Edward L. Ayers, *The Promise of a New South: Life after Reconstruction* (New York: Oxford University Press, 1992).

72. Dennis C. Rousey, "Cops and Guns: Police Use of Deadly Force in Nineteenth-Century New Orleans," *American Journal of Legal History* 28 (1984): 65.

73. Edward L. Ayers, *Vengeance and Justice: Crime and Punishment in the 19th Century American South* (New York: Oxford University Press, 1984), esp. 167–69, 250–55, 260–61; Brundage, *Lynching in the New South,* 81–84.

8

Southern Politicians, British Reformers, and Ida B. Wells's 1893–1894 Transatlantic Antilynching Campaign

Sarah L. Silkey

As the United States and Great Britain grew closer together at the end of the nineteenth century, British social leaders placed pressure on their American counterparts to uphold common social, economic, and political standards. While minor deviations might be forgiven, American leaders needed to demonstrate the general respectability of American society in order to be treated as trusted business partners. The issue of American lynching, therefore, became increasingly problematic during the 1890s as the obvious disparity between British images of American lynching as "frontier justice" and the harsh reality of southern attacks on African Americans increased. Ida B. Wells's 1893–94 transatlantic antilynching campaign highlighted this incongruity and encouraged British reformers to place pressure on American leaders, particularly southern state governors, to denounce lynching.[1] As the global economic crisis that became known as the Depression of 1893 developed, southern leaders struggled to balance domestic and international interests within an increasingly transnational society. When Wells's campaign elicited expressions of British moral outrage, the complex social, political, and economic landscape of the 1890s placed southern leaders in a difficult position—needing to uphold white supremacy, while simultaneously suppressing the mob violence it inspired in order to court outside investment.[2] Once maintaining this precarious balance became untenable under British scrutiny, southern leaders were forced to choose whether to embrace the rhetoric of white supremacy to please their white constituents, seek to impose law and order to reassure prospective international investors, or generate a viable strategy to abrogate Wells's campaign.

Despite fears of the potential social chaos it might foster, the practice of mob violence had been tolerated by Europeans—particularly Britons—as a peculiarity of American society throughout most of the nineteenth century. The British public had long embraced claims made by American lynching apologists that extralegal violence was necessary to maintain order in frontier communities. American newspaper reporters and social commentators wrapped mob violence in the language of American exceptionalism, claiming that Europeans, with their long histories and established traditions, simply could not understand the new social customs necessitated by life on the American frontier. In the first half of the nineteenth century, Americans (and their British sympathizers) argued that lynching supported the establishment of law and order in a young society by ensuring that swift and certain justice was delivered to those who would disrupt the common peace. The romantic appeal of this frontier justice narrative made it difficult to oppose, and the image persisted throughout the nineteenth century.[3]

Reinforcing these images, popular British publications relayed encounters with lynch mobs as colorful adventure stories about rural American folkways in the years after the Civil War. For example, in an 1887 edition of *MacMillan's Magazine,* a British traveler, A. H. Paterson, recounted his participation in a calm, confident lynch party, comprised of the area's most respected citizens, formed to protect their small western community from the threat of murderous anarchy. It is important to understand that lynching was not considered a secret or criminal act and, as such, did not require anonymity to be discussed in public. To British authors, lynching as "frontier justice" offered no moral ambiguity. Paterson was proud of the role he played in the lynching and defended lynching as a necessary evil that maintained order in a fragile frontier society.[4] Such thrilling tales of heroic lynch mobs became so thoroughly engrained in popular depictions of frontier life that Buffalo Bill Cody even incorporated depictions of lynching in his traveling Wild West show during his "Farewell Visit to Europe" in 1892. British audiences were "entranced by these vivid representations of lynch law" targeting horse thieves and other desperados "in the Far West."[5]

While frontier justice might be celebrated in transatlantic popular culture, the reports of American lynching that reached Europe by the early 1890s no longer fit this description. Lynchings in settled areas were becoming ever more frequent, and fears that lynching might undermine the judicial system began to trouble British observers.[6] Such fears appeared justified after the March 14, 1891, lynching of Italian nationals in a New Orleans prison. Thousands of local citizens, displeased with the verdict of a murder trial, "broke" into the city jail and killed eleven Italian immigrants. Sparking an international controversy and creating a diplomatic crisis between the United States and Italy, the New Orleans lynching shocked Great Britain. This was not some remote frontier community with limited access to the court system; New Orleans was a thriving port city with a population of more than 240,000 residents. Several of the victims had been legally tried and acquitted but remained in jail awaiting trial on lesser charges. Claims made by lynching apologists that extralegal violence maintained social order appeared ludicrous when that violence nullified the authority of a working judicial system.[7]

Despite threats and appeals from the Italian government for legal redress against the lynchers, the federal government washed its hands of the affair, maintaining it had no constitutional mandate to interfere in what was essentially a matter for the state of Louisiana. U.S. secretary of state James G. Blaine provoked angry responses from the international community when he argued that the murdered Italians had been afforded the same rights and privileges as any American citizen. Indignant British journalists derided the secretary's position, asking whether "liability to lynch law" should be considered "a right and privilege" that all foreign visitors must "enjoy."[8]

Still reeling from the social and political aftermath of the New Orleans lynching, Britons were stunned to hear reports of another horrific lynching. On February 1, 1893, Henry Smith, a black man accused of raping and murdering a four-year-old white girl, was tortured and burned alive in front of a crowd of ten thousand spectators in Paris, Texas. The British press detailed the elaborate preparations made by the town: announcements had been made days in advance, special excursion trains were arranged to bring spectators from neighboring districts into the town, schools were dismissed, and a scaffold was built to provide an unobstructed view of the proceedings. The family of the alleged victim was given the honor of torturing Smith with red-hot irons for forty minutes before setting him alight. Although Americans claimed that such terrible violence was required to satisfy community outrage over the violation of white women and children by black men, the bloodthirsty revelry of the crowd scandalized British readers and left them more confused than ever.[9] If lynching was not an act of frontier justice, if crowds numbering in the thousands could witness these deaths without hesitation, then what exactly, British audiences wondered, was going on in America? The search for answers created an opportunity for Ida B. Wells, an African American journalist from Memphis, to offer an alternative explanation.

In response to the Paris, Texas, lynching, Wells was invited to act as a spokesperson for the Society for the Recognition of the Brotherhood of Man (SRBM), a nascent British anti-imperialist organization. An outspoken civil rights activist, Wells had gained notoriety when a Memphis mob destroyed her newspaper in response to her protests against the myth of the "black beast rapist." By the 1890s, white southern social and political leaders frequently asserted that lynching was used primarily to suppress black rapists who, in their uncontrollable lusts, preyed upon innocent white women and girls.[10] As a new generation of educated young black men and women came of age outside the rigid social structure of slavery, they asserted the right to pursue new professional opportunities and enjoy the benefits of middle-class status. In the eyes of many southern whites, these African American gains were made at the expense of traditional southern society. White southerners employed the lynching-for-rape mythology to justify the restoration of a more familiar social and economic order.

Lynching also provided a cheap and effective object lesson in the costs of "stepping out of place." For example, the owners of the People's Grocery Company were lynched in Memphis in 1892 because their successful black-owned business provided unwelcome competition for a local white merchant. These three successful black businessmen were respected Memphis community leaders who had not been accused of any sexual transgressions. For Wells and other Memphis residents who knew the mob's victims, the People's Grocery Company lynching was obviously motivated by personal greed and a desire to prevent the upward mobility of African Americans, not rape. Disgusted by the white community's complicity in the lynching of her friends, Wells began to rail against the "lynching for rape" rhetoric used to justify public tolerance of mob violence against African Americans. In her protests, Wells encouraged black residents to boycott the streetcars and to leave Memphis and start over if better prospects could be found elsewhere.[11]

As white business leaders struggled to cope with the economic impact of black protest, Wells became determined to expose the underlying economic, political, and social functions of mob violence from her position as editor of the *Memphis Free Speech*. Compiling statistical and anecdotal evidence from white newspaper reports of lynchings, Wells determined that fewer than one-third of all lynching cases involved accusations of any degree of sexual misconduct; of those cases in which rape, attempted rape, or some other sexually based transgression was noted, the details of the cases and the relationship between the parties did not always correspond. In one inflammatory editorial, Wells accused white southerners of using "the old threadbare lie that Negro men rape white women" to save face when clandestine consensual relationships between white women and black men were exposed. Incensed by the allegation that southern white women might dishonor themselves and their race by willingly engaging in sexual relations with black men, a mob composed of Memphis's leading white citizens destroyed Wells's press, physically assaulted her business partner, and threatened Wells with assassination if she should return to the South.[12]

The mob's attack destroyed her livelihood, but it provided Wells with firsthand evidence of the ideological inconsistencies of lynching and launched her career as an antilynching agitator. Wells found temporary employment writing for T. Thomas Fortune's *New York Age* and used her exile from the South to promote her antilynching agenda. Through public speaking engagements and the publication of *Southern Horrors,* her first exposé on lynching, Wells attracted the attention of American and British reformers, including Catherine Impey and Isabella Fyvie Mayo, the cofounders of the SRBM, who invited Wells to travel to Britain in 1893 to provide personal testimony about the horrors of mob violence.[13] Still unsettled by the New Orleans controversy and stunned by the cruelty of the brutal lynching in Texas, British audiences were primed to hear Wells's critique of American race relations. If lynching were no longer a practical necessity of frontier justice, what had it become? Through her published writings, speaking engagements, and newspaper interviews in Britain, Wells offered a ready answer: lynching was nothing more than a racist act of violent oppression used to deny African Americans their civil rights.

Wells argued that British intervention was necessary because southern lynching had insidiously demoralized the entire nation, making it impossible to voice dissent without appearing to support the violation of white women. The silence of good Americans, "their tacit encouragement, their silent acquiescence," had allowed "the black shadow of lawlessness in the form of lynch law" to spread "its wings over the whole country."[14] If, Wells insisted, the true cause of lynching were in fact rape, then white men, who controlled the mechanisms of law enforcement, legislature, and courts, had nothing to fear. "Make your laws as terrible as you like against that class of crime," Wells pleaded; "devise what tortures you will . . . but prove your criminal a criminal first. Hang, shoot, roast him, if you will—if American civilisation demands this—but give him a trial first!"¹⁵

Unlike Americans, the British public had not been seduced by the lynching-for-rape narrative. As S. J. Celestine Edwards reminded readers in his introduction to Wells's pamphlet *United States Atrocities,* British colonial experiences did not reflect the wild assertions of southern lynching apologists. As a popular British lay preacher of Afro-Caribbean descent, Edwards was well positioned to address the concerns and racial stereotypes held by British reformers. "We do not find similar charges brought against the West Indian Negroes," he asserted; nor did the missionaries in Africa complain of black licentiousness, although they worked with "Negroes who are much more savage than those in the South." Even "if it is true that Negroes thus misconduct themselves," Edwards demanded, "what right have white men to withhold a fair trial in a Court of Law, or brutally Lynch men who could be easily convicted, if the charges are true?" Similarly, Philip C. Ivens, a sympathizer with Wells's campaign, lamented in the *Sun* that "even the Inquisition gave a man some sort of a trial, and an opportunity to clear himself of an accusation, but 'Southern Chivalry' evidently does not see the necessity of giving a nigger a fair trial." Britons, he observed, had not found it "necessary to burn negroes alive to ensure due protection to white women," even in colonies with majority black populations. All lynching accomplished was to inflict "the most dreadful tortures on men who may be quite innocent of any crime."¹⁶

Through personal interviews, networking with newspaper editors, and hard-fought correspondence battles against lynching apologists, Wells won the editorial support of an increasing number of British newspapers. After weighing her testimony, the *Bradford Observer* determined that "there seems to be nothing irrational or impossible in the plea that [African Americans] ought not to be branded and burned alive and rolled in nailed casks, or even hanged on a tree, at the whim and sport of a mob." The *Newcastle Daily Leader* sneered at America's "boasted forwardness in civilisation," which in reality amounted to a "chamber of horrors" for African Americans. The *Daily Chronicle* did not pull punches in its denunciation of the South. The editor deemed that "race prejudice, and even a slight mixture of cruelty, is one thing; the horrible tortures, not only described by Miss Wells, but admitted and almost gloried in by the Southerners themselves, are quite another. When we read of such atrocities," the editor concluded, "we ask ourselves whether the Southern States are really fitted for self-government."[17]

Such powerful indictments of American society did not go unchallenged by American social and political leaders, but Wells's tactic of using southern white newspaper reports to substantiate her claims made it difficult to question the veracity of her evidence. For example, when Georgia governor William J. Northen wrote a letter to the editor of the *Daily Chronicle* attacking Wells's character in an attempt to undermine her campaign, the editor admonished Northen for his futile attempt to deflect attention from the real problem: the prevalence and brutality of American lynching. When the American press "literally teemed with accounts of the most brutal lynchings," he warned, Americans had already indicted themselves before the world.[18] The vehemence of American attacks upon Wells's campaign prompted British editors to sympathize with her cause and refuse to entertain the rebuttals of southern leaders. Northen complained bitterly that "the English people have declined and refused to be properly informed about our laws and the conduct of our Government" and that British newspapers had "declined time and time again to publish statements made to them in defense of the South."[19]

Protecting the national and international reputation of the South became an important priority for southern leaders as they sought to court investors at the end of the nineteenth century. Following the devastation of the Civil War and the social and political upheaval of Reconstruction, southern politicians hoped to not only transform the South's economy but also restore traditional race, class, and gender hierarchies by embracing white supremacy. "New South" leaders sought to move away from dependence upon cotton exports in order to develop diversified agricultural and industrial centers fully integrated into transatlantic markets. The efforts of southern politicians and businessmen took on a new sense of urgency after widespread agricultural failures in the late 1880s thrust the South into yet another economic decline, several years ahead of the rest of the nation. Even without wartime losses, the South's infrastructure had lagged far behind that of the North and Midwest. Southern leaders believed the key to the South's development lay in attracting outside investment for infrastructural improvements and industrial production, including the creation of new railroads, textile mills, and mines, as well as tempting desirable immigrants to move to the South.[20]

The need to cultivate investment capital placed New South governors like William J. Northen in a difficult position. Like that of many southern states, Georgia's economy, hit hard by economic depression and agricultural failures, desperately needed to attract investment capital from within the Atlantic economy that integrated Atlanta markets into those of Bristol, Birmingham, Liverpool, and London.[21] As the global Panic and Depression of 1893 took hold, the pool of available capital shrunk precipitously, thus dramatically increasing the competition for investors. British capital, which accounted for approximately 75 percent of all foreign investment in the United States, evaporated as new capital issues dropped by two-thirds during the height of the economic crisis.[22] With fewer resources to invest, British businessmen might perceive the region as a high-risk investment unless southern communities could demonstrate their ability to maintain law and order.

Recognizing that mob violence was bad for business, Northen worked to suppress lynching throughout his career as the governor of Georgia. He offered substantial rewards for the arrest and conviction of lynch mob participants, placed pressure on local sheriffs to defend their prisoners from mob attacks, and pushed for legislation to hold local law-enforcement officials accountable for the safety and security of their jails. Northen modeled his antilynching legislation after the determined efforts of Montgomery County sheriff George W. Dunham, who prevented the lynching of three black men accused of murder by enlisting the assistance of a conference of Methodist ministers to calm the growing mob, lodging the prisoners in a distant jail, arranging for a special session of court, and convincing the train engineer to skip the stop at the victim's hometown when transporting the prisoners to trial. After the Georgia Assembly passed "An Act to Prevent Mob Violence" in 1893, outlining penalties for local sheriffs and deputized citizens who failed to defend prisoners against mob attacks, Northen promoted the legislation as evidence that Georgia provided ample legal protection for life and property rights, thus making it an ideal place "to invest capital and to live in."[23]

Other New South governors embraced similar law-and-order platforms to encourage outside investment. Alabama governor Thomas Goode Jones denounced lynching as a stain upon the honor of Alabama "and a great obstacle to our healthy progress and prosperity."[24] In his inaugural address,

Jones argued that the maintenance of a state militia was essential for the economic future of the state. "Labor will not work, nor capital invest," he warned, "unless the laws are enforced and the peace assured." When local authorities could not maintain the peace, Jones believed it was their duty to call in the state militia. He praised the citizen soldiers who offered "themselves a living sacrifice if need be against lawless commotion and violence" to preserve the honor of Alabama against the disgrace of mob violence.[25]

Like Northen, Jones believed that, in order to suppress lynching, local sheriffs must be determined to defend their jails. Jones had vigorously defended the Birmingham jail from a drunken angry mob as a colonel in the Alabama National Guard and held no sympathy for the "cowardice" of local sheriffs who refused to use force of arms in defense of their prisoners.[26] When incidents of lynching did occur, Jones investigated the circumstances, placing pressure on local sheriffs to explain their failure to protect their prisoners or request help from the state. In 1893, Jones even hired the famous Pinkerton Detective Agency to investigate when Pickens County sheriff J. T. Hamiter could not provide a satisfactory explanation for the lynching of three black men taken from his custody in the Carrollton jail.[27]

Similarly, Governor Charles T. O'Ferrall led the charge against lynching in the Commonwealth of Virginia by placing pressure on local officials to forestall lynchings and dispatching militia units to areas threatened by mob violence. Elected shortly after an 1893 lynching riot in Roanoke left eight people dead and at least twenty-five wounded from clashes with the militia, O'Ferrall was determined to prevent similar incidents of lawlessness from disgracing the state. Shortly after taking office, O'Ferrall sent troops to Manassas at the request of the local sheriff, J. P. Leachman, to prevent the threatened lynching of James Robinson and Ben White in February 1894. O'Ferrall called out the militia again two months later to parade in front of the Staunton opera house at the request of Sheriff N. C. Watts to deter the lynching of Lawrence Spiller, a black man accused of raping and murdering a white girl. In both cases, armed soldiers ensured that the accused survived to stand a brief trial, conviction, and legal execution—a tactic famously dubbed "legal lynching" by the International Labor Defense during the Scottsboro trials of the 1930s. Such speedy "justice" was seen by many southern governors as the remedy for lynch law, for if conviction and execution were deemed certain, communities would have no reason to take the law into their own hands, and financiers might have confidence in the security of their southern investments.[28]

In exchange for infrastructural and industrial investment, southern states promised to provide a steady supply of labor. The wave of violent strikes that stretched from Coeur d'Alene, Idaho, to Homestead, Pennsylvania, in 1892 had demonstrated the potential investment risks associated with organized labor. Southern leaders hoped to compete against the industrialized North and the rich mineral resources of the West by offering investors something those regions struggled to provide: a cheap, cooperative, English-speaking labor force to support new railroads, mines, and factories. The southern system of white supremacy could be used to discourage labor organization and biracial coalitions; limit Populist Party political challenges to the status quo; and reinforce strict class, race, and gender boundaries. When the southern racial hierarchy was challenged by successful African Americans like the owners of the People's Grocery Company in Memphis, communities could use lynching to buttress white supremacy. The potential social, political, and economic benefits derived from white supremacy were considerable; nevertheless, its violent manifestation in the form of lynch law undermined legal protections for personal and property rights and risked deterring potential immigrants and investors. Therefore, southern leaders sought to suppress mob violence through appeals for "law and order" that remained largely uncritical of the system of white supremacy that perpetuated lynching.[29]

Since the majority of African Americans were confined by poverty, poor educational opportunities, rural isolation, and racial discrimination to agricultural and domestic work, southern states sought to secure their industrial labor force by attracting northern white migrants and western European immigrants. As with other indicators of development, the South lagged far behind other regions in attracting immigrants. Although the South accounted for approximately 30 percent of the national population, it housed less than 6 percent of the foreign-born population. In contrast, New York attracted nearly three times the number of immigrants as fifteen southern states combined.[30] Given the widespread ethnic conflicts and labor strife plaguing the major immigrant centers of the North and West, British immigrants were highly valued for their ability to easily assimilate into America's largely Protestant, English-speaking society. Yet the supply of British immigrants contracted during the Depression of 1893–97. As the total number of immigrants to the United States dropped by over 50 percent during the height of the Depression, the proportion of British immigrants fell from approximately one in five before 1890 to less than one in twelve by 1894.[31] This placed southern states in steep competition with northern industrial centers and western mining and agricultural regions for British investment capital and immigrant laborers.[32]

As British reformers and newspapers increasingly turned their attention to the problem of lynching, New South governors and other advocates of southern immigration and investment began to fear the potential economic consequences of Wells's campaign. By casting the South as a lawless, violent, and uncivilized region, Wells might deter potential investors and discourage intending emigrants. As the *Christian Register* warned, "People will refuse to invest capital and to live in a country in which there is no adequate protection by law for life and property."[33] But beyond concerns that a violent reputation might frighten off squeamish investors, the black citizens of Memphis had demonstrated in the wake of the People's Grocery Company lynching that economic boycotts and selective migration could be used as effective tools in the campaign against mob violence. Wells advocated withholding capital and labor from the South to force American communities to end lynching because, as she cynically observed, appeals "to the white man's pocket" have "been more effectual than all the appeals ever made to his conscience."[34] As Wells's campaign gained momentum and she increasingly won the support of liberal British newspaper editors, the potential impact of British antilynching sentiment on the South's economy became a palpable threat.

Rumors circulated of a conspiracy launched by western land developers to use "the colored problem" to direct capital and immigration away from the South. As one visiting Englishman reportedly explained: "The excitement of immigration has to be kept up, or values will tumble. . . . Immigration must not be diverted south, or anywhere else, until those interests in the west shall have saved themselves." Governor Northen feared that capitalist consortiums employed speakers like Wells to turn people against the South. "The business of slandering the southern people" was, according to Northen, well organized. "Innocent, but meddlesome, people . . . are artfully called together to listen to a speaker. Typewritten resolutions are ready, with . . . talkative men primed to second them. They are passed with a rush" and sent out that same night. "By a curious coincidence . . ." Northen alleged, "many of the recipients of such resolutions . . . received by the same mail gorgeously printed maps and circulars describing the west as home for intending emigrants."[35] Although it may have been easier to focus on invented conspiracies than to address the realities of lynching, southern leaders were forced to address Wells's campaign if they wished to win desirable immigrants and corporate investors in an increasingly competitive international market.

The formation of a new British organization during the summer of 1894 provided southern leaders with a welcome opportunity to attack British antilynching activism without appearing to openly support mob violence or needing to devise a compelling response to Wells's rhetoric. The London Anti-Lynching Committee pressured American political leaders, particularly state governors, to investigate reported lynchings by attempting to shame them into taking action against these "outrages . . . whose inhumanity, lawlessness, and cowardice cannot fail to compromise the reputation of Americans generally."[36] The success of the committee's tactic relied in part on the influence of its distinguished membership of prominent British politicians and social reformers, including Sir John Eldon Gorst, members of Parliament Sir Joseph Pease and Justin McCarthy, and the Duke of Argyll. By focusing on the immorality of lynching and the disgrace such outrages brought—or should bring—on American communities, rather than attacking the underlying causes of lynching, the committee's tactic divorced British antilynching activism from Wells's critique of southern race relations and made the moral authority of the committee's membership a central part of the debate.[37]

When the London Anti-Lynching Committee sent a delegation led by Sir John Eldon Gorst to the United States to investigate lynching in September 1894, a furious wave of American indignation was unleashed. The *New York World* telegraphed state governors throughout the Midwest, South, and West asking for reactions to the British investigation. Eighteen responded denouncing the impertinence of the British committee, and their reactions were reprinted by newspapers across the country.[38] Arkansas governor William Meade Fishback was outraged that England would "assume the role of a missionary to teach us our duty" and warned that "the officious intermeddling of outsiders" would only make it more difficult for "the better class of people to suppress" lynching. Virginia governor Charles T. O'Ferrall believed it was "the quintessence of brass and impudence" to have "a lot of English moralists sticking their noses into our internal affairs," while Missouri governor William J. Stone declared it "an exhibition of superb cheek." Indiana governor Claude Matthews regarded the committee's "meddlesome interference" as "wholly unwarranted, and not deserving of even courteous or tolerant treatment by our people." "We have no need for English committees in this country," South Dakota governor Charles H. Sheldon stormed, "when the purpose is to give peculiar emphasis to the English idea of English superiority."[39]

South Carolina governor Ben Tillman offered the British committee a chance to gain firsthand knowledge of lynching by visiting his state: "the Englishmen are welcome to come to South Carolina and learn the truth. . . . I will afford them every facility to get at facts." Tillman's "invitation" could be interpreted as a veiled threat to teach the committee an object lesson in lynching. Southern newspapers picked up on this nuance and echoed Tillman's words with their own offers. The *Rome* (Georgia) *Tribune* invited the committee to "come south and stay with us a while." The *St. Louis Republic* suggested "the way to cure the visitors is to take each one into an agricultural community in one of the black belts and bid him or her wait until something happens."[40] Such equivocal statements were an essential component of Tillman's political strategy. While he publicly championed the beleaguered farmer and denounced black criminality, even famously pledging to lead a lynch mob if necessary in order to defend white women's virtue, Tillman nevertheless strove to enforce law and order during his term as governor. Like Northen, Jones, and O'Ferrall, Tillman pressured local sheriffs to bring accused criminals to trial and repeatedly sent troops to prevent outbreaks of mob violence. In his 1890 inaugural address, Tillman called for the power to remove any sheriff who allowed a prisoner to be taken from his custody. If mob violence were eliminated, Tillman argued, "all classes and colors" might finally compete "with each other in friendly rivalry to make the State prosperous and happy." Like most New South governors, Tillman promoted the cause of white supremacy to gain electoral support, while simultaneously fighting to suppress lynching in order to maintain good relations with outside investors.[41]

The debate over American lynching quickly moved from the underlying causes of mob violence to the impertinence of British moral interference. White southerners convinced themselves that foreign investigators possessed no useful understanding of their society. "While we have irregularities at the South," Northen conceded, "and negroes are sometimes lynched, they are never slaughtered by wholesale, as Englishmen sometimes destroy them." "Possibly the English committee can do some good in the South," speculated Illinois governor John P. Altgeld. "If it does, then the Southern people should return the compliment and send a committee to Ireland to stop the outrages there."[42] Unable to denounce mob violence while public attention focused on Wells's campaign and the committee's investigation, American governors abandoned their law-and-order campaigns to decry British hypocrisy and cheek.

Thus, the tactics of the London Anti-Lynching Committee, not lynching, became the new focus of debate. Because the controversy surrounding the committee's tactics pushed Wells's arguments to the side, those who opposed Wells's campaign finally found room in the transatlantic debate for their voices. The *Times,* which had both ignored Wells's campaign and refrained from participating in the British debate on lynching, eagerly published Alabama governor Thomas Goode Jones's indignant rebuttal to the London Anti-Lynching Committee's request to investigate a lynching reported in his state. As "a sturdy foe of mob violence," Jones warned there could be "no more formidable hindrance" to efforts to end lynching "than the attempt of a committee of British subjects to constitute themselves an international moral tribunal" and "arrogate the right to summon States to defend their civilization." "The laws, the efforts of the authorities, and the force of public opinion," Jones insisted, "are solving the problem and the good work can be retarded, but not hastened by your present method." Such impertinent interference could only serve to generate resentment that would hinder the efforts of progressive southern leaders to end mob violence.[43] Diminishing the importance of the antilynching campaign and demonstrating its general disdain for liberal reformers, the editor of the *Times* ridiculed every aspect of the committee's protest, including the writing skills of the committee's secretary, mockingly lamenting that "it would be such a pity if Miss [Florence] Balgarnie were lynched by a mob of enraged grammarians." By infuriating white Americans with their sanctimoniousness, the *Times* warned, the committee's interference likely "multiplied the number of negroes who are hanged, shot, and burnt by paraffin . . . throughout the Southern States."[44] The *Daily Telegraph* joined the debate, attacking the committee's lack of deference to the governor's office and expressing its sympathy for southern white men who were "inflamed to madness by outrages on their wives, their sisters, or their daughters, committed by negroes."[45]

Expressions of conservative British disapproval for the activism of the London Anti-Lynching Committee received enthusiastic coverage in the American press. The London correspondent for the *New York Times* was delighted by the *Times'*s declaration that, although it had "little or no sympathy for lynching," it had "none whatever with anti-lynching." The correspondent believed this was "almost the first expression . . . of a big majority of sensible Englishmen who resent the meddlesome antics of a little and noisy minority." Similarly, the *New York Times* reprinted the *London Truth*'s denunciation of British reformers "who take upon themselves to regulate the conduct of the whole world" and the *Saturday Review*'s praise for the "very good snub" of the London Anti-Lynching Committee administered by Jones.[46] Finding supportive coverage in the *Times, Pall Mall Gazette, Westminster Gazette, Globe, London Society, Sun,* and *Daily Telegraph,* the *Montgomery Daily Advertiser* was pleased to announce that the governor's letter had "Cut to the Quick."[47]

Despite the tactical miscalculation that resulted in this sudden burst of negative British press, the supporters of Wells's campaign interpreted the efforts of southern leaders to denounce their protests as a sign of progress. Florence Balgarnie, secretary of the London Anti-Lynching Committee, responded to the appearance of Jones's letter in the *Times* with enthusiasm "as a herald of good tidings, for it evinces a certain hopeful sensitiveness to outside opinion which augurs well for the ultimate and universal suppression of lynching."[48] Her sentiments were echoed by William Lloyd Garrison Jr., son of the famed abolitionist, who claimed "the very denunciation of foreign criticism by the Southern offenders demonstrates its potency." According to Garrison, Americans who recognized the evils of mob violence were no longer intimidated into silence. While only "a year ago the South derided and resented Northern protests[,] today it listens, explains, and apologizes for its uncovered cruelties."[49] By the following year, the committee's annual report celebrated the "changed attitude of the Southern Press" and the actions taken by several governors, judges, and state legislatures to denounce and ultimately suppress lynching.[50]

By expanding her antilynching campaign to Great Britain in 1893 and 1894, Wells had seized a valuable opportunity to critique the role of lynching in American society during a period when southern leaders were desperate to court international investment, and British commentators were searching for a satisfying explanation for the prevalence of mob violence in the United States. As British social leaders rejected southern excuses for lynching, southern governors struggled to avoid the appearance that they condoned lynching, giving new urgency to their efforts to suppress mob violence despite the increasing internal pressure they felt to embrace the rhetoric of white supremacy used to support lynching. As British reformers took charge of the antilynching campaign, southern leaders found an outlet to please their constituents by rallying nationalist sentiment against the unwelcome intrusion of meddling foreigners. Unfortunately, by permitting southern leaders to avoid addressing the true purpose and nature of American lynching, British reformers lost valuable momentum, and the backlash white southern leaders generated in response to the London Anti-lynching Committee's investigation eventually stalled the British antilynching movement. Nevertheless, by changing the way British reformers understood American lynching and encouraging them to hold southern leaders accountable for the lawless excesses of their constituents, Wells's antilynching activism had increased the perceived international "costs" of lynching for the South during a critical period of social and economic upheaval.

Notes

This essay has been published by permission of the University of Georgia Press and was supported by a Professional Development Grant from Lycoming College. Portions of this essay have been previously published in Sarah L. Silkey, "Redirecting the Tide of White Imperialism: The Impact of Ida B. Wells's Transatlantic Antilynching Campaign on British Conceptions of American Race Relations," in Angela Boswell and Judith N. McArthur, eds., *Women Shaping the South: Creating and Confronting Change* (Columbia: University of Missouri Press, 2006).

1. Although there has been considerable scholarship published on Wells's antilynching activism, traditional interpretations have not approached Wells's campaigns from a transnational perspective and largely ignore the impact of British antilynching activism. See Mildred I. Thompson, *Ida B. Wells-Barnett: An Exploratory Study of an American Black Woman, 1893–1930* (Brooklyn: Carlson Publishing, 1990); Patricia A. Schechter, *Ida B. Wells-Barnett and American Reform, 1880–1930* (Chapel Hill: University of North Carolina Press, 2001); Paula J. Giddings, *Ida: A Sword among Lions* (New York: Amistad, 2008); Mia Bay, *To Tell the Truth Freely: The Life of Ida B. Wells* (New York: Hill & Wang, 2009).

2. The ultimate resolution of post-Reconstruction tensions through disfranchisement, segregation, and other "reform" measures designed to rationalize southern society through the lens of white supremacy became known as "Southern progressivism." See C. Vann Woodward, *Origins of the New South, 1877–1913* (Baton Rouge: Louisiana State University Press, 1951); Jack Temple Kirby, *Darkness at the Dawning: Race and Reform in the Progressive South* (Philadelphia: Lippincott, 1972); Stephen Kantrowitz, *Ben Tillman and the Reconstruction of White Supremacy* (Chapel Hill: University of North Carolina Press, 2000).

3. For early examples of the frontier justice narrative, see Frederick Marryat, *A Diary in America, with Remarks on Its Institutions* (Paris: Baudy's European Library, 1839), 1: 314–16, 1: 323–24; Francis J. Grund, *The Americans in*

Their Moral, Social and Political Relations (1837; rpt., with introduction by Robert Berkhofer Jr., New York: Johnson Reprint Corp., 1968), 165, 166, 168, 179–80; Charles Summerfield, *Illustrated Lives and Adventures of the Desperadoes of the New World: Containing an Account of the Different Modes of Lynching . . . Together with the Lives of the Most Notorious Regulators and Moderators in the Known World* (Philadelphia: T. B. Peterson, 1849), 11–13. For evidence of continuing British acceptance of the frontier justice narrative, see "Lynching in America," *Chambers's Journal*, May 17, 1890, 317; N. J. D. Kennedy, "Lynch," *Juridicial Review*, July 1891, 218–19. For a discussion of the evolution of American lynching definitions, see Christopher Waldrep, *The Many Faces of Judge Lynch: Extralegal Violence and Punishment in America* (New York: Palgrave MacMillan, 2002), 49–66.

4. A. H. Paterson, "Lynch Law," *MacMillan's Magazine*, Mar. 1887, 342–50. A similar example may be found in R. B. Townshend, "A Trial by Lynch Law," *Nineteenth Century*, Aug. 1892, 243–55.

5. Buffalo Bill's "Wild West" Advertisement, *Graphic* (London), Aug. 6, 1892; "Fresh Attractions at the 'Horty,'" *Penny Illustrated Paper*, July 30, 1892.

6. For a well-articulated example, see "Lynching in America," May 17, 1890, 317–19.

7. Kennedy, "Lynch," 216; "The Lynching Affair at New Orleans," *Spectator*, Mar. 21, 1891, 401; Jessie White (Vedova) Mario, "Italy and the United States," *Nineteenth Century*, May 1891, 703; Michael R. Haines, "Population of Cities with At Least 100,000 Population in 1990: 1790–1990," table Aa832–1033, in Susan B. Carter et al., eds., *Historical Statistics of the United States, Earliest Times to the Present: Millennial Edition* (New York: Cambridge University Press, 2006), 1: 111. See also Stefano Luconi's essay "The Lynching of Southern Europeans in the Southern United States: The Plight of Italian Immigrants in Dixie," in this volume.

8. N. J. D. Kennedy, "Lynch II—Its International Aspect," *Juridicial Review*, Jan. 1892, 46, 48; "Lynch Law," *Saturday Review*, May 30, 1891, 643.

9. "Lynch Law in the United States: Horrible Atrocities," *Reuter's Journal*, Feb. 2, 1893; "Sensational Lynching Affray in State of Texas," *Glasgow Herald*, Feb. 2, 1893; "Lynch Law in Texas," *Daily News* (London), Feb. 3, 1893.

10. Joel Williamson, *The Crucible of Race: Black-White Relations in the American South since Emancipation* (New York: Oxford University Press, 1984), 184.

11. Linda O. McMurry, *To Keep the Waters Troubled: The Life of Ida B. Wells* (New York: Oxford University Press, 1998), 130–34; Alfreda M. Duster, *Crusade for Justice: The Autobiography of Ida B. Wells* (Chicago: University of Chicago Press, 1970), 47–52, 61–65; Mary Church Terrell, *A Colored Woman in a White World* (New York: G. K. Hall & Co., 1996), 105–6.

12. Ida B. Wells, *United States Atrocities: Lynch Law* (London: Lux, 1893), 1–3, 10–13; Duster, *Crusade for Justice*, 61–67.

13. Duster, *Crusade for Justice*, 61–63, 69–72, 77–86.

14. Wells, *United States Atrocities*, 9, 19–21.

15. Wells quoted anonymously in Charles F. Aked, "The Race Problem in America," *Contemporary Review* 65 (June 1894): 823–25, 827; "Lynch Law in America," *Daily Chronicle* (London), Apr. 28, 1894.

16. S. J. Celestine Edwards, "Introduction," in Wells, *United States Atrocities*, vi; Philip C. Ivens, "Colour Prejudice," letter to the editor, *Sun* (London), July 9, 1894.

17. Editorial, *Bradford Observer*, May 11, 1894; "Lynching in the United States," *Newcastle Daily Leader*, Apr. 20, 1894; Editorial, *Daily Chronicle*, Apr. 28, 1894.

18. William J. Northen, letter to the editor, *Daily Chronicle*, June 5, 1894; A. E. Fletcher, editor's note, *Daily Chronicle*, June 5, 1894.

19. "Get Out Englishmen!" [Sept. 1894], scrapbook clipping, William J. Northen Papers, 1865–1929, ac 1941-0354M, Georgia Archives (hereafter WJNP).

20. Don H. Doyle, *New Men, New Cities, New South: Atlanta, Nashville, Charleston, Mobile, 1860–1910* (Chapel Hill: University of North Carolina Press, 1990), 313–18; James C. Cobb, *Away Down South: A History of Southern Identity* (New York: Oxford University Press, 2005), 67–73, 76–78.

21. David F. Godshalk, "William J. Northen's Public and Personal Struggles against Lynching," in Jane Dailey, Glenda Elizabeth Gilmore, and Bryant Simon, eds., *Jumpin' Jim Crow: Southern Politics from Civil War to Civil Rights* (Princeton: Princeton University Press, 2000), 141–42; William J. Northen, *To the General Assembly of Georgia. Inaugural Address of Gov. Wm. J. Northen* (Atlanta: Southern Cultivator and Dixie Farmer, 1890).

22. Douglas O. Steeples, *Democracy in Desperation: The Depression of 1893* (Westport, CT: Greenwood Press, 1998), 27–28.

23. William J. Northen, "Lynching in the South," *Christian Register*, May 10, 1894, 291–92; "An Act to Prevent Mob Violence," Dec. 19, 1893, box 3, WJNP.

24. Thomas Goode Jones, "Mob Violence," *Montgomery Daily Advertiser*, Feb. 7, 1893.

25. Thomas G. Jones, *Inaugural Address of Thomas G. Jones, Governor of Alabama, Delivered before the General Assembly, December 1st, 1890* (Montgomery: Brown Printing Co., 1890), 15.

26. Thomas Goode Jones, "Mob Violence," *Montgomery Daily Advertiser*, Feb. 7, 1893; "Executive Messages," *Montgomery Daily Advertiser*, Feb. 7, 1893; Thomas Goode Jones, "Report to the Governor (1883)," in Christopher Waldrep, ed., *Lynching in America: A History in Documents* (New York: New York University Press, 2006), 136–37.

27. W. M. Waltrip to Thomas G. Jones, Apr. 3, 1891, Alabama Governor (1890–1894: Jones), Administrative Files, SG8, 415, Reels 5–13, Alabama Department of Archives and History, Montgomery (hereafter AFTGJ); W. R. Carter to Thomas G. Jones, Apr. 3, 1891, AFTGJ; J. K. Jackson to J. T. Hamiter, Sept. 20, 1893, AFTGJ; J. T. Hamiter to Thomas G. Jones, Sept. 22, 1893, AFTGJ; W. A. Pinkerton to Thomas G. Jones, Nov. 24, 1893, AFTGJ; W. A. Pinkerton to

Thomas G. Jones, Nov. 27, 1893, AFTGJ; W. A. Pinkerton to Thomas G. Jones, Nov. 29, 1893, AFTGJ.

28. Fitzhugh Brundage, *Lynching in the New South: Georgia and Virginia, 1880–1930* (Urbana: University of Illinois Press, 1993), 166–68, 173; George A. Mushbach to Charles T. O'Ferrall, telegram, Feb. 8, 1894, Executive Papers of Charles T. O'Ferrall, 1894–1897, Accession 43210, The Library of Virginia, Richmond (hereafter EPCTO); N. C. Watts to Captain of the Monticello Guards, telegram, Apr. 29, 1894, EPCTO; "Staunton's Brutal Tragedy," *Roanoke Times,* May 2, 1894; "Spiller Quickly Convicted," *Richmond Times,* May 3, 1894; editorial, *Richmond Planet,* May 5, 1894; Waldrep, *Many Faces of Judge Lynch,* 163.

29. Steeples, *Democracy in Desperation,* 91–92; Cobb, *Away Down South,* 71.

30. Southern states include Delaware, Maryland, West Virginia, Virginia, North Carolina, South Carolina, Georgia, Florida, Kentucky, Tennessee, Alabama, Mississippi, Louisiana, Oklahoma, Texas, and the District of Columbia. See Michael R. Haines, "Population, by Sex, Nativity, and Citizenship Status: 1890–1990," table Ad280–318, and Susan B. Carter, "Geographic Concentration of the Foreign-Born Population—Top Three States and the South: 1850–1990," table Ad696, both in Carter et al., *Historical Statistics,* 1: 598, 1: 613.

31. Susan B. Carter and Richard Sutch, "U.S. Immigrants and Emigrants: 1820–1998," table Ad1–2, and Robert Barde, Susan B. Carter, and Richard Sutch, "Immigrants, by Country of Last Residence—Europe: 1820–1997," table Ad106–120, in Carter et al., *Historical Statistics,* 1: 541, 1: 561.

32. Northen, "Lynching in the South," 291; William J. Northen, *The Negro at the South: Letters by Gov. W. J. Northen* (Atlanta: Franklin Printing and Publishing Co., 1894).

33. "Lynch Law in the South," *Christian Register,* Apr. 12, 1894, 225.

34. Wells, *United States Atrocities,* 16; Charles F. Aked, "One Woman's Work," *Christian World,* July 19, 1894.

35. "Tis Miss Ida," *Constitution,* July 28, 1894, scrapbook clipping, box 5, WJNP.

36. "Lynching in America," *Times* (London), Oct. 6, 1894; Florence Balgarnie, "Anti-Lynching Committee," letter to the editor, *Manchester Guardian,* Aug. 4, 1894.

37. Editorial, *Times,* Oct. 6, 1894.

38. Balgarnie, "Anti-Lynching Committee," *Manchester Guardian,* Aug. 4, 1894; "Sir John Gorst's Report," *New York Times,* Sept. 10, 1894; "Governors Speak Out," *New York World,* Sept. 14, 1894; "Get Out Englishmen!"

39. "Get Out Englishmen!"

40. Ibid.; "Our English Invaders," [1894], scrapbook clipping, box 5, WJNP.

41. *Inaugural Address of B. R. Tillman, Governor of South Carolina, Delivered at Columbia, S.C., December 4, 1890* (Columbia: James H. Woodrow, 1890), 6; Kantrowitz, *Ben Tillman,* 156–57, 162–70, 174–81. For Wells's criticisms of Tillman's record on lynching, see "Black versus White," *Labour Leader,* May 12, 1894.

42. "Our English Invaders."

43. "Lynching in America," *Times,* Oct. 6, 1894.

44. Editorial, *Times,* Oct. 6, 1894.

45. Editorial, *Daily Telegraph* (London), Oct. 8, 1894; Editorial, *Times,* Oct. 6, 1894.

46. "London Week of Excitement," *New York Times,* Oct. 7, 1894; "Lessons for Busybodies," *New York Times,* Oct. 15, 1894; "Impertinence That Amazes Labouchere," *New York Times,* Oct. 20, 1894; "Anti-Lynching Committee's Snubbing," *New York Times,* Oct. 25, 1894.

47. "It Cut to the Quick," *Montgomery Daily Advertiser,* Oct. 25, 1894.

48. Florence Balgarnie, letter to the editor, *Times,* Oct. 8, 1894.

49. William Lloyd Garrison Jr., letter to the editor, *Times,* Nov. 9, 1894.

50. "Anti-Lynching Committee," *Times,* Dec. 20, 1895.

9

Transatlantic Fundamentalism

Southern Preachers in London's Pulpits during World War I

William R. Glass

In 1911, Rev. A. C. Dixon left the famous pulpit of the Moody Church in Chicago, founded by the late nineteenth-century evangelist Dwight L. Moody and in some ways the Vatican of American nondenominational evangelicalism, and moved his ministry to an equally esteemed, conservative platform in London: the Metropolitan Tabernacle, a church led for nearly forty years by Charles Haddon Spurgeon. Two years later, another American preacher assumed the pastorate of Christ Church, a congregation that combined evangelical preaching from the pulpit with a variety of social programs intended to meet the needs of its community. In his first sermon, Leonard G. Broughton acknowledged this heritage and outlined an ambitious program to revitalize and expand these programs. Both of the churches were in London's Southwark district, within a mile of each other. Both men were from North Carolina, one was born before the Civil War, the other just after it ended, and both were Baptists. Though not obvious, the selection of southerners as pastors represented a minor example of the healing of nineteenth-century divisions from the American Civil War as both churches had connections to the abolitionism of the 1850s. More important, though, both Dixon and Broughton contributed to the development of American Protestant fundamentalism, and their moves to London represented one small part of a web of connections involving people and ideas that contributed to a fruitful exchange between conservative Protestants in Great Britain and the United States. In short, they were representatives of the transatlantic nature of the emerging fundamentalist movement.[1]

A. C. Dixon was the older and more noted of the two.[2] Born in 1854 in Shelby, North Carolina, and converted at age twelve, Dixon graduated from Wake Forest College in 1874 and had a year of theology school before serving churches in Chapel Hill and Asheville. On leaving North Carolina in 1883 for Baltimore's Immanuel Baptist Church, he began a steady ascent to larger, more prestigious, and more conservative congregations and to a national reputation as an effective evangelist, Bible teacher, and controversialist. After seven years in Baltimore (1883–90), he moved to Hanson Street Baptist in Brooklyn for ten years (1890–1900), then to Boston's Ruggles Street Church for five (1901–6), with his last U.S. pastorate before London being the nondenominational Moody Church in Chicago (1906–11). While pastoring these churches, he spoke at Bible conferences, conducted evangelistic services in secular auditoriums, and published newspaper columns denouncing modern thought and affirming traditional interpretations of Christian doctrine. These experiences paved the way for him to play a pivotal role in shaping the emergence of American fundamentalism through editing the first five volumes of *The Fundamentals*.[3] Published in 1910–15, this series of twelve pamphlets not only contributed to naming this conservative movement in American Protestantism but also defined its agenda. With these credentials, Dixon seemed a natural fit for London's Metropolitan Tabernacle.

This church was known throughout the world due to the ministry of Charles Haddon Spurgeon, one of the great preachers of the nineteenth century.[4] Not only blessed with great oratorical skills, Spurgeon was renowned for his conservative exposition of the Bible in his sermons. His fame was such that Dixon applied to Spurgeon's pastor's college when he was considering options for theology school. Spurgeon gently rejected the application, suggesting that Dixon take his training in the country where he would be ministering.[5] Moreover, Spurgeon and the Tabernacle were no strangers to controversy, political or theological. For example, Spurgeon's account of the Tabernacle's history did not mention any tradition of antislavery activity,[6] but in February 1860, in response to charges that he edited out abolitionist content for American editions of his sermons, he wrote a letter denying the accusation. He noted that his congregation had no slave owners, so he "would be beating the air" if he attacked slavery in his Sunday sermons, "for this is the very last crime" the Tabernacle's members "would commit." But he was unequivocal: "I do from my inmost soul detest slavery anywhere and everywhere, and although I commune at the Lord's table with men of all creeds, yet with a slaveholder I have no fellowship of any sort." As a parting shot, he affirmed, in words destined to inflame southerners, "John Brown is immortal in the memories of the good in England, and in my heart he lives."[7] When news of his remarks circulated in the United States, southerners banned and burned his books, with one newspaper suggesting that "the works of this greasy cockney vociferator may receive the same treatment throughout the South; and if the Pharisaical author should ever show himself in these parts, we trust that a stout cord may speedily find its way around his *eloquent* throat."[8] The sales of his books and pamphlets dropped precipitously, a not insignificant price to pay as Spurgeon used this money to support the charity work of the Tabernacle.[9] No evidence, though, can be mustered to suggest that these comments were part of an ongoing campaign against American slavery conducted by Spurgeon and the Tabernacle.

The most noted theological dispute of Spurgeon's career was the "Down Grade" controversy of the late 1880s, in which Spurgeon railed against the doctrinal deviation of some of his fellow Baptists: "We have before us the wretched spectacle of professedly orthodox Christians publicly avowing their union with those who deny the faith."[10] Because the Baptist Union refused to discipline those members who questioned traditional Baptist doctrine, Spurgeon left the Union, believing that "to pursue union at the expense of truth is treason to the Lord Jesus."[11] For Spurgeon, the course of action was obvious: "The bounden duty of a true believer towards men who profess to be Christians, and yet deny the Word of the Lord, and reject the fundamentals of the gospel, is to come out from among them."[12] One way of looking at this controversy is to see it as British Baptists' "fundamentalist moment," as Spurgeon's rhetoric and separation were not that different from that of American fundamentalists in the denominational battles of the 1920s.[13]

While the impact of Spurgeon's crusade was rippling out, the members of the Tabernacle became acquainted with Dixon in 1889. He had followed the controversy and used the occasion of a Sunday-school convention to come to London. While there, he gave the "long prayer" at a morning service in the Tabernacle, followed by short sermons at Monday-evening prayer meetings.[14] When Archibald Brown, one of Spurgeon's successors as the Tabernacle's pastor, resigned in October 1910, effective at the end of the year, the Board of Deacons invited Dixon to fill the pulpit for January 1911, an opportunity Dixon accepted.[15] The preaching extended into February, and by the end of the month some 225 members had signed a petition requesting that the board ask Dixon to become the permanent pastor.[16] In March, the church issued a formal call, which mentioned the ways the Tabernacle benefited from Dixon's ministry: "increasing congregations both on the Lord's Day and in the week have been brought together, the children of God have been edified, strengthened, comforted and taught, and sinners have been brought home to God."[17] After some dithering, Dixon accepted, noting that both the "blessing of God on the preaching of His word in the Tabernacle . . . and the door of service for Christ" that the church afforded "convince me that your invitation voices the call of God."[18] He took up full-time duties as the Tabernacle's pastor in June 1911, and within a month, the *South London Press* noted, "Dr. A. C. Dixon is worthily upholding the great preaching traditions of the Metropolitan Tabernacle."[19]

While Dixon's career took him outside the South, Leonard G. Broughton, apart from the time in London, remained more closely tied to his native region. Born in December 1865 in rural North Carolina, Broughton had a conversion experience after hearing Dixon preach in 1879 but took an unusual path to the pastorate.[20] He, too, graduated from Wake Forest College but, instead of theology school, continued his education in medical school in Kentucky.[21] He came back to North Carolina and built a fairly successful practice in the Piedmont. A bout of typhoid fever left him bedridden for six months and led him to give in to the feeling that he was called to preach, which he had stifled since his conversion.[22] After serving churches in North Carolina and Virginia, he accepted a call in 1897 to Atlanta's Third Baptist Church, where he met resistance from some of its members over his plans to relocate the congregation to a more central location and enlarge its ministries beyond the traditional worship services and Sunday school. He left Third Baptist with about two hundred members to establish Tabernacle Baptist. In five years, it had a new auditorium seating over two thousand and membership of thirteen hundred, hosted an annual Bible conference attracting nationally and internationally known preachers, and had started a nursing school and infirmary that eventually became the Georgia Baptist Hospital.[23]

The Bible conference was probably the connection that led Broughton to London. One of the speakers was F. B. Meyer, pastor of Christ Church, London, and well known on the Bible-conference circuit for his teaching of Keswick holiness doctrines.[24] Meyer filled the pulpit of Christ Church from 1892 to 1907 and spoke at the Tabernacle conference in 1901, 1905, and 1912. It is likely Meyer saw Broughton and Christ Church as a good match, as the church had an extensive program of social services for its neighborhood, including a nursing auxiliary; Broughton, with his medical training and emphasis on balancing community service with gospel preaching, could effectively lead Christ Church, despite the congregation's legacy of opposition to slavery.[25] It does not seem that the congregation and its pastors were involved in a significant way with British abolitionism, but beginning with the pastorate of James Sherman in 1836, the church began supporting the cause of ending southern slavery.[26] Sherman wrote an introduction to the British edition of *Uncle Tom's Cabin* and hosted an appearance of Harriet Beecher Stowe in the church during her European tour.[27] Christopher Newman Hall, Sherman's successor, was a vocal supporter of the North and an outspoken critic of British government policies toward the American Civil War. He believed that the government should support the North as he saw the war as the means of ending slavery.[28] After the war, at the suggestion of some Americans living in London, he toured the United States to raise money for the erection of a memorial to Lincoln in London.[29] In July 1874, the American ambassador laid the cornerstone, and two years later, on July 4, 1876, the church dedicated the Lincoln Tower, a two-hundred-foot Gothic spire rising above Christ Church's sanctuary at the corner of Westminster Bridge Road and Kennington Lane.[30]

Nonetheless, probably at Meyer's urging, Londoners began courting Broughton as early as 1910, but he was in the midst of a campaign to enlarge the Atlanta Tabernacle's sanctuary and felt he could not leave the job unfinished. Christ Church renewed its call in 1912, and Broughton accepted, leaving the South after the 1912 Bible conference.[31] The congregation in London welcomed him in a ceremony that included Americans Dixon and William Bell Riley and Englishmen G. Campbell Morgan and F. B. Meyer, all of whom spoke at a podium festooned with the Stars and Stripes and the Union Jack.[32] The following Sunday, he outlined his ambitions to revitalize the church by renovating the facilities, capitalizing on the Sunday School and its large attendance, training teachers for the Sunday School, starting a Bible conference, and establishing medical dispensaries in each of the nine branches of the church. A newspaper dryly commented, "He will bring to the work all the energy, all the go, all the push, that our American cousins possess. We English are a wee bit rusty; Dr. Broughton is going to polish and brighten us up."[33]

In this sermon, Broughton also addressed the antislavery heritage of Christ Church. He acknowledged the work that Hall did in "freeing the slaves" and the reality of the Lincoln Tower, describing Lincoln as "one of the world's greatest statesmen." Calling his presence in Christ Church's pulpit "a remarkable coincidence," he explained, "Here I am today, . . . the son of a slave-holder and an officer in the Army of the Confederacy. . . . Born just about the close of the great war between the States, born of Southern parents, with Southern blood coursing through every vein of my body, and Southern sentiments and sympathies from my childhood engraved upon my heart. . . . However it goes to show how time changes thoughts and conceptions, and how the grace of God heals every breach and makes us one of all His creatures."[34] These words express a nice sentiment but a vague one, as Broughton left unexplained who or what had changed. Broughton probably meant that he accepted the abolition of slavery, but he was also comfortable with Jim Crow: "I don't believe in the mixing of races," he wrote in a published collection of his sermons, "but I do believe . . . we are children of one common Father in the spiritual sense."[35] He publicly condemned lynching, resulting in him being burned in effigy and the Atlanta Tabernacle vandalized, but Atlanta's African Americans were barred from attending sessions of his Bible conference.[36] What reconciliation meant for his London congregation is unclear, but for Broughton it meant accepting emancipation while maintaining white supremacy. To this extent, Broughton reflects the tragic bargain the nation made to reconcile the regions.[37]

Dixon and Broughton moved in the circles that contributed to the development of Protestant fundamentalism, circles that included a variety of transatlantic connections. In his groundbreaking study of the origins of American fundamentalism, George Marsden identifies four theological streams that fed into shaping fundamentalism: a defense of the authority and inspiration of the Bible; support for evangelism and world missions; holiness; and premillennialism, particularly of the dispensational variety.[38] Of these four, the last two were British imports. More precisely, the holiness teachings were of American origin but took root in England and were popularized through conferences held in Keswick in the Lake District before coming back to the United States and gaining a fervent following.[39] John Nelson Darby of the Plymouth Brethren movement developed dispensational premillennialism as an explanation of the prophetic passages of the Bible.[40] In the last quarter of the nineteenth century, both Keswick holiness and dispensationalism found U.S. adherents among conservative Protestants who attended Bible conferences, such as those sponsored by the evangelist Dwight L. Moody in Northfield, Massachusetts. Both Dixon and Broughton attended and preached at these meetings.[41]

While these four theological streams sound a lot like conservative southern Protestantism, one must be careful not to read current perceptions into southern religion of the early twentieth century. What distinguished this emerging fundamentalist interpretation from mainline southern Protestantism was the way in which fundamentalists wove the stands together into a tighter, reinforcing system and were more willing to go to the barricades to defend it. Southern Protestants at the turn of the twentieth century, to borrow Rufus Spain's description of southern Baptists, were "at ease in Zion."[42] In different ways, Dixon and Broughton tried to break through this southern complacency and draw southern Protestants into transatlantic fundamentalism.

Dixon's major contribution was through editing the first five volumes of *The Fundamentals.* In *Fundamentalism and American Culture,* Marsden suggests, "At the center of the interdenominational anti-modernist movement were the evangelists and Bible teachers of the dispensational and Keswick movements," a description that certainly fits Dixon.[43] Moreover, Marsden classifies the essays in *The Fundamentals* into three broad categories, one vindicating the inspiration of the Bible; a second defending traditional Christian doctrines; and the third covering a variety of topics like missions, Christian living, and personal testimonies.[44] The first two represented traditional Christian apologetics, though here the defense was not against attacks from unbelievers but against Christians who went too far in accommodating Christian doctrine to modern science and higher criticism. The last group seemed aimed more at encouragement than argument. Even in the more polemical essays of the first two groups, a moderate tone dominates, with debatable issues like the interpretation of prophecy and the Holy Spirit avoided. As Marsden notes, dispensationalists and Keswick teachers "showed remarkable restraint in promoting the more controversial aspects of their views."[45] The authors Dixon recruited for the first five volumes reflected the transatlantic character of the movement: slightly less than half (twelve of the twenty-six) were from the British Isles, Canada, and Germany. Including Dixon, only three of the contributors were southern: E. Y. Mullins, president of Southern Seminary in Louisville, and J. J. Reeve, a professor from Southwestern Seminary in Fort Worth.[46] Financed by two southern Californian oil millionaires, the Stewart brothers, individual volumes of *The Fundamentals* were sent to pastors and workers at the Young Men's Christian Association (YMCA), including those in the South.

If Dixon's work on *The Fundamentals* was more well known and only incidentally directed at southern Protestants, Broughton's contribution should not be underestimated, as he played a more direct role in introducing his fellow southerners to this developing system of fundamentalist doctrines. He organized a Bible conference in Atlanta's Tabernacle Baptist that took place every year from 1898 through 1914, and the transatlantic element was a prominent part.[47] The conference was usually held in late February or March, lasted for seven to ten days, and featured three to six sessions per day. Interspersed with meetings about Sunday schools, reports from missionaries, Bible studies, and prayer meetings were sermons explicating one of the fundamentalist doctrinal themes, and transatlantic preachers were featured in this part of the conference program. For example, British authors F. B. Meyer and Charles Inwood spoke on holiness, while Irish evangelist George Needham used a premillennial interpretation of history to refute postmillennialism. The largest crowd to attend a conference session, some fifteen thousand people, came to hear G. Campbell Morgan, a London pastor, give an evangelistic address in 1911. A crude measure of Broughton's appreciation of the British connection is that Morgan appeared at seven of the conferences, more than any other speaker.[48] Moreover, the large crowd at Morgan's sermon suggests a way of evaluating the significance of Broughton's conference. It was not a small affair but attracted regional participation, as newspaper accounts mentioned pastors and laypeople from outside Atlanta coming to the city for the conference. The success of the conference inspired imitation as other cities such as Galveston, Birmingham, Nashville, and Gainesville hosted conferences. Once in the South, the speakers at these conferences often added other stops in the region to their itinerary. Thus these conferences and the preaching tours of their participants helped build a southern constituency for fundamentalist teachings and alerted fundamentalists in the North and across the Atlantic to the reality that the South was a region where cultural values still supported a conservative interpretation of Christianity.

There is little evidence that Broughton's and Dixon's ministries in London had much impact on the development of British evangelicalism. For Broughton, his stay was too short (not quite three years: April 1912–February 1915) to have much of an impact; he seems to have been too busy trying to implement his ambitious program and was sufficiently troubled by illness that he did not have many opportunities to make connections with British evangelicals outside of London. In fact, he promised his congregation, "It is not my purpose to scatter my work throughout the country. I shall content myself with building up and maintaining my preaching and teaching centre at Christ Church."[49] Dixon, on the other hand, was in London for almost eight years (June 1911–March 1919), but the opportunity to play a role in redirecting British evangelicalism in a more fundamentalist direction was not realized as Dixon was, first, caught up in internal disputes with his congregation over ending the practice of pew rentals and using a piano instead of an organ to accompany congregational singing.[50] This is not to suggest that Dixon's energies were expended in squabbling over trivial matters, but besides the normal pastoral duties of Sunday-morning sermons and midweek Bible studies, he took on a variety of additional duties, not the least of which was editing the Tabernacle's monthly publication, *The Sword and the Trowel.* The first four to six pages were comments by the editor. To the extent that this magazine circulated among British evangelicals, Dixon indeed was propagating his American fundamentalist views on culture and theology, but he did not use his comments to rally British evangelicals to a specific cause or course of action in quite the same way that Spurgeon used *The Sword and the Trowel* during the Down Grade Controversy.[51] The largest obstacle, though, to Dixon developing contacts with British evangelicals and pushing them in a more fundamentalist direction was that in August 1914 he became consumed with shepherding his congregation through the trauma of war.

The impact of the war years on Dixon, though, provides a good illustration of what Marsden and other scholars of American fundamentalism have observed: that the war radicalized fundamentalists; that the irenic spirit that permeated *The Fundamentals* was replaced by a militant, confrontational stance toward doctrinal and cultural change.[52] Dixon had not shunned controversy earlier in his career: while in Brooklyn, he attacked Henry Ward Beecher for incorporating evolution into his theology, and in Boston, he labeled the hometown religious movement Christian Science "a sham imitator of the truth, transferred from India."[53] What the war seemed to do for Dixon was not change his thinking, but offer direct, dramatic, vivid proof of cultural decline sourced in modern thought. Whether it was the German invasion of Belgium, the sinking of the *Lusitania,* the slaughter in the trenches, or zeppelin attacks on civilians, Dixon saw these events as evidence of the fatal consequences of Germany's domination by a "might makes right" philosophy sourced in evolutionary theory. Responding to the Bryce Report, issued by the British government about German atrocities in Belgium, Dixon commented that "the story of lust, rapine and fiendish cruelty surpasses in horror the tortures of the Spanish Inquisition and the brutality of savages. The use of asphyxiating gases, the poisoning of wells, and the sinking of passenger vessels without warning all contrary to international law have been prompted by the same spirit."[54] For Dixon, that spirit had led Germany astray and came from a rationalism divorced from revelation: "Nietzsche and his school have taught her to repudiate the Decalogue, the Sermon on the Mount and everything else that is Theistic or Christian. Her conscience has, therefore, been made not by the preacher in the church, but by the scientist in the laboratory. It has become a coldly scientific conscience. Scientific skill is its standard of right and wrong."[55] Thus on his return to the United States in 1919, Dixon added his voice to the fundamentalist critique of 1920s America, offering his observations from his front-row seat in London of the effect on society and its moral values of Darwinian ideas.

Both men finished their careers in the United States. Broughton left London in February 1915, citing the deleterious effects of London's weather on his health.[56] Despite the affirmations of goodwill and appreciation of his ministry at Christ Church, the newspaper accounts of Broughton's time in London convey a sense that the pastor and the congregation were not as well matched as had been hoped.[57] Perhaps Broughton's ill health deprived him of the energy needed to polish the rusty membership of Christ Church. In any case, he abruptly resigned, leaving almost immediately and without the traditional farewell service. He returned to the South, accepting the call of First Baptist Church, Knoxville. Broughton served several other churches in the South over the remainder of his career, including another term at Atlanta's Tabernacle. He died in 1936.[58] Dixon left in early 1919, accepting an offer from the Stewart brothers, the financers of *The Fundamentals,* to support Dixon for a year of preaching around the world in exchange for three months of teaching at the Bible Institute of Los Angeles. This opportunity appealed to Dixon, then sixty-five and having been a pastor for forty-five years, because it would relieve him of the weekly administrative and pastoral duties of leading a congregation.[59] The *South London Press* offered a mixed assessment of Dixon's tenure. The newspaper believed that Dixon "moulded a religious influence, equal to that, perhaps, with which the late Mr. Charles Spurgeon was so closely identified," but also noted that the Tabernacle had no net increase of members while Dixon was its pastor and that the current membership was little more than half the five thousand members the church had when Spurgeon died.[60] Returning just once to the Tabernacle, in 1923, while on his way to the Baptist World Congress in Stockholm, Dixon divided the remainder of his years between evangelistic work in China and preaching in the University Baptist Church in Baltimore, ending his career in the region he had left some thirty years earlier. He died in 1925.[61]

The stint of these two Baptist sons of the South in London pulpits was part of a long historical tradition of theological exchange among British and American evangelicals. From George Whitefield touring the colonies in the 1740s, raising money for an orphanage in Georgia, to southern-born-and-bred Billy Graham preaching to crowds of sixty thousand in Wembley Stadium in 1955, the exchange between British and American evangelicals in general, and conservative southern Protestants in particular, waxed and waned over the years, with both the degree and the direction of the influence difficult to determine with certainty. Dixon and Broughton were reflective of the dynamics of this exchange in the second decade of the twentieth century: both subscribed to the way fundamentalists formulated the doctrines of holiness, premillennialism, and the Bible's inspiration and promoted these doctrines in their preaching and writings. Both had warm, close relations with British evangelicals and imported representatives to speak in their American pulpits and conferences. In a way, they were both too late and too early: too late in the sense that their basic theological orientation had been set before going to London and in that the time for a fundamentalist crusade had passed in Great Britain. The brevity of Broughton's tenure and the necessity of being a wartime pastor for Dixon limited their opportunities to push British evangelicals in the fundamentalist direction that their American cousins were heading. And in that way, they were too early: their work in introducing American Protestants to British preachers and evangelists and the doctrines circulating in this transatlantic exchange only began to bear fruit in the fundamentalist battles in northern denominations after World War I and in southern denominations after World War II.

Notes

1. The transatlantic element is apparent in even the most cursory readings of the major historical studies of American fundamentalism, but it has not been isolated and analyzed with the same rigor that Richard Carwardine gave to discussing

the revivals of the antebellum era in *Transatlantic Revivalism: Popular Evangelicalism in Britain and America* (Westport: Greenwood Press, 1978). In "Fundamentalism as an American Phenomenon, a Comparison with English Evangelicalism," *Church History* 46.2 (June 1977): 215–32, George Marsden analyzed the social, cultural, theological, and ecclesiological differences between British evangelicalism and American fundamentalism to suggest why fundamentalism flourished in America but not in Britain. Most of this article was incorporated into his *Fundamentalism and American Culture: The Shaping of Twentieth-Century Evangelicalism, 1870–1925* (New York: Oxford University Press, 1980*)*, 221–28.

2. The best source for basic biographical information on Dixon is Helen C. A. Dixon, *A. C. Dixon: A Romance of Preaching* (1931; New York: Garland Publishing, 1988), from which the following summary was taken.

3. In *Fundamentalism,* 118–23, Marsden analyzes the content and significance of the entire series without evaluating the specific contribution of Dixon.

4. On Spurgeon, see Arnold Dallimore, *Spurgeon* (Chicago: Moody Press, 1984); and Mike Nichols, *C. H. Spurgeon: The Pastor Evangelist* (Didcot: Baptist Historical Society, 1992).

5. H. C. A. Dixon, *A. C. Dixon,* 39. A. C. Dixon confessed, "It was from the sermons of Charles Haddon Spurgeon I gathered my first inspiration to preach the Gospel" ("Dr. Dixon at the Tabernacle," *South London Press* [hereafter *SLP*], June 23, 1911, 11).

6. See C. H. Spurgeon, *The Metropolitan Tabernacle: Its History and Work,* reprint ed. (Pasadena, TX: Pilgrim Publications, 1990).

7. "Mr. Spurgeon on American Slavery," *Liverpool Mercury,* Feb. 20, 1860, 4. Cf. Nichols, *C. H. Spurgeon,* 119–21. Note: all references to British newspapers (except for the *SLP*) were taken from the digitized versions available online at the British Library, British Newspapers, 1800–1900, http://newspapers.bl.uk/blcs/start.do.

8. Unidentified quote from a southern newspaper in "The Slave Owners Burning Mr. Spurgeon's Books," *Leeds Mercury,* Apr. 7, 1860. See also "Mr. Spurgeon's Sermons Burnt by American Slaveowners" *Belfast News-Letter,* Apr. 6, 1860, n.p., and "Miscellaneous," *Derby Mercury,* Apr. 25, 1860, 3. The bonfires continued into the summer in Virginia, according to *Leeds Mercury,* July 24, 1860, 2.

9. Nichols, *C. H. Spurgeon,* 120.

10. "Withdrawal of Mr. Spurgeon from the Baptist Union," *Pall Mall Gazette* (London), Oct. 27, 1887, 7.

11. Ibid.

12. C. H. Spurgeon, "Notes," *Sword and the Trowel* (hereafter *S&T*), Oct. 1888, reproduced at the Spurgeon Archive, "The Down-grade Controversy," http://www.spurgeon.org/misc/dwngrd.htm. Similar language can also be found in C. H. Spurgeon, "The Case Proved," *S&T,* Oct. 1887, "Notes," *S&T,* July, Aug., Sept. 1888, and "Mr. Spurgeon's Confession of Faith," *S&T,* Aug. 1891, all at the Spurgeon Archive.

13. See Marsden, *Fundamentalism,* 171–84. A basic outline of the controversy can be found in Dallimore, *Spurgeon,* 206–11. Marsden's conclusion is that Spurgeon's efforts to rally Baptists to battle liberalizing tendencies had little effect ("Fundamentalism as an American Phenomenon," 222).

14. H. C. A. Dixon, *A. C. Dixon,* 104, 107–9. Spurgeon was so impressed with Dixon's work that he offered Dixon a position on the Tabernacle's staff. Dixon declined, citing a sense of obligation to his American congregation.

15. Minutes of the Board of Deacons, Metropolitan Tabernacle, London, United Kingdom, Oct. 17, Dec. 12, 1910. I wish to express my gratitude to the staff at the Tabernacle for the opportunity to examine these records.

16. Ibid., Jan. 20, Feb. 27, 1911. The church had a membership of around twenty-seven hundred in 1911: Minutes of the Meeting of the Congregation, Metropolitan Tabernacle, London, United Kingdom, Feb. 2, 1912.

17. Minutes of the Meeting of the Congregation, Mar. 21, 1911.

18. A. C. Dixon to the Deacons and Members of the Metropolitan Tabernacle Church, Apr. 26, 1911, in ibid., May 23, 1911.

19. "Dr. Dixon at Work," *SLP,* July 7, 1911, 5.

20. H. C. A. Dixon, *A. C. Dixon,* 202, mentions Broughton's conversion under her husband's preaching and later quotes Broughton: "I was converted under his [Dixon's] ministry while a lad in High School in Raleigh, North Carolina" (282).

21. "Leonard Gaston Broughton," in *Baptist Biography,* ed. B. J. W. Graham (Atlanta: Index Publishing Co., 1917), 46.

22. Leonard G. Broughton, "Divine Reciprocity in Matters of Benevolence," *Golden Age,* Mar. 16, 1911, 15.

23. Broughton has not had a biography written about him. This outline of his life has been gleaned from a variety of sources, including Leonard G. Broughton, "Tabernacle Tenth Anniversary," *Golden Age,* Mar. 11, 1909, 1; Vivian Perkins and William F. Doverspike, "The Baptist Tabernacle," in James L. Baggott, ed., *History of Atlanta's Baptist Churches* (Atlanta: privately published, n.d.), 5; "The Baptist Tabernacle," *Atlanta Constitution,* Oct. 12, 1908; and James Adams Lester, *A History of the Georgia Baptist Convention* (Nashville: Curley Printing Co., 1972), 333–35, 345–47. Additional details can be found in William R. Glass, *Strangers in Zion: Fundamentalists in the South, 1900–1950* (Macon: Mercer University Press, 2001), 37–39.

24. On Meyer and his career at Christ Church and the various social ministries of the church, see Bob Holman, *F. B. Meyer: "If I Had a Hundred Lives, They Should Be at Christ's Disposal"* (Fearn: Christian Focus Publications, 2007), 73–99.

25. "The Rev. Newman Hall's Church," *Leeds Mercury,* July 5, 1876, 5, notes these ministries: "a school society, a mission, a benevolent society, a nursing auxiliary, a Christian instruction society, a city mission auxiliary, a school of industry for the training of domestic servants, almshouses for 23 women, a temperance society, clothing societies, penny banks, etc.," and adds that the church "intended

also to hold open-air services, concerts, lectures, and other counter attractions to the gin palace."

26. To be precise, Christ Church was the continuation of a congregation that began meeting in Surrey Chapel on Blackfriars Road in 1783. It moved to its current location in the 1870s. See Holman, *F.B. Meyer*, 71–72.

27. See this edition: Harriet Beecher Stowe, *Uncle Tom's Cabin* (London: H. G. Bohn, 1852). See also "The Whitsun Week of Amusements," *London Lloyd's Weekly Newspaper*, May 22, 1853, 8; and "Mrs H. Beecher Stowe," *Leeds Mercury*, June 4, 1853, 1.

28. See Newman Hall, *The American War* (New York: Anson D. F. Randolph, 1862). This pamphlet was a reprint of a lecture Hall gave in London forcefully condemning the British government for not supporting the North. For a contemporary account of the lecture, see "The Rev. Newman Hall on the American Question," *London Daily News*, Oct. 23, 1862, 3.

29. "Christ's Church Kennington: The Lincoln Tower," *Leeds Mercury*, July 11, 1874, 12.

30. Ibid. See also, "The Lincoln Tower," *Portsmouth Hampshire Telegraph and Sussex Chronicle*, Oct. 2, 1875, 8; "The Rev. Newman Hall's Church," *Leeds Mercury*, July 5, 1876, 5; and "Mr. Newman Hall's New Church" *Pall Mall Gazette* (London), July 5, 1876, 8. Cf. Holman, *F. B. Meyer*, 71–72.

31. Glass, *Strangers in Zion*, 49.

32. "Dr. Len G. Broughton's Welcome," *SLP*, Apr. 12, 1912, 8.

33. "Dr. Len Broughton Begins His Ministry," *SLP*, Apr. 19, 1912, 5. See also Len G. Broughton, *The Future of Christ Church, London* (London: Hodder and Stoughton, n.d), 30–31. This pamphlet is a printed version of Broughton's first sermon at Christ Church.

34. Broughton, *Future of Christ Church*, 5–6.

35. Leonard G. Broughton, *Up from Sin: The Rise and Fall of a Prodigal* (Chicago: Fleming H. Revell, 1909), 117.

36. Broughton, "Tabernacle Tenth Anniversary," 3.

37. In *Race and Reunion: The Civil War in American Memory* (Cambridge: Harvard University Press, 2001), David W. Blight notes, "Reconciliation joined arms with white supremacy in Civil War memory at the semicentennial in an unsteady triumph" (397).

38. Marsden, *Fundamentalism*, 32–39, 48–55, 72–80, 103–23.

39. In *Holiness in Nineteenth-Century England: The 1998 Didsbury Lectures* (Carlisle: Paternoster Press, 2000), David Bebbington traces the American origins of Keswick teachings and offers a provocative interpretation of their affinities with Romanticism (73–90).

40. In *The Roots of Fundamentalism: British and American Millenarianism, 1800–1930* (Chicago: University of Chicago Press, 1970), Ernest Sandeen details the development of this movement and its immigration to the United States (59–80).

41. H. C. A. Dixon, *A. C. Dixon,* 81, 141, records that her husband first attended a Northfield conference in 1885 and later became a regular speaker at them. Broughton claimed that "no greater influence ever operated on my life" than the experience of attending these conferences. See "Big Conference Is On at the Tabernacle," *Atlanta Constitution,* Mar. 16, 1901, 7.

42. Rufus B. Spain, *At Ease in Zion: A Social History of Southern Baptists, 1865–1900* (Nashville: Vanderbilt University Press, 1967). A brief but expanded version of this argument is in the preface to Glass, *Strangers in Zion,* vii–xix.

43. Marsden, *Fundamentalism,* 121.

44. Ibid., 121–22. Sandeen, *Roots of Fundamentalism,* 203–6, has a similar categorization of topics.

45. Marsden, *Fundamentalism,* 121.

46. This analysis of Dixon's authors was done by inspecting volumes 1–5 of *The Fundamentals: A Testimony to the Truth* (Chicago: Testimony Publishing Co., n.d.), available at the Internet Archive, http://www.archive.org/details/fundamentalstest17chic.

47. A detailed analysis of Broughton's work with the Tabernacle conference is in Glass, *Strangers in Zion,* 39–61.

48. Dixon also preached at seven conferences (ibid., 42).

49. Broughton, *Future of Christ Church,* 30–31. Despite his promise, he did find time to travel to conferences in Mudesly, Northfield, and Atlanta and published a collection of sermons from these trips. See Len G. Broughton, *Christianity and the Commonplace* (London: Hodder and Stoughton, 1914).

50. In "Fundamentalism as an American Phenomenon," Marsden reaches the same conclusion (222), but without discussing the specific circumstances that affected Dixon's time in London. On pew rents, see Minutes of the Board of Deacons, Oct. 9, Nov. 6, 1911, Sept. 9, 1912. The Minutes of the Meeting of the Congregation, Feb. 17, 1913, notes that the members voted eight hundred to four to abolish pew rents, but it seems to have been mainly a victory in terminology, as the same vote also approved a system of "seat subscriptions."

51. One exception to this observation is a series of articles attacking Christian Science beginning in the Apr. 1912 issue (see "Christian Science," *S&T,* Apr. 1912, 150), which he then delivered as a series of sermons in 1915 (see "Christian Science Assailed," *SLP,* Jan. 15, 1915, 5).

52. Marsden, *Fundamentalism,* 141–64.

53. Quoted in H. C. A. Dixon, *A. C. Dixon,* 149; on Beecher, see ibid., 126–28.

54. A. C. Dixon, "The German Conscience," *S&T,* June 1915, 263.

55. Ibid. See also A. C. Dixon, "The Ethical Bankruptcy of Modern Philosophy," *S&T,* Mar. 1915, 167–68; A. C. Dixon, "The Fury of Harnack," *S&T,* June 1915, 264; A. C. Dixon, "Zeppelins," *S&T,* Oct. 1915, 4; A. C. Dixon, "Two Civilizations in Conflict," *S&T,* June 1917, 161–62; A. C. Dixon, "Giant Bodies, Pygmy Souls," *S&T,* Feb. 1918, 34; and A. C. Dixon, "Darwin and Lincoln," *S&T,* Mar. 1918, 66–67.

56. In "Dr. Len G. Broughton," *S&T,* Mar. 1915, 169–170, A. C. Dixon wrote that Broughton had the flu every winter, with each year's case being worse than the previous, which contributed to weakening his heart. *SLP* first reported that Broughton missed some services due to an operation for tonsillitis ("Dr. Broughton Indisposed," Nov. 13, 1914, 5), then recorded, "He is suffering from an acute nervous breakdown associated with great cardiac feebleness" ("Dr. Len Broughton and His Flock," Jan. 1, 1915, 6).

57. In "Dr. Len G. Broughton," Dixon has this odd comment about Broughton's prospects on leaving Christ Church for a southern congregation: "Dr. Broughton will find himself on his native heath among friends who love and admire him for his own and his work's sake" (170), which could imply that Londoners did not appreciate his efforts. Furthermore, *SLP* recorded that the church had a "serious financial deficit" at the beginning of 1915 and noted that some members seemed not to care for Broughton's "American stories" ("Dr. Len Broughton and His Flock," 6).

58. James L. Baggott, *Meet 1000 Atlanta Baptist Ministers, 1843–1973* (Atlanta: James L. Baggott, 1973), 33–34.

59. "Dr. Dixon Resigns," *SLP,* Jan. 24, 1919, 5; cf., H. C. A. Dixon, *A. C. Dixon,* 239.

60. "Dr. Dixon's Farewell," *SLP,* Apr. 4, 1919, 5. An inspection of the Minutes of the Meeting of the Congregation, which recorded the membership gains and losses, confirms the newspaper's account: 1,054 people joined the church during Dixon's pastorate (some three-quarters by baptism or profession of faith), while 1,238 left (34 percent transferred to a different church, 19 percent were removed from membership for nonattendance, and 37 percent died).

61. H. C. A. Dixon, *A. C. Dixon,* 242–95.

10

Europeans Interpret the American South of the Civil War Era

How British and French Critics Received *The Birth of a Nation* (1915) and *Gone With the Wind* (1939)

Melvyn Stokes

Since World War I, the market for films in Europe has been dominated by films produced in the United States. This has often been seen as exemplifying a process of "Americanization" in which American ideas, culture, values, and lifestyle have spread across the globe. Yet "America" on film is very much a generalized construct on the part of non-Americans. American films have often foregrounded diverse cultural and ethnic differences and regional diversities. One of the most obvious expressions of the latter has been the ways in which the South has been represented in the movies as a very distinctive region. The South's own history provided the basis for this representation. It resisted the American national narrative, first, by clinging to its "peculiar institution" of African American slavery for many years after it had been abolished in the North; second, by attempting to break up that national narrative completely by seceding from the United States; and third, by resisting the will of the federal government during the Reconstruction era that followed the war. Far from effectively being "reconstructed," the South emerged from the war shorn of slavery but with its society, politics, and culture still for the most part very different from elsewhere in the United States.

The Birth of a Nation (1915) (*La naissance d'une nation*) and *Gone With the Wind* (1939) (*Autant en emporte le vent*) were the two most commercially successful American films of their time and perhaps, if adjusted for inflation, of all time. This essay will analyze how British and French critics and commentators interpreted the ways in which both films represented the South in the Civil War era. British and French reviewers of *The Birth of a Nation* and *Gone With the Wind* inevitably explored the two films—and especially their presentation of race in the South—through the perspective of their own societies and cultures. There were a number of reasons why the two films, with their representation of the American South, should have been of particular interest in France and Britain. Both countries were colonial powers with large empires. They governed millions of people from different races. Both were pioneers in the abolition of African slavery: France initially in 1789 and, following its restoration by Napoleon, definitively in 1848; Britain in 1833. Both had a traditional interest in the American South: many British and French writers—including Frances Trollope, Fanny Kemble, Charles Dickens, François-René de Chateaubriand, and Alexis de Tocqueville—had traveled in and written about the region. Both countries, moreover, had fought as allies in World War I and (more briefly) in World War II.

This latter point is of considerable relevance because the manner in which British and French critics read the two films—and the different sensibilities this revealed—had much to do with the times when they were viewed. Both these films dealing with the American Civil War period were themselves made against a background of war. David W. Griffith, the director of *The Birth of a Nation,* began shooting his film on July 4, 1914, a week after the assassination of Archduke Franz Ferdinand in Sarajevo triggered the chain of events that led to World War I. Principal photography on *Gone With the Wind* began on January 26, 1939, and production ended on November 11, ten weeks after the start of World War II. *The Birth of a Nation,* which premièred in Los Angeles on February 8, 1915, was first shown in Britain seven and a half months later. It was not actually released in France until eight years later, in the summer of 1923. The French time lag in respect to *Gone With the Wind* was even greater. It had its Atlanta première on December 15, 1939, and opened in London on April 18, 1940. It was not released in France until May 1950, just over a decade later. The first point to make, therefore, is that each of these films—dealing with the Civil War and its aftermath—was shown in Britain during a war that heavily influenced the manner in which it was received and interpreted. Equally, each was released in France during a postwar era that also considerably influenced how it was constructed by French reviewers and spectators.

The Birth of a Nation in Britain

The Birth of a Nation is the story of two American families, the Camerons from the South and the Stonemans from the North, set principally in the South against the backcloth of the immediately antebellum period, the Civil War, and the Reconstruction era. Early in the film, two Stoneman brothers, Phil and Tod, visit the Camerons' slave plantation. Dr. Cameron, the head of the family, is described as "the kindly master of Cameron Hall." Clearly, it is suggested, he treats his slaves with compassion and thoughtfulness. This point is underlined when the visiting Stonemans are taken to see the slave quarters. An intertitle emphasizes that the slaves have "a two-hour interval for dinner, out of a working day from six till six." The slaves are obviously not exploited by the Camerons and respond with affection to their benevolent care. Subsequently the Civil War (presented by the film as a clash between state sovereignty and the "coming nation") breaks out. The young men of the Cameron and Stoneman families go off to fight and—in the case of three of them—die for their section. The final part of the film deals with the Reconstruction period. With the supposedly benign restraints of slavery gone, black and mulatto men are in charge of the political process. But they also lust after white women. In the end, led by the eldest surviving Cameron son, the white-clad "heroes" of the Ku Klux Klan emerge to protect white southern womanhood and restore white supremacy in general.

For all its astonishing qualities as a filmic entertainment, the release of *The Birth of a Nation* provoked vigorous controversy in the United States. The National Association for the Advancement of Colored People (NAACP) launched a long campaign to have it suppressed, and it was banned for some time in Ohio and Kansas and, rather more briefly, in a number of cities.[1] There was little or no similar controversy when the film arrived in the UK. The national British Board of Film Censors asked for no cuts and awarded it a "U" (universal) certificate on August 5, 1915. This decision, James C. Robertson would later write, "is not easy to reconcile with the BBFC's new-found sensitivity to racialism within the British Empire as well as its aversion to excessive violence."[2] But, Michael Hammond argues, what was missing in the popular reception of the film in Britain—as opposed to the United States—was "a dissenting voice, a counter-argument. There were . . . no well publicized debates or objections to the film's racist representations, no attempts to censor or ban the film at local exhibitions and no public disturbances such as those which accompanied the film in the United States."[3] There may, in fact, have been more opposition to the film than Hammond believed: black South African Sol Plaatje was "horrified" when he saw *The Birth of a Nation* in London and—together with radical suffragists Jane Cobden Unwin and Georgiana Solomon ("who on at least one occasion publicly harangued cinema audiences about the iniquity of the film")— wrote protesting the film to the home secretary, Sir John Simon.[4]

To British film critics, *The Birth of a Nation* offered an instructive lesson in American history. Almost all of them accepted the central premise of the film's title: that a new and united nation had been created through the experience of Civil War and the attempted Reconstruction of the South. "The evolution of the nation's soul, the progress of a people's development— its conception in blood and tears, its stormy, passionate travails, and its ultimate birth—this is the real thrust of Mr. Griffith's picture," observed a writer in the *Bioscope,* a cinema trade journal.[5] Curiously, for those brought up in Britain who might be expected to be aware of this, critics ignored the obvious point that the American nation had really been born as a result of the American Revolution. In terms of the film's more general representation of history, critics singled out four issues for especial comment: the cause or causes of the war, the war itself, the process of Reconstruction, and the rise of the Ku Klux Klan.

It appears probable that cultural memory of the origins of the American Civil War in Britain was heavily conditioned by the legacy of the long antislavery tradition. "Most people in this country," wrote a critic in the *Pall Mall Gazette,* "would define the cause of the American Civil War as a struggle for the abolition of slavery. The conception is, however, inaccurate and misleading, and . . . [*The Birth of a Nation*] throws new light on this darkest chapter of American history."[6] Although Griffith's film begins with a shot of a slave auction followed by one of an abolitionist meeting, its main view of slavery is the one advanced in the sequences on the Cameron plantation: it was a benign system, presided over by benevolent masters, that kept blacks from giving expression to their more primitive passions (as they would do, with slavery now abolished, in the second half of the picture). So *The Birth of a Nation* undercut the idea of slavery as an unmitigated evil. It also offered the traditional "southern" view of the war as a struggle between states' rights and the growing power of the federal government. Consequently, observed the movie critic of the *Daily Telegraph,* while the film did not ignore slavery, "historical emphasis is laid at the same time on the issue of national unity on the one side against states sovereignty on the other."[7]

The same critic speculated that the scenes dealing with slavery would prove less interesting to the British public than those dealing with Civil War battles in the South. Judging by the response of other British commentators on the film, he was right. As late as March 1916, a commentator in the *Bioscope* observed that World War I "is being waged in virtual secrecy. Save for brief official narratives and vague newspaper reports, the darkness of Armageddon has been unrelieved for the spectator by any really graphic verbal description of its dreadful but heroic course."[8] To a people starved of visual images of how World War I was being fought, *Birth of a Nation* offered in its first part what many took to be realistic impressions of modern warfare. It depicted, declared one reviewer, "the shock of hostile forces in trench fighting and in the open field, the bursting of shells, the red glare of burning countryside."[9] The very scale of the film—what another critic called "thousands of uniformed combatants struggling and swaying in long, locked lines over miles of territory"—gave many writers what appeared an accurate impression of the Western Front. To a number of critics, *Birth of a Nation* was also very effective in bringing home the personal tragedies of the war: the family told that a son had fallen in battle, the anxiety of those waiting at home, the "human wreckage" in a field hospital, and the "chaotic desolation" of bodies in a ditch—a shot described in an ironic intertitle as "War's Peace."[10]

There was a general agreement among reviewers that the second part of the film, dealing with the Reconstruction era, would be even less familiar to British spectators than the first. It introduced a historical episode, pointed out the critic of *Reynolds's Newspaper,* that was "comparatively so recent, and of which the average well-educated Englishman probably knows less than he does of the Punic Wars."[11] In the light of this ignorance, there was little or no resistance to the view that Reconstruction had reversed traditional relationships between blacks and whites, according African Americans what the *Times* called "a temporary dominance."[12] Most British critics seemed to have accepted the assumption of white supremacy: to the reviewer of the *Sunday Times,* Reconstruction had been a "vain effort to raise black to the equal of the white." They sympathized with what the

Times termed "the incredible sufferings of the whites at the hands of the liberated and deluded blacks."[13] It seemed clear to several reviewers that African Americans fresh from the cotton fields were incapable of exercising political power—one described the film's sequence set in the South Carolina legislature as "the riotous assembly of negroes from the Southern plantations."[14]

Critics were nearly unanimous in their enthusiasm for the visual appeal and what they perceived as the justifiable behavior of the Ku Klux Klan. The *Times* critic wrote of "the formation of that strange, romantic, somehow intensely American affair, the Ku Klux Klan, whose members, disguised in strange medieval garments—something of the Knight Templar, something of the brother of the Miserere, and something of the ordinary ghost—rode to and fro about the country on the new crusade of rescuing the oppressed whites from their horrible tyrants."[15] To the *Observer,* they were "that wonderful secret society . . . which delivered the white people from the tyranny of the blacks." The *Bioscope* hailed "the untameable spirit of these nineteenth-century Crusaders," and the *Era* praised their doings as being, like the whole film, "magnificent" in scale.[16] Only one critic seems to have restrained his enthusiasm for the Klan and its campaigns: the reviewer for the left-wing *Reynolds' Newspaper* commented of the film's portrayal of a race war in the South that "I fancy it is a wee-bit one-sided, and that the Ku Klux Klan is idealized."[17]

The Birth of a Nation in France

If *The Birth of a Nation* had been released at the same time in France as in Britain, it is likely that it would have been screened without difficulty. But by the time it was announced for exhibition in France a year later, in September 1916, a new wartime system of censorship had been introduced.[18] The French censors refused to grant the visa that would have permitted the film to be shown. Since the records of their deliberations have not survived, we can speculate that the realistic pictures of warfare that appealed to a number of British critics had the opposite effect on French censors. There were, indeed, strong antiwar tones to several sequences that could well have disturbed the censors. They were probably also aware of the large number of colored soldiers fighting in the French army: a total of 449,000 combatants had been recruited from the colonies, compared to a total mobilization of 7,948,000 from mainland France. The possible impact of *Birth of a*

Nation's unflattering representation of blacks on race relations (and hence on the ability of the French army to fight) may have been a factor in their decision to withhold a visa.[19]

It would not be until over six years later—in December 1922—that a new censorship commission issued a visa allowing *Birth*'s exhibition.[20] There was then a delay of several months more before the film was finally released. On August 17, 1923, *The Birth of a Nation* finally began to be shown to ordinary moviegoers at the Salle Marivaux cinema in Paris's second arrondissement. Business was brisk: at this and the next three performances, hundreds of customers were turned away. But on the morning of August 19, a large squad of police arrived at the theater with an order from the prefect of police banning the film as a threat to public order.[21]

The immediate background to the suppression of the film was the rapid expansion of postwar tourism. The year 1923 saw thousands of American tourists arriving in Paris. Many came from the South.[22] But whichever part of the United States they came from, it is clear that many brought with them some fairly intolerant racial views. They objected to having to meet and socialize with black people in nightclubs, bars, restaurants, and cabarets. Consequently, the summer of 1923 saw a series of racial incidents. There were a number of fights between white and black Americans when the former tried to throw the latter out of bars.[23] White Americans also frequently attacked colored people from the French colonies, prompting a major political storm.

In an article published on July 24, Georges Boussenot, a black deputy from Réunion, issued a public appeal to American tourists to respect French laws on equality, including that of race. In the process, he evoked memories of World War I as "the epoch when white American soldiers and colored French troops lived together on the front line, side by side, subject to the same tests, the same dangers, getting along with one another in a spirit of brotherhood that ignored issues of race." Boussenot went on to reference specific examples of this interracial fighting alliance: at Rheims, Chateau Thierry, and Longpont. How could white Americans, he asked, out of "simple racial prejudice," see it as undesirable to mix with colored Frenchmen who had once been their allies and neighbors? In his public appeal, Boussenot connected with the lingering French sense of gratitude to troops from the colonies who had fought for France in the war. But he also presented a heavily overidealized view of race relations in France. The warm welcome accorded by the French during the war to colonial troops had not been matched by the treatment of the three hundred thousand colonial subjects who came to France as workers rather than soldiers. Concentrated in camps outside major cities, they experienced racial prejudice and, at times, racial violence.[24] In the wake of Boussenot's article, however, the French government responded: on July 31, 1923, the Ministry of Foreign Affairs released an official statement warning that, if such incidents continued, "sanctions will be taken."[25]

The first performances of *The Birth of a Nation* just over two weeks later consequently took place in a highly charged racial and political atmosphere. Two black members of the National Assembly, Boussenot himself and Gratien Candace from Guadeloupe, attended one of the first showings and promptly complained about the film to ministers.[26] There was clearly intense political pressure on the government to have the film banned as a production that justified the kind of color-line segregation some American tourists were attempting to introduce in Paris.[27]

As was common practice in France in the early 1920s, *The Birth of a Nation* had been previewed to film critics from newspapers and the cinema trade press on June 6, ten weeks before it opened at the Marivaux Theatre. Even more so than their British counterparts, many French critics accepted that *The Birth of a Nation* was historically accurate. Jean de Mirbel, in a long review in *Cinemagazine,* recounted the narrative of Griffith's film as if it actually *was* history. Other critics followed the same path.[28] In the daily arts newspaper *Comoedia,* Jean-Louis Croze differed in one respect: he saw the Civil War (referred to in France as the "War of Secession") not as a struggle between nationalism and states' rights but as the inevitable result of the South's determination to keep slavery and the North's wish to abolish it. Otherwise, Croze depicted the devastating nature and consequences of the war: it had been "an implacable struggle, [expressed in] bloody battles with their procession of ruins, despairs and bereavements. Hatred bred hatred."[29] Lincoln's attempt to bind up the nation's wounds had ended with his assassination. Instead of conciliation, radical Congressman Stoneman had given power in the South to blacks. Completely accepting (like other French film critics) Griffith's version of events, Croze asserted that this resulted in "an ignorant and pleasure-loving people profiting from extraordinary circumstances to satisfy their thirst for vengeance and bestial instincts." However, a courageous opposition—the Ku Klux Klan—was organized by the whites and after "heroic and perilous exploits" succeeded in restoring "law and reason."[30]

Like Croze, other reviewers challenged the "states' rights" view of the causes of the Civil War presented in Griffith's film. The anonymous critic for *Le Matin* saw the Civil War as a struggle in which "outraged idealism sought the ultimate safety of a race debilitated by ignorance and dark hatreds." It began "when . . . the North, resonant with liberty, stood up against the South and all those who . . . served the abominable school of slavery."[31] Some reviewers such as Emile Vuillermoz in *Le Temps* noted the contemporary relevance of Griffith's depiction of the Klan: *The Birth of a Nation,* he wrote, referring to the rise of the refounded Klan in the early 1920s, "also relates curiously to current events in that it shows us the historical origins of the strange brotherhood of 'Ku-Klux-Klans' which, for some time, has again become a subject for discussion in America."[32] Although Vuillermoz was less vitriolic in his comments on the role of blacks during Reconstruction than Croze, he clearly also accepted both the inferiority and the guilt of African Americans as portrayed in Griffith's film. "The Ku-Klux-Klans," he wrote, "would [originally] have been organized by some psychologically-aware patriots who, aware of the childish and superstitious mentality of the black race, had decided to strike the imagination of their persecutors with the aid of a theatrical production. As soon as a black man had committed a crime, he saw the ghostly riders appear, coming to punish him mercilessly. These riders, dressed in long white robes, . . . played the role of exterminating angels and terrorizing the blacks so that they were made little by little to return to order."[33]

With the suppression of *The Birth of a Nation* by the French government in August, the terms of debate on the film changed. In his letter to Minister of the Interior Maurice Maunoury that helped prompt the ban, deputy Boussenot accused the latter part of *The Birth of a Nation* as constituting "a diatribe that is as violent as it is unjust against the black race. It is not a question, we should understand, of representing individual and isolated crimes—the looting of houses, attempts at raping white women, etc.—committed by a number of people belonging to this race. No. It is a whole people who find themselves, in the final part of the film, shown in an absolutely ridiculous and odious light."[34] Reviewer Jean Clair challenged Boussenot's critique in *L'Ère Nouvelle.* Dismissing the view of *The Birth of a Nation* as an indictment of a whole race, he defended it as "an impartial page of filmed history." Only Americans, he argued, could say whether "the facts related in the film are not a precise and rigorous reconstruction of what happened after the Civil War." The fact that U.S. reviewers had greeted the film with "unanimous praise" clearly suggested its historical accuracy. That Clair could assert this demonstrated his ignorance of the attacks on the truthfulness of the "history" recounted in *The Birth of a Nation* by a significant number of American critics. But he also arrived independently at some of the arguments advanced by those who had defended the movie in the United States. The crimes committed by blacks during Reconstruction, he argued, had been done at the instigation of white politicians (an argument advanced by Griffith himself).[35] It was also possible to believe that the black race—many of whom had fallen fighting for France in the war— was now "respectable," and no valid comparison could be made between "our colonial population of today" and American blacks of a period sixty years earlier. This argument, that blacks had been accurately depicted in *The Birth of a Nation* but had since made considerable social progress, was exactly, the same as that offered in the "Hampton Epilogue," a short film distributed by the producers of *Birth of a Nation* and shown after it in some American cities.[36]

There were a number of parallels in how British and French critics commented on *The Birth of a Nation*. Both accepted seemingly without challenge the film's deeply racist argument that a new nation had been born when whites from both North and South came together to defend their civilization against aggressive blacks. Since the true "birth of a nation" had been the Revolutionary War (1776–83), in which Americans—with French assistance—had secured their independence from Britain, this demonstrated a lack of familiarity with history. Both British and French writers also demonstrated similar ignorance of the Reconstruction period after the Civil War, offering no objection to the film's erroneous suggestions that the positions of the white and black races had effectively been reversed and that the newly dominant African Americans had persecuted whites. Finally, critics from Britain (with one mildly dissenting voice) and France accepted without question the distorted view of the Ku Klux Klan in *The Birth of a Nation* as an organization dedicated to the rescue of southern whites from black tyranny.

British and French reviewers differed in their comments on *Birth of a Nation*'s explanation for the outbreak of the Civil War. The film seems to have convinced many British critics that the war had not been fought over the existence of slavery (itself shown as entirely benign), but over the South's insistence on protecting states' rights against the growing power of the federal government. Among French critics, there was a clear consensus that the principal cause of the war had been slavery rather than states' rights. Analysis of the Civil War sequences also differed. In Britain, the shots of southern battles and fighting seemed to offer critics some hint—in the light of a dearth of both official and unofficial information on the conduct of World War I—of how a modern war was fought. By 1923, these sequences of the film had lost much of their impact: French critics tended to comment on the devastating physical and human consequences of the Civil War but paid little attention to the actual representation of conflict since, after a plethora of images about World War I in newspapers, magazines, books, and newsreels, these parts of Griffith's film now seemed much less original.

In the eight years after *The Birth of a Nation* was first shown in London in 1915, race became a major issue for the governments of both Britain and France. It was not yet apparent that this would happen in the United Kingdom in 1915. Soldiers from India fought for Britain in the trenches on the Western Front in France in 1914–15 but were withdrawn and posted to Egypt and Palestine toward the end of 1915. Raising black regiments from the West Indies only began after major losses in France.[37] Soldiers from the British colonies fighting in Europe during the war in any case attracted little publicity in the early stages of the war. There was no real comparison with the deep sense of French gratitude to colonial soldiers who had fought in France. It was only after the war was over that British officials began to demonstrate concern over the racial impact of *The Birth of a Nation* in overseas colonies: in 1923, the government asked Will Hays, recently appointed head of Hollywood's Motion Picture Producers' Association, to block the exhibition of the film in racially tense South Africa.[38] In the same year, *The Birth of a Nation* was banned by the French government from being shown in mainland France. It was suppressed, remarked one reviewer, because it "treated the relations between whites and blacks in a manner contrary to the ideas of the government."[39]

Gone With the Wind in Britain

Gone With the Wind, like *The Birth of a Nation,* is set in the Civil War era, covering the antebellum South, the war itself, and the Reconstruction era. Unlike *The Birth of a Nation,* there are no sequences set in the North and little reference to politics in the film. In essence, *Gone With the Wind* tells the story of the era through the experiences of Scarlett O'Hara (Vivien

Leigh), moving from southern plantation life before the war through the struggles of the Civil War (shown indirectly rather than directly, as in *The Birth of a Nation*), to the impact of Reconstruction on native southern whites. The brutal and threatening blacks of *The Birth of a Nation* have gone, replaced by loyal house slaves who continue to serve their former masters once slavery has gone. The devastation and poverty brought about by the war are shown more graphically than in *The Birth of a Nation*. Reconstruction is presented initially as a struggle for survival on the part of Scarlett and the old plantation class, later as an era in which Yankee-type materialism triumphs for those like Scarlett who are determined never to be poor again. There is no suggestion of blacks dominating the South in the Reconstruction era—the principal threats to southern whites appear to come from northern "carpetbaggers," together with the white and black vagrants living in Shadytown. There is no Klan, only a vigilante attempt to "clean out" Shadytown. Ultimately, *Gone With the Wind* is about survival: by the end of the film, Scarlett has saved the family plantation, Tara; built up a thriving lumber business; been widowed twice; watched her daughter die in a riding accident; lost her best friend, Melanie (Olivia de Havilland); realized her long-time love for Ashley Wilkes (Leslie Howard) has only been an illusion; and been deserted by her husband Rhett Butler (Clark Gable). Yet she remains indomitable, planning to bounce back once she has renewed her strength by returning to Tara.

Several of the British critics of 1940 who reviewed *Gone With the Wind* obviously had Griffith's spectacular film of 1915 in mind by way of comparison. Griffith, noted the writer for the *Manchester Guardian,* "would have been proud to have directed" many of the action sequences.[40] But *Gone With the Wind,* as the critic of the London *Evening Standard* remarked, "presents not the birth of a nation, but the death of the old South," a world characterized by "elegant gentlemen and ladies, colonial houses, horses, hounds, [and] contented slaves."[41] The film's opening sequences, pointed out the *Daily Mirror,* are set "on a sunny plantation in Georgia." Yet this "carefree South" (the *Illustrated London News*) seemed already static and doomed (the *Daily Mail* commented that the sequences at Tara appeared more like a picture postcard than a motion picture).[42] To the *Guardian,* the film's representation of the "Old South" emphasized its "chivalrous profligacy that dragged a dead civilisation into war."[43]

The British reception of *Gone With the Wind* in 1940 demonstrated considerably more awareness of the social realities underpinning the antebellum South than that of *Birth of a Nation* a quarter of a century earlier. The left-wing *Reynolds' News* commented that, in its treatment of the gracious world of the plantations, "the rotten reality of slavery [was kept] way off in the far, far distance." The opening part of the film, according to the communist *Daily Worker,* was "given over to nostalgic admiration of the airs and graces of the Southern slaveocracy." Yet this indictment of slavery as an institution spread across the political spectrum. The South shown in *Gone With the Wind,* remarked the more right-wing *News of the World,* was "peopled with aristocrats living luxuriously on the labours of their negro slaves."[44]

In terms of *Gone With the Wind*'s representation of the Civil War, some critics took the film to task for its one-sided view. George Pitman of *Reynolds' News* argued that seeing the war simply as "the murderous devastation of the chivalrous and suffering South" offered an entirely "false picture of one of the greatest progressive struggles in history." Not only are the North and its war aims (preserving the Union and, eventually, the abolition of slavery) completely disregarded, but "the only Yankee soldiers who appear in person are either gamblers, blockheads, or looters." Jane Morgan of the *Daily Worker* similarly accused the movie of "ignoring the true nature of the war."[45]

Both Pitman and Morgan demonstrated that they were also viewing *Gone With the Wind* from the perspective of a nation that was itself now at war. Both described blockade runner Rhett Butler in contemporary parlance as a "war profiteer."[46] Other critics argued that some of the representations of war in the film were too harrowing for Britain in 1940. Two scenes in particular were regarded as especially disturbing: the hundreds of wounded and dead in the railroad yard at Atlanta and the (indirect) shot of the man having his leg amputated in the Atlanta hospital without an anaesthetic.[47] Yet some reviewers were perceptive enough to point out that there are no sequences of the film showing actual fighting—the Civil War provides only a background to the drama of the O'Hara and Wilkes families, which makes up the basis of the plot.[48] Seton Margrave of the *Daily Mail* noted that "the 35-day siege of Atlanta is dismissed in a sub-title," while Dilys Powell of the *Sunday Times* observed that "the military scenes which were the best part of Miss [Margaret] Mitchell's . . . novel have been omitted or hurried over."[49]

Powell had clearly read Margaret Mitchell's book. Many other reviewers equally clearly had not, since they insisted that producer David O. Selznick and director Victor Fleming had brought the novel to the screen just as she had written it.[50] It was not only that the film had removed much of Mitchell's detail on the Civil War. It also vastly simplified her story of Reconstruction after the war. *Gone With the Wind* the movie showed the "harsh, cruel aftermath" of the war. The South was "ravaged." The gracious world of the great plantations had been replaced by "grim poverty." In the "chaos" following the war, Scarlett and her dependents have to toil and struggle to survive.[51] In foregrounding the personal struggles, however, the critic for the *Manchester Guardian* pointed out, the film largely ignored all the historical ones.[52]

Gone With the Wind in France

Twenty-two days after the London première of *Gone With the Wind,* German forces launched the campaign that would lead to the armistice with France, effectively a French surrender, on June 25, 1940. *Gone With the Wind,* like other Hollywood productions, could not be released in France during the war.[53] But whereas many other American movies would be exhibited there immediately after the war ended, *Gone With the Wind* had to wait until 1950. This delay, according to *La Cinématographie Française,* was partly caused by the economic situation: the price of cinema seats was frozen (which severely reduced potential profits to MGM, the movie's distributor), and the cost of paying for Technicolor prints (in dollars) was prohibitively high. France, moreover, had a rule that foreign films older than two years could not be dubbed into French, and it took time to secure a dispensation allowing this to be done.[54]

When critic Jean Thevenot published his review of *Gone With the Wind* in 1950, he cautioned that 1950 was not 1939. Color films had become considerably more common in the eleven years since the film's first release. He also warned that the acting might now seem a little out of date.[55] Thevenot's anxieties were misplaced: French moviegoers were not put off by the film. Indeed, they flocked to see it in numbers that made it the most successful film to be released in France until 1966.[56] Yet many critics approached the movie, like Thevenot, with a strong sense of awareness that time had passed since its 1939 release. The war had claimed the life of Leslie Howard (Ashley Wilkes), shot down by the Luftwaffe over the Bay of Biscay in 1943.[57] Both the director of the movie, Victor Fleming,[58] and the author of the book on which it was based, Margaret Mitchell, had died in 1949.[59]

French reviewers, like most of the British critics a decade earlier, saw the film as a close reflection of Mitchell's work. Thevenot, for example, praised "the extraordinary fidelity of the adaptation, which translates the novel more or less word for word."[60] But the French critics failed to understand that the film differs in significant ways from the book in its representation of the historical South. The reviewer for *Le Canard Enchainé*, for example, suggested that—according to the novel—Georgia in 1860 "was a country of proud and indolent aristocrats, who drank punch in beautiful mansions constructed on the model of Greek temples, while their 'good negroes' sang songs in the cotton fields."[61] Such a view owed something to the film version of *Gone With the Wind;* more to other "historical" Hollywood films about the South such as *So Red the Rose* (1935) and *Jezebel* (1938); and very little to Margaret Mitchell, who disliked any notion of an "aristocratic" South.

Mitchell's novel balances the experiences of the Civil War against the private stories of the O'Hara and Wilkes families. In the film, the impact of the war is conveyed by a very small number of sequences. The few scenes the critics could recall are much the same as those identified by British reviewers: the shot of the wounded and dying in the railroad yards of Atlanta, the burning of Atlanta, and the amputation of the soldier's leg without chloroform.[62] These sequences are the only ones to hint at the true cost of the war to the South in human terms. Indeed, as the critic of the left-wing journal *Action* remarked, the famous crane shot of the wounded in the railroad yards was the sole moment in the film when it seemed to him "as if the Civil War was neither a heroic cavalcade nor simply a setting invented for 'a beautiful love story.'"[63]

Finally, the French critics echoed their British counterparts in not appreciating the extent to which the film alters Mitchell's interpretation of the Reconstruction period. To the French, the essence of Reconstruction was Scarlett's struggle to preserve her family's plantation. Her connection with the land proved especially seductive in a country that still gave a high priority to agriculture. To *Le Canard Enchainé,* Scarlett "does not hesitate to work her hands to the bone in order to cultivate the land of her ancestors." Pierre Berger wrote of Tara, the O'Hara family estate, that it "sticks to the heart of Scarlett and gives her, sometimes, a human dimension." More cynically, perhaps, Claude L. Garson hailed the appeal of a character "who becomes head of the family through the War of Secession and who, for love of the land, sells herself to three different husbands."[64] What none of the

French reviewers—any more than the British—noticed is that the political aspects of Reconstruction (the radical Republican regimes in the South) are reduced in the film to one mention of taxation (the three hundred dollars owed on Tara) and a single carpetbagger (Jonas Wilkerson). The Klan of Mitchell's novel is eliminated completely, replaced by oblique references to a "political meeting."[65]

This essay has examined the ways in which British and French film critics accepted or questioned constructions of the American South in the two best-known "historical" movies about that region in the Civil War era: *The Birth of a Nation* and *Gone With the Wind*. As Janet Staiger has pointed out, it is virtually impossible to know what individual members of movie audiences made of particular films at particular times. Yet through the analysis of how reviewers make sense of films and the meanings they attribute to them, it is possible to gain some insight into "how politics and culture interweave" and establish "not the so-called correct reading of a particular film but the range of possible readings . . . at historical moments."[66] Film critics bring their own national, social, cultural, and political identities to what they write and, in complex and mediated ways, often reflect the values of their time.

British critics of 1915–16 appreciated that *The Birth of a Nation* had changed the terms of debate over the origins of the American Civil War. The representation of the Civil War itself in Griffith's movie was reinterpreted in the light of British reviewers' perceptions of World War I. There was little inclination on their part, however, to question the account of southern Reconstruction in the second part of the film, with its depiction of the rule of ignorant and vicious blacks finally overthrown by the Ku Klux Klan. These thoroughly racist elements of the film probably accounted for its suppression by French wartime censorship and subsequent delay in its exhibition in France. When French critics finally got to see the film in 1923, like their British counterparts they constructed the Civil War sequences through the perspective conferred by World War I and accepted without challenge Griffith's account of the Reconstruction era. Several French critics, however, took issue with the film's explanation for the outbreak of the Civil War, insisting that the South's desire to keep slavery—rather than its championing of states' rights against northern nationalism—had been the essential cause of the conflict. On this issue, therefore, British and French critics commonly disagreed.

To British critics of 1940, *Gone With the Wind*'s interpretation of the history of the South until 1865 was far more questionable. Several reviewers criticized the "Old South" of aristocratic plantations as a society condemned to inevitable death by its own static, unchanging character. They also saw the gracious way of life of the white planter class as rooted on the exploitation of black slaves. To some, the film's concentration on the wartime sufferings of the South gave a biased and false impression of a Civil War that resulted in the preservation of the Union and the abolition of slavery. This more critical view of the South may have reflected a wider transformation in British attitudes toward race in general since 1915—and the changes accompanying the outbreak of World War II. Critics of the film would have known that the British declaration of war seven and a half months before *Gone With the Wind*'s first screenings in London had also brought much of the multiethnic British Empire into the conflict on the Allied side. The impact of this was probably much greater than in 1915: ten weeks after *Gone With the Wind* began its run in Britain, France surrendered, and Britain and its empire and commonwealth were left fighting alone, facing the Axis powers of Germany and Italy. In sharp contrast with commentary on *The Birth of a Nation* in 1915, some critics found the Civil War sequences too harrowing for a nation now itself at war. When it came to the representation of the Reconstruction era, only one British critic noted that the film had effectively bowdlerized Margaret Mitchell's novel by eliminating the historical struggles in order to concentrate on the personal ones.[67]

French critics, writing a decade later, did not question the film's historical depictions of the plantation South and the system of slavery in the way their British predecessors had done (although one reviewer criticized the stereotypical way in which servile African American characters were shown). Perhaps influenced by memories of the German occupation and the liberation of France (together with the knowledge that France was now fighting a "dirty war" against Vietnamese nationalists), French critics were much less disturbed than their British counterparts by the Civil War sequences. Some, indeed, actually saw them as too mild and unrealistic. In terms of Reconstruction, French reviewers no more noticed the absence of politics and controversial issues such as the Klan than British critics of *Gone With the Wind* had done.

Film critics from Britain and France may be forgiven for failing to come to grips with the realities of the Reconstruction period as a whole and how they were distorted in *The Birth of a Nation* and *Gone With the Wind*. The dominant American school of historiographical interpretation of Reconstruction, Bernard A. Weisberger noted as late as 1959, forty-four years after the first release of *The Birth of a Nation* and twenty years after that of *Gone With the Wind,* was still "the prejudiced view laid down around the turn of the century by [James F.] Rhodes, [John W.] Burgess and [William A.] Dunning, developed by [Walter L.] Fleming and some of the individual state historians of the period, and widely popularized, in 1929, by Claude Bowers' zestful work of imagination, *The Tragic Era.*" Although Weisberger drew attention to the work of a number of American scholars, both black and white, who had criticized the "Tragic Era" legend, he also observed that disproving its representation of Reconstruction as an era when corrupt carpetbaggers and native white Republicans ruled the South, blacks were illiterate and aggressive, and the South owed a huge debt to the restorers of white supremacy was "a challenge not yet met by academic historians."[68]

In the case of slavery, however, it can be argued that British critics of 1940 anticipated the historical revisionism of the 1950s, as epitomized by Kenneth Stampp's book *The Peculiar Institution* (1956).[69] Stampp attacked the historiographical tradition associated with southern historian Ulrich B. Phillips that perceived slavery as a benign and paternalistic institution, accepted by slaves as well as masters. Stampp saw slavery as an exploitive system that was resisted by slaves themselves. Where masters looked after slaves benevolently, this was only to weaken dissent or shield themselves from prosecution. The reception of *The Birth of a Nation* saw no challenge to the benign Phillips view of slavery from British or French critics. By 1940, however, several British reviewers—long before the publication of Stampp's book—emphasized that the elegant white plantation world represented in the first part of *Gone With the Wind* rested on the forced labor of black slaves. French critics did not address the same point (though one attacked Hollywood's traditional representation of African Americans generally). The world of 1950 was very different from that of 1940: the grip of France on much of its empire had been weakened by the war, and the postwar years saw growing pressure for decolonization. Protests at French rule had been bloodily suppressed in Algeria in 1945 and Madagascar in 1947–48. In Vietnam, France was fighting an increasingly successful guerilla insurgency. Film critics may have believed that, in 1950 France, race was an issue best avoided.

Notes

1. Melvyn Stokes, *D. W. Griffith's "The Birth of a Nation": A History of "The Most Controversial Motion Picture of All Time"* (New York: Oxford University Press, 2007), chap. 6.

2. James C. Robertson, *The British Board of Film Censors: Film Censorship in Britain, 1896–1950* (London: Croom Helm, 1985), 11.

3. Michael Hammond, "'A Soul Stirring Appeal to Every Briton': The Reception of *The Birth of a Nation* in Britain (1915–1916)," *Film History* 11 (1999): 353–54.

4. Brian Willan, *Sol Plaatje: A Biography* (Raven Press: Johannesburg, South Africa, 1984), 193–94. My attempts to research this protest were undermined by the Rhodes House Library at Oxford, which was unable to locate the relevant box of papers belonging to the Anti-Slavery Society.

5. "'The Birth of a Nation': An American Odyssey," *Bioscope,* Sept. 9, 1915, 1114–15.

6. "Scala—'The Birth of a Nation,'" 6.

7. "The Birth of a Nation," *Daily Telegraph,* Sept. 28, 1915, 6.

8. "Peeps at the Hidden War," *Bioscope,* Mar. 23, 1916, 1234.

9. "Birth of a Nation," *Daily Telegraph,* Sept. 28, 1915, 6.

10. "'The Birth of a Nation': An American Odyssey," 1115; cf. "The Birth of a Nation," *Sunday Times,* Oct. 3, 1915, 3.

11. "The Scala," *Reynolds' Newspaper,* Oct. 3, 1915, 8.

12. "The Birth of a Nation," *Times,* Sept. 28, 1915, 5.

13. "Birth of a Nation," *Sunday Times,* Oct. 3, 1915, 3; "The Birth of a Nation," *Times,* Mar. 23, 1916, 11.

14. "Birth of a Nation," *Times,* Sept. 28, 1915, 5.

15. "Birth of a Nation," *Times,* Mar. 23, 1916, 11.

16. "Two Famous Films," *Observer,* Oct. 3, 1915, 3; "'Birth of a Nation': An American Odyssey," 1114–15; "The Birth of a Nation," *Era,* Sept. 29, 1915, 7.

17. "Scala," *Reynolds' Newspaper,* Oct. 3, 1915, 8.

18. "Echoes," *Ciné-Journal* 370, Sept. 16, 1916, 7; Neville March Hunnings, *Film Censors and the Law* (London: George Allen and Unwin, 1967), 332–37; Jean Bancal, *La censure cinématographique* (Paris: Jose Conti, 1934), 94–97.

19. Jacques Chastenet, *Histoire de la Troisième République, vol. 4, Jours inquiets et jours sanglants, 1906–1918* (Paris: Librairie Hachette, 1957), 340, 342–43; Georges Sadoul, *Histoire d'un art: Le cinéma des origines à nos jours* (Paris: Flammarion, 1949), 119.

20. L[ouis] D[elluc], "A quoi servent donc les visas," *Ciné-Journal/Le Journal du Film* 731/n.s. 29 (Aug. 31, 1923): 9.

21. "La préfecture de police interdit un film," *Le Petit Parisien,* Aug. 20, 1923, 3; "Color-Line Discussion Has Sequel in Ban on 'Birth of a Nation,'" *New York Herald* (Paris ed.), Aug. 20, 1923, 1.

22. "Many Southerners Stopping in Paris," *New York Herald,* Aug. 11, 1923, 2.

23. *Chicago Defender,* Aug. 23, 1923, cited in Harvey Levenstein, *Seductive Journey: American Tourists in France from Jefferson to the Jazz Age* (Chicago: University of Chicago Press, 1998), 264.

24. Tyler Stovall, "The Color Line behind the Lines: Racial Violence in France during the Great War," *American Historical Review* 193.3 (June 1998): 737–69.

25. "Respect aux hommes de couleur," *Le Journal,* Aug. 1, 1923, 1; "No 'Color Line' in France Tourists Told," *Chicago Tribune* (Paris ed.), Aug. 2, 1923, 3.

26. Auguste Nardy, "Les incoherences d'Anastasie," *Le Courrier Cinématographique,* Aug. 25, 1923, 7; "Suit Threatened in Banned Movie," *New York Herald* (Paris ed.), Aug. 22, 1923, 1.

27. The day after the banning of the film, it was reported that the police had received their instructions to suppress it directly from French prime minister Raymond Poincaré. See "Un film américain interdit," *Le Matin,* Aug. 20, 1923, 1.

28. Jean de Mirbel, "The Birth of a Nation," *Cinémamagazine,* June 22, 1923, quoted in *Cinéopse* 48 (Aug. 1923): 626; Robert Perline, "La naissance d'une nation," *Lumière* 42.9 (June 1923): 5–6; Georges Dureau, "Où l'exces de prudence paraît être une faiblesse coupable," *Ciné-Journal/Le Journal du Film* 731/n.s. 29 (Aug. 31, 1923): 1.

29. J[ean]-L[ouis] C[roze], "'La Naissance d'une Nation' de D.W. Griffith," *Comoedia,* June 15, 1923, 4. Jean Clair also evidently had World War I in mind when he wrote about the film's "extraordinary deployment of men and horses, the frantic flight of populations under a hail of bullets, the burning of cities, the layout of battlefields, disconcerting in their rigorous precision, their implacable logic, the impressions of life that they release." See Jean Clair, "La naissance d'une nation," *L'Ère nouvelle,* June 10, 1923, 3. Emile Vuillermoz, by contrast, believed that Griffith's "tableaux of battles magisterially treated" was now passé, having been "'surpassed' by the war." See Emile Vuillermoz, "Courrier Cinématographique-'La Naissance d'une nation,'" *Le Temps,* June 9, 1923, 5.

30. C[roze], "'La Naissance d'une Nation' de D. W. Griffith," 4.

31. "Cinema—Les grands films—La Naissance d'une nation," *Le Matin,* June 8, 1923, 5.

32. Vuillermoz, "Courrier Cinématographique," 5. The day after the première of *The Birth of a Nation* in France, *Le Figaro* reported that President Warren Harding had given his support to state governments fighting violence committed by the new Klan, refounded in 1915. See "Le président Harding contre le Ku-Klux-Klan," *Le Figaro,* June 7, 1923, 3.

33. Vuillermoz, "Courrier Cinématographique," 5.

34. Boussenot's letter was republished in Jean Clair, "La politique et le cinéma: Le film interdit—Erreurs de bonne foi," *L'Ère Nouvelle,* Aug. 22, 1923, 2.

35. Ibid.; "Defends Film Production," *New York Times,* May 9, 1921.

36. Clair, "La politique et le cinéma," 2; Stokes, *D.W. Griffith's "The Birth of a Nation,"* 144–45, 224–25.

37. See Jeffrey Greenhut, "The Imperial Reserve: The Indian Corps on the Western Front, 1914–1915," *Journal of Imperial and Commonwealth History* 12.1 (1983): 54–73; George Jack, "The Indian Army on the Western Front, 1914–15: A Portrait of Collaboration," *War in History* 13 (2006): 329–62; Rozina Visram, "The First World War and the Indian Soldier," *Indo-British Review* 16.2 (1989): 17–26; Arthur A. Cipriani, *Twenty-Five Years After: The British West Indies Regiment in the Great War, 1914–1918* (London: Karia Press, 1993); C. L. Joseph, "The British West Indies Regiment, 1914–1918," *Journal of Caribbean History* 2 (1971): 94–124.

38. As usual in such cases, Hays explained that he had no legal grounds for doing so but gave assurances that the American producers would decline to distribute the film there. See John Trumpbour, *Selling Hollywood to the World: U.S. and European Struggles for Mastery of the Global Film Industry, 1920–1950* (Cambridge: Cambridge University Press, 2002), 146 nn1, 2.

39. Clair, "La politique et le cinéma," 2.

40. C. R., "'Gone With the Wind'—A Long Film," *Manchester Guardian,* Apr. 18, 1940, 4. In fact, producer David O. Selznick had considered asking Griffith to direct some of the scenes revolving around the evacuation of Atlanta but decided that he was still too controversial a figure. See David O. Selznick to Wm. Wright, Jan. 5, 1937, in Rudy Behlmer, ed., *Memo from David O. Selznick* (New York: Modern Library, 2000), 158.

41. Ian Costner, "The Story Hollywood Could Not Improve," *Evening Standard,* Apr. 20, 1940, 8.

42. Reginald Whitley, "Love Story Cost £950,000—Worth It," *Daily Mirror,* Apr. 18, 1940, 8; Ivor Brown, "The World of the Kinema," *Illustrated London News* 196.5271, Apr. 27, 1940, 574; Seton Margrave, "4-Hour Film a Money-Maker," *Daily Mail,* Apr. 18, 1940, 7.

43. C. R., "'Gone With the Wind'—A Long Film," 4.

44. George Pitman, "History, Forward Please!" *Reynolds' News,* Apr. 18, 1940, 10; Jane Morgan, "A French Revolutionary Film," *Daily Worker,* Apr. 22, 1940, 3; "Technical Perfection of 'Gone With the Wind,'" *News of the World,* Apr. 21, 1940, 8.

45. Pitman, "History, Forward Please!" 10; Morgan, "French Revolutionary Film," 3.

46. Pitman, "History, Forward Please!" 10; Morgan, "French Revolutionary Film," 3.

47. A. Jympson Harman, "Films Will Be Longer," *Evening News,* Apr. 19, 1940, 4; Margrave, "4-Hour Film," 7; "Very, Very Wicked, But—," *Daily Mirror,* Apr. 19, 1940, 13; A. M., "Famous Novel Makes 4-Hour Film," *News Chronicle,* Apr. 18, 1940, 7; T. H. Palmer, "Four-Hour Film Is Worth Every Second of the Times," *Daily Herald,* Apr. 18, 1950, 5; Isolene Thompson, "220 Minutes of Colour, Drama," *Sunday Express,* Apr. 21, 1940, 8; Dick Richards, "And the New Films," *Sunday Pictorial,* Apr. 21, 1940, 19.

48. Pitman, "History, Forward Please!" 10; Whitley, "Love Story Cost £950,000," 8.

49. Margrave, "4-Hour Film," 7; Dilys Powell, "A Film Endurance Test," *Sunday Times,* Apr. 21, 1940, 3.

50. Harris Deans, "Vivien Leigh's Great Triumph," *Sunday Graphic,* Apr. 21, 1940, 17; Thompson, "220 Minutes of Colour, Drama," 8; Costner, "Story Hollywood Could Not Improve," 8; "'Gone With the Wind' To-Night," *Evening News,* Apr. 18, 1940, 2; "Margrave on the New Films," *Daily Mail,* Apr. 19, 1940, 7; Harman, "Films Will Be Longer," 4.

51. Palmer, "Four-Hour Film," 5; Whitley, "Love Story Cost £950,000," 8; Paul Holt, "Vivien Shines in Biggest Part Ever Tackled," *Daily Express,* Apr. 18, 1940, 7; "'Gone With the Wind' as Film," *Daily Telegraph and Morning Post,* Apr. 18, 1940, 4; A. E. Wilson, "A Great Film," *Star,* Apr. 18, 1940, 4.

52. C. R., "'Gone With the Wind'—A Long Film," 1940, 4. Cf. C. A. Lejeune, "Gone With the Wind," *Observer,* Apr. 21, 1940, 9; Pitman, "History, Forward Please!" 10.

53. It was, however, shown to an invited audience in Paris shortly after the city's liberation in Aug. 1944. Critic Jean Thevenot, who was present on that occasion, remembered that the film was entirely in English, with no French subtitles, and that the screening was interrupted several times by power cuts. He also recalled that Clark Gable, playing Rhett Butler, strongly resembled Pierre Laval, a collaborator who had twice been prime minister under the Vichy regime. See Jean Thevenot, "Souvenirs d'un amnésique à propos de: *Autant en emporte le vent,*" *L'Ecran Français* 255 (May 22, 1950): 7–8.

54. "Sortie au Biarritz de 'Autant en emporte le vent,'" *La Cinématographie Française* 1364 (May 20, 1950): 14. Also see "'Autant en emporte le vent': Le superfilm aux 7 'Oscars,' sort à Paris après onze ans d'attente," *France-Soir,* May 17, 1950, 4.

55. Thevenot, "Souvenirs d'un amnésique à propos de," 7–8.

56. See Simon Simsi, *Ciné-Passions: 7e art et industrie de 1945 à 2000* (Paris: Editions Dixit, 2000), 2–44.

57. "'Autant en emporte le vent' au Biarritz," *Le Monde,* May 20, 1950, 9; "Autant en emporte le vent," *Le Canard Enchaîné* 1544 (May 24, 1950): 3; "Autant en emporte le vent," *Le Populaire,* May 22, 1950, 2; Pierre Berger, "'Autant en emporte le vent' empêchera peut-être Hollywood d'être oublié un jour," *Paris-Presse/L'Intransigeant,* May 21–22, 1950, 4; "'Autant en emporte le vent' a révélé deux femmes: Margaret Mitchell et Vivien Leigh," *Cinémonde* 823 (May 15, 1950): 11.

58. "'Autant en emporte le vent': Une belle réussite," *Le Figaro,* May 20–21, 1950, 6; "Autant en emporte le vent," *Le Canard Enchaîné* 1544 (May 24, 1950): 3; Berger, "'Autant en emporte le vent,'" 4.

59. "Autant en emporte le vent (C'est le cas de le dire)," *L'Action* 295 (May 29–June 4, 1950): 5; "'Autant en emporte le vent' a révélé deux femmes,'" 11.

60. Thevenot, "Souvenirs d'un amnésique à propos de," 8; "Autant en emporte le vent," *Le Canard Enchainé* 1544 (May 24, 1950): 3; "Autant en emporte le vent," *L'Observateur* 7 (May 25, 1950): 22; "Autant en emporte le vent," *Le Populaire,* May 22, 1950, 2; Berger, "'Autant en emporte le vent,'" 4.

61. "Autant en emporte le vent," *Le Canard Enchainé* 1544 (May 24, 1950): 3.

62. "'Autant en emporte le vent' au Biarritz," *Le Monde,* May 20, 1950, 9; "Autant en emporte le vent," *Le Canard Enchainé* 1544 (May 24, 1950): 3; "Sortie au Biarritz de 'Autant en emporte le vent,'" 14.

63. "Autant en emporte le vent (C'est le cas de le dire)," 5.

64. "Autant en emporte le vent," *Le Canard Enchainé* 1544 (May 24, 1950): 3; Berger, "'Autant en emporte le vent,'" 4; Claude L. Garson, "En quatre heures de technicolor 'Autant en emporte le vent' ne nous apporte plus aucune surprise," *L'Aurore,* May 18, 1950, 5.

65. The lack of knowledge of French critics about the Reconstruction period is perhaps surprising. One major French politician had a view of Reconstruction that was very different from that advanced in *The Birth of a Nation.* Georges Clemenceau, French prime minister, 1906–9 and 1917–20, had lived in the United States in the late 1860s. Between 1865 and 1870, he published a series of articles in the newspaper *Le Temps,* supporting the attempts of radical northern Republicans to extend rights and opportunities to former slaves. Five years after the controversy over *The Birth of a Nation,* these articles were published in book form. See Georges Clemenceau, *American Reconstruction, 1865–1870, and the Impeachment of President Johnson,* ed. Fernand Baldenspeger, trans. Margaret MacVeagh (New York: Dial Press, 1928).

66. Janet Staiger, "The Handmaiden of Villainy: Methods and Problems in Studying the Historical Reception of a Film," *Wide Angle* 8.1 (1986): 20. Also see Janet Staiger, *Interpreting Films: Studies in the Historical Reception of American Cinema* (Princeton: Princeton University Press, 1992), esp. 15, 93.

67. Powell, "Film Endurance Test," 3.

68. Bernard A. Weisberger, "The Dark and Bloody Ground of Reconstruction Historiography," *Journal of Southern History* 25.4 (Nov. 1959): 428, 447. It would not be until the 1960s that historical revisionism in relation to Reconstruction finally undermined the "Tragic Era" legend. See Kenneth M. Stampp, *The Era of Reconstruction, 1865–1877* (New York: Knopf, 1965).

69. Kenneth M. Stampp, *The Peculiar Institution: Slavery in the Ante-bellum South* (New York: Knopf, 1956).

11

Gunnar Myrdal
and Arthur Raper
in the Jim Crow South

Louis Mazzari

A unique relationship between two social scientists, collaborating at the start of World War II, provides a view of a particular intersection between Europe and the American South during a time of great crisis and change in both—a relationship that developed substantial and lasting benefits for both, pushing a wedge into southern race relations at a time of ferment and offering lessons about the resiliency of American democracy to a gravely imperiled Europe and an uncertain postwar world.

In the mid-1930s, race in America was so highly charged an issue that, when the Carnegie Corporation decided to fund an exhaustive analysis, it sought the most detached perspective it could find. Instead of going to New York or Chapel Hill or Tuskegee for its scholarship, Carnegie president Frederick Keppel sought the proverbial man from Mars, a social scientist from a nation with "no background or traditions of imperialism which might lessen the confidence of the Negroes in the United States as to the complete impartiality of the study and the validity of its findings." The most knowledgeable American researchers would be enlisted, but the corporation looked for a director of research from a nation "of high intellectual and scholarly standards," wrote Keppel—but a nation with no legacy of race conflict. "Under these limitations, the obvious places to look were Switzerland and the Scandinavian countries, and the search ended in the selection of Dr. Gunnar Myrdal, a scholar who had already achieved an international reputation as a social scientist and economist, a professor in the University of Stockholm, an economic adviser to the Swedish Government, and a member of the Swedish Senate."[1]

Myrdal was one of the architects of the Swedish welfare state, propos-
ing new policies concerning economic planning, women's rights, birth control, child care, public housing, and agricultural modernization. He would
go on to work on economic problems in the postwar reconstruction of
Europe, for which he was awarded the Nobel Prize in Economics in 1974.
In Myrdal, Carnegie had chosen someone known for his theoretical work
in social planning and the application of research and the development
of public policy. In the summer of 1937, when the corporation extended
Myrdal its invitation to head the most comprehensive study of race ever
conducted in America, it told him his research should be "undertaken in a
wholly objective and dispassionate way as a social phenomenon." Carnegie
claimed the aim of objectivity, but it had hired a liberal progressive and a
prominent and vocal critic of race-biology science in Sweden to study the
racial caste system in the most tradition-bound region of the United States.

And Myrdal took the South back to Sweden as proof of the durability of what he called the "American creed." In *Kontakt med Amerika,* he
intended to convince his own people of the resilience that accrued to the
American "national conscience," at a time when Sweden's finely wrought
democracy was being threatened by Nazism.[2] "The secret," he wrote,

is that America, ahead of every other country in the whole Western
world, large or small, has a living system of expressed ideals for
human cooperation which is unified, stable, and clearly formulated. The political belief system is not simply as among us, latent,
unpracticed principles which—in degrees of compromise—find
expression in the nation's laws and political order. Furthermore,
the principles have been made conscious and articulate in all social
levels. Every American has had them stamped in his consciousness.
In America we referred to "the American Creed" . . . in our conversations with both the learned and unlearned. . . . A poor farmer
in Minnesota, an ordinary immigrant in Chicago, a Negro school
teacher in the South can all give a full, satisfactory account of the
Constitutional civil rights and freedoms of the citizen. Each of
these people knows what the Constitution is and he knows which
parts of it are important to him personally.[3]

Published in 1941, with the Nazis looming, *Kontakt med Amerika* became a
Swedish bestseller. Norwegians read it as a "resistance book," writes Myrdal's

biographer, Walter A. Jackson, "prophesying the end of Nazi supremacy." Myrdal became the country's foremost authority on American society and politics. Europeans might see Americans as naïve, he wrote, but America was a heterogeneous, multiethnic, continental nation living in peace, while Europe was abandoning democracy and convulsing in war.[4]

At the same time, the turn of the 1940s was a critical time, not only for Europe's struggle between democracy and totalitarianism but also for America's race relations. While the transformation of Europe filled every newspaper, the American South was changing more quietly, but the Great Migration of rural black southerners to the urban cities of the North had come to comprise an immense force of great consequence.

Myrdal arrived in New York in September 1938 to begin work on *An American Dilemma,* and he quickly decided to pursue a project very different from what Keppel had in mind. He considered the American race problem so systemic, and blacks so central to the national identity, that he knew he needed to conduct a study not of a racial subculture but of American society as a whole. Myrdal's immediate experience and fear of Nazism sensitized him to the political elements of the racism he was seeing. "I was shocked and scared to the bones by all the evils I saw," he later wrote, "and by the serious political implications of the problem which I could not fail to appreciate from the beginning."[5]

Myrdal's study would be clear about its values. There was no such thing as a wholly dispassionate perspective, he believed. The best approach a social scientist could make would be to define and acknowledge the particular values he brought to a project. Myrdal was, in part, rebelling against the positivism of his preceding generation of social scientists, rejecting the notion that an accumulation of facts would yield an objective result. Part of what he considered "modern" social science was the investigation not only of data but of researcher bias. No way existed to eliminate bias, but it was critical to the usefulness of that science that the nature of those biases be determined. In the case of the American South, biases were endemic to the issue of race. Myrdal wrote to his researchers that "everybody seems to be aware of the fact that a great part of the scientific literature on the American Negro is 'biased.' . . . It, therefore, must be of importance for us to search critically the existing literature for biases. . . . Every 'practical conclusion'—every appraisal of the existing situation and every recommendation of change in it—assumes *premises of value* as well as premises of facts, and social sciences are by necessity dominated by practical purposes even in their theoretical stages." Myrdal's approach meshed with that of any number of American sociologists and researchers at the time, both North and South.[6]

W. E. B. Du Bois, Walter White, and Howard Odum would contribute to Myrdal's project, along with pioneering anthropologists Melville J. Herskovitz, Ruth Benedict, and Franz Boaz; pioneering sociologists including Robert Park, Charles S. Johnson, John Dollard, Hortense Powdermaker, Rupert Vance, and Guy Johnson; and a number of other prominent figures, including Clark Foreman, Will Alexander, and Alain Locke. Many prepared monographs specifically for the study.[7] Among this group, recommended by Odum and Alexander, was also a North Carolinian named Arthur Raper.

Raper hailed from a white, southern family that farmed the rolling Piedmont of Winston-Salem, where his Methodist father grew tobacco, and his mother had grown within the communitarian tradition of the German Moravians. After high school, in the late 1910s, Raper had left the farm for Chapel Hill and eventually joined the circle of sociologists around the progressive Odum at the University of North Carolina. Of the so-called Chapel Hill school, Raper's politics were the most liberal, and he went on to work in the later 1920s and the 1930s with the Commission on Interracial Cooperation, researching and writing books that became classics of southern nonfiction. *Tragedy of Lynching* had an immediate impact nationwide, because of its provenance. It was the first study written by a white southerner to analyze and condemn race violence. And *Preface to Peasantry* used modern social science to puncture the moonlight-and-magnolias idylls of southern agrarianism in an assemblage of documentary research and observation on race and class in the rural South. He took time, too, to work with a number of New Deal agencies looking for ways to identify and address the region's social and economic inequalities for both black and white farm families.[8]

Raper was extraordinarily interesting to Myrdal because of Raper's work with the police and court system through his research for *Tragedy of Lynching*. In 1930, as the Great Depression took hold of the nation, it dredged up the old scourge of lynching. After falling through the 1920s, the number of southern lynchings spiked in the Depression's first year. The Commission on Interracial Cooperation, a private philanthropic foundation aimed at racial accommodation, wanted to investigate the social correlation between the dire economic conditions and the increase in lynchings.

So Raper spent a year traveling the South, investigating each of the twenty-one race murders—a liberal foundation's private eye, discovering the sociology of small-town racial violence in its most intimate detail, whose findings became a standard reference on lynching for the next fifty years. It was exactly this kind of research that Myrdal wanted for his study, and Raper was just the kind of southerner Myrdal wanted to work with to produce it.

Myrdal's experience as a magistrate in the Stockholm police court made him focus on the role of the police in the southern legal order.[9] And he saw an interest in the law as part of his own cultural patrimony of progressive European democratic traditions. As he wrote Raper, "Being a Swede, I, of course, attach a very much greater importance to the problem of law and order than ordinarily American writers on the Negro problem do." In *An American Dilemma,* he would state, "The Negro's most important public contact is with the policeman. He is the personification of white authority in the Negro community." He was appalled by much of what Raper presented to him: "These good-natured policemen based their view on what they conceived as their own 'experiences' of the Negro. Their way of handling the people was more distant from modern rational pedagogics than anything I have hitherto seen." And their interactions with the police were indicators of the institutions of law more generally: "This particular element of race relation would seem to me equally important in a study of the American Negro, irrespective of whether the problem was related to practical questions of possible reforms in the field of the race relations, or merely to the task of objectively interpreting the actual situation. It raises problems of how police officers are educated, how they are appointed, how their prevailing philosophy is created and maintained, etc.—all of them more general as they relate to the police institution in America."[10]

Myrdal wanted Raper to study those officials, who had been designated to carry most of the weight of southern race relations—"the Southern policeman who has been awarded this crucial position in the caste society." To Raper, the cop on the beat stood not only for civic order but also as the embodiment of the whole set of social customs associated with white supremacy. Especially in the South, a transgression of caste that aggrieved any individual white was conceived of as an aggression against white society and, indeed, as a potential threat to every other white American. "It is demanded that even minor transgressions of caste etiquette should be punished," wrote Raper in the finished study, "and the policeman is delegated to carry out this function. Because of this sanction from the police, the caste order of the South, and even the local variations of social customs, become extensions of the law."[11] He studied the symbolism and reality of black relations with the police and the various court systems. And he asked questions about the sociology of law enforcement. Who becomes a policeman in a southern town? What work did he do before he became a cop? What were their official and casual relationships with blacks? Had they killed any blacks? In what specific ways did the courts serve the racial caste system? How did Jim Crow work in prison? What extralegal pressures supplemented the legal system?[12]

In terms of shifts in the sociology of race, Myrdal and Raper agreed that technology was changing southern race relations by driving urbanization, while industrialization was eroding traditional social structures. And so were New Deal agricultural programs, shifting the structure of the southern agricultural economy by inadvertently pushing black and white sharecroppers and tenants off the land. By altering the economics of the cotton plantation system, the New Deal had struck the root of southern racism, the perceived need for a permanent farm peasantry. The decline of King Cotton had allowed other forces to weaken the foundation of the caste system.

Myrdal and Raper approached the project from opposite ends of the cultural spectrum. Raper researched the South from within. In a sense, though, Myrdal and Raper were equally confusing to most southerners they encountered. Few had heard a Swedish accent before or a white southerner's accent speaking with such conviction about racial equality. And yet Raper had a knack for disarming, rather than provoking, white conservatives, because he spoke the way they did. He just did not agree with them. At forty years of age, Raper had been preparing his whole career for *An American Dilemma*. And Myrdal, too, found in this project a culmination of all his social research and interest. His daughter Sisela Bok recalled his saying the book was "all that I had lived for!"[13]

Once Myrdal had recruited Raper and secured his leave from the Commission on Interracial Cooperation, the gregarious Swede and the droll southerner hit it off immediately. "He was a grand and glorious guy to work with," Raper recalled with enthusiasm. "One of the most resourceful I've ever seen." The more Raper talked with Myrdal, the more he felt they understood each other. "He was interested in what I could do," Raper said, "and I was interested in what he wanted me to do."[14]

Myrdal emphasized to his researchers the importance of constructing a comprehensive picture of the dynamics of social forces, focusing on the agency of each group of social actors. Like the Chapel Hill sociologists, Myrdal had an organic conception of sociology that required consideration of the parts and the whole at the same time. "The study," Myrdal explained in his introduction, "might properly be conceived, therefore, as an effort to interpret American culture from the viewpoint of the nation's most disadvantaged racial minority."[15]

Having worked in the South for many years, Raper had been reluctant to state so clearly in his writing his own perspectives on race and class, and neither Howard Odum at Chapel Hill nor Will Alexander at the Commission on Interracial Cooperation had pushed him to. But Myrdal was different. "How are you going to guide this person who's going to read this thing?" Myrdal demanded of his researchers. The genius of the Carnegie Corporation's choice of a foreign social scientist to lead the study was that Myrdal was not motivated by the idea of reducing racial tensions, as was the Commission on Interracial Cooperation. Rather, he took as his goal the task of measuring the practice of race relations in America against its principles of equality.[16]

In response, Raper gave fuller rein in his writing to his bent toward sarcasm and cultural criticism than he ever had before, and he employed the significant detail in narrative descriptions of the day-to-day, emotional landscape of black and white southerners as they lived out the intricate patterns of race and class and gender. "Funny to the white people, are the situations in which Negro men can get themselves," he observed at the start of a story that combined documentary and parable, "but the greatest levity comes when Negro women are involved," he noted, disconsolately, before telling the story of eighteen-year-old Bertha Nelson, who one day in 1940 stood timidly before the judge of the Atlanta Police Court, accused of stealing fruit at the municipal market.

> While the judge was writing the sentence on her card—$12 or twenty days—he turned with mischievous eyes to the arresting officer and said, "Is that big black cell downstairs empty?"
> "Which cell, Your Honor? That pitch dark hole in the ground?"
> "That's right. The one with the alligator in it."
> "Yes, Your Honor. I think it's empty."
> "Well, you run down there and reserve it for Bertha."
> While this farce was carried on, Bertha stared solidly and im-

passively ahead, and dignity lay in a young Negro girl in front of the bench rather than in the snickering judge behind it.[17]

Raper said he had never seen anyone treat white southerners the way Myrdal did. And for the rest of his life, Raper would remember his days with Myrdal down to the last detail. "I've seen a lot of people interview folks, and I've done a good deal of it myself," Raper recalled. "But Myrdal, here was a new dimension for me." Myrdal could get away with conversation that no American—northerner or southerner—could consider making. He took advantage of his status as a European; Myrdal's foreignness was treated by normally guarded southerners as simple curiosity.[18]

Alongside his pose of innocence, Myrdal had honed a keen ear for irony and hypocrisy that greatly appealed to Raper, who recalled an example of Myrdal's method. "We get down to Lowndes County, Alabama, and he says, 'Let's go talk to the sheriff.'" They bustled up to his office, and Myrdal seated himself in a chair across from the sheriff and started right in. "I'm Gunnar Myrdal. I'm from Sweden. We have nearly no Negroes in Sweden. I just wonder. I'm trying to understand—I'm here studying for the Carnegie people about race relations in the South—and I just wonder if you would tell me this. Why is it you're so afraid of them?" "Leading questions, just right to the gut," laughed Raper. "Now, if I had asked that question, the man would have said to me, 'You're baiting me,' having a Southern drawl somewhat. If I'd been from the North and asked it, why, I'd have been cursed for meddling."[19]

Myrdal played the innocent abroad, and his apparent lack of guile made his blunt questions palatable. He was simply wondering about this situation, and would the sheriff set him straight? "And the man sat there for two hours," said Raper, "and explained to him about why they didn't want their daughters to marry niggers." The sheriff explained why he had to shoot one every now and then. He told him why they had to lynch one every now and then and make a public spectacle. And why plantation owners had to rig their commissary books the way they did, and on and on. And when he was through, Myrdal graciously thanked him very much. He had been most helpful.[20]

"I saw him do that over and over again." Myrdal emphatically did not, as Raper said, "come around to it after you had gotten through with the family, and the weather, and this, that, and the other. He came right straight to the point. "'Why do you call them niggers? Do they like it? Does it do you good to call them niggers?' He asked them all." And their curiosity about him made them more open to his line of questioning. In just a few years, by the end of the war, gone would be the frankness with which the official South acknowledged and explained Jim Crow to a stranger from anywhere, even Sweden or Mars.[21]

Myrdal and Raper talked often about their confidence in the capacity of social science to advance rational self-government. Swede and southerner both subscribed to Enlightenment values and rational planning in a welfare state, as well as a practical bent in regard to sociology. Myrdal called science "nothing but highly sophisticated common sense." And he found in the Carnegie study a chance to advance "the old American faith in human beings which is all the time becoming fortified by research as the trend continues toward environmentalism in the search for social causation." The American attitude of boundlessness attracted him, its optimism matching his own confidence about the power of social engineering. "In a sense," he wrote, "the social engineering of the coming epoch will be nothing but the drawing of practical conclusions from the teaching of social science that 'human nature' is changeable and that human deficiencies and unhappiness are, in large degree, preventable."[22]

Myrdal was speaking of himself, too, and his faith in democratic institutions, and his attraction to the idea of a pragmatic America, when he wrote in *Dilemma* that "the ordinary American is the opposite of a cynic. He is on the average more of a believer and a defender of the faith in humanity than the rest of the Occidentals. . . . We recognize the American, wherever we meet him, as a practical idealist. Compared with members of other nations of Western civilization, the ordinary American is a rationalistic being, and there are close relations between his moralism and his rationalism."[23]

Myrdal would test both its moralism and its rationalism for himself, when he, Raper, and Ralph Bunche, the renowned Howard University political scientist, planned a car trip through Georgia and Alabama in the fall of 1939. Raper and Bunche, coguides on the trip, would end up contributing the most material among Myrdal's many researchers and writers. But the trip netted them several adventures, as well. The first told Myrdal a lot about what was possible and what was not in the Jim Crow South. And Raper's notes from their trip reveal that Myrdal's work in the American South informed Myrdal's views of European democracy during its fight against fascism.[24]

In early October, Myrdal and Bunche drove south to Atlanta, where

Raper lived and worked. The three spent a long day interviewing in the city, then had dinner at Raper's house in Decatur and drove the couple of hours to rural Greene County, where Raper had spent years working with black and white farm families. They planned to visit John Donald Wade, the southern Agrarian and professor of English, who lived near Greensboro, before traveling on to Macon, Tuskegee, and Montgomery.

In Atlanta, Myrdal had interviewed Dr. Hiram Wesley Evans, imperial wizard of the Ku Klux Klan, then spoke with Mrs. J. E. Andrews, who chaired the Society for the Preservation of the White Race. Andrews also wrote for the racist *Atlanta Woman's World* and Eugene Talmadge's race-baiting *Statesman*. Years later, Raper remembered Myrdal returning agitated from his interview with Andrews. Myrdal said she had returned again and again to the threat of widespread and increasing numbers of sexual relations between white girls and Negro men. Looking for proof, Myrdal had asked whether she knew any such white women. Andrews kept insisting in general terms on the prevalence of interracial sex. Myrdal was skeptical. "To make his point more strongly," Raper recalled, "he stopped her and said, 'Well, have *you* ever had intercourse with a Negro man?' This, he said, at first non-plussed her, and then she became very, very angry and could hardly go on with the interview."[25]

Myrdal had explained this over dinner to an incredulous Raper and Bunche, and afterward, the three drove out to the small town of Covington in Greene County in preparation for the following day's interviews. Myrdal and Raper walked Covington's quiet main street, now close to midnight, and Myrdal questioned Raper. "Why don't you run for governor here?" Myrdal demanded. "At first, I laughed," Raper recalled. "He kept pressing the matter, saying that even though at first a southern liberal would not perhaps get very many votes, that there was no other choice except for folks like me to get into politics. We talked about this at some length, and every time the subject was shifted to something else, shortly he would be back again insisting upon the importance of liberals taking an active part in politics."[26]

The next day, Myrdal talked with town officials, and they visited the county jail, but when they got back to their hotel at the end of the afternoon, they found Raper's wife had been trying to reach them: Mrs. Andrews had taken action against Myrdal for his indiscreet question. Her friend the sheriff had told her the insult to her honor was indeed a chargeable offense, so she had sworn out a warrant to arrest the Swedish senator and scientist. Raper called the county's leading lawyer, who told them the Greene County sheriff would have no choice but to serve the warrant.

"Gunnar turned to me," said Raper, "and asked what I thought the court would do in case they did arrest and try him. I told him, it was my thinking, on the basis of what he had told me, that it was highly unlikely that an Atlanta jury would do other than find him guilty." The whole problem, he said, "was more or less in keeping with things we were up against all the time." At that, Myrdal said they needed to leave, as quickly as possible. "The arrest and trial would be international news," Myrdal told Raper. "The study would be ruined."[27]

As they sped off toward the state line, the European social democrat talked about having gained a deeper appreciation for the intricacies and raw emotions surrounding southern race relations. Long into the dead of night, they crossed the Chattahoochee River into Alabama and out of harm's way. And Raper wryly noted that nowhere along the long ride or through the excited talk "did Gunnar reiterate his insistence that I run for governor."[28]

Stopping at a small-town hotel near Tuskegee, "we went to bed with the roosters already beginning to crow." But at ten o'clock the next morning, Myrdal stomped into Raper's room yelling about Runnymede. "Now Raper, tell me what in the hell does Magna Carta say?"

"Well, Gunnar, it says you can not be arrested without a warrant," Raper told him, "but Mrs. Andrews *has* a warrant." Raper remembered, "We talked then at some length about the means by which civil rights and personal liberties can be wholly ignored by a manipulation of the court procedures by persons intent upon using the court to further their racialistic interests." It had become as clear to Myrdal, firsthand, as it had been to Raper his whole life, that the courts themselves could often serve those racist interests.[29]

Largely because of such insights, *An American Dilemma* had an immediate and lasting impact when it was published in 1944. William Cooper and Thomas Terrill call it "the single most important book ever written about American race relations, a source and a stimulus for the civil rights revolution in the post–World War II South." A decade later, the Supreme Court cited its findings in their ruling on *Brown v. Board of Education*. In large measure, much of its influence came from its powerful statements of principle and values that abandoned the moderate course most white liberals had charted in an effort to keep peace with conservatives. Myrdal had started from the premise that, as Raper said, "people are people, and that one's as important as another, and that if we don't devise ways and means to see that none of them are handicapped and all of them are given development opportunities, the South and the nation will pay the bill."[30]

Thus, Raper's pragmatic idealism, as Myrdal would phrase it, considered America's race problem as a problem in the fulfillment of its democracy. "The main importance of the Myrdal materials, as I see them," Raper wrote soon after finishing the study, "is that they thoroughly document the well-known proposition that the Negro problem throws into relief and magnifies all our American shortcomings." And the very fact of the Carnegie study—a probing self-scrutiny of the flaws in its democracy—would stir encouragement to the pragmatic idealist in Myrdal struggling to support his own nation's democracy in Europe. He brought back to Swedes the exhortation that such an ideal, even fitfully realized, is worth honoring and fighting for.[31]

Myrdal found his outlook on economics changed by the project. Early in his career, his approach had been theoretical, focusing much more heavily on economics than on social factors. By the time he finished working with Raper and completed the Carnegie project using a sociopolitical approach—more pragmatic and American, so to speak—Myrdal had changed his perspective.[32] He would come to look back at his time in the South and write, "From then on, more definitely, I came to see that in reality there are no economic, sociological, psychological problems, but just problems, and they are all mixed and composite. In research the only permissible demarcation is between relevant and irrelevant conditions. The problems are regularly also political and have, moreover, to be seen in historical perspective. . . . It was during this study that I first came to realize the inadequacy of the equilibrium approach and to understand that the essence of a social problem is that it concerns a complex of interlocking, circular, and cumulative changes."[33]

Myrdal's work with Raper on *An American Dilemma* informed the rest of his career, including his subsequent development studies for the United Nations. Looking back from the standpoint of the 1970s, Myrdal saw the UN as having become less effective than expected in terms of its power to adjudicate political and military questions, but it had become more useful in the kind of work that he and Raper had studied together: the effects of inequality in rural and agricultural societies. In his Nobel acceptance speech, addressing development in the Third World, Myrdal continued to echo the convictions and holistic approach to social and economic problems that he and Raper had shared through their collaboration on *An American Dilemma*.

For his part, since the mid-1930s and the initiation of New Deal agricultural policies, Raper had been focusing on agricultural reform, observing the dynamic between a people's culture and the way they use their land, in what he called "man-land" relations. Myrdal would come to share Raper's socio-environmentalism and his belief in rural democratization. "Most important is to change 'the relation between man and land,'" Myrdal would claim in the Nobel speech, "creating the possibilities and the incentives for man to work more, work harder and more efficiently and to invest whatever he can lay his hands on to improve the land, in the first instance by his own labors. There are a number of auxiliary reforms—in regard to market organizations, extension service, credits, etc.—but without a land reform, which has been botched in most underdeveloped countries, they have proved ineffective to reach the masses of agriculturalists."[34]

By 1940, the New Deal was fading away, along with most of the rural activism of the region. Raper felt as if he were at the end of an era, believing that "things in the South were sort of running out." The once-energetic fields of regionalism and white southern activism had lost steam in the face of outmigration, increasing mechanization and corporatization, and an emphasis on war preparedness. Raper joined the Department of Agriculture and, at the end of the war, became part of the reconstruction of Japan, where he applied the same principles of land redistribution within a system of social justice to Japanese rice paddies that he had honed in Georgia cotton fields. From there, he traveled the Middle East and Africa during the 1950s, extending the lessons of the New Deal in Third World nations.

When Myrdal came to focus on Third World development, he found his belief in the power of social science had been bolstered by the results he had seen in the American South. Through his American experience, informed by his work with Raper, Myrdal brought home to Europe evidence of the ability of sociology to effect positive social change. He would come to claim that Raper and the rest of his collaborators,

> though often asserting in all good faith that their findings and teaching could not have any great practical effects on the development of interracial relations in America—were actually all the time efficiently bringing together and organizing the rational arguments for a fundamental social change. Indeed, they were making

it increasingly difficult for educated white people to continue to hold some of the stereotyped opportunistic views which were basic to segregation and discrimination. It is my conviction . . . that the work of American social scientists during the prewar period contributed mightily toward producing the driving forces for the dynamic development of interracial relations.[35]

And for the rest of his career, Myrdal would feel supported, his optimism buoyed, by the evidence he saw that the social science he practiced in the America South had helped create the conditions for the momentous changes of the civil rights movement. And his rapport with Raper—built on mutual feelings about democracy and humanity—endured as well. "I can quite see you," Myrdal wrote to Raper, once their work together was through, "talking kindly to everybody and finding out their sorrows and their secrets."[36]

Notes

This article is adapted from my biography of Arthur Raper, *Southern Modernist: Arthur Raper from the New Deal to the Cold War* (Baton Rouge: Louisiana State University Press, 2006), and uses source materials from the Southern Historical Collection at the University of North Carolina at Chapel Hill.

1. Gunnar Myrdal, *An American Dilemma: The Negro Problem and Modern Democracy* (New York: Harper & Bros., 1944), xlix.

2. Ibid., 124.

3. Walter A. Jackson, *Gunnar Myrdal and America's Conscience: Social Engineering and Racial Liberalism, 1938–1987* (Chapel Hill: University of North Carolina Press, 1990), 148. For a discussion of concepts surrounding the "American creed," see David Kennedy, *Freedom from Fear: The American People in Depression and War, 1929–1945* (New York: Oxford University Press, 1999).

4. Jackson, *Gunnar Myrdal*, 147.

5. Myrdal, *American Dilemma*, xxv. For background on Myrdal's project, see Jackson, *Gunnar Myrdal*, xi–xix, 312–29.

6. "Intra-staff memorandum on Chapter B in the introductory section: 'Critical survey over the history and present status of the research on the Negro in America,'" Arthur F. Raper files, University of North Carolina Southern Historical Collection, Chapel Hill (hereafter SHC).

Contemporary works of southern progressivism and racial activism in the Depression South, works whose views were similar to those of Raper, include Virginia Dabney, *Liberalism in the South* (Chapel Hill: University of North Carolina Press, 1932); Howard Odum, *An American Epoch: Southern Portraiture in the National Picture* (New York: Henry Holt, 1930); and Howard Odum, *Southern Pioneers in Social*

Interpretation (Chapel Hill: University of North Carolina Press, 1925). John Dollard's *Caste and Class in a Southern Town* (New Haven: Yale University Press, 1937) was a prime example of liberal sociology at work in the Depression South.

7. A number of involved social scientists and activists were progressives associated with the American regionalist movement, whose southern center of gravity was Howard Odum's Sociology Department at Chapel Hill. See W. T. Couch, ed., *Culture in the South* (Chapel Hill: University of North Carolina Press, 1934); Robert L. Dorman, *Revolt of the Provinces: The Regionalist Movement in America, 1920–1945* (Chapel Hill: University of North Carolina Press, 1993); Jack Temple Kirby, *Rural Worlds Lost: The American South 1920–1960* (Baton Rouge: Louisiana State University Press, 1987); Alexander Karanikas, *Tillers of a Myth: Southern Agrarians as Social and Literary Critics* (Madison: University of Wisconsin Press, 1966); and Willmarth W. Drake, *The New Frontier, based on American Regionalism, by Howard W. Odum and Harry E. Moore* (Chapel Hill: University of North Carolina Library Extension Publication, vol. 6.1, Oct. 1939).

8. Harvard Sitkoff makes an effective case for the efficacy of governmental and university efforts on behalf of black southerners during the Roosevelt era in *A New Deal for Blacks: The Emergence of Civil Rights as a National Issue, Volume I: The Depression Decade* (New York: Oxford University Press, 1978).

9. Beyond his focus on the police and law, Myrdal was accustomed to operating exclusively within government-initiated and -sponsored social programs; in the South, however, he saw in southern liberalism a knack for working through often-contradictory sources of power. For instance, the Southern Tenant Farmers' Union's (STFU) relations with the government proved both an alliance and adversarial at the same time. As Patricia Sullivan writes, "The STFU, in conjunction with its sympathetic supporters in the Roosevelt administration, succeeded in broadening the debate over federal farm policy and compelling the government to address the issues of rural poverty and displacement." See Patricia Sullivan, *Days of Hope: Race and Democracy in the New Deal* (Chapel Hill: University of North Carolina Press, 1996), 58.

10. Myrdal to Raper, Apr. 29, 1940, Raper files, SHC; Myrdal, "Introduction," in *American Dilemma;* "Excerpt from Dr. Myrdal's 'Memorandum on the Disposition of the Study of the American Negro,'" Oct. 5, 1939, Raper files, SHC.

11. Myrdal, *American Dilemma,* 535.

12. For *An American Dilemma,* Raper prepared an unpublished manuscript, "Race and Class Pressures," which covers the tenant system of agriculture, the legal system, prisons, lynching, the police and the courts, Jim Crow laws on trains, and labor unionizing in more than fifty cities.

13. Sisela Bok, "Introduction," in Gunnar Myrdal, *The Essential Gunnar Myrdal,* ed. Orjan Appelqvist and Stellan Andersson (New York: New Press, 2004), ix.

14. Daniel Singal, "Interview with Arthur Raper," Jan. 18, 1972, Raper files, SHC.

15. Gunnar Myrdal, "Memorandum to staff members and collaborators," Feb. 8, 1940, folder 1008, Raper files, SHC. Southern liberalism during the Depression has been the subject of numerous studies, often considering race and class issues as aspects of a similarly organic whole. See John Egerton, *Speak Now against the Day: The Generation before the Civil Rights Movement in the South* (New York: Alfred A. Knopf, 1994); John Hope Franklin, *From Slavery to Freedom: A History of Negro Americans* (1947; rpt., New York: Knopf, 1967); Richard H. King, *A Southern Renaissance: The Cultural Awakening of the American South, 1930–1955* (New York: Oxford University Press, 1980); Daniel Singal, *The War Within: From Victorian to Modernist Thought in the South, 1919–1945* (Chapel Hill: University of North Carolina Press, 1982); Morton Sosna, *In Search of the Silent South: Southern Liberals and the Race Issue* (New York: Columbia University Press, 1977); and Sullivan, *Days of Hope.*

16. Raper to Will Alexander, June 11, 1940, folder 92, Raper files, SHC.

17. Raper, "Race and Class Pressures," June 1, 1940, 103–4, Raper files, SHC. Raper had developed a documentary form of sociological research, which he applied in his work for Myrdal. In a memo to Myrdal, Raper proposed to present "a typical day at police court" through "a series of word pictures": "We would arrange to get verbatim all that is said, and pay particular attention to inflections, the manner in which orders are given, and other subtleties which make words meaningful. These court scenes will realistically relate the accused to police, judge, attorneys, bondsmen, witnesses, and courtroom audiences. . . . [for] all types of interracial and interclass situations in metropolitan, industrial, town, hillside farm areas and plantation counties." See "Proposed Study for September to June," Raper to Myrdal, June 1, 1939, Raper files, SHC.

18. Singal, "Interview with Arthur Raper," Jan. 18, 1972.

19. Ibid.

20. Ibid.

21. Ibid. Raper's collaboration with Myrdal, he wrote, "is the best piece of work I've done. I may have worked on it too hard, for I packed more than a year's work into a little over nine months. . . . It sort of rounded out, in broad outlines at least, my earlier research efforts—and such merit as it may have rests largely upon my earlier opportunity to get a rather comprehensive picture of the relation of race to economics and politics." See Raper to Will Alexander, June 11, 1940, Raper files, SHC.

22. Gunnar Myrdal, "Objectivity in Social Research," quoted in Myrdal, *Essential Gunnar Myrdal,* 72; Myrdal, *American Dilemma,* 1023.

23. Myrdal, *An American Dilemma,* introduction, lxxviii.

24. While compiling the project, Myrdal wrote to Raper, "I have had very much use of your manuscript; indeed, next to Ralph's voluminous studies, more of yours than of any other memorandum, as you will find from the published report. Being a Swede, I, of course, attach a very much greater importance to the problem of law and order than ordinarily American writers on the Negro problem do, and I

found a lot of stuff in your work. I think it would be highly valuable if you, in the future got the necessary time to write a comprehensive and penetrating study of the faltering system of justice in the South." See Myrdal to Raper, July 29, 1942, Raper files, SHC.

25. "Lest I Forget," unpublished manuscript, Nov. 10, 1949, Raper files, SHC.
26. Ibid.
27. Ibid.
28. Ibid.
29. Ibid.
30. William Cooper and Thomas Terrill, *The American South: A History* (New York: Knopf, 1991), 654; Singal, "Interview with Arthur Raper," Jan. 18, 1972.
31. Raper to "Mr. Causey," Dec. 2, 1940, Raper files, SHC.
32. For a broad sense of the American pragmatism Myrdal came to admire, see Dorothy Ross, *The Origins of American Social Science* (Cambridge: Cambridge University Press, 1991); and Robert Westbrook, *John Dewey and American Democracy* (Ithaca: Cornell University Press, 1991).
33. Gunnar Myrdal, *Rich Lands and Poor* (New York: Harper, 1957), 14–21.
34. Gunnar Myrdal, "The Nobel Speech," in Myrdal, *Essential Gunnar Myrdal,* 13.
35. Myrdal, *Rich Lands and Poor,* 14–21.
36. Myrdal to Raper, Nov. 25, 1941, Raper files, SHC.

12

Explaining Jim Crow to German Prisoners of War

The Impact of the South on the World War II Reeducation Program

Matthias Reiss

During the first half of the twentieth century, service in the armed forces was "a common form of popular mobility and the only form of mass travel the masses could afford."[1] For millions of soldiers in World War II, serving in uniform meant going to places few had ever been to—or sometimes even heard of—before. For many German soldiers, sailors, and airmen, the travel experience continued after they fell into enemy hands. By the end of the war, German prisoners of war (POWs) were interned all over the world, from Siberia to California and Great Britain to Australia. The last of them would only return home in 1956.

Over 371,000 of these accidental tourists ended up in the United States. The first large wave arrived after the surrender of the Army Group Africa (Heeresgruppe Afrika) in Tunisia in May 1943, and the last group was shipped back to Europe in July 1946. During these three years, most of them got at least a cursory impression of the South and its society. In 1945, for example, some 244,000 German POWs were interned in camps below the Mason-Dixon line, and several thousands more lived and worked in the Border States.[2] A large number of prisoners experienced repeated transfers between camps, so that the vast majority of them spent at least some time in the American South during their sojourn in the United States.

Security concerns were one of the reasons why so many POWs were brought to the South. The scarcity of big cities and the often-hostile land-scape made escapes difficult and offered few opportunities for sabotage. Financial considerations also played a role. The region already contained a large number of military installations or abandoned Civilian Conservation Corps camps that could be used to house enemy prisoners of war, and the warm climate kept maintenance costs low. Under international law, enlisted prisoners could be made to work for their captors, thereby offsetting some of the costs of their internment, and the War Department early on made plans with this regard. Already in October 1942, when there were merely 130 German POWs in the United States, a decision was made to build new POW camps in agricultural areas that suffered a shortage of labor and could therefore use POWs.[3] Many of these areas were in the South, as African American workers had been drafted or had migrated out of the region in search of better jobs, higher pay, and greater freedom.

The story of the "Nazi Prisoners of War in America," to quote the title of Arnold Krammer's standard work on this topic, has been researched in greater depth since the 1970s.[4] Recent controversies about the treatment of enemy prisoners at Guantanamo Bay, Iraq, and other places have led to a new wave of publications on how the United States has dealt with its captives throughout history.[5] Despite this long-standing interest in the history of prisoners of war and the fact that so many German prisoners were interned in the South during World War II, surprisingly little has so far been written about how the latter experienced this region. Most authors have shunned the regional perspective in favor of a state-centered focus, although the latter had no administrative relevance in the American POW system.[6] The Germans' perception of the Jim Crow system and their interaction with African Americans have also attracted very little scholarly attention so far, and most historians only point to the obvious fact that racial discrimination made the United States vulnerable to charges of hypocrisy.[7] In a similar fashion, historians discussing the situation of African Americans in World War II have focused on and uncritically accepted the popular wartime claim that the Germans were better treated than African Americans on account of their race.[8] The only work approaching the presence of German POWs in the United States from a regional southern perspective is still Morton Sosna's 1991 article "Stalag Dixie."[9] This excellent study discusses the impact of the South on the German novelist Alfred Andersch in greater detail but otherwise focuses on how the prisoners fitted into southern society. In contrast, this article examines how the prisoners' firsthand experience of Dixie and its economy shaped their view of the United States.

The Reeducation Program: Reasons and Aims

The U.S. government did attach some significance to what German POWs thought about the United States. Already in March 1944, over a year before Germany's unconditional surrender, U.S. secretary of state Cordell Hull argued in a letter to his colleague Henry L. Stimson in the War Department that the German prisoners' attitude toward the United States represented "a most important part of our problems of post-war security."[10] It was assumed that the POWs would "have a powerful voice in future German affairs," and a secret reeducation program was therefore started to "encourage an attitude of respect on their part for American institutions, traditions, and ways of life and thought."[11] In other words, the concern for America's standing among the German POWs confined within its borders was not the result of patriotic vanity, but part of a drive to increase American postwar national security by spreading U.S. liberal-democratic values around the world.

This article argues that the German prisoners' firsthand experience of southern society and Jim Crow was crucial in shaping their response to the United States and to the War Department's reeducation program. Since the late nineteenth century, many Germans had studied the United States in an effort to come to terms with the rapid modernization of their own society and to sharpen their sense of national identity.[12] As a supposedly backward part of the United States, the South had played very little role in the German imagination. German immigrants usually avoided it, and news about lynching further confirmed the impression that the South was "uncivilized," as the famous German professor Heinrich von Treitschke put it in a lecture W. E. B. Du Bois attended as a student in Berlin.[13] It was the fast-paced densely populated urban industrialized North with its consumerist culture that fascinated Germans, or its antithesis, the western frontier, which provided the setting for the hugely popular novels of Karl May. Respect for the United States' industrial capacity and high standard of living was mixed with disdain for the supposedly materialistic and volatile nature of American society. Nazi propaganda explicitly tried to strengthen these negative stereotypes while downplaying positive perceptions of the United States as the "land of unlimited opportunities," which also existed in German society, but with limited success.[14] When the U.S. Army's Psychological Warfare Division questioned newly captured German soldiers about their attitudes toward the United States, it found that "the average German P/W's ideas about America are a mixture of Karl May (extremely popular German writer of Wild West stories) and Josef Goebbels, with the whole picture overshadowed by a huge dollar sign."[15] However, it also added that such distorted notions were "usually somewhat tempered by a certain realism due to the fact that very many German families have relatives or friends in the USA."[16] The vast majority of prisoners of war realized that many Americans were better off than their German counterparts, but the "admission of America's high standard of living will be accompanied by a comparison of the number of 'Dichter und Denker' [poets and philosophers] produced by Germany and the U.S. respectively."[17] Most of the interviewed prisoners thought that Americans were driven by self-interest and the desire for profit: "Nothing is further from the German mind than to ascribe to Americans any idealism, either individually or collectively. . . . To him it is a country ruled by bankers and gangsters."[18] These negative images were, however, not deeply rooted. The Psychological Warfare Division concluded that "America has remained the land of opportunities and the object of sympathetic curiosity. 'Man moechte sich doch das Alles mal wirklich selbst ansehen' [One really would like to see all that with one's own eyes], is a phrase often heard by interrogators."[19]

Those who got the chance to do so were clearly excited about the prospect of going to America. As one of them put it later, "such a journey to the so-called New World, and that even for free, was something special during this time."[20] According to Reinhold Pabel, who was the first POW to publish his memoirs after the war, nearly all POWs were "quite curious to find out by own experience what the United States would really be like," although he admits that they all were "somewhat prejudiced."[21] The prospect of crossing the Atlantic often triggered a form of *Reisefieber* (travel disease). A German officer who was captured in Africa in 1943, for example, wrote in his diary after learning the news: "Thrilled expectation fills us, a tingling feeling of curiosity and uncertainty. . . . For hours we forget about the war and only have one thought: How will it be during the crossing, how will it be in America!"[22]

American officials were quick to recognize that this curiosity could be exploited. As Hull pointed out, the prisoners in America provided a link between the war and the postwar world. Eventually, they would return to

Germany and tell their stories, thereby shaping the image of the United States abroad. Plans to promote a positive perception of American society among German prisoners were discussed in the War Department as early as March 1943, two months before the Allies captured the first significant numbers of German soldiers in North Africa. However, the provost marshal general (PMG) who ran the POW program in the United States strongly opposed this idea. Among other things, PMG Allen Gullion argued that such a program was unnecessary because "the association of prisoners of war with American homes and their equipment and luxuries, through employment procedures, would do more to impress the prisoners 'than a teacher in a classroom or a lecturer from a platform.'"[23]

The idea of a reeducation program continued to float around, however, and it was eventually launched in November 1944, five months after Gullion had left office. As already said, the program's aim was to convince Germans of the superiority of the American way of life before they returned home. Assistant PMG Blackshear M. Bryan summarized it neatly when he told his subordinates: "Each man that we send back should be the expert on the United States for his home town so he can tell the people back home the United States does things. If he knows what kind of country we've got, he can't help but respect it; so it is our job to tell him the facts about America and not to beg him or coddle him into liking us."[24]

Sharing Hardships

The reality proved to be a bit more complicated. Gullion had failed to recognize that the German POWs often came into contact with American citizens whose homes were neither well equipped nor luxurious. As the Psychological Warfare Division reported with a noticeable sense of annoyance, even newly captured prisoners in Europe were quick to raise the issue of racial discrimination in the South when interrogated, despite lacking "the slightest idea of the historic, social and economic background of this problem."[25] The POWs who came to the United States to work were well aware that they mainly performed jobs usually reserved for African Americans. "While we were in America, we did the Negro-work. The slave-work," one of them recalled after the war, adding that the farmers treated them in a similar way: "We replaced the Negroes, nothing else. . . . We were treated like the Negroes over there."[26] Another one recalled: "For the farmers we had a status similar to the one colored work-slaves had down there in the southern states."[27]

Under international law, prisoners of war were protected from doing menial or degrading tasks, and some tried to argue that work traditionally performed by black people fell into this category. "The prisoners object to working, saying that white men do not work in the fields in Texas," a State Department official for example noted in June 1943, and an American officer in Georgia reported a few months later that some "German prisoners had refused to work on the peanut harvest, stating . . . it is menial work since it usually is performed by negroes."[28] By the end of 1943, however, the POW work program was firmly established, and the Germans worked side by side with African Americans in the fields, factories, and food-processing plants.

The newspapers the prisoners produced and published in their camps frequently reported on work details and thereby reminded their readers which work they were doing. After visiting a box factory in Texas, for example, the editor of Camp Maxey's *Echo* informed his readers that "Negroes, by the way, represent a large part of the workforce, and I was told that the work which is now done by the prisoners of war had been largely done by Negroes."[29] German prisoners were quick to realize that the lives of African Americans were often hard. The POW newspaper of Camp Fort Bragg, North Carolina, for example, reported about the prisoners' work in a fertilizer plant that "never before had employed white workers" and criticized the extremely poor sanitary conditions there.[30] Reports from neutral observers confirm that the working conditions for prisoners were "the same as those for the civilian workers, most of whom are negroes."[31]

The work the prisoners clearly hated the most was harvesting cotton. "We picked cotton the length of the Mississippi," Corporal Hein Severloh recalled after the war. "I know how to handle hard work, but there it was truly very, very hard. It was terribly hot, and we had to bend over all day. We had nothing to drink. . . . There were a great number of Blacks on the plantation. . . . For them it was worse than for us. And you have to see how they lived. Their farms: very ugly, very primitive. These people were so exploited."[32] Severloh was not the only one to comment on the poor living conditions and economic prospects of African Americans. Another former prisoner who worked in the sugar-cane fields contrasted the economic plight of black farmers with the compassion they showed for their POW workers: "he constantly brought ice water, he bought cake, the Negro, and he only had equipment which was antiquated and the shack, it was only made from the wood of egg boxes . . . that was his farm. He was in a pitiful situation; he was driven hard and cheated by the whites."[33] Working together obviously created a sense of solidarity between the two groups. All the evidence suggests that the Germans and the African Americans got along very well and frequently talked with each other at work.[34] When the reeducation program finally started in November 1944, many German prisoners therefore had a fairly good idea of the problems African Americans faced in the rural South.

Reeducation and the Issue of Race

The task of explaining the discrepancy between America's egalitarian creed and the reality of racial discrimination especially in the South rested to a large degree on foreign-born shoulders. The reeducation program was developed and administered by the newly created Special Projects Division (initially the Special Projects Branch) in the Office of the Provost Marshal General. It was headed by Lieutenant Colonel Edward Davison, a recently naturalized immigrant from Scotland who, like most of his subordinates, spoke very little German and had only limited knowledge of German culture.[35] Further, only about 15 percent of all German POWs in America had a working knowledge of English.[36]

To reach the prisoners, the Special Projects Division therefore had to produce material in their native language. The most important of these publications was the newspaper *Der Ruf* (The call), which was sold in all German prisoner of war camps. The person in charge of this side of the program was German-born captain Walter Schoenstedt. A writer and former communist, Schoenstedt had fled his home country in 1933 and arrived in the United States via France two years later. The other German immigrant on the team was the educational advisor Henry Ehrmann, who had only come to the United States in 1940.[37] The Special Projects staff was supported by a hand-picked group of around eighty-five German prisoners who were assembled in a special camp, the so-called Factory, where they produced and analyzed German-language material.[38] Among them were a number of writers who would later become famous in postwar Germany, such as Alfred Andersch and Hans-Werner Richter. In addition, German immigrant scholars were given permission to lecture on American history and society in the POW camps. In other words, the reeducation effort was very much a joint German-American endeavor. The only African American involved was, in the words of one Special Projects member, "a very competent black typist, universally known as Maggie."[39]

One of Special Projects' most basic problems was the widespread racism that existed within the U.S. Army. Already the first draft of the reeducation program warned that "Nazi prisoners of war have been trained to look for vulnerable points in other people's views and attitudes. After overhearing prejudicial talk about Negroes or Jews, they have been known to come back with their own theories on racial questions and to point out that American ideas are not dissimilar."[40] This warning was repeated several times, which indicates how widespread and serious the problem was.[41] In November 1944, the War Department even addressed this topic in one of its "Facts vs. Fantasy" pamphlets, which were designed to counter enemy propaganda by providing American GIs with the truth. However, the pamphlet could only stress that each individual in the United States was "guaranteed the same rights regardless of his race, religion or creed."[42]

Prisoners who pointed out that African Americans often had their guaranteed rights violated were quickly branded Nazis and troublemakers. One former POW recalled that he and his comrades became "stubborn" after having been forced to watch a documentary on the concentration camps after the war: "If we are accused of racism, we reply with the Negro problem or with the extermination of the Indians. Then we find helpless Americans who react in a stereotypical way and call all who are not of their opinion 'Nazis.'"[43]

To avoid such problems, the reeducation personnel tried to withhold information on discrimination against African Americans from the prisoners. This measure was covered by the guidelines of the reeducation program, but the irony of teaching democracy with the help of censorship was not lost on the Special Projects Division.[44] Davison defended the decision by claiming that "German prisoners of war are intellectually and ideologically adolescent" and therefore in need of "intellectual protection and guidance."[45] Although he conceded that it was "impossible to reject every book which deals in a realistic and not demagogic way with such questions as the Negro problem," a number of officers on the ground tried to do just that. In some POW camps, classics such as *Uncle Tom's Cabin* were banned, as well as the works of famous American historians such as William E. Woodward and Charles and Mary Beard. Publications of the National Catholic Welfare Conference and the Young Men's Christian Association's (YMCA) War Prisoners Aid that dealt with racial discrimination in the United States likewise attracted the wrath of some camp reeducation officers.[46]

The censorship did not go unnoticed. In June 1945, Andre Vulliet of the International YMCA warned that this approach was bound to fail. Vulliet had regularly visited German POW camps since America's entry into the war and correctly pointed out that the prisoners had already seen "race discrimination in the South, sharp contrasts everywhere between extreme wealth and utmost poverty, between splendid buildings and adjoining slums," while working outside of their compounds.[47] Shortly afterward, his permission to visit German POW camps was revoked on the grounds of accusations that he was a fascist sympathizer and that his German-born wife was engaged in espionage.[48] Although the War Department became considerably less conciliatory toward aid agencies after Germany's unconditional surrender and the liberation of all Allied POWs in Europe, this sudden and drastic action against a high-profile member of the International YMCA nevertheless came as a surprise, and it is tempting to see a connection with Vulliet's candid criticism of the reeducation effort. If this was the case, Vulliet had the same experience as many of the prisoners, who were also classified as Nazis after openly challenging the reeducators in the camps.[49]

Eventually, however, the members of the Special Projects Division developed a semiofficial line for how to explain the social reality of racial discrimination to their German students. In the special Reeducation Schools at Fort Getty and Fort Wetherill, the topic was presented as an opportunity to exercise free speech and develop critical thinking. These schools were created to train a small number of POWs for employment with the U.S. military government in occupied Germany. One of the teachers was Texas-born Thomas V. Smith, a highly respected professor of philosophy at the University of Chicago. Smith later claimed that he addressed the topic in a straightforward manner: "I was content (1) to point to its history, (2) to parade the progress that the Negroes have made since slavery, and (3) to ask for suggestions from them as to how we Americans can move faster and more securely in solving our major 'minority problems.' There was never any pretense on my part that 'democracy' is not fascism to our Negroes in certain sections and at certain times."[50] In a similar fashion, Henry W. Ehrmann stated that the issue was used to develop the critical faculties of the students in these schools. According to Ehrmann, it was "never attempted to gloss over social injustices and race prejudices; as the majority of the prisoners had been working in the cotton fields of the South and in the canneries of the Southwest it would not have been easy to do so."[51]

The print material that was produced for the rank-and-file prisoners in the camps, however, rarely dealt with the issue. *Der Ruf* published an article entitled "The Economy of the Southern States" in its first issue that acknowledged the "hard work" the prisoners were doing in the region. The article mentioned that cotton demanded cheap labor and that many white farmers had also been reduced to sharecroppers after the abolition of slavery but argued that the South was at a turning point and that its future looked bright. Dixie's racial tensions were not addressed.[52] The reeducation's flagship publication dealt with this aspect of southern life only indirectly in its first issue by publishing an excerpt from Stephen Vincent Benét's book *Amerika*. The prisoners were allowed to buy a "special translation and edition" of this book in their camps, "provided to fit the needs of the prisoners of war," and *Der Ruf* chose to print a passage that it thought would capture the interest of its readers.[53] In that excerpt, Benét stressed that the United States was "no heaven on earth, no paradise, nor a perfect state." Yet even that acknowledgment was balanced with a claim that Americans did not believe in a master race and that loyal Americans were the sharpest critics of their own country.[54] The only time *Der Ruf* directly addressed the issue of racial discrimination in the United States was in a review of Richard Wright's autobiography *Black Boy* in July 1945. Similar to the approach used by T. V. Smith, the review's anonymous author acknowledged that racism existed in American society but argued that its effects were curtailed by the right to free speech. Unlike in Germany, it was at least possible to discuss and criticize such problems in a democratic society.[55]

As already pointed out, this statement did not match the experience of many POWs—or African Americans, for that matter. Nevertheless, the reeducation publication with the widest distribution pursued a similar line of argument. The brochure "Kleiner Führer durch Amerika" (Small guide to America) was given free of charge to all German POWs in the United States, although they had to sign for their copy and buy a new one if they lost it.[56] The brochure acknowledged that African Americans had not yet achieved full economic and social equality in all regions of the United States and that there was still a lot to do, even though blacks had made remarkable progress since the abolition of slavery. Lynching was portrayed as an expression of still-existing racial antagonisms, but it was claimed that these incidents were not very common and were viewed with disgust by many whites. Persecution of or discrimination against blacks could be punished by law and was condemned by the federal government in the sharpest possible way. The United States was no "paradise of justice," but problems were made public, and many Americans were committed to correcting them.[57]

Most people on the Special Projects staff were liberal white academics, and their faith in the self-healing powers of American democracy is therefore hardly surprising. Immigrant scholars from Germany who were also allowed to lecture in the camps were apparently more critical. One of them was Professor Helmut Kuhn of the University of North Carolina, Chapel Hill. Born in Berlin, Kuhn gave lectures on American history and society in Camp Butner, North Carolina, and his notes have survived. Kuhn openly talked about racial segregation, as well as the economic exploitation of blacks and the fear of miscegenation among white Americans.[58] Like T. V. Smith, Kuhn also explained the situation of African Americans with regard to the long-term effects of slavery, thereby blaming the problem on earlier generations. Because of slavery, Kuhn argued, the vast majority of African Americans had remained in a childlike state—a widely held view that resembled Davison's claim that the Nazi regime had left the Germans in a state of adolescence. African Americans, Kuhn continued, were usually distrustful and hostile toward whites, but it was possible to break through this hostile barrier by approaching them in the spirit of brotherhood. Then one could find that they possessed "all the treasures of the human spirit . . . such as magnanimity, a willingness to make sacrifices, and childlike trust."[59]

Kuhn's explanations would have made sense to the German prisoners. In their diaries and memoirs, as well as in interviews after the war, the Germans consistently describe Africans Americans as good-natured, friendly, trusting, and caring, and almost all former prisoners claim that they had a special and friendly relationship with them.

Historians have usually portrayed the prisoners' criticism of the way African Americans were treated as a conscious resistance strategy against the reeducation program. Arnold Krammer, for example, acknowledged that the discrimination against African Americans during the war was "deplorable" but nevertheless thought it "ludicrous" that "it was exploited by the soldiers of a government which was, at that moment, exterminating people by the millions."[60] Such an interpretation neglects to take into account that the prisoners did not just criticize racial discrimination against African Americans. The economic exploitation of the latter, which the prisoners witnessed firsthand during their stay in the South, was at least as important. While the Germans' ability to use facilities for "whites" in the segregated South reassured them that their racial status as Caucasians was unquestioned, their present and future social status was much more in doubt. According to the POWs' memoirs and recollections, African Americans were eager to convince them that they were all victims of the same system. "And the Blacks!" one former POW later exclaimed. "They were always saying: 'We are just like you: Prisoners; Oppressed; Second-class men.'"[61] Former POW Wilhelm Gensmantel, who was interned in Louisiana, spoke for many other veterans when he asserted in 1995: "There the Negroes did not count any more than us. We were on the same level as they were there."[62] What probably convinced the prisoners more than anything else that they had been reduced to the same level as African Americans was their delayed repatriation to Germany. When they left the United States in 1946, the POWs' uniforms were dyed black, and some 178,000 of them were handed over to France, Great Britain, and other Western European states as forced laborers. Most of them had only one word for this measure: "slave-trading."[63]

As already noted, the depiction of American society as heartless and materialistic had a long tradition in German culture. "Contempt of America as a country without its own 'culture,' without a 'soul,' a country which is only interested in making money, is widespread among all classes of Germans," the Special Projects Division observed, summarizing the stereotypes it had to fight against in October 1944.[64] Talking about African Americans allowed German prisoners to voice such negative perceptions while using the democratic values and language the reeducators were trying to promote. Even decades after the war, German prisoners portrayed African Americans as anything but materialistic: they enjoyed music and laughter, had created a distinct culture, and were capable of profound and genuine emotions. They were not part of American society but part of the land—a role Native Americans had played in the popular novels of Karl May. In the eyes of many POWs, African Americans were the antithesis of the fast-paced materialistic American way of life they were uncomfortable with and that the victorious U.S. troops were bringing with them to Germany.

The portrayal of African Americans as the positive antithesis of a materialistic society had a long tradition in Germany, and even Nazi propaganda sometimes used them in this way.[65] Probably the best example is Alfred E. Johann's semifictional travel account *Das Land ohne Herz* (The land without heart), which was published in 1942. In this book, the poverty of the rural population in the South—black and white—is portrayed as a direct result of the capitalist system. According to Johann, whose real name was Wollschläger, only African Americans had managed to withstand the degrading effects of poverty. The book, of which half a million copies were distributed by Goebbels's Ministry for Propaganda in Germany, claims that southern blacks "had remained human, had, especially the old among them, preserved a simple, beautiful dignity, did not really notice how miserable and hopeless their existence was, the cheerfulness of their hearts remained unmarred. And this is why they were still able to sing, able to sing a song, and this is probably the most un-American activity there is."[66]

Music was a marker of culture, the only field in which Germans always felt superior to the rising superpower on the other side of the Atlantic. The POWs in the United States also clung to the notion of German cultural superiority, especially in the hour of defeat. Their focus on the exploitation of African Americans was just another way to portraying the United States as a materialistic "land without heart" that was unsuitable as a model for German society. The fact that the new West German state opted for a social market economy in 1949 shows that they were not alone in their rejection of American-style capitalism.

Notes

1. Eric J. Leed, *The Mind of the Traveler: From Gilgamesh to Global Tourism* (New York: Basic Books, 1991), 2.

2. Morton Sosna, "Stalag Dixie," *Stanford Humanities Review* 2.1 (1991): 61n1.

3. Internment of POWs, To Assistant Chief of Staff, G-1, through Chief of Administrative Services, from Brig. Gen. Bryan, Assistant PMG, Mar. 17, 1943, 2, National Archives and Records Administration, Record Group 389, Entry 452, Box 1395 (hereafter NARA, RG . . . , E . . . , B . . .), "383.6 General P/W #3 Jan. 16, 1943–March 1943." Numbers are from George G. Lewis and John Mewha, *History of Prisoners of War Utilization by the United States Army, 1776–1945* (Washington, DC: Department of the Army, 1955), 90–91.

4. Arnold Krammer, *Nazi Prisoners of War in America* (1979; Chelsea: Scarborough House, 1991). One of the first American historians to point out the potential of the topic was Jake W. Spindle, "Axis Prisoners of War in the United States, 1942–1946: A Bibliographical Essay," *Military Affairs* 39.2 (Apr. 1975): 61–66. Earlier studies were written by former officials of the POW program or remained unpublished. The "Maschke Commission" (Wissenschaftlichen Kommission für deutsche Kriegsgefangenengeschichte) in Germany started to work on the topic

in the 1950s, but access to its publications was restricted until Dec. 1975, and the volume dealing with the POWs in the United States was only completed in the early 1970s: see Hermann Jung, *Die deutschen Kriegsgefangenen in amerikanischer Hand—USA* (Zur Geschichte der deutschen Kriegsgefangenen des Zweiten Weltkrieges, vol. 10.1; Munich: Gieseking, 1972).

5. Harry P. Riconda, *Prisoners of War in American Conflicts* (Lanham, MD: Scarecrow Press, 2003); Paul J. Springer, "American Prisoners of War Policy and Practices from the Revolutionary War to the War on Terror" (PhD diss., Texas A&M University, 2006); Robert C. Doyle, *The Enemy in Our Hands: America's Treatment of Enemy Prisoners of War from the Revolution to the War on Terror* (Lexington: University Press of Kentucky, 2010); Stephanie Carvin, *Prisoners of America's Wars: From the Early Republic to Guantanamo* (London: C. Hurst & Co. Publishers Ltd., 2010); Antonio S. Thompson, *Men in German Uniform: POWs in America during World War II* (Knoxville: University of Tennessee Press, 2010).

6. See, for example, Anita Albrecht Buck, *Behind Barbed Wire: German Prisoners of War Camps in Minnesota during World War II* (St. Cloud, MN: North Star Press of St. Cloud, 1998); Robert D. Billinger Jr., *Hitler's Soldiers in the Sunshine State: German POWs in Florida* (Gainesville: University Press of Florida, 2000); David Fiedler, *The Enemy among Us: POWs in Missouri during World War II* (St. Louis: Missouri Historical Society Press, 2003); Robert D. Billinger Jr., *Nazi POWs in the Tar Heel State* (Gainesville: University Press of Florida, 2008).

7. See, for example, Judith M. Gansberg, *Stalag, U.S.A.: The Remarkable Story of German POWs in America* (New York: Crowell, 1977), 128–29; Krammer, *Nazi Prisoners of War, 93.* Exceptions are Matthew J. Schott, "Prisoners like Us: German POWs Encounter Louisiana's African Americans," *Louisiana History* 36.3 (Summer 1995): 277–90; and Matthias Reiss, *"Die Schwarzen waren unsere Freunde": Deutsche Kriegsgefangene in der amerikanischen Gesellschaft 1942–1946* (Paderborn: Schöningh, 2002).

8. For a discussion of the topic and the historiography, see Matthias Reiss, "Icons of Insults: Prisoners of War in African American Letters during World War II," *Amerikastudien/American Studies* 49.4 (2004): 539–62.

9. See note 2. James E. Fickle and Donald W. Ellis, "POWs in the Piney Woods: German Prisoners of War in the Southern Lumber Industry, 1943–1945," *Journal of Southern History* 56.4 (Nov. 1990): 695–724, also has a regional perspective but focuses only on one industry.

10. Secretary of State Cordell Hull to Secretary of War Henry L. Stimson, Mar. 30, 1944, NARA, RG615, E43, B572, "383.6."

11. Intellectual Diversion Program, to Commanding Generals, 1st–9th Service Commands and Military District of Washington, from Brig. Gen. Dunlop, Acting Adjutant General, Nov. 9, 1944, NARA, RG319, E47, B941, no folder title.

12. H. Glenn Penny, "Atlantic Transfers: Recent Work on the German-American Exchange," *German History* 26.4 (2008): 563; Christof Mauch and Kiran Klaus Patel, eds., *The United States and Germany during the Twentieth*

Century: Competition and Convergence (Cambridge: Cambridge University Press, 2010), passim.

13. Kenneth D. Barkin, "'Berlin Days,' 1892–1894: W. E. B. Du Bois and German Political Economy," *boundary 2* 27.3 (Autumn 2000): 86.

14. Günter Moltmann, "Nationalklischees und Demagogie: Die deutsche Amerikapropaganda im Zweiten Weltkrieg," in Ursula Büttner, ed., *Das Unrechtsregime. Internationale Forschung über den Nationalsozialismus*, vol. 1, *Ideologie—Herrschaftssystem—Wirkung in Europa* (Hamburg: Christians, 1986), 219–42. All translations from the German are the author's own.

15. Summary Report on the Attitudes of German Ps/W towards the United States. SHAEF, Psychological Warfare Division, Intelligence Section, June 19, 1945, 4, NARA, RG165, E179, B711, no folder title.

16. Ibid., 1.

17. Ibid., 2.

18. Ibid.

19. Ibid., 4.

20. Heinz R., "Thirty Years of Memory" (unpublished ms., Oberaudorf, c. 1974), 27 (copy from the author).

21. Reinhold Pabel, *Enemies Are Human* (Philadelphia: Winston, 1955), 147.

22. "Spannende Erwartung erfüllte uns, ein kribbliches Gefühl der Neugier und Unsicherheit. . . . Wir haben für Stunden den Krieg vergessen und denken nur eines: Wie wird das auf der Überfahrt, wie wird es sein in Amerika!" Hansjörg P., "Tagebuch: 13.5.1943–22.3.1944" (unpublished ms.), 25 (copy from Hansjörg P.).

23. George McCracken, "The Prisoner of War Re-Education Program in the Years 1943–1946" (unpublished study of the U.S. Army, Washington, DC, 1953), 6–15, esp. 15 (copy from the author).

24. Address on the Intellectual Diversion Program for Enemy POWs in the United States by Brig. Gen. Bryan, Jr., Assistant PMG before 5th Orientation Conference, Fort Slocum, NY, May 25, 1945, 2, NARA, RG389, E459A, B1630, "337 General."

25. Summary Report on the Attitudes of German Ps/W towards the United States, SHAEF, Psychological Warfare Division, Intelligence Section, June 19, 1945, 3. It is worth noting that some historians have taken a similar view. Judith Gansberg, for example, claims that the issue of racial discrimination "bewildered" the German POWs "in its complexity" (*Stalag, U.S.A.*, 128).

26. "Solange wir da waren in Amerika, haben wir die Negerarbeit gemacht. Die Sklavenarbeit. . . . Wir waren anstelle der Neger dort, nichts anderes. . . . wir sind so wie die Neger dort drüben behandelt worden, nichts anderes": Harry S., interview with Matthias Reiss, Aug. 3, 1996 (audiotape).

27. "Wir waren also im ähnlichen Status im Ansehen der Farmer wie die farbigen Arbeitssklaven unten in den Südstaaten," WKU-258, 26, Bundesarchiv-Militärarchiv Freiburg, B205/v.242b.

28. Use of POWs in Harvesting Peanuts in Georgia, Memo for Director, POW

Division, from Major Edwards, Assistant Director, POW Division, n.d. [Sept. 1943], 1, NARA, RG389, E467C, B1563, "Miscellaneous Reports"; Report of Visit to Camp Huntsville, TX, by Willy Bruppacher and Emil Greuter, Swiss Delegation, June 29, 1943, 13, NARA, RG59, ELot58 D7, B29, "Huntsville."

29. "Neger stellen uebrigens einen grossen Teil der Belegschaft der Fabrik dar und ich habe mir sagen lassen, dass die Arbeit, die heute von den Kriegsgefangenen geleistet wird, zum groessten Teil von Negern verrichtet wurde": "Wir besuchen Kameraden bei der Arbeit," *Echo* (Maxey, TX), Aug. 21, 1945, 15.

30. "Wir in Amerika," *Der Drahtberichter* (Fort Bragg, NC), Apr. 15, 1945, 49–50.

31. Report of Visit to Florence Army Air Base, SC, by Dr. Bubb, International Committee of the Red Cross, July 6, 1945, NARA, RG59, ELot 58 D7, B29, "Fort Jackson, South Carolina."

32. Krammer, *Nazi Prisoners of War,* 92–93.

33. "Der hat laufend Eiswasser rangebracht, der hat Kuchen gekauft, der Neger, und er hatte selbst nur also Geräte, die vorsintflutlich waren, und die Baracke, das war nur aus Eierkistenholz zusammen . . . das war seine Farm. Der war arm dran, der wurde von den Weißen getriezt und beschissen": Harry S., interview with Matthias Reiss, Aug. 3, 1996 (audiotape). See also Schott, "Prisoners like Us," 285.

34. Reiss, *"Die Schwarzen waren unsere Freunde,"* 231–81; Schott, "Prisoners like Us," 278–80; Sosna, "Stalag Dixie," 49–53.

35. Ron Robin, *The Barbed-Wire College: Reeducating German POWs in the United States during World War II* (Princeton: Princeton University Press, 1995), 44.

36. In Feb. 1945, Davison claimed that "only 15% of the prisoners of war can use English as a tool. They may be able to understand the caption on a comic strip and read a bit perhaps, but that is all. 30% are learning, but from the point of view of using English as an intellectual tool, I very much doubt more than 15% would count." See Conference on Prisoner of War Activities, Col. Davison, Headquarter, 1st Service Command, Feb. 23, 1945, NARA, RG389, E459A, B1630, "337 General."

37. Robin, *Barbed-Wire College,* 46–49, 51–52.

38. The Factory was started on Oct. 31, 1944, in Van Etten, NY, and moved to Fort Kearney, RI, on Mar. 1, 1945. See "Der 'Ruf' in America: Aus dem Lebenserinnerungen von Dr. Gustav René Hocke," transcript of a Radio Broadcast, WDR 2, Sunday, Dec. 10, 1972, 10–10:30 p.m., 2.

39. Howard Mumford Jones, quoted in Robin, *Barbed-Wire College,* 57.

40. Reorientation of German POWs, Memo for the Chief of Staff, Army Service Forces, from Maj. Gen. Lerch, PMG, Aug. 23, 1944, 11, in Special Projects Division, "Re-Education of Enemy POWs (unpublished study, Washington, DC, 1945), attachment no. 4.

41. Intellectual Diversion Program, to Commanding Generals, 1st–9th Service Commands and Military District of Washington, from Brig. Gen. Dunlop, Act-

ing Adjutant General, Nov. 9, 1944, 3; "Facts vs. Fantasy," War Department Pamphlet No. 19–2, Nov. 20, 1944, 16–19, NARA, RG389, E459A, B1649, "461 Gen. (Facts vs. Fantasy)"; "The Mission and Meaning of POW Special Projects Program," speech, Lt. Col. Davison, Conference on POW Activities, Headquarters, 1st Service Command, Feb. 23, 1945, 5, NARA, RG389, E459A, B1630, "337 General"; Notes on German Propaganda, Lt. Kunzig, Dec. 11, 1944, 1, NARA, RG389, E459A, B1631, "337 (4th Training Conference) Gen."

42. "Facts vs. Fantasy," 17.

43. "Wir werden störrisch und 'schalten auf stur.' Wirft man uns Rassismus vor, kontern wir mit dem Negerproblem oder mit der Ausrottung der Indianer. Dann finden wir hilflose Amerikaner, die stereotyp reagieren und alle, die nicht ihrer Meinung sind, als 'Nazis' bezeichnen": Heinz Wittmann, "Das zweite Gesicht der Niederlage: Wie deutsche Soldaten in amerikanischer Kriegsgefangenschaft den Krieg noch einmal verlieren," *Rheinpfalz*, May 4, 1985 (copy from the author).

44. The aim of the reeducation program was "not only to select and make available materials that will promote its purpose but also to assure the rejection of such materials as are harmful, indifferent, or alien to it." See Intellectual Diversion Program, to Commanding Generals, 1st–9th Service Commands and Military District of Washington, from Brig. Gen. Dunlop, Acting Adjutant General, Nov. 9, 1944, 1.

45. "Memo from State Department Concerning Censorship of Books for POWs," [Draft of] Memo for Gen. Bryan, from Lt. Col. Davison, Director, Special Projects Division, May 10, 1945, 4, NARA, RG389, E459A, B1647, "461 General #15."

46. Directions for the Reviewing of Books, Supplementary Memo No. 15, attachment to: Criteria for the Selection of Books. Office Memo No. 15, Major Davison, Chief, Special Projects Branch, Oct. 20, 1944, NARA, RG389, E459A, B1602, "008 Policy Questions."

47. Andre Vulliet, "Notes and Impressions about POW Camps in the United States" (unpublished ms., June 1945), 9, NARA, RG389, E459A, B1606, "080 (War Prisoners Aid, YMCA) Gen."

48. Andre Vulliet, Memo for Col. Tollefson, Director, POW Operations Division, from Col. Miller, Director, Security and Investigations Division, PMG's Office, June 11, 1945, NARA, RG389, E452, B1402, "680.2 General P/W April 1945-Dec. 1945."

49. The accusations against Vulliet and his wife are not mentioned in the literature on German POWs, and the work of the international agencies for the POWs still needs to be studied in greater detail.

50. Gansberg, *Stalag, U.S.A.,* 129.

51. Henry W. Ehrmann, "An Experiment in Political Education: The Prisoner-of-War Schools in the United States," *Social Research* 14 (1947): 313. Ehrmann added, maybe as a gesture to his American readers: "But it was possible to point

out to them that this is not a society that gives primary concern to the question who is superior to whom, and who is subordinate" (ibid.).

52. M. Bayer, "Die Wirtschaft der Südstaaten," *Der Ruf: Zeitung der deutschen Kriegsgefangenen in USA,* Mar. 1, 1945, 7.

53. Justification of the Selection for the First Series of the Buecherreihe Neue Welt, Memo for Chief Review Branch, from Henry W. Ehrmann, Apr. 3, 1945, 1, NARA, RG389, E459A, B1645, "461 General #9."

54. "Es ist kein Himmel auf Erden, kein Paradies, noch ein vollkommender Staat": Stephen Vincent Benét, "Amerika: Wie sieht der Amerikaner sein Land?" *Der Ruf,* Mar. 1, 1945, 6.

55. Anonymo., "Black Boy," *Der Ruf,* July 15, 1945, 4. The review is not signed, but Sosna claims that it was written by Andersch ("Stalag Dixie," 51). The paper also published three pieces that expressed general opposition to racist ideas: "Zwischenrufe," *Der Ruf,* Sept. 1, 1945, 4; "Der Rassenwahn," *Der Ruf,* Dec. 15, 1945, 1; and "Hautfarbe und Rasse," *Der Ruf,* Mar. 1, 1946, 3.

56. The pamphlet was also a popular souvenir with American soldiers, and some twenty thousand copies disappeared on their way to the POW camps. See Proposed Little Guide Book to the United States for POWs, Memo for Gen. Bryan from Lt. Col. Davison, Director, Special Projects Division, Mar. 22, 1945, NARA, RG389, E459A, B1638, "383.6 General"; Distribution of Publication to POWs, To Commanding General, 9th Service Command, Attn: Director, Security and Intelligence Division, from Major McKnight, Acting Director, Special Projects Division, June 26, 1945, NARA, RG389, E459A, B1597, "000.76 General #6"; Printing of the Small Guide to America, Memo for Gen. Bryan, from Lt. Col. Davison, Director, Special Projects Division, Aug. 11, 1945, NARA, RG389, E459A, B1647, "461 General #13"; Status Report of the Review Branch, Major Richards, Chief, Review Branch, Aug. 30, 1945, NARA, RG389, E459A, B1647, "461 General #13." Other individuals and organizations also came up with the idea of a souvenir book for German POWs. The War Department rejected these proposals, although the request of German POWs in Kentucky was approved provided that "no publicity be given [to] the project and no copies of the booklet be circulated outside the camp." See Major Richards, Acting Director, Special Projects Division, Commanding General, 5th Service Command, Fort Hayes, Columbus, OH, Sept. 8, 1945, NARA, RG389, E459A, B1647, "461 #14."

57. "Kleiner Führer durch Amerika" (pamphlet, 1945), 39–40.

58. "Die amerikanische Wirklichkeit," talk, Professor Helmut Kuhn, University of North Carolina, Camp Butner, NC, Nov. 2, 1945, 6, NARA, RG389, E459A, B1635, "350.001 (Camp Butner) General."

59. "Wenn es aber gelingt[,] dem Neger bruederlich entgegenzutreten, ihn aus seinem Misstrauen herauszulocken, dann findet man, dass alle die Schaetze des menschlichen Geistes wie im gewoehnlichen Menschen, wie Grossmut, Opferfreudigkeit und kindliches Vertrauen vorhanden sind" (ibid., 8). A similar argu-

ment was made by a Professor Muelder, who lectured at Camp Grant, IL. See "Das Negerproblem," *Lagerstimme* (Grant, IL), Jan. 12, 1946, 11, 13.

60. Kramer, *Nazi Prisoners of War,* 93.

61. Quoted in ibid. See also Schott, "Prisoners like Us," 279.

62. "Da galten die Neger nicht mehr als wir auch. Wir konnten uns dort den gleichstellen": Wilhelm Gensmantel, interview with Harald Leder, Aug. 10, 1995, Williams Center for Oral History, Louisiana State University.

63. WKG-123, "Reisebericht (Europa, Afrika, Amerika): Aufzeichnungen über Kriegsgefangenschaft in Tunesien, den USA und Großbritannien, 1943–1947," in Kurt W. Böhme and Helmut Wolff, eds., *Aufzeichnungen über die Kriegsgefangenschaft im Westen* (Munich: Gieseking, 1973), 157.

64. Criteria for the Selection of Books, Office Memo No. 15, Major Davison, Chief, Special Projects Branch, October 20, 1944, NARA, RG389, E459A, B1602, "008 Policy Questions."

65. Earl R. Beck, "German Views of Negro Life in the United States, 1919–1933," *Journal of Negro History* 48 (1963): 22–32.

66. "Sie waren Menschen geblieben, hatten, besonders die Alten unter ihnen, eine einfältige, schöne Würde bewahrt, nahmen es eigentlich gar nicht zur Kenntnis, wie elend und hoffnungslos ihr Dasein war, die Heiterkeit ihrer Herzen blieb ungetrübt. Und deshalb konnten sie noch singen, konnten ein Lied singen, und das ist wohl die unamerikanischte Beschäftigung, die es gibt": Alfred Ernst Johann, *Das Land ohne Herz: Eine Reise ins unbekannte Amerika* (Berlin: Deutscher Verlag, 1942), 177.

13

Britain, the American South, and the Wide Civil Rights Movement

Clive Webb

Here are two incidents that seem familiar to any student of the civil rights movement. First, white police officers use dogs to dispel black people from the streets in a city where racial confrontation has attracted international media attention. Second, demonstrators gather in the nation's capital in support of "Jobs and Freedom" for African Americans. To most readers, these snapshots appear to describe respectively the civil rights demonstrations that occurred during May 1963 in Birmingham, Alabama, and the March on Washington that took place three months later. In the context of this essay, however, they refer to events on the other side of the Atlantic: namely, a race riot in the British East Midlands city of Nottingham in August 1958 and a sympathy protest in London held simultaneously with the March on Washington.[1]

The transatlantic connections between the struggles for racial equality in Britain and the American South are the focus of this essay. It assesses the ways in which the southern civil rights movement provided an interpretative framework for understanding the race problems that afflicted the United Kingdom in the decades following World War II. Britain had long defined itself as an exemplar of racial progress, not only domestically but also internationally. British political commentators buttressed this self-mythologizing by contrasting the supposed liberalism and tolerance of their own country with the racial discrimination and violence of the United States, especially the Jim Crow South. The racist reaction to the arrival in Britain of unprecedented numbers of Caribbean migrants, the most dramatic expression of which was a series of racial disorders in the late 1950s

243

and early 1960s, threatened the comforting illusion that the nation was immune to the racial bigotry and brutality that had for so long beset the southern states. The southern civil rights struggle had a significant influence in shaping public policy on race relations in Britain during these years. It had an effect on the growth of organized protest by both racist reactionaries and liberal reformers and also helped shape the legislative reforms enacted by the British government to improve conditions for the migrant population.

In recent years the concept of a "long civil rights movement" has gained increasing credibility among scholars of the African American freedom struggle. Historians such as Jacquelyn Dowd Hall and Glenda Gilmore place the direct-action protests of the 1950s and 1960s in a longer tradition of activism that dates back to the interwar era.[2] This essay assesses whether it is appropriate to broaden our understanding of the geographic as well as temporal dimensions of the African American crusade for racial equality. The civil rights movement was as wide as it was long in the sense that African Americans provided a crucial stimulus to the British campaign for racial equality. Yet there were limitations to the diffusion of American influences on the United Kingdom. Although some aspects of the southern civil rights movement transferred to Britain, albeit with necessary adaptations to local context, others became lost in translation somewhere across the ocean. British activists undoubtedly drew inspiration from the other side of the Atlantic, but the different racial dynamics of the United Kingdom ultimately negated the growth of a southern-style grassroots movement based on a strategy of nonviolent direct action. White racists in Britain also drew inspiration from the other side of the Atlantic but were similarly unable to build a mass-based movement. The limitations of southern influences are therefore revealing of the distinctiveness as well as the similarities of race relations on either side of the Atlantic.

It is important to stress from the outset that transatlantic influences worked in both directions, at least in terms of the political advantage that southern segregationists took of the rise of racial tensions in Britain. White southerners historically had a cordial attitude toward the British. This opinion had survived despite Britain's abolitionist movement having spearheaded international condemnation of southern slavery and the British government refusing to grant diplomatic recognition to the Confederacy during the American Civil War.[3] The military alliance between Britain and the United States during World War II fostered a renewal of affection. To a certain extent practical considerations influenced southern attitudes, Britain remaining one of the largest importers of southern trade exports. This accounts for the enthusiastic support of southern politicians for postwar loans to rebuild the shattered British economy. Yet, according to sociologist Alfred Hero, white southerners also retained a "sentimental identification with the British" rooted in a racist construction of Anglo-Saxon brotherhood. It was this belief in the racial kinship between the two peoples that accounts for the bitter sense of betrayal felt by white southerners at popular support in Britain for the civil rights movement.[4]

Confronted by increasing international criticism of Jim Crow, white southerners retreated during the postwar era into isolationism. A cartoon published in the newsletter of the Citizens' Council, the preeminent segregationist organization, encapsulates this hostility toward world opinion. It depicts a confrontational figure clutching newspaper sheets with headlines such as "Racial Integration" and "Little Rock" as he stands astride a globe labeled "International Badgering," presses his index finger into the nose of a second character representing the United States, and screams "Tell You What You've Got To Do!"[5]

The figurative digit pressed most accusingly into the faces of white southerners belonged to Britain. A survey of West European countries conducted by the United States Information Agency in 1956 found that the harshest opposition to Jim Crow came, along with the Netherlands, from Britain.[6] The British press provided extensive coverage of the civil rights movement that emphasized the moral integrity and physical bravery of black activists. Alistair Cooke, Godfrey Hodgson, Hella Pick, and William J. Weatherby were among the many journalists whose reporting from the frontlines of the black freedom struggle stirred the hearts and minds of readers. British newspapers lauded the Supreme Court ruling in *Brown v. Board of Education* mandating the desegregation of public schools, reported sympathetically on the Montgomery bus boycott, and lamented the ineffectual leadership of the Eisenhower administration in promoting racial equality. An editorial in the *Manchester Guardian* acclaiming the *Brown* decision alluded not only to the ethical dimension of the civil rights cause but also to the strategic concern of the British government that its Cold War ally had compromised the containment of communist expansion by allowing the practice of racial discrimination to tarnish its position as leader of the free world. According to the paper, "the United States will rest on firmer foundations than it did, and will face the world with the happy consciousness of having put behind it what has long been its worst reproach."[7] Diplomatic and moral considerations informed the particularly outspoken criticism by the British press of the Little Rock school crisis, which focused both on demagogic Arkansas governor Orval Faubus for precipitating the conflict and on the federal government for not enforcing desegregation sooner.[8]

According to the *Observer,* the British should nonetheless be wary of claiming the moral high ground in their criticism of American race relations. "What happened in Little Rock could not happen in Britain. But it could happen in Kenya or Central Africa, where the British government has certain rights and duties comparable to those of the Federal Government in relation to the sovereign State of Arkansas. Before joining in a holier-than-thou attitude towards the American President's dilatoriness, we should be sure we intend to discharge our own comparable responsibilities."[9] The paper was only half right. Britain could not afford to be complacent about racial matters. Yet potential conflict existed not only overseas in nations seeking independence from British colonial rule but also much closer to home.

Between 1948 and 1958, 125,000 Caribbean migrants settled in the United Kingdom. The migrants were pushed from the West Indies by economic deprivation and pulled toward Britain by the prospect of work in an economy struggling with serious labor shortages.[10] As British subjects, they expected to be welcomed by their "Mother Country." The optimistic sentiments expressed in the title of calypso singer Lord Kitchener's "London Is the Place for Me" soon proved, however, to be out of tune with reality.[11]

The violent racist reaction to the arrival of the "Windrush Generation" (named after the ship carrying Jamaican passengers that docked in the United Kingdom in June 1948) shook Britain's self-righteous assumptions about its more tolerant attitude toward minorities. Racial disorders in Liverpool in August 1948 and in Deptford in July 1949 largely slipped under the radar of the American media. There was an altogether different response, however, to the race riots that erupted in Nottingham and London during August and September 1958.[12] The violence received extensive coverage in an American press relieved for once to report on racial troubles that afflicted another country. As a report published on behalf of Britain's Institute of Race Relations affirmed, to many Americans "it was gratifying that Britain, usually so sanctimonious about racial intolerance and violence, had herself proved to be no better than she should be."[13]

Southern segregationists, long on the defensive against international censure, made considerable capital out of the situation, castigating the hypocrisy of British critics of Jim Crow. According to the *Charleston News and Courier,* "If white and colored British subjects don't stop rioting in London and thereabouts, perhaps the NAACP will persuade President Eisenhower to land paratroopers to keep order in England. He didn't respect the sovereignty of the State of Arkansas, so why should English soil be exempt from integration-by-bayonet?"[14] A cartoon published by the Citizens' Council also captured the vengeful spirit of segregationists. It depicts John Bull tut-tutting the United States for the racial disorder that erupted during the Little Rock school crisis of 1957. In a second caption, an impudent adolescent representing the Nottingham rioters administers a retributive boot to the backside of John Bull while in the background appears an image of Britain's exploding inner cities.[15] Southern segregationists continued to emphasize the racial problems that beset their overseas critic by publicizing further outbursts of racial unrest in Middlesborough in 1961 and in the West Midlands industrial town of Dudley the following year. Such news stories attempted to deflect criticism of segregationists by demonstrating that racial conflict was a global phenomenon rather than a regional problem confined to the southern states.[16] As British historian Arnold Toynbee concluded, the reaction of segregationists to the racial unrest on the other side of the Atlantic was "a punishment for self-righteousness."[17]

Ironically, however, the comparison segregationists drew between Little Rock and London actually made it easier for British policy makers to deny that there was a serious racial problem in their country. British political commentators conceded that black immigrants faced problems such as inadequate housing and restricted educational and employment opportunities but emphasized that segregation and discrimination had no basis in law. Since Britain had no formal system of segregation comparable to Jim Crow, officials could dismiss the riots as an unfortunate aberration that only temporarily upset the prevailing liberal consensus. They claimed that those responsible for the violence were social and political deviants, disaffected young white males or members of the fascist lunatic fringe, in no way representative of broader public opinion. The arrest and conviction of these rioters demonstrated that Britain, in contrast to the American South, did not tolerate violent discrimination against racial minorities.[18]

British authorities also claimed that racial problems in their country were less deeply rooted in history than was the case in the American South and therefore less intractable. If there was a parallel between Britain and the United States, then it was less with the South than with the North, where thousands of black migrants struggled with similar problems of over-crowding and unemployment. What British analysts failed to foresee was that the northern inner cities would also become the focus of fierce racial conflict. Their attention should have focused less on Little Rock than on another race riot that occurred almost simultaneously in Levittown, Penn-sylvania, where state troopers had to dispel a mob attacking a black family that moved into an all-white housing development.[19]

This refusal to recognize that Britain had a serious and growing racial problem persisted despite the accumulation of evidence to the contrary. The British government also endured uncomfortable comparisons between race relations on either side of the Atlantic following the murder of Kelso Cochrane. On May 17, 1959, a gang of whites in Notting Hill Gate stabbed to death Cochrane, a thirty-two-year-old Antiguan migrant. The Commit-tee for African Organisations sent an open letter to Prime Minister Har-old Macmillan comparing the murder with the recent lynching of Mack Parker in Poplarville, Mississippi. In making this comparison, the signato-ries encouraged British authorities to demonstrate that they were less toler-ant of racial violence than white officials in the American South. No one, however, was ever convicted of the crime. The police insisted that the moti-vation for the murder was robbery rather than racial hatred, a further illus-tration of officials' state of denial about the depth of prejudice in Britain.[20]

Escalating racial tensions nonetheless induced British authorities to seek guidance from across the Atlantic. During the 1960s, the British gov-ernment enacted antiracist legislation that emulated American civil rights laws. Political debate about the proposed law similarly echoed the United States, with opponents in both instances arguing that no statute could change the hearts and minds of those who refused to accept black people as their equals. In 1965, Parliament nonetheless narrowly passed a Race Rela-tions Act that outlawed discrimination in public places on the "grounds of colour, race, or ethnic or national origins." British legislators drew inspi-ration from Titles II and III of the Civil Rights Act, signed into law by President Lyndon Johnson a year earlier. One important area in which they failed to follow the American federal government, however, was in prohib-iting the exclusion of racial minorities from work opportunities. Parliament redressed this issue with a second Race Relations Act in 1968, which out-lawed employment discrimination on similar lines to Title VII of the Civil Rights Act. The new law also drew on the more recent Civil Rights Act, enacted only months earlier, in providing for equal housing opportunities regardless of race or national origin.[21]

To assist in the planning of this legislation, British politicians furthermore sought the counsel of American civil rights activists. Bayard Rustin, Martin Luther King's principal adviser, traveled to London in the summer of 1965 to meet with a group of parliamentarians whom he advised on the appropriateness of American-style civil rights reform in Britain.[22] Rustin also addressed a two-day conference on racial equality in employment sponsored by the National Committee for Commonwealth Immigrants (NCCI) in February 1967.[23]

Rustin's presence provoked angry responses from British racists who resented what they perceived as American interference in the domestic affairs of their country.[24] These whites resisted the arrival of Rustin because they believed it would promote racial integration. Ironically, although the NCCI invited the civil rights activist to address its conference, it too attempted to control public debate on the race issue by excluding all but a few carefully selected representatives of Britain's own black communities. Dominated as it was by pillars of the white political establishment—its chairman was the Archbishop of Canterbury—the NCCI acted as a political gatekeeper that kept potentially more militant black voices out of the discussion on how to improve race relations. The organization also contained grassroots rebellion by placing its strategic emphasis on political lobbying rather than direct action. As antiracist activist Michael Dummett asserted, "Merely by coming into existence, the NCCI had delivered one of its most damaging blows to the embryo civil rights movement" in Britain.[25]

These criticisms of the NCCI point to one explanation for the failure to create a British civil rights movement. This lack of success was not, however, for lack of trying to emulate southern blacks. Antiracist activism in the United Kingdom owed much to the African American crusade against Jim Crow. Scholar Paul Gilroy has emphasized the cross-pollination that occurred as a result of the transmission of cultures throughout what he calls the Black Atlantic. In terms of the relationship between civil rights activists in Britain and the United States, the transmission of a black protest culture was not mutual but unidirectional. The movement for racial equality in Britain was essentially imitative of the United States.[26]

Southern race relations served as a means by which West Indian migrants to Britain contextualized their situation. Despite the hardships they endured, some migrants comforted themselves that race relations were far better in Britain than the United States, especially the South. Black Britons' conception of the southern states stemmed not only from media coverage of the civil rights struggle but also, in some cases, from personal experience accrued as migrant laborers.[27] The Trinidadian calypso singer Mighty Terror emphasized the virtues of Britain by contrasting them with the vices of both apartheid South Africa and Jim Crow. Referencing specific acts of racism such as the Little Rock school crisis, Mighty Terror proclaimed more broadly that "in the South with its Jim Crow laws / The black and the white is always having war / No civilization of any sort." This admonishment of white southerners contrasted with his enthusiasm for life in his adopted homeland. "There's no better place for a coloured man," he concluded, "In the universe better than Great Britain."[28]

Yet for other West Indian migrants the issue of whether life in Britain was much better than in the American South remained unresolved. These West Indians saw through the complacency and self-deception of white Britons, who sanctimoniously denounced the state of southern race relations. Conditions in the American South may have been intolerable, but at least whites there were honest in their hatred of blacks compared with Britons, who proclaimed an abstract belief in equality but seldom honored it in practice. Sam Selvon's poignant novel *The Lonely Londoners* conveys this tension during a scene in which recently arrived Galahad asks the more seasoned migrant Moses whether race relations are as bad in Britain as on the other side of the Atlantic.

> "That is a point the boys always debating," Moses say. "Some say yes, and some say no. The thing is, in America they don't like you, and they tell you so straight, so that you know how you stand. Over here is the old diplomacy 'thank you sir' and 'how do you do' and that sort of thing. In America you see a sign telling you to keep off, but over here you don't see any, but when you go in the hotel or the restaurant they will politely tell you to haul—or else give you the cold treatment."[29]

In seeing their domestic struggle for racial equality as part of a larger global resistance movement against white racism, black activists in Britain predominantly drew inspiration from anti-imperialist forces in Africa and the Caribbean. The civil rights struggle in the United States had nonetheless long been an important inspiration. The preeminent civil rights organization of the interwar era, the League of Coloured Peoples, adopted and adapted its name, strategy, and integrationist ideology from the National Association for the Advancement of Colored People.[30] Black Britons also owed much of their burgeoning political consciousness in the 1950s and 1960s to the crusade for racial equality in the United States. Events on the other side of the Atlantic received extensive media coverage in Britain, including the pioneering black newspaper the *West Indian Gazette,* edited by Claudia Jones. This reportage facilitated black Britons' consciousness of a global struggle against racism by collapsing the distance of time and space between themselves and civil rights campaigners on the other side of the Atlantic.[31] Black and white activists in Britain expressed their solidarity with the African American freedom struggle through lobbying, marching, and raising funds. Most dramatically, in an event timed to coincide with the March on Washington in August 1963, antiracist activists under the auspices of the Committee of Afro-Asian Caribbean Organisations demonstrated outside the American Embassy at Grosvenor Square in London.[32]

The ideology and tactics of African American activists also informed black protest against racial discrimination in Britain. The clearest example of this is the boycott of buses in Bristol, organized by black youth worker Paul Stephenson during the summer of 1963. This protest emulated the actions of African Americans in Montgomery, Alabama, seven years earlier in an effort to secure employment of nonwhite bus crews.[33] Although inspired by black activism on the other side of the Atlantic, the Bristol bus boycott nonetheless dramatized that the nonviolent direct-action tactics used to defeat Jim Crow were not especially adaptive to racial conditions in Britain. While black activists took their case against segregated seating on Montgomery buses to the U.S. Supreme Court, in Britain the absence of either a written constitution or law prohibiting racial discrimination in employment rendered it impossible to mount a similar legal challenge against the Bristol Omnibus Company. In Montgomery, the bus boycott had a crippling financial impact because African Americans constituted the overwhelming majority of passengers. By contrast, the nonwhite population of Bristol was much smaller and therefore had far less economic leverage. Although the bus company had by late August 1963 agreed to eliminate its color bar, this owed less to the direct economic impact of the boycott than to political pressure stemming from adverse publicity.[34]

The history of the most influential civil rights organization in Britain, the Campaign Against Racial Discrimination (CARD), similarly illustrates that while activists on the other side of the Atlantic drew inspiration from the African American freedom struggle, they could not successfully implement its tactics. CARD owed its existence to Martin Luther King's visit to London in 1964 (following earlier trips to the United Kingdom in 1957 and 1961), en route to receiving the Nobel Peace Prize in Stockholm. In a speech delivered to an audience that filled the aisles at St. Paul's Cathedral, King warned that unless action was taken to address housing, education, and employment discrimination, "festering sores of bitterness" on the part of the black community would precipitate a racial crisis in Britain comparable to the United States.[35] "I think it is necessary," he concluded, "for the colored population in Great Britain to organize and work through meaningful nonviolent direct action approaches to bring these issues to the forefront of the conscience of the nation."[36] The result was CARD, founded in January 1965 using an organizational model loosely similar to the Southern Christian Leadership Conference (SCLC). That the organization saw itself as the British equivalent of African American protest groups such as the SCLC is evident from the newsletter of one of its local branches, which proclaimed, "C.A.R.D. is to Britain what the Civil Rights Movement is to the U.S.A." A meeting at London's Conway Hall in 1967 at which Bayard Rustin was the keynote speaker strengthened the parallels between, and ties to, southern civil rights activists.[37] Yet CARD was ultimately unable to emulate the SCLC. Although the organization initially acted as an effective lobbying group, it never recruited a mass membership and by late 1967 had been reduced, in the words of one black community leader, to "an empty shell" as a result of infighting between radical and moderate activists.[38]

As the fates of both the Bristol bus boycott and CARD suggest, it proved impossible in Britain to implement the nonviolent direct-action model of civil rights protest pioneered in the American South. Why then were British civil rights activists unable to emulate their American counterparts in mobilizing mass resistance to racism? According to the Guianan-born author Mike Phillips, although African American activists provided inspiration to black Britons, "their style remained irreducibly alien," so much so that by the late 1960s "it was clear that if there was a way of being black in London we would have to create it ourselves."[39] Outlining the differences that shaped social and political protest in Britain and the American South not only helps explain why no mass movement against racism emerged in the United Kingdom but also casts further perspective on the distinctive historical factors that produced the American civil rights movement.

Several factors account for the relative failure of civil rights activism in Britain. First, the migrant community was proportionately much smaller than the black population of the southern states. Some commentators have also observed that at least initially few of the migrants possessed a strong political consciousness. Most concerned themselves only with their individual need to secure employment and housing and acculturate to their new environment rather than the promotion of their collective interests. Some also refrained from pushing for racial equality because they did not see Britain as their permanent home.[40] In the Jim Crow South, African Americans created parallel institutions that later provided them with the means to mobilize grassroots resistance to white rule. Black Britons' lack of numbers as well as their recent arrival in the country rendered it more difficult for them to create comparable community centers and associations.[41] In particular, the church did not serve as a focal point for black mobilization in Britain in the same way that it provided African Americans with a source of leadership and finance as well as a secure meeting space. The American civil rights movement enlisted many of its foot soldiers from among the women who made up the preponderance of black church congregations. This contrasted with Britain, where the black population was, at least initially, preponderantly male and less religiously observant. Black social protest in Britain, unlike the United States, was not therefore imbued with the power of the divine.[42]

Second, the heterogeneity of the migrant population complicated efforts to forge a united front. Other than their status as nonwhite immigrants, West Indians had little in common culturally with the Pakistanis and Indians who also settled in Britain during the postwar decades. The lack of contact between their respective community organizations reduced what could potentially have been one movement into a series of splinter groups. These interest groups pursued parallel lines of activism that seldom converged. Intra- as well as intercultural differences further divided the nonwhite migrant population. Although collectively categorized as "West Indians," there were often few close cultural ties between the migrants from the numerous islands of the Caribbean. Many of these migrants defined themselves more in terms of their island of origin or their status as British subjects than as members of a single nation-state. The failure of the West Indies Federation, an effort to amalgamate the Caribbean islands into a single governmental unit, is emblematic of this cultural and political diversity.[43]

Third, Britain did not produce a charismatic black leader equivalent to Martin Luther King. Although King galvanized black activism when he visited the United Kingdom, no native activist with the same moral authority and personal appeal emerged to assume control of that movement once he had returned to the United States. This absence of political leadership was the subject of a conversation between West Indians in the Brixton district of London, recalled by black journalist Donald Hinds. "Show me who we got to lead us," uttered one of the men. "The Americans got Malcolm X and Luther King, it do not matter whether you like them or not. They are there, but who have we got?" This political vacuum made it all the more difficult to unite the factionalized immigrant community in the way that King sustained the American civil rights coalition.[44]

Fourth, in contrast to the American South, racial discrimination in Britain was not maintained by law and therefore proved a less tangible issue to dramatize. In this sense race relations were more comparable to the de facto discrimination of America's northern cities than to the de jure segregation of the southern states.[45]

Although the effort to replicate southern civil rights protest in Britain had limited success in promoting equality for the black migrant population, the inspiration and counsel of African American activists was of considerable importance to a broad array of social and political movements. That influence was not limited only to racial issues. The Campaign for Nuclear Disarmament (CND), for instance, emulated the nonviolent direct-action tactics of the civil rights movement and appropriated "We Shall Overcome" as its anthem. Bayard Rustin also met with CND activists in January 1964, although his commitments meant he had to decline an invitation to lead a protest march in London.[46]

More significant still was the political capital that Martin Luther King provided Britain's anti-apartheid movement. British activists campaigning against the white supremacist regime in South Africa hoped to channel some of the respect and sympathy that the public had for African Americans struggling against Jim Crow. In May 1963, S. Abdul Minty, the honorary secretary of the Anti-Apartheid Movement, invited Dr. King to address activists celebrating South Africa Freedom Day in London. "Your activities in Birmingham have drawn the attention of the whole world to the racial injustice which prevails in the Southern States of the U.S.A.," enthused Minty. "We know how much encouragement it would bring to the millions of non-whites who are now living under the most vicious form of racial oppression."[47] Although King could not fit the event into his relentless schedule, his return to the United Kingdom the following year did foster public perception of the campaigns against Jim Crow and apartheid as two facets of a common fight for human dignity. Anti-Apartheid Movement publicist Anne Darnborough informed the American Committee on Africa that King had been "causing a stir all over the place," including a speech in which he "made a loud strong call for sanctions, blaming the U.S. and Britain for their complicity in the South African crime." To encourage the British public to draw parallels between the Jim Crow South and apartheid South Africa, Darnborough requested help soliciting an article for publication in her organization's newsletter by an African American civil rights leader. The American Committee on Africa proposed Congress of Racial Equality director James Farmer.[48]

The analogies drawn between the American South and South Africa stemmed less from political opportunism on the part of British anti-apartheid activists than a sincere conviction that they formed two fronts in a larger global conflict against racism. Anglican bishop Trevor Huddleston, who later served as president of the Anti-Apartheid Movement, met Martin Luther King during a trip to the United States in 1957. The experience helped inform his conception of an interconnected matrix of antiracist activism. A speech on race relations Huddleston delivered at the University of Cambridge in 1960 used the examples of Little Rock, Sharpeville, and Notting Hill to construct a triangulated network of global resistance to white supremacy. "We are getting used to a *shrinking world*," the bishop opined. "And, as the world gets smaller against the background of a vast universe, so we become more and more conscious of our relationship with those who—till now—were far from us."[49] Huddleston reiterated this point in an address delivered at Mansion House in London shortly after Martin Luther King's assassination. Citing W. E. B. Du Bois's observation that "the problem of the twentieth century is the problem of the color-line," the bishop affirmed that racial discrimination affected not only the United States but also the entire world. "It has passed from being a local problem," he asserted, "to being an international world problem."[50]

As this speech demonstrates, King's violent death brought home to British antiracist activists the moral and political urgency of combating discrimination both domestically and internationally. A Martin Luther King

Foundation and Memorial Fund established in 1968 had the explicit purpose to "give moral and material support to non-violent movements for civil
rights in any part of the world."[51] The notion that Britain's racial problems
were intertwined with those not only of the United States but also of all
nations was underlined by an address King's widow, Coretta, gave on a visit
to London in March 1969, "There was a time when one could talk of the
racist oppression of coloured peoples as though it were simply an American problem," stated Mrs. King, "but I understand that as the population
of non-white peoples began to increase in England, the response has also
tended to be oppressive."[52] A memorial event for King staged by the Caribbean Artists Movement similarly emphasized the global dimensions of the
race struggle by featuring speakers from Ghana, Jamaica, Trinidad, South
Africa, and the United States.[53]

While its influence may have been more inspirational than practical,
the African American freedom struggle was therefore integral to British
activists' awareness of the worldwide dimensions of the race struggle. The
rise of British racism from the late 1950s demonstrated a similar global consciousness on the part of white reactionaries that brought them into closer
contact with southern segregationists. Yet the opponents as well the proponents of civil rights reform in Britain would learn the limited adaptability
of southern politics and protest.

The British press reported in the late 1950s that the Ku Klux Klan was
attempting to exploit racial tensions by establishing its first overseas branch
in London.[54] Although there is little evidence that this initiative succeeded,
southern and British white supremacists may have collaborated in sending
death threats to Dr. David Pitts, a black physician who ran as a Labour candidate for the parliamentary seat of Hampstead in the autumn of 1959.[55]
The Klan also briefly capitalized on the dramatic rise of British racism in
the mid-1960s. A series of Klan-style cross burnings that occurred in communities throughout London and the Midlands during 1965 encouraged
Imperial Wizard Robert Shelton to declare his intention to travel to Britain
in order to recruit support. The British Home Office announced it would
refuse him entry to the country, however, and the threatened visit never
occurred.[56]

British racism appropriated ideas and rhetoric that were ironically in
decline among white southerners. In attempting to resist the *Brown* decision, many southern segregationists had eschewed explicitly racist arguments and emphasized the doctrine of states' rights. By the mid-1960s

white southerners had further toned down their rhetoric, abandoning massive resistance for a strategy of minimum compliance with court orders to desegregate public facilities. What to many southern segregationists seemed anachronistic arguments in defense of white supremacy now gained greater currency in Britain as intellectual racism moved from the margins to the center of political discourse. Conservative candidate Peter Griffiths won the parliamentary seat of Smethwick in 1964 with a campaign commitment to defend local whites against immigrants settling in the constituency. This included his endorsement of the slogan "If you want a nigger for a neighbour, vote Labor," which he claimed was a legitimate expression of popular sentiment. Griffiths also drew explicitly on the example of the American South to support his claims about the impossibility of implementing racial integration. A cartoon in the *Spectator* commented on Griffiths's resort to crude race-baiting tactics comparable to those traditionally used by white supremacists in the South. As a hooded Klansman walks through the public entrance of Parliament, a policeman standing guard outside explains to his colleague, "I think he's come to see the new member for Smethwick."[57]

Although British reactionaries dissociated themselves from southern racists, they shared many similar rhetorical tropes. African American journalist Charles L. Sanders observed that, other than a few idiomatic differences, the racist headlines published by the British press seemed to have been cut and pasted from southern segregationist newspapers. "They are stories that would be tedious for Americans to read," he asserted, "for they seem to have been plagiarized from the pages of American history itself. All that one has to do is substitute the word 'Negro' for the word 'Coloured,' and sprinkle in such familiar words as 'Bogalusa,' 'Deacons for Defense,' and 'Ku Klux Klan.'"[58]

This appropriation of southern segregationist rhetoric reached to the higher levels of British intellectual life. Cambridge historian and Conservative peer Godfrey Elton argued against civil rights legislation on the grounds that it would not change the attitudes and customs of a white population that wanted to preserve racial segregation. He further emulated the reasoning of southern segregationists by using the supposed hypocrisy of liberals in the northern United States to support his position. It was, he insisted, "remarkable how often the very Americans who most warmly applaud the determination of their Government to put an end to legal segregation in the South will bitterly resist any attempt to diminish extra-legal segregation in the North."[59]

The influence of the South on British understanding of race relations is further emphasized by press reaction to Conservative MP Enoch Powell, who in April 1968 delivered his infamous anti-immigrant "Rivers of Blood" address. Powell saw the racial disorders that afflicted the northern inner cities of the United States during the late 1960s as a prophetic warning of the racial turmoil that faced Britain unless it imposed tighter controls on immigration. "The tragic and intractable phenomenon which we watch with horror on the other side of the Atlantic, but which there is interwoven with the history and existence of the States itself," he exclaimed, "is coming upon us here by our own volition and our own neglect."[60]

Although it was the northern United States that provided his point of reference for warning of racial calamity, the demagogic language used by Powell led to the press comparing him to southern white supremacists, specifically George Wallace. The personalities of the erudite classical scholar and the plainspoken southern politician appeared to be poles apart, but both men espoused a reactionary form of populism that exploited white working-class resentment toward black people and the liberal elites who supposedly accorded them preferential treatment.[61] A cartoon published in the *Daily Telegraph* further illustrates how the British media continued to use the American South as an interpretative lens through which to analyze domestic race relations. As Powell walks like a farmer through a field, sowing his hate-filled seeds, hooded Klansmen start to grow out of the ground.[62]

By the late 1960s it was nonetheless not the civil rights conflicts of the South but rather the urban crises of the northern United States that informed both sides of the debate about race in Britain. White reactionaries warned of the need for restrictions on immigration to avert violence on the scale of the ghetto uprisings in cities such as Newark and Detroit. The rise of overt racism in turn fueled increasing anger, resentment, and militancy among black Britons. As the influence of the southern nonviolent direct action movement ebbed, a new tide of social and political protest shaped by northern Black Power was about to sweep through Britain. While Martin Luther King continued even in death to be a powerful inspiration to Britain's black community, militant leaders such as Malcolm X and Stokely Carmichael came to exert a similarly strong influence. The militant activism of black Britons in the late 1960s and early 1970s would further demonstrate the global diffusion of African American protest.

Notes

1. These events are further discussed later in the essay.

2. Jacquelyn Dowd Hall, "The Long Civil Rights Movement and the Political Uses of the Past," *Journal of American History* 91 (2005): 1233–63; Glenda E. Gilmore, *Defying Dixie: The Radical Roots of Civil Rights, 1919–1950* (New York: W. W. Norton, 2008). For a robust criticism of this interpretation of the black freedom struggle, see Eric Arnesen, "Reconsidering the 'Long Civil Rights Movement,'" *Historically Speaking* 10 (2009): 31–34.

3. Michael O'Brien, "On the Irrelevance of Knights," in Joseph P. Ward, ed., *Britain and the American South: From Colonialism to Rock and Roll* (Jackson: University Press of Mississippi, 2003), 220.

4. Alfred O. Hero Jr., *The Southerner and World Affairs* (Baton Rouge: Louisiana State University Press, 2005), 91; Joseph A. Fry, *Dixie Looks Abroad: The South and U.S. Foreign Relations, 1789–1973* (Baton Rouge: Louisiana State University Press, 2002), 226–27.

5. *Citizens' Council* 5.9 (June 1960): 2, South Caroliniana Library, University of South Carolina, Columbia. The cartoon originally appeared in the *Nashville Banner.*

6. Laura A. Belmonte, *Selling the American Way: U.S. Propaganda and the Cold War* (Philadelphia: University of Pennsylvania Press, 2008), 170. See also Hazel Erskine, "The Polls: World Opinion of U.S. Racial Problems," in Michael L. Krenn, ed., *Race and U.S. Foreign Policy from the Colonial Period to the Present: A Collection of Essays* (New York and London: Garland, 1998), 275–88.

7. *Manchester Guardian,* May 18, 1954. After 1959 the name of the newspaper changed to the *Guardian.*

8. *Observer,* Sept. 7, 1958.

9. *Observer,* Sept. 29, 1957. For more on British criticism of Jim Crow, see Mike Sewell, "British Responses to Martin Luther King, Jr. and the Civil Rights Movement, 1954–68," in Brian Ward and Tony Badger, eds., *The Making of Martin Luther King and the Civil Rights Movement* (Houndmills, Basingstoke, and London: Macmillan, 1996), 197, 198, 202.

10. For further analysis of the factors motivating migration, see Ceri Peach, *West Indian Migration to Britain: A Social Geography* (London: Oxford University Press, 1968).

11. This song is available on the compilation album *London Is the Place for Me: Trinidadian Calypso in London, 1950–1956* (Honest Jon, HJRCD2, 2002).

12. The most extensive analysis of the racial disorder that affected Britain is Edward Pilkington, *Beyond the Mother Country: West Indians and the Notting Hill White Riots* (London: I. B. Tauris, 1988).

13. J. A. G. Griffith, Judith Henderson, Margaret Usborne, and Donald Wood, *Coloured Immigrants in Britain* (London: Oxford University Press, 1960), vii. See also Nicholas Deakin, ed., *Colour and the British Electorate 1964: Six Case Stud-*

ies (London: Pall Mall Press, 1965), 1. For evidence of American press reaction, see the editorial "Notting Hill and Little Rock," *Los Angeles Times,* Sept. 3, 1958.

14. *Charleston News and Courier,* Sept. 3, 1958. In the same edition, the newspaper also took aim at French critics following reports that city authorities in Paris, fearing that the contagion of racial violence could spread from England, had urged North African immigrants to stay off the streets at night. "This racial discrimination may bring down the wrath of the NAACP, the Dept. of Justice and the commander-in-chief of the United States of America," the newspaper observed sarcastically. "Failure to make the Champs Elysees safe for all races could stir enmity in Asia and Africa, and create a victory for communist propaganda. At least that's what is said when American communities try to separate the races for the peace and order of all concerned."

15. *Citizens' Council,* Oct. 1958, 2. For a similar assessment of British embarrassment over the race riots, but from the opposite end of the political spectrum to the Citizens' Council, see *Jet,* Sept. 25, 1958; Philip King, "A New Immigrant Comes to Britain," *Crisis* 67.1 (Jan. 1960): 15–16.

16. *Citizens' Council* 4.3 (Dec. 1958): 3; *Charleston News and Courier,* Aug. 22, 1961; *Gettysburg Times,* Aug. 4, 1962. For further analysis of the Middlesborough disorder, including the dismissal by the local press of any connection between events in that city and in Little Rock, see Panikos Panayi, "Middlesborough 1961: A British Race Riot of the 1960s?" *Social History* 16 (May 1991): 139–53, esp. 146.

17. *New York Times,* Aug. 7, 1960.

18. "Clashes in the Streets: More Than Race Issues Involved," *Times,* Sept. 5, 1958; Robert Miles and Annie Phizacklea, *White Man's Country: Racism in British Politics* (London: Pluto, 1984), 34–36.

19. On the Levittown riot, see "Introduction: The End of Southern History," in Matthew D. Lassiter and Joseph Crespino, eds., *The Myth of Southern Exceptionalism* (New York: Oxford University Press, 2010), 4–5.

20. *Manchester Guardian,* May 19, 1959. The African American press reported on the British police's claim that the murder was not racially motivated but did not pursue the matter. See, for example, *Chicago Defender,* May 30, 1959. The case is the subject of Mark Olden, *Murder in Notting Hill* (London: Zero Books, 2011).

21. For a comparative analysis of the American Civil Rights Act of 1964 and the British Race Relations Act of 1965, see *New York Times,* Apr. 18, 1965.

22. Melvin L. Bergheim, Governmental Affairs Institute, to Bayard Rustin, June 30, 1965, box 22, folder 11, Bayard T. Rustin Papers, Library of Congress, Washington, DC.

23. "Racial equality in employment," conference agenda, Feb. 23–25, 1967, box 22, folder 11, Rustin Papers; *Guardian,* Feb. 26, 1967; *Times,* Feb. 27, 1967.

24. Mrs. G. Horton to Bayard Rustin, Feb. 28, 1967, and J. R. Wilson to Bayard Rustin, Mar. 1, 1967, both box 22, folder 12, Rustin Papers.

25. Michael Dummett, "The Travails of a British Civil Rights Movement," *Patterns of Prejudice* 2 (1968): 11.

26. Paul Gilroy, *The Black Atlantic: Modernity and Double Consciousness* (Cambridge: Harvard University Press, 1995).

27. Donald Hinds, *Journey to an Illusion: The West Indian in Britain* (London: Heinemann, 1966), 153.

28. Mighty Terror and his Calypsonians, "Heading North." This 1958 recording is available on the *Trojan Calypso Boxset* (Trojan Records, TJETD033).

29. Sam Selvon, *The Lonely Londoners* (London: Penguin, 2006), 20–21.

30. Peter Fryer, *Staying Power: The History of Black People in Britain* (London: Pluto Press, 1984), 327–32.

31. Bill Schwarz, "'Claudia Jones and the West Indian Gazette': Reflections on the Emergence of Post-Colonial Britain," *Twentieth-Century British History* 14 (2002): 270, 280.

32. Dilip Hiro, *Black British White British* (London: Eyre & Spottiswoode, 1971), 53–54.

33. Madge Dresser, *Black and White on the Buses: The 1963 Colour Bar Dispute in Bristol* (Bristol: Bristol Broadsides, 1986); Paul Stephenson, *Memoirs of a Black Englishman* (Bristol: Tangent Books, 2011).

34. Rosalind E. Wild, "'Black Was the Colour of Our Fight': Black Power in Britain, 1955–1976" (PhD diss., University of Sheffield, 2008), 53–58.

35. *Guardian*, Dec. 7, 1964; *Times*, Dec. 7, 10, 1964. The capacity audience that turned up for the speech is described in Joseph Robinson, "Man and Cathedral," in Ian Henderson, ed., *Man of Christian Action: Canon John Collins—the Man and His Work* (Guildford: Lutterworth Press, 1976), 13.

36. *Jet*, Aug. 8, 1968.

37. CARD Islington Newsletter, May 1967, John La Rose Collection, George Padmore Institute, London, JLR/3/10: CARD. For an example of an African American activist from the North meeting with black Britons, see the invitation to invite New Yorker Bill Epton to address the West Indian Standing Conference in "Minutes of the Monthly General Meeting Held on Sunday, 1st, January, 1967 at the West Indian Students' Centre, 1 Collingham Gardens, Earls Court, London, S.W.5.," John La Rose Collection, JLR/3/1/33.

38. The most extensive history of CARD, albeit one that has been much criticized, is Benjamin W. Heineman Jr., *The Politics of the Powerless: A Study of the Campaign against Racial Discrimination* (London: Oxford University Press, 1972).

39. Mike Phillips, *London Crossings: A Biography of Black Britain* (London: Continuum, 2001), 45.

40. Alastair Buchan, "Multicolored Britain," *International Journal* 23 (Autumn 1968): 521; Dummett, "Travails of a British Civil Rights Movement," 8; Hinds, *Journey to an Illusion*, 136.

41. Allen D. Grimshaw, "Factors Contributing to Colour Violence in the United States and Britain," *Race and Class* 3 (1962): 13.

42. Griffith et al., *Coloured Immigrants in Britain*, 75.

43. Griffith et al., *Coloured Immigrants in Britain*, 49; Paul B. Rich, *Prospero's*

Return? Historical Essays on Race, Culture and British Society (London: Hansib, 1994), 159.

44. Hinds, *Journey to an Illusion,* 155.

45. David Dabydeen, John Gilmore, and Cecily Jones, eds., *The Oxford Companion to Black British History* (Oxford: Oxford University Press, 2007), 495; Anthony H. Richmond, *The Colour Problem* (Harmondsworth, Middlesex: Penguin, 1961), 259.

46. Michael G. Long, ed., *I Must Resist: Bayard Rustin's Life in Letters* (San Francisco: City Lights Books, 2012), 288.

47. Abdul S. Minty to Martin Luther King Jr., May 10, 1963, Archive of the Anti-Apartheid Movement, 1956–98, Bodleian Library of Commonwealth and African Studies at Rhodes House, University of Oxford, MSS AAM 2331.

48. Anne Darnborough to Mary-Louise Hooper, Dec. 9, 1964, Anne Darnborough to Mary-Louise Hooper, Jan. 25, 1965, and Ruth Vaughn to Anne Darnborough, Feb. 8, 1965, all Archive of the Anti-Apartheid Movement, MSS AAM 2331.

49. Handwritten notes for speech, "Race Relations," Cambridge University, 1960, Correspondence and Papers of Archbishop Trevor Huddleston, Bodleian Library of Commonwealth and African Studies at Rhodes House, University of Oxford, MSS Huddleston 371. For a brief reference to Huddleston's visit to the United States, see Piers McGrandle, *Trevor Huddleston: Turbulent Priest* (London: Continuum, 2004), 108.

50. "Notes for Address on Race Relations," July 23, 1968, Mansion House, Correspondence and Papers of Archbishop Trevor Huddleston, MSS Huddleston 371.

51. Christian Action, undated memorandum, Michael Ramsey Official Papers, V01.135, f.272, Lambeth Palace Library, London.

52. The Martin Luther King Foundation, *Towards Racial Equality and Racial Harmony* (London: Martin Luther King Foundation, n.d.), 6–7, Lambeth Palace Library. See also Rev. Wilfred Wood's Address at Central Hall, Westminster, Mar. 17, 1969, at Public Meeting "Coretta King Speaks," John La Rose Collection.

53. Advertisement, "The Caribbean Artists Movement Presents an Evening of Poetry and Prose from the Third World in Memory of Dr. Martin Luther King," West Indian Students' Centre, July 5, 1968, Caribbean Artists Movement Collection, George Padmore Institute, London, CAM 2/24 (1).

54. *Daily Sketch,* Apr. 29, 1957; *Daily Worker,* Aug. 28, 1958; Colin Holmes, "Violence and Race Relations in Britain, 1953–1968," *Phylon* 36 (1975): 113.

55. *Chicago Defender,* Sept. 22, Oct. 3, 1959.

56. *Los Angeles Times,* June 16, 1965; *Chicago Defender,* July 19, 1965; Hiro, *Black British White British,* 58; A. Sivanandan, "From Resistance to Rebellion: Asian and Afro-Caribbean Struggles in Britain," *Race and Class* 23 (1981): 124–25; unidentified newspaper clippings, Ku Klux Klan Collection, box 1, folder 13, Archives and Special Collections, J. D. Williams Library, University of Mississippi.

57. Peter Griffiths, *A Question of Colour* (London: Leslie Frewin, 1966). The cartoon can be seen at http://www.politicalcartoon.co.uk/gallery/artist/trog-wally-fawkes-b1924_91.html (accessed Sept. 1, 2011).

58. Charles L. Sanders, "Race Problem in Great Britain: Bias Forces 'Coloureds' to Band Together for Survival as in U.S.," *Ebony* (Nov. 1965): 154–55.

59. Lord Elton, *The Unarmed Invasion: A Survey of Afro-Asian Immigration* (London: Geoffrey Bles, 1965), 67.

60. William E. Nelson, *Black Atlantic Politics: Dilemmas of Political Empowerment in Boston and Liverpool* (Albany: State University of New York Press, 2000), 199.

61. For examples of the parallels drawn by the UK press between Powell and Wallace see *Guardian,* Oct. 7, 1968; *Daily Mirror,* Mar. 21, 1969. Similar comparisons by U.S. newspapers include *Sarasota Herald-Tribune,* Apr. 21, 1968; *Boston Globe,* Apr. 23, 1968; *Christian Science Monitor,* Sept. 23, 1968.

62. *New York Times,* Dec. 15, 1968; *Daily Telegraph,* Jan. 19, 1970.

14

Resisting the Wind of Change

The Citizens' Councils and
European Decolonization

Daniel Geary and Jennifer Sutton

"Will Western Europe Be Driven Out of Africa?" So worried Medford Evans in a 1978 article in the *Citizen,* the official publication of the leading white segregationist organization, the Citizens' Councils of America (sometimes known colloquially by its original name, the White Citizens' Councils). Evans quoted the 1910 edition of the *Cambridge Modern History,* which claimed that the "colonies of France, Britain, Portugal, Germany, and Italy" had made Africa an "annex of Europe." "There is no indication," Evans reflected, "that the learned historian had any idea that fifty years later—that is, in 1960, the African possessions of those West-European nations would begin a chain-reacting process of 'liberation' and 'independence' which seemed to leave the continent not an annex of Europe, but a disconnected shambles."[1] The Citizens' Councils strongly identified with an ideal of a racially homogeneous Europe, yet they sharply criticized European decolonization measures, which they perceived as an abandonment of civilization to the anarchy of majority black rule.

In the mid-twentieth century, the relationship of white southern segregationists to Europe pivoted on its policies toward former colonies in Africa. Segregationists such as Evans identified most strongly with whites in former British colonies of southern Africa, whom they believed were in an embattled position analogous to their own. As seen in the pages of the *Citizen,* American segregationists in solidarity with whites in Africa resisted the "wind of change" that British prime minister Harold Macmillan identified in his famous 1960 speech indicating a shift in British policy in favor of decolonization in Africa. During the 1960s and 1970s, British colonial policies strained segregationists' affinity for Britain. However, by the 1980s their hostility toward Britain gave way to a more positive view of metropolitan Britain under its new prime minister, Margaret Thatcher. They perceived her as committed to advancing the interests of whites in Britain, southern Africa, and, through her close affiliation with Ronald Reagan, the United States.

The agendas of white supremacists in the American South have too easily been assumed to focus on highly local concerns—matters of school boards and lunch counters—rather than global ones. Most historians have overlooked those whites who couched their resistance to racial equality in international frameworks. In contrast, many scholars have shown that resistance to segregation and racism promoted associations during the mid-twentieth century among African Americans and colonial peoples around the world.[2] Historians also have demonstrated how Cold War imperatives shaped American policy makers' responses to the civil rights movement in the United States, as Jim Crow proved an embarrassment to Americans seeking to win the support of the new nations of Africa.[3] In comparison to the scholarship on the international dimensions of antiracist protest and government policy making, only a few scholars have considered the international dimensions of white resistance to racial equality. Similar to how African Americans understood the outcome of the civil rights struggle to be linked to the outcome of African struggles for independence, international-minded segregationists merged their cause with that of whites in decolonizing African states and, later, with that of metropolitan Britons affected by an influx of nonwhite immigrants from the former empire.

Even one of the best of the few scholarly works on the international views of southern segregationists, Thomas Noer's "Segregationists and the World," stops short of fully recognizing the international dimensions of white supremacist outlooks. Noer contends that "segregationists used selected international issues largely to gain support for their major domestic goal of defeating the civil rights movement."[4] To be sure, southern segregationists' public opposition to decolonization in Africa reinforced their arguments for segregation at home by demonstrating the perils of black rule. In addition, as Noer demonstrates, segregationists framed their arguments against decolonization in Cold War terms that facilitated alliances with anticommunist American conservatives outside of the South. Yet an examination of the sustained engagement of the *Citizen* with decoloniza-tion in Africa suggests that their international concerns went beyond an interest in defending American segregation to an intense identification with embattled whites in Africa's European outposts.

Noer's account concludes with the third-party presidential campaign of segregationist George Wallace in 1968, but the international concerns of white segregationists continued long past that date.[5] Indeed, an examina-tion of the *Citizen* suggests that white segregationists' interest in interna-tional affairs increased just at the moment in the mid-1960s when it was clear they had lost the battle to maintain segregation. With exclusive white rule doomed in the American South, they focused their efforts on preserv-ing it in the one part of the world where it still held sway, in the former British colonies of southern Africa. Some of the major stories followed by the *Citizen* thus were international: the defense of the white government in Rhodesia following its preemptive declaration of independence from Britain, the anti-immigration struggle in Britain, and the imposition of sanctions on South Africa. The organization's political activities regarding U.S. foreign policy reflected these international concerns. This essay, which focuses on the *Citizen* during the 1960s, 1970s, and 1980s, demonstrates sustained engagement by American white supremacists with foreign affairs, particularly those related to European decolonization.

Citizen writers described their battles as part of an international strug-gle to maintain both democracy and the primacy of white civilization. The connections they made between ideas of political liberty and whiteness had a long history for Americans. These issues had been linked in the early nineteenth century in the form of racial Anglo-Saxonism, a form of white supremacy that asserted the superiority of British and American political institutions and the inferiority of peoples not of British descent. In the mid-nineteenth century Americans used racial Anglo-Saxonism to justify American westward expansion and the conquest of Native Americans and Mexicans.[6] At the end of the century, overseas imperialism employed the evolving logic of racial Anglo-Saxonism, which privileged people of English descent above other whites. By then, racial Anglo-Saxonism was increas-ingly conflated with whiteness, as Rudyard Kipling famously captured in his poem "The White Man's Burden." In the early twentieth century, so-called white men's countries like South Africa and the United States, especially the South, rejected the idea of a multiracial democracy, often subverting national or imperial policies through ostensibly nonracial criteria such as literacy tests.[7]

The affinity that writers for the *Citizen* showed for defenders of white rule in southern Africa in the mid-to-late twentieth century drew on this longer history of white supremacy. Their denial of the possibility of white and nonwhite liberty coexisting reflected earlier international fantasies of a white-dominated world, if not a specifically English-speaking one. White southerners' longstanding Anglophilia and the legacy of racial Anglo-Saxonism accounts for the *Citizen*'s intense interest in British decolonization and domestic politics, often to the exclusion of developments in other European countries and colonies.[8] Yet writers for the *Citizen* developed friendships and lent moral support to Dutch-descended Afrikaner state and business leaders in South Africa. The terms they used to describe settlers in Africa (or their descendants) were *white* and *European*. They were less concerned with "Europe" as a geographic region than they were with the status of people of European descent all over the world.

The White Citizens' Councils formed in 1955 to fight desegregation following the Supreme Court's 1954 ruling in *Brown v. Board of Education* that racially segregated schools were unconstitutional. The first White Citizens' Council was founded in Indianola, Mississippi, and similar organizations quickly spread across the South. Councils aimed to recruit respectable, educated, middle-class southerners. Many members were leading businessmen involved with Kiwanis, Rotary, and other civic groups. At its zenith in 1956, the national organization claimed more than 250,000 members, but it soon entered a gradual decline.[9] There is little doubt that the organization lost relevance as segregationists lost the fight to retain Jim Crow during the 1960s, yet it survived desegregation to remain an influential organization with close links to the national conservative movement. In 1968, it built a new office building for its headquarters in Jackson, Mississippi. Many of the original leaders of the Citizens' Councils, including Medford Evans, William J. Simmons, and organizational founder Robert Patterson, wrote regularly for the *Citizen* into the 1970s and 1980s.

The Citizens' Councils distinguished itself from the Ku Klux Klan and other extremist white supremacists by recruiting an educated membership and eschewing vigilante violence. To that end, the *Citizen* conferred intellectual respectability on the Citizens' Councils, as well as promulgating its views. Beginning in 1955, the Association of Citizens' Councils of Mississippi published a four-page tabloid, the *Citizens' Councils*. The national organization, the Citizens' Councils of America, adopted the newspaper as its official publication in 1961. It replaced the paper in 1966 with a monthly journal, its name shortened to the *Citizen,* that combined original articles with reprintings from like-minded media.[10] The publication had an approximate circulation of forty-five thousand in 1961 and twenty-five thousand in 1969.[11] Wanting to move past a stereotype of segregationists as parochial rednecks whose worldview could not see past Dixie, the *Citizen* strove to create a body of readers well informed about world affairs with a particular interest in Africa. An analysis of the *Citizen* reveals a level of reporting of events in southern Africa, albeit heavily biased, that easily outpaced national news sources.[12]

From the 1950s to the 1980s, the *Citizen*'s coverage of international events focused primarily on issues related to European decolonization in Africa, signaled by Macmillan's 1960 "Wind of Change" speech. When Macmillan delivered his address to the South African Parliament on February 3, 1960, he had just completed a tour of Africa. He shared his impressions of African nationalism on the eve of decolonization, just days after Belgium had agreed to withdraw from the Congo within six months. Macmillan suggested that the changes he had seen in central Africa would come to affect southern Africa. He expressed a preference for "one-man, one-vote" principles, or majority rule, and he made it clear that the British government would no longer support apartheid. The timing of this speech was significant for South Africa as well. Hardly two weeks prior, the South African cabinet had decided to pursue status as a republic. Though South African leaders initially sought to join the British Commonwealth, the "Wind of Change" speech signaled that South Africa as a white minority-rule state would not be tolerated by other Commonwealth members.[13]

Though Macmillan addressed South Africans and spoke about African issues, his message reached a world audience and grabbed American segregationists' attention. British withdrawal of support for white minority rule in southern Africa became a flashpoint for them because of the connections they saw between their positions and those of white settlers and their descendants in Africa. Segregationists were interested specifically in the region of southern Africa that editors of the *Citizen* defined for readers as the Republic of South Africa, "its mandated territory of South West Africa," Rhodesia, Mozambique, and Angola. They explained that the region of southern Africa specially interested them because it "is the only one on the continent that remains under the control of white governments," distinguishing "White Africa" from "Black African" countries.[14]

The *Citizen*'s editors saw segregationists' position in the South as analogous to that of whites in Africa in terms of how the outside world regarded their resistance to democratic change. As southerners who felt their case for segregation had been judged before northern, federal courts of white opinion, they recognized early on that the future of white minority rule in southern Africa would also be shaped by the global North—the United States and Europe—and in international organizations such as the United Nations. Articles discussing southern Africa in the *Citizen* mainly sought to shift the debate from "one-man, one-vote" issues to a focus on the material success of "White Africa" in ways that portrayed white rule as ultimately benefiting Africans. When economic sanctions were imposed on Rhodesia and later South Africa, the *Citizen* pointed to the economic costs of the sanctions, bitterly noting their effects on both whites and blacks in those countries.

In 1966, the *Citizen* devoted a special issue to "southern Africa," following a three-month expedition to that region by members of the Citizens' Council of Mississippi. Commenting on the trip, *Citizen* editor William J. Simmons asked, "What effects have resulted from the campaign to loose the 'winds [*sic*] of change?'"[15] He linked the battle to maintain white supremacy in southern Africa to the similar losing battle at home. He also expressed a deep identification with the positions of whites in southern Africa. For instance, discussing his visit to Salisbury (now Harare), Rhodesia, he noted the town's similarities to his hometown of Jackson, Mississippi.

Simmons saw the effects of decolonization as not only comparable to racial changes in the American South but also connected. Regarding whites in southern Africa, he asked, "What . . . do we share with them? How does their situation affect us? And how does ours affect them? Finally, what portents are there for our future?"[16] Simmons's questions were partly prompted by the internationalization of antiracist struggles. As he declared, "The 'liberals' and leaders of the Negro Revolution have made it increasingly clear to us that our destiny here in the South is intertwined with South Africa. If South Africa succeeded, our cause was helped. If she failed, our cause was hurt."[17]

Simmons returned from his tour of Rhodesia and South Africa with a new perspective on the world-historical significance of the struggle in the American South. Fighting to preserve southern segregation would help determine the "world's course." He declared, "we can stop the drive to impose a racial revolution on Rhodesia, on South Africa, and on ourselves."[18]

Macmillan's "Wind of Change" speech prompted segregationists' increased attention to southern Africa and angered them, but it was the refusal of Labour prime minister Harold Wilson's government to recognize Rhodesia's November 1965 declaration of independence that truly alienated segregationists from Britain. Wilson successfully lobbied the UN to impose sanctions on Rhodesia in 1965, which the United States observed.[19] Historian Clive Webb has noted that white southern segregationists who had long idealized Britain were shocked and embittered by the level of support given to the African American civil rights movement by the British government and public.[20] An examination of the *Citizen* shows that segregationists were also incensed by British policies toward its former colonies.

A 1967 article in the *Citizen* speculated that "the day is coming now when America must re-evaluate her true friends in the world."[21] In the *Citizen*'s view, America's true friend was no longer Britain, but Rhodesia. The *Citizen* sought to convince its readers that the United States should recognize the new Rhodesian government and lift the sanctions against it. The *Citizen* contended that U.S. recognition of other decolonizing African states but not Rhodesia demonstrated "favoritism" toward blacks.[22] This reasoning echoed earlier articles on decolonization that accused Africans of "prejudice" or "reverse racism."[23] *Citizen* writers also argued that failing to support "White Africa" was racial treachery. The United States and Great Britain "should have been bound . . . by ties of blood, culture, and political philosophy."[24]

In the context of the Cold War, the *Citizen* argued, white-led Rhodesia was a bulwark against communism. Articles by James Angus, Rhodesian minister of defense, published in the *Citizen* made this point bluntly: "Rhodesia today is in the front line of resistance to world communism. . . . If we fail, South Africa will fail too and then the whole of the West will be in great jeopardy."[25] The *Citizen* emphasized Rhodesia's importance as an ally against communism by citing its support of the U.S. war in Vietnam. It noted bitterly that American support for Britain's position on Rhodesia was not reciprocated by British support for the U.S. war in Vietnam. Such Cold War arguments would have appealed to right-wing anticommunists outside the South who were desirable allies for southern segregationists.

Ian Smith, the prime minister of Rhodesia, heavily emphasized these points in an interview he gave to *Citizen* editor William J. Simmons when they met on Simmons's 1966 tour. The Citizens' Council Forum made a thirty-minute sixteen-millimeter sound-film of this interview, available for rental "to responsible individuals and organizations" for twenty-five dollars. According to the *Citizen*, 350 U.S. radio stations broadcast the interview, and it was scheduled for television broadcast "in all sections" of the United States.[26]

The difference between British and Rhodesian positions on Vietnam entrenched southern segregationists against Great Britain. In an article reprinted in the *Citizen*, Jesse Helms wrote about why he opposed the UN actions against Rhodesia. Helms, a future U.S. senator from North Carolina and a vigorous opponent of sanctions against South Africa, was in 1967 a "broadcasting executive" with WRAL-TV in Raleigh. He praised Rhodesia as a bulwark against communism and cited Rhodesian support for American efforts in Vietnam. How, he asked, could the United States "help Great Britain in her efforts to crush Rhodesia—at the very time that Great Britain is trading with our communist enemies"? Helms concluded, "As long as we have 'friends' like the British . . . we don't need any enemies. We're being played for suckers."[27]

Like Helms, other conservative white Southerners echoed Citizens' Councils' support of Rhodesia. In 1966, the Friends of Rhodesia formed in the United States with financial assistance from the Rhodesian government; it had 122 branches and some twenty-five thousand members, mostly in the South. Southern senators such as Strom Thurmond of South Carolina and James Eastland of Mississippi were vocal supporters of Ian Smith's government, and anticommunist Republicans such as Barry Goldwater opposed sanctions against Rhodesia on Cold War grounds. Some white Americans even fought as mercenaries for the Rhodesian government in the civil war that broke out in 1971.[28] White segregationists including those in the Citizens' Councils remained strongly interested in events in Rhodesia throughout the 1970s. After Helms was elected to the U.S. Senate in 1972, he led a fight to lift U.S. sanctions against the Rhodesian government, culminating in his sponsorship of the Helms-Byrd Amendment of 1979. Helms, the *Citizen,* and their allies continued to push the Rhodesian government line that liberation fighters were communists and terrorists, though they failed to convince southern president Jimmy Carter.[29]

Editors of the *Citizen* were interested not only in European decolonization in Africa but also in related developments in Britain. They particularly followed conflicts over the growing immigrant populations of racial minorities from the Commonwealth, a development strongly connected to the decline of the British Empire. Clive Webb notes that southern segregationists found considerable *Schadenfreude* in rising racial tensions in Britain, which seemed to reveal the self-righteousness and hypocrisy of British stances toward the U.S. South.[30] The *Citizen* made this point and connected it to the perceived hypocrisy of British colonial policy. A 1978 article on Rhodesia speculated that "quite probably the British at home are not less racist than their cousins in Rhodesia; quite possibly they are more so. But they are not for *all* ethnic Britons, only those who still reside in Britain. To save the insular remnant, they are prepared to sacrifice their kinsmen abroad."[31]

Attitudes toward British politics that had been chilled by the "wind of change" and turned icy by Wilson's standoff with Rhodesia warmed to British opposition voices in the late 1960s, especially that of Conservative member of Parliament Enoch Powell. The *Citizen* appreciated Powell's opposition to international organizations that threatened national sovereignty such as the UN and the European Common Market; of course they also appreciated his opposition to sanctioning Rhodesia.[32] They celebrated his notorious 1968 "Rivers of Blood" speech, which attacked nonwhite immigration from the Commonwealth to Britain as driving a wedge into British culture. The *Citizen* even claimed that Powell was "assuming the mantle of Gov. George Wallace of Alabama."[33]

Similar to how *Citizen* editors created ties to Ian Smith of Rhodesia, they sought personal contact with Powell and interpreted his concerns in terms of southern experience. Powell visited the United States in 1967 and 1971, when he went to Jackson, Mississippi. There he attended a luncheon with members of the Citizens' Councils, other civic groups, judges, and "elected state officials."[34] Powell's remarks at this luncheon discussed the costs to white opportunity posed by immigrants from the former empire. Editors compared his comment that "whites are being held back to accommodate the Asiatics and blacks" to U.S. school busing practices that enforced integration.[35]

Illustrating the article on Powell's visit were photographs taken in Powell's district of Wolverhampton, representing the effects of nonwhite immigration to the British heartland. One image showed a younger and an older black woman walking in front of a typical Edwardian row of red-brick terrace houses. The caption noted that arriving black immigrants had "progressively occupied" these "workers' houses," suggesting it was a process similar to American "block-busting." In another image, South Asians gathered over pints at a pub table. At the center of the photo sat a man wearing a suit jacket and a turban characteristic of Sikhs. Although a white man sat at the table as well, the caption said pubs were experiencing "de facto segregation," implying that even such a mainstay of English life as pub culture was vulnerable to racial change.[36]

Photographs of Powell himself appeared repeatedly in the *Citizen,* alongside regular updates on his activities. He proved an especially compelling figure for the Citizens' Councils because his image and background as a scholar of classics seemed to refute the stereotype that conservatives were anti-intellectual. In a biographical profile of Powell, the *Citizen* noted his Cambridge degree and his early career as a scholar of Greek and juxtaposed the "erudite Mr. Powell" to the "liberal intelligentsia." Putting the matter in southern terms, they noted that it would be impossible to "dismiss him lightly or contemptuously as being a British equivalent of America's much-maligned 'redneck.'"[37]

The *Citizen's* praise of Powell helps explain why its writers came to embrace a more positive view of Britain after the election of Margaret Thatcher in 1979. The May 1978 cover featured Thatcher and declared that her vigorous leadership of the Conservative Party was one reason "Why There Should Always Be an England."[38] Published a year before Thatcher's election as prime minister, the feature praised Thatcher for saying that she would seek an "end to immigration" before Britain became "swamped by people of a different culture." The article celebrated her jump in the polls following a speech in which she "promised four times 'the prospect of a clear end to immigration.'" When editor George Shannon wondered whether Thatcher could "liberate" Britain, he specifically cited her opposition to immigration by "Blacks from Africa and the West Indies, along with Asian[s]." Shannon approvingly quoted Thatcher's statement that such immigration "threatened to destroy the British character."[39] The *Citizen* retained a strong interest in anti-immigration politics in Britain throughout the 1980s. One headline from 1983 asked, "Have the British Had Enough," and praised the Nationality Act introduced by the Thatcher government as "a new British law to halt invasion by non-whites."[40]

Despite this reconciliation to political developments on the British mainland, the *Citizen* remained outraged by what one writer saw as Britain's "betrayal" of Rhodesia.[41] After the establishment of Zimbabwe in 1980, the publication printed increasingly lurid articles describing violence involving blacks. In particular, it contained several articles by Father Arthur Lewis, an Anglican priest and founder of the Rhodesian Christian Group, which operated in South Africa, the United Kingdom, and the United States. In one typical article from 1982, Lewis reported, "The onslaught on the white man in Zimbabwe continues from all sides."[42] Lewis claimed that "the truth is that both civilization and Christianity were brought here by white people."[43] He urged readers to "never listen to the siren voice of 'world opinion,' regardless of whether it comes from Moscow, New York, or the WCC [World Council of Churches] in Geneva."[44] By defining the enemies as the United Nations, the WCC, and communists, Lewis offered a broad critique of international liberalism that he hoped would resonate with the conservative revival in the United States and the United Kingdom.

Despite events in Zimbabwe and increasing anti-apartheid activism in the United States, writers for the *Citizen* took heart from the policies of the Thatcher regime and the change of political climate in the United States marked by the election of Ronald Reagan, who reversed the Carter administration's focus on international human rights and began a policy of "constructive engagement" with South Africa.[45] The *Citizen* also viewed the Falklands War, in which the British government intervened to protect a small community of English settlers on islands off the coast of Argentina, as a sign that the British government would reverse course elsewhere and defend white settlers in its former colonies. The *Citizen* believed that the Falklands War had implications for British policy in the world region it cared most about, southern Africa. An editorial introduction to an article by the South African ambassador to the United States included the striking statement: "As of now, it [South Africa] is surely the main target in the war for the Southern hemisphere. Defense of the Falklands, objectively speaking, is also defense of South Africa."[46] In 1982, the journal printed a photograph of Reagan shaking hands with Thatcher following the Falklands War and expressed hope that the two could triumph over "irrational revolutionary forces."[47]

The *Citizen* favorably reported the Thatcher government's opposition to sanctions on South Africa while challenging growing popular American calls for sanctions. Indeed, the Citizens' Councils' identifications with whites in southern Africa culminated with its strong defense of the South African government in the face of growing international support for the anti-apartheid movement. They viewed support for apartheid as the final battle over the issue that always most concerned them: the preservation of exclusive white rule. Local Citizens' Councils reached out to support white South Africans. For example, after the United States imposed sanctions, the board of directors of the Metro-South Citizens' Council of St. Louis published an article in the Afrikaans-language newspaper *Rapport* entitled "Message to South Africans: Liberals in the United States Do Not Speak for Most Americans." The authors assured South African supporters of apartheid that "average Americans, in organizations like ours, are stepping up efforts to counter anti-South African propaganda."[48] South African government officials were aware of and encouraged by Citizens' Councils activities, as was evident in its publication of an article by South Africa's ambassador to the United States.[49]

Strikingly, many antisanctions articles in the *Citizen* in the 1980s eschewed overtly white supremacist arguments, relying instead on arguments such as the right to national self-determination, anticommunism, practical damage to the American economy, and the notion that Africans were well served by the South African government. This strategy made sense given the *Citizen*'s desire to influence broader public opinion in a national climate in which open racism was no longer tolerated as it had been in the 1960s. However, not far beneath the surface of *Citizen* articles were assumptions that only those descended from Europeans were fit to govern themselves. *Citizen* writers sometimes explicitly raised the specter of "black peril," the notion of black-on-white violence, should apartheid end. In October 1985, following anti-Indian riots in Durban, South Africa, that August, the journal's cover showed a photo of several dozen black men marching and carrying sticks captioned: "Savage Zulu mob on rampage against South Africa's Indians." The accompanying editorial described the Durban riots as "an orgy of destruction reminiscent of the burning of the Watts section of Los Angeles" and urged readers to consider what "might happen if South Africa's 20,000,000 blacks should suddenly gain control of 4,000,000 whites." The editorial cited the riots as furnishing "graphic examples of the horrors which lie ahead."[50]

Regular readers of the *Citizen* could easily have imagined "graphic examples" of black violence based on their recollections of the journal's many photographs of the late 1970s and 1980s illustrating articles about violence committed by Africans. These images fit racist themes of black savagery. In 1978, for instance, the journal ran photographs of a white missionary family murdered in Rhodesia, including images of a blood-covered body of a mother and her infant daughter and mutilated children. Showing white victims, though, was exceptional. Most photographs of victims depicted Africans. In a gory example, most of a man's head lay on a rock in a photograph closely cropped to include his shoulders: he had been shot in the temple.[51] Another photo showed a line of contorted bodies lying face-up, presumably following a mass execution in Rhodesia. When this image appeared in the *Citizen* for a second time, but not in connection to the same incident, the caption explained that editors "repeat[ed] it because it emphasizes the basic point that the struggle in Africa is not between black and white, but between productive and unproductive elements, with both black and white on both sides. On each side the main leadership is white, the majority of the sufferers are black."[52] Such images ostensibly demonstrated the risks to Africans of black rule. However, recurring depictions of mutilated or dead black bodies supported a more explicitly white-supremacist position with a long history.

During U.S. debates over apartheid in the 1980s, writers for the *Citizen* marshaled what they saw as the lessons of decolonization and its harm to Africans to refute arguments for sanctioning South Africa. In the article "Fruits of Misguided Liberalism," Robert Patterson blamed "the world's press, the world's liberals and the United Nations" for pressuring Europeans to abandon their African empires: "Uganda, a prosperous well ordered country as a British colony, has become a disease ridden killing field, and a place of unbelievable horror under 'Uhuru,' 'Freedom' or specifically, self-government by blacks." Patterson concluded, "When these primitive people of many diverse tribes with different cultures and beliefs are thrown together to govern themselves, chaos and genocide have inevitably followed. . . . The liberals and anti-colonialist do-gooders of the world should look with shame on what they have helped bring about in Africa."[53] Earlier examples of decolonization were seen as case studies of what would happen to South Africa under black rule.[54] Regular writer for the *Citizen* Bobbe Simmons described Zimbabwe as becoming "just another poor, helpless African country, governed by an arrogant black dictator, using foreign aid to perpetuate himself in office." Simmons asked, "And what about South Africa, the only peaceful and well-fed nation in Africa now? Let us pray."[55] In one article, Patterson asserted, "South Africa is one of the few African countries where blacks do not starve and are not murdered by the thousands in tribal or government wars."[56]

In the early 1980s, the Citizens' Councils, along with its conservative allies, successfully fought efforts to impose U.S. sanctions on South Africa. These arguments held sway within the Reagan administration. As Reagan's point man on Africa, Chester Crocker, told reporters, "All Reagan knows about southern Africa is that he's on the side of the whites."[57] In the U.S. Senate, Jesse Helms, who had long-standing ties to the Citizens' Councils, led the conservative attack against sanctions. The *Citizen*'s role in the debate over South African sanctions demonstrates the continued relevance of the Citizens' Councils in American debates, the organization's commitment to international issues, and the centrality of European decolonization as a political issue for council members.

Ultimately, the sanctions movement triumphed. Under pressure from anti-apartheid forces within the United States, Reagan signed an executive order imposing limited sanctions on South Africa in 1985 that effectively ended the policy of constructive engagement. In 1986, Congress passed the Comprehensive Anti-Apartheid Act over Reagan's presidential veto.[58] To Citizens' Councils members who had long treated their fight against desegregation as a cause tied to the preservation of apartheid, this loss appeared to have been the last major contest of American political resistance to preserving international white supremacy. Authors of subsequent articles in the *Citizen* rued their betrayal not only by the Reagan administration but even by the South African government as it began to dismantle apartheid.

Yet even after the anti-apartheid victory in the Congress, *Citizen* writers continued to romanticize South Africa and identify with South African whites. Some hinted that they saw South Africa as the last outpost of white civilization, given the political and racial changes in the United States and Europe. In 1987, the *Citizen* published the article "Why I Love South Africa," by an American émigré living in South Africa. Its author, Robert Hall, concluded, "it is my sad but candid opinion that America is well on the way to becoming a 'has-been' nation, and is reaching the end of the era. America today is a land beset with drug problems, morality problems, and corruption." South Africa reminded Hall of the United States during its earlier glory years, particularly his home state of California, "long before the hordes of people swamped the beautiful state." Sounding like a settler of earlier generations, he reflected, "Day to day life in South Africa has a quality unsurpassed in any like situation in America. The ethnic work force is enormous, and domestic and agricultural help is readily available." Speaking to more contemporary concerns, Hall claimed, "The socialist welfare state so predominant in Europe, the UK, and America has not been initiated here, and therefore a job is a very meaningful pastime."[59]

The end of the apartheid era in South Africa marked the last chapter of decolonization in Africa. It is perhaps fitting then that the *Citizen's* run as a journal ended in 1989, just as South Africa's new state president, F. W. de Klerk, began to end apartheid, symbolized in the release of Nelson Mandela in February 1990. For editors and readers of the *Citizen* who had followed events in southern Africa closely over the preceding decades and linked resisting racial equality to the preservation of apartheid, the regime's end was their final lost cause.

The global struggle against apartheid helped African Americans forge and strengthen black international connections.[60] For southern segregationists, decolonization similarly created international connections based on racial affinities and shared goals, though to an opposed end: maintaining white rule in the American South and southern Africa. While the role of decolonization in African American international politics has been recognized, white internationalism has often been assumed to relate directly and primarily to Europe and to be politically liberal in nature. Citizens' Councils' interest in British affairs from the 1960s into the 1980s, as evident in the *Citizen,* shows that a conservative white internationalism in this period addressed itself to colonial relations. In the 1960s and 1970s, white segregationists viewed Britain's policies toward its former colonies in Africa as examples of the same disastrous liberal policies that had desegregated the American South. By the 1980s, they took a last stand opposing anti-apartheid legislation in Congress. Scholars increasingly recognize that U.S. civil rights protest extended beyond the mid-1960s; so too did resistance to black rights.[61] From the 1960s to the 1980s southern white segregationists affiliated with the Citizens' Councils internationalized their fight to resist desegregation in ways that have gone unnoticed, spreading their resistance to include southern Africa, well past the commonly recognized end of the civil rights movement.

Notes

1. Medford Evans, "Will Western Europe Be Driven Out of Africa?" *Citizen* (July–Aug. 1978), 4.

2. See, for example, Penny Von Eschen, *Race against Empire: Black Americans and Anticolonialism, 1937–1957* (Ithaca: Cornell University Press, 1997); Nikhil

Pal Singh, *Black Is a Country: Race and the Unfinished Struggle for Democracy* (Cambridge: Harvard University Press, 2004).

3. Mary L. Dudziak, *Cold War Civil Rights: Race and the Image of American Democracy* (Princeton: Princeton University Press, 2000); Thomas Borstelmann, *The Cold War and the Color Line: American Race Relations in the Global Arena* (Cambridge: Harvard University Press, 2001). Recent works on U.S.-Africa relations in this period have stressed how African nationalism complicated Cold War frameworks. See Sue Onslow, ed., *Cold War in Southern Africa: White Power, Black Liberation* (New York: Routledge, 2009); Phillip E. Muehlenbeck, *Betting on the Africans: John F. Kennedy's Courting of African Nationalist Leaders* (New York: Oxford University Press, 2012).

4. Thomas Noer, "Segregationists and the World: The Foreign Policy of White Resistance," in Brenda Gayle Plummer, ed., *Window on Freedom: Race, Civil Rights, and Foreign Affairs, 1945–1988* (Chapel Hill: University of North Carolina Press, 2003), 141–62.

5. Ibid.

6. Reginald Horsman, *Race and Manifest Destiny: The Origins of Racial Anglo-Saxonism* (Cambridge: Harvard University Press, 1981).

7. Marilyn Lake and Henry Reynolds, *Drawing the Global Colour Line: White Men's Countries and the International Challenge of Racial Equality* (New York: Cambridge University Press, 2008), 2–9.

8. On southern Anglophilia, see Joseph A. Fry, *Dixie Looks Abroad: The South and U.S. Foreign Relations, 1789–1973* (Baton Rouge: Louisiana State University Press, 2002), 154–55.

9. Numan V. Bartley, *The Rise of Massive Resistance: Race and Politics in the South during the 1950's* (Baton Rouge: Louisiana State University Press, 1969), 84.

10. For information on the Citizens' Councils, see Neil R. McMillen, *The Citizens' Council: Organized Resistance to the Second Reconstruction, 1954–1964* (Urbana: University of Illinois Press, 1971); Bartley, *Rise of Massive Resistance.*

11. McMillen, *Citizen's Council,* 154.

12. For a statistical analysis of American media coverage of apartheid, see Donald R. Culverson, "The Politics of Anti-Apartheid Movement in the United States, 1969–1986," *Political Science Quarterly* 11 (Spring 1996): 127–49, esp. 144.

13. Harold Macmillan, "Address to the South African Parliament, 3 February 1960," in *Pointing the Way* (London: Macmillan, 1972), 473–82.

14. William J. Simmons, "Report on a Trip to Southern Africa," *Citizen* (July–Aug. 1966), 4.

15. Ibid., 8.

16. Ibid.

17. Ibid., 5.

18. Ibid., 14.

19. Andrew DeRoche, *Black, White, and Chrome: The United States and Zimbabwe, 1953–1988* (Trenton: Africa World Press, 2001), 97–142.

20. Clive Webb, "Britain, the American South, and the Wide Civil Rights Movement," in this volume.

21. Kenneth Tolliver, "Traveler's Report on Southern Africa," *Citizen* (July–Aug. 1967), 11.

22. William J. Simmons, "A Conversation with Ian Smith," *Citizen* (July–Aug. 1966), 19.

23. For example, see Robert C. Ruark, "Whites in Africa Victims of Prejudice," *Citizen* (Mar. 1962), 11–13.

24. "The 'Internal Solution'" (no author listed), *Citizen* (Mar. 1978), 6.

25. Angus Graham, "Defense Advice from Rhodesia," *Citizen* (Jan. 1969), 5. This quote comes from an article that presents excerpts of Graham's speeches. See also Angus Graham, "Rhodesia: Free World's Defense," *Citizen* (Mar. 1969), 5–7; Angus Graham, "A Letter from Rhodesia," *Citizen* (Nov. 1970), 21.

26. Simmons, "Conversation with Ian Smith," 15–21. See "Filmed Interview with Ian Smith Now Available," *Citizen* (July–Aug. 1966), 21; W. J. Simmons, "Notes on Africa," *Citizen* (July–Aug. 1966), 2.

27. Jesse Helms, "We're Being Played for Suckers," *Citizen* (Feb. 1967), 19–20.

28. Noer, "Segregationists and the World," 46; Borstelmann, *Cold War and the Color Line,* 198–99, 234.

29. William A. Link, *Jesse Helms and the Rise of Modern Conservatism* (New York: St. Martin's, 2008), 207–9; DeRoche, *Black, White, and Chrome,* 243–309; Nancy Mitchell, "Terrorists or Freedom Fighters: Jimmy Carter and Rhodesia," in Onslow, *Cold War in Southern Africa,* 177–200.

30. Webb, "Britain, the American South."

31. "Afterword" (no author listed), *Citizen* (Mar. 1978), 17.

32. George Shannon, "Enoch Powell in Jackson," *Citizen* (Nov. 1971), 16–23.

33. Ibid., 16. See also Ronald Bell, "Preposterous Nonsense," *Citizen* (Dec. 1972), 19–20.

34. Shannon, "Enoch Powell in Jackson," 17.

35. Ibid., 19.

36. Ibid., 18.

37. Ibid., 20–21.

38. The notion that "there will always be an England" was one that *Citizen* writers cherished. They repeated the phrase in a caption celebrating the birth of Prince William to Prince Charles and Lady Diana in 1982. See *Citizen* (Aug. 1982), 30 (caption).

39. George W. Shannon, "Can Margaret Thatcher Liberate Great Britain?" *Citizen* (May 1978), 12.

40. "Have the British Had Enough," *Citizen* (Apr. 1978), 13.

41. Bobbe W. Simmons, "Unfinished Tragedy in Southern Africa," *Citizen* (May 1980), 8.

42. Arthur Lewis, "The Crocodile Waits for You," *Citizen* (June 1982), 9.

43. Ibid., 12.

44. Ibid., 26 (emphasis removed).

45. Borstelmann, *Cold War and the Cold Line,* 259–62.

46. Donald B. Sole, "The Golden Prize in the War for the Southern Hemisphere," *Citizen* (July 1982), 16 (caption).

47. Ibid., 28 (caption).

48. "A Message to South Africans: Liberals in the United States Do Not Speak for Most Americans," *Citizen* (Oct.–Nov. 1986), 20.

49. Ibid.

50. George W. Shannon, "Black Savagery in South Africa," *Citizen* (Oct. 1985), 2, 29.

51. *Citizen* (Oct. 1980), 14.

52. *Citizen* (June 1978), 9.

53. Robert B. Patterson, "The Fruits of Misguided Liberalism," *Citizen* (Aug.–Sept. 1988), 16, 19.

54. Don Caldwell, "Black Rule Brings Chaos to Southern African Nations," *Citizen* (Dec. 1987–Jan. 1988), 4–8.

55. Bobbe Simmons, "Wreckage in Rhodesia: Aftermath of Freedom," *Citizen* (June 1983), 12–13.

56. Robert B. Patterson, "Civil Rights Cry Illogical," *Citizen* (Feb. 1985), 12.

57. As quoted in Borstelmann, *Cold War and the Color Line,* 260. Crocker had close ties to Rhodesia and was in fact married to a Rhodesian woman. See Gerald Horne, "Race from Power: U.S. Foreign Policy and the General Crisis of White Supremacy," in Plummer, *Window on Freedom,* 17.

58. DeRoche, *Black, White, and Chrome,* 333–42; David L. Hostetter, *Movement Matters: American Antiapartheid Activism and the Rise of Multicultural Politics* (New York: Routledge, 2006), 130–33.

59. Robert Hall, "Why I Love South Africa: Comments on Life in South Africa by an American Who Chooses to Live There Permanently," *Citizen* (Oct.–Nov. 1987), 4–8.

60. Singh, *Black Is a Country;* Francis Njubi Nesbitt, *Race for Sanctions: African Americans against Apartheid, 1946–1994* (Bloomington: Indiana University Press, 2004).

61. Jacqueline Dowd Hall, "The Long Civil Rights Movement and the Political Uses of the Past," *Journal of American History* 91 (Mar. 2005), 1233–63.

Acknowledgments

The essays in this volume were originally presented and discussed at the Roosevelt Study Center's Ninth Middelburg Conference of Historians of the United States, titled "The U.S. South and Europe," on April 27–29, 2011, and later revised into publishable essays. The conference and publication of the book were made possible by the generous sponsorship of the Roosevelt Study Center and the Provincial Government of Zeeland in Middelburg and the U.S. Embassy in The Hague, the Netherlands, as well as the Roosevelt Institute in New York.

In our capacity as organizers of the conference and as editors of this volume, we gratefully acknowledge the indispensable and most efficient services of the Roosevelt Study Center's management assistant Leontien Joosse throughout the project. We also acknowledge the enthusiastic support for this book's publication by Anne Dean Watkins, senior acquisitions editor at the University Press of Kentucky, who graciously guided the manuscript through the editorial and production process. We also want to thank our copyeditor, Carol Sickman-Garner, who did an excellent job. We are happy that our volume is part of the University Press of Kentucky's New Directions in Southern History series.

Contributors

Manfred Berg is the Curt Engelhorn Professor of American History at the University of Heidelberg, Germany. His research interests encompass the history of the African American civil rights movement, racial discrimination, popular violence, and criminal justice. His most recent books include *The Ticket to Freedom: The NAACP and the Struggle for Black Political Integration* (2005) and *Popular Justice: A History of Lynching in America* (2011). He coedited *Racism in the Modern World: Historical Perspectives on Cultural Transfer and Adaptation* (2011) and *Globalizing Lynching History: Vigilantism and Extralegal Punishment from an International Perspective* (2011).

Thomas Clark is currently visiting professor for U.S. history at the American Studies Department of Goethe University, Frankfurt, Germany. He received his PhD at Frankfurt in 2001 and has subsequently held positions in the history departments of the universities of Kassel and Münster, Germany. He most recently published "'...let Cato's virtues fire': Das Catobild in der amerikanischen Revolution" in the Beiheft of the *Historische Zeitschrift* (2011) and coedited *Aufklärung, Konstitutionalismus, atlantische Welt* (2009). His current research project is entitled "Tocquevillian Moments: Transatlantic Visions of an American Republican Culture."

Don H. Doyle is McCausland Professor of History at the University of South Carolina. He has published several books on the American South and the United States, including *New Men, New Cities, New South* (1990); *Faulkner's County* (2000); *The South as an American Problem,* edited with Larry Griffin (1995); *Nationalism in the New World,* edited with Marco Pamplona (2006); and *Secession as an International Phenomenon* (2010). He is currently writing a book on "America's international civil war" and has contributed several essays to the *New York Times'* "Disunion" series that draw on his current research. He was a Fellow at the National Humanities Center in 2011–12.

Daniel Geary is the Mark Pigott Assistant Professor of U.S. History at Trinity College, Dublin. He is the author of *Radical Ambition: C. Wright Mills, the Left, and American Social Thought* (2009) and is currently writing a history of the Moynihan Report controversy, tentatively entitled *Splitting Liberalism*.

William R. Glass is a professor of American social history at the American Studies Center of the University of Warsaw, Poland. In addition to teaching courses about the American South, religion, and film, he coedits the *Americanist*, the journal published by the center. He has published articles on religion in the South in a variety of journals and one book: *Strangers in Zion: Fundamentalists in the South, 1900–1950* (2001). Currently he is working on a monograph tentatively titled *Laughing in War/Laughing at War: The Service Comedy as Genre*.

Kathleen Hilliard received her PhD from the University of South Carolina in 2006. She is an assistant professor of history in the Department of History at Iowa State University in Ames. Her book *Masters, Slaves, and Exchange: Power's Purchase in the Old South* will be published in 2013. She is currently at work on her next project, entitled *Planters' Jubilee: Mastery, Honor, and Contest in the Old South*, which examines agricultural fairs and contests as places where deeply subjective understandings of Old South honor came into conflict with ostensibly objective calculations of agricultural productivity and reform.

William A. Link is Richard J. Milbauer Professor of History at the University of Florida. He is the author of eight major books on the history of the South, including *Roots of Secession: Slavery and Politics in Antebellum Virginia* (2003); *Righteous Warrior: Jesse Helms and the Rise of Modern Conservatism* (2008); *North Carolina: Change and Tradition in a Southern State* (2009); and *Atlanta, Cradle of the New South: Race and Remembering after the Civil War* (2013).

Stefano Luconi teaches U.S. history at the universities of Padua, Florence, and Naples L'Orientale, Italy. His publications include *From Paesani to White Ethnics: The Italian Experience in Philadelphia* (2001); *The Italian-American Vote in Providence, Rhode Island, 1916–1948* (2004); and *Gli afro-americani dalla guerra civile alla presidenza di Barack Obama* (2011). He also edited, with Dennis Barone, *Small Towns, Big Cities: The Urban Experience of Italian Americans* (2010). His current research focuses on how Student Nonviolent Coordinating Committee leaders relied on the networks of civil rights organizations to launch their own careers in politics.

Louis Mazzari is on the faculty of the Department of Western Languages and Literatures at Bogazici University in Istanbul, Turkey, and teaches in Bogazici's Department of History. He is the author of *Southern Modernist: Arthur Raper from the New Deal to the Cold War* (2006). He also wrote a new introduction to Raper's 1936 study of the American South, *Preface to Peasantry*, republished in 2005. Mazzari was a primary contributor to the *Encyclopedia of New England* (2005) and has coedited and contributed to *American Turkish Encounters: Politics and Culture, 1830–1989* (2012) and several journals.

Lawrence T. McDonnell teaches U.S. history at Iowa State University in Ames. He has published essays on slavery, secession, and American labor history and is currently completing two book-length studies, *Politics, Chess, Hats: The Microhistory of Disunion in Charleston, South Carolina* and *The Death and Rebirth of John C. Calhoun*. His long-range project, *Bloody Work: The Civil War and the Making of the American Working Class, 1846–1877*, examines the crisis of the Union as a process of class formation and Civil War combat as a site of class struggle.

Cornelis A. van Minnen is the director of the Roosevelt Study Center in Middelburg, the Netherlands, and a professor of American history at Ghent University, Belgium. His books include *American Diplomats in the Netherlands, 1815–1850* (1993) and *Van Loon: Popular Historian, Journalist, and FDR Confidant* (2005). He is the editor and coeditor of many volumes, most recently *Teaching and Studying U.S. History in Europe* (2007), *Political Repression in U.S. History* (2009), and *Four Centuries of Dutch-American Relations, 1609–2009* (2009). He was a fellow at the National Humanities Center in 2010 and is working on a book on the post-1960s U.S. South and the "southernization" of America.

Daniel Nagel studied history, political science, and public law at the universities of Mannheim and Heidelberg, Germany, and at the University of North Carolina at Asheville. His PhD dissertation *Von republikanischen Deutschen zu deutsch-amerikanischen Republikanern: Ein Beitrag zum Identitätswandel der deutschen Achtundvierziger in den Vereinigten Staaten*

(1850–1861) was published as his first book in 2012. He teaches at the University of Mannheim and works as a freelance historian and journalist. His current research interests include the history of republicanism in the nineteenth century.

Matthias Reiss is a senior lecturer in modern history at the University of Exeter, Devon, UK. His research interests are the history of street protest, unemployment, African American history, the history of prisoners of war, and visual history. He has written, among other things, *"Die Schwarzen waren unsere Freunde": Deutsche Kriegsgefangene in der amerikanischen Gesellschaft 1942–1946* (2002) and edited *The Street as Stage: Protest Marches and Public Rallies since the Nineteenth Century* (2007) and *Unemployment and Protest: New Perspective on Two Centuries of Contention* (2011). He is currently writing a monograph on the National League of the Blind, a trade union of blind workers in the UK.

Sarah L. Silkey is an assistant professor of history at Lycoming College in Williamsport, Pennsylvania. She is the author of "British Public Debates and the 'Americanization' of Lynching," in *Swift to Wrath: Lynching in Global Historical Perspective* (2013), and "Redirecting the Tide of White Imperialism: The Impact of Ida B. Wells's Transatlantic Antilynching Campaign on British Conceptions of American Race Relations," in *Women Shaping the South: Creating and Confronting Change* (2006). She received her PhD from the University of East Anglia in Norwich, England, and served as a Carter G. Woodson Institute Fellow at the University of Virginia.

Melvyn Stokes is reader in Film History at University College London. He is the author of *D. W. Griffith's* The Birth of a Nation: *A History of "The Most Controversial Motion Picture of All Time"* (2007), *Gilda* (2010), and *American History through Hollywood Film* (2013). He has edited or coedited eleven books, including four for the British Film Institute on audiences for Hollywood films (1999–2004) and *The State of U.S. History* (2004). He has served as president of SERCIA, the European film organization, since 2008 and is director of the AHRC-funded project on "Cultural Memory and British Cinema-going of the 1960s." He is currently completing a book on Charlie Chaplin's French reception.

Jennifer Sutton received her PhD in U.S. history from Washington University in St. Louis in 2012. Her dissertation studied relationships among Americans, Europeans, and South Africans at the start of the early twentieth century. Her research examines U.S. history from transnational, global, and imperial perspectives.

Clive Webb is a professor of modern American history at the University of Sussex in Brighton, England. He is the author of *Fight against Fear: Southern Jews and Black Civil Rights* (2001) and *Rabble Rousers: The American Far Right in the Civil Rights Era* (2010). Webb is coauthor with David Brown of *Race in the American South: From Slavery to Civil Rights* (2007) and with William D. Carrigan of *Forgotten Dead: Mob Violence against Mexicans in the United States, 1848 to 1928* (2013). He is also the editor of *Massive Resistance: Southern White Opposition to the Second Reconstruction* (2005). Webb is currently researching U.S. influences on British race relations.

Index

abolition/abolitionists, 88; Europe and, 112–15, 182, 244; France and, 114, 182; German "Forty-Eighters" and, 59, 60; London fundamentalist churches and, 165, 166–67, 169–70, 178n28; United Kingdom and, 15, 23–24, 26, 113–14, 182, 244. *See also* slavery

Action (journal), 195

Adams, Henry, 105

Africa, 4. *See also* Rhodesia; South Africa; Zimbabwe

African Americans, 4, 154, 279; *Birth of a Nation* portrayal during Reconstruction and, 185–86, 188, 189, 190, 192, 196; escaping slavery, 23, 24–26; German POWs in U.S. South and, 11, 224, 227, 228–29, 233–34, 235; Italian Americans and, 127–28, 129, 130, 135; lynching and, 130, 147–48, 153, 155, 248, 260n20; migration to the north, 1940s, 207, 224; racism in northern United States and, 12, 25, 26, 248, 258; travel to Europe and, 16–17, 23–29. *See also* Jim Crow; slavery

Aiken, Joseph Daniel, 80–81

Aiken, Wyatt, 17–18

Alabama, 152–53, 243

Alabama in Africa (Zimmerman), 4

Albano, Angelo, 126, 134, 135

Alexander, Archibald, 21

Alexander, Will, 208, 211

Altgeld, John P., 157

American Committee on Africa, 255

"American creed," 206

American Dilemma, An (Myrdal),

10–11, 207, 209, 213; Raper and, 210, 215, 216–17, 219n12

Amerika (Benét), 232

Amsterdam News, 130

"An Act to Prevent Mob Violence" (Georgia), 152

Andersch, Alfred, 224, 229, 240n55

Andrews, J. E., Mrs., 214

Angus, James, 271

anti-apartheid movements, 254–55, 275–76, 278, 279

apartheid, 250, 255, 269, 276, 277, 278, 279

Applebome, Peter, 1

Arctic (paddle-steamer), 21

Argyll, Duke of, 156

Association of Citizens' Councils of Mississippi, 268–69, 270

Atlanta Woman's World, 214

Atlantis, 55

Aus dem schwäbischen Pfarrhaus nach Amerika (Weil), 44

Austrian uprising, 1848, 40, 41

Balgarnie, Florence, 158, 159

Baptists, 165, 166, 167, 168, 171, 175, 177n13

Barnwell, Robert, 80, 81

Barthes, Roland, 95

Beard, Charles, 230

Beard, Mary, 230

Beauvallet, Léon, 76

Beecher, Henry Ward, 173

Beecher, Lyman, 22

Benedict, Ruth, 208

Benét, Stephen Vincent, 232

Benjamin, Judah P., 111, 112

Berendt, John, 2

Berger, Pierre, 195

Civil War *(cont.)*
 of, at beginning, 108–10; German
 "Forty-Eighters" and, 8, 66–67;
 Gone With the Wind and, 182,
 191–96, 197; reconciliation
 meaning white supremacy at end
 of, 170, 178n37; slavery causing,
 108, 188, 189, 190–91, 196;
 southern chivalry causing, 89, 98,
 99n17; states' rights causing, 10,
 20, 185, 188, 189, 190, 191, 196;
 travel to Europe and, 15–16; Union
 public diplomacy and, 115–16;
 Union victories, 20, 117. *See also*
 Confederate States of America;
 secession
Clair, Jean, 189–90
Clark, Thomas, 6, 7
Cobden, Richard, 26, 27
Cochrane, Kelso, 248, 260n20
Cody, Buffalo Bill, 146
Cold War, 266–67, 271, 272, 280n3
Comer, James, 22
Comer, Laura Beecher, 22
Commission on Interracial
 Cooperation, 208, 210, 211
Committee for African Organisations,
 248
Committee of Afro-Asian Caribbean
 Organisations, 251
communism, 271, 272
Comoedia, 188
Comprehensive Anti-Apartheid Act of
 1986, 278
Compromise of 1850, 54
Confederate States of America:
 beginning of Civil War and, 106,
 107, 108; cotton and, 107–8,
 111, 112, 117; diplomacy during
 Civil War, 4–5, 8–9, 105, 108–9,
 110–12; France and, 107, 111,
 116–19; Gettysburg, Battle of, and,
 20; international recognition and,

4, 106–7, 111–13, 115, 119–21,
 244; propaganda campaign and, 9,
 115–19, 120; slavery and, 114–15,
 120–21; United Kingdom and,
 105, 106, 107, 109, 112, 244
Congress of Racial Equality, 255
Conjectures of Order (O'Brien), 16
conservatism, 1, 10, 20, 39–40,
 210, 215; American Protestants
 and, 10, 166, 170–71, 172, 175;
 Citizens' Councils of America
 and, 268, 272, 274, 278, 279;
 fundamentalism and, 165, 166,
 175; German immigrants and,
 52, 61; southern chivalry and, 89,
 90–92, 96, 97
Cooke, Alistair, 245
Cooper, James Fenimore, 74, 75, 80,
 81
Cooper, William, 215
Cooper Union, New York City, 23
Corriere della Sera, 135
cotton, 4, 210; Confederacy and,
 107–8, 111, 112, 117; German
 POWs in U.S. South and, 228,
 231; transport of, 17–18. *See also*
 King Cotton diplomacy
cotton famine, 107
Crimean War (1853–1856), 91, 110
Crocker, Chester, 278, 282n57
Croze, Jean-Louis, 188
Cruger, Henry, 74, 80, 81, 83n4
Crystal Palace Exposition, 21–22
Cuba (Cunard steamer), 22
Cunningham, George, 129
Cutler, James Elbert, 128

Daily Chronicle, 150–51
Daily Mail, 192, 193
Daily Mirror, 192
Daily Telegraph, 158, 159, 185, 258
Daily Worker, 193
Darby, John Nelson, 170

German "Forty-Eighters." *See* Forty-
Eighters
German POWs in U.S. South, 223–
25; African Americans and, 11,
224, 227, 228–29, 233–34, 235;
asking about racial discrimination,
227, 231–32; censorship and,
230–31, 239n44; interest in
United States and, 226–27; Jim
Crow perceptions and, 11, 224,
225, 234; "Kleiner Führer durch
Amerika" (Small guide to America)
and, 232–33, 240n56; as laborers,
224, 227–29; newspapers of, 228;
reeducation plans for, 225, 227,
229; reeducation program, 11,
229–33, 234, 238n36, 239n44,
239–40n51; research on, 224,
235–36n4
German Revolution of 1848–1849, 40,
52, 57
Germany, 23; cultural superiority and,
8, 11, 226, 235; Du Bois and, 27,
28, 225; materialism of United
States and, 234–35; U.S. South
and, 4, 225; World War I and,
173–74
Gettysburg, Battle of, 20
Gilmore, Glenda, 244
Gilroy, Paul, 249
Gladstone, William, 112
Glass, William R., 9–10
Globe, 159
Goldwater, Barry, 272
Gone With the Wind (movie, 1939),
201n40; British perceptions of,
191–94, 197; France and, 182,
194–96, 202n53; Reconstruction
portrayal and, 192, 194, 195–96,
197–98; slavery and, 193, 197, 198;
World War II and, 10, 182–83,
193, 194, 197
Gorst, John Eldon, 156

Graham, Billy, 175
Grand Tour, 15, 24
Grant, Madison, 127
Grayson, William J., 91
Great Britain. *See* United Kingdom
Great Depression, 208
Greenville Mountaineer, 82
Griffith, David W., 182, 184, 188,
189, 192, 196, 201n40
Griffiths, Peter, 257
Grubb, James, 79
Guardian, 2. See also *Manchester
Guardian*
Gullion, Allen, 227

Hahnville, LA, 133, 136
Hall, Christopher Newman, 169,
178n28
Hall, Jacquelyn Dowd, 244
Hall, Robert, 278
Hamiter, J. T., 153
Hammond, James Henry, 73, 80, 94,
107
Hammond, Michael, 183–84
"Hampton Epilogue" (short film), 190
Happoldt, Christopher, 17, 18
Harmonist utopian community, 44, 47
Harper's New Monthly Magazine, 75,
76
Harper's Weekly, 129
Harvard University, 27, 28
Harvey, Paul, 2
Hays, Will, 191, 201n38
Hegel, Georg Wilhelm Friedrich, 54
Heinzen, Karl, 59, 61, 62
Helms, Jesse, 272, 278
Helms-Byrd Amendment of 1979, 272
Hennessey, David, 126, 129, 131, 132,
135–36
Hero, Alfred, 245
Herskovitz, Melville J., 208
Higham, John, 129
Hilliard, Kathleen, 6, 8

Hinds, Donald, 254
Hodgson, Godfrey, 245
Hofstadter, Richard, 129
Honeck, Mischa, 53
Hope, Alexander Beresford, 110
Houston, James D., 132
Howard, Leslie, 192, 194
Howard University, 213
Huddleston, Trevor, 255
Huger, Alfred, 88
Hughes, John, 115
Hugo, Victor, 26, 27
Hull, Cordell, 225, 226
Hunter, Robert, 110–11

ideal theory, 54
Illustrated London News, 192
Il Progresso Italo-Americano, 126, 127
il Risorgimento, 19
Immanuel Baptist Church, Baltimore, 166
immigration: German immigrants, 1850s and, 51, 52; late nineteenth century and, 154–56; rights of immigrants and, 62–63; as solution to slavery, 58. *See also* Caribbean immigrants to UK; Forty-Eighters; Italian Americans
Impey, Catherine, 149
Institute of Race Relations (Britain), 246
International Labor Defense, 153
international law, 106–7
International Peace Congress (1849), 26, 27
International Red Cross, 110
Inwood, Charles, 172
Italian Americans: African Americans and, 127–28, 129, 130, 135; labor relations and, 134–35; lynchings and, 9, 125–27, 128–29, 130–33, 137, 138n8, 138–39n9, 147; marginalization of, 130, 132; as

non-white, 127, 128, 129, 130, 135, 136; racism and, 127–28, 130, 136–37; Sicilians, 9, 125–27, 128, 129, 130, 131–33, 135, 137; threatened with lynching, 133–34; "whitening" of, 130
Italian Mezzogiorno, 74
Italian unification, 81–82
Italy, 19–20, 74, 84n7, 110; U.S. lynchings and, 126, 129, 130–31, 135, 147; Venice, 8, 73–75, 76, 77–83
Ivens, Philip C., 150

Jackson, Andrew, 43
Jackson, Walter A., 207
Japan, 217
Java (schooner), 17
Jim Crow, 170, 213, 215, 250, 266, 268; African American activism against, 245, 249, 251, 253; German POWs in U.S. South and, 11, 224, 225; United Kingdom criticism of, 243, 245–47, 273. *See also* segregation
Johann, Alfred E., 234
Johnson, Charles S., 208
Johnson, Guy, 208
Johnson, Lyndon, 248
Jones, Claudia, 251
Jones, Kate, 21–22
Jones, Thomas Goode, 152–53, 157, 158, 159
jousting, 8, 88, 89, 98n2. *See also* knights; tilting; tournaments

Kansas-Nebraska Act of 1854, 55
Kapp, Friedrich, 55–57, 58, 59
Keitt, Lawrence, 78, 89, 98
Keller, Christian B., 53
Kenner, Duncan, 120
Kentucky, 38
Keppel, Frederick, 205, 207

United Nations, 216, 271, 272, 273, 275

United States Atrocities (Wells), 150

United States Information Agency, 245

University of North Carolina, Chapel Hill, 2, 10, 18, 233; Chapel Hill school, 208, 211, 219n7

Unwin, Jane Cobden, 184

U.S. Army: Psychological Warfare Division, 226, 227; racism and, 230; Special Projects Division, 229–33

U.S. Census Bureau, 5–6

U.S. Constitution, 57

U.S. South: African American migration to north from, 1940s, 207, 224; African Americans and travel to Europe and, 16–17, 23–29; Anglophilia and, 268, 274, 281n38; British racial unrest, post-World War II and, 11–12, 246–48, 249–50, 272–73; against capitalism, 89, 96–97, 99–100n18; civil rights demonstrations and, 243, 245, 246, 247, 248; delineation of, 5–6; as distinct from the north, 1, 34, 35, 37, 42, 47–48, 66, 181; European interest and, 1–4, 5, 6, 7, 182, 225; vs. European political systems and, 74, 84n7; European travelers to, 33–34, 37–48, 206–15; immigration, late nineteenth century and, 154–56; Old World vs. New World and, 35–36, 39, 43–44; race and, 6–7, 10–11, 182; recent economic revival, 1, 2, 3; vs. Republicanism, 57–59, 64, 65; southern identity and, 2, 34–35, 39–40, 43; as stagnating and backward, 1, 5, 35, 41–42; Tocqueville and, 7, 33, 36–40, 42, 45, 46, 47, 49n12, 49n29; travel to Europe and, 7,

15–29, 29–30n2, 73, 80–81, 187; United Kingdom relations and, 4, 152, 155, 244–45, 271–73; as unstable and revolutionary, 37–39, 46; women traveling to Europe and, 16, 20–23. *See also* chivalry; Citizens' Councils of America; Civil War; conservatism; Forty-Eighters; German POWs in U.S. South; Jim Crow; lynching; New Orleans; racism; slavery; South Africa; South Carolina; white supremacy

U.S. Supreme Court, 215, 245, 251, 268

U.S. War Department, 224, 225, 227, 230, 231

Vance, Rupert, 208

Venice-Charleston comparison, 8, 73–75, 76, 77–83

Venice Preserved (Otway), 75

Victoria, Queen, 91–92

Vietnam, 197, 198

Vietnam War, 271, 272

Villarosa, Federico, 128–29

Virginia, 21, 41, 57, 70n42, 90, 153

virtue, 51, 53, 54, 62, 65

Vuillermoz, Emile, 189

Vulliet, Andre, 230–31, 239n49

Wade, John Donald, 214

Wallace, George, 258, 267

Ward, Samuel Ringgold, 23–24

War of 1812, 43

Washington, George, 117

Watts, N. C., 153

Weatherby, William J., 245

Webb, Clive, 6, 11, 126, 271, 273

Weed, Thurlow, 115

Weil, Louise, 7, 36, 43, 44–47

Weisberger, Bernard A., 198

Wells, Ida B.: antilynching campaign

New Directions in Southern History

Series Editors
Michele Gillespie, Wake Forest University
William A. Link, University of Florida

The Lost State of Franklin: America's First Secession
Kevin T. Barksdale

Bluecoats and Tar Heels: Soldiers and Civilians in Reconstruction North Carolina
Mark L. Bradley

Becoming Bourgeois: Merchant Culture in the South, 1820–1865
Frank J. Byrne

Cowboy Conservatism: Texas and the Rise of the Modern Right
Sean P. Cunningham

A Tour of Reconstruction: Travel Letters of 1875
Anna Dickinson (J. Matthew Gallman, ed.)

Raising Racists: The Socialization of White Children in the Jim Crow South
Kristina DuRocher

Lum and Abner: Rural America and the Golden Age of Radio
Randal L. Hall

Mountains on the Market: Industry, the Environment, and the South
Randal L. Hall

The New Southern University: Academic Freedom and Liberalism at UNC
Charles J. Holden

Entangled by White Supremacy: Reform in World War I–era South Carolina
Janet G. Hudson

Bloody Breathitt: Politics and Violence in the Appalachian South
T. R. C. Hutton

Cultivating Race: The Expansion of Slavery in Georgia, 1750–1860
Watson W. Jennison

De Bow's Review: *The Antebellum Vision of a New South*
John F. Kvach

Remembering The Battle of the Crater: War as Murder
Kevin M. Levin

The View from the Ground: Experiences of Civil War Soldiers
edited by Aaron Sheehan-Dean

Reconstructing Appalachia: The Civil War's Aftermath
edited by Andrew L. Slap

Blood in the Hills: A History of Violence in Appalachia
edited by Bruce E. Stewart

Moonshiners and Prohibitionists: The Battle over Alcohol in Southern Appalachia
Bruce E. Stewart

*The U.S. South and Europe: Transatlantic Relations in the Nineteenth
and Twentieth Centuries*
edited by Cornelis A. van Minnen and Manfred Berg

Southern Farmers and Their Stories: Memory and Meaning in Oral History
Melissa Walker

Law and Society in the South: A History of North Carolina Court Cases
John W. Wertheimer

Family or Freedom: People of Color in the Antebellum South
Emily West

www.ingramcontent.com/pod-product-compliance
Lightning Source LLC
Chambersburg PA
CBHW020335100426
42812CB00029B/3135/J